EARLY HISTORY OF THE
CHRISTIAN CHURCH

By Monsignor LOUIS DUCHESNE

EARLY HISTORY OF THE CHRISTIAN CHURCH

FROM ITS FOUNDATION TO THE
END OF THE FIFTH CENTURY.
RENDERED INTO ENGLISH FROM
THE FOURTH EDITION

VOL. I. — To the End of the
Third Century.

VOL. II. — The Fourth Century.

VOL. III. — The Fifth Century.

EARLY HISTORY OF
THE CHRISTIAN CHURCH

FROM ITS FOUNDATION TO THE END OF THE FIFTH CENTURY

BY MONSIGNOR LOUIS DUCHESNE

DE L'ACADÉMIE FRANÇAISE

HON. D.LITT. OXFORD, AND LITT.D. CAMBRIDGE
MEMBRE DE L'INSTITUT DE FRANCE

RENDERED INTO ENGLISH
FROM THE FOURTH EDITION

VOLUME II

LONDON
JOHN MURRAY, ALBEMARLE STREET

FIRST EDITION	.	.	.	.	*June* 1912
Reprinted	.	.	.	.	*August* 1922
Reprinted	.	.	.	.	*April* 1931
Reprinted	.	.	.	.	*April* 1950
Reprinted	.	.	.		*December* 1957

Made and printed in Great Britain by Butler & Tanner Ltd., Frome and London
and published by John Murray (Publishers) Ltd.

PREFACE

I PREFACED my first volume with the mention of Eusebius. And it is again under the patronage of the Bishop of Cæsarea that the present one begins. The last three books of his *Ecclesiastical History*, and the four books of his *Life of Constantine*, deal with nearly the whole of the subject-matter of my first five chapters. Faithful to his custom of reproducing his authorities, Eusebius has preserved to us, for the time in which he himself lived, a great number of official documents. We should have been glad if he had more often given expression to his own recollections and impressions; but unfortunately, the nearer the events which he relates approach to his own time, the more afraid he seems to be of seeing them clearly, and above all of relating them. With the exception of the general glorification of the Church, and the special eulogy of Constantine, everything else in his pages is enveloped in so much reserve, with so many oratorical safeguards, and so many things hinted at rather than affirmed, that we have often a difficulty in finding out what he really means.

After Eusebius, the history of the Church remained for a long time neglected. Rufinus of Aquileia was the first to give himself anew to the task. To his translation of the *Ecclesiastical History*, executed at the time when Alaric was devastating Italy, he added two supplementary books, in which the narrative was continued to the death of Theodosius (A.D. 395). His work is a sufficiently mediocre production, hastily put together and devoid of interest save for the last pages, where the author relates events of which he had himself been witness.

vii

The subject was again taken up at Constantinople, shortly before the middle of the 5th century,[1] by two men of the world, Socrates and Sozomen. The first of these, at least, availed himself of the account of Rufinus, which a certain Gelasius had translated into Greek. About the same time, Theodoret, Bishop of Cyrrhos, in the province of Euphratesia, also undertook the task of continuing Eusebius. And finally, Philostorgius, an Arian of the most advanced type, a Eunomian, or Anomœan, applied himself to the same work, in the spirit of his own sect. His book has not been preserved : we have only extracts from it—very copious ones, it is true—in the *Bibliotheca* of Photius. Philostorgius is interesting in one respect— namely, that he allows us to hear the voice of a party conquered and thereby reduced to a silence deeper than history could have wished. Theodoret preserves to us traditions, anecdotes, and legends of Antioch ; Socrates and Sozomen render us the same service for Constantinople and its neighbourhood. Socrates had had much communication with the Novatians of the capital, and they had given him many curious details respecting their Church. But the most important point is that the three orthodox historians have worked over collections of official documents, that they often reproduce original sources, and that, even when they do not reproduce or quote them, they betray the use they have made of such documents by the details of their narrative. The result of this is, that although when they speak for themselves, or as simply following oral traditions, their authority is weak, they afford serious guarantees for their statements when we are able to recover underlying their text the testimony of contemporary documents. This distinction must always be made ; it has guided me, it is hardly necessary to say, in the use I have made of these

---

[1] The priest Philip of Side had published, about the year 430, under the title of *Christian History*, an immense compilation, destitute of order or method. It is now lost ; but what Socrates (*Hist.* vii. 27) and Photius (cod. 35) say of it is not of a character to make us regret its loss very keenly.

authors; it must never be lost sight of in estimating the
references which I make to their works.

If a great many original documents were within the
reach of these authors, it was because various collections
of them had been made, in which it was easy to find them.
St Athanasius compiled one of these, about the year 350,
in his *Apology against the Arians*, a pleading *pro domo*,
in which — reinstalled, in fact, in his see of Alexandria, but deposed in law, in the eyes of his adversaries—
he set himself to show the baselessness of his sentence of
deposition, and to establish the fact that it had been
annulled by more authoritative decisions. Other documents had been added by him to his treatise *The Decrees
of the Council of Nicæa*, which is of rather later date than
his *Apology*.[1] His *History of the Arians, addressed to the
Monks*, also contains more than one document which is
both authentic and interesting. Finally, in the year 367,
when he was in the fortieth year of his episcopate, he
caused to be made a kind of history of the vicissitudes
through which the Church of Alexandria had passed since
the Great Persecution. Documents of great interest were
included in this. The collection has not been preserved in
Greek; but, in a collection of canons, known by the name
of *The Collection of the Deacon Theodosius*, important
fragments of a Latin translation remain to us.[2]

Moreover, Athanasius had not been the first, nor was
he the only person who in this way gathered together
documents. Even before the Council of Nicæa, Arius and
Alexander had brought together the letters of their
respective adherents, and had made use of them in their
polemics. Towards the end of the 4th century, Sabinus,
Bishop of Heraclea for the "Macedonian" party, had also
compiled a collection (Συναγωγή) of various documents
relating to Councils of the Church, from quite another
point of view from that of Athanasius.

---

[1] *Cf.* G. Loeschcke, in the *Rheinisches Museum*, vol. lix., p. 451, who
thinks that he is able to identify this collection with the enigmatical
Synodicon of Athanasius; E. Schwartz, in the Göttingen *Nachrichten*,
1904, p. 391.   [2] *Cf.* page 132, *infra*.

Socrates was acquainted with this collection and also with the others. He openly quotes Sabinus. Sozomen, who re-edited Socrates and at the same time completed his work, did not confine himself to reproducing his quotations. He studied the documents for himself, and made a larger and more judicious use of them, but without quoting the collection—a characteristic method of procedure. We know that although he follows Socrates he gives the reader no sort of notice of this, so that we cannot spare him the reproach of plagiarism.

It was not only in the East that controversy was carried on by means of historical *dossiers* and collections of official documents. In the West also the same method was observed. About the time when the long career of Eusebius of Cæsarea was drawing to its close, the Catholics of Africa, harassed by the Donatists, and ill defended against them by the imperial authorities, conceived the idea of influencing public opinion by making known, through a series of indisputable documents, the conditions which had given rise to that lamentable schism. With this end in view was drawn up the collection called *Gesta purgationis Caeciliani et Felicis*, which long served as a text-book for the anti-Donatist polemics, and was made use of afterwards by St Optatus and St Augustine. As in the Greek collections, a brief commentary bound the pieces together, and formed a kind of historical thread of connection.[1]

It was a collection of the same kind that St Hilary of Poitiers formed in 360, at Constantinople, at the moment when the Nicene orthodoxy appeared to have become obscured in the unfaithfulness, more or less enforced, alike of the Latin and the Greek episcopates. Hilary relates once more, in opposition to the partisans of the Council of Rimini (Ariminum), the series of events which had happened since the Council of Sardica in 343. In the fragments of his compilation which have come down to

[1] *Sylloge Optatiana*, following St Optatus in the Vienna edition, vol. xxvi., p. 206 ; *cf.* my memoir, "Le dossier du Donatisme," in the *Mélanges de l'École de Rome*, vol. x. (1890).

us are to be found documents of later date than the original edition, which proves that it must have been retouched after 360, no doubt by others than the author himself.

Besides these collections of documents, upon which rest, though with gaps, the statements of later historians, the latter had at their disposal, as we ourselves have, often in a larger measure, a considerable body of literature on these subjects. Hilary, Athanasius, Basil the two Gregorys, Epiphanius, Ambrose, and Jerome only to mention the most celebrated, have left us an entire library on which historical learning has drawn for centuries.

It is upon this whole *corpus* of texts that my own account rests. I refer to them with moderation, confining myself, as in the first volume, to indicating, here and there, the authorities to be consulted upon certain debatable questions. If I had gone more deeply into bibliography and critical discussions, the notes would have taken up so much room that I do not see what would have been left for the text. And yet this includes the whole period which corresponds to the six volumes of the late Duke Albert de Broglie, *L'Église et l'empire romain au IVième Siècle*, a book which I have not cited, since I cite only first-hand authorities or special treatises; but one which I could scarcely omit to mention here, were it only to beg of charitable readers not to remember his book too much while they are reading mine.

ROME, *March* 25, 1907.

CONTENTS

CONTENTS

CHAPTER III

THE SCHISMS RESULTING FROM THE PERSECUTION

CHAPTER IV

ARIUS AND THE COUNCIL OF NICÆA

CHAPTER V

EUSEBIUS AND ATHANASIUS

CHAPTER VI

THE EMPEROR CONSTANS

CHAPTER VII

THE PROSCRIPTION OF ATHANASIUS

CHAPTER VIII

THE DEFEAT OF ORTHODOXY

CHAPTER IX

JULIAN AND THE PAGAN REACTION

CHAPTER X

AFTER ARIMINUM

CHAPTER XI

BASIL OF CÆSAREA

CHAPTER XII

GREGORY OF NAZIANZUS

CHAPTER XIII

POPE DAMASUS

CHAPTER XIV

THE MONKS OF THE EAST

CHAPTER XV

THE WEST IN THE DAYS OF ST AMBROSE

CHAPTER XVI

CHRISTIANITY IN THE EAST UNDER THEODOSIUS

CHAPTER XVII

CHRISTIANITY, THE STATE RELIGION

EARLY HISTORY OF THE CHRISTIAN CHURCH

CHAPTER I

THE GREAT PERSECUTION

Accession of Diocletian : the Tetrarchy. Persecution decided upon: the four edicts. Crisis of the Tetrarchy : Constantine and Maxentius. Application of the first edict in Africa. The Terror of 304. The canons of Peter of Alexandria. The beginning of Maximin's reign. Death of Galerius : his edict of toleration. The religious policy of Maximin : his end. Licinius at Nicomedia : edicts of pacification. The martyrs of Palestine, of Egypt, and of Africa. Literary controversies : Arnobius, Hierocles, Lactantius.

1. *The Emperor Diocletian.*

WHEN Gallienus was assassinated (March 22, 268), the Empire, invaded and torn in pieces, was at its lowest. A two-fold task was imposed upon the heirs of the son of Valerian — the reconstruction of the frontier, and the restoration of unity. The upright princes who succeeded one another during the following sixteen years, Claudius II., Aurelian, Tacitus, Probus, and Carus, laboured at this task conscientiously and not without success. Aurelian recovered Gaul from the native princes whom it had chosen, and deprived the Queen of Palmyra of the government of the eastern provinces. As to the frontier, its re-establishment was without doubt achieved, but only by drawing it farther back. The Empire was lopped of everything beyond the Rhine and the Danube : it lost, in Upper Germany, the *Agri Decumates* (Swabia and the Black Forest), and in the region of the Carpathians the entire province of Dacia, with the parts of the two Mœsias which lay beyond the Danube. And even after these readjustments had been made, a feeling of perfect security did not exist in the interior of the Empire. The towns surrounded themselves with walls raised in haste ; and it was necessary to fortify Rome itself. The enclosure which protected it during the whole of the middle ages preserves the name of Aurelian.[1]

In the East, war with the Persians was almost incessant. The Emperor Carus perished in it in 284, leaving two sons, one of whom, Carinus, entrusted with the government of the West, had remained in Italy. The other, Numerian, had followed his father beyond the Euphrates. He was bringing home the army, when, in the neighbourhood of Byzantium, he was found dead in his tent. The generals, without troubling themselves about Carinus, elected one of their own number in the place of Numerian, and it was in this way that Diocletian, commander of the imperial guard (*comes domesticorum*), was raised to the throne (September 17, 284). Carinus marched against the usurper, came up with him in Mœsia, and inflicted a few defeats upon him ; but in the end he was abandoned by his troops, who passed over to Diocletian.

Diocletian had long dreamed of the sovereign power. Trained in the school of Aurelian and his officers, he was a real soldier and, better still, a clever organizer. When he had the Empire in his hands, it was not of enjoying it that he thought, but rather of restoring it. Before all things, stability was necessary. Diocletian deemed that the revolutions and rivalries for power were caused by the impossibility of a single man governing a territory of such vast extent, and above all directing the operations of armies, separated by such great distances from one an-

---

[1] Homo, *Essai sur le règne de l'empereur Aurélien*, p. 214 *et seq.*

other. In order to avoid rivals, he gave himself colleagues.
In the year 285, one of his companions-in-arms, Maximian,
was adopted by him, invested with the title of Cæsar, and
sent to Gaul to repress the insurrection of the Bagaudæ.
In the following year, he made him Augustus and entrusted
to him the government of the West. In 293 the system
was perfected : each of the two Augusti was provided with
an auxiliary emperor, who had the title of Cæsar and a
definite jurisdiction : Constantius the Pale (Chlorus) in
this way governed Gaul and Britain, with Maximian ;
while Galerius relieved Diocletian of the care of watching
over the Danube frontier.

All these princes were natives of Illyricum, and of low
origin. Maximian and Galerius remained under the
imperial purple the men they had always been, coarse
soldiers, cruel on occasion, without education and without
morals ; Constantius seems to have been more civilized.
Diocletian was not anxious that his colleagues should have
too many recommendations. He had given to Maximian
the title of *Herculius*, and assumed for himself that of
Jovius, thus indicating plainly his own part in the imperial
Olympus, and the kind of service he expected from his
assistants. It is assuredly to him that we must refer the
whole policy of the Dyarchy and the Tetrarchy, especially
the whole of the reforming legislation, by which he
endeavoured to restore order in the finances, in the army,
and in the general management of public affairs.

The leading idea of his system was an absolute central-
ization, the suppression of all local political life, of every
vestige of ancient liberties : in one word, Autocracy. Diocletian is the founder of the Byzantine *régime*. It was
indeed no very considerable change. The reformer did
but consecrate by appropriate institutions the tendencies
of the situation and usages which were already established.
Such a system had the same results that it always has :
the centralizing organ was developed at the expense of the
body which it was supposed to direct ; the fiscal system at
the expense of general prosperity ; and management at
the expense of energy. The Empire was soon a prey to

the malady of its government; the time was to come when
it died of it.

The supreme head of this immense hierarchy of
functionaries, all ornamented with the most high-sounding
titles, was necessarily obliged to rise entirely above the
ordinary conditions of humanity. The person of the
Emperor was sacred, divine, eternal; his house was also
divine (*domus divina*). Therein reigned a pomp worthy
of Susa and of Babylon; the *Jovius* of Nicomedia was
scarcely more accessible than his celestial patron. Things
had travelled far from the simple life and familiar manners
which Augustus had maintained in his house on the
Palatine.

And it was not in Rome itself that this Asiatic pomp
was displayed. The ancient mistress of the world was
nothing now. Her senate, deprived of political power and
closed, since the time of Gallienus, to veteran warriors,
was now only a great town council. For the crowd which
still thronged in the enclosure of Aurelian, games continued
to be given and baths to be opened; but they no longer
saw their emperor. Diocletian reigned at Nicomedia; his
lieutenants had their official residences at Milan, at Trèves,
at Sirmium. No doubt it was well that the emperors
should not be too far away from the frontiers; but there
were other reasons. These soldiers of fortune, born in the
least cultured provinces, and brought up in the camps
on the Danube, cared nothing at all for Rome. Her
traditions were tiresome, her populace always ready for
seditious movements; her senate might remember that it
had once been supreme, and might still wish to be of some
consequence. On the death of Aurelian, it had come to
life for a brief moment, and had tried to take part in
public affairs. It was far better to keep at a distance from
this uncomfortable city of Rome, and, since the Empire
had become an Oriental monarchy, to instal its capital in
the Orient. Diocletian well understood this, and so did
Constantine after him.

Amongst the reforms introduced at this time, it is
fitting to mention here the new distribution of the

provinces. Diocletian increased their number. Before his
time, there were already sixty of them : he left ninety-six.
It is true that this partition was compensated for by the
creation of *dioceses*, more comprehensive divisions, in each of
which several provinces were included. Each diocese was
governed by a *vicarius*—that is to say, by a representative
of the prefect of the imperial prætorium. This organization was in many places appropriated for the ecclesiastical
use. In the East, from the time of the Council of Nicæa,
the groupings of bishops corresponded almost everywhere with the new provincial divisions : the bishop of the
city in which the governor resided, of the metropolis, as it
was called, was the head of the episcopate of the province.
It was he who presided over the elections, when a see
became vacant, who convened his colleagues in council and
presided over their meetings. This system was adopted
later on in a great part of the West. These imperial
dioceses also served, in a certain measure, to settle the
boundaries of the ecclesiastical jurisdictions. It was in
this way that Diocletian appears as of some importance in
the organization of the Church. But he has claims of a
very different character to figure in its history.

2. *The Edicts of Persecution.*

During the long peace which followed the persecution of Valerian, the Christian propaganda had made
enormous progress. Not to speak of Edessa and the
kingdom of Armenia, where Christianity was already
the dominant religion, there were regions in the
Empire in which it was not far from representing
the half, or even the majority, of the population. This
was the case, for instance,[1] in Asia Minor. In northern
Syria, in Egypt, and in Africa, the Christians were also
very numerous. At the councils of the time of St Cyprian
we find as many as ninety bishops mentioned, which

[1] Dr Harnack, *Die Mission und Ausbreitung des Christentums*,
p. 539 *et seq.* (2nd ed., vol. ii., p. 276 *et seq.*), gives more precise
estimates, including a certain amount of conjecture, but of a very
probable kind.

presupposes a much greater number of churches at
that time, and in the forty or fifty years which followed
many more must have been organized. The sixty
Italian bishops assembled in 251 by Pope Cornelius
allow of a similar estimate with regard to the Italian
peninsula. In the south of Spain and of Gaul, in Greece,
and in Macedonia, the spread of the Gospel, without
perhaps having made so much progress, must nevertheless
have obtained important results. In other countries, such
as central and southern Syria, the north of Italy, the
north, centre, and west of Gaul, in the island of Britain,
in the mountains of the Alps, the Pyrenees, and the
Hemus, the situation was quite different. The ancient
cults were still in favour, and groups of Christians were
only to be found by way of exceptions.

This is a general account of the state of things, but
in each country the situation varied according to local
circumstances. Not far from Edessa, notable for its
Christianity, Harran adhered obstinately to its old Semitic
religion, which it preserved until the advent of Islam.
Certain towns of the Lebanon, such as Heliopolis, or of
the seaboard of Syria, such as Gaza, contained either
a very small number of the faithful, or none at all. In
Phrygia were to be found small towns, where everyone,
including the magistrates, professed Christianity. Christian
duumvirs and *curators* were not rare; there were even
Christian *flamens*.[1] The bishops were in frequent communication with the governors and the financial officials;
they were treated with respect; much favour was shown
them. And further, they had no longer any difficulty
in rebuilding the old churches, in laying the foundation
of new ones, and in holding largely attended meetings
on festivals.

And there was something more significant still, from
the point of view of the progress of Christianity and the
liberty of action which it enjoyed, in the fact that not
only municipal functions, but even the government of

---

[1] See vol. i., p. 378.

provinces was often entrusted to Christians. The palace itself, the divine dwelling of the imperial Jupiter, was full of Christians; they occupied there the superior positions of the central administration. Several of them—Peter, Dorotheus, and Gorgonius—figure in the number of the persons most highly placed in the favour of the emperor. The government offices, and the employments attached to the personal service of the sovereign, were, to a large extent, occupied by Christians. The Empress Prisca herself and her daughter Valeria seem to have had very close relations with Christianity.

But it was not so with Diocletian himself. Whatever may have been his toleration for the opinions of his subjects, his officials, and his family, he, for his part, preserved his attachment to the old customs of the Roman worship. He frequented the temples and sacrificed to the gods, without any mystic ideas, without ostentation, but with a deep devotion, deeming, no doubt, that he was thus fulfilling his duty as a man and, above all, as a sovereign. Such a state of mind could not make him really favourable to rival religions. " The immortal gods," he says in his rescript against the Manicheans " have condescended, in their providence, to entrust to the enlightenment of wise and good men the responsibility of deciding as to that which is good and true. No one is allowed to resist their authority: the old religion must not be criticized by a new one. It is a great crime to go back on anything which, having been established by our forefathers, is now in possession and in use."

It was comparatively easy to apply these principles to Manicheism, which had been quite recently imported from abroad. But with regard to the Christian beliefs the same might already be said as of the old Roman cults : *statum et cursum tenent ac possident.* Besides, they were already too extensively propagated to allow any reasonable hope of extirpating them. Decius and Valerian had tried to do so ; and it was known how unsuccessful their efforts had proved. Since then the position of Christians had grown and had been reinforced : a new attack upon them could only meet with still greater obstacles.

For a long time the good sense of the emperor led him to avoid any kind of persecution. At length, however, his ideas underwent a change. It is possible that, like so many other reformers, he was led astray by the chimera of religious unity, a baleful and lusty chimera, which still claims its victims. However, the details which have remained to us with regard to his attitude do not indicate any such point of view. Diocletian seems to have discovered, from a certain definite point of time, that there were too many Christians in his palace and in his army. To remedy this inconvenience, there was really no necessity to declare a war of extermination on Christianity. A few personal measures, a few dismissals, would have settled everything. Even among the Christians themselves such a course would have found supporters. There were not wanting among the faithful those who disapproved of military service,[1] and who did not look at all favourably upon those of their brethren who were engaged in public offices. The matter might well have ended here. But Diocletian was old : his power of resistance to external influence was enfeebled, and he was surrounded by a powerful party which clamoured for radical measures. Its head, the ferocious Cæsar of Illyricum, found means of bending the aged Augustus to his ends, and of making him commit the enormity to which his name remains attached.

---

[1] It is to holders of this view that there belong several African martyrs of this time, in regard to whom we possess authentic documents. Maximilian, a conscript, was executed for refusing military service, at Theveste, on March 12, 295. The proconsul Dion in vain adduced in opposition to him the Christians who served in the imperial army. "They know what they ought to do," replied Maximilian. "I am a Christian, and I cannot do what is wrong." At Tangier, the centurion Marcellus who refused to continue his military service, and the clerk of the court, Cassian, who refused to write the sentence rendered against Marcellus, also suffered (October 30 and December 3 : the year is uncertain).

Lactantius[1] gives as the origin of the persecution an event which is said to have happened in the eastern provinces. Diocletian was about to sacrifice, and to consult the entrails of the victims, when some Christians among his attendants made the sign of the Cross. The *haruspex*, whose operations that day had led to no result, observed the gesture, and informed the emperor of it, complaining of the profane persons who thus disturbed his ceremonies. Diocletian was furious, and at once commanded that not only the actual offenders, but all the officers of his palace should be compelled to sacrifice, and that, in case of refusal, they should be beaten with rods. Letters were immediately despatched to the various military commanders, to the effect that all soldiers were to sacrifice, under pain of being excluded from the army.

Whatever influence the fact just related may have had upon the emperor's decision, it is certain that measures were taken to eliminate from the army the Christian element which it contained.[2] A *magister militum*, named Veturius, was specially appointed to carry out this order. A very large number of Christians were thus forced to renounce the profession of arms and accepted the situation. There was no other penalty attached; only in one or two cases, Eusebius tells us, was death inflicted as a punishment, no doubt on account of special circumstances. This was in the year 302.

On his return from the East, Diocletian passed the whole winter at Nicomedia. Galerius rejoined him there, and devoted himself with all his energies to inducing the emperor to sanction more severe measures. It is said that he was incited to this by his mother, an aged and very devout Pagan with an implacable hatred of Christians.[3] Diocletian resisted. "What is the use," he

---

[1] *De mortibus persecutorum*, 10.

[2] *Ibid.*, 10; Eusebius, *H. E.* viii. 1, 4; *Chronicon*, ad ann. 2317.

[3] Lactantius does not say, but we may suspect, that there was here a conflict of feminine influences. The princesses of Nicomedia were Christians or favourable to the Christians; this was quite

said, "of causing trouble everywhere, and shedding
torrents of blood? The Christians have no fear of
death. It is quite sufficient to prevent the soldiers and
the people about the palace from following their religion."
Galerius persevered, and returned incessantly to the
subject. At last the emperor made up his mind to
summon a council of friends, military officers and civil
functionaries. Opinions were divided. As usual, those
who were urgent in the matter—behind whom might be
detected the influence of Galerius, the Cæsar of to-day,
the Augustus of to-morrow — drew over those who
hesitated to their side. Yet the wise old emperor still
refused to yield. It was at last agreed to consult the
oracle at Miletus, the Didymean Apollo. The priestess,[1]
as can easily be imagined, did not fail to unite her
inspiration to the wishes of Galerius and his party. And
the conflict was decided upon.

If Galerius could have had his own way entirely,
extreme measures would have been taken at the outset,
and the stakes would have been lighted everywhere
But Diocletian did not wish for bloodshed ; and, for the
moment, his will prevailed. An edict was prepared in
accordance with his views. On the day before its
proclamation (February 23, 303), police officers proceeded
at daybreak to the church of Nicomedia, a large edifice
in full view of the imperial palace. The sacred books
were seized and thrown into the fire, the furniture was
given up to pillage, and the church itself demolished from
top to bottom.[2]

On the next day (February 24) the edict was
published. It commanded that throughout the whole
Empire the churches should be demolished, and the
sacred books destroyed by fire. All Christians in
enough to make the ladies of the rival imperial establishment wish
for the condemnation of Christians to death.

    [1] It is, I think, to this consultation that the recollections of
Constantine refer, as we have them in Eusebius, *Vita Constantini*, ii.
50, 51.

    [2] Lactantius, *De mort. pers.*, 13 ; Eusebius, *H. E.* viii. 2 ; *Martyr.
Pal.*, preface.

possession of public offices, dignities, or privileges, were deprived of them; they lost also the right of appearing in a court of justice to accuse anyone of injuries, or adultery, or theft. Christian slaves might no longer be set free.[1]

No sooner was the edict posted up than it was torn in pieces by a Christian of Nicomedia, whose name has not been preserved, but who paid for his daring by dying at the stake. A few days afterwards a fire broke out in the palace. Galerius at once accused the Christians of having kindled it; they repudiated the accusation, saying that he wished in this way to excite Diocletian's anger against them. While the emperor was making enquiries to obtain light on the affair, a second fire broke out. Galerius, although it was winter-time, made haste to leave Nicomedia, declaring that he did not wish to stay there to be burnt alive.

Convinced at last, Diocletian determined to recommence the horrors of Nero's reign. The whole of the palace suffered in consequence. His wife and daughter were forced to sacrifice; Adauctus, the head of the fiscal administration; the eunuchs most in favour, Peter, Dorotheus, and Gorgonius; the Bishop of Nicomedia, Anthimus; priests, deacons, Christians of every age, even women, were burnt or drowned wholesale. Thus was expiated the crime, clearly a faked one, of having set fire to the sacred palace and attempted to destroy two emperors at once.

But measures did not stop with this local repression. Seditious movements having occurred in the direction of Melitene and in Syria, they were declared to be the work of Christians. Other general edicts followed the first[2]: they began by commanding the arrest of all the heads of the Churches, bishops, priests, and other clerics; and then that they should be compelled to sacrifice by every means available.

---

[1] This first edict reached Palestine towards the end of March, just when the Feast of Easter was being celebrated (Eusebius, *H. E.* viii. 2).

[2] Eusebius, *Martyr. Pal.*, preface.

On September 17, 303, began the twentieth year of the reign of Diocletian. On this occasion an amnesty was granted to condemned criminals[1]; but we have no reason to think that it included the imprisoned confessors, who, in the eyes of the law, were neither prisoners awaiting trial nor condemned criminals, but rebels. The aged emperor resolved to celebrate at Rome the feast of his *vicennalia*. It took place on November 20. The construction of his celebrated baths was not sufficiently advanced for the ceremony of their ˎdedication to be possible; it was therefore postponed. Besides, Diocletian was never happy on the banks of the Tiber. His Oriental magnificence, his austere and melancholy manners, made no impression on the turbulent Roman populace: they wearied him so much with their familiarities and pleasantries, that he did not even stay in Rome till January 1, the day on which he was to inaugurate his ninth consulate, but set out, in the depth of winter, for Ravenna. In the course of this unseasonable journey, he contracted an illness which lasted a long time, and became more severe on his return to Nicomedia. In this condition of affairs, he himself, the East, and in some ways the whole Empire, were in the hands of Galerius. The war against Christians was waged with still more fury. A fourth edict appeared. This time, there was no longer any question of special classes of persons: all Christians, without distinction, were commanded to sacrifice. After following Nero, a return had been made to the policy of Valerian; now it was the work of Decius that was resumed.

3. *The Dislocation of the Tetrarchy.*

It was a terrible year, not only for the Christians, but also for the emperor. His health went from bad to worse. In the middle of December, it was reported that he was dead; he was not dead, but when he showed himself again in public, on March 1, 305, he could scarcely be recognized. Weakened in body and spirit, he allowed himself to be

---

[1] Eusebius, *Martyr. Pal.* 2.

persuaded by Galerius, that the time had come for him
to resign. Galerius had suggested the same idea to
Maximian Herculius, at the same time threatening him
with civil war. This double abdication entailed the
elevation of Constantius and Galerius to the position of
Augusti. Galerius appointed the two new Cæsars—
Severus, a drunken soldier, and Daia, a rough-hewn
barbarian, who was called *Maximinus* to disguise him as
a Roman. With two such colleagues as these, the new
Augustus of the East hoped to be almost the sole head of
the Empire; for Constantius, far away and pacific in
character, and besides of enfeebled health, would be no
obstacle. Maximin Daia was set over the diocese of the
Orient—that is to say, over Syria and Egypt. Galerius
united to his own Illyricum the dioceses of Thrace, Asia,
and Pontus; Spain was added to the jurisdiction of
Constantius; Italy and Africa fell to the lot of Severus.

This satisfactory arrangement was disturbed by the
revolt of the natural heirs. If Diocletian and Galerius had
no male children, it was not so with Constantius and
Maximian, and their natural heirs did not at all relish
the new system of succession. Constantine, the son of
Constantius, was at Nicomedia when the change was made;
he was a hostage given by Constantius.[1] The latter, now
become Augustus, demanded the return of his son, and
Galerius was obliged to let him go, though he did it with
much reluctance. What he feared, actually happened.
The Emperor Constantius died soon after at York; in
his last moments, he commended his son to the soldiers
as his successor, and these, as soon as he had breathed his
last, acclaimed the young prince as emperor (July 25,
306). It was a serious annoyance to Galerius; but as
York was a long way from Nicomedia, and as Constantine was not without adherents, he was obliged to recognize him. At the same time, the title of Augustus was
not conceded; Galerius proclaimed Severus as Augustus
in the place of Constantius Chlorus, and Constantine as

---

[1] Eusebius (*V. C.* i. 19) had seen him journeying through Palestine
in the train of the Emperor Diocletian.

Cæsar in the place of Severus. The Tetrarchy was reconstituted with the two Augusti, Galerius and Severus, and the two Cæsars, Maximin and Constantine.

At the same time as Constantine succeeded his father, Maxentius, the son of Maximian, profiting by the state of abandonment in which the emperors had left Old Rome, seized upon the government there, without troubling himself at all about the Tetrarchy. Notwithstanding his dissolute morals, which recalled the days of Commodus, this young man knew how to please the Romans. As a protest against the new capitals, he reinstated the old forms of worship and the ancient legends in their former position of honour ; he restored the Forum and the Sacred Way, and near the latter he raised a magnificent basilica. Severus tried in vain to dispute the position with him ; his soldiers deserted him. They were soldiers of the old Maximian, and rallied all the more readily round his son because Maximian himself, issuing from his retreat, had just reassumed the purple, with the title of " Augustus for the second time " (*bis Augustus*). This reappearance of Maximian put the last touch to the disorder. Severus had been driven to suicide; Galerius hastened to avenge him ; but, as he drew near to Rome, the attitude of his soldiers decided him to return home. Maxentius, now feeling his hands free, proclaimed himself Augustus (October 27, 307). However, the old Maximian, having now quarrelled with his son, betook himself to Gaul and joined Constantine. There he tried, by making use of his support, still to play a part ; then abandoned his protector, returned to him again, betrayed him, and finally was either put to death, or forced to be his own executioner by the advice of his host (310).

Galerius, in search of a second Augustus, had thought (November 11, 308) of giving this title to Licinius, one of his old companions-in-arms. Maximin at once protested : from his distant diocese, he saw with jealousy this newcomer attaining supreme honours at one stroke. Constantine might well have raised the same objections. Galerius, to pacify them, gave them both the new title of "son of the Augusti"; some months later, he went the whole way and made them full Augusti. There were thus four emperors of the first rank.

When Galerius died, in May 311, Licinius and Maximin hastened to claim his inheritance; however, an arrangement was concluded, by virtue of which the Bosphorus became their common boundary. In this way the empire of Maximin comprehended Asia Minor, with Syria and Egypt; that of Licinius stretched from the Bosphorus to the Alps: theoretically, it extended also to Italy and Africa; but, as a matter of fact, these countries obeyed Maxentius, an illegitimate emperor from the point of view of the law of the Tetrarchy, but in reality firmly established in his power.

Constantine, meanwhile, kept his position in Gaul, manœuvring skilfully in the midst of all these conflicts, and no doubt meditating the design which he soon accomplished—that of annihilating all his rivals, by making use of some in order to rid himself of the others.

It was with Maxentius that the process of simplification began. After making sure of the moral support of Licinius, to whom Maximin was causing some useful feelings of alarm, Constantine invaded Italy, inflicted several defeats upon the partisans of the "tyrant," and finally met him in the ever-famous battle near the Milvian Bridge (October 28, 312). Maxentius perished in the waters of the Tiber; Constantine entered Rome, and was at once recognized throughout the whole of Italy and in Africa. The following year, the hands of Licinius were free to attack Maximin. The infamous Daia, defeated in Thrace on April 30, recrossed the Bosphorus, and then the Taurus, and finally poisoned himself at Tarsus.

There remained now only two emperors, Constantine and Licinius, the one at Rome, the other at Nicomedia.

4. *The Persecution down to the Edict of Galerius.*

We must now return to the enactments of persecution. The first edict, besides the degradations and disqualifications which it pronounced against certain classes of Christians, commanded the demolition of the churches and the burning of the sacred books. Such are, at any rate, the proceedings which are known to us directly; but we know also that the real property of the Christian communities was confiscated, and that, ere the religious edifices were destroyed, the furniture of them was seized. These operations were carried out according to regular forms; in certain places, authentic inventories were made; some of these were preserved for a very considerable period. It was thus that the Donatists were able, in 411, to produce the formal records of the seizure of the churches of Rome.[1] These have been lost since then; but we are still able to read those which were drawn up at Cirta in Numidia. More summary accounts remain to us with regard to the application of the edict in other localities, in Africa and elsewhere. It would have been very difficult to resist the seizure of the Church properties. But at least the clergy did everything in their power to save the furniture, and especially to save the Holy Scriptures. Some women of Thessalonica fled to the mountains with a quantity of books and papers.[2] The Bishop of Carthage, Mensurius, had succeeded in concealing the sacred books; in their place, he left in one of his churches a collection of heretical books, which were seized and destroyed by the unheeding police. The officials, indeed, were not always very observant. Some decurions of Carthage, having obtained knowledge of Mensurius' deception, denounced him to the proconsul: the latter took no notice of their disclosures. If this was the case in the large towns, we can imagine what would happen in the smaller localities. There were places where the Christians were in bad repute, and where the municipal government was in the hands of their adversaries; but in other places they had to deal

---

[1] Augustine, *Breviculus Collationis cum Donatistis*, 34-36. Several members of the clergy, among others a deacon Strato, are there mentioned as giving up to the magistrates the ecclesiastical furniture; the prefect speaks of them as *hortatores vanissimae superstitionis*.

[2] The Passion of SS. Agape, Chionia, and Irene (April 1)—an important document.

with magistrates who were Christians themselves, or who, at least, were sympathetic. Ways out of the difficulty were often found. As in Carthage, other books were seized in the church instead of those of the Bible,[1] and if the search was extended even to the bishop's house, there were still means of evading it. Sometimes, instead of entirely destroying the churches, the police contented themselves with burning the doors. Moreover, the bishops and clergy often showed themselves accommodating, and gave up their holy books, thinking, doubtless, that it would be easy later on to obtain new copies. But this complaisance was not accepted by general opinion, especially, as can readily be understood, when the persecution was over, and when one could be unyielding without risk. It was then that the heroism of certain bishops was remembered, e.g., of Bishop Felix of Thibiuca, who had paid with his head for his refusal to give up the Scriptures.[2] Miracles also, were reported, like that which occurred at Abitina, where, as the sacred books, which had been given up by the Bishop Fundanus, were thrown into the fire, a terrible storm burst over the flames and inundated the whole country.

In those provinces which were governed by the Cæsar Constantius, the destruction did not extend beyond the edifices themselves. The churches were seized and destroyed; but the same treatment was not enforced in regard to the Scriptures.

If destruction thus befell the churches in which the Christians assembled under the eye of the authorities there was, of course, far more reason for forbidding clandestine meetings. This was a necessary consequence of the first edict, and we are justified in believing that such

---

[1] At Aptonga (for the orthography of the name of this town, see the texts collected in the Latin *Thesaurus*), some *epistolae salutatoriae* (?) were seized in this way ; at *Calama*, some books on medicine ; at *Aquae Tibilitanae*, papers of some sort.

[2] The Passion of this Saint, authentic on the whole, was provided, later on, with additions, which transferred its *dénouement* to Italy. See *Analecta Bollandiana*, vol. xvi., p. 25.

a prohibition was expressly formulated in it. This follows also from an African document, in which figure some fifty Christians of the little town of Abitina, who are accused of having met for service ("collect") under the presidency of a priest called Saturninus. The second edict, which ordered the imprisonment of the clergy, was aimed indirectly at the meetings for worship; for how could they be held without religious leaders?

Up to this time, for those who obeyed the edicts, who accepted their legal disqualifications, who allowed their Scriptures to be burnt and their churches to be seized, who abstained from taking part in the assemblies for worship henceforth forbidden, there was still some measure of safety. In Nicomedia, it is true, recourse was had at once to the most extreme measures; but that was on account of special circumstances. The more sanguinary form of persecution had not yet attacked the simple profession of Christianity. It was different when the government renewed, for the clergy first and then for all the faithful, the obligation of taking part in the ceremonies of the official form of worship; when they no longer confined themselves to proscribing, but endeavoured to convert.

At this stage the same state of things was repeated as had been already experienced in previous persecutions. Excited enthusiasts rushed to martyrdom, denounced themselves, made an uproar before the tribunals, and insulted the police. Wise and strong characters waited quietly until they were arrested, and then met the commands of authority with a calm and persevering resistance, which, in many cases, triumphed over imprisonment and torture, and was maintained unto death. There were also many apostates, most of them in a great hurry to do whatever they were told to do, in order to escape from danger; others resisting at first, and then weakening, overcome by the horror of the dungeons and the anguish of the torture.

Many fled, or hid themselves, at the sacrifice of all their possessions. There was a great difference between various kinds of Christians. We can study them in the penitential letter of Bishop Peter of Alexandria, written in 306, in the canons of the Council of Ancyra (314), in the accounts given by Eusebius, and in certain fragments of hagiography. Many deceived the police, sent their slaves or their pagan friends to sacrifice in their stead, and thus obtained their certificate of sacrifice. Others followed a simpler method still, and bought this certificate, if they could find anyone disposed to sell it to them. Among the stout hearted there were some who could not get their confession of faith accepted. Some of the magistrates cared far less for executions than for apostasies. There were even some who, when the term of their office had expired, boasted of not having put a single Christian to death.[1] In the matter of the pagan actions required, the authorities were very easily satisfied; sometimes they registered people against their will as having complied with the law. Sometimes it happened that inconsiderate friends, Christians or pagans, absolutely determined to save from death a believer whom they knew to be resolute, dragged him to the altars, with his hands and feet bound, gagged him to stop him from crying out, and forced him, even at the cost of burning his hands if necessary, to throw a few grains of incense upon the sacred fire.

Lactantius complains,[2] and with reason, of other judges, more to be feared on account of their pretended clemency, who did not wish to kill their victims, but invented tortures so exquisite that they often overcame the most intrepid resistance. He prefers those judges who were openly cruel, either from natural ferocity, or that they might stand well with the superior authorities. There were some of them who did not hesitate to go beyond their instructions, like the judge in a little town of Phrygia, the inhabitants of which were all Christians, who set fire to the church in which the whole population was assembled, and burnt it to the ground with those in

---

[1] Lactantius, *Institutiones*, v. 11.   [2] *Loc. cit.*

it, including the town council and the magistrates of the place.[1]

The change of emperors, brought about by the abdication of Diocletian and Maximian, had the effect of extending, in the West, the field of action of Constantius Chlorus. Spain, annexed to his immediate jurisdiction, shared from that time in the relative peace which Christians had hitherto enjoyed in Gaul and in Britain. His lieutenant Severus does not seem to have been distinguished in Italy and Africa by a special zeal for the edicts of persecution. After the death of Constantius, Constantine showed himself even more favourable to the Christians than his father had been[2]; Maxentius also was tolerant. We may say, then, that rigorous persecution lasted scarcely more than two years (303-305) in the western provinces. It was quite otherwise in Illyricum, in Thrace,[3] Asia-Minor, and the Orient, where nothing was opposed to the will of Galerius and of Maximin, his creature. In these men natural ferocity was at the service of a kind of religious conviction: Galerius was devout, Maximin a fanatic, The latter combined an unbridled, brutal, and despotic licentiousness with an extraordinary zeal for the worship of the gods. At the beginning of his reign, as the persecution seemed to him to have somewhat abated.

---

[1] Lactantius, *loc. cit.; cf.* Eusebius, *H. E.* viii. 11. Eusebius says that the town itself (πολίχνην) was burnt, with the *curator*, the *duumvir*, and the other magistrates; Lactantius speaks only of the church, but he also relates that the whole population perished: *universum populum cum ipso pariter conventiculo concremavit.*

[2] *Suscepto imperio Constantinus aug. nihil egit prius quam christianos cultui ac Deo suo redderet.*—Lactantius, *De mort. persec.* 24.

[3] With regard to the victims of the persecution in the dominions of Galerius we possess several important and trustworthy traditions, contained in documents sufficiently near the date of the events themselves. They allow us to determine the current application of the edicts, but they cannot be used to define the special action of the prince who presided over their execution in these countries. I am speaking here of the accounts relating to St Philip of Heraclea, with the priest Severus and the deacon Hermes (October 22); to the three holy women of Thessalonica, Agape, Chionia, and

he took care to revive it at once, and imposed afresh the obligation to sacrifice.[1]

The police, armed with lists of names, went from street to street calling upon the inhabitants to appear, and forcing everyone, even women and children, to repair to the temple, and there perform the prescribed ceremonies. However, after the lapse of a certain time, dating from the year 307, a more lenient state of things was introduced. The penalty of death, in ordinary cases, was replaced by that of hard labour in the mines, with this aggravation, that the confessors were previously deprived of the sight of the right eye, and maimed in the left leg by cauterizing the tendon. A little later, in 308, after a short respite, the provincial and municipal authorities were again set to work. The Cæsar ordered the old temples to be rebuilt everywhere, and everyone, even the little children, was obliged to take part in the sacrifices; the wine of the libations was to be poured over the victuals in the market; and at the doors of the public baths altars were erected upon which all those who entered were compelled to throw incense. There were still many evil days to come and go.

Irene (April 1); to the martyrs of Dorostorum, Pasicrates, Valention (May 25), Marcian, Nicander (June 17), Julius (May 27), Hesychius (June 15); to the priest Montanus of Singidunum (March 26); to the Bishop of Sirmium, Irenæus (April 6); to the hermit Syneros, belonging to the same town (February 22); to Pollio, chief of the lectors of Cibales (April 28); to the Bishop of Siscia, Quirinus (June 5; cf. Jerome, *Chronicon*, a. *Abr.* 2324); to the Bishop of Poetovio, Victorinus (November 2; cf. Jerome, *De viris illustribus*, 74); to St Florian, of Lauriacum in Noricum (May 4), etc. This enumeration must not be taken as exhaustive; I have only selected some names among those of the martyrs of these countries which can be safely referred to the persecution of Diocletian rather than to any other. The Hieronymian Martyrology contains many other names under the heading of the Danubian provinces, especially of the Lower Danube, from Sirmium onwards; it is very probable that the greater part of these were victims of the last persecution rather than of the preceding ones.

[1] Eusebius, *Martyr. Pal.* iv. 8. If we were to believe Maximin himself (Eusebius, *H. E.* ix. 9, 13), he was never a persecutor.

However, the first author of the persecution was already struggling with the terrible malady which was to overcome his ferocity. It began almost with the opening of the year 310; and for some eighteen months the wretched Galerius fought against it, wearying his physicians with his complaints, and the gods with his fruitless supplications. At last there came to him an idea —surely of all the strangest—of interesting in his health the Christians, whom for years he had hunted down, and the God whose worship he had sworn to exterminate. From Sardica, no doubt, where he then was with Licinius, a proclamation was sent through all the provinces in the name of the four sovereigns.[1] It declared that the emperors, with the general intention of reform, had wished to bring back the Christians to the religious institutions of their ancestors,[2] but that they had not been able to succeed, the Christians having persisted, in spite of the severities of which they had been the victims, in obeying the laws which they had made for themselves. Under these conditions, as they would not honour the gods of the empire, and since they could not practise their own form of religion, it was necessary to make provision by indulgence for their situation. In consequence, they were allowed to exist once more, and to reconstitute their assemblies, on condition, however, that they did nothing contrary to discipline.[3] The magistrates were informed that another imperial letter would explain to them what they were to do. "In return for our indulgence," the edict con-

---

[1] Lactantius (*De mort. persec.* 34) has preserved the original text, but without the title; this is only known to us through the version of Eusebius (*H. E.* viii. 17). It only mentions Galerius, Constantine, and Licinius; the name of Maximin is omitted, either because his memory was officially abolished, or from the fault of the copyists.

[2] These recitals have a singular resemblance to those of the edict with regard to the Manicheans.

[3] *Ut denuo sint christiani et conventicula sua componant, ita ut ne quid contra disciplinam agant.* We must observe that the term *conventiculum* signifies, like the word *ecclesia*, both the assembly itself and the place where it is held.

cluded, "the Christians are to pray to their God for our health, for the State, and for themselves, that the commonwealth may enjoy perfect prosperity, and that they may be enabled to live at home in security."

What a change! The emperor and the empire recommended to the prayers of the Christians, and this by the very man who was responsible for all the calamities which they had endured for eight years!

5. *The Persecution of Maximin.*

The edict was published at Nicomedia [1] and in all the provinces belonging to Galerius, Licinius, and Constantine. In the empire of Constantine it was really only an official consecration of a liberty already re-established as a matter of fact. Maxentius restored to the bishops the places of worship which had hitherto remained in the hands of the treasury. Maximin showed himself less prompt. He did not publish the edict; but, by his orders, his prætorian prefect, Sabinus, communicated it to the governors of the provinces, commanding them to let the municipal magistrates know that the emperors had given up the idea of converting the Christians to the State religion, and that they were no longer to be punished for their resistance. This was sufficient in the eastern provinces, as in Asia-Minor; the gaols were opened; the mines yielded up their prisoners; the Christians who had disguised their religion, took courage and showed themselves as they were. The confessors were welcomed with enthusiasm, the penitent apostates were received back to the fold. Upon the high roads resounded the joyous canticles of the liberated prisoners and the exiles returning to their homes. The religious assemblies, after an interval of eight years, were held again as of old. The Christians were specially attached to those which took place in the cemeteries, over the graves of the martyrs.

But these joys of religious peace were not of long

---

[1] The publication of the edict at Nicomedia took place on April 30, 311.

duration. No sooner was Galerius dead than Maximin transported to Nicomedia the seat of his tyranny and the scandal of his debaucheries, and along with them his fanatical zeal for the service of the gods. In the preceding years, he had caused all their temples in the Orient to be restored; now he reorganized the priestly colleges. Taking a hint from the Christian hierarchy, he established in each city a chief priest, and in each province a high priest, giving them authority over their colleagues, and loading them with honours and dignities. These pagan bishops and archbishops[1] were designated, of course, to take care that the gods should have no cause to complain of the liberty granted to the Christians. Spurious *Acts of Pilate* were fabricated, filled with blasphemies against Christ. An official having procured, by infamous means, pretended revelations with regard to the morals of Christians and the horrors of their assemblies, the greatest publicity was given to all these documents; they were placarded in all the cities and villages, and were imposed as text-books in the elementary schools.[2]

The *curator* of Antioch, a certain Theotecnus, conceived the idea of procuring an oracle against the Christians, by means of the god Zeus Philios, whose worship he had restored. The god demanded that the impious persons should be driven from the city and its surrounding territory. This demand, when brought to the knowledge of Maximin, pleased him greatly. At Nicomedia a similar request was presented to him by the magistrates of the town. The people of Tyre were unwilling to be behind-hand; to the petition which they sent him, the emperor replied by a letter full of unction and of gratitude. We still possess it, for Eusebius procured a copy of it, and inserted it in Greek in his *History*.[3]

---

[1] This organization had nothing to do with that of the cult of Rome and of Augustus. In the latter, the municipal priest of Rome and Augustus had no authority over his colleagues of the other cults, any more than he was himself under the authority of the provincial priest. Here, we are dealing with a general grouping of all the priestly colleges : such an attempt had never before been made.

[2] Eusebius, *H. E.* ix. 5.   [3] *Ibid.* ix. 7.

The movement spread : the municipal councils and the provincial assemblies hastened to follow an example thus encouraged in high quarters. The officials, besides, were on the spot, to stir up zeal. We still possess,[1] in part at least, the text, inscribed on stone, of the petition addressed to Maximin by the provincial assembly of Lycia and Pamphylia, and also of the emperor's reply. We see in the reply, as in the letter to the people of Tyre, that the petitioners were regarded with high approval, and that the greatest rewards were promised to them.

Thus strengthened by imperial approbation, the municipal magistrates could give themselves up with an easy mind to hunting the Christians. Soon troops of wretched beings were to be found wandering upon the public roads in search of a refuge. Yet still the edict of toleration had not been officially recalled. The magistrates confined themselves to forbidding meetings in the cemeteries, and the rebuilding of churches.[2] The Government did not acknowledge that anyone was punished for the simple fact of being a Christian. Constantine, moreover, intervened by means of letters, and set himself to restrain the frenzied zeal of his eastern colleague. But in the state of mind in which Maximin was, we can well imagine how easily he found pretexts for getting rid of the troublesome Christians. It was in this way that the Bishop of Emesa, Silvanus, was put to death, being thrown to the beasts with two companions; Peter, Bishop of Alexandria, was beheaded, without even the pretence of a trial; and several Egyptian bishops were treated in the same fashion. Lucian, the celebrated priest of Antioch, who had retired to Nicomedia, was arrested there, and, in

---

[1] *Corpus Inscriptionum Latinarum*, vol. iii. No. 12132, found at Arycanda in Lycia. The petition is addressed, according to the opening, to the three legitimate emperors, Maximin, Constantine, and Licinius. Yet the name of Constantine has not been reproduced on the marble : the place for it is left blank.

[2] Upon this point, the instructions of Maximin to the prætorian prefect, Sabinus, went beyond the edict, for the edict allowed the Christians *componere conventicula sua*.

spite of the eloquent speech which he made in his own defence, was executed in prison.

These are examples of the kind of treatment to which the Churches of Asia-Minor, of the Orient, and of Egypt had to submit, during the two years that the tyranny of Maximin lay heavy upon them. To these miseries was added also, in Syria at least, the scourge of famine and that of contagious disease. Eusebius has left us[1] affecting details on this subject. The Christians around him distinguished themselves at this time by their charity to the sick and starving, without any distinction of religion, as well as by their assiduous care in burying the dead. They thus disarmed the hostility of many of their enemies. During this time, Maximin attempted to interfere in the religious affairs of the Armenians, who were friends and allies of the Empire,[2] and to force them to "sacrifice to idols." The Armenians rose in revolt, and war once more drenched the eastern frontiers with blood.

But the days of Maximin were numbered. At the beginning of the year 312, he heard that the war between Constantine and Maxentius, a war foreseen and expected ever since the death of Maximian,[3] had at last broken out; that Constantine was in Italy, marching from one success to another; that he had betrothed his sister to Licinius, and concluded an alliance with him. The Nicomedian Emperor then understood the danger which threatened him. He, the legitimate prince, consecrated by the choice of Galerius, and invested with the imperial insignia by Diocletian, entered into a secret treaty with the "tyrant," against whom had fulminated, for six years, all the

---

[1] *H. E.* ix. 8.

[2] In these Armenians (Eusebius, *H. E.* ix. 8) we must recognize, I think, the inhabitants of the five satrapies beyond the Tigris, annexed to the empire by the treaty of 297 (Mommsen, *Römische Geschichte*, vol. v. p. 445). They had not been reduced to provinces; they remained under the authority of their national chiefs. These were Christians, on account of the change of religion which had for some time been in process in the kingdom of Armenia.

[3] Constantine had pronounced against Maximian the *damnatio memoriae* ; on the contrary, Maxentius had declared him *divus*.

thunders of the Tetrarchy. When the news reached him
of the battle of the Milvian Bridge, he felt that it was he
himself who was defeated. Constantine had found in
Rome statues of Maximin placed side by side with those
of Maxentius, and—a more serious matter still—he found
letters which confirmed the alliance and the treason.
However, he did not at once take up a hostile attitude, but
he assumed for himself, or allowed the senate to give him,
the first place in the imperial triumvirate, a place which
had, until then, been accorded to Maximin. It was an
evil omen for the latter. He was officially informed of the
defeat of Maxentius, and at the same time he was invited
to leave the Christians in peace. He made a pretence of
compliance. In a new letter,[1] addressed to his prætorian
prefect, Sabinus, he reminded him that ever since his
accession to power (305) he had endeavoured to mitigate,
in the provinces of the Orient subject to his authority, the
severities enjoined by Diocletian and Maximian against
the followers of the Christian religion; that, when he
became emperor at Nicomedia (in 311), he had, it was true,
received favourably the requests presented to him against
the Christians by the inhabitants of that town and of many
others; that, nevertheless, he had not intended that anyone
should be ill-treated on account of his religion, and that it
was necessary to write to that effect to the officials of the
provinces.

This document was lacking in precision. The
Christians mistrusted it; they abstained from holding
assemblies in public, and from rebuilding their churches.
The new edict did not specify that they were authorized
to do so. The whole thing did not amount to more than
a purely formal satisfaction given to Constantine.[2] In
reality, things remained in the condition in which Maximin
had maintained them for the past two years.

[1] Eusebius, *H. E.* ix. 9.

[2] So far as Constantine was concerned, Maximin had not ceased
to be a regular emperor. On April 15, 313, fifteen days before the
battle of Adrianople, a letter from the proconsul of Africa to
Constantine still bears at the head the names of the three emperors
St Augustine, *Ep.* 88).

6. *The End of the Evil Days.*

This was the position in the spring of 313, when Maximin opened his campaign against Licinius. Being defeated on April 30, near Adrianople, he recrossed the Bosphorus, disguised in borrowed clothes, passed through Nicomedia, and did not stop until he reached the Taurus. There, in Cilicia, he was again in his former empire. But Licinius was following him closely; he forced the passes, and at last Maximin, in despair, poisoned himself at Tarsus. He died in frightful suffering. Before killing himself, he had thought for a moment that resistance was still possible, and, to conciliate the Christians whom he had so eagerly persecuted, he had an idea of issuing a fresh edict, giving them full and complete toleration.[1] But with him cruelty never lost its sway. At the same time as he granted liberty to the Christians, he ordered the execution of a number of pagan priests and diviners, whose oracles had induced him to engage in this disastrous war.

His edict, as regards its practical part, was absolutely similar to that which Licinius had hastened to publish at Nicomedia,[2] of which the following is the text :—

"Inasmuch as we have long considered that liberty of religion could not be refused, and that everyone ought to have granted to him, according to his opinions and wishes, power to act as he pleases in the practice of divine things, we had already given orders that every person, including the Christians,[3] may remain faithful to his religious principles.[4] But since different provisions

---

[1] Eusebius, *H. E.* ix. 10.

[2] The Latin text is in Lactantius, *De mort. persec.* 48, but without the prologue ; a complete translation in Greek is in Eusebius, *H. E.* x. 5.

[3] Greek, ἕκαστον κεκελεύκειμεν, τοῖς τε χριστιανοῖς, τῆς αἱρέσεως καὶ τῆς θρησκείας τῆς ἑαυτῶν τὴν πίστιν φυλάττειν. Unless a few words are lost, the original Latin ought to run, as nearly as possible, thus : *unumquemque iusseramus, non exceptis christianis, sententiae et religionis propriae fiduciam servare.*

[4] The edict of April 311.

have been added to the text by which this concession was granted to them,[1] it seems speedily to have come to pass that some of them have not been able to profit by it.

"While [2] we were happily together at Milan, namely, I, Constantine Augustus, and I, Licinius Augustus, and while we were consulting together upon all that relates to the public welfare and safety, amongst the things which appeared to us useful to the greatest number, we decided that the first place must be given to that which concerns the worship of the Divinity, by granting to the Christians and to everyone else perfect liberty to follow the religion which he prefers, in order that whatsoever Divinity there be in the celestial mansions may be favourable and propitious to us,[3] and to all those placed under our authority. Wherefore we have decided, being influenced thereunto by wise and just reasons, to refuse liberty to no man, whether he be attached to the religious observances of the Christians, or to any other religion which he finds suitable to him; in order that the Supreme Divinity, whom we serve in all freedom, may grant us, in all things, his favour and benevolence. Therefore, be it known to Your Devotedness,[4] it has pleased us to remove absolutely all the restrictions contained in the letters previously addressed to your offices regarding the Christians, as odious restrictions, incompatible with our clemency; and to allow every person who wishes to observe the Christian religion the pure and simple liberty to do so, without being troubled or molested. We have thought fit to dignify this expressly to Your Solicitude, that you may have full knowledge of our intention to give the Christians perfect and entire liberty to practise their religion.

"In making this concession to them, we wish also, and Your Devotedness will understand this, that others too should have the same entire liberty with regard to their religions and observances, as the peace of our own times requires, in order that everyone may have free

---

[1] The additional and restrictive provisions of Maximin.
[2] Here begins Lactantius' text.   [3] *Placatum ac propitium.*
[4] The document is addressed to an official.

licence to adore whatever he pleases. We have made this rule, in order that no dignity and no religion should be diminished.

"As concerns the Christians, we have decided in addition, that the places in which they were accustomed to assemble, and regarding which letters addressed to your offices have previously given instructions, if some of them have been bought by our imperial treasury or by anyone else, are to be restored to the Christians gratis and without asking any price for them, without seeking any pretexts or raising any doubtful questions; and that those to whom such places may have been given, must also restore them to the Christians, with as little delay as possible. These buyers, however, and those who have received such places as a gift, may address themselves to our benevolence, to obtain some compensation, for which our clemency will provide. And since the Christians possessed, not only their places of assembly, but others also, belonging to their corporate bodies, that is to their churches, and not to private individuals, these properties also you will cause all to be restored, on the conditions expressed above, without ambiguity or dispute, to these same Christians, that is to say to their corporations and conventicles, subject to the reservation already announced that those who thus restore them, without exacting any price for them, may rely upon an indemnity from our benevolence. In all this, you are to lend to the said body of Christians the most efficient assistance, so that our orders may be executed with the briefest possible delay, and that thus, through our clemency, provision may be made for public tranquillity. Thus, as we have already said, the Divine favour, of which we have had experience in such grave conjunctures of affairs, will continue to sustain our success, for the public weal.

"In order that the purport of this decision of our benevolence may come to the knowledge of all, you shall take care to publish this edict by means of placards posted up everywhere, and also give notice of it to everyone, that no one may be ignorant thereof."

This edict, in the name of the two emperors, Constantine and Licinius, but emanating immediately from Licinius, was undoubtedly addressed to the prætorian prefect of the Orient, who was charged with the duty of publishing it, and communicating it to the governors of provinces and other magistrates competent to execute it. It represented, first of all, the abolition, by Licinius, of all those restrictions by which, for eighteen months, Maximin had tried to impede the application of the edict of toleration; in the second place, it represented an addition decided upon at Milan, between Constantine and Licinius, which addition was directed to two points: (1) to religious liberty in general, which it declared to be full, entire, and absolute for Christians as for others, for others as for Christians; (2) to ecclesiastical properties apart from the buildings used for purposes of worship: it prescribed the immediate restitution of these, whether they had remained in the hands of the imperial treasury or had been disposed of, either by sale or gift, to private individuals.

Following upon the interview at Milan, another edict, earlier than this one, must have brought these liberal arrangements to the knowledge of the public in the West, and in Illyricum: we no longer possess the details of it, and it is only by its Eastern adaptations [1] that we are able to judge of it. As a matter of fact, thanks to these extensions to the edict of Galerius, the Christians, as individuals and as a body, were restored, by a kind of *restitutio in integrum*, to the position in which they found themselves before the persecution. But this position they had at that time only enjoyed by a tacit toleration: the new arrangements gave them a legal title.

7. *The Effects of the Persecution.*

At last, then, religious peace reigned; it was complete, without reservations, and extended to the whole Empire.

---

[1] Eusebius has preserved to us a letter addressed by the emperors to the proconsul of Africa, Anulinus, relating to the restitution to the churches of their confiscated properties (*H. E.* x. 5, Ἔστιν ὁ τρόπος).

The Christians breathed again; the Churches were re-organized in the full light of day; the sacred edifices were rebuilt, and the interrupted meetings were resumed. In this re-awakening to life, the memory of the dark days was soon obliterated, and then effaced entirely. It would almost have been lost to history, if the indefatigable Eusebius had not taken care to record some details of it at once. And even he did not think it expedient to present a general picture of the persecution. Leaving to others [1] the task of relating what they had witnessed around them, he confined his special enquiries to his own province of Palestine, contenting himself, so far as the other provinces were concerned, with reporting a few names and indicating a few general features of the situation. Unfortunately, however, the "others," upon whom he had relied, nowhere took up the pen, and it is only for Eusebius' own province that we possess exact information.

His book, *The Martyrs of Palestine*, written in the year 313,[2] just when the persecution was drawing to an end, enumerates forty-three persons condemned to death and executed by order of the governors of Palestine during the ten years 303-313. We must remark, first of all, that this number does not include the name of a single bishop, although there were, at that time, at least some twenty [3] episcopal sees in the province. The most distinguished of these dignitaries, Agapius, Bishop of Cæsarea, passed through the whole of the crises unscathed Eusebius [4]

---

[1] *H. E.* viii. 13.

[2] There are two recensions of this book : one, the shorter of the two, which in the majority of the manuscripts is attached to Book VIII. of the *Ecclesiastical History* ; the other and longer recension, of which the Greek text has only been preserved partially, or in an abridged form. There is a Syriac version of it, in a very full form, in a MS. of the year 411. (W. Cureton, *History of the Martyrs in Palestine*, 1861). Dr Bruno Violet (*Die Palästinischen Märtyrer des Eusebius*, in the *Texte u. Untersuchungen*, vol. xiv. 1896) has given a German version of it, making use of earlier texts and treatises. It should be completed by *Anal. Boll.*, vol. xvi., p. 113.

[3] Eighteen Palestinian bishops were present, in 325, at the Council of Nicæa.   [4] *H. E.* vii. 32, § 24.

praises his alms-giving and his talent for administration, but that is all.   Hermon, Bishop of Ælia, also came safely through all.   The only Palestinian bishop who made the supreme sacrifice at that time was a Marcionite bishop, Asclepios, martyred in 309.   With regard to priests, we hear only of Pamphilus, the learned and celebrated disciple of Origen, and a priest of Gaza, called Silvanus. Moreover, the last named was only sent to the mines, and, if he died there, it was not by sentence of the governor of Palestine.   Several deacons, exorcists, and readers[1] represent the lower ranks of the clergy rather more largely.

Nevertheless, we must not think that those whose names do not appear among the victims, properly so-called, remained absolutely untouched.   Eusebius, who is by no means well disposed to the bishops of his own country, relates[2] that, since they had not known how to lead the Lord's sheep, they were made leaders of camels, or set to look after post-horses.   These details evidently refer to persons who had survived, and into whose history it was better not to enquire.   Eusebius adds that, as regards the sacred vessels of the churches, they were submitted to many outrages on the part of the officials of the imperial treasury.

Another observation which the accounts given by Eusebius suggest to us, is that, in many cases, the persons executed were executed, not for the simple refusal to sacrifice, but for having complicated their refusal by words or actions calculated to aggravate it, for instance, by having made demonstrations in favour of those condemned, or assisting the confessors with too much zeal.   Enthusiastic believers, as always happens, lost no opportunity of distinguishing themselves.   Procopius, a reader at Scythopolis, thought it wrong that there should be four emperors,

---

[1] Romanus, rural deacon of Cæsarea, who was martyred at Antioch ; Valens, deacon of Ælia ; Zacchæus, deacon of Gadara ; Romulus, sub-deacon of Diospolis ; Alphæus, lector of Cæsarea ; Procopius, lector of Scythopolis.

[2] *Martyr. Pal.* 12.

and quoted to the audience a verse from Homer, in which *monarchy* was commended. Others spoke, in this connection of Jesus Christ as the only true King.[1] The governor, Urbanus, was going one day to the amphitheatre, where, it was said, a Christian was to be thrown to the beasts ; he met a group of six young men, who presented themselves before him with their hands bound, declaring that they also were Christians, and ought to be thrown into the arena.[2] Eusebius and Pamphilus had received into their house a young Lycian, Apphianus by name, a prize-winner of the schools of Berytus, and so fervent a Christian that he could not endure to live with his parents, who were still pagans. Pamphilus used to instruct him in the Holy Scriptures ; but, one day, he heard shouting in the street. The Christians were being summoned to a pagan ceremony. Apphianus could no longer restrain himself, made his escape without any warning to his hosts, rushed to the temple, where the governor was, sprang upon him, seized his hand, and tried to prevent him from offering sacrifice to the idols.[3]

Apphianus had a brother, Ædesius, a Christian like himself and a disciple of Pamphilus, a youth of superior culture and an ardent ascetic. He had been several times arrested, and was at last condemned to the mines of Palestine ; he escaped from them, fled to Alexandria, and lost no time in frequenting the audiences of the prefect. This official was a certain Hierocles, a great devourer of Christians.[4] Appointed to the government of Lower Egypt, he there applied his principles with the greatest severity. Ædesius heard him condemn some Christian virgins to a treatment which was far worse to them than death, and which was, besides, illegal. This was quite enough. Protesting against the sentence, he sprang upon the tribunal, gave the judge two resounding boxes on the ears, threw him on the ground, and trampled him under-foot.[5]

[1] *Martyr. Pal.* 1.   [2] *Ibid.* 3.   [3] *Ibid.* 4.
[4] Lactantius, *Institutiones.* v. 2 ; *De mort. persec.* 16.
[5] *Martyr. Pal.* 5.

A virgin of Gaza, threatened with the same shameful fate, protested against the tyrant who caused himself to be represented by such abominable magistrates. She was immediately put to the torture. In indignation a poor woman of Cæsarea, Valentina by name, caused an uproar and overturned the altar. The two women were burnt together.[1] Three Christians, Antoninus, Zebinas, and Germanus, imitated the exploit of Apphianus, and assaulted the governor during a religious ceremony: they were beheaded.[2]

From these accounts it may be concluded, I think, that the governors of Palestine, though much abused by Eusebius, must not be regarded as having displayed any special ferocity. They may have made examples, and severely chastised several Christians, who were in too great a hurry to declare themselves as such, or guilty of having infringed some special prohibitions. But we are not told of any of those wholesale executions, or of those refined and revolting tortures which we find in other provinces.[3]

After the year 307, the punishment of death was generally replaced by that of condemnation to the mines. But, by way of compensation, the punishment was applied very largely to considerable bodies of persons : for instance, to a whole assembly of Christians, who were surprised by the vigilant police of Gaza. The confessors were sent to the copper-mines at Phæno, to the south of the Dead Sea. It was a very desolate place. Thither also were sent, in large troops of a hundred or a hundred and thirty persons at a time, many Egyptian Christians, for whom a place could no longer be found in the quarries of their own country. Phæno ended by becoming a Christian colony. The condemned, apart from their work, enjoyed there a certain amount of liberty ; they assembled themselves together in various places, transformed into churches. Priests and

---

[1] *Martyr. Pal. 8.*   [2] *Ibid.* 9.

[3] We may notice also, that in addition to the forty-three martyrs mentioned by Eusebius, there were about ten Egyptians, who were arrested accidentally at Ascalon or at Cæsarea.

bishops were to be found amongst them, and presided over these assemblies. We may mention among them the Egyptian bishops, Nilus, Peleus, and Meletius; and also Silvanus, a veteran of the army, who had entered the service of the Church. At the time when the persecution broke out, he was exercising his priestly functions in the neighbourhood of Gaza; he was a past confessor. He was ordained bishop at Phæno itself.[1] There also officiated the Reader John, who had long been blind, and who knew the whole Bible by heart, and used to recite it without a book in the meetings of the confessors. These meetings were not always peaceful ones: even in prison they found means of quarrelling with one another. So much liberty displeased the governor, Firmilian. After a visit paid to these quarters, he informed Maximin of the state of affairs, and by the emperor's command the colony of Phæno was dispersed in other mines. Several executions took place at the same time; Nilus and Peleus were burnt, with a priest and the confessor Patermouthios, a personage highly esteemed for his zeal. This execution was ordered by the military commandant. There only remained thirty-nine infirm persons, incapable of real work; in this group were to be found the Bishop Silvanus and the Reader John. They were got rid of by cutting off their heads.

In Egypt the persecution was far more severe, especially in Upper Egypt, in the Thebaïd. Eusebius visited these regions while the persecution was still going on. He heard of wholesale executions, of thirty, sixty, or even a hundred martyrs who died each day, either by being beheaded or burnt alive; he heard of abominable tortures — of women suspended, naked, by one foot only, of confessors attached by their legs to branches of neighbouring trees which were forcibly brought close together: then, when the rope was cut, the branches flew back to their former positions, quartering the poor victims. It was all in vain; no amount of torture could

---

[1] This was, no doubt, one of the irregular ordinations performed by Meletius.

terrify these Egyptians, always severe in their life, and inspired by their enthusiasm and their resistance. The more executions there were, the more eagerly fresh victims presented themselves. In Lower Egypt, Peter, the Bishop of Alexandria, kept himself hidden, but with a watchful eye over his flock; several of his priests, Faustus, Dius, and Ammonius, figured among the victims. The first of these had already confessed his faith, nearly half a century before, when he was deacon to Bishop Dionysius[1]; he had now attained extreme old age. Some bishops also were arrested and put to death, after long confinement in prison. We hear of Hesychius, Pachymius, Theodore, and, above all, of Phileas, the learned Bishop of Thmuis. Before he became bishop he had filled high offices; he was a very rich man, and was surrounded by a numerous family. His relations and friends, and even Culcianus,[2] the prefect himself, did all in their power to save him from death, but in vain. He remained unshaken. With him died also Philoromus, the head of the financial administration in Egypt. From his prison, Phileas had written to his flock at Thmuis a letter in which he described to them the torments suffered by the martyrs of Alexandria. Eusebius has preserved a fragment of this letter.[3] As in the Thebaïd, there were executions of numbers at a time. Besides the martyrs of whom Phileas speaks, we hear of thirty-seven who, divided into four groups, perished on the same day, by means of different punishments — beheading, drowning, fire, and crucifixion.[4] Several of them were clerics, of various orders.

It was not only in their own country that the Egyptians

---

[1] Eusebius, *H. E.* vii. 11 ; viii. 13.

[2] This Culcianus was prefect from the year 303, as we learn from a papyrus published in 1898 by Grenfell and Hunt, *Oxyrhynchus Papyri*, Part I., p. 132. Hierocles, of whom we have spoken above, must have been his successor.

[3] Eusebius, *H. E.* viii. 9, 10. The Passion of SS. Phileas and Philoromus, published by Ruinart, may have been retouched here and there from Rufinus, but it contains parts which are certainly genuine.

[4] Compare the homily published by the Bollandists (January 18), and by Ruinart, under the title *Passio ss. xxxvii. Martyrum Ægypti-*

confessed the faith.   Several are mentioned by Eusebius
as having found martyrdom in Palestine and elsewhere.
He himself saw some of them, in the amphitheatre at
Tyre, who were thrown to the wild beasts, and whom
the beasts refused to devour.   When it was decided to
send recalcitrant Christians to the mines, the confessors
of the Thebaïd were despatched to the porphyry quarries,
near the Red Sea.   But this prison was not large enough
for all of them : and gangs of Christian convicts were
continually sent to Palestine, to Idumea, to the island of
Cyprus, and to Cilicia.

Besides Egypt and the Thebaïd, where the persecution
lasted so long, Eusebius mentions the African and
Mauritanian provinces,[1] in which it was of short duration,
as among the countries where Christians had most to
suffer.   The commentary on these words is furnished to
us by the long lists of Egyptian and African martyrs,
preserved in the Martyrology attributed to Saint Jerome.
With regard to Africa especially, groups of thirty, fifty,
and a hundred names recur very frequently all through
the calendar.   It is, apparently, to Diocletian's persecution,
rather than to any of the preceding ones, that these
hecatombs must be referred.[2]   The same impression

orum, with the text of the Hieronymian Martyrology for February
9 and 14, as well as for May 18.   The charming story of Didymus
and Theodora (*Boll.*, April 28, and Ruinart) is very doubtful as a fact.
St Ambrose, who had heard it related (*De virginibus*, ii. 4) places the
scene of it at Antioch.   Cf. *Bibliotheca hagiographica latina*, p. 1169,
1304.

[1] *H. E.* viii. 6.

[2] In the matter of descriptive documents, the Passion of Crispina
of Thagura (Theveste, December 5, 304) is the only one from the
hand of a contemporary.   Others, such as those of the three saints,
Maxima, Secunda, and Donatilla (Tuburbo Lucernaria, July 30,
mentioned also in the *Passio Crispinae* ; see *Anal. Boll.* vol. ix. p. 110) ;
of St Mammarius and his companions (*Vagenses*, June 10 ; *cf.*
Mabillon, *Analecta*, iv. 93 ; this Passion is by the same author as
the preceding one) ; of St Martienna of Cæsarea (July 11) ; of St
Fabius of Cartenna (July 31, *Anal. Boll.* vol. ix. p. 123) ; of St
Typasius of Tigava (January 11, *ibid.* p. 116) ; all belong also to the
persecution of Diocletian, but they were written fairly late in the
4th century.

may be deduced from the Martyrology as concerns Nicomedia, where the persecution raged very cruelly.

As to the other countries of the Orient, our information is very inadequate. We know from Eusebius that Silvanus, the Bishop of Emesa, suffered under Maximin, in the amphitheatre of his episcopal city; that Tyrannion, the Bishop of Tyre, and Zenobius, a priest of Sidon, confessed the faith at Antioch; that the former was thrown into the sea, and that Zenobius died under the agonies of the rack.[1]

The Bishop of Laodicea, Stephen, apostatized shamefully. Like his predecessor, Anatolius, he was a man of great culture, well versed in literature and philosophy, but either of weak character or a hypocrite, as his fall proved.[2]

At Antioch also suffered, quite at the beginning of the persecution (303), a certain Romanus, rural deacon of Cæsarea in Palestine, who was passing through the Syrian metropolis, and made himself conspicuous by his vigorous protests against the apostates. As to the clergy and the faithful of Antioch, we do not know what happened to them.[3] But the persecution was severe.

---

[1] Tyrannion and Zenobius must have been arrested outside their own cities, for they were under the jurisdiction, not of the governor of Syria, but of the governor of Phœnicia. It is also strange that Eusebius speaks of the Bishop of Tyre as having been thrown into the sea (θαλαττίοις παραδοθεὶς βυθοῖς) at Antioch, which was not a maritime town.

[2] Eusebius, *H. E.* vii. 32, § 22.

[3] Eusebius, in his Chronicle, places the death of Bishop Cyril in 301-302, before the persecution, and says, in his *Ecclesiastical History*, vii. 32, § 1, that the persecution reached a head (ἤκμασεν) under Tyrannus, his successor. It is impossible that he could have been mistaken to the extent to which he would have been, if we were to admit, on the faith of a document of very little authority, that Cyril had been condemned to the mines in 303, and sent to Pannonia to work in the marble quarries. The Passion of the Four Crowned Ones (October 8) mentions, it is true, a bishop *in custodia religatum, nomine Cyrillum, de Antiochia adductum, pro nomine Christi vinctum, qui iam multis verberibus fuerat maceratus per annos tres*, who had died in prison at the same quarries. But so grave a fact as the confession and exile of the chief Bishop of the Orient could not have

Eusebius [1] tells us of pyres on which the martyrs were burnt gradually over a slow fire, and of the altars on which, when commanded to drop grains of incense, they allowed their hands, flesh and bone alike, rather to be devoured by the flame. Without mentioning the names, he recalls the remembrance, apparently known to his readers, of two young girls, two sisters, distinguished by their birth and fortune as much as by their virtue, who were thrown together into the sea; and also the story of a noble lady, who, when the persecution broke out, fled with her daughters, no doubt beyond the Euphrates. Their retreat being discovered, they were being brought back to Antioch. But at the crossing of the river, in despair at the thought of the treatment, worse than death, which awaited them on their return, they escaped from their escort and threw themselves into the current. [2]

With regard to other countries, what Eusebius has preserved is the recollection of extraordinary punishments; in Arabia, Christians were killed by being hewn in pieces by a hatchet; in Cappadocia, their legs were broken; in Mesopotamia, they were suffocated, hung by their feet over a brazier; in Pontus, sharp-pointed reeds were driven under their nails, or the most sensitive parts of their bodies were sprinkled with molten lead. Certain officials distinguished themselves by their ingenuity in combining torture and obscenity.

If such horrors as these had come to our knowledge escaped the knowledge of Eusebius, and he had no reason for concealing it. We have spoken of his theological animosities. But, when he wrote, he could have had no cause for exhibiting them to such an extent. Peter of Alexandria was certainly not of his way of thinking. But has Eusebius kept silence as to his virtues, his learning, and his martyrdom?

[1] *H. E.* viii. 12.

[2] The lawfulness of suicide, in such a case, was recognized by the Church. There is a homily of St John Chrysostom in honour of these saints, *Hom.* 51; *cf.* Augustine, *De civitate Dei*, i. 26. St John Chrysostom gives the name of the mother as *Domnina*, and of the daughters as *Berenice* and *Prosdocia*. St Ambrose, *De virginibus*, iii. 7, and *Ep.* 37, also speaks of this story, with which he associates the name of St Pelagia.

through legendary stories, we could never have sufficiently distrusted the exaggeration of the narrators; in the present case, the man who relates them was in a position to be well informed, and little inclined to pervert the meaning of the documents which had been transmitted to him. When Eusebius wrote, the fires were scarcely extinguished: their ashes were still warm. We must therefore believe him. And, moreover, have we not other stories, less ancient and as well attested, to tell us that in matters of this kind anything and everything is possible?

As regards all the special occurrences, of which the recollection was consecrated in each country by religious observance, and cultivated by local hagiography, it would be impossible to enumerate them here. Among the documents which treat of them, there are very few on which we can rely for the details of the circumstances. Of the features which we can really gain from them, those which are of general interest are already known to us through Eusebius and Lactantius: the others have no importance except for local history.

8. *Literary Polemics.*

To the strife of laws and police was added that of literary controversy. This, indeed, had never really ceased. After Tertullian, Minucius Felix and St Cyprian had again set before public opinion the exposition and the defence of Christianity; to the Greek Apologies of the 2nd century had succeeded various writings, of which we still possess the text, but without knowing who were the authors of them.[1]

When Porphyry's book against the Christians appeared, Methodius and Eusebius had answered it at once. The persecution had excited the zeal of people who delighted—it is a characteristic of every age—in crushing the conquered. An African rhetorician, Arnobius, an official professor at Sicca Veneria, had for

---

[1] *Cf.* vol. i., pp. 153-4.

a long time attacked the Christians, when, suddenly
touched by divine grace, he became a Christian himself.
The bishop of that place, who did not believe in his
conversion, asked him for guarantees of it, and Arnobius
gave one of the most striking kind, by publishing a
searching attack upon paganism.[1] While he was thus
engaged in refuting himself, he seems at the same time
to have had in view a certain Cornelius Labeo, the author
of writings hostile to Christianity. His work bears the
mark of the haste with which it was composed; the style
of it is very careless; and with regard to the soul, its
origin and its immortality, the language of the author is
that of a neophyte inadequately instructed.

Arnobius had among his disciples at Sicca Veneria
another African who was to take a much more prominent
place as a Christian apologist.[2] This was Lactantius
(*L. Caecilius Firmianus Lactantius*), who had acquired as
a rhetorician a reputation sufficient to induce the Emperor
Diocletian to invite him to Nicomedia, and to entrust him
with an official professorship of Latin oratory. He had
begun life as a pagan, and was so still, to all appearance,
at the time of his promotion. At Nicomedia he was
converted. The persecution deprived him of his position;
he was reduced to private teaching, which was little
remunerative to a professor of Latin in this Greek city,
and especially to a Christian in such times. He employed
his enforced leisure in writing in the defence of his
beliefs. He was a man of ability. Happily for his
literary fame, he did not take Arnobius as his model, and
tried rather to imitate Cicero. Of his writings there are
preserved to us two little treatises: one on the nature of
man (*De opificio Dei*), the other on certain anthropo-
morphisms (*De ira Dei*); but also, and more important,
a great apologetic work, the *Divine Institutions* in seven

---

[1] *De errore profanarum religionum.* With regard to this book,
see Monceaux, *Histoire littéraire de l'Afrique chrétienne*, vol. iii.,
p. 241 *et seq.; cf.* Martin Schanz, *Geschichte der röm. Litteratur*,
Nos. 611, 749, *et seq.*

[2] Monceaux, *loc. cit.*, p. 286; Schanz, *loc. cit.*, p. 445.

books, of which he himself made a summary (*Epitome*).
It was the attacks of his enemies which made him take up
his pen. While the executioners were doing their worst
against the Christians, a certain sophist, whose name he
has not preserved, attacked them in his lectures. An
eloquent apostle of theoretical poverty, he could be seen
walking about in a short mantle, with his hair in disorder ;
but it was well known that his possessions were constantly
increasing, thanks to the favour of highly placed personages, that at his house a better dinner was served than in
the imperial palace, and also that no kind of austerity
was practised there. He preached to the public that the
duty of philosophers was to correct the errors of men,
and to guide them in the right way ; he praised the
emperors highly for having undertaken the defence of the
old religion and violently attacked the new, of which he
knew next to nothing, as was easily perceived. The
public, moreover, agreed that the time was ill chosen for
this kind of rhetorical display, and that it was discreditable
to trample in this way on the fallen. The sophist was
hissed.

After him another enemy of Christianity entered the
lists, Hierocles, formerly governor of Phœnicia, then
vicarius, and finally governor of Bithynia. He was a
very great personage and a councillor of the emperor ;
he had been a member of the famous council in which
the persecution was decided upon. He published a work
in two books with the title : *To the Christians, the friend
of truth*.[1] Lactantius considers it very well informed, and
especially familiar with the difficulties of Holy Scripture.
This can easily be explained. Hierocles had stolen
largely from Porphyry. On certain points, however, he
followed his own path. I do not know whence he had
obtained the information that Jesus, after being driven
away by the Jews, put Himself at the head of a band of
nine hundred brigands. The romance of Philostratus had
suggested to him the idea of making numerous com-
parisons between the Saviour and Apollonius of Tyana.

[1] Φιλαλήθης.

On this point he was attacked by Eusebius, who devoted a special book to him. When, later on, he became governor in Egypt, he had to do with an apologist of a different kind.[1]

As for Lactantius, a saddened witness of these cowardly attacks, they furnished him with the idea, not of measuring his own strength against that of the aggressors—for he did not think they were worth the trouble—but of taking up again, against all the adversaries of Christianity and with an appeal to the opinion of cultivated persons, the task which Tertullian and Cyprian had assumed before him. The first of these, he thought, had written with too much polemical ardour, the second had made use of arguments which appealed to Christians themselves rather than to their pagan adversaries. A calm statement in good style, and resting upon the ground of philosophy and literature common to all well-educated persons: this was what Lactantius intended to compose, and what he succeeded in producing. He was the Cicero of Christianity.

He was the Christian Cicero even to the Philippics; for it was certainly he (the fact is now scarcely disputed) who was the author of that spirited pamphlet, *The Death of the Persecutors*, published in 313, just when Licinius was posting up, on the walls of Nicomedia, the edict of freedom. Lactantius, who during the evil days had seen his friends massacred or tortured, and had found himself obliged to leave Nicomedia, returned there to enjoy the religious peace. He was still unhappy. It was only some years later that fortune smiled upon him: Constantine summoned him to the West, and entrusted him with the education of his son Crispus (about the year 317). He was then far advanced in years.

---

[1] This is the same Hierocles of whom we have spoken above, p. 34.

CHAPTER II

CONSTANTINE, THE CHRISTIAN EMPEROR

Conversion of Constantine. Religious measures in the West. The
Pagans tolerated and the Christians favoured. Licinius and his
attitude towards the Christians. The war of 323 : Constantine
sole emperor. Development of his religious policy. Measures
against the temples and the sacrifices. Foundation of Churches :
the Holy Places of Palestine. Foundation of Constantinople.
Death of Constantine.

1. *Constantine, Emperor of the West.*

THE victory of Constantine over Maxentius was universally
considered as an extraordinary event, in which the
intervention of the Divinity could scarcely fail to be
recognized. The senate expressed this idea by causing
to be engraved upon the arch raised in commemoration
of the event the two famous words: INSTINCTV
DIVINITATIS. The pagans, many of whom were also
fighting under the banners of the conqueror and in his
train, attributed their success to the abstract Divinity
which they honoured in their gods, or even to the
intervention of celestial legions, led by the deified
Emperor Constantius Chlorus.[1] But the general impression was that the catastrophe in which Maxentius and his
brilliant army had perished was the work of the God of
the Christians. Before the battle, the "tyrant" had
appealed to all the resources of pagan religion : oracles,
aruspicy, sacrifices, divination, all had been resorted to

[1] *Panegyricon*, ix. 2 ; x. 14. M. Boissier justly compares these
various interpretations with those regarding the Thundering Legion
(*La fin du paganisme*, vol. i., p. 44) ; *cf.* Vol. I. of this *History*, p. 182.

with extraordinary completeness. While marching against him, the soldiers of Constantine had displayed upon their shields the sign ☧, formed from the first two letters of the name of Christ. This was in consequence of a dream of their prince,[1] who had commanded them to depict this strange emblem upon their arms. Maxentius had relied upon the assistance of the ancient gods : Constantine had placed himself and his army under the protection of the Christian God.

The battle at the Milvian Bridge confirmed him in his reliance, and decided his definite adhesion to Christianity. But this reliance had its roots already in the past. It is probable that Christianity had gained some footing in the family of Constantius Chlorus, just as it had in that of Diocletian ; one of the sisters of Constantine had received the entirely Christian name of Anastasia. Although the edicts of persecution had borne the name of Constantius, as well as those of his imperial colleagues, he himself in his own dominions[2] had shed no Christian blood. Eusebius represents him as being himself a Christian at heart. Yet we cannot admit that he had made the formal declarations of adhesion involved in admission among the catechumens, and especially in baptismal initiation. Brought up in a family where Christianity was, if not actually practised, at least regarded favourably, Constantine had the opportunity during his stay at Nicomedia, of seeing how the faithful were treated there. The instigator of the persecution, Galerius, was his father's enemy and his own. When he became master in the western provinces, he immediately assumed a favourable attitude towards those who were being persecuted elsewhere. Nevertheless, it was still a long step from these tolerant inclinations to personal conversion, and the latter was in no wise suggested by the political circumstances. The Christians were far less numerous in the West than in Asia-Minor and the East. The Emperor of the Gauls, so far as he could be affected by the religious opinions of his subjects, had no reason for abandoning the old gods, and no

---

[1] Lactantius, *De mort. pers.* 44.　　　[2] *Vita Const.* i. 17.

political interest in declaring himself a Christian. But
this is what Constantine did. At the moment when he
undertook his expedition against Maxentius, anxious to
enlist on his side, not only all possible military support
and precaution, but also all divine assistance, he
bethought himself that the attitude of his father and
himself had certainly deserved the favour of the God of
the Christians; that he had even an assurance of it
already in the success which had always hitherto attended
them, while the other sovereigns, the enemies of Christianity,
Maximian, Severus, and Galerius, had all met with a most
tragic end. These reflections, which seem to have been
familiar to him, for he often refers to them in his letters,
he communicated to Eusebius later on, adding that, to
assist him in coming to a decision, he asked God to
enlighten him by some marvellous sign. Shortly afterwards, he saw in the sky, and his whole army saw it with
him, a Cross of light, with these words : " In this sign,
conquer "[1]; finally, Christ appeared to him in a dream,
holding in His hand the same sign which he had seen
shining in the heavens, commanding him to reproduce it,
and make use of it as a defence against his enemies. He
summoned the Christian priests, and asked them what was
this God who had appeared to him, and what was the meaning of the sign. It was then that he obtained instruction
in the Christian religion and openly professed it.

It is difficult to admit that Constantine could have
been down to that time so ignorant of Christianity.
The story, on this point at least, reveals a little arrangement. As to the visions, by day and by night, we have
no reason to doubt Eusebius when he tells us that they were
related to him by Constantine ; but it is difficult for the
historian to appreciate the exact value of such testimony,
and, speaking generally, to investigate with any profit into
such personal matters. Leaving, therefore, to mystery
the things which belong to mystery, we will confine
ourselves here to stating facts known as facts, and
to acknowledging that Constantine undertook the war

[1] Τούτῳ νίκα.

against Maxentius, and in particular the encounter at the Milvian Bridge, in the firm conviction that he was under the protection of the Christians' God, and that, from that time he always spoke and acted, in religious matters, as a convinced believer. The monogram of Christ, painted upon the shields of his soldiers, displayed at the top of the military standards (*labarum*), soon stamped upon the coins, and reproduced in a thousand different ways, gave an unmistakeable expression of the opinions of the emperor.[1] There were many others. Only a few months after the battle at the Milvian Bridge, we find, among his personal suite, a sort of ecclesiastical councillor, Hosius, Bishop of Cordova. Several letters, despatched in the name of the emperor about the year 313, give evidence of a lively feeling of Christian piety.[2]

In fact, the event had happened which Tertullian had declared to be impossible — a Christian emperor.[3] Constantine could already have signed himself, as his Byzantine successors did, $\pi\iota\sigma\tau\grave{o}\varsigma$ $\beta\alpha\sigma\iota\lambda\epsilon\grave{v}\varsigma$ $\kappa\alpha\grave{\iota}$ $\alpha\grave{v}\tau\text{о}\kappa\rho\acute{a}\tau\omega\rho$ $^\prime P\omega\mu\alpha\acute{\iota}\omega\nu$, "Christian prince and Emperor of the Romans." And it was not merely a question of private and personal opinions, the consequences of which might never have spread beyond the family circle or the private chapel. The change wrought in Constantine, whatever its degree of sincerity, was connected with external events of the highest importance, the defeat of persecution, and the downfall of Maxentius. It was impossible that they

[1] Upon this subject see especially Boissier, *La fin du paganisme*, vol. i., p. 11 *et seq.*

[2] We cannot admire too much the artless simplicity of certain critics, who approach this imperial literature with the preconceived idea that it was impossible for an emperor to have religious convictions ; that men like Constantine, Constantius, or Julian, were in reality free-thinkers, who, for political exigencies, openly proclaimed such and such opinions. In the 4th century, free-thinkers, if there were any, were *rarae aves*, whose existence could not be assumed or easily accepted.

[3] "Sed et Caesares credidissent super Christo, si aut Caesares non essent saeculo necessarii aut si et christiani potuissent esse Caesares.' —*Apol.* 21.

should not have produced a reaction in the management of the empire, that the "Emperor of the Romans" should not be inspired by the "Christian prince." This was felt immediately. The pagans deemed themsélves threatened; it was necessary to reassure them, and we have a proof of this desire in the edict which followed the interview at Milan.[1] In this it was expressly declared that religious liberty was not intended for the Christians only, but for everybody.

This was also guaranteed by the very fact that, if one of the two emperors was a Christian, the other was not. It is true that before the battle of Adrianople Licinius himself had also had a dream from heaven, and that in the moment of combat, he had caused his soldiers to invoke the "Supreme God" (*summus Deus*).[2] It is true that on the day after his victory he hastened to proclaim religious liberty. But, after the year 314, he was at war with Constantine, and his devotion to the *summus Deus* must soon have suffered from his irritation against his Christian colleague.

We must not think of the empires of Constantine and Licinius as two separate states, absolutely independent of each other; they were merely two parts of the same Roman Empire, governed by two imperial persons as colleagues. Under these conditions, if there were differences, and even very great ones, in administrative measures and in the distribution of favours, there was no result with regard to legislation and institutions as a whole.

Constantine allowed all the old religious institutions previously existing to remain as they were—the temples, the priestly offices, colleges of pontiffs, quindecemvirs, and vestal virgins; he himself preserved the title of *Pontifex Maximus*, and even the prerogatives of this office, in so far as they did not imply any personal compromise with pagan ceremonies. The public mint continued for

---

[1] *Supra*, p. 29.

[2] Lactantius (*De mort. pers.* 46) even gives us the words of this prayer, which, he says, an angel (*angelus Dei*) had revealed to Licinius during his sleep.

II   D

some time to strike coins upon which appeared, with the imperial effigy, an image of the Sun or some other divinity. All this may seem strange, and difficult to reconcile with serious convictions. But we must not forget that already, under preceding emperors, it was possible to be a municipal magistrate, governor of a province, a royal chamberlain, the head of the central departments of administration, and even a *flamen* of a city or a province, and at the same time to be a Christian, and that it was easy to secure dispensation from any religious ceremony incompatible with this profession. It was said that the supreme office had already been filled by a Christian in the person of Philip. All this was arranged by means of contrivances which might displease, and did actually displease, those who took strict views, but they were practised all the same. Constantine, who was the master, had no difficulty in reconciling his beliefs with his position ; and it was from this position that he hastened to enable his co-religionists to profit.

We have already seen that the measures agreed upon at Milan between the two emperors assured to the Christians the most complete religious liberty, as well as the restoration to the churches of their confiscated possessions. Constantine did not stop there. Understanding perfectly that the restitution of their real property was far from compensating them for all the havoc caused by the persecution, he tried to supply, by generous alms-giving, the more pressing needs of the impoverished communities ; he also wished that indemnities should be granted to persons who had suffered from the persecution. Bishop Hosius was appointed to arrange the details and to distribute the funds.[1]

Clerics were exempt from burdensome public functions —that is to say, especially, from municipal office and from statute labour.[2] Such exemptions had for a long time

---

[1] Eusebius, *H. E.* x. 6, Letter from Constantine to Cæcilian, Bishop of Carthage : Ἐπειδήπερ ἤρεσε ; cf. *V. C.* i. 41, 43.

[2] *H. E.* x. 7, Letter from Constantine to the proconsul Anulinus : Ἐπειδὴ ἐκ πλειώνων. This decided many ecclesiastical vocations ; it

been granted to physicians, to professors, and to persons
who had filled expensive priestly offices.   Constantine considered that the services rendered by the Christian clergy
deserved the same immunity.

There is no doubt that from these early days his piety
was displayed in the foundation of churches.   In Rome,
the old dwelling-place of the Laterani, on the Cœlian Hill,
which had several times been confiscated, belonged at this
time to Fausta, the sister of Maxentius and the wife of
Constantine.   The episcopal residence was transferred
to it: and in the autumn of 313 Pope Miltiades held a
council there.   It was not long before the construction of
a basilica annexed to this *domus ecclesiae* was commenced,
the existing church of the Lateran.   Others were raised,
by the care of the emperor, over the tombs of St Peter, St
Paul, and St Laurence.[1]   The princesses of Constantine's
family, who willingly took up their abode in Rome, also
built churches.   Helena, the emperor's mother, lived sometimes at the *domus Sessoriana*, beyond the Lateran, quite
on the outskirts of the city, sometimes at the villa *Ad duas
Lauros*, on the Labican Way.   Near the latter was a
Christian cemetery, in which slept the martyrs Peter and
Marcellinus, victims of the last persecution; Helena built
a small basilica in their honour.   When, later on, she
visited Palestine, and there recovered the relics of the
Passion, she reserved part of them for the *Sessorium*, which
soon became like a little Jerusalem, and even took its name.
Constantina, the daughter of Constantine, had a special
affection for another imperial villa, situated on the Via
Nomentana, near the cemetery in which was the tomb of
St Agnes; she raised a basilica there with a baptistery[2]

became necessary to forbid the clerical profession to members of
municipal bodies and to persons who were in a position to become
members.

[1] The Constantinian basilicas of St Paul and St Laurence were
very small, far below the dimensions of the churches of the Lateran
and of St Peter.

[2] It was in this baptistery that Constantina and her sister Helena,
the wife of Julian, were buried, in a large sarcophagus of porphyry,
which is now in the museum of the Vatican.   Another sarcophagus,

which still exists. Lastly, it is possible that the church of Anastasia, at the foot of the Palatine, derives its name from one of the emperor's sisters. This lady very nearly became empress. She had been married to an important personage, Bassianus, whom Constantine wished to make a Cæsar. He would have assigned Italy to him as his jurisdiction: Anastasia would have sat enthroned on the Palatine. Unfortunately, it was soon discovered that Bassianus and his brother Senecio were in too close relations with Licinius. Bassianus was got rid of,[1] and the surrender of Senecio, who had taken refuge with Licinius, having been demanded in vain, war broke out between the two emperors. Licinius was defeated at Cibales, in Pannonia, and afterwards in Thrace, and finally purchased peace by the sacrifice of Illyricum (end of 314).

This peace was only a truce. It lasted eight years (315-323). Of this period there remain to us several laws made by Constantine which testify to his good intentions towards Christians. He forbade the Jews, under penalty of being burnt, to stone members of their religion who were converted to Christianity[2]; he allowed the manumission of slaves to be recorded in church in the presence of the bishop and the clergy[3]; he ordered Sunday to be kept as a day of rest in all tribunals, public offices, and workshops of the cities[4]; he proclaimed liberty to make a will in favour of the churches.[5] As to paganism, he preserved to it its freedom, confining himself to the prohibition, in private houses, of the practice of divination; in the temples he allowed these ceremonies, and even, in certain cases, prescribed them.[6]

exactly similar to this one, received the remains of Helena, the empress-mother. This also has been transported to the Vatican. There are still to be seen, at Tor Pignattara, on the Labican Way, the imposing ruins of the mausoleum of Helena.

[1] "Convictus et stratus est," says the *Origo Constantini* (Anon. Valesii, ed. Mommsen, *Chronica minora*, vol. i., p. 8).

[2] *Codex Theod.* xvi. 8, 1.

[3] *Cod. Just.* i. 13, 2 ; cf. *Cod. Theod.* iv. 7, 1.

[4] *Cod. Just.* iii. 12, 2.   [5] *Cod. Theod.* xvi. 2, 4.

[6] *Cod. Theod.* ix. 16, 1, 2, 3 ; xvi. 10, 1.

But the good will of the emperor was soon sorely tried by the internal dissensions amongst his *protégés*. The Church of Africa gave him a great deal of trouble from the very beginning. There, two religious parties had been formed, both of which claimed to be the Catholic Church. The persecuting princes had made no distinction between Christians; heretics and orthodox believers had been proscribed together, and more than one among the dissidents had given his life for the common faith. But Constantine, for his own part, wished to bestow his support and favour exclusively upon the authentic Church; he had no wish to protect everyone indiscriminately. This at once furnished an urgent motive for his interest in the African dispute. The "Christian prince" wished to know where in Africa his brothers in religion were to be found. As to the "Emperor of the Romans," he had another reason for intervening, the quarrel having reached such proportions that public order was disturbed. Therefore it is not astonishing that he did all in his power to minimize the quarrel: that he brought about assemblies of bishops, and ordered official enquiries; that he himself assumed the position of arbitrator, and then carried out the execution of sentences decided upon, with mingled leniency and severity. The public officials were set to work, and post-carriages were used to carry the bishops to the places of the councils. We need not regard this as a special mark of favour to the episcopate. It was assuredly not for their own pleasure that the bishops took long journeys, at his invitation, to Rome, to Arles, or Milan; it was to assist the emperor in restoring order. In providing carriages for the bishops, Constantine was actuated by State reasons, just as Diocletian had deemed himself to be in imprisoning them.

2. *The East under the Government of Licinius.*

Under Licinius also there were meetings of bishops. The Christians, finally delivered from Maximin, breathed again, resumed their assemblies, restored the ruins of their churches—ruins both material and moral. Numerous

must have been the dedication festivals at that time, like
that of the great church of Tyre, at which the historian
Eusebius, already bishop of Cæsarea, was present. He
pronounced there a great formal oration, and, that this
might not be lost to posterity, he inserted it in the
last edition of his *Ecclesiastical History*.[1] Of two councils
held during the reign of Licinius, one at Ancyra, the
other at Neocæsarea, the canons and the signatures
remain to us. The canons belong, generally speaking,
to the ordinary category of ecclesiastical legislation—cases
of penitents, rules with regard to ordinations, and other
matters of that kind. But more than half the canons
of Ancyra treat of situations resulting from the recent
persecution; it was still quite close, and therefore it is
probable that this council was held about the year 314.
In the canons of Neocæsarea, there is no longer any
trace of the persecution. The two councils included the
bishops of Asia-Minor, Cilicia, and Syria; at both of
them there were present the Bishops of Antioch and of
Cæsarea in Cappadocia, Vitalis and Leontius.

The tranquillity, which such assemblages of bishops
imply, did not last long. Any influence which Constantine
may have had over Licinius, either directly or by means
of his sister Constantia, was soon destroyed by jealousy
and the spirit of intrigue. A time came when Galerius'
old companion-in-arms thought it necessary to prepare
his revenge for the campaign of 314. Constantine
became, for him, the enemy. In this state of mind
he could but distrust the Christians, of whom his rival
was the benefactor in the West and the hope in the
East. He began, as Diocletian had done, by dismissing
all Christians from his personal service and from palace
appointments. Then came the turn of the army: either
military service or Christianity must be renounced.[2]

---

[1] *H. E.* x. 4.

[2] With regard to the persecution of Licinius, see especially
Eusebius, *H. E.* x. 8, and *V. C.* i. 49-56; Council of Nicæa,
c. 11-14; Constantine's edict directing reparation for damages
caused, in Eusebius, *V. C.* ii. 24-35.

Everyone was forbidden to visit or assist the prisoners
—a measure which, especially at such a moment, was a
serious blow to the free exercise of Christian charity.
Though little inclined to severity in his own morals,
Licinius discovered that it was unseemly that women
should take part in public worship, or be catechized by
men; and even when men only were admitted to the
Christian meetings, they seemed to him too numerous
to be allowed in the towns: religious services had to
be conducted outside the walls. He had a particular
objection to episcopal assemblies as composed of
persons whom he suspected of being far too favourably
inclined towards his western colleague: councils were
forbidden, and many bishops were individually persecuted,
under various pretexts.

These regulations and proceedings did not, so far,
constitute an overt persecution. The profession of
Christianity and the exercise of public worship, apart
from certain restrictions, were allowed to private individuals. But as to soldiers, *employés*, officials, and
anyone who desired the imperial favour, it was no longer
the same. This was enough to cause many apostasies;
the Council of Nicæa, after Licinius, like that of Ancyra,
after Maximin, had to legislate upon this subject. There
were not only apostates: there were also confessors and
martyrs. Several bishops lost their lives, notably amongst
them Basil of Amasia.[1] The region of Pontus was treated
with special severity; in many places the churches were
closed, and even destroyed. It was at Sebaste, in
Armenia-Minor, that there took place the celebrated
drama of the forty martyrs of the frozen pool. We
still possess a touching document, the testament[2] of
these Christian soldiers; in it they took leave of their
friends, and bequeathed to them the only thing they
could dispose of—their own remains. Other episodes
have been preserved and cultivated by hagiographical

[1] Amasia was the metropolis of the province then called
Diospontus, later *Helenopontus*.

[2] Gebhardt, *Acta martyrum selecta*, p. 166.

tradition; it is safer to confine oneself to generalities, as they are enumerated by Eusebius, an eye-witness, and by Constantine, in his edict of reparation.[1] Many Christians lost their positions and honours, whether in the army or in the various public offices; saw their goods confiscated; were unjustly attached once more to the municipal bodies, exiled, banished to the islands, condemned to the mines, to the public workshops, to the *corvées*. They were made slaves of the imperial treasury, were even sold to private persons; and many of them, accused under one pretext or another, paid for their attachment to Christianity by the sacrifice of their lives.

The story of these sufferings resounded through the West. To borrow the language of Eusebius, that part of the empire which was still enveloped in darkness turned with longing eyes towards the countries where the light shone brightly. The tension between the two emperors steadily increased. It was not only the Christians who had cause for complaint. Licinius, a coarse and brutal soldier, was transforming himself more and more into a typical Asiatic tyrant. Constantine uttered remonstrances; but they were ill received. In this state of smothered hostility, peace was very precarious. Then an incident occurred. Licinius had charge of the frontier on the Lower Danube; he neglected this duty. The Barbarians crossed the river and spread themselves throughout Thrace. Constantine was then at Thessalonica; he marched against them, drove them back, and forced them to sue for mercy. But this operation had brought him into the territory of Licinius, to whom the "diocese" of Thrace belonged. Licinius was enraged: war broke out. Defeated near Adrianople (July 3, 323) and besieged in Byzantium, the Emperor of the East watched the arrival of the victorious fleet, commanded by Crispus, Constantine's son. He recrossed the Bosphorus, and again engaged in battle at Chrysopolis (Scutari) on September 18, 323; he was again defeated. His wife interceded for him, and his life was

[1] *V. C.* i. 30-35.

spared.   He was sent to Thessalonica, where doubtless he soon resumed his intrigues, for the soldiers demanded his head, and Constantine granted their request.[1]

The Emperor of the West entered Nicomedia : we can imagine the acclamations of the Christians.

3. *Constantine, sole Emperor.*

Constantine lost no time, and hastened to promulgate two edicts.   In the first,[2] he provided for the necessities of the situation, recalled the exiles, opened the prison doors, restored to the confessors the liberty, property, dignities, and positions of which they had been deprived ; Christian soldiers might, according to their choice, re-enter the army or remain at home with the *honesta missio* ; the inheritances of the martyrs and confessors were restored to their next-of-kin, or, if there were none, presented to the Churches ; the confiscated property of the latter was given back to them, but not the profits accrued ; in short, everyone was re-established in the state he had been in before the persecution, so far as possible.   In another edict,[3] Constantine openly proclaimed himself a Christian, recalling the memory of his victories over the persecuting emperors, and attributing them to succour from on High ; he expressed his wish to see all his subjects also embrace the faith, but declared that he would constrain no one, and that those who held other opinions were free to profess and practise their forms of worship in the temples, which would remain open.   At the same time he encouraged [4]

---

[1] *Origo Constantini* (Anon. Valesii), *M. G.   Auct. Ant.* vol. ix., p. 9 ; *cf.* p. 232.   With regard to the year, see Mommsen, *Hermes*, vol. xxxii., p. 545, and E. Schwartz, *Nachrichten*, p. 540 *et seq.*

[2] Eusebius has given this to us, according to the copy addressed to the inhabitants of the province of Palestine, ἐπαρχιώταις Παλαιστίνης (*V. C.* ii. 24 *et seq.*).

[3] Eusebius, *V. C.* ii. 48-59, has translated it from the Latin copy addressed "to the Easterns."

[4] Letter to Eusebius, *V. C.* ii. 46 ; this is only a specimen. Eusebius says that he was the first person to receive such a letter.

the bishops to rebuild their ruined churches, and to construct larger ones ; he gave orders to his financial agents to make them large grants from the public funds. Public officials were, from that time, principally chosen from among Christians ; if they were pagans, they were not allowed to take part officially in the ceremonies of their religion.[1]

These were the immediate measures. Constantine lived for nearly fourteen years longer. Nothing remained now of the Tetrarchy. He was henceforth sole master of the whole empire. His religious policy showed the effects of this. The idea of a certain equilibrium between the two religions is often attributed to him ; he maintained them both, it is said, holding them in mutual respect for each other, and dominating both ; being supreme pontiff of paganism by the very fact of being emperor, he extended his cognizance to Christianity, and thus presided over the whole religious system of his empire. This way of looking at things does not appear to me to have any foundation. Even over the pagan cults the emperor had no direct authority : his title of *Pontifex Maximus* corresponds to certain defined prerogatives, sufficiently limited, as a matter of fact, and in no way capable, in any case, of being extended to the government of the Church. But, apart from his sacerdotal titles and his religious sphere, the emperor was, for Christians as for pagans, the supreme lawgiver, the defender of public order, the distributor of favours. It was not an unimportant matter whether this enormous power leant towards one side or the other, or maintained its equilibrium.

There may have been equilibrium at the beginning. It was a great advantage for the Christians to find themselves in the same position as before the persecution, to be certain of their liberty, and even of indemnities for the losses they had sustained. At first they had no idea of claiming any more. This was already one guarantee for the pagans, and another was furnished them by their numbers, which in many of the western provinces greatly exceeded

[1] Eusebius, *V. C.* ii. 44.

those of the Christians. Finally, Licinius, who had never made any adhesion to Christianity, represented, as joint-emperor, the followers of the old religious traditions. From this resulted a certain parity between the two parties, independent of any political design and even of the private inclinations of the two imperial rulers.

I do not know what were the real convictions of Licinius. We have not a single writing of his which can throw any light upon his religious feelings. The case is otherwise with his colleague. Constantine was a convinced Christian, a somewhat lax one, perhaps, and holding a rough-and-ready theology. The Supreme Being, the *summus Deus*, the Emperor of Heaven, the antithesis to the pagan pantheon, complicated and confused as it was, appealed to him far more than speculations with regard to the Incarnate Word. But his monotheism was not simply a philosophical matter: it was essentially a religious monotheism, and religious in a Christian way— a monotheism revealed and manifested in Jesus Christ, a monotheism of salvation, the benefits resulting from which the Church preserved and propagated by its teaching, its discipline, and its worship. Penetrated by this belief, Constantine could see no reason why it should not be accessible to and accepted by everyone. Like Diocletian and so many others, he dreamed of religious unity. But, unlike his predecessors, he no longer deemed it possible with paganism, while he thought that it could be realized with the religion of Christ. Hence arose the decided and declared favour for the latter, which was manifested at once and steadily increased, and which was, no doubt, the cause of many conversions, thus modifying the numerical proportion of the conflicting parties. Hence arose also, to a certain extent, the pagan reaction under Licinius in the eastern provinces, in spite of the fact that it would have been to his interest in every way to conciliate the Christians.

Victorious in the final struggle, Constantine had no longer any rival to fear; in Nicomedia he found himself supported by a Christian opinion far more powerful than that of the Latin countries, and this opinion, alienated by memories of Galerius and Maximin, and recently exasperated by the brutalities of Licinius, was quite ready to support the Christian emperor in measures of retaliation. Many at that time must have thought and said that it was necessary to make an end of these sacrifices, so often insisted upon with violence, of these altars which had witnessed so many enforced apostasies, of these temples of idols, which were no longer taken seriously by anyone, and were now only frequented by persons who engaged in questionable conferences or unhallowed orgies. *Cesset superstitio!*

It is true that Constantine promised liberty to the pagans, but in what terms! "As to those who hold themselves aloof from us, let them keep their lying temples, if they wish. . . . There are some, it is said, who pretend that the use of the temples is forbidden them. . . . Such would have been my wish; but, to the detriment of the public welfare, this lamentable error still resists too strongly in certain persons."[1] The liberty thus reluctantly granted was evidently, in the mind of Constantine, only a precarious and temporary liberty. During the years which followed, various partial measures were adopted. Certain temples, notorious for the immorality of their worship, were prohibited and demolished; such were those of Aphaca, in the Lebanon, of Aegae in Cilicia, of Heliopolis (Baalbek) in Phœnicia. Others, notably that at Delphi, were deprived of their beautiful statues in bronze and marble, and of their other artistic treasures; all of these were transported to Constantinople, and served for the embellishment of the new capital.[2]

It appears that still further measures were taken. Eusebius[3] speaks of a law which forbade the erection of idols, the practice of divination, and finally all sacrifices.[4]

---

[1] Eusebius, *V. C.* ii. 56, 60.

[2] *V. C.* iii. 54-58; *cf.* the *Chronicle* of St Jerome, a. Abr. 2346 (332): *Dedicatur Constantinopolis omnium paene urbium nuditate.*

[3] *V. C.* i. 45; *cf.* iv. 23, 25.   [4] μήτε μὴν θύειν καθόλου μηδένα.

In 341, a rescript of the Emperor Constans,[1] addressed to the *vicarius* of Italy, refers to a law of Constantine against those who dared "to offer sacrifices." As we have not the text of Constantine's law, it would be difficult to affirm that it forbade sacrifices without reserve or distinction. Perhaps it was a question, as with regard to aruspicy, of ceremonies forbidden in private houses, and tolerated only in the temples.

Moreover, in many places, there was no occasion for the government to take any steps: the populace, converted *en masse* to Christianity, themselves broke their idols and destroyed their temples. This is what took place at Antaradus (Tortosa) on the coast of Phœnicia; the emperor strongly approved of this resolution, and rebuilt the town, giving it his own name.[2] The port (Maïouma) of Gaza did the same; Constantine gave it the name of his sister Constantia, and raised it to the rank of city.[3] To renounce the ancient gods was the surest way to win the favours of the sovereign.[4] We can easily imagine how many conversions, individual or in masses, were the natural result of this. Yet there were some who resisted. In spite of the example of Maïouma, Gaza preserved its temples and remained pagan. At Heliopolis, after having destroyed the temple of Venus, the emperor set to work to convert the population. But it was in vain that he multiplied his letters of exhortation, erected a great church, sent a whole staff of clergy, and organized large distributions of charity; it was labour lost: no one was converted to Christianity.

Among the various manifestations of imperial favour, one of the most striking was the official honour paid to the Holy Places mentioned in the Gospels and the Old Testament. Pious curiosity had long been directed

---

[1] *Cod. Theod.* xvi. 10, 1. *Cf.* St Jerome, *Chron.*, a. Abr. 2347 (333): *Edicto Constantini templa eversa sunt.*

[2] Eusebius, *V. C.* iv. 39 ; *cf.* Theophanes, p. 38 (De Boor).

[3] *V. C.* iv. 38.

[4] It was exactly the same situation as in the last years of Maximin, save that the imperial favour was reserved for Christians instead of for pagans.

towards the places mentioned in the Holy Scriptures. Revolutions, wars, vicissitudes of every kind, had never succeeded in effacing the memory of the Temple of Israel; notwithstanding all the transformations of Jerusalem, the Christians still knew where Jesus had been crucified and laid in the tomb. The church of Ælia, the edifice in which Narcissus, Alexander, and the bishops who succeeded them, were wont to assemble the faithful, marked, so it was believed, the site of the house where the Lord had celebrated the Last Supper, and where the disciples had assembled during the early days of Christianity. Other traditions were localized around the city, and throughout the whole of Palestine. In the 2nd century, Bishop Melito came from Asia into the land of the Gospel[1]; later on, Alexander of Cappadocia and his successor, Firmilian, were also attracted by veneration for the Holy Places.[2] Julius Africanus, a native of Ælia,[3] displayed an extraordinary zeal in seeking out Biblical memories in Palestine and elsewhere.[4] It was the same with Origen: among other monuments of the Gospel, he mentions, at Bethlehem, the grotto of the Nativity.[5] At the instigation of his friend, Paulinus of Tyre, Eusebius devoted a whole series of works to Biblical geography—a translation in Greek of the names of peoples mentioned in the Hebrew Bible; a description of Ancient Palestine, with its distribution into tribes; a plan of Jerusalem and of the Temple; an explanation of the names of places mentioned in Holy Scripture.[6]

[1] There is a letter from him in Eusebius, *H. E.* iv. 26.

[2] *H. E.* vi. 11 ; Jerome, *De viris,* 54.

[3] Grenfell and Hunt, *Oxyrhynchus Papyri,* n. 412.

[4] Vol. I., p. 333.   [5] *In Johannem,* vi. 24 ; *Contra Celsum,* i. 51.

[6] This last part only has been preserved, in Greek as well as in a Latin recension executed by St Jerome (See the edition of Klostermann in the third volume of the "Eusebius" published by the Berlin Academy). The works of Eusebius must have served as a basis for the curious map of Palestine, with a plan of Jerusalem, which was discovered on a mosaic pavement at Medaba, beyond Jordan (Stevenson, *Nuovo Bulletino,* 1897, p. 45 ; Schulten, "Die Mosaikkarte von Madaba," in the *Abhandlungen* of the Society of Sciences at Göttingen, Phil.-hist., new series, vol. iv. (1900).

The appearance of such works had already shown the interest awakened by the Holy Places.   Pilgrimages, which had, no doubt, begun before the Great Persecution,[1] were resumed as soon as peace was restored.   About the year 333, a pilgrim from far-off Gaul compiled, from his notes of his journey, a complete itinerary, outward and homeward, from Bordeaux to Jerusalem, one of the most precious documents of Roman geography.   When he arrived in Palestine, he took note there of all the sacred memories pointed out to him in the different localities. He is the most ancient witness of the magnificent buildings by which the piety of Constantine and his family had enriched the Holy Places at that time.

The colony of Ælia Capitolina, founded by Hadrian on the site of the ancient Jerusalem, consisted of [2] two distinct parts, separated by a valley.   On the east, upon enormous foundations, extended an oblong, rectangular platform, surrounded by porticoes ; this comprised the site of the ancient Temple, upon which now stood the Capitol ($\tau\rho\iota\kappa\acute{a}\mu\alpha\rho\sigma\nu$) dedicated, as all the provincial Capitols were, to the three Roman divinities, Jupiter, Juno, and Minerva. On the other side of the valley, upon the western hill, the town, properly-so-called, underwent a development almost exactly parallel to the buildings of the Temple.   According to custom, a wide street, bordered by colonnades, traversed it from one end to the other ; at its extremities were the public buildings.   About the middle, on the western side, this colonnade was broken to give access to a platform upon which was erected the temple of Venus. According to tradition, this platform had been constructed immediately over the place consecrated by the Crucifixion of the Saviour and by His tomb.   The Bishop of Ælia, Macarius, who was present at the Council of Nicæa,

---

[1] Observe that Eusebius, in his *Demonstratio Evangelica* (vi. 18), written before Constantine came to the East, speaks of Christian pilgrims, who came from all parts of the world to pray at the cave on the Mount of Olives, near which had taken place the Ascension of the Saviour.

[2] With regard to the topography of Jerusalem, I refer to the excellent articles of P. Germer-Durand in the *Echos d'Orient*, 1903-4.

obtained from the emperor the necessary authorization to make excavations. The buildings of the temple were demolished, as well as the platform which supported them; the earth, which had been used to level the ground, was removed; and finally, a tomb hollowed in the rock was brought to light again: it was recognized as that which they were seeking.[1] The exact spot of the Crucifixion and even the Saviour's Cross were also identified.[2] The emperor, informed of these discoveries, gave orders for the erection of a monument in this place, which should be worthy of such memories. Upon the enlarged site of the temple of Venus arose first an immense basilica, in front of which was a vestibule; its façade looked towards the East.[3] Behind this came a

---

[1] In the time of Jesus, Golgotha and the tomb were outside the city; shortly afterwards, the boundaries of the city having been re-arranged by Herod Agrippa, they were included in it; they were also inside the new enclosure of Ælia, which, on this side, appears to have coincided to a considerable extent with that of Herod Agrippa. With regard to questions of topography and history relating to these sacred sites, see, amongst others, the work of Major-General Sir C. Wilson, *Golgotha and the Holy Sepulchre*, London, 1906. I am less doubtful than he is about the value of the tradition.

[2] Eusebius, who in his *Life of Constantine* describes minutely the excavations of Macarius, says not a word of the True Cross. Yet the oratory of the Cross was then already in existence; he had himself mentioned it in his discourse of the Tricennalia (*De laudibus Constantini*, c. 9, p. 221, Schwartz), as well as the two other parts of the monument: οἶκον εὐκτήριον παμμεγέθη (the basilica), νεών τε ἅγιον τῷ σωτηρίῳ σημείῳ (the oratory of the Cross), μνῆμά τε (the Holy Sepulchre). Observe that even here he speaks of the Cross as a sign, not as a relic, σημείῳ not ξύλῳ. Perhaps he had some doubt upon the identity of the object. But whatever may have been his scruples, the wood of the Cross was soon publicly venerated in Jerusalem, and fragments of it were detached and dispersed by devotion throughout the whole world. This is attested about 347, twenty years after the discovery, by the *Catecheses* of St Cyril, delivered upon the very spot (iv. 10; x. 19; xiii. 4); an inscription of the year 359 found at Tixter, in the neighbourhood of Setif in Mauritania, mentions, in an enumeration of relics, a fragment *de ligno crucis* (*Mélanges de l'École de Rome*, vol. x., p. 441). Thenceforward, similar testimonies abound.

[3] With regard to this orientation, see Clermont-Ganneau, in the *Compte-rendus de l'Académie des Inscriptions*, 1897, p. 552.

great square court, ornamented with porticoes, where, in a special shrine, the relic of the Cross was preserved ; beyond this court, towards the west, was the holy tomb, contained in a building of circular form (*Anastasis*).

In spite of her great age, the Empress Helena, attracted by a pious curiosity, undertook the pilgrimage to Palestine. We can imagine her interest in her son's buildings. She herself began to search for other holy places. The grotto at Bethlehem, and another grotto upon the Mount of Olives, where, it was said, the Lord had often conversed with His disciples [1] and had taken leave of them just before His Ascension, were also enclosed in splendid basilicas.

Following the example of the emperor's mother, his mother-in-law also, Eutropia,[2] widow of Maximian Herculius, and mother of Maxentius and Fausta, was distinguished by her devotion to the Holy Places. She was especially interested in the monuments of Hebron. There were to be found the mysterious tombs of the patriarchs, Abraham, Isaac, and Jacob, with their wives, Sarah, Rebecca, and Leah. At some distance from the town, on the road to Jerusalem, was shown the well, dug by the Father of the Faithful, and also an enormous terebinth, so old that it was deemed to go back to the creation of the world.[3] It was, according to the legend, the famous oak of Mamre, under which Abraham had received the visit of the three heavenly messengers, one of whom was none other than the Divine Word. This old tree was the object of universal veneration. Every summer festivals were celebrated there, and a great fair was held : Jews, Christians, and pagans also, came thither in crowds. It was at this fair that, in the reign of Hadrian, the greater part of the prisoners after the Jewish insurrection were sold,[4] a bitter remembrance, which did not, however, over-

---

[1] *Supra*, page 63, note 1.

[2] Eutropia was mother-in-law of Constantius Chlorus, as well as of Constantine. To the first, she had given her daughter Theodora, the issue of a former marriage ; to the second, Fausta, daughter of Maximian.

[3] Josephus, *Bell. Jud.* iv. 9, 7 ; *Chronicon Paschale*, Olymp. 224, 3.

[4] St Jerome, *in Jerem.* xxxi. 15 ; *in Zachar.* xi. 5.

II   E

shadow that of the great patriarch. Eutropia discovered that near the sacred terebinth were idols and a heathen altar; she informed Constantine of this, and he gave the necessary orders to the bishops of Palestine and Phœnicia, that these relics of paganism should be replaced by a church.[1]

At Antioch also, at Nicomedia, and in many other towns, new churches were erected—imposing monuments of imperial favour. At Antioch, the principal Christian place of worship was in the old part of the city[2]; it was believed that this old church[3] dated from the time of the Apostles. Constantine constructed another, octagonal in form, with a high cupola dominating an immense court surrounded by porticoes.[4]

But of all the foundations of Constantine, the most important, alike in itself and in its consequences, was that of Constantinople. A thousand years before, some Greek colonists, coming, it was said, from Megara, had discovered, near the opening of the Bosphorus into the Propontis, the place where the deep cleft opens which has ever since been called the Golden Horn. Upon the actual spot where the Seraglio now stands, they traced out the place for a settlement, which they called Byzantium, from the name of a Thracian hero, no doubt honoured in that locality. It was an admirable situation, on a promontory easily fortified, surrounded on all sides by the deep sea, at the mouth of the Euxine, upon one of the most important commercial highways of the ancient world![5] Then began a long history of negotia-

---

[1] Eusebius, *V. C.* iii. 51-53.

[2] τὴν ἀποστολικὴν ἐκκλησίαν τὴν ἐν τῇ καλουμένῃ Παλαιᾷ διακειμένην (Theodoret, *H. E.* ii. 27).

[3] After the construction of Constantine's basilica, the title of Old, Palæa (παλαιά), was transferred from that part of the city to the building itself, the ancient church (Ath. *Tom. ad Ant.* c. 3).

[4] Eusebius *V. C.* iii. 50. The church was not dedicated until 341.

[5] Some years before Byzantium, Chalcedon had been founded on the other side of the Bosphorus, but in a position much less advantageous. Its founders were ridiculed by the whole ancient world for not having preferred the situation of Byzantium.

tions and wars, the episodes of which were mixed up with the ordinary life of the Greek world, at the time of its independence, then under the Macedonian kings, and finally under the empire of Rome. Severus, at war with Niger, had besieged Byzantium for three years, and then, having chastised it, had ended by reconstructing and enlarging it. Even in the recent war it had played its part; it had been necessary to oust Licinius from it. Constantine resolved to transfer to it the seat of the eastern empire, to make it a city really his own; for he would found it afresh, and it should bear his name, and, at the same time, it should be a city without a rival, a second sanctuary of the Roman power, a new Rome. The Tetrarchy had only possessed capitals of the second rank: Nicomedia, Sirmium, Milan, Trèves. Constantinople should be quite another thing, and this sovereign city should be a Christian capital.[1] The emperor had seen Rome in 312; he had returned there in 315 for his Decennalia, in 326 for his Vicennalia. He must have discovered that the old cults were still too full of life there to be easily uprooted or set aside. Upon the Bosphorus his hands would be free.

Byzantium had already possessed for a long time a Christian colony. It was from there that the famous heresiarch, Theodotus,[2] came to Rome towards the end of the 2nd century. According to somewhat vague traditions, the Christian settlements had been at first in the outskirts of the city, on the eastern shore of the Golden Horn.[3] Later on, these were transferred to the city; at the beginning of the 4th century there was a church in those parts called the Church of Peace[4]

---

[1] According to accounts collected by Zosimus (ii. 30) and Sozomen (ii. 3), he had first thought of the site of Troy. This is very improbable.   [2] See Vol. I., p. 217.

[3] Socrates, vii. 25, 26; *cf.* Pseudo-Dorotheus in Lequien, *Oriens christianus*, vol. i., p. 198; churches of Argyropolis (Foundoukly), of Elea (Pera), of Sycæ (Galata).

[4] Socrates, i. 16; ii. 16. The church of Hippo also bore the name of Church of Peace; the Council of Hippo, in 393, assembled *in secretario basilicae Pacis.*

(Irene, St Irene), which was no doubt the seat of the first bishops, Metrophanes and Alexander.[1]

The Church of Irene was near the market-place of Byzantium (*agora*), not far from which rose two important buildings of Severus, the baths of Zeuxippus and the Hippodrome; the latter had remained unfinished. Constantine carried the market farther west,[2] finished the Hippodrome, restored the baths, and, between the two, began the construction of his imperial palace, and of another palace for the new senate. The Church of Irene was restored at first and enlarged; but it was soon found insufficient, and another church was commenced, at a short distance, the Church of the Wisdom (Σοφία, St Sophia). St Sophia, the Senate, the Palace, and the Hippodrome enclosed a vast square, the Forum of Augustus, in which, as at Rome, a milestone of gold was erected. A long colonnade, which also dated from the time of Severus, led to the new market-place, the Forum of Constantine, near the principal gate of the enclosure of Severus. Beyond extended the new quarters, traversed by two great roads, one of which, parallel with the sea, followed westward the line of the old *Via Egnatia*, and ended in the Constantinian enclosure, at the Golden Gate; the other, more to the north, ran in the direction of the gate of Adrianople. Near the latter, and within it, the emperor built a large church in honour of the Apostles[3]; it was in the form of a cross, and rose in the midst of a court surrounded by colonnades. Eusebius, who saw it when quite new, was much struck by the

[1] These are the bishops whose names appear at the head of the most ancient episcopal lists; other catalogues are suspect, especially that of the Pseudo-Dorotheus, which gives Metrophanes twenty-one predecessors. There is every appearance that before Metrophanes the Christians of Byzantium were attached to the Church of Perinthus-Heraclea. The union of two towns under one bishop lasted for a long time in these parts (Vol. I., p. 382).

[2] The Forum of Constantine: his statue towered from the summit of an enormous column, the ruins of which still remain (the Burnt Column).

[3] The mosque Mohammedieh stands now upon this same site.

reflection of the sun upon its cupola of bronze. In the same court was the imperial mausoleum. Constantine had placed there twelve representative tombs, deemed to be those of the Twelve Apostles; his own sarcophagus occupied the centre.[1]

Besides these edifices, Eusebius[2] mentions other churches, both within and without the city; these were dedicated to the martyrs. He says also that, in this city to which he was giving his own name, Constantine would not suffer any idols in the temples, or any sacrifices upon the altars.[3] But "idols" were not wanting in the public squares and elsewhere. Many works of art and celebrated statues, the ornaments of temples and of cities, were brought to Constantinople at this time and employed in its decoration.[4] Some of them still remain; after so many centuries and revolutions, there is still to be seen, upon the site of the Hippodrome, the base of the celebrated tripod consecrated at Delphi by the Greek cities in thanksgiving for their victory at Platæa.

On May 11, 330, the dedication of the new city was celebrated with great pomp. Great expedition was shown in executing the emperor's orders; in fact, there was too great haste; for these hasty erections lasted but a short time. They were replaced by others, for the city "guarded by God"[5] was not destined to an ephemeral existence. Energetic measures had been adopted from the outset to attract the populace to it, by privileges, obligations of residence, official supplies of food, and gratuitous distribution of alms. Yet time was necessary

---

[1] *V. C.* iv. 58-60. Constantine, in the Greek Church, is a saint; he is given the title of ἰσαπόστολος, "equal to the Apostles."

[2] *V. C.* iii. 48.

[3] This is perhaps an exaggeration, or rather applicable only to the new city, the pagan worship being possibly tolerated in the ancient parts.

[4] Upon this subject, see Allard, *L'art païen sous les empereurs chrétiens* (Paris: 1879), p. 173. The *Scriptores originum Constantinopolitarum* have been brought together by Dr Th. Preger, in the little Teubner Collection, 1901 (1st part).

[5] θεοφύλακτος.

before the new Rome could attain the greatness of the old.[1] In this, as in other things, Constantine had opened the way, leaving to his successors the care of continuing his task. In this they succeeded. The original enclosure of Constantine was filled; it became necessary to construct another, much larger. The new Rome was developed, to confront, to the detriment, and at the expense of the ancient one. It furnished a magnificent centre of authority and an invincible fortress to the Roman power, then broken in the West. Behind its walls, the dynasties of the Middle Ages continued the succession of the Cæsars, and maintained against barbarian Slavs and Arabian fanaticism, the tradition of the old mistress of the world, a tradition which may have been weakened and confused to any extent, but which was a tradition all the same. From the religious point of view, it resisted Islamism for eight centuries, and propagated the Gospel among the invaders who attacked it from the Ural and the Danube. Unfortunately, from its very importance, it early became a grave menace to Christian unity. The Hellenized Rome of the Bosphorus could never succeed in coming to an understanding with the old Rome, which remained, or had become once more, Latin. History is filled with the accounts of their conflicts; their separation, which seems beyond all remedy, is one of the gravest disasters which has ever befallen the religion of the Gospel.

After the ceremonies of the dedication, the emperor took up his residence in Constantinople, and scarcely ever left it again. After the Festival of Easter, in the year 337, he experienced certain ailments for which he tried a course of hot baths; afterwards, he visited Helenopolis, where the memory of his mother was preserved as well as the cult of the martyr Lucian. Here his malady assumed such a serious form that he feared his end was approaching.

[1] According to Julian, *Orat.* i. 8, Constantinople as much surpassed all other cities as it was itself surpassed by Rome: τοσούτῳ τῶν ἄλλων ἁπασῶν μείζονα ὅσῳ τῆς Ῥώμης ἐλαττοῦσθαι δοκεῖ.

He removed to the imperial villa of Achyron, near Nicomedia, and, as he had not yet received Baptism, he asked the bishops to give it to him. The ceremony was presided over by the bishop of the place, Eusebius, a personage of somewhat grievous notoriety, as we shall soon see.[1] Constantine died on May 22. His three surviving sons were all absent; the one nearest to him, Constantius, came to superintend his funeral, and carried his body to the Apostoleion at Constantinople. The succession was not decided without some difficulty; affairs of State were still conducted in the name of the deceased emperor until September 9, 337, on which day his three sons were proclaimed Augusti.

Constantine has been, and still is, the subject of various estimates. The main fact of his reign, the conversion of the emperor and the empire to Christianity, has procured for him the enthusiasm of some, and the severity of others; for it is in the nature of men that their present passions display their fierceness even in their manner of representing ancient times. Unfortunately for Constantine, there was too much bloodshed in his history. We might pass over the death of Maximian and of Licinius, who were restless and inconvenient rivals; but his son Crispus, and the son of Licinius, and his wife Fausta! We have very little information with regard to these horrible affairs. Constantine wished that the details of them should be unknown; perhaps, by this imposed silence, he may have suppressed extenuating explanations. But, whatever may be the truth with regard to these domestic tragedies, it is not only the Church which has reason to rejoice in the first Christian emperor: the Empire also benefited under his government. So long as he lived, he secured to it religious peace, a wise administration, the safety of the frontiers, and the respect of neighbouring nations. It was no inconsiderable achievement.

[1] Eusebius, *V. C.* iv. 60-64. *Cf.* Jerome, *Chron.*, a. Abr. 2353.

CHAPTER III

THE SCHISMS RESULTING FROM THE PERSECUTION

Pope Marcellinus and his memory. Disturbances at Rome with
regard to apostates : Marcellus, Eusebius. Egyptian quarrels :
rupture between Bishops Peter and Meletius. The Meletian
schism. Origins of the Donatist schism. Council of Cirta.
Mensurius and Cæcilian, Bishops of Carthage. Schism against
Cæcilian : Majorinus. Intervention of the Emperor. Councils
of Rome and of Arles. Imperial arbitration. Resistance of the
Donatists : organization of the schism.

1. *The Roman Schism.*

AT the time when the persecution broke out, the
Roman Church had had at its head, for nearly seven years,
Bishop Marcellinus.[1] The edict of confiscation of ecclesiastical property, whether real or personal, was applied
without difficulty in Rome. The Christian community
there was so considerable, and so well known, that any
kind of disguise would have been not only dangerous but
impossible. The formal records regarding this seizure
were preserved for a long time, thanks to the belief of
the Donatists that they could find weapons in them
against their adversaries. Certain clerics were called
upon to make the surrender of the things confiscated—
there is no mention of the Holy Scriptures—and, when this
case of conscience presented itself in Africa, great stress
was laid upon their share in the transaction. Then came
the order to arrest the members of the clergy : it appears

---

[1] His name is mentioned in an inscription of the cemetery of
Callistus, anterior to the persecution. (De Rossi, *Inscriptiones
christianae*, vol. i., p. cxv.)

that they must have evaded a too severe application of
this order.   Only one priest, Marcellinus, and one exorcist,
Peter, are mentioned as having died at this time.   The
bishop escaped the first measures of severity, as did those
of Carthage, Alexandria, and Antioch ; but he died on
October 24, 304, at the moment when Diocletian arrived
in Rome, and when the persecution was everywhere raging
in its full severity.

For a person of such importance, it was sufficiently
unfortunate, at such a time, to die in his bed.   The memory
of Marcellinus was much ill-treated by the Donatists
during the course of the 4th century.   They included
him in the number of the *traditores* without bringing
forward any very clear proofs.   Several of them[1] went
farther, and charged him with a much more serious offence :
that he had offered incense upon pagan altars.   This last
accusation seems to have been admitted in Rome, at
least by the general public, towards the end of the 5th
century.   We have no other documents respecting it than
two apocryphal ones : the spurious Council of Sinuessa, a
composition a little later than the year 501, and the Life
of Marcellinus in the *Liber Pontificalis*.   These two documents agree in representing Marcellinus as having rehabilitated himself.   According to the council, a numerous
assemblage of bishops had established his fault and his
repentance, but had refused to condemn the sovereign
bishop ; according to the legend of the *Liber Pontificalis*,
the erring Pope, being once more arrested by his persecutors, showed more courage, and shed his blood for the
Faith.

Taken by themselves and reduced to their real value,
such testimonies would not be very compromising.   There
was in Rome, during the 4th century, a colony of
Donatists, who may well have spread abroad among the
people the idea of a Pope unfaithful to his duties at a
time of persecution, an idea which may have fructified,
later on, in the hands of those fabricators of false legends
and false councils, who were so active at the beginning

[1] Aug., *Contra litteras Petiliani*, ii. 202 ; *De unico baptismo*, 27.

of the 6th century. But we must take account of a fact, serious in another way because it throws light, not upon popular rumours, but upon the opinions of the superior clergy in Rome, and that immediately after the persecution. The Roman Church in the time of Constantine possessed a calendar in which were marked the anniversaries of the Popes and of the principal martyrs. From the time of Fabian (250) until that of Mark (335), all the Popes appear there, with only one exception, that of Marcellinus. Such an omission,[1] which cannot be accounted for by any errors in copying or other excuses of the same kind, cannot have been without reasons. In his *Ecclesiastical History* Eusebius confines himself to saying that, when the persecution began, Marcellinus was bishop; it is a simple chronological note. He is, otherwise, very little informed of what was taking place in Rome in his own time. In fact, something unpleasant must have happened; but we do not know exactly what it was.

Disorganized by the persecution, and saddened by the death of its bishop, the Roman Church passed through a crisis of considerable danger, less, perhaps, on account of the persecution than of the internal dissensions which followed it. The violence of the persecution appears to have diminished greatly after the abdication of Diocletian; when Maxentius was proclaimed emperor, it must have ceased altogether.[2] Yet the Christians in Rome were in no hurry to elect a new bishop. Maxentius was a usurper, a rebel. His good-will did not guarantee that of Galerius, who was then in open hostility against him and might at any moment become once more master of the situation. Nevertheless, when, after the death of Severus, Galerius had been driven back from Rome, and when Maxentius,

---

[1] Marcellinus is only omitted in the calendar; the Philocalian collection, which has preserved the calendar for us, contains a catalogue of the Popes, in which Marcellinus appears in his proper place.

[2] Eusebius, *H. E.* viii. 14, goes so far as to say that at the outset he pretended to be a Christian "to please the Roman people"; he adds, what is more probable, that Maxentius commanded his subjects to moderate the persecution : Τὸν κατὰ Χριστιανῶν ἀνεῖναι προστάττει διωγμόν.

then on fairly good terms with Constantine, appeared to have established his power, it was decided to incur the risk of the election. Towards the end of June 308, Marcellus was enthroned as Pope, after a vacancy of nearly four years.

He found that the question of the apostates had already come to the front, and was being discussed.[1] The danger over, the apostates were returning to the Church, and claiming even to enter it without conditions; while the authorities, the new Pope at their head, faithful to traditional principles, insisted that they should submit to penitential expiation. The number of apostates was legion, and the conflict which they let loose degenerated into a kind of sedition. From the temporary edifices where Christian assemblies were held, the churches not having as yet been given back, the dispute soon spread into the street, and public order was endangered. The government of Maxentius intervened, and, on the accusation of an apostate,[2] Marcellus was adjudged responsible for the disorder and banished from Rome.

He was succeeded, either in the same year (309), or in the year following (310), by Eusebius. This time, the election was not unanimous. Another candidate, Heraclius, was acclaimed by the party opposed to the infliction of penance. The schism was complete: troubles began once more. At the end of four months, the police again interfered, arrested the two leaders, and drove them out of Rome. Eusebius, banished to Sicily, died there shortly afterwards.

The edict of Galerius must have been known in Rome by the month of May, 311. Although Maxentius did not show himself unfavourable to the Christians, he had

---

[1] As to what follows, we have no other documents than the epitaphs of Popes Marcellus and Eusebius, composed long afterwards by their successor Damasus. The description they give of the state of things in Rome agrees very well with what we know to have happened at Carthage and at Alexandria.

[2] Damasus does not give his name, but says he had denied Christ in time of perfect peace (*in pace*)—that is to say, before the persecution. He was an apostate before the time.

maintained the confiscations carried out in 303. It seems
that he did not wish to be behindhand with Galerius in
the matter of toleration, and that his favourable attitude
towards Christianity was increased in consequence. The
Roman Church, after a vacancy of one or two years, again
gave itself a bishop, in the person of Miltiades (July
2, 311), and he obtained from Maxentius the restitution
of the confiscated places. The "tyrant" and his prætorian
prefect issued letters, with which the deacons of Miltiades
presented themselves before the prefect of Rome : the
churches were officially restored to them, and a formal
record of this proceeding was drawn up.[1]

This time, persecution was really over; the Roman
Church enjoyed external peace. It seemed further as
though internal peace were also successfully established,
for we hear no more, after that time, of the schism with
regard to penance. Other Churches were agitated by it
for a longer period.

2. The Meletian Schism.[2]

In Egypt, as elsewhere, the question of the apostates
gave rise to various opinions, and thereby, having regard
to the ecclesiastical usages of the time, to quarrels.
Religious peace was still very far off, when, in the spring
of 306, the Bishop of Alexandria issued a formal ruling
upon the matter, inspired by sentiments of mercy.

---

[1] This formal record, as well as that regarding the confiscation,
was brought forward by the Donatists at the conference of 411.
(*Coll.* 499-514 ; Aug. *Brev.* iii. 34-36 ; *Ad Don.* 17.)

[2] Upon the Meletian schism, see—(1) The canons in the letter of St
Peter of Alexandria, with the additions in the Syriac text, edited by
Lagarde in his *Reliquiae iuris ecclesiastici antiquissimae,* and retrans-
lated into Greek by E. Schwartz, "Zur Geschichte des Athanasius,"
in the Göttingen *Nachrichten,* 1905, p. 166 *et seq.* ; (2) Several extracts at
the end of the *Historia acephala* of St Athanasius contained in the
collection attributed to the deacon Theodosius (MS. at Verona, No.
LX.): (P. Batiffol, *Byzantinische Zeitschrift,* 1901, has carefully
republished them, and shown the link which connects them with the
Historia acephala) ; (3) Epiphanius *Haer.* 68, in which the original
history is already slightly illustrated with legends ; (4) Athanasius,
Apol. contra Arianos, 11, 59 ; *Ad episcopos Aegypti et Libyae,* 22, 23.

He had not the slightest idea of receiving apostates to communion without penitence; but in his judgment on particular cases, and in his estimate of the amends to be made, he gave evidence of a certain compassion for the sinners, as well as a certain eagerness to fill up the ranks of his Church, considerably thinned by so many apostasies. The opposition which he foresaw,[1] when publishing his tariff of penance, was not slow in manifesting itself.   A bishop of Upper Egypt, Meletius of Lycopolis, well known for his uncompromising severity, protested with considerable vigour, declaring that such a course was inopportune, that, before holding out a welcoming hand to the apostates, the end of the persecution should be waited for, and that then severe conditions should be imposed upon them. He did not go so far, as Novatian had done half a century earlier, as to deny to the fallen any hope of being restored to the communion of the Church.   Between him and Bishop Peter there were only questions of degrees and of the proper amount of penance.   But they were sufficient to lead to extremities.

After the short respite, which the Bishop of Alexandria had wrongly imagined to be the dawn of real peace, persecution was revived in the East.   Peter concealed himself again, and his representatives in the "great city" did the same.   Meletius travelled through Egypt, went from church to church, stirring up agitation upon the question of penance, and intruding himself to perform ordinations, in place of the Pastors whom the persecution kept in separation from their flocks, and of those whom they had chosen to fulfil their duties.   He even ordained bishops, without any respect for the rights of the metropolitan, Peter, who alone had authority in such matters. He thus drew down upon himself a severe letter from four of his colleagues, Hesychius, Pacomius, Theodore, and Phileas, then imprisoned together in Alexandria.[2] The Bishop of Thmuis and his three companions died soon after.   Nevertheless, the unmanageable Bishop of

---

[1] *Nachrichten*, 1905, p. 168.

[2] Migne, *Patrologia Graeca*, vol. x., p. 1565.

Lycopolis persisted in his attitude. He came to Alexandria, where he held communication with two ambitious
teachers, Isidore and Arius [1]—the latter an ascetic, the
other of more easy morals [2]—who disclosed to him the
place of concealment of the bishop's vicars. Meletius had
the audacity to replace them ; and chose, for that purpose,
two confessors, one of whom was in prison, and the other
at the mines, circumstances calculated to win for them
respect but not to facilitate the exercise of their ministry.

Peter, being soon informed of these vagaries, pronounced an excommunication against the Bishop of
Lycopolis, which was to last until a fuller examination
of the circumstances could be made. However, Meletius
was arrested and sent to the mines of Phæno, where he
found various persons of his own way of thinking, among
them another Egyptian bishop, called Peleus. They
sowed discord among the Christians of their own country
who were working in this prison. These unfortunate
beings, after labouring all day long, spent their nights
in anathematizing one another. When they were released,
in 311, their quarrels were not made up. They returned
to Egypt, with their hearts embittered, less against their
persecutors than against their brethren who did not share
their opinions. The martyrdom• of Bishop Peter did not
extinguish these angry feelings.[3] His successors were
restored in the possession of the churches ; an opposition
to them was started in conventicles, which were called
"churches of the martyrs"—a strange title, for, after all,
Phileas and his companions, and Bishop Peter himself,
credited with being the patrons of apostates, had laid down
their lives for the faith ; while Meletius, on his return from
the mines, ended by dying in his bed.

----

[1] Perhaps the celebrated heretic.

[2] *Moribus turbulentus*, according to the Latin version.

[3] Athanasius, *Apol. adv. Ar.* 59, says that Meletius was condemned
in synod by Peter of Alexandria, for various misdeeds and for having
sacrificed, ἐπὶ θυσίᾳ. This last imputation is very improbable. It
was not brought forward, or at least was not proved, before the
Council of Nicæa, which, if this had been the case, would not have
extended to Meletius such lenient conditions.

The schism continued; it ended in the establishment of an opposition hierarchy, which spread throughout the whole of Egypt, and lasted for one or two generations. We shall soon meet with it again.

3. *The Donatist Schism.*

Africa also was sorely troubled by schism; things even went considerably farther there than in Egypt.[1] As a consequence of the abdication of Maximian in 305, the African provinces came under the imperial jurisdiction of the Cæsar Severus. It was not without difficulty that Maxentius succeeded in obtaining recognition in that country. The *vicarius* of Africa, Alexander, vacillated between the "tyrant" of Rome and the other emperors, legitimate but remote. He ended by quarrelling with Maxentius; and, to extricate himself from the difficulties of his position, proclaimed himself emperor in 308. This African reign lasted three years; Maxentius put an end to it in 311, before engaging in his own war against Constantine. His prætorian prefect, Rufius Volusianus, sailed from Italy and overcame Alexander, who was taken prisoner and executed.

The persecution seems to have been quickly over in Africa. When the churches had been destroyed, and the Scriptures burnt (*dies traditionis*, 303), when, for more than a year (304), Christians had been hunted out to compel them to offer incense (*dies thurificationis*), the government began to leave them comparatively in peace. It was possible for them to assemble in secret without incurring very much danger, and even to provide for the replacing of their bishops who had disappeared. This is what took place at Cirta, in the spring of the year 305: about ten bishops[2] met together there in a private house,

---

[1] Upon the documents with regard to this affair, see my memoir, "Le dossier du Donatisme," in the *Mélanges* of the School of Rome, vol. x., 1890.

[2] Council of Cirta, formal record read at the conference of 411 (iii. 351-355; 387-400; 408-432; 452-470; Aug. *Brev.* iii. 27, 31-33). St Augustine gives a long fragment of it (*Adv. Cresc.* iii. 30); cf. *Ep.*

to give a successor to Bishop Paul. The latter, as we learn from the formal record of the seizure of his church, drawn up in 303, had not been a hero. And this was the case with the majority of the persons present. The president of the assembly, Secundus of Tigisi, the senior of the Numidian bishops, conceived the idea, quite praise-worthy in itself, of making enquiries as to the conduct of his colleagues. One of them had refused to burn incense, but, the year before, he had been a *traditor*; another had thrown the Four Gospels into the fire; others had given up various books to the police, but not the Scriptures. With regard to Purpurius, Bishop of Limata, many damaging rumours were in circulation; he was accused of having killed two of his sister's children. He was certainly not at all an estimable person, and his temper was very violent. He was in a great rage with Secundus, who became frightened, cut short his investigations, and passed a general condemnation upon the sins of his brother bishops.

He was not himself above suspicion. It was known that he had been called upon by the *curator* and the municipality to give up the sacred books; but how he got out of it was less clear. Purpurius, quick of tongue, did not hesitate to tell him so to his face. As for Secundus, he had his own version of the occurrence.[1] To the messengers of the *curator*, he had replied majestically: "I am a Christian and a Bishop; I am not a traditor." When still pressed to give up at least something, however small its value, he had equally refused.

It was in this way that he explained the matter to Mensurius of Carthage,[2] about the time of the meeting at Cirta. Mensurius had written to him—it is not known to what effect—perhaps to consult with him as to the measures

---

43, 3 ; *Contra litt. Petiliani*, i. 23 ; *De unico bapt.* 31 ; *Ad Donatistas*, 18 ; *Contra Gaudentium*, i. 47, etc. ; Optatus, *De schism.* i. 14.

[1] Aug. *Brev. Coll.* iii. 25.

[2] The letters of Mensurius and Secundus, read at the conference of 411 (iii. 334-343 ; *Brev.* iii. 25, 27), are also quoted by St Augustine, *Ad Don.* 18 ; *De unico bapt.* 29 ; *Contra Gaud.* i. 47.

to be taken after the persecution.   The Bishop of Carthage related in his letter how cleverly he had evaded the search and substituted heretical works for the Holy Scriptures.[1] He spoke also of certain enthusiasts, whom no one asked to give up the Scriptures, but who went to the police, of their own accord, boasting that they possessed the sacred books, and proclaiming that they would never give them up.   The ill-treatment they thus drew upon themselves did not at all recommend them to the bishop, who forbade any honour to be paid them.   He was not less severe with regard to certain Christians of evil repute, notorious criminals or public debtors, who found during the persecution a respectable way of putting themselves right, gaining an honourable reputation, and even living comfortably in prison, where the generosity of the faithful enabled them to amass a little fortune for themselves.

We know from other documents that Mensurius, whose clever evasions could scarcely have been known to the public, passed at Carthage as a *traditor*, and that, if the opinion of lax Christians ignored this, he was severely condemned in the prisons, where the confessors were suffering pain and misery while awaiting the last penalty. Mensurius had thought it necessary to interfere actively in restraining the zeal of the faithful.   His deacon Cæcilian, who was charged with this office, necessary perhaps according to the bishop's ideas, but in any case odious, was accustomed to lay wait for persons at the approaches to the prisons and to intercept the food which was being carried thither.   The martyrs retaliated to these harsh measures by the excommunication : " He who is in communion with *traditores*, shall have no part with us in the Kingdom of Heaven." [2]

We see, then, that in Carthage the situation was somewhat strained.   Once more, as in the time of Decius, the

---

[1] *Supra*, p. 16.

[2] Passion of *SS. Saturninus, Dativus*, etc. (Migne, *P. L.* vol. viii., p. 700, 701).   This is a Donatist document, written after the beginning of the schism.   It is possible that some features in it may be exaggerated.   I do not accept it entirely.

confessors were in conflict with their bishop; and
Mensurius was not Cyprian. The senior bishop of
Numidia, who was well acquainted with the position of
affairs, replied to his colleague by extolling the grand
examples given in his own province, the severity of the
persecution, the resistance it had met with, the courage of
the martyrs who had refused to give up the Holy
Scriptures and, on that account, had suffered death. They
had a worthy claim to the honour they received. He also
spoke of his own conduct, in the terms quoted above.
This letter strongly reminds us of the one which Cyprian
received from the Roman clergy, after the first days of
persecution.[1] The result was that a certain agreement of
view was very soon arrived at between the Numidian
episcopate and the most zealous Christians of Carthage,
especially with regard to their estimate of Bishop
Mensurius and his attitude. The consequences were not
slow to disclose themselves.

Among the persons compromised in the "usurpation" of Alexander, and diligently sought for, when the
Maxentian reaction ensued, was a certain deacon, Felix,
accused of having written a pamphlet against Maxentius;
he took refuge with the bishop. Being called upon to
give him up, Mensurius refused.[2] His position in
Carthage must have been an important one, for the
proconsul did not feel competent to proceed on his
own authority. He sent a report to the emperor, who
ordered that, if Mensurius persisted, he was to be sent to
Rome. The bishop was actually put on board, pleaded
his own cause, and gained it. Obtaining permission to
return home, he died before arriving at Carthage.

As soon as the death of Mensurius became known,
immediate steps were taken to proceed to the election of
his successor. The deacon Cæcilian was elected. Three
bishops from the neighbourhood of Carthage,[3] Felix of

---

[1] Vol. I., p. 291.

[2] This circumstance is honourable to Mensurius, and proves that
he was not deficient in character.

[3] This was already the custom in the time of Cyprian : *Quod apud*

Aptonga and two others, took part in his ordination.
Nothing could have been more regular. But, unfortunately, Cæcilian was seriously compromised in the eyes
of the fanatics. Like the deceased bishop, he was to
them a *traditor*, an enemy of the saints, an ecclesiastical
persecutor. An opposition party was formed at once.
Two priests, Botrus and Celestius, were ostensibly at the
head of it. It was afterwards related that, before his
departure for Italy, Mensurius, anxious about the treasures
of his Church, had entrusted a large number of valuable
things to two old men, and that, without informing them
of the fact, he had also given to an old woman a document
mentioning this deposit, with an inventory of the treasures.
If any misfortune were to happen to the bishop, she was
to wait until his successor was installed, and then to hand
over the document to him. She did so, and this greatly
annoyed the trustees, who had made up their minds to
be unfaithful, and transformed them into enemies of
Cæcilian. But his most formidable adversary was Lucilla,
a lady of high rank, very devout, rich, and influential, of
a quarrelsome disposition,[1] and an old enemy of the
archdeacon, who, even before the persecution, had opposed
her practices of devotion.[2] She seized the opportunity of
doing him an ill turn. We know what people of this kind
are capable of.

The opposition party organized itself, refused to
recognize Cæcilian, and invoked the support of the
Numidian bishops, with whom they had long been on
friendly terms. One of these prelates, Donatus of *Casae
Nigrae*, had been staying for some time in Carthage ; even

---

*nos quoque et per provincias universas tenetur ut ad ordinationes rite
celebrandas ad eam plebem cui praepositus ordinatur episcopi ejusdem
provinciae proximi quique conveniant* (*Ep.* lxvii. 5). In Rome also,
it was the Bishop of Ostia, assisted by several neighbouring prelates,
who consecrated the Pope.

[1] *Potens et factiosa femina.*

[2] She was accustomed, at communion, before drinking from the
chalice, to kiss a bone which, she said, had belonged to a martyr—
who in any case had not been recognized as such (*vindicatus*) by the
Church of Carthage.

before Cæcilian's ordination, he had openly professed the greatest dislike for him, and had already held aloof. In these early days of the struggle he played an important part. As to the senior bishop, Secundus, he assembled his forces, and hastened to Carthage, to meddle with what was certainly no concern of his.

Seventy bishops were thus assembled to wage war against Cæcilian. Although he had been regularly installed, they pretended not to consider him a legitimate pastor, and held their meetings outside the ecclesiastical precincts which Maxentius first, and afterwards Constantine, had restored to him. Lucilla and her friends joined them, with all the fanatics and enemies of the acting clergy in Carthage. Cæcilian was summoned to appear before them. Naturally, he refused,[1] not being in any way subject to the jurisdiction of this irregular assembly, whose first duty should have been to recognize him as its head. His case was judged by default. It was decided that Felix of Aptonga, who consecrated him, having been a *traditor*, his ordination was null and void; he was also condemned for his attitude, as deacon to Mensurius, with regard to the imprisoned confessors. As at the council of 256, each of the bishops present gave a vote with reasons assigned. Several bishops from the neighbourhood of Carthage were condemned with Cæcilian; and first and foremost, Felix of Aptonga; all on the ground that they were guilty of being *traditores*. Without adjourning, the bishops then elected and ordained, in place of Cæcilian, a reader called Majorinus, who belonged to the house of Lucilla. The latter, now finally revenged upon her bishop, did not fail to reward those who

---

[1] Optatus relates (*De schism.* i. 19) that Cæcilian, learning that the power of his consecrators to ordain him was disputed, exclaimed: "Very well! Let them ordain me themselves, then, if they think I am not a bishop." Purpurius had then thought of allowing him to come, and of laying his hands upon him, not as a bishop, but as a penitent, which would have meant excluding him from the clergy altogether. These ideas, or that of Purpurius at least, are sufficiently probable.

had helped her, and sent considerable sums to
Numidia.[1]

To anyone who really understood the circumstances,
this council must have presented a singular spectacle.
From authentic documents it is clear that several, and
those the most influential, of its members were
traditores whose guilt was established ; and that upon
others, and upon Secundus himself, rested very grave
suspicions in that respect. This did not prevent them
from posing as defenders of the saints, full of righteous
indignation at the position of Cæcilian's consecrator. But
their sins were not known in Carthage ; some ten years
had still to elapse before they came to the knowledge of
the public. In the eyes of many people at the time, they
had the appearance of being upright and zealous judges ;
Majorinus was soon surrounded by a powerful party.

However, the churches were in the power of Cæcilian.
It was he whom the government consulted in all the
negotiations relating to the settlement of the last crisis.[2]
In a letter, addressed to him by the emperor,[3] Constantine,
already acquainted with the divisions in the African
Church, invited Cæcilian to seek the support of the proconsul Anulinus and the *Vicarius* Patricius, against those
who were the cause of disturbances.

It was then the month of April, 313. One day the
proconsul was accosted in the street by a large crowd of
persons, the leaders of whom presented him with two
documents, one sealed, the other open. The first bore the
inscription : " Plaints of the Catholic Church against
Cæcilian, presented by the party of Majorinus." The
other was a brief petition, in the following terms : " We
appeal to you, our good Emperor Constantine, for you
come of a just race ; your father, unlike the other
emperors, never practised persecution, and Gaul remained
free from that crime. In Africa, quarrels have arisen
between us and the other bishops. We implore your

---

[1] Four hundred *folles* ; nearly sixty thousand francs (£2,400).
[2] Letters in Eusebius, *H. E.* x. 5, 6, 7.
[3] Eusebius, *H. E.* x. 6.

Piety to send us judges from Gaul. Given by Lucian,
Dignus, Nasutius, Capito, Fidentius, and other bishops of
the party of Majorinus."[1] The proconsul received these
documents, and forwarded them. Constantine thus found
himself in the same situation as Aurelian at Antioch,
forty years before, that of being made cognizant of a
dispute between two Christian parties, and interested by
his regard for public order that it should be cut short as
effectually as possible. But Constantine was personally
influenced in this affair by sympathies quite different from
those of Aurelian. Besides, he was not requested to
pronounce judgment himself upon the dispute, but to
submit it to the consideration of bishops in a specified
country. The dissenting Africans obtained the judges
they asked for. The emperor selected Rheticius, Bishop
of Autun, Maternus of Cologne, and Marinus of Arles.
At the same time, he thought it his duty to send them to
Rome, and entrust Pope Miltiades with the office of
presiding over and controlling the debates. To this end
he communicated to the Pope[2] the act of accusation
received by Anulinus, and took measures to arrange that
Cæcilian should come to Rome, with ten African bishops
of his own party and ten of the adverse party.

The tribunal assembled in the house of Fausta, at the
Lateran,[3] on October 2, 313; there were three sittings.[4]
By agreement with the emperor, the Pope had added to
the bishops from Gaul fifteen Italian prelates[5]; so that

[1] . . . *et caeteris episcopis partis Donati*, runs the transcription of
this document in Optatus i. 22. But here, the ending has been
retouched.

[2] Letter from Constantine to Pope Miltiades in Eusebius, *H. E.* x. 5.

[3] This is the first time that the Lateran is mentioned in ecclesiastical documents. Perhaps the house of Fausta had already been
ceded to the Roman Church, either as a gracious gift or in compensation for some confiscated property.

[4] The formal record of the first sitting was read at the conference
of 411 (iii. 320-336, 403, 540; *Brev.* iii. 24, 31). A large fragment in
Optatus, *De schism.* i. 23, 24; *cf.* Aug. *Contra ep. Parmen.* i. 10; *Ep.*
43, 5, 14; *Ad Donat.* 56, etc.

[5] The Bishops of Milan, Pisa, Florence, Sienna, Rimini, Faenza,
Capua, Beneventum, *Quintiana* (*Labicum*), Preneste, *Tres Tabernae.*

there were nineteen bishops in all. Donatus of *Casae Nigrae* led the chorus of the opposition. Requested to state what was their cause of complaint against Cæcilian, they declared that they had no personal objection to him, and postponed to another sitting the statement and the proof of the objections which they raised to his ordination.[1] Donatus, however, formulated some causes of complaint which he could not substantiate. This led to his being accused himself. It was shown that, even before the ordination of Cæcilian, he had been a fomenter of schism in Carthage; he admitted that he had performed rebaptism, no doubt upon apostates,[2] and that he had laid hands on bishops who were *lapsi*, both of them things contrary to the rules of the Church. No more was done on the first day. At the second sitting the adversaries of Cæcilian refrained from putting in an appearance: the third day was given up to the votes, which the judges pronounced one after the other, first against Donatus, and then in favour of Cæcilian. We still possess that of Pope Miltiades, who spoke last: "Whereas Cæcilian has not been accused by those who came with Donatus, as they had announced,[3] and as he has not been upon any point convicted by Donatus, I think it is right to support him entirely in his ecclesiastical communion."[4]

The schismatics were thus condemned and by the very

Ostia, *Forum Claudii*, Terracina, *Ursinum* (?); this last name may perhaps represent Bolsena (*Vulsinii*), perhaps Urbino (*Urvinum*).

[1] It is thus that we may reconcile two points in St Augustine's summary: *ubi accusatores Caeciliani qui missi fuerant negaverunt se habere quod in eum dicerent . . . ubi etiam promiserunt iidem adversarii Caeciliani alio die se repraesentaturos quos causae necessarios subtraxisse arguebantur.* I think they intended to direct the debate upon the consecrator, Felix of Aptonga.

[2] The rebaptism of heretics was still practised by everyone in Africa. There was no reason to complain of Donatus on that account. As to his laying hands on the bishops, we cannot quite see whether it was a case of reordination or readmission of penitents; both were inadmissible, according to received custom.

[3] *Juxta professionem suam*; these words are not very clear.

[4] That is to say, in his position with regard to communion with them, such as he had before the schism.

judges whom they themselves had demanded. They set out on their return to Africa, but did not consider themselves beaten, and soon appeared again to assail the emperor with their protestations. The affair, they said, had not been examined properly, and in detail. From that time, Constantine had very little respect for these disturbers of the peace; he had willingly concurred in the judgment of the Roman council. But the accounts which his officials sent him from Africa were not reassuring. A little spark had kindled a great fire. Division was raging everywhere. Some of the bishops recognized Majorinus, others Cæcilian; often, in the same town, two parties organized themselves, one against the other. There were two bishops at Carthage; and the same state of things reproduced itself elsewhere. The minds of men were excited to an extreme degree: the followers of Majorinus called themselves the *Church of the Martyrs*, as the Meletians of Egypt had done, and described the others as the party of "the traitors." In such an over-heated atmosphere as this, the Church quarrels soon degenerated into acts of violence and street fights. The government was therefore justified in interfering in this unfortunate affair, however paltry it might seem, and in endeavouring to settle it.

Constantine decided to have the case tried over again. To this end he convoked a great council in Gaul, at Arles, to meet on August 1, 314.[1] It actually took place.[2] The schismatics supported their cause there

[1] We still have the letter of summons, addressed to the Bishop of Syracuse, Chrestus (Eusebius, *H. E.* x. 5), and the order given to the *Vicarius* of Africa, Ælafius, to send to Arles a certain number of African bishops of both parties (Migne, *P. L.* vol. viii., p. 483).

[2] With reference to this council, we possess a letter addressed to Pope Silvester, of which several recensions exist. That of the *Sylloge Optatiana* (Vienna *Corpus scriptorum eccl. latinorum*, vol. xxvi., p. 206) gives the convening letter in full, and an abridgment of the canons of the council; it is otherwise in the recension of the collections of canons which also contains the signatures of the members of the assembly. The following Churches were represented

with their usual insolence, which produced a most unfavourable impression. The bishops could scarcely
recognize such enraged fanatics as Christians.[1] Not
only did they refuse to listen to their accusations, but
they condemned the accusers themselves. They also
laid down the principles which ought to decide the matter :
" Whoever shall have given up the Holy Scriptures or
the sacred vessels, or betrayed the names of his brethren,
ought to be removed from the ranks of the clergy ; always
provided that the facts against him be confirmed by
official documents (*actis publicis*), and not by mere
rumours. If any such person has conferred ordination,
and there is no cause of complaint against those he has
ordained, the ordination so conferred cannot prejudice
him who has received it. And, as there are some people
who, against ecclesiastical rule, claim the right of being
admitted as accusers, while supported by suborned
witnesses, such persons must not be admitted, unless,
as we said before, they can produce official documents." [2]

Nothing could be wiser. It was necessary to put
a stop to the accusations, by which, almost everywhere,
the clergy were threatened by the discontented, to punish
those who were really guilty, to secure peace to the
innocent, and to pass condemnation in doubtful cases.

The Council of Arles profited by this opportunity
to regulate various points of discipline. We may note
here the understanding which was then established,

---

at the Council of Arles either by their bishops or by other clerics.
Italy : Rome, Portus, Centumcellae, Ostia, Capua, Arpi, Syracuse,
Cagliari, Milan, Aquileia ; *Dalmatia* : a bishop, whose name is
lost ; *Gaul* : Arles, Vienne, Marseille, Vaison, Orange, Apt, Nice,
Bordeaux, Gabales, Eauze, Lyon, Autun, Rouen, Reims, Trèves,
Cologne ; *Britain* : London, York, Lincoln, and perhaps a fourth
Church ; *Spain* : Emerita, Tarragona, Saragossa, Basti, Ursona,
and another Church of Bætica ; *Africa* : Carthage, Cæsarea in
Mauritania, Utina, Utica, Thuburbo, Beneventum (?), Pocofeltis (?),
Legisvolumini (?), Vera (?).

[1] *Graves ac perniciosos legi nostrae atque traditioni effrenataeque
mentis homines pertulimus.* Letter to Silvester.

[2] Can. 13.

upon the question of the baptism of heretics, between the Church on the continent of Europe and the Africans, those of them, at least, who followed Cæcilian. The African Church renounced the custom, for which Cyprian had fought so ardently sixty years before, and promised to conform to the rule observed at Rome and in the other Churches of the West.[1]

The decision at Arles was not without effect; a certain number of the dissidents joined themselves to Cæcilian[2]; but the leaders remained obstinate. As little satisfied with the Council of Arles as they had been with the Council of Rome, they again hastened to appeal to the prince who had given them this twofold opportunity of justifying their position. Constantine was extremely irritated at their obstinacy. Nevertheless, he was willing to exhaust all means of conciliation, and accepted their appeal.[3]

Either before or after the Council of Arles,[4] it had been decided by both parties to investigate the affair of Felix of Aptonga and his "surrender." The Donatists[5] had conceived the idea of going to the fountain-head, and obtaining a certificate from the municipal magistrates of Aptonga to the effect that Bishop Felix had really surrendered the Holy Scriptures in 303. The *duumvir* who had then been in office, Alfius Cæcilianus, was still alive. To him was sent a certain Ingentius, with instructions to get the necessary document from him. Alfius was a respectable pagan, sufficiently astute to guess at

---

[1] Can. 8.   [2] Aug. *Brev. Coll.* iii. 37.

[3] Letter of Constantine to the bishops of the Council of Arles, *Aeterna, religiosa* (Migne, *P. L.* vol. viii., p. 487).

[4] The date is not so exact as we could wish. We know that the Council of Arles was convened for August 1, 314; but there is nothing to prove that it assembled exactly at that time, and we do not know how long the bishops remained assembled. However, it was certainly held in 314. (*Mélanges de l'École de Rome*, vol. x., p. 644).

[5] We may now employ that term, because the celebrated Donatus, from whom the party took its name, must by that time have succeeded Majorinus.

once that they desired to take advantage of him, and
he refused to speak. However, one of his friends,
Augentius, who had influence over him, was induced to
intervene, and he was told that Bishop Felix, having
received in trust several precious books which he did
not wish to give up, desired a certificate that they
had been burnt during the persecution. The honest
Alfius was scandalized at this disclosure:—"Here is a
sample," he said, "of the good faith of Christians!" But
he consented to write to Felix a letter in which he recalled
to him what had happened in 303; how he had, in the
absence of the bishop, seized the church, taken away
the bishop's throne, burnt the doors and the correspondence
(*epistolas salutatorias*). The Donatist agent was obliged
to be content with this not very compromising document.
When he returned home, he made haste to complete it
by a post-script of quite a different meaning.

This letter, however, did not constitute an official
document. To give it that character, it was planned to
obtain its authentication by the *curia* of Carthage. Taking advantage of a journey which the *duumvir* Alfius had
taken to the capital, they summoned him to appear—at
the request of a certain Maximus, another Donatist agent
—before "Aurelius Didymus Speretius, priest of Jupiter
Optimus Maximus, duumvir of the illustrious colony of
Carthage," in order to certify the notorious letter. It was
increased by the post-script; but whether because he was
not allowed to read the whole, or from some other cause,
Alfius declared himself to be the author of the document.
This formal appearance took place on August 19, 314.[1]

The government also instituted enquiries of its own.
By command of the emperor, the *vicarius* Ælius Paulinus
summoned the ex-*duumvir* Alfius and his recorder from
Aptonga. They had to wait a long time at Carthage,[2]
for Ælius Paulinus had just then been replaced, and his

---

[1] "Gesta purgationis Felicis" (*P. L.* vol. viii., p. 718 *et seq.*; *Corpus
scriptorum ecclesiasticorum latinorum*, vol. xxvi., p. 197 *et seq.*).

[2] It was perhaps during this stay that Alfius Cæcilianus appeared
before the *duumvir* of Carthage.

successor, Verus, fell ill, so that the proconsul Ælianus
was obliged to take charge of the matter. He summoned
before him, not only Alfius, but also a centurion named
Superius; a former *curator*, Saturninus; the *curator* then
in office, Calibius; and a public slave, Solon. These were
all carefully interrogated at the proconsular audience
on February 15, 315. Alfius, being summoned to identify
his letter, examined it more closely, and declared that the
clauses compromising Bishop Felix had been added later,
and had not been dictated by him. The forger, Ingentius,
also appeared; he was not put on the rack, because he
happened to be *decurion* of a small town; but he confessed,
without torture, that he had added the post-script to Alfius'
letter to revenge himself upon Bishop Felix, against
whom he had some grudge. The report was despatched
to the emperor, who summoned Ingentius to appear
before him.[1]

Constantine was much embarrassed by this affair, for
he saw quite plainly that there was no way of inducing
such fanatics to submit with a good grace. At first he
thought of sending some trustworthy persons to Africa,
after sending back there[2] the Donatist bishops who were
prosecuting the interests of their own party at his court.
Some days after, he changed his mind, kept them with
him,[3] and summoned both parties to Rome, where he
spent the summer. The Donatists came, but Cæcilian,
we do not know why, did not appear. The emperor was
very angry at this. He threatened to go himself to
Africa, and teach both parties "how the Divinity ought
to be worshipped."[4]

Another year passed by. Constantine succeeded in
bringing together the two leaders, Cæcilian and his rival
Donatus, the successor of Majorinus as head of the opposi-

---

[1] Letter of Constantine to the proconsul Probianus, successor of
Ælianus, *P. L.* vol. viii., p. 489.
[2] Before April 28, 315, the date of the document "Quoniam
Lucianum," *P. L.* vol. viii., p. 749; *Corpus*, p. 202.
[3] Letter "Ante paucos," *ibid.*, p. 489; *Corpus*, p. 210.
[4] Letter "Perseverare Menalium," *ibid.*; *Corpus*, p. 211.

tion Church. A formal debate took place, at the end of which the emperor declared himself in favour of Cæcilian. A communication of his decision was at once made to the *vicarius* of Africa, Eumelius.[1]

Nevertheless, the emperor wished to see if, in the absence of the two bishops, it would not be possible to reunite the two Churches. To this end, he kept Donatus and Cæcilian in Italy, and sent two commissioners to Carthage, the Bishops Eunomius and Olympius.[2] These spent forty days there, trying their utmost to bring about an understanding; but their mission of peace was opposed by the violence of the rebels. The bishops ended by declaring that those alone were Catholics who were in agreement with the Church spread throughout the whole world, and in consequence entered into communion with Cæcilian's clergy. The wiser spirits of the opposing party also came over to their side; but the majority remained inflexible. Donatus managed to elude the watch set over him, and returned to Carthage; Cæcilian did the same: and the religious war continued as fiercely as ever.

Constantine tried rude measures. The Donatists had possession of a certain number of churches in Carthage. He gave orders that these churches should be taken from them,[3] and, as they resisted, proceedings *manu militari* were resorted to. Nothing could have suited the enthusiasts of the party better: the champions of the martyrs could now look forward to becoming martyrs themselves. With regard to the impression made upon them by the execution of the law, we still possess a curious document relating to their eviction from three churches in Carthage.[4] During the first eviction, no blood was spilt, but the soldiers

---

[1] Letter of November 10, 316, produced at the conference of 411 (iii. 456, 460, 494, 515-517, 520-530, 532, 535 ; *Brev.* iii. 37, 38, 41). *Cf.* Aug. *Contra Cresc.* iii. 16, 67, 82 ; iv. 9 ; *Ad Don.* 19, 33, 56 ; *De unitate eccl.* 46 ; *Ep.* 43, 20 ; 53, 5 ; 76, 2 ; 88, 3 ; 89, 3 ; 105, 8.

[2] Upon this mission, see Optatus, i. 26.

[3] A law mentioned by St Augustine, *Ep.* 88, 3 ; 105, 2, 9 ; *Contra litt. Petiliani*, ii. 205 ; *cf. Cod. Theod.*, xvi. 6, 2

[4] "Sermo de passione SS. Donati et Advocati," *P. L.* vol viii., p. 752.

installed themselves in the church, and gave themselves to
riot and debauchery; in the second, the Donatists were
attacked and beaten; one of them, the Bishop of Sicilibba,
was wounded; in the third, there was a veritable massacre;
several persons were killed, notably the Bishop of Advocata.[1]
Summary executions of this kind took place, no doubt, in
many places; a certain number of people were exiled,
either by way of precaution, or for having resisted eviction.[2]

But all proved ineffectual. The schism spread from one
end of Roman Africa to the other, in spite of all the
decisions, and in spite of the futility of the original strife.
People made up their minds to being unsupported in
their opinions; as to the decisions of emperor or bishop, no
notice was taken of them; communion with the Churches
over the sea counted for nothing. The Church no longer
existed save in Africa, and in the party over which
Donatus presided. Donatus was not an ordinary man.
He was intelligent and well educated,[3] and of ascetic
morality; he ruled with a very high hand the strange
following whose chief he was, and among whom we are
a little astonished to find him. But, like Tertullian,
Donatus was very domineering, and in his own world,
such as it was, he reigned supreme. His followers, who
were very proud of him, treated him as a being of a
higher order than themselves.

If the schism flourished at Carthage, and in the proconsular province, this was nothing in comparison with

[1] If strictly pressed, all these things may have happened in the
same church; the account is more eloquent than lucid. *Cf.* the
conjectures of M. Gauckler (*Comptes rendus de l'Académie des Inscriptions*, 1898, p. 499), and of M. Gsell (*Mélanges de l'École de Rome*,
1899, p. 60) upon the name Advocata and of the bishop killed in this
affair.

[2] The *comes* Leontius and the *dux* Ursacius, who were concerned
in these reprisals, left a memory odious to the Donatists. Upon
these personages, see Pallu de Lessert, *Fastes des provinces africaines*,
vol. ii., pp. 174, 233.

[3] No writing of his has been preserved. St Jerome (*De viris*, 93)
knew of Donatus' many writings pertaining to his heresy (*multa ad
suam haeresim pertinentia*), and also a treatise on the Holy Spirit, in
conformity with Arian doctrine.

its success in Numidia. There, almost everyone was
Donatist. The Catholics in those parts had a very hard
life. They were forced to realize the emptiness of
official protection. No one wished to have anything to
do with them, not only from a religious point of view,
but even in ordinary life. No one spoke to them, no one
answered their letters; everyone sought occasions for
insulting them, and at a pinch for murdering them:
"What communication can there be between the sons of
the martyrs and the followers of traitors?"

The "sons of the martyrs" had a severe trial in 320.
In that year, a conflict arose between the Bishop of Cirta
(called at this time Constantina) and one of his deacons.
This bishop was Silvanus, one of the original supporters
and leaders of Donatism. The deacon Nundinarius had
been excommunicated by him—we do not know for what
reason; he claimed even to have been pelted to some
extent with stones. He went to complain to various
bishops in the district, threatening, if reparation were
not given him in Constantina, to reveal dangerous secrets.
The prelates, to whom he appealed, tried to intervene;
some of them were interested in securing the deacon's
silence. But they could not succeed in closing his mouth,
and the dispute ended in an official enquiry, over which
the *consularis* of Numidia, Zenophilus, presided in due
form. The government was not at all sorry to take the
great Donatist leaders red-handed in this way, and to
discredit them in the public opinion. The matter was
examined at a public hearing, at the request of
Nundinarius, on December 13, 320.

The formal record respecting the seizure of the church
at Cirta, in 303, was produced, and it appeared from this that
Silvanus, then a sub-deacon, had assisted his bishop in
giving up to the magistrates the sacred vessels of his
church. This enemy of *traditores*, who for years was
engaged in railing against them, had been himself a
traditor. The fact was established by evidence, that
Silvanus and Purpurius, the notorious and violent Bishop
of Limata, were thieves; that they had appropriated jars

of vinegar belonging to the fiscal authorities and deposited in a temple, one taking possession of the contents, and the other of the jars; that Lucilla, the great patroness of the schism, had rewarded the services of the Numidian bishops, or (and this was a still more serious matter) that some of them had appropriated the alms which she had entrusted to them for distribution among the poor; also, that Silvanus had received money for the ordination of a priest. Nundinarius also brought forward evidence with regard to the election of Silvanus, which proved the strong dislike with which it had been regarded by a section of the people, and in addition a strange record, in which the consecrators of that bishop confessed to having been guilty of various acts of *traditio*.[1]

As a result of this, a circumstantial account of the whole affair was drawn up, of which only a portion remains to us. Silvanus was exiled, it would be hard to say exactly for what reason; the misdeeds with which Nundinarius reproached him were, after all, mostly of an ecclesiastical character,[2] and did not fall under the operation of legal penalties; we are led to conclude that he was considered as an instigator of disorder, and that therefore, like several others, he was banished in the interests of public tranquillity. The Donatists in the time of St Augustine said that, during the "persecution" of Ursacius and Zenophilus, Silvanus was exiled for not having wished to unite with the rest of the Church (*communicare*).[3]

It was not long before he returned, and with him the other exiles. Constantine, finding it impossible to subdue them by severe measures, soon decided, on their request, to let them alone. The letter of May 5, 321, in which he notifies this decision to the *vicarius* Verinus,[4] is as severe

---

[1] A document already made use of above, p. 80.

[2] However, the theft of jars of vinegar was a crime according to common law.

[3] Aug. *Contra Cresc.* iii. 30.

[4] Petition of the Donatists, and letter to the *vicarius*: *Coll.* iii. 541-552; *Brev.* iii. 39, 40, 42; Aug. *Ep.* 141, 9; *Ad Don.* 56.

as it could possibly be to the Donatists. It is the same
with another letter which he wrote, a little later, to the
Catholic bishops, enjoining them to bear patiently with
the insults of their liberated enemies.[1]   The emperor loved
to persuade himself that the agitators were but few in
number, and could easily be gained by methods of
kindness.   A fond illusion in administrative affairs!   He
discovered only too soon upon what kind of gratitude he
could rely.   At Constantina, the episcopal city of the
notorious Silvanus, he had constructed, at his own cost, a
basilica for the use of Catholics.   As soon as the building
was finished, the Donatists took possession of it, and no
official summons, no judicial decisions, no imperial letters,
could induce them to give it up.   Constantine found
himself obliged to build another church.   The best proof
we have of the supremacy of the Donatist party in
Numidia is, that they had succeeded in depriving the
Catholic clergy of their immunity from the duties of the
curia, and other similar offices, a privilege which had
already been granted to them by the State.   For this
purpose also the emperor was obliged to interfere.   We
must add that, while he thus left the African Catholics to
their fate, he carefully preached to them, in the most
edifying terms, the forgiveness of injuries![2]   This must
have been small comfort in tribulations which were only
too real.

[1] Migne, *P. L.* vol. viii., p. 491 : *Quod fides.*

[2] Letter "Cum summi Dei," Sardica, February 5, 330 (*P. L.* vol.
viii., p. 531) ; law of the same day in the *Theodosian Code*, xvi. 2, 7.

CHAPTER IV

ARIUS AND THE COUNCIL OF NICÆA

The parishes of Alexandria. Arius of Baucalis: his doctrine. Conflict with traditional teaching. The deposition of Arius and his followers. Arius is supported in Syria and at Nicomedia. His return to Alexandria: his *Thalia*. Intervention of Constantine. Debate on the Paschal question. The Council of Nicæa. Presence of the Emperor. Arius again condemned. Settlement of the Meletian affair, and of the Paschal question. Compilation of the Creed. Disciplinary canons. The *Homoousios*. First attempts at reaction,

AFTER the martyrdom of Peter (†312), the Church of Alexandria had for a short time at its head Achillas, one of the former masters of the Catechetical School. His tenure of office lasted but a few months, and he was succeeded by Alexander. Both of them had cause of complaint against Meletius and his schism ; but Alexander had besides trouble with Arius, one of his priests, and this difficulty was a great event in the history of the Church.

The city of Alexandria contained at that time, and subsequently, several churches controlled with a certain measure of independence by special priests. St Epiphanius[1] mentions several of these churches—*e.g.*, those of Dionysius, of Theonas, of Pierius, of Serapion, of Persæa, of Dizya, of Mendidion, of Annianus, and of Baucalis, which, perhaps, do not all date back to the time of which we are now speaking. Over all the members of these churches, both clergy and laity, the bishop had superior authority. To

[1] *Haer.* lxix. 3.

ensure the maintenance of this, and to preserve the unity
of the flock, regular meetings assembled the priests and
deacons together around the supreme head of the local
Church.

But there were decentralizing influences at work. The
Alexandrian priests remembered the time when they
themselves ordained their bishop.[1] During the episcopate
of Alexander, one of them, named Kolluthus, asserted
once more this power of ordination, and began to hallow
priests and deacons, without any reference to his ecclesiastical superior. But quite another matter presented
itself.

About the year 318,[2] the priest of Baucalis, Arius,
began to excite much discussion. He had already been
talked about with regard to the Meletian schism, with
which he seems to have been mixed up for some time.
After somewhat wavering as to his course, during the
episcopate of Peter and Achillas, he ended by regaining
his balance under Alexander. He was an elderly man,
tall and thin, of melancholy looks, and an aspect which
showed traces of his austerities. He was known to be an
ascetic, as could be seen from his costume, which consisted
of a short tunic without sleeves, over which he threw a
sort of scarf, by way of a cloak. His manner of speaking
was gentle : his addresses were persuasive. The consecrated virgins, who were very numerous in Alexandria,
held him in great esteem ; among the higher clergy he
counted many staunch supporters.[3]

[1] See Vol. I., p. 69. Some traces of this custom must have
remained, for it is still mentioned in the 5th century. (*Apophthegmata
Patrum*, ii. 78 ; Migne, *P. G.* vol. lxv., p. 341).

[2] This is all we can say, for the chronology of these early times
is very inexact. As it is impossible to place all the events between
the victory of Constantine over Licinius and the Council of Nicæa,
we have to go back to a period before the persecution of Licinius.

[3] With regard to the beginnings of the affair of Arius, apart from
the official documents, which will be quoted later, we have hardly
any serviceable information. The historical accounts are generally
of late date, hasty, and confused. Yet some details can be gleaned
from St Epiphanius (*Haer.* lxix.), and especially from Sozomen, i. 15,

Indeed, he had a party and a doctrine of his own. In Alexandria, it was not at all an exceptional thing to have a doctrine of one's own. We have seen before what could be taught, in the days when Clement and Origen ruled over the Catechetical School. That school was still in existence, and had abandoned neither the ideas nor the methods of its former masters. But still it was only a school; the teaching of Arius was given in the name of the Church. And the Church recognized at once that it raised difficulties. Later on, the Meletians claimed to have had their part in the recognition of this, and said that it was they who had awakened the bishop's attention. It seems more probable that the opposition against Arius originated with Kolluthus, one of his colleagues, perhaps the same man with whom we have just been concerned.

But however that may be, Arius was called upon for an explanation. During his youth, he had attended, in Antioch, the school of the celebrated Lucian. It was from this quarter that he had derived his system, which can be summarized in a few words.

"God is One, eternal, and unbegotten.[1] Other beings are His creatures, the Logos first of all. Like the other creatures, the Logos was taken out of nothingness ($\dot{\epsilon}\xi$ οὐκ ὄντων) and not from the Divine Substance; there was a time when He was not ($\mathring{\eta}ν$ ὅτε οὐκ $\mathring{\eta}ν$); He was created, not necessarily, but voluntarily. Himself a creature of God, He is the Creator of all other beings, and this relationship justifies the title of God, which is improperly given to Him. God adopted Him as Son in prevision of His merits, for He is free, susceptible of change (τρεπτός), and it is by His own will that He

who had before him documents which we do not possess in their entirety. According to him, Arius belonged at first to the party of Meletius; having then joined Bishop Peter and been ordained deacon, he again quarrelled with his superior. Under Achillas, he may have resumed his functions, and may even have been promoted to the dignity of the priesthood. *Cf. supra*, p. 78.

[1] In those days scarcely any difference was recognized between γενητός (become) and γεννητός (begotten), any more than between their contraries ἀγένητος and ἀγέννητος.

determined Himself on the side of good. From this sonship by adoption results no real participation in the Divinity, no true likeness to It. God can have no like. The Holy Spirit is the first of the creatures of the Logos ; He is still less God than the Logos. The Logos was made flesh, in the sense that He fulfilled in Jesus Christ the functions of a soul."

This idea of the Word as a creature, however remote from received tradition, was yet not without connection with certain theological systems professed at an earlier date.

From the time of Philo to that of Origen and Plotinus, leaving, of course, Gnosticism out of account, all religious thinkers formulated the idea of the Word with cosmological prepossessions in their minds. Their abstract God, their Being in Itself, ineffable and inaccessible, was so absolutely opposed to the world of sense, that there was no means of passing from one to the other, except through an intermediary who should participate in both. The Word proceeded from God, from the Divine Essence; but as He contained in Himself, in addition to the creative power, the idea, the pattern of the creation, He fell, in certain respects, within the category of the created. However like the Father He might be represented as being, there were none the less between them differences of capacities. Under such conditions, the problem was not resolved, but merely changed from one point to another. The two ideas of Infinite and Finite were confronted with each other, and in conflict, in the intermediate Person. The Word was linked to God by a mysterious procession, upon which there were many discussions with much use of figurative language, but which no one could clearly define. It could not easily be reconciled either with pure Monotheism or with the idea of a distinct Person, two essential data furnished by tradition, and based upon Scripture.

At the time of which we are now speaking, it is remarkable that everyone seemed to be in agreement to escape from this *impasse*. The followers of Lucian resolutely sacrificed the obscure idea, in favour of a clearer one; they no longer affirmed any Procession from the Substance. The whole Divinity was contained in the Father; He alone was truly God. The Word was the First of creatures, but a creature. He was no longer God, He was essentially distinct from God. It was thus that they thought to save Monotheism, and also the personality of the pre-existing Christ. The philosophical difficulty was eliminated, but with it had disappeared the very essence of Christianity. In complete contradiction to Arius, Alexander and Athanasius held firmly to the absolute Divinity of the Word. At the risk of appearing to agree with the Modalists, they cut short all idea of procession from without, paid no heed to the asserted necessities of cosmology, maintained, as best they could, the distinction of Persons, but preserved first and foremost the identity of the Word with God. The religious aspect of the question dominated everything. The heavenly Being, incarnate in Jesus Christ, must be God without qualification, and not approximately so, or as a way of speaking. Otherwise, He would not be the Saviour. That such ideas were difficult to translate into the philosophical language of that day, is a matter which they perhaps took into consideration, but they scarcely troubled themselves on that account; they were not concerned with cosmology, but with religion; not with scientific pro-prieties, but with tradition.[1] Besides, in treating of these Divine matters, is one called upon to explain everything? *Generationem eius quis enarrabit?*

This state of mind was not peculiar to the Bishop of Alexandria. We have seen instances of it elsewhere, and for a long time past. Side by side with scholastic theories, there had always been, even among highly cultivated persons, an opinion which respected these mysteries of

---

[1] Alexander was still influenced, more or less, by his Origenist training. We see traces of this in his two letters. He was like Eusebius of Cæsarea, an Origenist who had sacrificed one of the two halves of the system; but he had kept the good half—that which was commended by its agreement with tradition.

religion, which held fast to the essential doctrines, and distrusted persons who threatened to compromise these under pretence of reconciling them with other notions, or throwing more light upon them. Bishop Peter had already given an example of this state of mind, on the throne of Alexandria. After Alexander, it was very clearly maintained by Athanasius, who was already, at the time when our present narrative begins, a deacon and adviser of his bishop.

The doctrines of Arius were discussed first in the assemblies of the Alexandrian clergy, under the presidency of Alexander, who appears to have directed the debates with much moderation and kindness. The teaching given in certain churches of the city was brought forward, and it was shown to be contrary to tradition. The incriminated priests, being first entreated, and then commanded, to renounce their innovations, obstinately refused. The situation became grave. Upon one point of principal importance, the superior clergy of Alexandria were divided; some, with their bishop, taught the absolute Divinity of Christ; others, with Arius at their head, would only accord him a divinity which was relative and secondary.

Such a state of things could not continue. From the moment that Arius and his followers refused to accept the teaching of their bishop, they ought to have resigned their functions. They did nothing of the kind, imagining no doubt that, in view of the independent position of the Alexandrian priests, they were rulers of the Church, quite as much as their bishop was, and had no need of his instructions. And as their number was comparatively large, Alexander thought it his duty to reinforce the authority of his decision, by summoning the whole of the Egyptian episcopate to his assistance. These indeed were beginning to be excited; Arius had supporters amongst them. The affair was not exclusively an Alexandrian affair: it was beginning to interest all within the metropolitan jurisdiction. Nearly a hundred bishops rallied round Alexander: two of them, Secundus of Ptolemais in Cyrenaica, and Theonas of Marmarica, deserted, and ranged themselves on the side of Arius. They were deposed, and with them six priests and six deacons of Alexandria: the priests Arius, Achillas, Aeithales, Carpones, another Arius, and Sarmatas ; and Euzoïus, Lucius, Julius, Menas, Helladius, and Gaius, the deacons. Mareotis also, a rural district surrounding Lake Mareotis, was represented in the list of the proscribed : either at the council, or shortly afterwards, two priests from that district, Chares and Pistus, and four deacons, Serapion, Parammon, Zosimus, and Irenæus, openly professed their sympathy with Arius, and were deposed, as he was.[1]

There were not many defections in the Egyptian episcopate as a body; but the Alexandrian clergy were very considerably affected. Arius and his followers, like Origen in bygone days, decided to leave Egypt, passed over to Palestine and settled at Cæsarea. And, still like Origen, they met there with a warm welcome. For several years the learned Eusebius had presided over that Church. His reputation was great: his historical works and his apologies had had time to make their way. In theology, his Origenism had not remained unyielding. In particular, he had sacrificed the eternity of creation, and, therefore, Origen's reason for maintaining the eternity of the Word. At bottom, he thought like Arius; but in proportion as the latter was clear and precise in his explanations, so did the Bishop of Cæsarea excel in clothing his ideas in a diffuse and flowing style, and in using many words to say nothing. We can form an idea of this from the elaborations with regard to the generation of the Word, which figure at the beginning of his *Ecclesiastical History*.[2] Other bishops in Palestine, Phœnicia, and Syria held the same opinions.[3]

---

[1] See Alexander's encyclical letter, 'Ενὸς σώματος, and the document annexed, Κατάθεσις 'Αρείου (Migne, *P. G.* vol. xviii., pp. 573, 581). The encyclical was signed by seventeen priests and twenty-four deacons of Alexandria, nineteen priests and twenty deacons of Mareotis. At the head of the priests of Alexandria signs a certain Kolluthus, who may well have been the person of whom mention has already been made.

[2] *H. E.* i. 2.

[3] In his letter to Eusebius of Nicomedia, Arius mentions, besides

The Bishop of Cæsarea was not at that time, as he became afterwards, a personage in favour at court, and of assured position. This part was filled by another Eusebius, an aged prelate well versed in intrigue, who had succeeded in transferring himself from Berytus, where he had first exercised his episcopal functions, to the more important see of Nicomedia. There, in close proximity to the court, in high favour with the Empress Constantia, the sister of Constantine and the wife of Licinius, he had made for himself a position, the strength of which was soon felt. He was besides a theologian, and a disciple of Lucian of Antioch. He shared all the ideas of Arius, and for a long time had been on the coldest of terms with his colleague of Alexandria. The party could never have dreamed of more powerful patronage. Arius wrote to Eusebius from Palestine,[1] and lost no time in joining him.

The Bishop of Nicomedia set himself at once to work : he inundated the Orient and Asia-Minor with letters addressed to the bishops,[2] in order to persuade them to range themselves on the side of Arius, and to support him against his own bishop, by demanding of the latter a reversal of his decision. Arius drew up an explanation of his doctrine, in the form of a letter addressed to Alexander[3]; and this was circulated in the hope of gaining many adhesions. Eusebius of Cæsarea interposed several times on his behalf with the Bishop of Alexandria.[4]

the Bishop of Cæsarea, those of Lydda (Aetius), of Tyre (Paulinus), of Berytus (Gregory), of Laodicea (Theodotus), of Anazarba (Athanasius), "and all the Easterns." Yet he himself admits that the bishops of Antioch (Philogonius), of Jerusalem (Macarius), and of Tripoli (Hellanicus) were opposed to him. There were others also.

[1] Epiphanius, lxix. 6 ; Theodoret, i. 5. It is in this letter that he gives Eusebius of Nicomedia the name of *collucianist* (συλλουκιανιστά).

[2] One of these letters, addressed to Paulinus of Tyre, has been preserved in Theodoret, *H. E.* i. 5. Paulinus seems to have had some difficulty in taking a side.

[3] Athanasius, *De synodis*, 16 ; Epiphanius, lxix. 7, 8.

[4] Letter mentioned by Eusebius of Nicomedia, in the document quoted above, note 1 ; another letter, of which some fragments appear in the *Acts of the VIIth Œcumenical Council*, Mansi *Concilia*, vol. xiii., p. 317. *Cf.* Sozomen, i. 15 *ad fin.*

Alexander, meanwhile, had not been idle. He wrote
to all the bishops, protesting against the interference of
Eusebius of Nicomedia, "who deems himself entrusted
with the care of the whole Church, ever since, abandoning
Berytus, he cast his spell over the Church of Nicomedia,
without anyone daring to punish him for so doing," and
poses as the protector of Arius and his party. Alexander
then gave the names of the condemned persons, and
summarized, in a brief outline, the principal features of
their teaching, "more pernicious than the heresies of the
past, the fore-runner of Antichrist." To this letter were
added the signatures of all the clergy who had remained
faithful, both in Alexandria and Mareotis.[1] A copy was
sent to Pope Silvester[2]; others to the Bishop of Antioch,[3]
Philogonius, to Eustathius, Bishop of Berea, and to many
besides. Just as Arius was collecting signatures for his
profession of faith, so in the same way the messengers of
Alexander were obtaining signatures everywhere for his
protest against it. He gained many adherents from Syria,
Lycia, Pamphylia, Asia, Cappadocia, and the neighbouring
countries. He wrote[4] a little later to another Alexander,
Bishop of Byzantium, to obtain his support also. In this
letter he complains of the disturbances which the followers
of Arius are causing him in Alexandria. Women were
mixing themselves up with the affair; I have already said
that Arius was in high favour with the virgins. These
obstinate and argumentative ladies raised one quibble after

---

[1] It is this letter ('Ενὸς σώματος) (*P. G.* vol. xviii., p. 572) which is
called the *Tome* of Alexander. Dr E. Schwartz (*Nachrichten*, 1905,
p. 265) wishes to reserve this title for a document preserved in a
Syriac MS. in the British Museum (*Add.* 12, 156, copied in 562), and
published by P. Martin (Pitra, *Analecta Sacra*, vol. iv., p. 196;
Schwartz gives a Greek translation of it). This document seems to
be derived from a copy of the *Tome*, addressed to a Bishop Meletius
(he can hardly be the person spoken of by Eusebius, *H. E.* vii. 32,
who speaks of him as if he were dead; see rather Athanasius, *Ep.
ad episcopos Aegyptios*, 8); topographical references of a very doubtful character have been added to it, as well as the signature, also
suspect, of the Bishop of Antioch, Philogonius.

[2] Quoted in a letter of Liberius, in 354 (Jaffé, 212).

[3] Theodoret, *H. E.* i. 3.   [4] *P. G.* vol. xviii., p. 548.

another against their bishop. They held schismatical
meetings. In short, the general disorder, which the
exodus of the condemned persons had not appeased,
became every day more extreme.[1]

The return of Arius brought matters to a crisis. A
synod, assembled in Bithynia by the efforts of Eusebius of
Nicomedia, had pronounced that the dissenting party
ought to be admitted to communion, and that Alexander
should be entreated to receive them. As he still refused,
the supporters of Arius in Phœnicia and in Palestine,
Eusebius of Cæsarea, Paulinus of Tyre, Patrophilus of
Scythopolis, and several others, in their turn assembled in
council, and authorized Arius and his adherents to resume
their functions, while remaining, however, at the same time
under obedience to their bishop.[2]

This latter condition was difficult to fulfil. Arius and
his friends returned, counting apparently upon the number
and energy of their supporters to force the hand of their
ecclesiastical superior. Nothing was neglected which could
excite the populace and secure their support for the
opposition party. Pamphlets were circulated, and even
songs. Arius had composed a long rhapsody, in which
the beauties of his metaphysics were extolled. This is
what is known as his *Thalia*, and several fragments of it
have been preserved. It begins as follows :—

> According to the faith of God's elect,
> Who comprehend God,
> Of the holy children,
> The orthodox,
> Who have received the Holy Spirit of God,
> This is what I have learnt
> From those who possess wisdom,
> Well-educated people,
> Instructed by God,
> Skilled in all knowledge.
> It is in their footsteps, that I walk, even I,
> That I walk as they do,

---

[1] Arius had perhaps already returned, when the letter was written.

[2] Sozomen, i. 15, summarizes here synodical documents which
have not come down to us.

> I, who am so much spoken of,
> I, who have suffered so much
> For the glory of God,
> I, who have received from God
> The wisdom and knowledge which I possess.

The dock-labourers, the sailors, all the idle and the rabble in the streets, knew these songs, and shouted them into the ears of Alexander's faithful followers. Hence ensued brawls without end.

Outwardly, the episcopate was greatly divided. Each of the two parties boasted of adhesions received. Letters in favour of Arius were formed into a collection[1]; the same was done with those in support of the Bishop of Alexandria.[2] A rhetorician of Cappadocia, called Asterius, who had apostatized during the persecution, and could not enter the ranks of the clergy on that account, spent his time travelling through the East, giving lectures to explain and defend the new theology. The public began to take interest in these questions, even the pagan public, who, of course, took advantage of this opportunity to amuse themselves at the expense of the Christians and of their beliefs. The quarrels of Arius and Alexander were even echoed in the theatres.[3]

It was in this state of disturbance that Constantine found the Eastern Church, when his victory over Licinius brought him into close relations with it.

On his arrival at Nicomedia, he had at first intended to visit the "Orient"[4] immediately; and among the reasons which prevented him, these ecclesiastical disputes held an important place. The accounts given him with regard to that at Alexandria astonished and distressed him. He had counted upon the assistance of the Greek episcopate to help him in reducing the African schism,

---

[1] Athanasius, *De synodis*, 17.

[2] I cannot accept as authentic the Council of Antioch in 324, of which Dr E. Schwartz (*Nachrichten*, 1905, p. 171 *et seq.*) publishes a supposed synodical letter addressed to Alexander of Byzantium (Νέας Ρώμης) from a Syriac MS. at Paris, No. 62.

[3] Eusebius, *V. C.* i. 61.

[4] By which is meant here, Syria and Egypt.

which was a grievous anxiety in his religious policy,
and lo! the Greek bishops were themselves divided. And
why? For a mere nothing. Alexander had been imprudent enough to puzzle his priests with idle questions
respecting a text from the Bible[1] upon subjects of no
religious importance; and Arius, instead of keeping his
own opinions to himself, had expressed and defended
them with extreme obstinacy. Was this of all others
the time to devote oneself to such disputations? Could
they not let such irritating and insoluble questions sleep,
and live at peace in Christian brotherhood?

The emperor wrote a letter in this sense, addressed
jointly to Alexander and to Arius. It was carried to
them by the hand of his faithful adviser in matters
ecclesiastical, Hosius, Bishop of Cordova, who had followed him to the East. Constantine implored them both,
in moving terms, to be reconciled with each other, and
so to restore peace to the Church, and tranquillity to
their sovereign.

In Constantine's method of dealing with this affair,
we recognize at once the ruler and administrator favourable towards the Christian religion, desirous even that
the whole world should accept it, and that in this way
a moral unity (he expressly says so) might be established,
but at the same time quite incapable of interesting himself in metaphysical questions. The kind of Christianity
which the government wanted at the time was the
religion of the Supreme Being (*summa divinitas*), crystal-
lized in the faith in Christ as Revealer and Saviour, and
in the observance of the religious and moral precepts
inculcated by the Church in His name. As for puzzling
one's brains with regard to the *summa divinitas*, and
its intimate relationship with Christ, it might be all very
well as a subject of study for private individuals; different
opinions might be held on such a subject; but what
was the use of producing them in public, and especially
with such persistence as to provoke opposition and to

[1] Proverbs viii. 22.

give rise to quarrels?[1] The State could be interested in such matters only in so far as they affected the public welfare.

Hosius, who was a practical man, may have been, at bottom, of the same opinion as the emperor. Nevertheless, when he arrived at his destination, he at once perceived that the imperial exhortation was not sufficient to calm the troubled spirits. It might perhaps have succeeded with Westerns, whose theological needs were limited. But with Greeks, who were born thinkers, talkers, and wranglers, it was quite another matter. The question could not be suppressed; it was necessary to decide it.

However, advantage was taken of the visit of Hosius, to settle certain local affairs. It was undoubtedly at that time that Kolluthus was condemned and his ordinations declared invalid. At all events, among them was annulled that of a certain Ischyras, who came to the surface again later and made some stir.[2]

On his return to Nicomedia, Hosius informed the emperor of the state of affairs, and Constantine decided to summon a great council, which, as they both thought, would succeed in restoring peace.

The affair of Arius was not the only one which excited trouble. There were also the schism of Meletius in Egypt and the dispute on the calculation of Easter. The substance of the latter question may be stated as follows[3] :—

The dispute in Pope Victor's time between the Church of Rome and the Churches of Asia had ended in

---

[1] We may note, in the imperial letter, this curious comparison: "Philosophers themselves (of a school) are all in agreement as to their way of looking at things (δόγμα); if sometimes they are divided with regard to some proof, this difference of opinion does not prevent them from agreeing as to essentials" (Eusebius, *V. C.* ii. 71).

[2] Athanasius, *Apol. contra Ar.* 74. According to Socrates, iii. 7, Hosius was consulted then upon the questions of essence and of hypostasis, with regard to the Sabellians and their dogma.

[3] See my memoir, "La question de la Pâque au concile de Nicée," in the *Revue des questions historiques*, vol. xxviii. (1880), p. 1.

favour of the Roman use. Everybody agreed that the
Feast of the Resurrection of Christ should take place
on the Sunday after the Jewish Passover. At Antioch
they allowed the Jews to fix the time of the 14th of
Nisan—that is, of the full moon at which the feast
was celebrated. The month of Nisan being the first
lunar month, it might be placed differently, according as
the preceding year had consisted of twelve or thirteen
months. This latter point was decided by the Jewish
authorities according to their own methods. At Alexandria they did not trouble themselves about the Jews;
they made their own calculations for Easter, and the
fluctuation of the first lunar month was put an end to
by the special regulation that the feast celebrated
after the full moon must be celebrated also after the
vernal equinox, fixed at March 21. As the Jews—at
that time, at least—took no account of the vernal equinox,
the result of this was that their 14th of Nisan might occur
a month before that of the Alexandrians, and that the
Church of Antioch, which was accustomed to adopt it,
might also find itself a month in advance of the great
metropolis of Egypt. Both of the rival methods of
calculating had their adherents, and, strange as it may
appear to us, even passionate adherents.

Great councils were no novelties to the Eastern
episcopate.[1] They had seen many of them in the middle

---

[1] The formal records of the Council of Nicæa, if any were drawn
up, have not been preserved. The account given by Eusebius (*V. C.*
iii. 22), is the only one emanating from a witness who was present;
Eustathius of Antioch (Theodoret, i. 7), and Athanasius (especially
the *De decretis Nicaenis* and the epistle *Ad Afros*), who had also
been present at the council, report but few details regarding it.
Under the Emperor Zeno (476-491), a certain Gelasius, a native of
Cyzicus, compiled in Bithynia a history of the council, in which he
inserted a number of official documents. The narrative part of his
collection is borrowed from Eusebius, from Rufinus (a Greek
Rufinus translated by another Gelasius), from Socrates, and from
Theodoret. These authors (with the exception of Rufinus) have
supplied him with many documents; he has also borrowed a certain
number from a previous collection, made by a priest named John,
but otherwise unknown. He had, besides, at his disposal, extracts

of the 3rd century, and since then, at which the bishops of Eastern Asia-Minor and of the Syrian provinces had assembled at Antioch or elsewhere. Alexandria itself had also witnessed from time to time assemblies of the Egyptian and Libyan episcopate; one of these local councils had been summoned specially with regard to Arius. These two groups, however, had never been united; the "Eastern" bishops had never deliberated with those of Egypt. On the present occasion, the assemblage was much larger. To the Egyptians and to the Easterns were added bishops from the whole of Asia-Minor, alike from the ancient province (now a *diocese*) of Asia, and from Cappadocia, Pontus, and Galatia. The provinces beyond the Bosphorus were also represented, although in a smaller proportion. Still less numerous was the representation of the Latin countries: one Pannonian bishop; one from Gaul, the Bishop of Die; one bishop from Calabria; the Bishop of Carthage; and finally,

made by himself during his life at Cyzicus, from a book which had belonged to Dalmatius, the Bishop of that city, and a member of the Council of Ephesus in 431; this book was an artificial composition, claiming to be an exact reproduction of conversations between various philosophers and the members of the council. See, on this subject, Gerhard Loeschcke, *Das Syntagma des Gelasius Cyzicenus*, a study which appeared in the *Rheinisches Museum*, 1905, 1906; the author is much too favourable to Gelasius and to the book of Dalmatius. The text of Gelasius was divided into three books; the first two are in Migne's *Patrologia graeca*, vol. lxxxv., pp. 1192-1344; for the third, of which Mai (*Spic. Rom.* vol. vi., p. 603) has only given the table of contents, with some insignificant fragments, we must have recourse to Ceriani, *Monumenta sacra et profana*, vol. i., p. 129. That which Migne gives as Book III. consists of three letters of Constantine, the first of which is really an extract from this book, as Mai's index describes it and as Ceriani has published it. It seems to have been longer (*cf.* Photius, *cod.* 88), and may have comprised the two others. As to the signatures of Nicæa, of which recensions exist in various languages (*Patrum Nicaenorum nomina*, ed. Teubner [Gelzer, Hilgenfeld, Cuntz], 1898), they come to us, when completely analyzed, not from an official record simply recopied, but from an arrangement in which the names have been distributed in their geographical order. This arrangement appears to belong to the end of the 4th century.

Hosius of Cordova, whom we may consider as the representative of the Spanish episcopate, and two Roman priests, sent by Pope Silvester. Even from countries situated on the extreme frontiers, from the Black Sea and from Persia, came several bishops. Thus there were to be seen at Nicæa the Bishop of Pityus, in the Caucasus, the bishop from the kingdom of Bosphorus,[1] two from Armenia Magna, and lastly, one from the kingdom of Persia.

The exact number of the members of the Council of Nicæa was not fixed at the outset by official documents. Eusebius of Cæsarea,[2] who took part in this assembly, says that there were more than 250; another member of the council, Eustathius of Antioch,[3] speaks of 270, Constantine of more than 300.[4] This last figure is that of St Athanasius, of Pope Julius, and of Lucifer of Caliaris. In the course of time it was increased a little, to arrive at the symbolic number of 318, which was that of the servants of Abraham in his struggle against the confederate kings,[5] and tradition has so fixed it. The lists which have come down to us only mention 220 names, fourteen of which are the names of *chorepiscopi*. It is possible that these lists may be incomplete, and, in particular, that the names of episcopal sees, the occupants of which were only represented by simple priests or other clerics,[6] were not preserved at all, except in the case of the Church of Rome.

[1] This is no doubt the Scythia of which Eusebius speaks, *V. C.* iii. 7.

[2] *V. C.* iii. 8.   [3] *In Prov.* viii. 22 (Theodoret, i. 7).

[4] Letter to the Church of Alexandria, Socrates, i. 6.

[5] Genesis, xiv. 14.

[6] The great authority of the First Œcumenical Council caused it soon to become a theme for legends. By the end of the 4th century, various things, more or less doubtful, were related with regard to it ; and these again, in the following century, already found a place in books of history. The private legislators, to whom we owe so many apocryphal collections of canon law, at first sheltered themselves under the pretended authority of the apostles (*cf.* Vol. I., p. 388) ; now, we shall see them also claim authority from the three hundred and eighteen Fathers.

II   H

In the spring of the year 325, all this multitude was making its way, either in the carriages of the imperial post, or on horses supplied by the emperor, towards the appointed meeting-place, which was the town of Nicæa, in Bithynia, close to the imperial residence at Nicomedia.

These prelates were of widely different degrees of education. The most learned was undoubtedly Eusebius of Cæsarea. Several others, such as Alexander, Eustathius of Antioch, and Marcellus of Ancyra, are known to us from writings in the anti-Arian controversy; these questions, which had already been discussed for several years, must have been familiar to the greater part of them. Some of the number, like Leontius of Cæsarea in Cappadocia, and James of Nisibis, were celebrated for their virtues. But those who were looked for most eagerly were the confessors during the Great Persecution, Paul of Neocæsarea in Syria, with his burnt hands, Amphion of Epiphania, and the Egyptians Paphnutius and Potamon, both blinded in one eye and lame from their sufferings in the mines. If this great convocation excited the curiosity of the faithful, and even of the pagans, it could not have produced a slighter impression upon those who composed it. Never before had the Church seen such a review of its official rulers.

But, although he was an actual witness and actor in this scene, Eusebius scarcely gives us any information as to the details of it. What seems to have struck him most of all was the appearance of the emperor at the first meeting, and the State banquet at which he entertained the members of the council.

In a great hall of the palace, seats were placed to right and left; the bishops took their places there, and waited. Soon appeared several Christian officers, and then the emperor, clothed in the purple and in the magnificent costume which was then in fashion. It was indeed a solemn moment—this meeting between the head of the Roman State and the representatives of the Christian communities, who had been so long and so severely persecuted. Now the evil days were over: Galerius,

Maximin, Licinius, all the enemies of Christ, were dead.
But of the blows which they had struck the recollection
was still vivid, and of those present more than one bore
the marks of them.   The emperor of to-day, the puissant
prince who for twenty years had defended the frontiers and
kept the barbarians at a distance, who had but just now
restored the unity of the empire, and was holding it
complete and undivided in his hand, was also the restorer
of religious liberty—nay more, he was the protector and
the friend of the Christians.

Constantine took his place at the head of the hall.
The bishop nearest to him, on his right hand,[1] perhaps
Eusebius of Cæsarea, perhaps the Bishop of Antioch,
better entitled to it by the superiority of his See, then
spoke, and expressed to him the feelings of the assembly.
The emperor replied in Latin, and his speech was
immediately translated into Greek.[2]   After this the
debates began.   The emperor followed them carefully,
and sometimes joined in them.

In the intervals, the members of the council were his
guests at the festivities by which he celebrated the
twentieth year of his reign.   On this occasion, Eusebius
of Cæsarea pronounced an eloquent panegyric.   The
emperor gave a great banquet to the bishops.   On their
way to it, the guard presented arms; the confessors
saw, as they had seen in other days, the glint of steel,
but now there was no longer cause for fear.   Many of

---

[1] Eusebius does not specify the name.   The author of the index
of the chapters of his *Life of Constantine* (iii. 11) thought that it was
the Bishop of Cæsarea himself; Theodoret (i. 6) mentions Eustathius
of Antioch.   Hosius, as one of the immediate attendants on the
emperor, was scarcely marked out for this honour.   The Bishop of
Antioch had already presided over the Councils of Ancyra and
Neocæsarea; it was natural that he should preside over that of
Nicæa.   There were not yet any fixed rules of precedence; later on,
Alexandria, in these meetings, took precedence of Antioch.   At the
time we are now speaking of, Antioch was the residence of the *Comes*
of the *Oriens*, a sort of viceroy to whom Egypt was subject as well as
Syria.
[2] Eusebius, *V. C.* iii. 12, has preserved the emperor's speech.

them asked themselves if it were all a dream, or if they were already in the kingdom of Christ.

Apart from these celebrations, the council was busy at work. The affair of Arius came first. The question at issue was to know whether the sentence already passed upon him by his own bishop would be confirmed. Being called upon to justify himself, Arius and his followers explained their position very frankly, so much so that Alexander had no difficulty in proving how well-founded his decision was. The support which the Bishop of Nicomedia and his other partisans gave to the priest of Alexandria proved no help to him. Few persons in that assembly were disposed to listen calmly to such propositions as these: "There was a time when the Son of God was not; He was taken out of nothing; He is a creature, a being susceptible of change," etc. The sentence of Alexander was not only sustained, but confirmed. The condemned ecclesiastics held firm; it was not possible to reclaim one of them.

Another Egyptian affair, that of Meletius and his schism, was then examined. The council recognized that Meletius was most seriously in the wrong. Nevertheless, in its desire for peace—a desire which was certainly favoured by the emperor—an arrangement was adopted, by which the Meletian clergy might still be allowed to exercise their functions, and to work with Alexander's clergy, but in subordination to him. At the same time, if the bishop appointed by Alexander were to die, the bishop set up by Meletius might replace him, provided always that he were elected according to rule, and with the approbation of the Metropolitan of Alexandria. As to Meletius himself, having regard to his special culpability, he was only allowed to retain the title of bishop, but was absolutely forbidden to exercise any pastoral functions.

It was not by the advice of Athanasius that the Meletians were treated so mercifully. He knew well the kind of people with whom they were dealing, and foresaw that there would be trouble on their account in the future. The event justified his opinion.

As to the reckoning of Easter, the Bishop of Antioch and his Eastern colleagues consented to conform to the use of Alexandria, and to celebrate Easter at the same time as the other Churches.

These decisions were communicated to all the Churches interested in the matter, not only by the council, but also by the emperor,[1] who had made it his special duty to exercise pressure upon the dissenting party in order to bring them back to Catholic unity.

It also appeared to be necessary, in view of the divisions which the affair of Arius had introduced amongst the bishops, to come to some mutual agreement upon a formula which, being admitted by everyone, might prevent a repetition of the theological movements of which there had been reason to complain. The only doctrinal synthesis which the Church recognized at that time was the baptismal creed, which had its origin in Rome, but which had been modified here and there, in various ways, since the very early times when it had begun to be current. Eusebius of Cæsarea thought the opportunity a good one for avenging here the defeat sustained by his Egyptian friends; he presented to the council the text of the creed in use in his own Church. It was accepted, he says, in principle: it contained nothing that could startle anyone. But since in regard to the special points which had been matter of dispute it remained absolutely indefinite, it was modified by introducing into it certain additions, and suppressing certain useless words. It was thus[2] that the celebrated Creed of Nicæa was drawn up :—

---

[1] Letter of the council to the Church of Alexandria, Ἐπειδὴ τῆς τοῦ Θεοῦ, Socrates, i. 9 ; Theodoret, i. 8 ; Gelasius, ii. 34. Letter of Constantine to the Church of Alexandria, Χαίρετε ἀγαπητοί, Socrates, i. 9 ; Gelasius, ii. 37. Letter of Constantine to the Easterns, Πεῖράν λαβών, Eusebius, *V. C.* iii. 17-20 ; Socrates, i. 9 ; Theodoret, i. 9.

[2] According to St Basil, *Ep.* 81 (*cf.* 244, 9), the drawing up of this creed was entrusted to Hermogenes, who became later Bishop of Cæsarea in Cappadocia. He was undoubtedly a priest or deacon of that Church, who had, like Athanasius, accompanied his bishop to the council.

"We believe in one God, Father, Almighty, author of all things, visible and invisible; and in one Lord, Jesus Christ, the Son of God, the only begotten[1] of the Father—*i.e.*, of the essence of the Father, God of God, Light of Light, Very God of Very God; begotten and not made, consubstantial with the Father, by whom all has been made; Who for us men, and for our salvation came down, was incarnate, was made Man, suffered, was raised to life the third day, ascended into heaven, and will come to judge the living and the dead; and in the Holy Ghost.

"As to those who say: There was a time when He was not; Before He was begotten, He was not; He was made of nothing, or of another substance or essence[2]; the Son of God is a created being, subject to change, mutable; to such persons, the Catholic Church says Anathema."

In addition to this creed, the council also drew up a certain number of ecclesiastical regulations, which it formulated in twenty canons.

The internal crises of the preceding century had left in the East traces which the council endeavoured to remove. The Novatians were to be met with, more or less, throughout Asia Minor; at Antioch, and perhaps elsewhere, Paulianists were to be found, followers of the doctrines of Paul of Samosata. With regard to the Novatians, the council (*c.* 8) showed itself very conciliatory. It enjoined that they should be admitted to communion, on the simple promise to accept Catholic dogmas and to hold communion with persons who had been twice married[3] and apostates who had repented. Their clergy might perform their duties in places where there were no Catholic clergy, and were merged in the latter when there were any. As to the Paulianists (*c.* 19), their baptism was declared invalid; they were obliged to submit to rebaptism. Their clergy also, if they wished to continue their functions, which the council admitted as a possibility, were obliged to be reordained.

---

[1] γεννηθέντα μονογενῆ.   [2] ἐξ ἑτέρας ὑποστάσεως ἢ οὐσίας.

[3] Of course, it is here a question of two marriages in succession—of second marriage, and not of simultaneous bigamy.

The persecution of Licinius was still of recent date; several canons (*cc.* 11-14) were devoted to legislation with regard to cases of penance arising from it.

With regard to clerical discipline, the council forbade the ordination of voluntary eunuchs (*c.* 1), of neophytes (*c.* 2), or of penitents (*cc.* 9, 10); it forbade priests and bishops to transfer themselves from one Church to another[1] (*cc.* 15, 16); it forbade the clergy in general to practise usury (*c.* 17), and to keep under their roof any women who might give cause for suspicion (*c.* 3). Bishops, in each province, were to be installed by all their colleagues; and if any of these were unable to be present, their approval was at least necessary; the installation was to be confirmed by the bishop of the principal city, the metropolitan (*c.* 4). No bishop was allowed to receive, and certainly not to promote, clerics who had deserted their own Church (*c.* 16), or to reinstate persons who had been excommunicated by his colleagues. As there might be occasion, with regard to this point, to revise the episcopal sentences, the bishops of each province were invited to assemble twice a year in council to deliver judgment in cases of appeal (*c.* 5).

In thus laying down its rules for the provincial relations of bishops, the council had no intention of diminishing the dignity of positions consecrated by long custom, notably that of the Bishop of Alexandria[2] with regard to the Churches of the whole of Egypt, of Libya and the Pentapolis; for all these Churches the Bishop of Alexandria was the immediate superior of the local

---

[1] This decision affected the Bishops of Nicomedia and Antioch, transferred, one from Berytus, the other from Berea; but the law had not a retrospective effect.

[2] Here, the council brings forward the custom of Rome: ἐπειδὴ καὶ τῷ ἐν τῇ Ῥώμῃ ἐπισκόπῳ τοῦτο συνηθές ἐστιν. Actually, the Pope exercised at that time the authority of a metropolitan over the bishops of the whole of Italy. In certain Latin versions of this canon a closer definition has been attempted by restricting the metropolitical juris-diction of the Pope to the *suburbicaria loca*—that is to say, to those Churches not included in the jurisdictions of Milan and Aquileia, established after the Council of Nicæa.

bishop : there was no other metropolitan but himself. The ancient customs of Antioch and elsewhere were also to be maintained ; the Bishop of Ælia, also, was to preserve his traditional prerogatives—without prejudice, however, to the metropolitical rights of Cæsarea (*cc.* 6, 7).

Such is the ecclesiastical legislation of Nicæa,[1] legislation without synthetic character, entirely determined by circumstances, as was always the case with the legislation of the councils. It represented certainly not the general regulation of ecclesiastical relations, but simply the solution of a certain number of cases, to which the attention of the assembled members happened to have been called. Up to that time the Church had existed either upon unwritten traditions, or upon collections of rules claiming the authority of the apostles or their disciples, but without any title which could be verified. The Councils of Elvira and of Arles were never acknowledged in the East; those of Ancyra and Neocæsarea waited a long time before they were recognized in the West: the canons of Nicæa were accepted everywhere, from the first, and were everywhere placed at the head of the authentic records of ecclesiastical law.

The canons relating to discipline do not appear to have met with much opposition. It was quite otherwise with the creed. The precision of the negative formulæ with which it concluded, and such expressions as " begotten of the Essence of the Father, Very God, begotten and not made, consubstantial with the Father," absolutely excluded Arianism in doctrine. The supporters of Arius, whether they came from the Lucianic school, like Eusebius of Nicomedia, or from among the Origenists who had joined their forces, like Eusebius of Cæsarea, could not sign such a profession of faith without detracting from their principles. They raised great objection, in particular, to the word *consubstantial*, finding fault with it as not taken

---

[1] For the sake of completeness, we may mention further two other canons, one against the encroachments of deacons (*c.* 18), the other against the custom of kneeling at prayers on Sunday and during the Paschal season (*c.* 20).

from Scripture, and as having been repudiated by the
Council of Antioch, in the time of Paul of Samosata. To
this the orthodox party replied, that several ancient and
weighty authors, Theognostus, Origen, and especially the
two Dionysii, the one of Alexandria and the other of
Rome, had all made use of the word in dispute, which was
not, it is true, scriptural, but which clearly expressed what
it was desired to teach. This last point was open to
dispute, for, in itself, the word "consubstantial" was not so
very clear, and, as a matter of fact, it has not always been
taken in the same sense.[1] But, in the creed, the truth
which it was meant to express was that the Son of God
belongs in no wise to the category of created beings, and
that, whatever may be the mystery of His generation, His
Essence is truly divine. This is the meaning of the
formula, "begotten of the Essence of the Father," ἐκ τῆς
τοῦ Πατρὸς οὐσίας, which has disappeared from the text
at present in use, and which forms really a mere repetition
in conjunction with the ὁμοούσιος. Athanasius, to whom
the formula ἐκ τῆς τοῦ Πατρὸς οὐσίας is very familiar, does
not often use, for his own part, the word *consubstantial*. It
was certainly not he nor his bishop who suggested it to
the council. It appears rather as if the suggestion came
from the Roman legates. For in Rome, as a matter of
fact, the word was in current and official use; sixty years
before the Council of Nicæa, Dionysius of Alexandria had
been reproved for his hesitation in employing it.[2] Since
the days of Zephyrinus and Callistus, the Roman Church
had always been more concerned to maintain the doctrine
of absolute Monotheism and the absolute Divinity of Jesus
Christ than to develop methods of reconciling these two
data. This primary concern was shared by the Modalists;
and those minds with a tendency towards Sabellianism
among the members of the council were attached to it
in advance, notably Marcellus, the Bishop of Ancyra, of

---

[1] For instance, when it is said that Christ, consubstantial with
God by His divine nature. is consubstantial with us by His human
nature.

[2] See Vol. I., p. 352.

whom we shall soon hear more. Such supporters of the *homoousios* were not very likely, it must certainly be admitted, to recommend it to the minds of people who, ever since the time of Origen, had waged incessant war against Modalism.

Indeed, the *homoousios* only won acceptance with considerable difficulty; it was imposed rather than received. Hosius patronized it with much energy; and so did the Bishops of Alexandria and Antioch. The emperor made no secret of his agreement with it; and this, for many, was a supreme argument. Opposition grew weaker; even that of Eusebius of Cæsarea, even that of the Bishops of Nicomedia and Nicæa, as well as of the whole Lucianic party. Everyone signed, except the two Libyans, Theonas and Secundus, who refused to separate themselves from their party. And, by the action of the government, they were confined in Illyricum, with Arius and his Alexandrian followers.[1]

How their former protectors explained their complete change of front, we can form some idea from reading the pitiful and insincere letter which the Bishop of Cæsarea wrote without a moment's delay to his own Church. Athanasius, who was no friend of his, and with reason, took care to transmit this document to posterity, by annexing it to the work which he afterwards published on the decrees of Nicæa. It must have weighed heavily upon the conscience of its author. However, he dared not rebel openly, and waited for the hour of retaliation.

Eusebius of Nicomedia and Theognis of Nicæa showed themselves less prudent. At the actual time of the council they had had a narrow escape, for the emperor, knowing their responsibility in the disturbances, wished to treat them like Arius and the others. However, nothing more was done than to force them to sign. But their opinions were unchanged; and this was soon evident. The decisions of the council resulted at Alexandria in executive action which gave rise to many protests. "The Egyptians alone," says Eusebius, "continued, in the

[1] Philostorgius, *Supp.* (Migne, *P. G.* vol. lxv., p. 623).

midst of the universal peace, to wage war upon each other."[1] Like the Donatists, after the Council of Arles, those who were condemned, whether Arian or Meletians, began afresh to importune the emperor. Constantine again assumed the *rôle* of arbitrator, summoned the party leaders before him, and tried to reconcile them. Eusebius and Theognis profited by this opportunity, welcomed the dissentients, as they had welcomed Arius, and vigorously undertook their defence. This was too much. The emperor could not allow a controversy scarcely extinguished to be fanned again into flame; and, besides, he had a grudge against Eusebius, who was regarded as having shown but a short while before too strong an attachment to Licinius. He seized the two bishops and sent them to Gaul. Then he wrote to their Churches, proposing that new bishops should be chosen[2]; and this was done. The Bishop of Laodicea in Syria, Theodotus, a notorious Arian, apparently held anti-Nicene opinions. The emperor wrote also to him to explain from the example of Eusebius and Theognis what would be the consequences of his attitude.

The emperor had fully made up his mind to admit no compromise in regard to the council. It was his very own council: he had been present at it; he had even in some measure directed it; he held resolutely to its decisions.

It seemed then that everything was finished, and as if there still remained only a small group of opponents, upon whom the imperial police had their eye and their hand. But it was not so in reality; the real struggle

---

[1] Eusebius mentions this affair, *V. C.* iii. 23; the general terms of which he makes use hardly allow us to discover whether it was a question of Arians or Meletians, or of both parties together. The same indefiniteness is displayed in the letter of Constantine mentioned below. There has been much exaggeration, in our own times, in assuming from this incident a second session of the Council of Nicæa. Eusebius in no way speaks of a new convocation of the whole episcopate, but merely of an invitation addressed to the "Egyptians."

[2] The letter to the Church of Nicomedia is preserved in Theodoret, i. 20, and in Gelasius of Cyzicus, i. 10.

was only beginning. In the 2nd century, after various alarms, the Gnostic crisis had ended by subsiding of itself. Christianity had eliminated the morbid germs by the mere reaction of a vigorous organism. Later on, the Modalist movement, after having agitated the Churches everywhere to a certain extent, in Asia, at Rome, in Africa, Cyrenaica, and Arabia, had gradually been extinguished or confined to a few adherents. There had been no necessity for council, or emperor, or creeds, or signatures. The dispute between Origen and his bishop, vigorous enough at the outset, had ended by settling itself without external interference. But in this affair with Arius the strongest measures were called into requisition; and the only result was a truce of very short duration, followed by an abominable and fratricidal war, which divided the whole of Christendom, from Arabia to Spain, and only ceased at last, after sixty years of scandal, by bequeathing as a legacy for generations to come the germs of schisms, the effects of which the Church still feels.

CHAPTER V

EUSEBIUS AND ATHANASIUS

Eusebius of Cæsarea: his learning, his relations with Constantine
The *homoousios* after the Council of Nicæa. Deposition of
Eustathius of Antioch. Reaction against the Creed of Nicæa.
Athanasius, Bishop of Alexandria. First conflicts with the
supporters of Meletius and of Arius. Submission of Arius:
his recall from exile. New intrigues against Athanasius.
Council of Tyre. Deposition of Athanasius. His first exile.
Death of Arius. Marcellus of Ancyra: his doctrine, his deposi-
tion. Writings of Eusebius of Cæsarea against Marcellus.

CONSTANTINE, in coming into contact with the episcopate
of the East, had been able to form a judgment of their
divisions, of the bitterness with which their disputes were
maintained, and yet at the same time of the great respect
which was felt among them for his own person and
authority. Of this feeling of respect he did not fail to
take advantage to calm troubled spirits, to waive aside
inopportune complaints, and in everything to show himself
favourable to peace and unity. The bishops at Nicæa
were not dismissed without many exhortations, for
Constantine was the greatest preacher of sermons in his
empire. He strongly recommended them not to tear each
other to pieces, and especially to support those of their
colleagues who were distinguished by their learning and
wisdom, and to consider this great gift of some of their
number as an advantage to them all.

It is not without cause that Eusebius[1] has selected for

---

[1] Eusebius, *V. C.* iii. 21.

notice this detail, which concerned himself so nearly.   The
emperor had immediately singled out this great scholar,
regarding him with justice as an ornament to Christianity
and to the episcopate.   He could not disguise from
himself that the Bishop of Cæsarea's reputation had
suffered from his defeat at the council, and, no doubt, the
easy witticisms which were current with regard to him,
in consequence, had come to the emperor's ears.
Constantine covered him with unchanging marks of
favour.

Eusebius was a man of elaborate learning.   He knew
everything : history, biblical and profane, ancient literature,
philosophy, geography, mathematical computation, and
exegesis.   In his great works, the *Praeparatio Evangelica*
and the *Demonstratio Evangelica*, he had explained
Christianity to the educated public ; by his *Chronicle* and
his *Ecclesiastical History*, he had drawn up its Annals ; he
had defended Christianity against Porphyry and Hierocles.
And, although already advanced in years, he continued
to write.   He commented upon Isaiah, the Psalter, and
other books also.   Was anyone in need of explanations
upon the difficult question of Easter, in which exegesis,
ritual, and astronomy were inextricably involved ?   He was
there to give them.   Public attention was then beginning
to be attracted towards the Holy Places.   Eusebius, who
knew Palestine and the Bible thoroughly, explained the
names of the places and of the peoples who figure in Holy
Scripture, described Judæa, and reconstructed the ancient
topography of the Holy City.   He excelled in formal
discourses.   He was the orator marked out for great
ceremonial occasions, for solemn dedications, or imperial
panegyrics.   It was to him that the emperor had recourse,
whenever he needed copies of the Bible well copied and
perfectly correct.   Once he asked him for fifty of these at
one time, for the churches of Constantinople.[1]

Thus highly esteemed by his sovereign, Eusebius was
in no way behindhand on his side, and took little pains
to conceal his enthusiastic admiration for Constantine.

[1] *V. C.* iv. 36.

He has been reproached severely for this, but most unjustly, for it was a sincere and disinterested enthusiasm. His position had been an assured one before he came in contact with Constantine, and the emperor could only add his personal favour. Constantine never set foot in Palestine. We have no knowledge of Eusebius having been near him on any other occasions but those of the Council of Nicæa (325), and the Tricennalia (335). Cæsarea was a long way from Nicomedia, and the bishop was no longer of an age to take long journeys without a special reason.

The years following the Council of Nicæa were sad enough for him. He could ill stomach his discomfiture, and, to speak candidly, he was not the only person who looked with a very moderate approval upon the new creed. The *homoousios* insisted upon by the Romans had but few adherents in the East, unless it were in the ranks of the Sabellians, or those suspected of an inclination towards their doctrines. In Egypt, the term had a very clear meaning : it signified that the Arians were heretics ; but, beyond that, the explanations of it which were given did not shine by their lucidity. In the East, properly so-called, it had also an independent signification, *viz.*, that the seventy or eighty bishops who, in 268, had condemned Paul of Samosata, had made a mistake on an important point. The result was that, notwithstanding the promises of mutual agreement and discretion made to the emperor from various quarters, the quarrels soon recommenced. Eusebius of Cæsarea and his colleague, Eustathius of Antioch, exchanged bitter letters,[1] which threw little light upon the debate, and soon made it still more venomous. Eustathius was a great enemy of Origen, and an enemy of a very militant kind. This was no recommendation to him at

---

[1] Socrates, i. 23, says that he had seen episcopal letters on this subject : Ὡς δὲ ἡμεῖς ἐκ διαφόρων ἐπιστολῶν εὑρήκαμεν, ἃς μετὰ τὴν σύνοδον οἱ ἐπίσκοποι πρὸς ἀλλήλους ἔγραφον, ἡ τοῦ ὁμοουσίου λέξις τινὰς διετάραττε κ. τ. ἑ. St Jerome, *De viris*, 85, was also acquainted with letters of Eustathius in great numbers, *infinitae epistolae*.

Cæsarea.[1] At Antioch the clergy were greatly divided. Down to that time, the episcopal throne had been occupied by prelates unfavourable to the Arians; but Antioch was the real home of Arianism: it was there that Lucian had held his school. His spiritual posterity was not entirely dispersed in other dioceses; some had remained on the spot. This was clearly to be seen when Bishop Eustathius, quick enough himself in retort,[2] began to be a subject for discussion. The quarrel grew fiercer, and ended by producing between Eustathians and anti-Eustathians a conflict of the most savage kind. Accusations of Sabellianism and of Polytheism were freely flung at each other's heads. Eustathius reproached the Bishop of Cæsarea with betraying the faith of Nicæa; Eusebius protested that it was not so at all, and that if Eustathius asserted it, it was because he was himself a Sabellian.

Things came to such a point that a synod appeared necessary. We do not know by whom it was convoked. It was held at Antioch, and, as in the time of Paul of Samosata, the decision was given against the bishop of that great city. We do not possess its *Acts*; the authorities give different accounts of it.[3] According to the opponents whom Eustathius had upon the spot, it was for his teaching that he was condemned, Cyrus, his successor in the see of Berea, having laid against him an accusation of Sabellianism.[4] Theodoret, who wrote a century after the event, speaks of a woman who is represented as falsely accusing the bishop of

---

[1] See the treatise of Eustathius upon the Pythian priestess and Origen's explanations with regard to that story. *Cf. Bulletin critique*, vol. viii., p. 5.

[2] Besides the treatise on the Pythian priestess, a fragment relating to the Council of Nicæa, preserved by Theodoret, i. 7, enables us to form an idea of his style.

[3] Socrates here complains of the bishops, who, he says, deposed people as impious, without stating in what their impiety consisted.

[4] Socrates, i. 24, gets this from George of Laodicea, a notorious Arianizer who seems to reproduce a remark of Eusebius of Emesa. Cyrus himself might have been deposed upon the same doctrinal pretext.

having seduced her.[1] Athanasius gives another reason:
Eustathius, it is alleged, was accused to the emperor
of having insulted his mother. In this there may well
have been a foundation of truth. Helena visited the
East in the time of Eustathius. We know that she had
a great devotion to St Lucian, the celebrated priest of
Antioch, whose body, being thrown into the sea off
Nicomedia, had been carried by the currents—according
to the legend, by a dolphin—to the exact spot on the
shore at Drepanum, where the empress was born, and
where, no doubt, she had a residence. Lucian was her
own special martyr; she built a magnificent basilica in
his honour. He had left a memory in Antioch which
was the subject of controversy: the Arians held him
in great veneration; their adversaries were less enthusiastic. It is quite possible that on this subject Eustathius
may have let fall some indiscreet words. Later on, as
we shall see, St Ambrose does not hesitate to say that
Helena had been a servant girl at an inn, *stabularia*,
which, considering the customs of that age in matters
of hospitality, implied a great many things. In the days
of Constantine it was not wise to push one's enquiries
into early history of this kind.

I should not like to affirm that the council considered
this a reason for deposition, and I would rather accept,
as the ground for the ecclesiastical condemnation, the
motive suggested by George of Laodicea, *viz.*, Sabellianism.
But the measures taken by Constantine lead us to believe
that he saw in this affair something other than a theological question, and that he took note of the remarks
made about his mother. Helena was empress (*Augusta*);
it was a case of *lèse-majesté*. Eustathius was arrested
and brought before the emperor, who, after having
listened to his defence,[2] exiled him to Trajanopolis, in

---

[1] Theodoret, i. 20, 21. The council seems to have admitted this
assertion without any other guarantee but the woman's oath; and
she confessed later that her child was indeed the son of a Eustathius,
but a blacksmith and not the bishop. All this is very doubtful,
and reads like legend.   [2] *V. C.* iii. 39.

Thrace, and then to Philippi, with a certain number of priests and deacons. He died shortly afterwards.[1]

It was not easy to find his successor.[2] Eustathius had many supporters; he had also bitter enemies, for he had been very severe to the opponents, more or less avowed, of the condemnation of Arius. Antioch was in a state of effervescence; the *curia* and the magistrates were divided in their opinions. A little more, and they would have come to blows in the matter. Paulinus, the unattached Bishop of Tyre,[3] who was a native of Antioch, was for some time at the head of the Church there, perhaps as provisional administrator. He died at the end of six months; then a certain Eulalius was elected bishop; but his tenure of the see was also short, and the agitation began again. Constantine sent a *comes* of his personal suite to Antioch, and a comparative calm succeeded; a great many votes were collected in favour of Eusebius of Cæsarea.

Eusebius was not at all anxious to leave for the

---

[1] St Jerome, in his *De viris*, says that Eustathius was exiled to Trajanopolis, and that his tomb was still to be seen there. It was, however, from Philippi (see the chronicles of Victor and Theophanes) that the remains of Eustathius were brought back to Antioch about the year 482. Socrates (iv. 14), followed by Sozomen (vi. 13), represents him as living till the time of Valens; but there must be a confusion in this. Eustathius is never mentioned again in the documents of the time of Constantine and Constantius, in which appear the names of so many bishops in a similar situation; besides, we know, from Theodoret (iii. 2), that Eustathius was dead when Meletius was elected Bishop of Antioch in 360.

[2] For this, see especially Eusebius, *V. C.* iii. 59-62.

[3] Paulinus had been, we know not why, replaced by another as Bishop of Tyre; it was Zeno who signed in that capacity at the Council of Nicæa. Eusebius dedicated to him (shortly afterwards, it would seem) his *Onomasticon*. In his work against Marcellus (i. 4), Eusebius says that the Church of Antioch had claimed him as a possession of its own; the lists of bishops of Antioch agree in placing, either before or after Eustathius, a certain Paul or Paulinus to whom they assign an episcopate of five years; St Jerome, in his *Chronicle*, also mentions a Paulinus, and places him *before* Eustathius. Theodoret (i. 24) does not speak of him. Philostorgius (iii. 15) is very precise: he places Paulinus immediately before Eulalius, and says that he died after six months of authority.

inferno of Antioch his peaceful bishopric and his comfortable library. He protested that the canons of Nicæa, in conformity with sound ecclesiastical usage, forbade the translation of bishops. The emperor commended him much for his modesty and his respect for rules; he signified to the Syrian bishops that they must choose another candidate.[1] He himself indicated to them two such candidates — Euphronius, a priest of Cæsarea in Cappadocia, and George, who was at that time a priest of Arethusa, but who had formerly been ordained, and then deposed, by Alexander of Alexandria.[2] They decided upon Euphronius. He was a man of the same opinions as Eulalius and Eusebius. The see of Antioch was, therefore, secured for a long time to the adversaries of Council of Nicæa—secret adversaries, of course, for Constantine would never allow it to be attacked openly.

The organizer of this concealed reaction was Eusebius of Nicomedia. His exile had only lasted three years,[3] and there is no doubt that he and his friend Theognis had already returned at the time when Eustathius was deposed (c. 330). The causes of this return, so big with consequences, are not easily discernible.[4] A complete change was really brought about in the inclinations of Constantine, with whom, henceforth, Eusebius of Nicomedia appears to have possessed considerable influence.[5] Not only were

---

[1] Letters to the people of Antioch, to Eusebius, to the bishops (Theodotus, Theodore, Narcissus, Aetius, Alphius, and others), *ibid.*

[2] It was he who afterwards became Bishop of Laodicea.

[3] This is the number given by Philostorgius.

[4] I should be inclined to suspect that the account of Rufinus (i. 11, *vide infra*), as to the recall of Arius, really refers to that of Eusebius. Constantia had no special reason for being interested in Arius. On the contrary, Eusebius, as bishop of the city in which the emperor lived, must have been known to her for a long time; he was also distantly connected with the imperial family. We can easily understand that the widow of Licinius was distressed at the exile of Eusebius, her spiritual father and her friend.

[5] Following Tillemont and many others, I feel myself obliged to reject the letter, which Socrates (i. 14) gives us as having been written by Eusebius and Theognis to the most important bishops (τοῖς κορυφαίοις τῶν ἐπισκόπων) to stir them up to demand their recall

the two prelates recalled from exile, but they were also reinstated in their bishoprics, and their temporary successors were ousted.

In Egypt, the aged Bishop Alexander died on April 18, 328.[1] His deacon, Athanasius,[2] already a very prominent person, both on account of the confidence placed in him by Alexander and the part he had played at Nicæa, was immediately acclaimed as bishop, and consecrated on

from exile. See the discussion in Tillemont, vol. vi., p. 810. On the other hand, it is not easy to explain the origin of this document. Perhaps Socrates may have been deceived with regard to its authors. It would suit well enough Bishops Secundus and Theonas ; in any case, it assumes Arius as rehabilitated by the bishops, an event which only took place in 335.

[1] A passage of St Athanasius (*Apol. contra. Ar.* 59), in which it is said that Alexander died scarcely five months after the Nicene Council, seems to contradict this date, which is furnished by the Paschal Letters and their Chronicle. On close examination, it seems to me that this interval is indicated as starting, not from the Council of Nicæa, but from the reception of the Meletians. Between the decision of Nicæa and the end of the schism in Egypt a certain time may have elapsed, and there is every appearance (*vide supra*, p. 123), that after the council there were renewed discussions upon this subject. Matters of this kind are always very delicate to arrange. I should allow, then, that the schism may have dragged on until towards the end of 327. *Cf.* Eusebius, *V. C.* iii. 23. On the objections made to this date, see Gerhard Lœschcke, *Rheinisches Museum*, 1906, pp. 45-49.

[2] Upon the history of St Athanasius, apart from his *Apologies* and his *History to the Monks*, we possess two chronological documents of great importance : the *Chronicle of the Festal (Paschal) Letters*, and what has been called the *Historia acephala*. The collection of the Paschal letters of Athanasius has come down to us, in an incomplete form, in a Syriac manuscript. On this text two versions have been made : one in Latin (Mai, *Nova Patrum Bibliotheca*, vol. vi., p. 1 ; Migne, *P. G.* vol. xxvi., p. 1351), the other in German (Larsow, *Die Festbriefe des heil. Athanasius*, 1852) ; they leave much to be desired. At the head of each letter, various chronological indications are given, as well as the Paschal date ; then, all these chronological prefaces are repeated in another recension, and united at the head of the collection of letters. In this other recension, which has come down to us entire, appear, here and there, historical notes. The *Historia acephala* was first published by Maffei, from a Latin collection of canons preserved at Verona (*Veronensis* 60), the collection

June 7.[1] "He is an upright man and a virtuous, a good Christian, an ascetic, a real bishop!" Such were the cries of the multitude. We must notice his description as ascetic. It secured for Athanasius, destined as he was for so much strife, the support of the Egyptian solitaries, who now began to be a religious power in that country. But his greatest source of strength lay in his own character. In addition to his gifts as an experienced pastor, God had endowed him with a clear intellect, and a wide vision of Christian tradition, of current events, and of men; and with all this, he possessed a character of absolutely undaunted courage, tempered by perfect sweetness of manner, but incapable of weakening before anything or anybody. The orthodoxy of Nicæa had found its representative. Already threatened at this time, it was soon to pass through many terrible crises. At certain times, it seemed to have no other support but Athanasius. But that was enough. Athanasius had against him the empire, its police, the councils, and the episcopate: the parties were still equally balanced, while such a man stood firm.

He was neither an unlettered man, nor a professional scholar. At the time when he was elected bishop, he had

known as that of the deacon Theodosius (Migne, *P. G.* vol. xxvi., p. 1443; there is a much better edition by Batiffol, in the *Mélanges Cabrières*, vol. i., 1899, p. 100). It is clear, and Mgr. Batiffol has established the fact (*Byzantinische Zeitschrift*, vol. x., 1901, p. 130 *et seq.*), that other parts of the Theodosian collection join on to the fragment of Maffei, and, like that, are derived from a sort of apologetic *dossier*, drawn up at the instigation of Athanasius, in 367, and then continued until his death. Mgr Batiffol has proposed (*Byz. Zeitschr., l. c.*) to identify this *dossier* with the *Synodicon* of Athanasius, mentioned by Socrates (i. 13); this is very disputable. Upon these two documents, see E. Schwartz, *Zur Geschichte des Athanasius*, in the Göttingen *Nachrichten*, 1904, p. 333 *et seq.*

[1] His enemies dared, later on, to raise difficulties with regard to his election. They are refuted by the Egyptian Council of 340 (Athan. *Apol. contra. Ar.* 6), which quoted a letter addressed to the emperors by the opposition party; doubtless the same letter which Sozomen saw (ii. 17). It was a matter of course that Athanasius did not have the votes of the supporters of Arius, of Meletius, and other schismatics.

already published two books of apologetics,[1] remarkably well put together and admirably clear. But he willingly left to others the task of unravelling philosophical enigmas, or exploring the secrets of learning. It was enough for him to know how to write, and not to lose the documents which interested him. From this talent and this care his enemies fared ill.

The struggle soon commenced. By the beginning of the year 330, Athanasius found himself already at variance with his flock, an estrangement due to the ill-will of the "heretics." He complains of this in his Paschal charge, but without specifying the particular intrigues which were troubling him. The little Meletian Church had joined forces with Bishop Alexander, on the conditions laid down by the Nicene Council. But on Alexander's death[2] it did not come to terms with Athanasius, and disagreements made themselves felt. The head of the party, after the death of Meletius, was a certain John Arkaph, Bishop of Memphis. The supporters whom Arius had left in Alexandria also began to agitate. At the beginning of 331, when Athanasius had to write the pastoral letter,[3] by which the Bishops of Alexandria were accustomed to announce the Feast of Easter, he again found himself estranged from his flock and once more on account of the "heretics."[4] Athanasius imposed conditions for their return to the Church which seemed to them extreme. Eusebius

---

[1] The two treatises, Καθ' Ἑλλήνων and Περὶ ἐνανθρωπήσεως. In the first, he shows the emptiness of paganism; in the other, he presents the justification of Christianity; the authenticity of these books has only been disputed on worthless grounds.

[2] Five months after the reconciliation, according to Athanasius (*Apol. contra Ar.* 59), which must, therefore, have taken place towards the end of the year 327. Between the close of the Nicene Council and the reunion of the Meletians there was an interval of about two years.

[3] *Letter* No. 3. The chronicle at the head of these letters says that Athanasius sent this letter during his journey from the court (*comitatus*) to Alexandria; but there must be some confusion, on this subject, between the letter of 331 and that of 332.

[4] Τοὺς περὶ Ἄρειον, says St Athanasius (*loc. cit.*); the reference here cannot be to Arius himself and his companions in exile.

of Nicomedia encouraged them from his distant diocese, and sent to the young bishop written remonstrances and verbal threats. He contrived to induce Constantine to order Athanasius to readmit to communion all those who desired it, under penalty of being himself banished from Alexandria.[1] Whether these threats were beginning to be executed, or some outbreak warned him to withdraw himself for a short time, it is certain that he was obliged to leave his episcopal city. He wrote to the emperor in justification of his attitude; but the Meletians at once entered the lists. Three of their bishops, Ision, Eudæmon, and Callinicus,[2] set out for the court to complain of Athanasius. He had, they said, imposed upon the Egyptians, a tribute of linen shirts. Two of his own priests, Apis and Macarius, who happened to be at court, refuted this accusation; but the emperor commanded the bishop to appear before him. Two other accusations were then brought forward. The priest Macarius, acting upon the responsibility of his bishop, had broken a chalice during a pastoral visitation in Mareotis. And Athanasius himself had sent a large sum of money to a certain Philomenus, a person suspected of evil intentions towards the emperor's person. This last accusation was specially grave.

Athanasius had in Nicomedia one powerful and faithful friend, the prætorian prefect, Ablavius. He was able to justify himself: his accusers were driven from court, and he himself, after suffering from the inclement winter, was able to return to Alexandria before the Easter of 332.[3]

[1] Athanasius (*Apol. contra Ar.* 59) has preserved for us a fragment of this imperial letter; he says that it was brought to him by the "palatines," Syncletius and Gaudentius. If this is not a *lapsus memoriae*, we must allow that these officers took the same journey twice, for later on we shall find them the bearers of other imperial letters.

[2] *Apol. contra Ar.* 60. Cf. *Festal Letter* No. 4; in this document, he adds to the three other accusers "the ridiculous Hieracammon, who, ashamed of his name, calls himself Eulogius."

[3] The *Chronicle of the Festal Letters*, which advances this journey by a year, mentions a very singular cause for it; the enemies of Athanasius had accused him of having been made a bishop when too young. That is all that it knows of in the way of accusations. Our best plan is to trust to the *Apology against the Arians*.

He brought with him a letter from the emperor, in which, after a long homily on concord, were to be found a few words of commendation in reference to the bishop, while no definite censure was inflicted on his accusers.[1] Athanasius reassumed the government of his Church and the usual course of his visitations as metropolitan.[2]

During all this time, Constantine still maintained, not only his fidelity to the Nicene Council, but also his absolute repudiation of Arius, his adherents, and his sympathizers. What he wanted in the East was a Christianity at once peaceful and uniform. Shortly after the deposition of Eustathius, he published an edict[3] commanding severe measures to be taken against the dissenters of long standing, Novatians, Valentinians, Marcionites, Paulianists, Montanists, and in general against all heretics, forbidding their assemblies and confiscating their places of worship. In 332 or 333, Syncletius and Gaudentius, officials of the imperial secretariat (*magistriani*), brought to Alexandria two letters from the emperor, addressed, one to the bishops and the faithful,[4] the other to Arius and the Arians.[5]

The latter, that to the Arians, which was of considerable length, was officially read at the palace of the prefect, whose name at that time was Paterius. It is a very strange document; if its authenticity were not guaranteed by so many outward indications, we should scarcely believe that so violent an invective against an unhappy exile could ever have been written by any sovereign, or in his name. But there is no room for doubt. We learn, in consequence, that at this time Constantine was still as hostile as possible to all those who had caused trouble in the Church of Alexandria, and throughout the Eastern empire. However, at the end, after threatening the heretics with certain penalties of a pecuniary character in

[1] *Apol. contra Ar.* 61, 62.

[2] In 329-330, he visited the Thebaïd; in 331-332, the Libyan provinces (Pentapolis, the oasis of Ammon); in 333-334, Lower Egypt (*Chronicle of the Festal Letters*).

[3] *V. C.* iii. 64, 65.

[4] Τοὺς πονηρούς . . .   [5] Κακὸς ἑρμηνεύς . . .

case they obstinately continued to support Arius, he addressed himself directly to the latter, inviting him to come and explain his position to the "man of God," as he styled himself.

Arius required pressing before he would comply. He had sources of information at court. The ex-Empress Constantia,[1] widow of Licinius, was well disposed to the *protégés* of her old friend, Eusebius of Nicomedia. She died about this time; but before her death she recommended to her brother, the emperor, a priest who was in her confidence.[2] This priest speedily suggested that Arius was not so far from accepting the doctrines of Nicæa as was generally believed. The emperor allowed himself to be convinced, and repeated his invitation in less hostile terms.

Arius came, with Euzoius, one of his companions in exile. He had an interview with Constantine, and at last succeeded in satisfying him by giving him a profession of faith, which, though vague, was comparatively orthodox, and capable of being reconciled with the Creed of Nicæa.[3] The emperor declared himself satisfied with it. He imagined that, henceforth, everyone being in agreement, nothing more remained to be done than to restore Arius and his followers to communion with the Bishop of Alexandria. But this Athanasius refused,[4] a refusal which could not fail to be displeasing in high places.

[1] Here we are reduced to a narrative by Rufinus, i. 11, reproduced by Socrates, i. 25, and Sozomen, ii. 27. *Cf.* p. 131 of this volume, note 4.

[2] Gelasius of Cyzicus (iii. 12) has preserved his name; he was called Eutocius.

[3] This was the beginning of it: "We believe in one God, Father, Almighty, and in the Lord Jesus Christ, His Son, born (γεγενημένον) of Him before all ages, God the Word, by Whom everything has been made. . . ." The phrase ἐξ αὐτοῦ γεγενημένον, taking account of the synonymy which still prevailed between γενητός and γεννητός, might be considered as equivalent to ἐκ τῆς τοῦ Πατρὸς οὐσίας. It certainly excluded creation *ex nihilo*. The Nicene *homoousios* is not pronounced, but Arianism is practically excluded.

[4] *Apol. contra Ar.* 59. We are tempted to regret this refusal, when we think of what followed.

The intrigues began again. The story of the broken chalice was revived. This chalice, it was alleged, belonged to a priest, one Ischyras, who had a church in Mareotis. There was actually in those parts a certain Ischyras who had been ordained in former days by Kolluthus, but whose ordination had not been recognized as valid, so that the people of Mareotis would not allow him to exercise his ministry, and he confined himself to officiating in his own family. It was alleged that Athanasius had caused his altar to be overturned, and had broken his chalice. The truth of the matter was that, when the representatives of the bishop went to visit Ischyras, they found him ill and confined to his bed; there could have been no opportunity for disturbing any form of Divine Service. When Ischyras returned to a better state of mind, he certified in writing that he knew nothing of the whole story. Athanasius was also accused of having put to death a Meletian bishop, Arsenius of Hypsele, after having caused his hand to be cut off. This Arsenius was afterwards found alive and in possession of both his hands. The Meletians had hidden him in a monastery, but Athanasius managed to discover his hiding-place. Arsenius, like Ischyras, asked pardon in writing. It was time, for Constantine had already instructed his half-brother, the censor Delmatius, to hold a criminal investigation in the matter. The trial was abandoned; a synod which had been summoned in this connection, and had already assembled at Cæsarea in Palestine, was also countermanded, after a long delay. The Bishop of Alexandria received a fresh letter from the emperor, couched in more explicit terms, against the intriguers who had tried unsuccessfully to ruin him. It was now the year 334.[1]

[1] Documents relating to this affair are to be found in the *Apol. contra Ar*: (1) Retractation of Ischyras (*c.* 64), presented to Athanasius in the presence of six priests and seven deacons; (2) Letter of Pinnes, a priest of the monastery of Ptemencyris, in the Anteopolitan nome, to John Arkaph (*c.* 67); (3) Letter of Arsenius to Athanasius (*c.* 69); (4) Letter of Constantine to Athanasius, Τοῖς παρὰ τῆς σῆς . . . (*c.* 68); (5) Letter of Alexander of Thessalonica to Athanasius (*c.* 66); (6) Letter of Constantine to John Arkaph (*c.* 70).

John Arkaph, the archbishop of the Meletians, had become temporarily reconciled to Athanasius, and was congratulated upon the fact by the emperor, who invited him to court. It was a fatal inspiration. The Meletian chief fell into bad company at court. In the following year (335), the whole business was on the point of beginning again. The Meletians were once more at variance with Athanasius, and leagued in their opposition to him with the Arians and their protectors.

The time was drawing near when the emperor would enter upon the thirtieth year of his reign. He resolved to celebrate this event by a great religious festival, the dedication of the basilica of the Holy Sepulchre, which was at last completed. A great number of bishops were summoned to assist at the ceremony. It was suggested to Constantine that this would be a good opportunity for finally putting an end to the Egyptian dissensions, so continually renewed, and for settling them by an episcopal decision. This had already been contemplated in the preceding year; since the emperor's solution of these affairs had not succeeded in restoring peace, it was quite natural that the idea of a council should again be taken up. Was it not much to be desired that, before celebrating this festival at Jerusalem, the ministers of the Lord should first be reconciled with one another? The emperor adopted this idea, and the city of Tyre was proposed as a meeting-place. All the enemies of Athanasius in the whole empire arranged to be present, hoping to obtain at Tyre their revenge for the abortive Council of Cæsarea, and to find means of getting rid of the troublesome Bishop of Alexandria. An imperial letter[1] exhorted the council to fulfil its task of peacemaker, assuring it that the resources of the government would ensure that all those whose presence would be useful should appear before it. This assurance referred especially to Athanasius. He was invited to be present, and threatened with compulsion if he refused. The priest Macarius was brought to Tyre, loaded with chains. A

[1] Eusebius, *V. C.* iv. 42.

high official, Count Dionysius, was sent on a special mission to the council.

Athanasius submitted.[1] Knowing well that he was going to appear before a meeting of his enemies, he took with him about fifty Egyptian bishops. But, as these had not been summoned, their names did not appear amongst the judges.[2] These had been chosen with care. Not one of the enemies of Athanasius was absent. Even two young Pannonian bishops were there, Ursacius of Singidunum (Belgrade) and Valens of Mursa (Eszeg), two disciples of Arius himself, who had taken advantage of his exile to recruit adherents in those distant countries. The Bishop of Antioch, Flaccillus, was present, and also Eusebius of Cæsarea, very much irritated at the failure of the council the year before. Several other prelates, either neutral or even fairly well disposed towards Athanasius, such as Alexander of Thessalonica, had also been invited. But the majority and the management of the whole affair were secured for the adversaries of the Bishop of Alexandria.

No question of doctrine was raised.[3] The Arians and their party did not take part in the proceedings, as such : the whole issue was between Athanasius and the Meletians. The Meletians had a cause of complaint against him which dated back to the time of his election : the bishops who took part in it had agreed not to ordain anyone before their differences had been arranged.[4] The ordination took

---

[1] His departure for Tyre took place on July 10, 335.

[2] According to Socrates, the council comprised (apart from the Egyptians) about sixty members.

[3] Sozomen (i. 25) had before him the "acts" of this council; and what he derives from them is very important. Athanasius' version of the facts is given in the *Apol. contra Ar.*, in which we find first an account of some length, contained in a letter from the Council of Alexandria in 340 (*cc.* 3-19), then another account by Athanasius himself (*cc.* 71-87), which contains several contemporary documents. We must not neglect the version of the other side, which we know through the synodal epistle of the Council of the Easterns at Sardica (Hilary, *Frag. hist.* iii. 6, 7) in 343. This document agrees fairly well with the summary of the "acts" given by Sozomen.

[4] At the time of the election, the Meletians were reconciled to the

place without any regard being paid to this agreement; and therefore they had separated themselves from communion with the newly-consecrated bishop. To force their return, he had employed violent measures, and in particular imprisonment. Five Meletian bishops, Euplus, Pacomius, Achillas, Isaac, and Hermæon, accused him of having caused them to be beaten with rods; Ischyras, again changing sides, had joined the Meletians; he complained that his chalice had been broken, and his chair overthrown; Athanasius had cast him into prison several times, and had calumniated him to the prefect Hyginus, alleging that he had thrown stones at the emperor's statues. Callinicus, the (Meletian) Bishop of Pelusium, having renounced communion with him on account of Ischyras' chalice, Athanasius had deposed him and replaced him by another. Arsenius was again spoken of. And finally, a memorandum was read of the popular outcries raised by persons at Alexandria, who refused to enter the churches on account of the bishop. In fine, what he was reproached for, was the strong measures he had considered himself obliged to take against those of the Meletian party who had relapsed.

Athanasius succeeded in justifying himself with regard to certain points; as to others, he asked for delay. Arsenius was still living, and owing to this fact the worst of the accusations fell to the ground. The council fixed upon the affair of Ischyras, the interrupted religious service and the broken chalice. An enquiry was decided upon. Athanasius offered no opposition to this, but he objected to his most notorious enemies being entrusted with the investigations.

These were exactly the persons who were chosen, not during a general meeting, but in a private conference. Moreover, as Ischyras claimed to be the head of a Meletian Church in Mareotis, and as everyone knew that Mareotis did not contain a single Meletian, the chiefs of this sect sent recruiters throughout Egypt to collect a group of

'Great Church.' It can only be a question here of secondary quarrels proceeding, however, from the previous separation.

parishioners for him.   All these intrigues awakened a
protest, not only on the part of the Egyptian prelates, who
rallied faithfully around their Pope,[1] but also from the
Bishop of Thessalonica, a highly-respected old man, and
from Count Dionysius himself, who held a similar position
in this council to that which Constantine had held at the
Council of Nicæa.   But all protest proved useless ; the
high commissioner had his hand forced, and the commission set out for Egypt.   The enquiry was concerned
with the evidence of only one side.   Not only was the
priest Macarius, who was directly implicated, detained at
Tyre, but not a single member of the Athanasian clergy,
whether belonging to Alexandria or to Mareotis, was
allowed to take part in it.   On the other hand, the prefect
of Egypt, Philagrius, lent his assistance to the commissioners sent by the council, and conducted matters with
so high a hand that they succeeded in obtaining the
depositions they wished.   The commission of enquiry
returned to Tyre with an overwhelming mass of evidence.[2]

As to the affair of Arsenius, which appeared at first to
be going contrary to the accusers of Athanasius, they
explained it by saying that a certain Plusianus, a bishop
of the party of Athanasius, had, by his orders, burnt the
house of Arsenius, caused him to be tied to a pillar and
beaten, and then shut him up in a small hovel.   Arsenius
had escaped through a window, and had succeeded in
concealing himself so well that the bishops of John
Arkaph's party, regretting the disappearance of a man so
distinguished and also a former confessor of the faith, had

[1] This term was at that time, and long remained, employed to
denote bishops, whoever they might be.   Later on, it was reserved
for the Bishop of Rome in the West, and the Bishop of Alexandria in
the East.   He still takes the title of Pope in his official style.

[2] At the same time, the records of this enquiry were so little to
the honour of the commissioners that the anti-Athanasian party tried
to conceal them as much as possible ; but it was known that they
were drawn up by a certain Rufus, who afterwards became *speculator*
to the Augustal prefecture.   Athanasius was able to invoke his
testimony.   Pope Julius also, to whom the documents were sent,
himself communicated them to Athanasius (*Apol. contra Ar.* 83).

believed him to be dead, and had caused a search to be
made for him by the authorities.[1]   It was therefore quite
excusable that they should have been mistaken.

The proceedings were taking an unfavourable turn for
Athanasius.   His enemies cried out upon him as a
sorcerer, a brutal ruffian, and declared him unfit to be a
bishop.   Such a tumult arose against the accused at the
hearing that the officials present were obliged to get him
away secretly.   He himself understood that no good
could be expected from such judges, and he embarked
for Constantinople.   The council pronounced sentence
of deposition against him in his absence, and forbade him
to remain in Egypt.   On the other hand, it admitted John
Arkaph and his followers to communion, considering them
as victims of an unjust persecution, and reinstated them in
their ecclesiastical positions.   Formal intimation of these
decisions was sent to the emperor, to the Church of
Alexandria, and to the episcopate in general.   The
bishops were entreated to have nothing more to do with
Athanasius; he had been convicted upon every point
which the council had been able to discuss; as to the
others, his flight proved that he did not feel himself in a
position to make any defence.   Already, during the
preceding year, he had refused to appear before the
Council of Cæsarea; this time, he had come, but
surrounded by a numerous and turbulent escort.   Sometimes he had refused to defend himself, sometimes he
insulted the other bishops, refused to appear before them,
and challenged their decision.   His guilt in the affair of
Mareotis had been established.

When this judgment had been pronounced, the
council proceeded to Jerusalem, and the dedication of the
Holy Sepulchre was celebrated, on September 14, with every
imaginable pomp of worship and eloquence.   Eusebius,

[1] In the letter of Arsenius, mentioned before (p. 138, note 1), Bishop
Plusianus is named, but no allusion is made to the story of the disappearance of Arsenius himself.   If Athanasius (c. 69) did not
expressly say so, we should not believe the letter to have been
written after his adventure.

the Metropolitan of Cæsarea, as was to be expected,
particularly distinguished himself. A further session of
the council was held, at Jerusalem itself, to adjudicate upon
the affair of Arius and his supporters. The profession
of faith presented to the emperor by Arius and Euzoius,
the one which Constantine had considered sufficient, had
been sent by him to the council : it satisfied the council also.
The Arians were admitted to communion ; the emperor
was informed of the fact, and it was also notified both to
the Church of Alexandria and the bishops of Egypt.[1]

Yet, on his arrival in Constantinople, Athanasius
succeeded in obtaining an audience. And, impressed by
his complaints, Constantine summoned the Council of
Tyre to his presence.[2] But no one obeyed the summons
except the most determined opponents of Athanasius—
prominent among them being Eusebius of Cæsarea, who
had to pronounce a set oration on the occasion of the
Tricennalia. Constantine heard them. According to
Athanasius, they were very careful not to enter on a new
investigation of the stories discussed during the council,
and no mention was made of the chalice or of Arsenius :
they had found something much better. Athanasius, they
told the emperor, was determined to hinder the transport
of Egyptian corn to Constantinople. What ! To starve
his own foundation, his beloved New Rome ! The
emperor made no further enquiries. Without waiting for
any new defence, he actually banished the Bishop of
Alexandria to a distant part of Gaul. Athanasius was
imprisoned at Trèves.[3]

When Athanasius was once more taken into favour,
people were very ready to say that, if he was exiled, it was
only to protect him from the fury of his enemies. It is
not at all probable that Constantine would accept without
verification the imputation regarding the transport of

---

[1] Fragment of the synodal letter in *Apol. contra Ar.* 84.

[2] Letter of Constantine, 'Εγὼ μὲν ἀγνοῶ (*Apol. contra Ar.* 86).

[3] This is Athanasius' account of this last sudden change of front
(*Apol. contra Ar.* 87 ; *cf.* 9) ; and he adduces the testimony of five
Egyptian bishops, who heard the assertion of his adversaries.

corn.   The best plan is to see the facts as the public saw
them at that time, and as Constantine himself explained
them in very weighty documents.[1]   The Bishop of
Alexandria had been judged and condemned by a great
assembly of his colleagues.   The Council of Tyre had
deposed him from his episcopal office, and forbidden him
to remain in Egypt.   Following up this sentence, the
civil government took the measures which were in its
province : it exiled Athanasius.

So ends the first act of the Athanasian tragedy.   We
may be tempted to think, at some points in it, that things
might have taken, both then and afterwards, a better turn,
if the young Bishop of Alexandria had treated the
Meletians with less severity, and if he had made it easier
for the party defeated at the Council of Nicæa to return
to the bosom of the Church.   Without sacrificing any
essential principle, he might then have avoided exasperat-
ing the opposing parties ; it would not have been so
easy for his enemies to represent him to the emperor
as a man impossible to deal with and an instigator of
troubles.   Later on, Athanasius became a man of peace
and a peace-maker ; but at the time we have now reached
he was, above all things, a fighter.   He was right ; but,
by the very fact that he was right, too many people found
themselves put in the wrong.

Arius remained at court.   The imperial favour had
recalled him from exile ; the decision of the Council of
Tyre had again opened to him the doors of the Church.
It only remained for him to make his official re-entrance.
According to later accounts,[2] he did return to
Alexandria, and then, because of the commotion caused
by his presence, was recalled to Constantinople.   It was
more in conformity with Constantine's usual ways to
remove all quarrelsome persons for the time being from
Alexandria, Arius as well as Athanasius.   However, as he

---

[1] See, below, the letters to St Antony.
[2] Rufinus, i. 11, 12 ; Socrates, i. 37 ; Sozomen, ii. 29.   Athanasius,
even in his letter to Serapion on the death of Arius, does not speak
of this journey.

II   K

considered the declarations of Arius to be sincere and
sufficient, he exerted his influence to persuade the Bishop
of Constantinople,[1] Alexander, to admit him. Alexander
did not look upon him with favour. But Arius died
suddenly; and Alexander was thus spared the mortification of receiving him in his Church. Athanasius had
already gone to his place of exile; but Macarius, one of his
priests, was at Constantinople at the time. It is from his
account that, twenty-five years later, Athanasius related
the mournful end of his adversary.[2]

At Alexandria the bishop's throne remained unoccupied.
No attempt was even made, for the time being, to appoint
a successor to the exiled bishop; either because the emperor
did not wish it, or more probably because the Christian
population did not appear disposed to agree to it.

There were disturbances.[3] The faithful continued to
demand the restoration of their bishop, both by public
manifestations and in the churches. Antony, the famous
hermit of the desert, was called upon to intervene, and
he wrote several times to the emperor. But all was in

---

[1] A letter of Constantine to Alexander, relating to this affair, has
been preserved in the collection of Gelasius of Cyzicus (iii. 15, in
Ceriani, *Monumenta sacra.*, vol. i., p. 145), not entire, but only in
extracts: Εἴπερ οὖν τῆς ἐν Νικαίᾳ ἐκτεθείσης ὀρθῆς καὶ εἰσαεὶ ζώσης
ἀποστολικῆς πίστεως ἀντιποιουμένους αὐτοὺς εὕρητε—τοῦτο γὰρ καὶ ἐφ᾽ ἡμῶν
φρονεῖν διαβεβαιώσαντο—προνοήσατε πάντων, παρακαλῶ. In the title, the
document is represented as addressed to Alexander, Bishop of
Alexandria. Ceriani, for this reason, pronounces it apocryphal;
Loeschcke (*Rheinisches Museum*, 1906, p. 44 *et seq.*) accepts it as
authentic, and tries to reconcile it with the facts known regarding the
episcopate of Alexander. But this is difficult, especially in view of
the fact that Arius and Euzoius are mentioned together in this letter,
just as they appear together in the proceedings of the year 333. The
best course, as it seems to me, is to remove the Gelasian rubric, or to
conjecture that, in its original form, it read only πρὸς Ἀλέξανδρον
ἐπίσκοπον, without Ἀλεξανδρείας. Neither the fragments of the text,
nor the place it occupies in the collection of Gelasius, give any
indication that it was addressed to Athanasius' predecessor.

[2] Arius is said to have died in a privy. Upon this event, see
Ep. ad Serapionem de morte Arii and *Ep. ad episcopos Aeg. et Libyae*,
c. 19.

[3] Upon this, see Sozomen, ii. 31; *cf.* Athan. *Apol. contra Ar.* 17.

vain. Four priests were arrested and exiled. Constantine wrote to the people of Alexandria, and especially to the clergy and the consecrated virgins, advising them to keep quiet, and declaring that he would not go back upon his decision or recall an instigator of disturbance who had been condemned in proper form by an ecclesiastical tribunal. To St Antony he explained that undoubtedly some of the judges might have been influenced in their decision by hatred or partiality, but that he could not believe that so numerous an assembly of wise and enlightened bishops could all have been so far mistaken as to condemn an innocent man. Athanasius was a presumptuous and over-bearing fellow, a man of strife.

The Meletians, restored to their position by the Council of Tyre, lost no time in seeking to reap the fruits of their success. They certainly did this with little restraint, for their leader, John Arkaph, was exiled like his opponents. The Egyptians, to whatever party they belonged, were certainly very difficult people to deal with. Ischyras alone had any reason to congratulate himself upon all these changes; for, as a reward for his labours, the Meletian party promoted him to the episcopate. In his own village,[1] so small that hitherto it had never even possessed a priest, they built him, at the expense of the State, a cathedral in which he could play the *rôle* of a bishop.

It was not in Egypt only that the victorious party followed up the advantage they had gained, assisted here and there by the excesses of zeal and the mistakes of their adversaries. Since the end of the Great Persecution, the Church of Ancyra had had as its bishop a certain Marcellus, a good man with some knowledge of theology. At the Council of Nicæa, he had attracted notice by the vigour of his opposition to the opinions of Arius, and so successfully that he had made a very favourable impression upon the legates from Rome. During the years

---

[1] 'Εν τόπῳ Εἰρήνης Σεκονταρούρου. Letter from the *Rationalis* of Egypt to the tax-collector of Mareotis (Athan., *Apol. contra Ar.* 85).

which followed, he continued to assail by his speeches the two Eusebii, Paulinus, and other more or less declared upholders of the defeated heresy. At that time, people did not run the risk involved in expressing their opinions in writing. The theology of the Arian party was only represented to the public by the addresses of Asterius,[1] which finally appeared in the form of a small book. As no one else seemed inclined to do so, Marcellus took the lecturer in hand and, to refute him, compiled a work of considerable proportions, in which he vigorously assailed the principal leaders of the opposite party, both living and dead, Paulinus, Narcissus, Eusebius of Cæsarea, Eusebius of Nicomedia, and the rest. Even Origen himself was not spared. Marcellus was present at the Council of Tyre, but refused to join in the condemnation of Athanasius and the restoration of Arius; he even refused to take part in the celebrations at the dedication of the Holy Sepulchre.[2] On the other hand, his book being finished, he went to present it to the emperor, with a dedication full of compliments. Constantine perhaps looked upon this gift with some suspicion; at all events, he commissioned the bishops who had assembled in Constantinople, after the ceremonies at Jerusalem, to examine the book and to make him a report upon it. This was to deliver Marcellus into the hands of his enemies. They discovered in his work lamentable traces of the Sabellian heresy. A sentence of deposition was pronounced against him, and then communicated to the emperor, to the Eastern bishops, and to the Church of Ancyra; Marcellus, after an episcopate of more than twenty years, was given a successor in the person of a certain Basil. The latter, as we shall see, will himself play a part of some importance in the future. However, as many people cried out against the proceedings as a scandal, and represented Marcellus as an innocent victim, the council asked the learned Bishop of Cæsarea to justify its decision by exposing and refuting the errors of the man whom they had condemned. This is the subject

[1] See p. 108 *supra*. [2] Socrates, i. 36; Sozomen, ii. 33.

of his two books *Against Marcellus*, which were immediately published. A short time afterwards, he resumed the same subject in a second work, dedicated to Flaccillus, the Bishop of Antioch, and divided into three books, entitled, *The Theology of the Church.*

To judge from Eusebius' extracts, which are of sufficient length to enable us to base an estimate upon them, the system of Marcellus did really approach Sabellianism, although, for all that, the two theologies were not identical. The Sabellians of that time [1] imagined God as a monad who extends Himself (πλατύνεται) in a Trinity. The designations, Father, Son, and Holy Spirit, mean three successive manifestations, three *rôles* (πρόσωπα, *personae*). As Father, God is the Law-giver of the Old Testament, as Son He manifests Himself in the Incarnation, as Holy Spirit in the sanctification of souls. These expansions are temporary: they are caused by the needs of the creature. When once this need has ceased, the expansion equally ceases, and the Divinity again draws itself in. This double movement of expansion and contraction (πλατυσμός, συστολή) may be compared to an arm which is stretched out and then drawn back again. The world, towards which these successive expansions are produced, is the work of God considered under another aspect, that of Word. The manifestation *Word,* differing therein from the other manifestations, is permanent: it lasts as long as the world lasts. The same cannot be said of the Son of God. The Sabellians were not agreed upon the subject of the Divine Sonship: some made it to consist in the humanity of the Christ (τὸν ἄνθρωπον ὅν ἀνέλαβεν ὁ Σωτήρ)[2]; others in the blend of the Word and humanity; others again said that the Word assumes the character of Son at the moment of the Incarnation. This Incarnation was transitory; it ceased before the

---

[1] This exposition is based on St Athanasius, in his fourth treatise against the Arians.

[2] In this explanation, however, the personality is attached to the divine element; it is not to be based upon the character of Son.

sending of the Holy Spirit[1]; the manifestation *Son* then came to an end; the divine arm was drawn back again. What, then, became of the humanity of Christ, when the Incarnation had once ceased? We have no information on this point.

Marcellus,[2] also, taught a kind of divine expansion ($\pi\lambda\alpha\tau\upsilon\sigma\mu\dot{o}s$). How could the monad have always remained a monad, and yet produce the world? The eternal Reason of God ($\lambda\dot{o}\gamma\sigma s$) proceeds forth outside the Godhead in some manner ($\pi\rho o\acute{\epsilon}\rho\chi\epsilon\tau\alpha\iota$) by an active energy ($\acute{\epsilon}\nu\epsilon\rho\gamma\epsilon\acute{\iota}\alpha$ $\delta\rho\alpha\sigma\tau\iota\kappa\hat{\eta}$) without ceasing to remain in God. In this way the Creation and the Incarnation are explained; a subsequent irradiation of the Logos produces the manifestation of the Holy Spirit.[3] These irradiations do not give rise to the production of distinct *hypostases;* there is only *One* divine hypostasis. At the end of all things, when once the reign of a thousand years is over, the irradiation will cease, and the Logos, as well as the Holy Spirit which emanated from Him, will return to the Bosom of God. Before the Incarnation, and here Marcellus invoked on his side the language of Scripture, there was only the Word. It was by the Incarnation alone that the Word became Son[4]; He will cease to be Son, when His reign on earth comes to an end.

With this system, embracing conceptions which were very ancient, and assuredly foreign to Origen's theology and anterior to it, Marcellus defended very stoutly the idea of the Divine *Monarchia*, the consubstantiality; and in this respect he was, from a polemical point

[1] We may notice how this feature agrees with the fact that, in Cyrenaica, at the time of St Dionysius of Alexandria, the Son of God was no longer preached (Athan. *De sententia Dionysii*, 5).

[2] On Marcellus, see the book of Th. Zahn, *Marcellus von Ancyra* (Gotha, 1867), and especially the memoir of Loofs in the Reports of the Berlin Academy, 1902, p. 764.

[3] Thus, up to this point, Marcellus' Trinity has only two terms; it is a " Binity."

[4] This opinion had the advantage of cutting short the Arian arguments as to the necessary priority of the begetter to the begotten; but it did away with any idea of Divine generation.

of view, on the same lines as the Roman Church, the Council of Nicæa, and St Athanasius.   But these allied forces were confronted with an opposition, the claims of which were not all destined to be overthrown.   Arius, Eusebius, and similar theologians had tradition against them, when they attacked the eternity of the Word and His absolute Divinity; but tradition was on their side, when they defended the real distinction of the hypostases.   Upon this point, their contention finally gained the day, after many struggles and eliminations, when men had at last grown weary of an impious warfare, when they consented to give each other the credit of being really sincere, and to listen to each other's arguments, and when, without actually expressing it in words, without proclaiming themselves victors or avowing themselves vanquished, they resigned themselves to combine together the consubstantiality and the three hypostases.   But that time of peace was still far away.   At the end of Constantine's reign, so far as the fighting propensities of the opposite parties had not been stifled by government pressure, they were determined to triumph over each other, and to exterminate one another *per fas* or *per nefas.*

Eustathius, Athanasius, and Marcellus, three of the principal champions of Nicæa, were already disqualified from taking further part in the battle, the last of them, at least, on account of heresy, a fact which was well calculated to throw obloquy on the term 'consubstantial,' and to prove that behind this formula, which was so strongly insisted upon, dangerous doctrines might be hidden. Other bishops succumbed to the malice of the victorious party.[1]   But, in spite of all, the Creed of Nicæa still held its ground.   At Tyre, no steps had been taken directly against it.   The restoration of Arius could not be interpreted as an abandonment of the celebrated formula: the

---

[1] St Athanasius (*Apologia de fuga,* 3; *Hist. Ar.* 5) mentions several of these: *Asclepas of Gaza,* who, according to the synodal letter of the Easterns at the Council of Sardica (Hil. *Frag. hist.* iii. 11), had been condemned seventeen years before, possibly in 326; *Hellanicus of Tripoli, Carterius of Antaradus, Cymatius of*

profession of faith delivered by the arch-heretic to the emperor was held to be equivalent to that of the three hundred bishops. Yet we cannot deny that by admitting the substitution of one formula for another a door was opened to many subterfuges.

In the meantime, Constantine died, on May 22, 337, after having been baptized in a villa near Nicomedia. It was the bishop of that city, the aged Eusebius, the indefatigable champion of Arius, who officiated at the final initiation of the first Christian Emperor. His colleague and namesake of Cæsarea began at once to compile the funeral oration in four books, known by the name of the *Life of Constantine*, an evidence of his enthusiastic admiration for what he considered the good actions of the deceased emperor, and of his skill in disguising the others. No trace is found there of the murder of Crispus and that of Fausta; the author has discovered a way of telling the story of the Councils of Nicæa and of Tyre, and the ecclesiastical events connected with them, without even mentioning the names of Athanasius and of Arius. It is a triumph of reticence and of circumlocution.

Paltus, Euphration of Balanea, Cyrus of Berea, in Northern Syria; *Diodorus (of Tenedos)*, in Asia; *Theodulus* and *Olympius (of Ænos)*, in Thrace, with two successive bishops of Adrianople, *Eutropius* and *Lucius*: the first was a declared enemy of Eusebius of Nicomedia, and Basilina, Constantine's sister-in-law, had a strong grudge against him; *Domnio of Sirmium;* and finally, the Bishop of Constantinople, *Paul,* who succeeded Alexander in 336.

CHAPTER VI

THE EMPEROR CONSTANS

The heirs of Constantine. Return of Athanasius. Intrigues of
Eusebius; the rivalry of Pistus. The Pope is made cognizant
of the Alexandrian affair. The intrusion of Gregory. Athanasius
in Rome. The Easterns and Pope Julius. Roman Council in
340. Cancelling of the sentences pronounced in the East against
Athanasius and Marcellus. Constans sole Emperor in the West.
Dedication Council at Antioch in 341. Death of Eusebius of
Nicomedia. Paul of Constantinople. Council of Sardica: the
Eastern schism. Negotiations. Condemnation of Photinus.
Athanasius recalled to Alexandria. African affairs. The Circum-
cellians. Mission of Paul and Macarius. Unity restored:
Council under Gratus.

CONSTANTINE had three brothers, the sons of Constantius
Chlorus and Theodora: Delmatius, Julius Constantius,
and Hannibalian. Having little in common with the
Empress Helena, as we can well understand, they remained
for a long time at a distance from the court. Their
residence was first at Toulouse, but in the end they drew
nearer to the emperor, and after the death of Helena
they attained high honours. Delmatius was appointed
consul in 333, and even invested with the office of censor,
which lay outside the ordinary course. In consequence of
this he had to occupy himself with the accusations made
against Athanasius. Julius Constantius also received in
335 the honour of the consulship. In regard to the third,
Hannibalian, we have no similar information; and it is
probable that he died early, and certainly before Constantine. Julius Constantius had four children—two sons
and a daughter by his first wife, and one son of his second
marriage with Basilina. This last son afterwards became

the Emperor Julian ; and one of the two others, Gallus, was Cæsar under Constantius. These children were still too young, at the time of Constantine's death, for him to have taken any account of them in his political arrangements. It was otherwise with the two sons of Delmatius. The one of these, also called Delmatius, was created Cæsar in 335 ; the other, Hannibalian, was provided, under the title of King of Pontus, with a sort of vassal sovereignty in the provinces bordering on Armenia. A new tetrarchy was to replace the united empire of Constantine. In the West, Constantine II. was to reign over Gaul, Britain, and Spain; in the East, Constantius with the vassal king, Hannibalian, was to govern Asia Minor, Syria, and Egypt; Italy, Africa, and the provinces of the Upper Danube were assigned to Constans, the third son of Constantine; and all the rest, as far as the Bosphorus, was to be the inheritance of the Cæsar Delmatius.

Such were Constantine's intentions ; but they were not entirely realized. After his funeral, events happened in Constantinople in regard to which we are badly informed : palace intrigues, barrack conspiracies, demonstrations of troops, seditions and massacres. Constantius, the only one of the three brothers then present in Constantinople, allowed many things to be done which he might have prevented. The emperor's brothers were massacred ; and so were the Cæsar Delmatius and King Hannibalian; the eldest son of Julius Constantius shared his father's fate; the two others, Gallus and Julian, escaped—Julian, thanks to the intervention of a Syrian bishop, Mark of Arethusa. The prætorian prefect, Ablavius, was also murdered, and so was the patrician Optatus, brother-in-law of the deceased emperor.[1] The pretext for these horrors was that only the sons of Constantine ought to have a share in the succession to him.

There were three children.. The eldest, Constantine II., was not yet twenty-one : the second, Constantius, was twenty : the third, Constans, was entering on his

[1] He had married Anastasia, one of the three daughters of Constantius Chlorus.

fifteenth year. In the course of the summer they all three met at Viminacium, on the banks of the Danube, and agreed together to allow Constans to inherit all the provinces left without a ruler by the death of Delmatius. Thus, the youngest of the three princes was the best provided for; however, Constantine II. claimed a sort of guardianship over him. All three assumed the title of Augustus on September 9, 337.

The sons of Constantine had been brought up in the Christian faith. Their interest was soon excited by religious questions. They agreed together to grant permission to all the exiled bishops to return to their flocks. In its wide extent, this measure of clemency was not without inconvenient consequences. Several of the recalled prelates had already been provided with successors : all had left behind them supporters and opponents; and their reinstatement gave rise to disturbances. This was the case in Adrianople, Constantinople, Ancyra, and Gaza.[1] A few days after the death of his father,[2] Constantine II. had set Athanasius free, and had written to the "Catholic" Church of Alexandria to announce this fact, and to say that the step was only the fulfilment of the wishes of the late emperor. At Viminacium Athanasius met Constantius, the prince with whom henceforward he had specially to deal. Constantius, notwithstanding his youth, was a stiff and solemn person, of overwhelming vanity. He could not have been specially pleased to see the return of a man who, for ten years, had had the reputation in the East of a sower of trouble. It was perhaps on account of his ill-will that Athanasius was so long on his homeward journey. Bishop and prince met again at Cæsarea in Cappadocia. Athanasius took good care not to speak to the emperor of his adversaries, Eusebius of Nicomedia and others. On his way to Egypt he was more than once mixed up with the quarrels provoked by the return

---

[1] *Ep. Oriental.* (Hil. *Frag. hist.* iii. 9).

[2] The letter is dated from Trèves, *xv. kal. jul.* (June 17) ; Constantine II. still bears in it the title of Cæsar, which he relinquished three months later for that of Augustus.

of the exiles. Later on, he was accused of taking a
prominent part in their reinstallation, and even of ordain-
ing new bishops in place of those already in possession.[1]
At Alexandria the conflict had already begun, even before
his arrival, and the authorities were obliged to intervene.[2]
At length Athanasius re-entered the city, on November 23,
337,[3] after an absence of more than two years.

His enemies took care not to leave him in peace there.
Eusebius of Nicomedia was in high favour with the new
sovereign of the East. He could not allow his revenge
to be snatched from his grasp nor the decisions of the
Council of Tyre to be lightly regarded. Athanasius, it
was true, had been warmly welcomed by his faithful flock,
and his popularity in Egypt was great. It would have
been more prudent not to continue the attack on this
energetic man, so fertile in resource. But was it possible
to think of yielding? "Let us rather annihilate everything: such is the Church's spirit," thought the aged
Eusebius, like Boileau's canon.

----

[1] "Per omnem viam reditus sui Ecclesiam subvertebat; damnatos
episcopos aliquos restaurabat, aliquibus spem ad episcopatus reditum
promittebat; aliquos ex infidelibus constituebat episcopos, salvis
et integris permanentibus sacerdotibus, per pugnas et caedes gentil-
ium, nihil respiciens leges, desperationi tribuens totum."—*Ep. Or.*,
loc. cit. 8.

[2] *Apol. contra Ar.* 3.

[3] The *Festal Chronicle* seems to indicate the year 338. Such
a delay would be inexplicable: but, as the Chronicle assigns to the
same year the death of Constantine and the return of Athanasius,
it is possible that it really refers to the year 337, just as, a little
before, it places the Council of Tyre in 336 instead of 335. The
Xth *Festal Letter*, for the Easter of 338, begins by complaints
of the afflictions to which Athanasius is exposed on the part of his
enemies, who are detaining him at the ends of the world, and prevent
him from celebrating Easter with his flock. It would seem, therefore,
as if during the winter, 337-338, Athanasius were still at Trèves. But
the letter ends by expressing the joy which the bishop feels at
the end of his persecution and the prospect of celebrating the feasts
in company with his Church as they had been wont to do. It is
evident that the beginning of one letter (that of 337) has been
joined on to the end of another (that of 338).

The first measures adopted were of a very clumsy character. The supporters of Arius, even before the death of their master, formed at Alexandria a well-organized group whom the excommunications of Athanasius kept excluded from the Great Church. It was decided [1] that they should be given a bishop of their own, and that an effort should be made to secure his recognition abroad as the legitimate head of the Church of Alexandria. With this end in view, they chose one of the earliest converts to Arianism, Pistus, formerly a priest in Mareotis, who had been deposed, at the same time as Arius himself, by Bishop Alexander. Secundus, the ex-Bishop of Ptolemais, condemned at the same time as he was, ordained him on the spot.[2] Everyone pretended to look upon Pistus as a brother, to conduct a considerable correspondence with him; and letters were written to various bishops, in order to induce them to enter into communion with him.[3] His friends even addressed themselves to Pope Julius, to whom a deputation was sent consisting of a priest named Macarius, with two deacons, Hesychius and Martyrius. These persons brought to Rome records of the proceedings of the Council of Tyre, in order to make it clear that Athanasius, having been deposed in due form, could no longer be regarded as Bishop of Alexandria.

Athanasius replied to this attack by a synodal letter of all the Egyptian bishops: the story of the Council of Tyre was there related from his point of view, and thoroughly sifted; at the same time, the existing position of affairs was described, the unanimity of the Egyptian episcopate, the reduction of the opposition, as usual, to the Meletian clergy and some few of Pistus' flock. Some Alexandrian priests set out for Italy with this document. They were tne bearers of letters not only to the Pope, but also to the

[1] This intrusion of Pistus may very well have been before the return of Athanasius.

[2] *Supra*, pp. 103, 122, and 131 (note 5).

[3] Letter of the Bishops of Egypt, *Apol. contra Ar.* 19; letter of Pope Julius, *ibid.* 24.

Emperors Constantine II. and Constans, with whom attempts were being made to damage the credit of Athanasius. It was alleged that his return had not been well received at Alexandria, and that the opposition of the people had had to be forcibly overcome by the police; that he was selling, for his own profit, the corn which the emperors were wont to entrust to the Bishop of Alexandria for distribution to the poor of Egypt and of Libya.[1] These innuendoes had been brought to the notice previously of Constantius himself, the more effectually to prejudice him.

It was about this time that Eusebius of Nicomedia, having succeeded for the second time in driving from Constantinople the unfortunate Bishop Paul, translated himself into his place, leaving the see of Nicomedia to Amphion, who had been appointed as a substitute to himself during his own exile. Eusebius of Cæsarea was perhaps no longer living; for, after the death of Constantine, we hear of him no more: he appears to have been swallowed up in the funeral oration of the great emperor, and in the observance of his memory.[2]

The arrival in Rome of the representatives of Athanasius was an unpleasant surprise for Macarius. He at once departed for the East, leaving behind him his two companions. The latter, seeing their assertions contradicted by the Alexandrians, took the initiative in a very grave step: they appealed to the Pope to convoke a synod, and to give judgment on the matter after hearing both sides. Julius would have hesitated to put the Eastern bishops to so much trouble; nevertheless, as the council was asked for in their name, he did not think that he ought to refuse it, and letters of summons were sent to the Bishop of Alexandria as well as to the Bishop of Constantinople and his party.

During these negotiations at Rome, the situation in Egypt was going from bad to worse. Eusebius and his followers, assembled in Antioch at the

---

[1] *Apol. contra Ar.* 3-5, 18 ; *Hist. Ar.* 9 ; *Apol. ad Const.* 4.

[2] Eusebius died on May 30, in a year that may have been 338, 339, or 340.

court of the Emperor Constantius, had recognized the impossibility of supporting Pistus, and resolved to send as bishop to Alexandria a man who, while agreeing with their opinions, had not been compromised in the disputes of the previous years.   Their choice fell upon a certain Eusebius, a native of Edessa, who, after having studied with Eusebius of Cæsarea and sojourned for some time in Alexandria, was living among the dependents of Flaccillus, Bishop of Antioch.   Eusebius refused, not wishing to brave the popularity of Athanasius.[1]   Failing him, they agreed upon a native of Cappadocia, called Gregory, who was at once consecrated and then despatched to Egypt.

Nothing could possibly have been more irregular. Even admitting the validity of the sentence of the Council of Tyre, and regarding Athanasius as no longer the lawful bishop, it was necessary at least that his successor should have been elected by the clergy and the faithful of Alexandria, and should then have been installed by the bishops within his jurisdiction as metropolitan.   But they did not trouble about one illegality more or less. Philagrius, under the patronage of the aged Eusebius, who had formed a high opinion of his zeal at the time of the Council of Tyre, was once more prefect of Egypt. He announced by edict, about the middle of March, 339, that Alexandria had a new bishop.   The Christian population flocked to the churches, raising protests.   The churches of Alexandria, in spite of all that had been done against the bishop, had remained in his power; during his exile, his priests continued to perform their functions there.   The problem now was to take these from them, in order to hand them over to the intruder.

The church of Quirinus[2] was the first to be attacked, on March 18; as a result, some were killed, others wounded, and lamentable scenes took place: finally, fire seized upon

----

[1] Socrates, *H. E.* ii. 9, following George of Laodicea, a contemporary and friend of Eusebius of Emesa.

[2] *Hist. Ar.* 10. The *Chronicle of the Festal Letters* gives the church of Theonas, which was, in 356, the theatre of similar scenes. There is perhaps some confusion here.

the building itself, and it was burnt together with the neighbouring baptistery. Four days afterwards, Gregory made his entrance into the city, guarded by an escort, and welcomed with cries of joy by pagans, Jews, and Arians. The bishop's palace was opened to him, but not without scenes of pillage. It was during the season of Lent, and Easter was drawing near. Gregory went from church to church, under police protection, and caused them, one by one, to be handed over to him. In one of them, on Good Friday, he caused thirty-four persons to be arrested, and they were flogged and cast into prison. Even on Easter Day, arrests were made. Athanasius still held out in one church. He knew that it was going to be attacked, and withdrew from it of his own accord, to avoid further scandals. Of course, the official reports laid to his account all the horrors of which Alexandria was at this time the theatre.

We can imagine his intense indignation. But there is not even need to imagine it, for we possess the indignant protest which he addressed at the time to the whole episcopate. It begins with a reference to the story of the Levite of Ephraim, who in days of old cut into small pieces the dead body of his outraged wife, and made use of these mournful fragments to excite the indignation of the tribes of Israel. His own Church of Alexandria, too, had been violated before his eyes : it had been torn from him bit by bit. Then follows the deplorable story of Gregory's intrusion. And finally, addressing himself to his colleagues, Athanasius appeals to them with unstudied eloquence :

"Behold the comedy which Eusebius is playing! Behold the intrigue which he has been so long fomenting, and which he has finally brought to a head, thanks to the slanders with which he besets the emperor. But that is not enough for him ; he would have my head ; he seeks to frighten my friends by threats of exile and of death. But that is no reason for bowing before his wickedness ; on the contrary, I must defend myself, and protest against the monstrous injustice of which I am the victim. . . . If, as you sit upon your thrones, presiding peacefully over the meetings of your flocks,—if all in a moment there came to you a successor appointed by authority, would you endure him? Would you not cry aloud for vengeance? Well! Now is the time for vigorous action; otherwise, if you keep silence, the present evil will spread to all the Churches; our episcopal seats will be the object of the meanest ambitions, and of disgraceful bargains. . . . Do not suffer such things to be done; do not allow the illustrious Church of Alexandria to be trampled under foot by heretics."

After launching this manifesto, Athanasius embarked for Rome. To do so was not a very easy matter, for the port was well watched; but he was popular among the sailors, and they let him pass. Almost at the same time as himself, Carpones, one of the Alexandrian priests deprived with Arius, also landed in Italy, bearing a letter from Gregory. Such a messenger was well calculated to confirm what was already known—that Gregory and those who had sent him were supporters of Arianism. In Rome, where the Council of Nicæa was alone recognized, that party could not hope for success.

Nevertheless, the Roman legates, Elpidius and Philoxenus, set out for the East. They were detained there for a long time on various pretexts: so much so, that they were not able to start on their return journey until January 340. They had not been much edified by the ecclesiastical world with which they had found themselves in contact. The invitation which they bore was refused; and they were given a very haughty letter, containing a protest against the idea of revising in the West the decisions of Eastern councils, and hinting that the Pope must choose between the society of such people as Athanasius and Marcellus and communion with the prelates of the East.

This document,[1] which is no longer extant, was dated from Antioch, and written in the name of the Bishops of

---

[1] Besides what the reply of Pope Julius tells us about it, Sozomen's analysis (iii. 8) should be consulted.

Cæsarea in Cappadocia (Dianius), of Antioch (Flaccillus),[1] of Constantinople (Eusebius), and of several other sees. The Pope was highly affronted by it; but it did not prevent him from holding the council. The assemblage, consisting of some fifty bishops, was held in the church (*titulus*) of the priest Vitus, one of Silvester's legates at the Council of Nicæa, during the summer or autumn of 340. Athanasius had no difficulty in justifying himself and unmasking the intrigues of which he was the victim.

His was not the only case. Every bishop throughout the East who had been deposed and hounded out of his see, hastened to Rome at the first mention of the council. From Thrace, from Asia Minor, from Syria, from Phœnicia, and from Palestine, the exiled bishops and priests alike poured into Rome. Marcellus of Ancyra made a long stay there. He also had been denounced to the Pope, who had invited his accusers, as he had invited those of Athanasius, to appear before him. In their absence, Marcellus explained his belief, and his language seemed satisfactory; Vitus and Vincent, the Roman legates to the Nicene Council, testified to the zeal he had then displayed against the Arians. In short, he was restored to communion and to his episcopal dignity.

These decisions were notified to the Eastern episcopate by a letter which Pope Julius[2] addressed to those who had signed the one brought by the legates from Antioch. The Pope's letter is one of the most remarkable documents in the whole affair. Although deeply wounded by the bitterness of the Orientals, and the insolent tone they had adopted towards him, he maintained an attitude in keep-

---

[1] Title of the reply: Ἰούλιος Δανίῳ καὶ Φλακίλλῳ, Ναρκίσσῳ, Εὐσεβίῳ, Μάρι, Μακεδονίῳ, Θεοδώρῳ καὶ τοῖς σὺν αὐτοῖς ἀπὸ Ἀντιοχείας γράψασιν ἡμῖν. Flaccillus and Dianius appear to have been rather poor creatures; Narcissus of Neronias and Macedonius of Mopsuestia, Cilician Bishops, as well as Maris of Chalcedon and Theodore of Heraclea in Thrace, were pillars of Eusebius' party.

[2] Preserved by St Athanasius in his *Apol. contra Ar.* 20-25. Sabinus the Macedonian had inserted in his collection the letter of the Eastern prelates to Julius, but not the latter's reply (Socrates, ii. 17).

ing with his position, and remained calm, pacific, and
impartial. If he had summoned the Easterns, it was at
the request of their own envoys; he would have done it,
in any case, on his own motion, for it was natural to take
cognizance of the complaints of bishops who said they had
been unjustly deposed. A revision of the decisions of
councils was not an unheard-of thing: when the Eastern
Churches received Arius and his followers, did they not
act in this way towards the Council of Nicæa? They
contested his right, by alleging that the authority of
bishops is not measured by the importance of their cities.
A strange argument in the mouth of persons who are
forever transferring themselves from one capital to another.
As for himself, the Pope said, stories about broken
chalices interested him much less than the unity of the
Church. He cannot fail to perceive that, beneath their
condemnation of the misdeeds of Athanasius and the
errors of Marcellus, the enemies of these prelates do but
ill conceal their intention of declaring the Arians innocent.
Yet his desire throughout has been to make a close and
thorough examination of the whole question. It is not
his fault if the accusers, after having besought his intervention, now try to escape from the enquiry, nor if the
prefect of Egypt prevents the bishops of that country
from embarking for Rome. He has decided the case
upon the information at his command, and in particular
upon the documents of the Council of Tyre, furnished by
the Easterns themselves. If they think that they can
prove that he is mistaken, let them appear; the accused
are always ready with an answer. But instead of presenting themselves at the requisition of the Bishop of Rome,
they have been guilty of outrageous proceedings, such as
the nomination of the intruder Gregory.

If they had been willing to conform to ancient usage,[1]
and, since the matter concerned bishops of importance
—the see of Alexandria, to address themselves at the
outset to the Roman Church, with a request that she

---

[1] Ἢ ἀγνοεῖτε ὅτι τοῦτο ἔθος ἦν, πρότερον γράφεσθαι ἡμῖν καὶ οὕτως ἔνθεν
ὁρίζεσθαι τὰ δίκαια (*Apol. contra Ar.* 35).

would decide what was right, things would not have come to this pass. They must get out of these scandalous quarrels, in which the bitter grudges of self-love give themselves rein at the expense of charity and of brotherly union.[1]

The Pope was abundantly justified. Yet this letter marks the beginning of an alliance which was to have very troublesome consequences, that of the Roman Church and of St Athanasius with Marcellus of Ancyra. Marcellus may have had the best intentions: his teaching, as we have seen before, laid itself open to criticism, even in those times when precision in theological language still left much to be desired. Athanasius, tossed about in so many storms, has never been accused on the score of his belief, even by his bitterest enemies. It was otherwise with Eustathius and with Marcellus. Eustathius soon disappeared; but Marcellus lived almost as long as Athanasius, and it is worthy of notice that—not to mention the Arianizers, whose special aversion he was—he was almost everywhere looked upon with suspicion. Two years after his death, St Epiphanius considered him a proper subject for his collection of heretics, and included him in it, though, it is true, with some reserve. He had questioned Athanasius himself upon the matter, and the old warrior, without either attacking or defending his former companion-in-arms, replied by a smile,[2] which Epiphanius interpreted as meaning that Marcellus had gone as near as possible to the danger-point, and had been obliged to justify himself.

He was already in this position at the time of which we are now writing. Pope Julius did not allow him to leave Rome, without asking him for a written profession of faith.[3] This document, skilfully worded, managed to

---

[1] This letter was carried to the East by a certain Count Gabianus (*Ap. c. Ar.* 20).

[2] Epiph. *Haer.* lxxii. 4: μόνον διὰ τοῦ προσώπου μειδιάσας ὑπέφηνε μοχθηρίας μὴ μάκραν αὐτὸν εἶναι, καὶ ὡς ἀπολογησάμενον εἶχε.

[3] The text is preserved by Epiphanius. *Haer.* lxxii. 2-3 It should be read in connection with the letters addressed to the bishops, evidently on the subject of Marcellus, and there is reason to believe

conceal the characteristic notes of the doctrine so strongly
attacked in the previous years by Eusebius of Cæsarea.
On reading it, one might think that Marcellus admitted
the eternity of the Word, not only as Word but as Son,
and that he accepted the formula, "His kingdom shall
have no end," in the same sense as the Gospel.[1] This
little artifice might succeed with the Western Church,
little versed in these theological subtleties; but the
Easterns, better informed, could not be so easily deceived.

During these negotiations, a great political change had
taken place in the West. The Emperors of Gaul and of
Illyricum, Constantine II. and Constans, were in conflict
with each other—Constantine not being satisfied with his
share of the empire, nor with the way in which his young
brother accepted his guardianship. They met in battle
near Aquileia: Constantine II. was defeated and killed.
The whole of the West, from the Ocean to Thrace, recognized Constans as its emperor (April 340), and his power,
being thus doubled, soon forced itself on the attention of
his Eastern colleague, Constantius.

The following year (341) there took place at Antioch
the solemn dedication of the principal church, the building
of which had been begun by Constantine. The solemnity
was the occasion of a large assemblage of bishops, about
a hundred in number[2]; the Emperor Constantius was
present. In spite of their attitude of lofty independence,
Eusebius and his party were exceedingly annoyed at the
whole course of the recent proceedings in the West. They
had hoped for, and even solicited, the support of the
Roman Church, and now that Church was upholding
their opponents. Their own sovereign, Constantius, was
favourable to their opinions; but Rome, the ally of
Athanasius, was under the protection of a prince of far
greater power than their own. They saw themselves
driven to act on the defensive. It was not only in Rome
that it was actually so attached to the letter of Pope Julius, of which
we have just spoken.

[1] St Luke i. 33.

[2] Ninety, according to St Athanasius; St Hilary and Sozomen
(Sabinus) give the total as 97.

and at the Court of Constans that they were represented
as defenders of Arianism and the Arians; this accusation
was also circulated in the East, even outside Egypt.
Everything that was happening in that unfortunate country
was known, in spite of police precautions; how the
intruder Gregory was everywhere waging war with those
Christians who had remained faithful to Athanasius,
assailing the churches, and even going so far as to include
among those thrown into prison confessors of the time of
Maximin. The aged Eusebius felt that the time was
come to defend himself. From the Council of the Dedication (*in Encaeniis*), there issued various letters,[1] one of
which contained the following words:—

"We are not followers (ἀκόλουθοι) of Arius. How
could we, being bishops, follow in the train of a priest?
We have no other faith than that which has been handed
down from the beginning. But having had occasion to
enquire into his own faith, and to form an estimate of it,
we have rather admitted it than followed it. You will see
this by what we are about to say." Then follows a sooth-
ing and conciliatory profession of faith,[2] containing neither
the technical terms of Nicæa, nor the final anathema; by
way of compensation, a few words are inserted with regard
to the eternal Reign of Christ, evidently directed against
Marcellus of Ancyra.

Another profession of faith, emanating from the same
synod, is more explicit upon the Divine prerogatives of
the Son of God; it even heaps up terms calculated to
enforce them [3] and, in a certain fashion, repudiates the

---

[1] Athan. *De syn* 22-25.

[2] Characteristic passages are the following : καὶ εἰς ἕνα υἱὸν τοῦ Θεοῦ
μονογενῆ, πρὸ πάντων τῶν αἰώνων ὑπάρχοντα καὶ συνόντα τῷ γεγεννηκότι αὐτὸν Πατρί . . . διαμένοντα βασιλέα καὶ Θεὸν εἰς τοὺς αἰῶνας.

[3] Τὸν γεννηθέντα πρὸ τῶν αἰώνων ἐκ τοῦ Πατρός, θεὸν ἐκ θεοῦ, ὅλον ἐξ ὅλου,
μόνον ἐκ μόνου, τέλειον ἐκ τελείου, βασιλέα ἐκ βασιλέως, κύριον ἀπὸ κυρίου, λόγον
ζῶντα, σοφίαν ζῶσαν, φῶς ἀληθινόν, ὁδόν, ἀλήθειαν, ἀνάστασιν, ποιμένα, θύραν,
ἄτρεπτόν τε καὶ ἀναλλοίωτον· τῆς θεότητος, οὐσίας τε καὶ βουλῆς καὶ δυνάμεως
καὶ δόξης τοῦ Πατρὸς ἀπαράλλακτον εἰκόνα, τὸν πρωτότοκον πάσης κτίσεως, τὸν
ὄντα ἐν ἀρχῇ πρὸς τὸν Θεόν, λόγον Θεόν. . . . Εἴ τις λέγει τὸν Υἱὸν κτίσμα ὡς
ἓν τῶν κτισμάτων, ἢ γέννημα ὡς ἓν τῶν γεννημάτων, ἢ ποίημα ὡς ἓν τῶν
ποιημάτων . . . ἀνάθεμα ἔστω.

expressions which were forbidden by the Council of Nicæa.
We find in it that the Son is "the image of the essence"
(οὐσία) of the Father, not that He is "of the essence" of
the Father. The three names, Father, Son, and Holy
Spirit are represented not as terms having no relation
with realities, but as characterizing the hypostasis
(ὑπόστασιν), the rank, the dignity of the Persons named;
thus, by hypostasis they are Three; by their mutual
agreement (συμφωνίᾳ) they make but One.[1]

A third formula, presented by Theophronius, the Bishop
of Tyana, was approved of. In its positive statements it
is absolutely colourless; but at the end it formally repudiates Marcellus of Ancyra, Sabellius, Paul of Samosata,
"and all those who are in communion with them."

These formulas certainly indicate a tendency to
modify in some degree the position of the party. Arius
was dead; and they were beginning to find him rather
embarrassing, and to extricate themselves from too close
an identification with his views. As a matter of fact, no
one, except a few fanatical disciples, now maintained his
system. On this point they drew back, step by step, and
without regret. They had discovered a better fighting-
ground—the struggle against Marcellus. It was on this
that the conflict was renewed. "You are Arians," so rose
the cry, without ceasing, from Rome and from Alexandria.
"You are Sabellians," was the reply from Antioch. And
this state of things was all the more serious because
Marcellus himself was not dead; and the Westerns kept
him in their ranks, recognized him as a bishop, and
defended him.

Athanasius, who has preserved for us the formulas of
Antioch, gives us no information as to the way in which
they were presented to the assembly, and approved by it.
It is possible that different bishops or different groups
may have availed themselves of this opportunity to obtain

---

[1] St Hilary (*De synodis*, 29, *et seq*.) gives a Latin text of this
formula, and explains it favourably; as does also Sozomen (iii. 5),
from whom we learn that this formula was, in the party, attributed to
the martyr Lucian.

certificates of orthodoxy. The Council of Nicæa, while decreeing a formula, had decided nothing as to the use to be made of it, nor on the question whether it was to be substituted for those previously in use in the various Churches for the ceremonies of Christian initiation. It even seems as if the council had no idea of such a substitution, for in that case, it would have completed the conclusion of it by mentioning therein the Catholic Church, the remission of sins, and the resurrection of the flesh. As a matter of fact, the Churches kept their old creeds. In the profession of faith which he sent to Pope Julius, Marcellus of Ancyra inserted word for word the text of the Roman symbol. In other places, the traditional text was modified, either according to the formula of Nicæa, or to others. Already, even in the time of Constantine, jealous as he was of the interests of his council, Arius had been able to submit to the emperor a profession of faith which did not reproduce word for word the symbol of Nicæa. It is not astonishing, therefore, that other formulas should have been presented or published. At the same time, it was a dangerous game to play—a fact which was soon perceived.

The Dedication Council[1] was the last in which

---

[1] It is customary to connect with the Dedication Council the 25 canons of a Council of Antioch which is mentioned in the oldest collections of canons. This attribution is very doubtful. According to the covering letter sent to those who were absent, and according to the signatures, the assembly which promulgated these canons was composed exclusively of bishops within the jurisdiction of Antioch, Syria, Mesopotamia, and Cilicia ; this was not the case as regards the Dedication Council, which certainly included other bishops. We know it was held after the Council of Nicæa, because it mentions that council, and before the year 359, when the new province of Euphratesia makes its first appearance in the documents. If the signatures were, in regard to the particulars given, better supported by evidence than they are, we should be inclined to date the Council of Antioch very shortly after the Nicene Council, for nearly all the signatures are common to the two councils. The enactments furnish hardly any indications : anti-Athanasian and anti-Eustathian pre-possessions were early discovered in them ; but there is not much evidence of this. I should be inclined to think that the council was before, rather than after, the year 341.

Eusebius took part. He seems to have died about the end of 341, being still in outward communion with the Church, for there was, as yet, no open schism between the East and Rome. If he had always minded his own business, and not had the fatal idea of intervening between Arius and his bishop, Arianism would have remained a purely Alexandrian controversy, and could have been suppressed without much difficulty. But Eusebius let loose upon the Bishop of Alexandria, first the Eastern episcopate, and then the emperor and the empire. The memory of this intriguing prelate, in whom one can find no single sympathetic feature, remains weighted with a heavy responsibility.

The Church of Constantinople, which he governed during his latter years, had also itself passed through strange periods of crisis—thanks to him. After the death of Alexander (336), a certain Paul, a native of Thessalonica, had been elected bishop there. He had been present, according to report, at the deposition of Athanasius,[1] and had associated himself with it by his signature. He was himself accused, soon afterwards, by one of his priests, Macedonius, deposed by the same council as Marcellus of Ancyra, and exiled to Pontus. His place had not yet been filled when Constantine died. He immediately returned to his Church, and for some time Macedonius maintained friendly relations with him. But the see of Constantinople tempted the ambition of Eusebius. The former accusations were again revived at the opportune moment. Paul saw himself ousted once more, and Eusebius installed in his place (either at the end of 338 or the beginning of 339). On Eusebius' death (341), Paul, who had fled to Trèves and been warmly welcomed

---

[1] *Paulus vero Athanasii expositioni interfuit manuque propria sententiam scribens, eum ceteris eum etiam ipse damnavit* (*Ep. Or.* Hil. *Frag. hist.* iii. 13). I cannot adopt the opinion of those who, from the evidence of this text, reject entirely the story of the death of Arius, in the time of Bishop Alexander, as it is related by St Athanasius. It is possible that Paul may have taken part in the Council of Tyre as the representative of his bishop, or that his signature may have been given at Constantinople a little later.

by Bishop Maximin, obtained through his mediation permission to return to his episcopal city. Eusebius had had time to organize a party, at the head of which Macedonius now found himself. The populace were divided between Paul and him, and disagreement degenerated into scenes of violence. Things went so far that a general, the *magister militum*, Hermogenes, was killed in a riot and his body dragged through the streets (342). However, the coercive power was still in the hands of the authorities. The prætorian prefect Philip succeeded, after a struggle, in which more than three thousand persons are said to have perished, in installing Macedonius. As for Paul, he was arrested, loaded with chains, and sent to Singar in the extremity of Mesopotamia on the Persian frontier. Thence he was transferred to Emesa, then to Cucusa, in the mountains of Cappadocia, where an attempt was made to starve him to death; and finally, as he persisted in living, the prefect Philip ordered him to be strangled.[1]

All this time the imperial court of the West continued to interest itself in the affairs of the Eastern Church, and the *protégés* of the Apostolic See. In consequence of some step on his part, it was decided at Antioch that a deputation of bishops should be sent to the young Emperor Constans. Four distinguished members of the Arianizing party were chosen for this purpose, Narcissus of Neronias, Maris of Chalcedon, Theodore of Heraclea, and Mark of Arethusa: the first two had taken part in the Council of Nicæa. They were the bearers of a creed,[2] differing from the three approved by the Dedication Council, and conceived almost in the same spirit. This document is important, for the Easterns adhered to it for

---

[1] The story of Paul is very difficult to unravel. The synodal letter of the Easterns (343) is the most ancient document on the subject, but it is inspired by too much passion to be taken literally. Next comes St Athanasius (*Hist. Ar.* 7; cf. *Apol. de fuga* 3), then St Jerome (*Chron.* ad ann. Abr. 2358). Socrates (ii. 6, 7, 12 *et seq.*), and Sozomen (iii. 3, 4, 7-9) give us the local tradition of Constantinople, but with much confusion. See the discussion by Dr Loofs in Hauck's *Encyclopädie*, s. v. "Macedonius."

[2] Athan., *De syn.* 25.

several years, and often presented it, especially to the
West, as the expression of their belief. It was vague
as to the procession of the Son, but precise as to the
eternity of His Reign, and it repudiated several of the
Arian expressions.[1]

The bishops were received at the court at Trèves, but
not by the Church. Bishop Maximin was devoted to
Athanasius: he refused to see his enemies.

It was no doubt as a sequel to this embassy that
Constans, on the advice of several Western bishops, came
to an understanding with his brother Constantius[2] that
a new council should be convoked, in which the bishops
of both empires should sit together and arrange their
differences. The place chosen for this great assembly
was the town of Sardica, the modern Sofia.[3] It was
the capital of inland Dacia (*mediterranea*) and the last
town of the Western empire on the borders of Thrace,
itself included in the jurisdiction of Constantius.[4]

Athanasius, apprised by the emperor, came to meet
him at Milan, afterwards in Gaul, where he had a meeting
with Hosius. The latter was then far advanced in years.
But no one had more information than he had upon the
controversies of the East, and no one was better qualified

---

[1] Τὸν πρὸ πάντων τῶν αἰώνων ἐκ τοῦ Πατρὸς γεννηθέντα θεὸν ἐκ θεοῦ, φῶς
ἐκ φωτὸς . . . λόγον ὄντα καὶ σοφίαν καὶ δύναμιν καὶ ζωὴν καὶ φῶς ἀληθινὸν . . .
)ὃ ἡ βασιλεία ἀκατάλυτος οὖσα διαμένει εἰς τοὺς ἀπείρους αἰῶνας. . . . Τοὺς δὲ
λέγοντας ἐξ οὐκ ὄντων τὸν Υἱὸν ἢ ἐξ ἑτέρας ὑποστάσεως καὶ μὴ ἐκ τοῦ Θεοῦ, καὶ
ἦν ποτε χρόνος ὅτε οὐκ ἦν, ἀλλοτρίους οἶδεν ἡ καθολικὴ Ἐκκλησία.

[2] Athan., *Ap. ad Const.* 4.

[3] In Bulgarian it is still called Sredec, which is the ancient name.

[4] The date of the Council of Sardica, formerly fixed as 347,
following a false clue in Socrates, is still not yet quite certain. We
may hesitate between the years 342 and 343. The first is indicated
in the Alexandrian section of Theodosius' collection : *Congregata est
synodus consulatu Constantini et Constantini* (read *Constantii et
Constantis*) *aput Sardicam* (Maassen, *Quellen*, vol. i., p. 548). The
Chronicle of the Festal Letters seems to indicate the year 343 (*Placido
et Romulo coss.*) ; but as the chronicler often reckons in Egyptian
years, beginning with Thoth 1 (August 29), this indication may well
be identified with the preceding one. There is nothing to prevent
the council having taken place in the autumn (September—October)
of the year 342. *Cf.* E. Schwartz, *Nachrichten*, 1904, p. 341.

to negotiate with its bishops.   He was deputed to conduct
the Western bishops to Sardica and to preside over the
assembly, just as he had directed, more or less, that at
Nicæa.

About eighty bishops gathered round Hosius, in the
autumn of 342 (or 343).   Half of them came from Greek
and Latin Illyricum ; the others from the West properly
so-called.   Pope Julius was represented by two priests,
Archidamus and Philoxenus, and by the deacon Leo.
There were at least ten bishops from Italy, and six from
Spain.   The Easterns arrived in about equal numbers.
They had all travelled together, under the escort of two
high officials, the Counts Musunianus and Hesychius.
The new Bishop of Antioch, Stephen, the successor of
Flaccillus, led this procession.   They had not set out in
very good spirits.   Of course it was necessary to obey the
Emperor Constantius, who was himself, in this matter,
yielding to the representations of his brother.   It is a long
journey from Antioch to Sardica.   In the evening, at
their various halting places in Asia Minor and Thrace,
they held consultations upon the attitude to be adopted
in face of these troublesome Westerns.   A large number
of the travellers were either indifferent, or even favourable
to Athanasius.   But, as always happens, the main body
was directed by a few leaders.   The two Eusebii were
gone, but there remained some of the early members of
the Eusebian party, former protectors of Arius, and some
members of the Council of Tyre.   They persuaded the
others to take no part in the synod, either as parties to
the disputes, or as judges : they would go as far as
Sardica, since the emperor wished it, but they would act
in such a manner as to get out of it as soon as possible,
and to avoid contact with the Westerns.[1]

This programme was carried out to the letter.   On
their arrival at Sardica, the Eastern bishops were confined
to their own rooms by their leaders, who feared defections.[2]

---

[1] *Apol. contra Ar.* 48.

[2] Two of them, however, had the courage to join Hosius : Asterius
of Petra, and Arius, another Palestinian Bishop.

When invited to join themselves to their Western brethren, they protested that they would do nothing of the
sort,[1] giving as an excuse that Athanasius, Marcellus,
and Asclepas, all three deposed by Eastern councils, were
treated by Hosius, by the Bishop of Sardica, Protogenes,
and by the rest, as lawful bishops.   This scruple was not
without some apparent foundation.   The Council of Rome
had, it was true, quashed the Eastern decisions.   But as the
Roman Council was not being adhered to, and an attempt
was being made to review the proceedings which that council
had settled, it would perhaps have been more prudent,
considering the unfavourable attitude of their opponents,
not to appear to prejudge any of the issues.   Hosius tried
to arrange matters in a friendly spirit.   In order to
persuade the Easterns to allow the case to be heard, he
promised them that, even if the innocence of Athanasius
should be proved, he would relieve them of his unwelcome
figure and take him with him to Spain.[2]   The Easterns
would listen to nothing : they held a council of their own ;
and then retired to Thrace, to Philippopolis, and from
thence returned to their homes.   But before leaving
Sardica,[3] they indited an encyclical letter, addressed to
the whole episcopate, to the clergy and to the faithful,
especially to Gregory of Alexandria, Donatus of Carthage,
Maximus of Salona, and several Italian bishops, whom
they knew, or imagined, to be favourable to their views.

The letter began with the subject of Marcellus, and a
condemnation of his heretical doctrines.   Then they gave
the history of Athanasius from their own point of view ;
his condemnation at Tyre, and the scenes of violence for
which his own return and that of others—Marcellus,
Asclepas, and Lucius—had everywhere been the signal.
They protested against the idea that such persons could

[1] According to Sozomen (iii. 11), this protest had been preceded by
another, sent from Philippopolis.

[2] Letter of Hosius, in Athanasius, *Hist. Ar.* 44.

[3] This letter purports to have been written at Sardica : *Placuit
nobis de Sardica scribere* (Hil., *Frag. hist.* iii. 23) ; Socrates (ii. 20)
speaks here of Philippopolis, but he deserves no confidence.   What
he says of the Council of Sardica is a tissue of errors.

be restored to the episcopate, at a distance from their own sees, by people unacquainted with the facts, and also against the claim of the Westerns to revise decisions of the Eastern bishops. On their arrival at Sardica, the Easterns had been met with the surprising sight of persons whom they had condemned, sitting in the midst of their Western brethren, as if nothing had happened, and as if they and some of their present protectors had not in former years been alike condemned. They had proposed to reopen the enquiry as to the affair in Mareotis; no notice was taken of this proposal.[1] From that time, they had separated from such colleagues as these (among whom, besides, there were several persons of doubtful reputation), and threw upon them the whole responsibility for the schism to which, in order to defend a few wretches, they were about to expose the whole Church. They maintain all the sentences of deposition which they have themselves pronounced; and in addition they declare the following persons to be deposed and excommunicated—Julius of Rome, Hosius of Cordova, Protogenes of Sardica, Gaudentius of Naïssus (Nisch), and Maximin of Trèves. Finally, as a protestation against the heresy of Marcellus, patronized by Hosius, they set forth their own faith. Here we find the creed already sent to Constans with a few additional anathemas.[2]

The Westerns, being abandoned in this fashion, resumed their examination of the proceedings against Athanasius, Asclepas, and Marcellus. So far as Athanasius was concerned, they did not consider that there was any occasion for a new enquiry. That of Tyre was sufficient for them; it had evidently turned against those who had

---

[1] They were well aware that, with Gregory at Alexandria and the prefect of Egypt on their side, the enquiry could not fail to turn in their favour.

[2] *Similiter et illos qui dicunt tres esse deos, aut Christum non esse Deum aut ante ea unum* (?) *non fuisse Christum neque filium Dei, aut ipsum Patrem et Filium et Spiritum sanctum, aut non natum Filium, aut non sententia neque voluntate Deum Patrem genuisse Filium* (Hil., *Frag. hist.* iii. 29). This text has been altered—like the whole document, for the matter of that.

instituted it, and had proved the innocence of the Bishop
of Alexandria. Asclepas produced the documents
relating to his own trial, drawn up at Antioch in the
presence of his accusers and of Eusebius of Cæsarea: the
course of this trial showed that he also was innocent.
As to Marcellus, his notorious book was read. It was
recognized, with too much leniency, that the objectionable passages were rather tentative propositions than
assertions maintained, and that, at bottom, his faith was
sound.[1]

As to the Easterns, their behaviour was severely
judged. In the opinion of the council, their abrupt
departure showed that they had but little confidence in
their previous decisions, and feared to be accused in their
turn; as would actually have happened, since many plaints
had been made against them. Their victims had presented
themselves in large numbers, with witnesses, proofs, and
even such damning exhibits as the instruments of torture
to which they had been subjected. All these alleged
wrongs were examined, and the council, so far as was in
its power, made provision for the reparation necessary in
each case. It also pronounced—for contumacy, just as the
Easterns had done—several sentences of deposition and
excommunication. These sentences were directed first
against the three successors wrongfully appointed in place
of the reinstated bishops, Gregory of Alexandria, Basil

---

[1] That in this Marcellus had imposed on the council is evident
from these remarks on his doctrine: "He has not said, as his
adversaries allege, that the *Word* of God derives His origin from the
Virgin Mary, nor that *His* kingdom would have an end; he wrote
that His kingdom is without end, as it is without beginning."
What the adversaries of Marcellus really charged him with,
was not the denial of the Eternity of the *Word*, but the assertion
that His existence as *Son* began with the Incarnation. They accused
him, not of setting limits to the Kingdom of the Word, as Word, but
to His Kingdom as Christ, as the Word Incarnate. On these two
points, he was certainly wrong. But Marcellus was skilful in
manœuvring. He had signed the Creed of Nicæa, in which the
generation of the Word, before the Incarnation, is clearly affirmed;
he placed an interpretation then on the term γεννηθέντα, which, in
his system, could only be applied to the Incarnate Word.

of Ancyra, Quintianus of Gaza; then the actual leaders of
the party, Stephen, Bishop of Antioch, Acacius of Cæsarea
in Palestine, Menophantus of Ephesus, Narcissus of
Neronias, Theodore of Heraclea, Ursacius of Singidunum,
Valens of Mursa; the last three had taken part in the
famous enquiry in Mareotis; Valens, as an aggravation,
had just distinguished himself by fomenting a sedition to
secure his own election as Bishop of Aquileia. Scenes of
violence had taken place there: a certain Bishop Viator
had been so seriously injured that he died three days afterwards. To this list of persons proscribed the council
added further George, Bishop of Laodicea in Syria, who
had not, however, accompanied the other Eastern prelates;
but they had this against him, that, being a priest at
Alexandria, he had been deposed by Bishop Alexander.

Besides these questions of individuals, the council also
wished, after the example of the Council of Nicæa, and as
the Eastern prelates had just done, to draw up a profession
of faith. With this intention, a composition of considerable length was prepared, which, for the most part, either
justified or disguised certain ideas for which Marcellus had
been blamed, and which affirmed the unity of hypostasis,
this word being taken, be it understood, in the sense of its
Latin equivalent *substantia*.[1] Hosius and Protogenes, who
approved of this rather tenuous creed, had even prepared
a letter to Pope Julius, to induce him to give it his
approval. However, the proposal miscarried. The council
was made to understand, and Athanasius seems to have
exerted himself strongly to this end, that there was already
quite sufficient difficulty in maintaining the Creed of
Nicæa, without complicating it with appendices, which
would only increase the centres of opposition to it; and
that therefore it was much better to keep to the text

---

[1] For people who translated ὁμοούσιος by *consubstantialis*, the terms
οὐσία and ὑπόστασις were equivalent. We must note carefully that the
word *essentia*, by which we translate οὐσία, was not at that time in
use; that, for the two Greek words, οὐσία and ὑπόστασις, there was but
one Latin term, *substantia*. We can therefore understand the Council
of Sardica being tempted to pass from the 'consubstantial' to the unity
of hypostasis.

unanimously adopted by that venerable assembly, and not
to imitate the opposing party, who every year brought out
a new creed.

Athanasius was quite right, as the sequel showed. The
Nicene Council, inspired solely by the desire to save the
absolute Divinity of Christ, had accepted the Western
homoousios, which really safeguarded the point assailed,
but gave no explanation of the personality of the pre-
existing Christ. Such a formula was incomplete in itself;
it was necessary to supplement it by that of the Three
Persons. This latter dogma the Western bishops at
Nicæa may have held in the spirit: Tertullian and
Novatian speak unhesitatingly of the *tres personae*. But
it had not been introduced into the Creed of Nicæa; and,
besides, the word *persona*, πρόσωπον in Greek, was not
sufficiently explicit. *Persona* has undoubtedly the sense
of rational individuality, but it equally well signifies a
character, a mask, a personage. The most orthodox
among the Easterns clung to a greater precision of
language. This they expressed by the term *hypostasis*,
which was itself inadequate, for its proper meaning is
substance, and, when one speaks of three divine hypostases,
one has the appearance at first of speaking of three divine
substances, of three gods. However, without really
comprehending what they were trying to explain—and
how can anyone comprehend such relations in the Infinite
Being?—they ended by acknowledging the one essence
and the three hypostases of the Easterns. It was finally
agreed that that which, in the Trinity, was common to the
Father, to the Son, and to the Holy Spirit, should be
called "essence" (οὐσία), and that which was proper to each
of them should be designated by the terms "hypostasis" or
"Person." But, at the time of which we are now writing,
that solution was still far off. It would certainly have
been compromised, if the Council of Sardica had prejudiced
it by proscribing the three hypostases. It was a wise
inspiration on the part of Athanasius to oppose such a
declaration.

Nevertheless, the idea of a creed was not lost sight of,

any more than the text of the letter which was to commend
it to Pope Julius[1]: and, later on, certain enthusiasts found
an opportunity for taking advantage of it. But the
encyclical addressed by the council to "all the bishops
of the Catholic Church," contained nothing of the kind.[2]
It concluded with an invitation to those addressed to
confirm by their signatures the definitions of the assembly
in which they had not been able to take part. The edition
of this encyclical inserted by St Athanasius some years
later in his *Apology against the Arians* actually contains
more than two hundred signatures which were thus added,
besides those of the members of the council.

The council was unwilling to separate without passing some disciplinary canons. For the most part, these
regulations were inspired by existing circumstances.
Thus, the first two forbid in the severest terms the translation of bishops from one see to another; we can perceive
here the impression left by the affair of Valens.[3] Others
condemn the constant journeys of bishops to the imperial
court,[4] or deal with incidents which had taken place at
Thessalonica[5]; others concern the ordinations of bishops,
law-suits of clergy, and the sojourn of bishops outside
their dioceses.[6] The most famous are the canons relating
to the condemnation of bishops.[7] Such condemnations
can only be pronounced by the council of the province to

---

[1] Both these are preserved in the Alexandrian *dossier*, which the
collection of the deacon Theodosius has preserved to us in Latin.
The Greek text of the creed is in Theodoret, *H. E.* ii. 6, pp. 844-888:
Ἀποκηρύττομεν δὲ ἐκείνους κ.τ.λ.

[2] Πολλὰ μὲν καὶ πολλάκις (Athan. *Apol. contra Ar.* 44 *et seq.*). The
council wrote also to the Church of Alexandria (*ibid.* 37), as well as
to the bishops of Egypt and Libya (*ibid.* 41), and finally to the
Churches of Mareotis, *Etiam ex his* (Collection of the deacon
Theodosius, Migne, *P. L.* vol. lvi., p. 848). Athanasius himself
wrote to the priests and deacons of Alexandria, as well as to the
priests and deacons of Mareotis (*ibid.*, pp. 852 and 850).

[3] A special report was addressed to the Emperor Constans upon
this affair.

[4] Can. 8-12 of the Latin text; 7, 8, 9, 20 of the Greek text.

[5] Lat. 20, 21; Gr. 16-19.

[6] Lat. 13-19; Gr. 10-15.   [7] Lat. 3, 4, 7; Gr. 3, 4. 5.

which the accused belongs.   And if he is not satisfied
with the decision given, his fellow-bishops of the province
are to write to the Bishop of Rome, who shall decide if
there is any occasion for revision, and if so, shall appoint
judges of appeal.   The appeal shall temporarily suspend
proceedings, and the appellant bishop shall not be able to
be replaced before the final decision has been pronounced.
The judges of appeal must be the bishops of a province
near to that of the first judges.   The Pope shall be able,
at the request of the accused, to cause himself to be
represented at their council by legates.   Here, what is
evidently in mind is the deposition of the Bishop of
Alexandria outside his own province, at the request of the
Eastern prelates ; the decision given by Pope Julius, and
the summoning of the Council of Sardica.

These canons, with the other documents relating to
the council, were despatched to Pope Julius,[1] with a letter[2]
signed by a majority of the members of the assembly ; the
legates were to give him information as to details.

Regarded as a whole, the Council of Sardica, which
was summoned with such excellent intentions, had failed
in its essential task—the pacification of the Church.   This
failure was primarily due to the unfriendly attitude of the
Eastern prelates, led throughout by the supporters of
Arianism, and throughout implacable in their animosity
against Athanasius.   We must also admit that certain
blunders had been made by the Western prelates, and
especially by Hosius.   This " Father of Councils," as he
was called, who had had a seat at the Council of Elvira in

---

[1] *Optimum et valde congruentissimum esse videtur*, says the
council (letter to Julius), *si ad caput, id est ad Petri apostoli sedem, de
singulis quibusque provinciis Domini referant sacerdotes.*

[2] Letter *Quod Semper* (Hil. *Frag. hist.* ii. 9-15).   In this letter we
must take note of the following phrase, which gives a peculiar signifi-
cance to certain pieces of information :—*Ipsi religiosissimi imperatores
permiserunt ut de integro universa discussa disputarentur, et ante
omnia de sancta fide et de integritate veritatis.*   Thus the two
emperors themselves decided the programme of the council.   Besides
the question of faith, there was that of the sentences unjustly passed
and that of the acts of violence attributed to the Easterns.

the days before the persecution, and who, under Constantine, had taken the principal part in the Council of Nicæa, was, nevertheless, not the kind of man needed to preside over such sessions. He was a true Spaniard, dictatorial, harsh, and inflexible. At Nicæa he had insisted upon the *homoousios*, without any consideration for the feelings of dislike which such a formula, presented without any saving clause, might excite in the East; now he had furnished his opponents with the very pretext they were seeking against the council, by allowing them to pose as defenders of correctness of procedure and even of orthodoxy.

The whole conduct of the proceedings, in short, represented a bad enough piece of business. Pope Julius ordered the canons of Sardica to be inscribed upon his registers, following those of Nicæa. And there they remained dormant.[1] After, as before, this legislation with regard to appeals, the Apostolic See continued to receive them; but there is no evidence to show that in this matter it conformed to the procedure laid down at Sardica. Instead of confining himself to quashing the decisions and appointing new judges, the Pope continued to decide the appeal himself. The West scarcely troubled itself about the new canons; the East only recognized them two or three centuries later, and even then rather as historical documents than as a code to which it owed obedience.

On their return from the council,[2] the Eastern bishops met with a very cold reception at Adrianople, where Bishop Lucius had already had occasion to complain of them. They were treated as runaways, and the Church refused to hold communion with them. They took their revenge by once more sending the bishop into exile, with a chain around his neck, and manacles upon his hands.[3] Ten workmen belonging to the armoury, who had been

---

[1] Pope Zosimus revised them a century later; and then they were the cause of a celebrated controversy.

[2] Athan. *Hist. Ar.* 18-20.

[3] He died shortly afterwards, at the place to which he had been exiled.

wanting in respect to them, were put to death on the application of their friend, Philagrius, now raised to the dignity of Count.   Several years afterwards, Athanasius, passing through Adrianople, had an opportunity of seeing their graves.   As to those bishops who had been restored to their former position by Hosius' council, they were forbidden, under pain of death, to show themselves again in their episcopal cities.   The Bishops Arius and Asterius, who had forsaken their colleagues to go over to the side of the Westerns, were arrested and banished to the wilds of Libya.   Some priests and deacons of Alexandria were deported to Armenia.   The condition of affairs throughout the East amounted almost to a reign of terror.

Nevertheless, Constans did not abandon those whom he had promised to protect.   No doubt he shared, just as his brother did, the opinions of his own bishops ; moreover, he would not be sorry to have a cause of quarrel with his imperial colleague : the exiles furnished him with this. Towards Easter, in the year 344,[1] two Western bishops, Vincent of Capua, the former legate at Nicæa, and Euphratas of Cologne, arrived at Antioch ; they were escorted by a general, the *magister militum*, Salianus, and were the bearers of letters from their emperor. Bishop Stephen made them the subject of a plot which can only be characterized as abominable.[2]   The house where they stayed was situated in a lonely spot.   The bishop's servants engaged the services of a common prostitute, and, making one of the attendants their accomplice, introduced

---

[1] This date follows from a narrative of St Athanasius (*Hist. Ar.* 21), who places the death of Gregory (June 25, 345) about ten months after certain events which followed closely upon the affair of Euphratas and the deposition of Stephen. This passage, in any case, prevents us from going back as far as the year 343, which would, besides, be inadmissible, if the Council of Sardica had really taken place in that year. If it was held in the autumn of 342, as seems probable, we must admit that the Western authorities waited some months to make sure as to the attitude of the Eastern emperor in regard to the restored prelates.

[2] Athan. *Hist. Ar.* 20 ; *cf.* Theodoret, ii. 7, 8.   Theodoret, who came from Antioch, has preserved some details as to the locality of the affair.

her by night into the chamber where the Bishop of
Cologne was sleeping. Euphratas awoke, and at once
called for help. The woman, who had expected from what
they told her to find a young man, herself took fright when
she saw that she was in the presence of an old man whose
appearance showed him to be a bishop. She too began
to call out. At that moment, some persons, who were
secreted in readiness, burst into the house. The bishops
did not lose their heads; their cries for help were answered,
the outer door was closed, and the result was the capture
of the woman and also of several of the organizers of the
plot. The next morning the general, Salianus, who had
lodgings elsewhere, appeared on the scene, and, without
waiting to listen to the bishops under his charge, who were
already beginning to show themselves mercifully inclined,
went at once to the palace to make a complaint and to
demand a formal enquiry. The Emperor Constantius,
greatly shocked, granted his request without demur.
Stephen's complicity in the affair was established: steps
were speedily taken to gather together a synod of neighbouring bishops, and he was deposed.

His place was filled by a native of Phrygia, Leontius,
a staunch supporter of the Arianizing party. Thus, while
the direction of ecclesiastical affairs changed hands,
the spirit which actuated it was unchanged. However,
Constantius, reflecting upon all that had just happened,
and listening also to his brother's expostulations, began
to relax the severities into which he had been led. The
clergy of Alexandria were recalled from their exile in
Armenia, and the Egyptian officials received orders to
leave the partisans of Athanasius in peace.[1]

But the chief matter was the schism, for there was
really a schism between the two episcopates. The pass
of Tisucis, between Sardica and Philippopolis, formed a
boundary between the two communions. On either side
of the frontier, people might differ in their opinions, but
they remained in religious communion one with another;
but, once over the border, it was not so.[2] Such a state

---

[1] Athan. *Hist. Ar.* 21.   [2] Socrates, ii. 22.

of things was intolerable. The Eastern prelates, no doubt as a reply to the affair of Vincent and Euphratas, or provoked in another way by delegates from their Western brethren, decided to send to the court of Milan four bishops—Demophilus, Eudoxius,[1] Macedonius, and Martyrius—with instructions to explain their faith to the Emperor Constans and his bishops, and to see if some kind of understanding could not be arrived at. They carried with them, besides the creed already presented in 342 and republished at Sardica, a long explanation, in ten articles.[2] This contained nothing that was unorthodox, and, if it had not been for its silence as to the *homoousios*, it might have given satisfaction. Naturally, it expanded at length the points compromised by the teaching of Marcellus and his disciple Photinus, or, as he was called, by a play upon his name, Scotinus.[3] This is the first time that we hear of him. Like his master, he was a Galatian, and, under Marcellus' instructions, had performed at Ancyra the functions of a deacon. He was now at the head of the bishopric of Sirmium, a very important position. The members of his diocese were much attached to him; they appreciated his learning, his eloquence, and his other qualities. Unfortunately, his doctrine left much to be desired. We may describe it with sufficient accuracy by saying that it was almost identical with that of Paul of Samosata. Besides, the principles of Marcellus, with his impersonal Word who became Son and a distinct hypostasis solely by His Incarnation, ended logically in the theology of the two Theodoti, a theology which was condemned at Rome by Pope Victor, and at Antioch in the time of Bishop Paul. The Easterns had abundant reasons for rejecting this theology, and even for charging the old Bishop of Ancyra

---

[1] Eudoxius and Demophilus succeeded one another, later on, in the see of Constantinople.

[2] Athan. *De Syn.* 26, who gives the date of it as three years after the Council of 341. He mentions three of these bishops, Eudoxius, Macedonius, and Martyrius.

[3] Φωτεινός is an adjective meaning "light"; Σκοτεινός means "dark" or "obscure."

with being the father of it. The plain speaking of his disciple put Marcellus in a difficult position. Athanasius, who was then not very far from Sardica, and was living in retirement at Nisch, began to see more clearly into the ideas of his colleague, and to recognize that they hardly differed from those of Photinus.

An understanding might have been arrived at in Milan. In fact, it was almost attained. The Western bishops, assembled around the emperor with the legates of the Roman Church,[1] made up their minds to condemn Photinus. But in return they demanded of the Eastern delegates the condemnation of the doctrines of Arius. This was refused, and the Eastern contingent finally departed in anger.[2] Ursacius and Valens, subjects of the Emperor Constans, had no qualms about it; they sacrificed themselves, and repudiated the Arian heresy.

Notwithstanding the ill-humour of the Eastern envoys, the Council of Milan thought it a duty to notify to those whom they represented what had been decided upon with regard to Photinus. The receipt of this letter was acknowledged; though, at the same time, it was carefully pointed out that, if Photinus was so deplorably heretical, it was because his education had been in the hands of his former bishop, Marcellus.[3]   To revive at

---

[1] Hil. *Frag. hist.* ii. 20 ; viii. 2.

[2] "Quattuor episcopi, Demophilus, Macedonius, Eudoxius, Martyrius, qui ante annos octo, cum apud Mediolanum Arii sententiam haereticam noluissent damnare, de concilio animis iratis exierunt." Letter of Liberius written in 354 (Jaffé, 212 ; Hil. *Frag. hist.* v. 4). "[Photinus] qui ante biennium iam in Mediolanensi synodo erat haereticus damnatus" (Hil. *Frag. hist.* ii. 19). Observe the expression *Arii sententiam haereticam.* It was scarcely possible to ask the Eastern delegates to condemn Arius in person, since, after he had given a satisfactory explanation to them, they had readmitted him to ecclesiastical communion.

[3] Hil. *Frag. hist.* ii. 22. St Hilary weakens his position here to show that Marcellus had not been formally condemned by any council since that of Constantinople. Unfortunately he was right. The Latins would have acted wisely in following the example of Athanasius, and refusing to recognize a compromising person. The support they gave him is a proof of their lack of insight.

such a time the delicate question of Marcellus, was evidence of feelings in which friendship was not conspicuous. But opposing parties not infrequently have too long a memory.

Athanasius, just about this same time, went some way of his own accord to meet the wishes of the Eastern prelates. He notified Marcellus that he could no longer hold relations with him; and it is certainly worthy of remark that Marcellus accepted the position and abstained from any rejoinder. As to Photinus himself, Athanasius, whose views had certainly not gone unconsidered in the deliberations at Milan, could only have a highly unfavourable opinion. However, the Bishop of Sirmium, protected by his local popularity, troubled himself very little at the censure of which he had been the subject at Milan, and stood his ground in the face of and in spite of everyone.

But at the end of two years, as his attitude was a cause of scandal, and as it was important from the point of view of relations with the East that the main body should not appear to be compromised by his heresy, a council was called together at Sirmium itself, with a view to getting rid of the bishop. But they tried in vain. Photinus, like Paul of Samosata, was a difficult person to dislodge. The intervention of the government was neither given nor even asked for; and the bishops, reduced to spiritual weapons, were obliged to return home without having met with any success.

However, a great event happened: Athanasius was reinstated at Alexandria. The intruder Gregory, who had long been ill, finally died on June 25, 345.[1] Constantius took advantage of this to yield to his

---

[1] As to this date there can be no doubt. The *Chronicle of the Festal Letters* mentions the day (2 epiphi = June 25). It is true that it speaks of the event under the year 346, but in relation to the return of Athanasius to Alexandria—which actually occurred on October 21, 346. We know, from the *Historia Arianorum*, that Athanasius, who was recalled immediately after the death of Gregory, delayed for more than a year.

brother's requests. He forbade the appointment of a
successor to Gregory, and recalled Athanasius. It was
more than a year before Athanasius would comply with
the summons. He mistrusted both Constantius and his
advisers. Who could tell whether, if the wind happened
to change, the memory of the Council of Tyre might not
be called up? No one said anything of formally annulling
the decision. But Constantius insisted; he even wrote
three times to the bishop, and made many of his intimates
write also, even his brother Constans; he swore that
everything was forgotten. At last Athanasius made up
his mind. From Aquileia, where he was at the time, he
journeyed to Rome, to take leave of Pope Julius, who
gave him a kind letter for the clergy and faithful of
Alexandria; he also went to see the Emperor Constans,
who had upheld him so effectually, and at last he set out on
his way to the East. His friends received him everywhere
with joy; some, who had not been so faithful as the
others in upholding him, were rather embarrassed. As
to his enemies, they found pretexts for not appearing at
all. At Antioch he met the emperor, and requested that
advantage might be taken of this opportunity to bring
him face to face with his accusers, and investigate once
for all their complaints against him.[1] His request was
not granted, and he continued his journey. The farther
he travelled, the more pronounced was the sympathy
shown to him. In Palestine—although the Metropolitan
Acacius, who had succeeded Eusebius, was one of his
most inveterate enemies — Maximus, the Bishop of
Jerusalem, assembled a council of sixteen bishops to do
honour to the exile. They gave him letters to the
Egyptian bishops and to the faithful of Alexandria.
At last he crossed the desert, and his triumph began;
the State officials themselves travelled as much as a
hundred miles to meet the outlaw. They had received
strict instructions: the emperor had given orders for the
destruction, in the official records, of everything which
might have been inserted against Athanasius and his

[1] Letter of Hosius, in Athan. *Hist. Ar.* 44.

followers.   On October 21, 346, the victorious bishop
found himself once more in the midst of his Alexandrians.[1]

The wind had decidedly changed.   This was the
subject of the reflections of Bishops Ursacius and Valens,
on the banks of the Danube.   They had already made a
move at the time of the Council of Milan, which apparently
had referred them to Pope Julius.   The Pope had demanded
substantial pledges, and there is no doubt that the two
bishops had hesitated some time before giving them.
In the end they submitted, and addressed the Pope, asking
pardon for their misdeeds and recognising the decisions
of the Council of Sardica.   It will be remembered that
they had there been deposed.   Wishing for peace, Julius
thought it best to give them back the government of their
Churches; but he summoned them first to his presence,
and made them sign a document, in which they retracted
everything they had said and done against Athanasius,
condemned Arius and his teaching, and promised to
have nothing more to do with these affairs, whether at
the invitation of the Easterns or of Athanasius, without
the consent of the Pope.[2]   They wrote also to the
Bishop of Alexandria, in order to put themselves again in
communion with him.[3]

Everything seemed to have been satisfactorily arranged.
Nothing remained to be settled, so far as the West was
concerned, but the question of Photinus, and this they
might hope to dispose of, some time or another, without
recourse to strong measures.   In the East they had been
too badly beaten by Athanasius not to bear him a grudge
in consequence.   But this also might come to an end,
provided the position of external affairs remained
unchanged.   The Emperor Constans now turned his

[1] Upon this, see *Apol. contra Ar.* 51-57; *Hist. Ar.* 21-23, with the
official documents; cf. *Apol. ad Const.* 4.   The exact date is given by
the Alexandrian chronicles.

[2] The letter was written by Valens, with his own hand, and signed
by Ursacius.

[3] The original letters are in Hil. *Frag. hist.* 20; cf. Athan., *Apol.
contra Ar.* 58.

attention towards Africa, where, for more than twenty-five years, two religious parties had been in conflict, and indeed in armed conflict, much to the detriment of public order.

We have already seen that Constantine, after trying his utmost to bring back the Donatists to unity, had ended by leaving them alone—a concession of which they had not failed to take advantage to stir up disturbances on all sides, and to ill-treat their opponents. The latter, left to their own resources, did the best they could, and tried to appeal to the good sense of the public, by enlightening it as to the origins of the dispute. To this end, they drew up a sort of apologetic *dossier*, in which there figured, side by side with the records of the enquiry on Felix of Aptunga and the trial of Silvanus,[1] various documents relating to the decisions of Rome, Arles, and Milan.[2] But the Donatists were hardly in a mood for a discussion of the issues. Entrenched behind the barriers of their sullen obstinacy, their only answer to arguments was in the form of curses or blows. Towards the end of his reign the emperor seems for a moment to have lost patience. The prætorian prefect of Italy, Gregory (336-337), undertook some measures of repression. Donatus protested against these with extreme violence : " Gregory, pollution of the senate, and disgrace of the prefecture!" such was the beginning of his letter. The prefect replied with patience, and in a style, says St Optatus, which would befit a bishop.[3] For all that, the Donatists

---

[1] *Supra*, pp. 90, 95.

[2] This is what I have called the *Sylloge Optatiana*, because it figures at the end of the work of St Optatus upon the Donatist schism. It is preserved, in a very incomplete form, in a Cormery MS. (*Parisinus*, 1711). But as it was certainly seen by St Optatus and St Augustine, who often refer to it, I have been able to recon-struct it completely. On this subject, see my Memoir, *Le dossier du Donatisme*, in the *Mélanges* of the French School at Rome, vol. x. 1890. The fragments contained in the Cormery MS. appear at the end of the text of Optatus in the Vienna *Corpus scriptorum ecclesiasticorum latinorum*, vol. xxvi.

[3] Optatus, iii. 3, 10.

inscribed his name, after those of Leontius, Ursacius, and Zenophilus, upon the list of their persecutors, and only became more and more insolent.

It was about this time that there was formed under their auspices the strange body called Agonistics, or Circumcellions. This name was given to bands of fanatics, who travelled all over the country, especially in Numidia, to lend a hand to the good cause and wage war against the *traditores*. They claimed to observe strict chastity, and this was why the Donatists, later on, compared them to the Catholic monks. Armed with stout cudgels, they appeared everywhere, on the public roads and in the markets, prowled about cottages, whence came their name of Circumcellions, and kept a strict watch over farms and country houses. It was not only in the quarrel of Donatus and Caecilian that they interested themselves. Sturdy redressors of wrongs, the enemies of all social inequalities, they eagerly took the part of small holders against proprietors, of slaves against their masters, and of debtors against their creditors. At the first call of the oppressed, or those who pretended to be so, and especially of the Donatist clergy when they found themselves hemmed in at close quarters by the police, the Circumcellions appeared on the scene in fierce gangs, uttering their war-cry: *Deo laudes!* and brandishing their famous clubs. One of their chief amusements, when they met a carriage preceded by running slaves, was to put the slaves inside the carriage, and make the masters run in front. Even for those who did not belong to any of the classes regarded with dislike by these extraordinary people, it was not at all pleasant to meet the Circumcellions upon lonely roads. The sons of martyrs often had the intention of being martyrs themselves; and as, to their uneducated minds, the meaning of martyrdom was simply and solely a violent death, they sought for it with the greatest eagerness. When the madness seized them, they appealed to passers-by, and endeavoured to compel them to kill them. If such an one refused, they killed *him*, and then hastened on to find someone who would be more obliging. If necessary, they procured martyrdom for themselves, burnt themselves alive, threw themselves into rivers or, very commonly, from precipices. Once dead, they were buried by their companions with the greatest respect; the plains of Numidia were studded with their tombs, to which the same honours were paid as to those of the real martyrs.

In Aures, where they were very numerous, they ended by becoming an organized body. Their principal chiefs, Axido and Fasir, were powers both dreadful and dreaded. But at last they made themselves unbearable, not only to their victims, but to the Donatist clergy themselves, upon whom public opinion fastened the responsibility for this brigandage under the guise of religion. The bishops adopted an attitude of disapproval of them, and then, when they gained nothing by it, made up their minds to declare the Circumcellions incorrigible, and addressed themselves to the military authorities. Count Taurinus sent his troops into the market-places, and made some arrests. In one quarter, called Octava, the soldiers met with determined resistance, as a result of which there were a good many killed and wounded. The dead, of course, were held up as martyrs; but this time the Donatist bishops refused them Christian burial.[1] This local and temporary repression only served to strengthen their fanaticism. The Circumcellions began again to swarm everywhere.

At length the Emperor Constans decided to undertake the work of pacification, which had baffled previous attempts. Two commissioners, Paul and Macarius, were despatched to Africa, well furnished with money, to try first if imperial subsidies, freely distributed among the common people, might not make them favourably disposed. At Carthage they presented themselves to Donatus, who received them majestically: "What can the emperor have to do with the Church?"[2] he said, and added that he

---

[1] Optatus, iii. 4. This event is not dated with sufficient definiteness; it seems that it must fall between 340 and 345.

[2] Optatus, iii. 3.

would write everywhere, commanding his people to refuse the proffered alms.

In spite of the opposition of the " Prince of Tyre," as Optatus calls him, the imperial emissaries began their circuit, which passed off quietly in Proconsular Africa, and was even in many places crowned with success. The alms were distributed, the people were exhorted in the name of the emperor, and an agreement was arrived at, without any too severe measures having been necessary. In Numidia the case was different. There, the Donatist bishops organized a savage resistance.[1] They rallied in great numbers around the Bishop of Bagaï, one of the most determined amongst them ; his name also was Donatus, like the great primate of Carthage. An appeal was made to the " chiefs of the Saints ": and from all the region of Aures the Circumcellions flocked to Bagaï, where the church was transformed into a store-house for provisions. Ten bishops were appointed to meet the two commissioners, who arrived by way of Theveste, with instructions to protest energetically against " the sacrilegious union." The meeting took place at Vegesela. The Donatist prelates spoke in such a manner to the emperor's representatives that the latter considered themselves obliged to chastise them without more ado. After being tied up to pillars and flogged, they moderated their tone. One of them, however, a certain Marculus, remained obstinate, and was kept a prisoner.

Being informed of the state of things at Bagaï, the commissioners did not think it prudent to venture there without an escort. The Count of Africa, Silvester, put his troopers at their service. Some of these, being sent on in advance to Bagaï, were received with showers of stones, and compelled to fall back on the main body, carrying with them a number of wounded. It is quite certain that matters did not end there. We have no exact details, but the measures of repression were prompt and severe.

[1] In what follows, I have combined with the information given in Book III. of Optatus some details from the *Passion of Marculus.*

Donatus of Bagaï lost his life as a result; Marculus,[1] after being taken for some time from one town to another, was finally thrown from the top of the rock at Nova Petra. The Donatists, as we may well imagine, honoured them as martyrs : their opponents alleged, on the contrary, that Marculus had cast himself down when there was no one with him, and that Donatus also had thrown himself into a well.[2]

Henceforth the operations of Macarius and Paul assumed a severer aspect. The imperial envoys travelled from town to town, accompanied by the Count of Africa's troopers. The Donatist clergy fled at their approach ; as to the faithful, they were persuaded to assemble in the church, which they entered not without fear, for they had been led to believe that Paul and Macarius were placing images on the altar—the reference no doubt was to portraits of the emperors—and that the Christian Sacrifice was about to be offered to these new idols.[3] Of course, nothing of the kind happened. The commissioners spoke, and explained in appropriate terms the object of their mission. In certain places, their success was

[1] " Ecce Marculus de petra praecipitatus est ; ecce Donatus Bagaiensis in puteum missus est. Quando potestates Romanae talia supplicia decreverunt, ut praecipitentur homines ? "—Aug. *In Joh.* xi. 15.

[2] *Passion of Marculus* (Migne, *P. L.* vol. viii., p. 760). This document itself betrays some perplexity : the Donatist author who compiled it does not disguise that the execution had no other witness but the executioner. Another document dealing with martyrdoms, the work of Macrobius, Donatist Bishop of Rome, relates the death of two Carthaginian Donatists, Isaac and Maximian. The latter had torn up a proconsular edict relating to union ; the other had uttered seditious cries before the judge. They were condemned to exile, and then died in prison. Their bodies were cast into the sea, but this was so unskilfully done that they were thrown back on the shore. The Donatists said that Maximian was still living when cast into the water. This happened, it seems, in August 347 (xviii. *kal. sept. die sabbato*), when the union, already an accomplished fact in Carthage, was no longer meeting with any difficulties except in Numidia (*P. L.* vol. viii., p. 767). It is possible that Macrobius may also be the author of the *Passion of Marculus.*

[3] Optatus, iii. 12 ; vii. 6.

complete, and effected a union which even included the
Donatist bishop, with whom his Catholic colleague found
means of coming to an arrangement, either by a division
of the parishes or in some other way.[1]

But such cases seem to have been rare. There was
much local resistance, which was repressed with severity.[2]
The name of Macarius remained an object of hatred
among the Donatists, and even the Catholics found the
recollection of his military reprisals becoming after a time
inconvenient.

Of those members of the clergy who had sought refuge
in flight, many died of fatigue and want : others hid themselves, or even succeeded in holding their ground, here and
there, under the protection of the Agonistics.   Those who
were captured—the bishops at least—were banished from
Africa. Donatus was among the number ; and he died in
exile. Persecution, as it always does, only fanned to fever-
heat the anger of the opponents.   One of these, a certain
Vitellius, published an eloquent book with the title: *The
Servants of God are hated of the World.* This book is
unfortunately lost ; but we still possess two *Passions* of
Donatist "martyrs," from which we can form an idea of
the state of mind of the persecuted sect.[3]

When, their task accomplished, the *operarii unitatis* re-
embarked for Italy, the Donatist Church had been abolished,
outwardly and officially. There remained but one body
of clergy and one Bishop of Carthage. Gratus, who was
at that time invested with this lofty dignity, called
together a great council, in 348, at which there were
present several Donatist prelates, who had been brought
into union during the preceding years. It is a curious
proof of the state of men's minds immediately after the
re-union. There had already been partial councils in the
provinces ; but for this one the letters of summons

---

[1] Council of Gratus, c. 12.

[2] Optatus again and again returns to this : *aspera, aspere gesta.*

[3] Gennadius, *De viris,* 4. Vitellius had already inveighed against
the pagans and the Catholics. Upon these two *Passions,* see p. 192,
note 2.

embraced the whole of Africa.[1]　The president began by giving thanks to God, who had inspired the Emperor Constans with the thought of this work of union, and with the choice of his representatives, Paul and Macarius. Then the council adopted several regulations to meet questions which arose from the situation; in particular, the repetition of baptism was forbidden [2] and the practice of honouring as martyrs persons who had been assassinated, or those who had killed themselves, either by throwing themselves over precipices or in other ways. Questions of general discipline were also dealt with.　In conclusion, Gratus revived and solemnly renewed the condemnations directed long before against the *traditores* and rebaptizers. The censure of the *traditores* was a satisfaction granted to the reconciled Donatists; that of the rebaptizers a condemnation, however indirect, of Donatism itself. Old disputes were allowed to sleep in peace. Caecilian, Felix, and Majorinus had long been dead: no further mention was made of them.

With the wise spirit, of which these decisions of the council bore witness, peace would in the end have been restored, if only, side by side with a close supervision of the unquiet element still remaining in the country, and the prolongation of the exile of its leaders, time had been allowed to extinguish feelings of resentment, and to accustom people to live together who had been cursing each other for nearly forty years. But unfortunately for Africa—and we may say so quite apart from any religious

---

[1] It is vexatious that we have not a complete list of signatures in connection with this council : it would have been of quite unusual interest.

[2] Canons 1, 2.　The Donatists maintained the old Cyprianic principle, that there is no baptism outside the true Church.　And as they did not accord this title to the Catholic Church, they were, of course, obliged, when a Catholic became a Donatist, to confer upon him the only baptism valid in their eyes, namely, their own.　We have already seen that the Catholic Church of Africa had abandoned, at the Council of Arles in 314, the custom formerly upheld by St Cyprian.　In these circumstances, it could not but recognize Donatist baptism.

prejudice in the matter—the attitude of the government was not maintained long enough. The fire was still smouldering under the ashes, when Julian, to do an ill turn to the Church, released the exiles and once more let loose the storm upon the African provinces.

CHAPTER VII

THE PROSCRIPTION OF ATHANASIUS

Assassination of Constans. The usurper Magnentius. Constantius makes himself master of the West. The two Cæsars, Gallus and Julian. Deposition of Photinus. New intrigues against Athanasius. The Council of Arles. Pope Liberius. Councils of Milan and of Béziers. Exile of Lucifer, Eusebius, Hilary, Liberius, and Hosius. Police riots at Alexandria. Assault on the Church of Theonas : disappearance of Athanasius. Intrusion of George. Athanasius in retirement.

THE religious policy of Constans had in some measure succeeded. 'Order was supreme' in Africa. It is true that on the Danube frontier the heretical bishop of Sirmium still held his ground; but, as the members of his diocese put up with him, the interruption of relations between him and his colleagues was only of local interest. In the East, the restoration of Athanasius had been secured, and this meant the pacification of Egypt. The Egyptians, it is true, remained more or less isolated in the episcopal world of the East, and the Eastern bishops were not in agreement with the Western Church. But some steps had been taken towards union; the bishops of Palestine and of the island of Cyprus had resumed communion with Athanasius; and there was reason to hope that, in process of time, these tendencies towards peace would increase, and East and West arrive at last at mutual understanding. But to ensure this it would have been necessary that the political equilibrium should remain such as circumstances had made it.

Unfortunately this was exactly what did not happen.

On January 18, 350, a military conspiracy broke out at Autun, and the Count Magnentius was proclaimed emperor in place of Constans, who was assassinated a few days afterwards at Elna, at the foot of the Pyrenees.

Against this attack upon the due succession in the line of Constantine, all the remaining members of his family instinctively set themselves in opposition. In the West, two daughters of Constantine were still living, Constantina and Eutropia, both of them widows, one of King Hannibalian, the other of the consular, Nepotianus. Constantina, who was residing at Sirmium, lost no time in setting up a rival to Magnentius, and proclaimed as Augustus an old general named Vetranio (March 1). Eutropia, who lived in Rome, was at first out-flanked by the rapid movement of Magnentius, who secured his own recognition in the ancient capital ; but she quickly rallied, and advanced her own son Nepotianus to the imperial dignity on June 3. So far as he was concerned, however, Magnentius had little difficulty in getting the upper hand. Before a month had elapsed, his general, Marcellinus, recaptured Rome after a fierce conflict, in which Nepotianus was killed. The conqueror did not show himself disposed to mercy ; Eutropia was put to death, and with her a large number of prominent members of the Roman aristocracy.

Constantius also did not lose hope. He had upon his hands, besides the catastrophes in the West, a never-ending war with the Persians. The city of Nisibis endured during this year a heroic siege, and its inhabitants, encouraged by their famous Bishop James, resisted for a space of four months all the attacks of King Sapor. In this quarter, the military operations were under the direction of the emperor's lieutenants. Constantius himself lost no time in gathering his forces and setting out on his march to the West. He had already come to some sort of understanding with Vetranio, who allowed him to pass through Illyricum. Vetranio did more than this : the son of Constantine managed to persuade him to resign the purple, succeeded him himself without a struggle, and sent him to end his days in peace at Prusias in Bithynia.

By this arrangement, Constantius gained the Balkan Peninsula and the Pannonian provinces, supposing always that Magnentius did not come to dispute them with him, a contingency which there was much reason to fear. In the meantime, Constantius took up his winter quarters at Sirmium. In the spring, he marched towards the Julian Alps; the "tyrant" came to meet him, and obliged him to fall back as far as the confluence of the Drave and the Danube. There, on September 28, 351, the battle of Mursa was fought, the result of which was unfavourable to Magnentius, and compelled him to recross the mountains.

When winter set in, the two rivals remained in their positions of the preceding year, Constantius at Sirmium, Magnentius at Aquileia. It was not till the following summer (352) that Constantius succeeded in crossing the passes and making his way into Italy: Magnentius was obliged to fall back upon Gaul. The victor entered Milan, where he married Eusebia, a beautiful and capable woman, who soon gained an immense influence over her husband. In 353, Magnentius, who had tried in vain to defend the Alps, beat a retreat upon Lyons. Seeing that he was on the point of being betrayed by the remnant of his forces, he killed himself on August 10. Constantius entered Lyons, and the unity of the empire was once more re-established.

None the less, like his predecessors, Constantius felt the need of sharing its burden. He could not at the same time conquer the West and carry on a struggle with the Persians. Already, in 351 (March 15), Gallus, one of the sons of Julius Constantius, had been brought out of his retirement and despatched to Antioch with the rank of Cæsar; a wife was found for him in the person of the emperor's own sister, Constantina, the widow of Hannibalian, the princess who a year earlier had made an emperor out of Vetranio. This enterprising person helped her husband to transform himself into an Asiatic tyrant ; and left to themselves they had soon succeeded in subjecting Antioch to an unbearable system of oppression. The cries of the victims were at last heard in Milan. Being summoned to appear before the master of the empire, Gallus sent his wife in advance, knowing her fertility in resource. She, however, died on the way,[1] so that he felt himself obliged to go in person. As he had not been able to assume the attitude of a rival, he speedily found himself in the position of a culprit before his judge. He was taken to Flanona, near Pola, and there condemned and executed (at the end of 354).

He had still one brother remaining, Julian. The latter, in the following year, was summoned to court and proclaimed Cæsar (November 6, 355). Gaul was entrusted to him, and he governed it well, gaining the gratitude of its people, especially for the bravery and skill with which he defended them against the barbarians beyond the Rhine.

But we must now return to the affairs of the Church. The news of the death of Constans had burst upon the East like a thunderclap. All the enemies of Athanasius in Syria and in Asia Minor had not, indeed, dared to show their joy openly (for that might have been imprudent and dangerous), but trembled with hopefulness. Some of them had even plucked up courage to talk once more of the Council of Tyre, and the necessity of adhering to its decisions. These were in too great a hurry : Constantius refused to listen to them. He wrote to Athanasius and assured him that the wishes of his dead brother would be respected, and that, whatever rumours might reach him, his mind might be at rest : he should always be supported.[2] The Egyptian officials received instructions to the same

---

[1] It was she who built at Rome the celebrated basilica of St Agnes, where this fact was commemorated by a metrical inscription, the text of which is still extant : *Constantina Deum venerans Christoque dicata*, etc. She was buried there, in a mausoleum which is still in existence (see above, p. 51, note 2). It is this Constantina whom legend has transformed into a holy Virgin Constantia, in spite of the fact that she had been married twice, and that in other ways her life bore only the most distant resemblance to the evangelical ideal.

[2] Athan. *Hist. Ar.* 23, 51.

effect. Athanasius, on his part, published in his own defence a brochure illustrated by documentary evidence, in which he set out, first, the decisions given in his favour by the Egyptian episcopate, by the Council of Rome, and by that of Sardica; and then traced once more in a series of official documents, joined together by a short outline of narrative, the whole story of the intrigues directed against him, down to the time of his recall by the Emperor Constantius, and the retractation of Ursacius and Valens. This is the work which we call the *Apologia against the Arians.* Up to this time, Athanasius had abstained from writing anything on the subject, for fear that, as had happened in the case of Marcellus, his words might be misconstrued. And even now, he himself scarcely came into the open, being content to allow the documents to speak for themselves.

There was another important person to whom the change of emperors must have seemed very unpleasant, namely, the Bishop of Sirmium. If he had become a cause of scandal to his colleagues of the West, we can imagine with what feelings he was regarded by those in the East. And the Eastern bishops were always represented among the personal attendants of Constantius. As soon as they saw him installed at Sirmium, they flocked thither and prepared to settle their old scores with " Scotinus," as they called him. But " Scotinus " was a man of resource. He succeeded at the outset in evading the council, and managed to arrange that a commission appointed by the emperor should decide between himself and those who criticized his teaching. Constantius, who delighted in this kind of disputation, appointed an Areopagus of eight officials, assisted by a staff of shorthand writers. Photinus appeared before them, and the opposing party chose as their speaker Basil, Bishop of Ancyra, a man of moderate opinions and a great talent for oratory. He, like Photinus, was a Galatian, and must have lived for a considerable time with him amongst the clergy of Marcellus. The story of Paul of Samosata was reproduced in all its details · Photinus and Basil resumed the duel between

the Bishop of Antioch and the priest Malchion.[1] St
Epiphanius had before him the formal record of this
discussion,[2] which makes it possible to form a fairly clear
idea of the errors of Photinus.   Then the council assembled;
the Bishop of Sirmium received an additional condemnation from the Eastern episcopate, and the emperor exiled
him.   His place was filled by a certain Germinius, who
was brought from Cyzicus, and who shared the views of
the party.   The Eastern bishops had recovered, on the
banks of the Danube, two old friends, Ursacius and
Valens, who had formerly been forced to desert them,
but who were now free to display their sympathy, and
hastened to rejoin the main body.

A retaliation was being prepared; but it was necessary
to display caution.   The Emperor Constantius was
engaged in conquering the West; and there were good
hopes that this political victory might result in complete
assimilation in religious matters.   But the Latins, as
experience had long shown, had prejudices which must be
reckoned with.   The council contented itself with publishing for the fourth time the Creed of Antioch, with an
appendix of twenty-seven doctrinal canons, specially
directed against Marcellus and Photinus, but without
mentioning either of them by name.   St Hilary,[3] who, as
well as St Athanasius, has preserved for us the text of this
document, finds in it nothing objectionable; and indeed,
if this creed had been presented through other hands, it
might have found acceptance in the West.   No doubt
there is no question in it of the *homoousios*; but was it so
certain that one could not dispense with this formula,
which gave rise to so many objections, and which, while
expressing but one aspect of the common faith, always
required so many additions and explanations?   Even good

---

[1] See vol. i., p. 342.   [2] *Haer.* lxxi. 1, 2.
[3] Hil. *De syn.* 38-62; Athan. *De syn.* 27. Socrates, *H. E.* ii. 29,
gives the date (351) of the assembly; and, notwithstanding the
monstrous blunders which he makes here, we must acknowledge that
the date he gives fits in well with the sequence of the facts as
ascertained.

honest persons might have difficulties in regard to it.   It
is true that the *homoousios* had been canonized at Nicæa.
But, without failing in respect for that venerable council,
which no one then dreamed of doing, was it forbidden to
interpret a little the words which it had decided upon?
Such thoughts must have passed through minds like that
of Basil of Ancyra.   They soon gained a great success,
but it was only a transitory one, for they were the thoughts,
not of all the Easterns, nor probably of the conscious or
unconscious majority of that party, but only of a group of
moderate persons.

In the meantime, while his enemies were agitating in
Illyria and preparing for the conquest of the West,
Athanasius felt their intrigues once more beginning to
twine around him.   The winter of 351-352 seems to have
been spent in a new attempt to get round the Emperor.
They assured him that Athanasius, during his stay
in the West, had maligned him to his brother, and
that he had concluded an alliance with Magnentius.[1]
Constantius was engaged in building at Alexandria a
great church, called the *Caesareum*; one day, during the
Easter Festival, the faithful, who were somewhat crowded
in the ordinary churches, betook themselves to it with
their bishop.   The enemies of Athanasius represented
this as a great crime; he ought to have waited until
the Emperor himself had celebrated its dedication.   In
short, Athanasius again became in his eyes a dangerous
person.[2]   The Eastern bishops ended by finding themselves

[1] An embassy, sent to the Eastern court by Magnentius in 350,
had, in order to avoid Vetranio, disembarked in Libya, and passed
through Alexandria.   Servasius, Bishop of Tongres, and Maximus,
another bishop, formed part of it.   *Apol. ad Const.* 9.

[2] Ammianus Marcellinus (xv. 7, 6), who reproduces the gossip of
the army, represents Athanasius as a sort of political sorcerer:
"*Athanasium episcopum eo tempore apud Alexandriam ultra professionem altius se efferentem scitarique conatum externa, ut prodidere
rumores adsidui, coetus in unum quaesitus eiusdem loci multorum,
synodus, ut appellant, removit a sacramento quod optinebat.   Dicebatur
enim fatidicarum sortium fidem, quaeve augurales portenderent alites
scientissime callens, aliquoties praedixisse futura.   Super his intende-
bantur et alia quoque a proposito legis abhorrentia cui praesidebat.*"

in a position to urge once more the idea that Athanasius
had not in reality any recognized position, since he had
been deposed by the Council of Tyre. Nothing therefore
remained to be done but to rid Alexandria of him, and
to secure his repudiation by the bishops of the West.

Just at this very moment the Western Church lost its
head: Pope Julius died on April 12, 352, about the
time that Constantius was marching against Aquileia.
His place was filled, a month later (May 17), by the deacon
Liberius, destined, under the *régime* which was beginning,
to meet with many misfortunes. Shortly after his
accession, various letters, emanating from Eastern and
Egyptian bishops,[1] reached him, denouncing Athanasius
and his crimes. Like all the superior clergy of Rome,
Liberius must have known what to believe. He read
the letters of the Eastern bishops " to the Church and the
Council,"[2] and answered them, without accepting accusations so often contradicted.[3] By "the council" we may
certainly understand the meeting of bishops which took
place every year at the Pope's *natale*; thus the date of it
would be May 17, 353. About the same time, there
arrived a deputation from the Egyptian bishops and the
clergy of Alexandria, headed by Serapion of Thmuis,
the most faithful lieutenant of Athanasius. These
persons brought a protest, signed by eighty bishops,
in favour of their persecuted brother.[4] The Pope then
addressed the Emperor, in the name of a large number of
Italian bishops, requesting that a great council should be

---

[1] The Meletians, no doubt.

[2] Hil. *Frag. hist.* v. 2. Letter from Liberius to Constantius, in
354 (Jaffé; 212).

[3] I omit here, as apocryphal, the famous letter *Studens paci*, preserved in the historical fragments of St Hilary (*Frag. hist.* iv.). It
cannot be reconciled with the attitude of Liberius in the following
years, and there is every appearance that St Hilary gives it as a
document fabricated by some member of the Eastern party.

[4] I connect the sending of this letter with the mission of Serapion
and his companions, which left Alexandria on May 18, 353, according
to the *Athanasian Chronicle*; see also the *Chronicle of the Festal
Letters*.

convened at Aquileia, to decide anew the controversy which was beginning to revive. Constantius had previously given him reason to hope for an assembly of this kind. The papal legates, Vincent of Capua and Marcellus, another Campanian bishop, met the emperor at Arles, where he was spending the inclement season (353-4). They found him in the middle of the celebration of his *Tricennalia*, surrounded by the bishops of the country, from whom he was demanding signatures against Athanasius.

The Eastern quarrels were but little familiar to the clergy of Gaul. Ten years previously, at the time of the Council of Sardica, some of the bishops had found themselves mixed up in these affairs: this was the case with Maximin of Trèves, Verissimus of Lyons, and Euphratas of Cologne. The first, an avowed partisan of Athanasius, had been dead for some little time, and perhaps the two others also. The signatures, to the number of about thirty, which had been collected in favour of the decisions of Sardica, had no doubt been added, for the most part, on trust, at the request of the Emperor Constans and of important bishops such as those of Trèves and Lyons. At the time of Constantius' arrival, all this was already rather ancient history. As to preceding events the bishops had but a faint idea ; even the Council of Nicæa was almost unknown. Hilary, Bishop of Poitiers, although a well-informed man, had never heard of the famous Nicene Creed, until Constantius had come to disturb the peace in which, on this subject, the Gallic episcopate was living. Possessed of but slight information on these matters and those which lay behind them, the bishops could scarce help following their natural inclination to do what so religious an emperor asked them. It was in vain that the Pope's representatives endeavoured to arrest this open action, to reserve the decision for the council which was to come, or, at least, to secure that, before condemning Athanasius, they should begin by reprobating the heresy of Arius. Their efforts were entirely unsuccessful The eloquence of Valens, the spokesman of the Eastern prelates, and the general enthusiasm for the son of Constantine, overcame all resistance. The Bishop of Arles, Saturninus, one of the first adherents secured, displayed great zeal. The legates themselves were carried away by the stream, and signed the condemnation of Athanasius. The Bishop of Trèves, Paulinus, alone had the courage to protest. He was deposed and sent into exile.[1]

The vessel which had brought Serapion to Italy had passed on the high seas, after leaving Alexandria, an official galley, from which, on May 22, there disembarked a messenger from the court, named Montanus. He seemed thwarted in his embassy, for his instructions were to bring back Athanasius himself. He handed the bishop an imperial letter by which he was authorized, "according to his request," to appear before his sovereign. Athanasius had made no request. Accustomed to the ways of the court, he scented a trap and excused himself. His own messengers were refused admittance to Constantius, and returned to Alexandria. The bishop no doubt thought that the order would be pressed, and that, sooner or later, he would be forced to appear before the emperor. In view of this contingency, he prepared a defence of himself, in a dignified style, worthy of being pronounced before the court. He had even gone so far as to anticipate the changes of countenance which his eloquence might provoke in his imperial auditor: "You smile, sire, and your smile shows that you agree . . ."[2] This fine speech was never delivered.[3] For more than two years the court pretended to know nothing of Athanasius.

But if, for the present, he was left at peace in Egypt, his enemies in Italy and Gaul continued their efforts to isolate him more and more. Irritated by the opposition

---

[1] Indignus ecclesia ab episcopis, dignus exilio a rege est iudicatus (Hil. *Frag. hist.* i. 6).

[2] *Apol. ad Const.* 16. Athanasius was very confident; for it was not at all an easy matter to bring a smile to the august lips of the Emperor Constantius.

[3] Athanasius took it in hand again later and published it, with additions supplied by the sequel of his tragic history. It is his *Apology to the Emperor Constantius.*

of Liberius, the Emperor had sent a proclamation to
Rome, in which the Pope was violently abused. He
was reproached for his ambition, his boasting, his blind
obstinacy, his spirit of discord. Liberius defended himself. Grieved as he was at the hostile attitude of his
sovereign and the weakness of his own legates, he did
not lose courage; he addressed himself a second time to
the emperor, in order to obtain a council, in which, after
a confirmation of the faith of Nicæa, all questions relating
to persons might be arranged by general consent.[1] His
letter was carried by fresh legates, men to whom fear was
unknown and from whom no weakness was to be feared,
but rather excess of zeal: these were Lucifer, Bishop of
Caliaris, the priest Pancratius, and the deacon Hilary.
Liberius tried at the same time to fortify around himself
the courage of the Italian bishops; he confided his anxiety
to Hosius of Cordova, the veteran warrior in these melancholy conflicts.[2]

Constantius, who had nothing to fear from so pliable
a body of bishops, listened to the Pope's suggestions, and
consented to the assembling of a council, which was
actually held, not indeed at Aquileia, but at Milan, in the
early months of the year 355. Liberius had commended
his legates to Eusebius, Bishop of Vercellæ, formerly one
of the Roman clergy, well known for the holiness of his
life and his strength of character. He also relied much
upon the Bishop of Aquileia, Fortunatian. When the
bishops were assembled, Eusebius, who was not at all
easy in mind as to their intentions, was in no hurry to
present himself; he needed to be summoned in the name
of the emperor, and to be entreated by the Roman legates
to appear, "as St Peter formerly did, to expose the wiles of
the Magician." At last he presented himself, escorted by
the legates. But, for ten days, the bishops had been
working incessantly: they were beginning to show signs
of weakness. Eusebius was implored to sign the condemnation of Athanasius. He declared that several of

---

[1] Jaffé, 212 (Hil. *Frag. hist.* v.).
[2] Jaffé, 209, 210 (Hil. *Frag. hist.* vi. 3).

the persons present appeared to him to be heretics, and that, to remove doubts on this point, every one must sign the Creed of Nicæa. As he said this, he drew out a copy of it, and handed it first to the Bishop of Milan, who took a pen and was on the point of signing it, when Valens threw himself on him, and tore pen and paper out of his hands, crying out that such a mode of proceeding could not be allowed. A great disturbance ensued. The faithful appeared on the scene, and threatened to interfere on behalf of their bishop. The deliberations were then transferred from the church to the palace, and soon changed their form. The bishops were asked to choose between signing and exile. Three only accepted exile —Lucifer, Eusebius, and Dionysius; all the others submitted.[1]

Further measures were taken with regard to those who were absent. Commissioners went from one Church to another, demanding signatures; some of the clergy of Ursacius and Valens accompanied the imperial envoys. In Gaul a council was held at Béziers in the following year (356), before which several belated laggards were summoned. Among their number was Hilary of Poitiers. Immediately after the Council of Milan, he had organized a protest in Gaul against the sentence of exile on the bishops, and, in general, against the intervention of the civil power in questions of faith and communion. His first *Apology to Constantius*[2] may be considered as the manifesto of this opposition. Hilary and his party had separated Ursacius, Valens, and Saturninus from their communion, and had called to repentance others who had given way at their instigation. He was compelled to present himself before the Council of Béziers. He absolutely refused to change his attitude, and carried with him by his example his colleague of Toulouse, Rhodanius,

---

[1] Upon this council, see especially Hilary, *Ad Const.* i. 8, completed by Athanasius, *Hist. Ar.* 32-34, Sulpicius Severus, *Chron.* ii. 39, and the letters collected by Mansi, vol. iii., p. 326 *et seq.*

[2] Of this document we only possess a mutilated text; Sulpicius Severus (*Chron.* ii. 39) had read the whole of it. The Cæsar Julian seems to have attempted to defend Hilary (Hil. *Ad Const* ii. 2).

a man of a more accommodating disposition, but one who. at the decisive moment, also made his choice in favour of exile.

Pope Liberius was treated in a more ceremonious manner. His attitude had not changed : he was for the exiles against the government. At the outset, he had written to Eusebius, Dionysius, and Lucifer, a touching letter, in which he expressed to them his regret at not being able to follow them yet, and his firm persuasion that his own turn would not be long in coming.[1] His envoys, the priest Eutropius and the deacon Hilary, were ill received ; they were both exiled, and the deacon had in addition to endure the torture of the lash.[2] The eunuch Eusebius, a trusted agent, was sent to Rome to induce the Pope to yield : his arguments met with no success. In vain he produced his purse ; in vain he emptied it at the tomb of St Peter : Liberius caused the money to be cast forth outside. The prefect Leontius was then instructed to send the rebellious pontiff to court. This was not an easy matter, for Liberius was much beloved by the populace ; it was necessary to seize him by night, and to adopt great precautions.[3]

However, it was at last accomplished. Liberius was carried off to Milan. Brought into the emperor's presence, he could only repeat the protest he had been making ever and anon for two years : he could not condemn persons unheard ; the decision at Tyre, not having been based on a discussion in which both sides had been listened to, could be of no value whatever ; it was necessary, first of all, to recall the exiles, and to make sure that everyone was in agreement with regard to the faith of Nicæa ; then, a meeting should be held at Alexandria, in the actual place where the facts in dispute had taken place. Of this interview we possess a kind of formal record,[4] in which the figures of the speakers—the

---

[1] Jaffé, 216 (Hil. *Frag. hist.* vi. 1-2).   [2] Athan. *Hist. Ar.* 41.
[3] Ammianus, xv. 7, 6. *Cf.* Athan. *Hist. Ar.* 35-40.
[4] Preserved by Theodoret, ii. 13 ; Sozomen, iv. 11, also had it before him. *Cf.* Athan. *Hist. Ar.* 39, 40.

Pope, the Emperor, the eunuch Eusebius, and Bishop Epictetus[1]—stand out in striking relief.

"Of what consequence art thou?" said the emperor, "thou, who alone takest the part of an impious man, and dost thus disturb the peace of the whole world?" "It is no matter if I do stand alone," replied the bishop, "the faith will lose nothing by that. In the days of old, there were but three, and they resisted." "How!" interrupted Eusebius, "dost thou take our emperor for Nebuchadnezzar!" "A great deal he cares," said Epictetus, "for the faith, or for ecclesiastical decisions! What he wants, is to be able to boast to the Roman senators that he has defied his sovereign." The conference ended by a final invitation to sign. The Pope was granted a delay of three days; he refused it, and also refused the financial assistance offered by the emperor and empress. He was then sent to Berea in Thrace, where he was put into the charge of one of the heads of the party, the Bishop Demophilus.

There still remained the "Father of the Councils," the living embodiment of the memories of Nicæa, the centenarian Bishop of Cordova. In spite of his years, Hosius was forced to come to Milan; but he remained deaf to all entreaties, and had perforce to be sent back to his distant diocese. There, he was again attacked by letters and messengers. He resisted them all, and wrote a most touching letter to the emperor. Among other things, he said that, having confessed the faith under the emperor's grandfather Maximian, he was not disposed to deny it now, to please the Arians; that he knew for a certainty the innocence of Athanasius and the bad faith of his accusers; that the emperor ought to occupy himself with his own affairs, and leave the bishops to deal with those of the Church.

But no eloquence was of any avail to move Constantius. He had among the bishops of Spain one man who was

---

[1] This Epictetus was a young ecclesiastical adventurer, whom the court party had caused to be elected Bishop of Centumcellae (*Civita-vecchia*), and charged to keep an eye on the Pope.

capable of anything, Potamius, the Bishop of Lisbon, who played in that country almost exactly the same part as Saturninus in Gaul, and who, for that reason, had been roughly treated by Hosius.   When he complained of this, Constantius again summoned the rebellious patriarch before him.[1]   They succeeded in transporting him as far as Sirmium, where the court was then in residence, and there he was kept in exile.

Now unity was accomplished.   Neither in the West nor in the East was there one single bishop in the possession of his see who had not declared against Athanasius.   This was the time to take formal action against him.   It seemed that there was nothing more to be done but to send him a sentence of exile, or to carry him off, as they had carried off Liberius.   But the Pope of Alexandria had around him a populace even more devoted and more unmanageable than that of Rome; and, besides, he had in his possession official letters, whereby Constantius had solemnly undertaken never to abandon him.   To get out of these difficulties, the government conceived the idea of forcing his hand.   They resolved to organize at all costs a disturbance in Alexandria.

The project was difficult of execution.   An imperial notary, Diogenes, arrived in the month of August 355, advised the bishop to go away, and began to work upon the clergy and the faithful.   But Athanasius sheltered himself behind the emperor's letters, protesting that he would not leave Alexandria without formal orders emanating from him; as to the people themselves, it was no use to be harsh with them, they would not submit to it.   At the end of four months Diogenes returned, leaving things exactly as when he arrived.

During the winter another attempt was made.   Troops were collected from the whole of Egypt, under the command of the Dux Syrianus, who was placed in charge of the business.   Athanasius made no movement, declaring

---

[1] *Marcellini et Faustini Libellus precum*, 32 (*Coll. Avellana*, ed. Günther, p. 15).

that a bishop could not desert his flock, unless for most
serious reasons; but that he would do so, if the emperor
really wished it, or even if the "dux" or the prefect of
Egypt would give him a written order to that effect.
The people supported his attitude, and asked permission
to send a deputation to the emperor. The tone of these
protests caused Syrianus to reflect; he declared that he
would write to the emperor himself, and that, in the meantime, he would take no action against the churches.

This promise was not kept.

On February 8, at midnight, the Church of Theonas
was surrounded on all sides. It was still the principal
church of the city: Athanasius was celebrating in it one
of the nocturnal offices, called vigils ($\Pi\alpha\nu\nu\nu\chi i\delta\epsilon\varsigma$), which
only attracted the more devout; hence, there was not a
great crowd. The Dux Syrianus caused the doors to be
forced; his soldiers, augmented by a disorderly rabble,
burst in, with drawn swords and trumpets sounding. Their
helmets gleamed in the light of the candles, their arrows
flew through the church. We can imagine the tumult
which ensued. The consecrated virgins were represented
by a large proportion in the devout congregation; they were
assailed with obscene cries; several were killed, and others
were outraged. Trampled under foot and crushed at the
exits, the faithful left many corpses upon the floor. In the
midst of all this, the bishop remained upon his seat;
monks and devoted laymen surrounded him. They
succeeded at last in getting him away, but it was not
without being severely bruised that he at last managed
to penetrate through the crowd. Those who were
seeking for him did not recognize him. Besides, they
scarcely wished to take him prisoner; what they wanted
was that he should take himself off, that he should seem
to have been driven away by a popular rising. They
had their wish. From that hour, Athanasius was seen
no more.[1]

---

[1] Later on (about 388), Palladius saw in Alexandria an old nun,
who, it was said, had given shelter to Athanasius, during the six years
of his disappearance. He had been concealed in her house, certain

When the day dawned, the Christians of Alexandria hastened to the authorities to protest. But the Dux Syrianus was already preparing the official version of the affair; there had been no occasion for scandal; Athanasius had passed judgment upon himself by leaving Alexandria of his own free will. In attestation of this signatures were demanded, and those who held back were beaten. But, on February 12, the people of Alexandria caused a second[1] protest to be posted up, in which the number of those killed was given, and the presence of the Dux in the Church of Theonas, accompanied by an imperial notary Hilary, was stated. The municipal *strategos* (duumvir), Gorgonius, was there also; and his testimony was appealed to. Besides, the swords, javelins, and arrows, which had been used, had been kept in the church; and were still being kept, as a proof of the violence employed. The prefect of Egypt and the police were entreated to bring these facts to the knowledge of the emperor and of the prætorian prefects; and the captains of vessels were asked to spread the news in other ports. Above all, it was added, let no one think of sending to the Alexandrians another bishop; they would not endure him, and would remain faithful to Athanasius.

No attention was paid to them. A Count Heraclius was sent to Egypt, as bearer of imperial letters to the senate and people of Alexandria. In these Constantius excused himself for having, out of consideration for his brother, tolerated for a time the presence of Athanasius in Alexandria; but now Athanasius was a public enemy; he must be sought for and found, at any cost.[2] On June

that no one would seek him in the house of a young woman as she then was. This story, improbable in itself, is contradicted by what St Athanasius himself tells us with regard to his wanderings as an exile. But it is possible that the person in question may have served as an intermediary for his correspondence, or may have given him hospitality from time to time during his secret visits to Alexandria (*Historia Lausiaca*, c. 64, ed. Butler).

[1] The text of this protest has been preserved; Athanasius included it in his *History of the Arians*.

[2] *Hist. Ar.* 48, 49.

14, the churches were taken from Athanasius' clergy and
handed over to the Arians. This was not done, as may
be imagined, without resistance. In the Cæsareum
especially, there were horrible scenes.[1] The opposing
party were not satisfied with seizing the churches; an
address was sent to the emperor, in which they declared
their readiness to accept any bishop he might deign to
send them. This petition was covered with signatures
of pagans and Arians. Strange to say, the pagans had
been warned that, if they did not take a side, their temples
would be closed.

Finally, on February 24, 357, the nominee of the
emperor and of his religious party made his entrance
into the city of Alexandria. He came from Antioch,
where he had been invested by a council of about thirty
bishops, from Syria, Thrace, and Asia Minor.[2] He was a
certain George, a native of Cappadocia, like so many
notable persons of the time. He had formerly held a post
at Constantinople in the department of finance, and
there, it was said, he had shown himself so honest that
they were obliged to part with him.[3] Since then, he had
led a wandering life, in the course of which he had come
into touch with the future Cæsar, Julian, and had even
lent him books. He had the reputation of being exceedingly fond of money. He was, besides, a hard, merciless
man, capable of going to any imaginable length with a
brazen face. This character suited well with the demands
of the situation which awaited him in Alexandria. It
remained to be seen, which would be stronger, the man or
these demands.

At first, all went as he desired. With him had been
associated a military commander well fitted for rough
measures, the Dux Sebastian, a Manichean in religion,
and a man difficult to soften. After a few weeks, the
ninety bishops of Egypt had become acquainted with
George : sixteen of them were exiled, thirty of them were

---

[1] *Hist. Ar.* 55-58.　　　　　[2] Sozomen, iv. 8.

[3] St Athanasius (*Hist. Ar.* 51) calls him a devourer of the treasury
(ταμειόφαγος); cf. *ibid.* 75 : σφετερισάμενον πάντα καὶ δἰ αὐτὸ τοῦτο φυγόντα.

obliged to flee; and the others were more or less disturbed. They were called upon to renounce communion with Athanasius, and accept it with George: those who held back were replaced without mercy. As to Alexandria itself, the slightest opposition was immediately repressed. Those of the clergy who remained faithful were sent into exile, or condemned to the mines; the terrible *metallum* of Phæno once more received confessors, as in the days of Maximin Daia. They were forbidden to hold meetings of any kind in the city, even for the mere distribution of alms. If they tried to assemble in the outskirts, near the cemeteries, the Dux Sebastian arrived with his troops; the meeting was broken up; the women, especially the consecrated virgins, who naturally figured at the head of the most zealous, were ill-treated, beaten with thorny branches, half-roasted on braziers, to make them declare allegiance to Arius and George. The dead remained on the ground and their relations had difficulty in obtaining permission to bury them; the prisoners, men and women, were deported through the desert, as far as the Great Oasis.

This reign of terror lasted eighteen months. The Christians were not the only ones who suffered from it. The new bishop began to speculate, making a "corner" in nitre, the salt works, and the marshes where the papyrus and calamus grew; even organizing a monopoly in funeral arrangements.[1] At the end of August 358, the Alexandrians, tired of his tyranny, rose in revolt, and proceeded to attack him, in the Church of Dionysius. It was not without difficulty that his friends succeeded this time in rescuing him from those who desired to do him injury. He departed a few days later, and for more than three years kept away from Alexandria. But the struggle continued after his departure. At one moment the Athanasians regained possession of their churches; but the Dux Sebastian compelled them to give them up. While Constantius lived, the coercive power remained with their opponents: so far as the government was concerned,

---

[1] Epiph. *Haer.* lxxvi. 1.

Athanasius had ceased to exist. For all that, from the
shelter of his hiding-places, he did not fail to disturb from
time to time the slumbers of those in office. It was in
vain that Constantius had congratulated the Alexandrians
on the "alacrity" (!) they had shown in driving Athanasius
away, and rallying to George.[1] The emperor did not
really feel comfortable about the matter. And, as a
stimulus to his uneasiness, Athanasius sent him his
Apology, which had long been prepared and was now
supplemented by appendices dealing with the recent
events. Since his eviction from the Church of Theonas,
he no longer appeared in public; for six years the police
sought for him in vain. Every respectable inhabitant of
Egypt was on his side. He was the defender of the Faith,
the lawful Pope, the common father; he was also—and it
was a great recommendation—the enemy, the victim, of the
government. The desert was kind to him: he could
knock without fear at the doors of monasteries and
anchorites' cells. With the exception of a few malcontents,
who only showed themselves under the protection of the
soldiery, the populace was entirely at his orders. He was
never betrayed; his movements were never tracked by
the police. Like the true Egyptian that he was, he was
not above playing them a trick now and then. One
evening as he was going up the Nile in a boat, he heard
behind him the sound of oars: it was an official galley.
They hailed his boat: "Have you seen Athanasius?"
"I think so," he replied, disguising his voice. "Is he
far off?" "No, he is quite near you, on ahead; row
hard." The galley darted southwards, and the outlaw,
turning about, quietly returned home.

The rumours from the outer world reached his ears:
his emissaries kept him carefully informed. He was no
longer afraid to write. Formerly, he had not done so
willingly, fearing to give a handle to his enemies and to
bring about his own ruin. But, now that the ruin had
come, there was no longer anything to lose. One day he
heard that at Antioch they were making jokes about his

---

[1] See the letter H μὲν πόλις (Athan. *Apol. ad Const.* 30).

flight. He seized his pen: "I hear that Leontius of Antioch, Narcissus of Nero's city,[1] George of Laodicea, and the other Arians are expending their lewd wit on me and tearing me to pieces; they treat me as a coward because I have not allowed them to assassinate me." This is how he begins the *Apology for his flight*; Leontius and company would have done better not to provoke its publication. The leisure afforded by his exile Athanasius employed in combating the heretics; it was then, I think, that he wrote his four treatises against the Arians, the fourth of which is really directed against Sabellianism old and new. To the good monks, whose guest he often was, he relates the life of their patriarch Antony, who had been a faithful friend to him, and who had just died. It was for them also, to put them in touch with the controversies of the time, that he wrote his curious *History of the Arians*,[2] in a lively and picturesque style, well calculated to please those big children. Observe how he dramatizes the situations, and makes his characters speak. The Easterns are arriving at Sardica: "There is a mistake," they say. "We travelled in company with counts, and the case is to be judged without them. Certes, we are condemned already. You know what the orders are: Athanasius has at hand all the documents relating to the Mareotis affair; by their means he will clear himself, and cover us all with confusion. Let us hasten to find some excuse, and to depart; otherwise, we are lost. It is better to incur the shame of a retreat than the confusion of being denounced as false accusers."[3] As Athanasius knows the stories of all his enemies, he cannot resist the pleasure of confiding some of them to the solitaries. Thus he tells them that if the Bishop of Antioch mutilated himself, some time back, in the same way as Origen did, it was for less creditable reasons.[4] Eunuchs never fail to excite his mordant humour. The court is full of them; they have supported all the intrigues of which he has been the victim. "How can you expect," he says, "such people to understand

---

[1] Neronias in Cilicia.   [2] The beginning is lost.
[3] *Hist. Ar.* 15.   [4] *Hist. Ar.* 28.

anything about the generation of the Son of God?"[1]
With the monks Athanasius felt himself entirely at home.
Of the emperor himself, that solemn and ceremonious
sovereign, he speaks with a marked absence of ceremony:
we are very far from the Apology to Constantius, with
its official adjectives.   The emperor is called simply
Constantius.   Athanasius even goes so far as to give him
a nick-name: "Costyllius," he says, 'who would dare to
call him a Christian?   Is he not rather the picture of
Antichrist?"[2]

Language of this sort could not be used anywhere but
in the desert.

[1] *Hist. Ar.* 38.   [2] *Hist. Ar.* ; *cf.* 8c.

CHAPTER VIII

THE DEFEAT OF ORTHODOXY

The Church of Antioch in the time of Bishop Leontius. Paulinus ; Flavian and Diodore : Aetius and Theophilus. State of parties in 357. The failing away of Liberius. The formulary of Sirmium accepted by Hosius. Anomœans and Homoïousians. Western protests. Eudoxius at Antioch : triumph of Aetius. Basil of Ancyra and the homoïousian reaction. Return of Pope Liberius. Success and violence of Basil : his defeat by the advanced party. Formula of 359. Councils of Ariminum and of Seleucia. Acacius of Cæsarea. Development of events at Constantinople : general prevarication. Despair of Hilary. The Council of 360. Eudoxius, Bishop of Constantinople. Meletius and Euzoïus at Antioch. Julian proclaimed Augustus. Death of Constantius.

THE city of Antioch, at the middle of the fourth century, was for the most part Christian. There were still temples and still pagans ; but the number of the latter was rapidly diminishing : the contagion of example—especially imperial example—peculiarly effectual in a city where the court often resided, denuded the ancient altars of worshippers, and filled the ranks of the Church. The time was already in sight when the Church would attract to itself the entire population ; and learned pagans, such as the famous rhetorician Libanius, already appeared as somewhat behind the times.

However, if the flock of Christ was receiving constant accessions, it left much to be desired from the point of view of unity and mutual understanding. To say nothing of old schisms, of Marcionites, Novatians, or Paulianists, the theological disputes of the period had resulted in the formation of various ecclesiastical cliques, which could with difficulty be brought to live together in peace. Of course, the mass of the people contented themselves with a rudimentary Christianity; they left "the doctors" to wrangle and hurl texts at each other, and councils to frame and reframe without ceasing the formulas of the creed; they followed the offices of the Church, and the distributions of alms, without troubling their heads much about the leanings of the superior clergy. When the time came for electing a bishop, they were told which name they ought to acclaim, and they acclaimed it on trust. Since the deposition of Eustathius, the people had taken part, under these conditions, in the installation of several bishops suggested by the Arians. At the time we have reached, they gathered themselves beneath the pastoral staff of Bishop Leontius, a man of scant sympathy with Athanasius, an Arian at bottom, or with Arian tendencies. In bygone days he had had not a few adventures; but age had now overtaken him, and was marked on the bishop's head by a beautiful crown of white hair. Now and again he was seen to pass his hand over it, and was heard to say: "When this snow has melted, there will be mud in Antioch." Who could have been better informed than he upon the divisions in his Church?

Already, a certain section had for a long time been holding themselves aloof. The deposition of Eustathius, in Constantine's time, had not been accepted by everyone; a party had been formed to support him and to demand his restoration. Eustathius had died in exile; but the Eustathians had not rejoined the main body. They continued to hold themselves apart, under the direction of a priest named Paulinus. This little group held resolutely to the Council of Nicæa, to the *homoousios*, without explanations or additions: of the three hypostases, a formula which was brought forward from time to time, they spoke only with horror. At bottom the theological position of this small section was closely akin to that of Marcellus of Ancyra, and the others did not fail to point out this affinity.

Other people, who combined the doctrine of the three

hypostases with that of the consubstantiality, and thus
anticipated the system of the future, had at their head two
laymen, highly distinguished for their knowledge and their
eloquence, Diodore and Flavian.   They also adhered to
the Creed of Nicæa; but, since the official Church did not
actually repudiate it in terms, they did not consider themselves justified in separating themselves from that body,
and continued in communion with the successors of
Eustathius.   Nevertheless, when they heard certain
preachers endeavouring to reproduce the heretical
opinions of Arius, they did not conceal their displeasure.
Moreover, in addition to the usual offices of the Great
Church, they had others which they celebrated among
themselves.   They gathered themselves together (apart
from the official meetings for service—mass and vigil) in
the cemeteries on the outskirts of the city, near the
tombs of the martyrs, and spent long hours in chanting
psalms antiphonally.   These chants, in which, thanks to
the use of refrains easily remembered, everyone could
take part, met with very great success.   The populace of
Antioch flocked eagerly to these new psalm-singings.
Leontius, disturbed at this rivalry, summoned Flavian
and Diodore before him, and persuaded them to transfer
their offices to the churches of the city.   They accepted
his offer, but the bishop was obliged on his side to make
several concessions.

Leontius had had for some time among those about
him a kind of Christian sophist, named Aetius, whose past
adventures and present attitude were not at all reassuring
to the orthodox.   Born at Antioch or in its neighbourhood, he had pursued many occupations, being, by turns, a
coppersmith, a goldsmith, a servant, and a physician.
Between times, and here he showed himself a true Greek,
he had cultivated his mind, and learnt dialectic and
theology.   In this latter study, his views were formed by
certain survivors of the Lucianic school, who were growing
old in the bishoprics of Cilicia, or amongst the clergy of
Antioch.   His mind was a subtle one, capable of the
finest hair-splitting, and of arguing for days together.

In this exercise he was at first beaten by a Borborian, a member of one of the obsolete Gnostic sects (there were still a few of them remaining). But he took his revenge, at Alexandria, upon a celebrated Manichean, a certain Aphthonius, whom he put so shamefully to silence that his opponent died of chagrin at his defeat. Aetius profited by his stay in Alexandria to perfect himself in the philosophy of Aristotle, and, on his return to Antioch, he did not shrink from attacking Basil, the Bishop of Ancyra, who had just covered himself with glory in a successful dispute with Photinus. This time, Basil himself was beaten; and Aetius quickly acquired the reputation of being invincible. To avenge his defeat, Basil tried to ruin him with the Cæsar Gallus; but Bishop Leontius intervened, and Gallus, instead of causing his legs to be broken, as he had threatened, admitted the doctor to his friendship; he even entrusted him with the honourable task of completing the religious education of his brother Julian, who was beginning to be a cause of anxiety.[1]

Julian was in good hands! We have already seen him borrowing books from George of Alexandria. Aetius was in a position to initiate him into Arianism of the purest and, one may add, the most arid type; for his speciality was to present heresy in syllogisms. We can form an idea of his method from a little treatise,[2] divided into short sections, in which he defends his opinions. It begins as follows :—

"If it is possible for the Un-begotten God to make the begotten become un-begotten, both substances being un-begotten, they will not differ from each other as to independence. Why, then, should we say that the one is changed, and the other changes it, when we will not allow that God produces (the Word) from nothing?"

This canticle contains no fewer than forty-seven couplets, all equally dry, all equally devoid of any religious meaning. Aetius, so we gather from St Epiphanius, had composed more than three hundred of them. Such eloquence must have given his ordinary listeners very

---

[1] Philostorgius, iii. 27.　　[2] Epiph. *Haer*. lxxvi. 11.

severe headaches; it was little suited to draw Julian away from the mysteries of Eleusis and the worship of Apollo.

The doctor returned to Antioch, where the easy-going Leontius at length promoted him to the diaconate, which gave him the right of preaching in church. The orthodox party protested. It was not the first time that they had had imposed upon them clerics of a doubtful past and advanced opinions; it was even traditional that no priest, no deacon, should be chosen from their ranks. But the clergy, thus badly recruited as they were, had still address enough to avoid dogmatic scandals. Aetius was not only a notorious, a professed, a militant Arian: he was known to be inflexible in his obstinacy; at every opportunity he was heard to protest against accommodations and those who made use of them. The bishop recognized that he had gone too far; Aetius was removed, and transferred himself to Alexandria, to the society of the intruder George, to whom he became, for several months, one of his most energetic advisers.

The affairs of his party did not suffer very much from his absence. Besides, he was not the only Anomœan celebrity to be met with at Antioch. There was living there a curious individual, one Theophilus the Indian, as his friends called him, Blemmyàs as other people styled him. He came from a distant island, called Dibous, from which he had been sent as a hostage in the reign of the Emperor Constantine. He was then quite young. Eusebius of Nicomedia had taken charge of his education, had initiated him in the purest Arian theology, and had raised him to the diaconate. He led the life of an ascetic, and among his acquaintances passed for a saint. His complexion, which was very dark, drew people's attention to him and made him popular. Long, long after, even in Theodosius' reign, he enjoyed an extraordinary reputation among the Arians. In the time of Bishop Leontius, he was in high favour at court with the Cæsar Gallus; Aetius profited greatly from his protection. When Gallus fell into disgrace, Theophilus, whom he treated as a sort of domestic saint, followed him to the

West, and undertook his defence before Constantius, whereby he earned a sentence of exile for himself. But the Empress Eusebia falling ill, it was necessary to recall the holy man; the empress got better, and Theophilus was sent on a mission to the king of the Homerites (Yemen), and the king of the Axoumites (Abyssinia); on this occasion he was consecrated bishop (about the year 356).

The further he went, the stronger became his Arianism and his obstinacy. He would never have approved of the half-and-half terms to which people resigned themselves at the bishop's palace at Antioch.[1]

Poor Leontius was greatly embarrassed by all these disputes. While looking after the affairs of his own party, he tried not to exasperate his opponents too far: the government was anxious that quiet should be maintained in the Churches. In the Divine Office, when the time came to recite the Doxology, the orthodox said, as they do to-day: "Glory be to the Father, and to the Son, and to the Holy Ghost"; the others: "Glory be to the Father, *through* the Son, *in* the Holy Ghost." The bishop, closely watched by both sides, began by saying: "Glory be to the Father" in a loud and intelligible voice; then he coughed or lost his voice for a moment, not recovering it till the conclusion: "world without end." This anecdote is a delightful illustration of the position of affairs.

But "the snow was going to melt, and the mud to appear." Bishop Leontius died towards the end of the year 357.

For some two years, the Church had been passing through a singular crisis. Orthodoxy, as represented by the Council of Nicæa, was everywhere dominant, in the sense that no bishop dared openly to confess himself hostile to that holy assembly; it was everywhere abolished, in the sense that no bishop in possession of his see dared to defend the creed which it had put forth. The tactics of the aged Eusebius of Nicomedia had completely succeeded.

---

[1] Upon Theophilus, see Greg. Nyss. *Ad Eunom.* (Migne, *P. G.*, vol. xlv., p. 264; Philostorgius, iii. 4-6; iv. 1, 7, 8; v. 4; vii. 6; viii. 2; ix. 1, 3, 18).

Pronounce an anathema upon the council! Who would ever have thought of such a thing? The memory of Constantine forbade it. Besides, did it not bear the signature both of Eusebius himself, of his namesake of Cæsarea, of Theognis, of Maris, of Narcissus, of Patrophilus, and the rest? All the great men of the Arian party figured in the number of the three hundred and eighteen Fathers. But Arianism, banished from the front door, could re-enter by the back, under the cloke of a prudent silence. This plan was adopted. Such dissimulations belong to all times and to all parties.

Prudence, for all that, is a virtue which is practised willingly enough during the time of conflict, but which is generally discarded, once success has been attained. When there were no longer Consubstantialists save in places of exile, people began to feel less acutely the need for remaining united. Up to that time, the battle had been rather for canon law than for theology. The Council of Nicæa was all very well; but there was also the Council of Tyre to be considered. As to Arius and his adherents, condemned at Nicæa, there had come to pass that which had pleased God and the Emperor Constantine. They had offered explanations; these had been accepted; this account was closed. But the Council of Tyre had condemned Athanasius, and even if he had succeeded in securing his vindication by the bishops of Egypt, who were suspect, and by the Westerns, who were ill-informed and incompetent, the Easterns had never relaxed the severity of the decisions which they had themselves given against him. Such was the essence of the position. When Athanasius sought to compromise the Eastern bishops by speaking of their Arian sympathies, there was produced, not exactly the Creed of Nicæa, but a Creed of Antioch, more vague, it is true, and not admitting the much-disputed term *homoousios*, but orthodox in itself, and having the advantage of being acceptable to almost everyone.

There remained, of course, the question of communion. At Sardica both parties had excommunicated each other.

But in the course of fifteen years many of the persons specifically condemned had disappeared. Julius of Rome was dead; so also were Theodore of Heraclea, Maximin of Trèves, and no doubt several others also. Stephen, the Bishop of Antioch, had been deposed; the Westerns repudiated Photinus. Moreover, at the Councils of Arles (353) and of Milan (355), the two episcopates had fraternized. One after the other the recalcitrants were yielding. Heremius of Thessalonica had signed the Eastern formula; Fortunatian of Aquileia likewise, notwithstanding the trust placed in him by Pope Liberius. He had even given Liberius counsels of accommodation—counsels which bore fruit. Once at Berea, in the heart of Thrace, the good Pope ended by feeling himself very far from Rome, from his people, from the senators who loved him, the matrons who received him with so much respect, and the churches where he was wont to deliver moving discourses. His keeper, Bishop Demophilus, also set himself to work upon Liberius. At the end of two years, his resistance was overcome. He did not abandon the Council of Nicæa. He signed, perhaps, a formula; but, at the time at which we have arrived, the formulas which the Easterns were accustomed to tender to the Westerns contained nothing contrary to the faith; the only objection that could be made to them was that they were not sufficiently precise.[1]

[1] The document upon which is based the admission that Liberius did sign a formula (see, however, the texts quoted in the following note), is one of the three letters preserved in the Fragments of St Hilary (vi. 5-11). These letters must have been written at Berea by the exiled Pope, to hasten his recall to Rome; they are addressed to the Eastern Bishops, to Ursacius, Valens, and Germinius, and finally to Vincent of Capua. Liberius reviews in them the concessions he had made, his repudiation of Athanasius, his entering into communion with the Eastern Churches, and the approval given to their formulary. In the Fragments of St Hilary these documents are accompanied by a narrative which condemns them severely; there are even here and there very harsh notes upon the most reprehensible passages. The author of text and notes evidently considered the letters to be authentic. He identified the formula signed by Liberius with one of the professions of faith previously produced by the Easterns. To

A matter which seems of graver character is the fact that he repudiated communion with Athanasius, and allied himself with that of the Easterns—people of every shade of opinion, we must confess, among whom were to be met, side by side with Ursacius and Valens, others like Basil of Ancyra and Cyril of Jerusalem, whose ideas were much less advanced.

This proceeding of Liberius involved the re-establishment of relations with the advocates of prudent silence. It meant the abandonment of the position which the Pope had maintained hitherto with most signal distinction —a position for which he had braved the anger of the emperor and the sorrows of exile. It was a weakening, a downfall.[1]

judge from the signatures which it bore and which the writer enumerates, it can scarcely be different from the formula put forth at Sirmium in 351. In any case, neither these signatures nor the date of the Pope's weakening allow us to believe that the formula subscribed by him could have been the one which Hosius signed during the summer of 357. When it was drawn up, the Easterns were still united, and their official creed was the fourth formula of Antioch. (*Vide supra*, p. 170.) It is surprising that St Hilary, elsewhere so well disposed to this formula (see p. 234), here treats it with such severity, and without any qualification or restriction includes among the heretics, Basil of Ancyra, one of its signatories. Thus we may ask ourselves if it is really St Hilary who is speaking in this passage. It might possibly be that this portion of the historical Fragments has been interpolated by some Luciferian. M. L. Saltet has put forward reasons for believing in such an interpolation (*Bulletin de littér. ecclés.* 1905, p. 222 *et seq.*). In that case, the letters would come to us from people to whom Liberius was specially hateful. But this would not prevent them being authentic ; we do not expect that such documents would have been published by Liberius or his friends.

[1] Not to speak of the Fragments of St Hilary, mentioned in the preceding note (cf. *in Const.* 11), the weakening of Liberius is attested by St Athanasius (*Apol. contra Ar.* 89), a passage added as a supplement, and *Hist. Ar.* 41. St Jerome, in his *Chronicle*, does not hesitate to speak of a formula signed : *in haereticam pravitatem subscribens.* The same is true of the Roman author of the preface to the *Libellus precum* : "*manus perfidiae dederat.*" From this document, and from St Athanasius, we learn that the Pope's action took place at the beginning of 357, about two years after his departure for exile.

The Emperor Constantius already knew of it when he came to Rome in May 357. A very short time afterwards, either in the summer or the autumn, the prince's visit to Sirmium was taken advantage of by the three doughty leaders of the Arian party in those parts, Ursacius, Valens, and Germinius, to aim a decisive blow at the Creed of Nicæa. Such an attempt had already been made at Milan, two years before; there had been produced, in the guise of an imperial edict, a theological statement so clearly heterodox that the people had perceived the heresy, and their protests had caused the failure of the attempt.[1] This time it took the form of an episcopal declaration, which, emanating from the bishops then at court, should afterwards be presented, in every province, for the acceptance of their colleagues. And—a thing scarcely to be believed—they selected as the person to "launch" this anti-Nicene document, a document in which the *homoousios* was demolished, none other than the great man of the Council of Nicæa, the inventor, if we may be permitted the expression, of the *homoousios*—the aged patriarch, Hosius of Cordova. Assisted by the Bishop of Lisbon, Potamius, apparently reconciled to him,[2] by Germinius of Sirmium, and the inevitable Ursacius and Valens, Hosius appended, at the end of this impious declaration, the same signature that had headed those of the three hundred and eighteen Fathers of the Council of Nicæa. It is evident that an unfair advantage had been taken of his great age and of the enfeeblement of his faculties, and that personally he was hardly a responsible agent in this sad story.[3] This is all the more probable because—a touching detail— no one could ever succeed in making him anathematize Athanasius. His poor brain grew confused, no doubt,

[1] Sulpicius Severus, *Chron.* ii. 39. Sulpicius here seems to be relying upon a lost passage of the Fragments of St Hilary.

[2] *Supra*, p. 210.

[3] Athanasius speaks of acts of physical violence used to the old man. He says also that he protested at the moment of death (*Apol. contra Ar.* 89, an appendix added subsequently, when the work was already published; *Hist. Ar.* 45).

by theological questions; but Athanasius remained for him a concrete personality, a friend, a companion in conflict; he clung to that, and they could not make him relax his hold.

The document in question[1] was not a confession of faith, but a simple theological declaration. "Some dissension having arisen in regard to the Faith, all the questions have been carefully considered and discussed, at Sirmium, in the presence of the holy bishops, our brethren, Valens, Ursacius, and Germinius. We believe that there is but One God, etc." The idea of the existence of two gods is set aside, and the terms "substance" and "essence" are repudiated; there must no longer be a question either of *homoousios* or *homoïousios*, expressions which are not in Scripture, and which, besides, presume to express in words relations which are inexpressible. The Father is greater than the Son; His attributes are described as those of the One Only God, while the Son is always placed below Him.

This document is, in episcopal language, a sufficiently clear expression of the doctrine which Arius had taught in bygone days, and which Aetius at Antioch was engaged in translating into syllogisms. At the period of which we are now speaking, attention was directed towards the idea of resemblance. In the time of Arius, they preferred rather to say that the Word was not eternal, that He was a creature; now stress was laid on the point that He did not resemble the Father; He was unlike Him ($\dot{\alpha}\nu\acute{o}\mu\omicron\iota\varsigma$) from whence was derived the name of Anomœans applied to the new Arians. Ranged against them, in the Christian world of the East, besides the general tone of feeling, which was little favourable to any one who attacked the absolute Divinity of Christ, were theological opponents, strong in numbers and of high authority. They rallied round the word *homoïousios*, "like in essence," a term

---

[1] The original Latin text is in Hilary (*De syn.* 11): the Greek in Athan. *De syn.* 28. This is what is often called the *second* formula of Sirmium; the first being represented by the profession of faith of the synod of 351.

sometimes employed by Alexander and Athanasius, and
one which, if it differed slightly from the Nicene *homoousios*,
embodied almost, granted the circumstances in which it
was employed, the same connotation.   Those who made
use of it through preference, and through fear of the
Sabellian meaning of which the *homoousios* remained
susceptible, had been at first confused with the Arians;
several among them, including the most distinguished, had
been waging war for thirty years against Athanasius, in
the ranks of the "Easterns."   But this personal hostility,
which drew upon them, from the orthodox party, rather
more hard knocks than they deserved for it, must not
prejudice us with regard to their theology.   People who
declared that the Son was, in essence, like to the Father,
and who meant to be and to remain Monotheists, found
themselves, when everything is considered, at the same
point as those who proclaimed the identity of essence
between the Father and the Son, while maintaining at the
same time the distinction of one from the other.   Ursacius
and Valens knew perfectly well what they were doing
when they clamoured for the repudiation of the *homoïousios*
as well as the *homoousios*.   As a protest against Arianism,
the two terms were of equal weight.

The astute impudence which made Hosius appear to
support an Arian interpretation of the Creed of Nicæa had
only a small success.   In Gaul and Britain it provoked a
very lively revulsion.   In these countries, where the
theology of the Emperor Constantius did not find a very
enthusiastic upholder in Julian, the bishops had a certain
latitude to say what they thought.   Ever since the
occurrences at Arles and Milan, they had a bitter grudge
against Saturninus of Arles, the courtier who was responsible for the disgrace which had befallen several of their
colleagues; they maintained no semblance of communion
with him.   When the declaration of Sirmium reached
them, one of their number, Phoebadius of Agen, published
a criticism of it,[1] of considerable vigour, undeterred by the
recommendation which the signature of Hosius seemed to

---

[1] Migne. *P. L.*, vol. xx. pp. 13-30.

give it. He and his colleagues came to an agreement, either in council or otherwise, to repudiate it. They communicated their decision to Hilary, the exiled Bishop of Poitiers, who, from his prison in Phrygia, was anxiously watching all these events.[1] The African bishops, also, protested in writing.[2]

It was just at this moment that the crisis foreseen by Bishop Leontius occurred in Syria. The see of Antioch was aimed at by two candidates, Eudoxius, Bishop of Germanicia, and George, Bishop of Laodicea. Eudoxius was the first to arrive on the scene. As soon as Leontius was dead, he secured for himself the provisional administration of the vacant Church, and managed things so well that he was acclaimed as bishop of the see. He installed himself without heeding the protests which were raised from Laodicea, Arethusa, and other neighbouring bishoprics. Eudoxius was, from a religious point of view, a very extraordinary person. There are still extant several samples of his eloquence, which are of a really scandalous character. St Hilary reports[3] the following statement of his, which was taken down in shorthand, and presented to the Council of Seleucia: "God was what He is. He was not Father, for He had not a Son. To have had a son, He must have had a wife. . . ."[4] His opinions had undergone some fluctuation: a homoïousian for one moment, he had allowed himself to be led back to the pure Arian doctrine,[5] which he knew how to dissemble

---

[1] We see, from the title of Hilary's reply (*De syn.* 1), that, with the exception of the district of the Rhone, of Vienne, and of Narbonne, the whole episcopate of Gaul was on the orthodox side. Toulouse had remained faithful to Rhodanius in exile, as Poitiers had to Hilary.

[2] Hil. *Adv. Const.* 26. It was Basil of Ancyra who had provoked this manifesto (Sozomen, *H. E.* iv. 24).   [3] *Adv. Const.* 13.

[4] The rest cannot be translated. The Latin text of St Hilary is as follows : *ut et femina sit, et colloquium et sermocinatio et coniunctio coniugalis verbi et blandimentum et postremum ad generandum naturalis machinula.* What bishops !

[5] Philostorgius, iv. 4. This historian tells us that Eudoxius was the son of a certain Cæsarius of Arabissos, in Armenia Minor, a man of profligate life, but one who, none the less, ended by dying a martyr, as we are told in regard to St Boniface.

when necessary.   Just now there was no occasion to
put a restraint upon himself.   Eudoxius sent his adhesion
to the new formula of Sirmium, and for his own part lost
no time in promoting to ecclesiastical positions, not only
Aetius himself, but a great number of his partisans or
disciples.   Among the latter figured a certain Eunomius,
whom he ordained deacon, and who speedily became one
of the pillars of the party.   The moderates, on the other
hand, and the orthodox, were at the same time very badly
treated.   George of Laodicea undertook their defence.
He addressed to Bishops Macedonius of Constantinople,
Basil of Ancyra, Cecropius of Nicomedia, and Eugenius of
Nicæa, a letter in most urgent terms, adjuring them to
come to the assistance of the Church of Antioch, and by
an episcopal demonstration as numerous as possible, to
force Eudoxius to get rid of Aetius and his gang.[1]

At this very moment Basil was holding a council at
Ancyra, on the occasion of a dedication festival.   He had
little need to be exhorted to march against Aetius and his
champions.   The sophist of Antioch was an old adversary
of his.   A formulary was speedily drawn up, approved in
council, despatched to the bishops of the various provinces,[2]
and finally conveyed to the court at Sirmium by Basil
himself and his colleagues, Eustathius of Sebaste and
Eleusius of Cyzicus.   It was then the spring of 358, for
the council had assembled just before Easter.   Basil, in
the presence of Constantius, met with an extraordinary
success.   The emperor had just given his approval of the
installation of Eudoxius at Antioch; he had even sent
letters to that effect to his delegate, a priest named
Asphalius.   He allowed himself to be turned completely
round.   Asphalius was enjoined to return the letters in
his possession; and in their stead others were sent to

---

[1] Sozomen, iv. 13.

[2] St Epiphanius, *Haer.* lxxiii. 2-11, has preserved to us the text of
the copy addressed to the bishops of Phœnicia, and in addition, cc.
12-22, that of another letter on the same subject, written in the name
of Basil and George.   St Hilary (*De syn.* 12-25) gives only part of the
document, twelve anathemas, which were detached from the whole,
and which received special publicity at Sirmium (cf. *ibid.* 90).

him, of a tenour highly unpleasant for Eudoxius, Aetius, and their party: " *We* did not send Eudoxius; let no one imagine such a thing. We are very far from wishing to support people of this kind." The emperor went on to express disapproval of bishops who changed their sees, and of adventurers like Aetius, who are bent upon corrupting the people by their heresies. As for himself, he had always been a *homoïousian*. The people of Antioch must remember the speeches he had made to them to that effect. They must banish the false doctors from ecclesiastical assemblies, and from the ranks of the clergy. If they persisted, they would see what would happen to them.

Having thus settled the affair in Antioch, Basil busied himself with the formula attributed to Hosius. It was withdrawn from circulation. Until a different one could be put forward by authority, two texts were united which had been adopted earlier, at Sirmium (351) against Paul of Samosata and Photinus and at Antioch (341) at the Dedication Council.[1] These texts were orthodox[2] in the main, except that the *homoousios* was passed over in silence. Hosius was no longer there to give them authority by his signature; he had been taken back to Spain, and perhaps was already dead. But Liberius, recalled from Berea, was still waiting at Sirmium for permission to return to Rome. He was asked to sign this third formula of Sirmium which was identical really with the first, already accepted by him. He consented to this, and thereby gave substantial support to the reaction, in an orthodox direction, which was making its appearance against the Anomœan intrigue. He even gave Basil a declaration, in which he excluded from the Church anyone who would not admit that the Son is like to the Father in substance and in everything. This declaration was not

---

[1] St Hilary, *De syn.* 29-60, reproduces the Creed *in Encaeniis*, the text of the (Eastern) Council of Sardica, and finally that of 351. The last two are identical with regard to the affirmative part (*Credimus*, etc.); they only differ in the anathemas.

[2] See the way in which St Hilary (*loc. cit.*) explains them.

unserviceable, for Eudoxius and his followers were
circulating the rumour that the Pope had signed the
formula of Hosius. It was in these circumstances that
the emperor at last made up his mind to yield to the
incessant demands of the Romans, and to send them back
their bishop. The prelates assembled at Sirmium wrote
to Felix and to the clergy to receive Liberius, and to
bury in oblivion all the dissensions caused by his banishment. Felix and Liberius governed the Apostolic Church
together.

The combination was an extraordinary one; but the
government was too deeply pledged to Felix to be able
to oust him openly. It counted, no doubt, upon the
populace forcing its hand; however this may be, this was
what actually happened. The system of having two
bishops at the same time was hissed in the Circus.[1] As
soon as Liberius presented himself, a riot broke out, and
Felix was driven forth; he retired to the outskirts, and
after an unsuccessful attempt on the basilica of Julius in
Trastevere, he made up his mind to live quietly in retirement. The emperor shut his eyes; it was the best
solution of the difficulty.

We must not think that the support given by Pope
Liberius to Basil[2] had been unfavourably regarded in
orthodox circles. Like him, the exiled Hilary and the
outlawed Athanasius applauded Basil's effort. Upon
the ground of doctrine, a reconciliation was in course of
being brought about; confronting the strictly Nicene

---

[1] Theodoret, ii. 14.

[2] Basil of Ancyra seems very probably to have been the author of
a treatise "On Virginity," which forms part of the apocryphal writings
of St Basil of Cæsarea (Migne, *P. G.* vol. xxx., p. 669). It is addressed
to a certain Bishop Letoïos, evidently the same, according to this
supposition, as the Letoïos who figures among the signatories of the
synodical letter of Ancyra, in 358 (*supra*, p. 251). This Letoïos is
described in the title of the treatise as Bishop of Melitene, and there
is nothing to prevent this being so, although we find another
bishop of that name, later on, in the list of bishops of Melitene. See
the memoir of Cavallera, "Le *De Virginitate* de Basile d'Ancyre," in
the *Revue d'hist. eccl.* (Louvain, 1905), p. 5 *et seq.*

orthodoxy, there was to be seen the gradual formation, in the camp of the enemies of Athanasius, of an orthodoxy almost equivalent to it.   The two parties must eventually come to a mutual understanding; and, meantime, they began to confer with each other and even to approve of one another. "Those," said Athanasius at this time,[1] "who accept everything that was written at Nicæa, although they may still retain scruples about the term *homoousios*, must not be treated as enemies. I do not attack them as mad Arians, nor as adversaries of the Fathers: I discuss matters with them as a brother with brothers, who think as we do, and only differ as to one word. . . . Among their number is Basil of Ancyra, who has written upon the Faith."   As to Hilary, he was then writing his treatise, " On the Synods and the Faith of the Easterns," addressed to the bishops of Gaul and of Britain, to give them information on the state of controversies in the East.   In this he exhibits a very friendly appreciation of the initiative just taken at Sirmium by Bishops Basil, Eustathius, and Eleusius; he shows, by reproducing and commenting upon their earlier formulas, not only that these documents do not represent a perversion of the Faith, but that certain circumstances have justified their existence.   He proves the equivalence of the terms *homoousios* and *homoïousios*, provided they are taken in the sense given to them by their respective patrons, the Council of Nicæa, and the friends of Basil. Addressing himself finally to the latter, he gently implores them to take one step more; since their own technical term is susceptible of the same sense as that of the Great Council, will they not consent to sacrifice it, and accept the formula of the three hundred and eighteen Fathers?

While Hilary was writing this message of peace, Basil, who was by nature combative, was taking steps against the Anomœans.[2]   He had succeeded in making Constantius believe that Aetius and his followers had, in the time of Gallus, been the supporters of intrigues against the

---

[1] *De syn.* 41.
[2] Upon what follows, see Sozomen, *H. E.* iv. 16.

supreme emperor.[1]   Constantius gave him the most
extensive powers. Aetius was banished to Pepuza, among
the Montanists; Theophilus to Heraclea in Pontus;
Eunomius, arrested at Ancyra, was imprisoned at Midæon
in Phrygia; Eudoxius retired to Armenia. Numerous
incidents of this kind were later brought up against the
leader of the Homoïousian party; we hear of more than
seventy sentences of exile, given at his request. Ursacius
and Valens, in a good position to see which way the wind
blew, had been among the first to submit, and, like Pope
Liberius, had signed Basil's declarations. In short, for
some months there was a reign of terror in the East, in
the interest of the orthodoxy of Ancyra and of Laodicea.

Basil took advantage of his favourable opportunities
to secure the assembling of a great Œcumenical Council,
which should revive the work of Nicæa and bring peace
to the Church. The first idea was to hold it at Nicæa
itself; then Nicomedia was suggested; but this town was
destroyed on August 24 (358) by an earthquake, and the
church collapsed upon the head of the Bishop, Cecropius.
There was no doubt, since the intervention of Hilary, that
this council would have brought to Basil the support of a
very large number of Westerns. Thus reinforced, the right
wing of the Eastern episcopate would assuredly have
prevailed: an understanding would have been arrived at,
in one way or another, upon the question of the *homoousios*
and the *homoïousios*, and Arianism would have been routed.
This result would have been obtained quite apart from
Athanasius, ever proscribed by the government, assailed
by one section of the episcopate, and abandoned by the
other. But it was written that the brave warrior who
had borne the brunt of the conflict should also share in its
honours. Basil's plan ended in a most lamentable failure.

There still remained, in the East, two Arian bishops
of the first generation, two personal friends of Arius, who
had indeed forsaken him at Nicæa, but had lent themselves to all the intrigues hatched for his restoration:

---

[1] This was probable enough, in view of the relations of Theophilus
and Aetius with the Cæsar of Antioch. *Vide supra*, p. 222.

these were Patrophilus of Scythopolis in Palestine, and Narcissus of Neronias in Cilicia. These two Nestors were sent as deputies to the court of Constantius, where they set themselves to represent Basil of Ancyra as a stirrer-up of strife, which was partly true, and to demand that, instead of one council, two should be assembled, one in the East, and the other in the West. The difference of languages justified this course, and also the consideration of the great expense which would be incurred by the transporting to the East of so many Latin bishops. Their appeal was listened to. The town of Ariminum (Rimini), on the Italian coast of the Adriatic, was selected for the Western council, and that of Seleucia in Isauria, near the seaboard of Cilicia, for that of the East. The Arians knew, from the experience of past years, that the Westerns were not proof against weaknesses and mystifications; in the East they felt pretty certain of obtaining a majority, not, of course, for a crude and undisguised Anomœanism, but for one of those non-committal declarations which had served them so well for the last thirty years.

Agreeably to this, the formula was prepared and accepted at a meeting of the court bishops, shortly before the time fixed for the opening of the councils, to both of which it was to be presented. It was Mark, the Bishop of Arethusa, who was appointed to draw it up. We possess the text of it [1] :—

" The Catholic Faith has been set forth, in the presence of our Master, the most pious and triumphant Emperor Constantius Augustus, eternal and venerable, in the consulate of the most illustrious Fl. Eusebius and Fl. Hypatius, at Sirmium, the xi. of the Kalends of June (May 22, 359).

" We believe in One Only True God . . . and in One Only Son of God, Who, before all ages, before all power, before all conceivable time, before all imaginable substance, was begotten of God, without passion . . . like to the Father who begat Him, according to the Scriptures. . . .

---

[1] Athan. *De syn.* 8 ; the signatures are in Epiph. lxxiii. 22.

"As to the term Essence ($o\dot{v}\sigma\acute{\iota}\alpha$) which the Fathers have employed in good faith, but which, being unknown to the faithful, has been the cause of scandal to them, since the Scriptures do not contain it, it has seemed good to suppress it, and to avoid entirely for the future all mention of Essence in reference to God, the Scriptures never speaking of Essence in reference to the Father and the Son. But we say that the Son is like to the Father in all things, as the Scriptures say and teach Him to be."

This formula no longer affirmed, like that of 357, the superiority of the Father over the Son; but, like the former creed, it repudiated the use of the terms *homoousios* and *homoiousios*. A serious blow, not only for the old Nicene orthodox party, but also for the neo-orthodox party, whose triumph Basil of Ancyra had brought about the year before! That prelate's influence had evidently declined in the changeable mind of the Emperor Constantius. However, the pure Arians had not obtained complete success: this was clearly seen, when the time for signature came. Valens of Mursa objected to employ the words $\kappa\alpha\tau\grave{\alpha}$ $\pi\acute{\alpha}\nu\tau\alpha$, "in all things," which seemed to him to include implicitly the likeness in essence. The emperor was obliged to insist on his introducing these words into his expression of adhesion. As to Basil, he would willingly have spoken of likeness $\kappa\alpha\tau'$ $o\dot{v}\sigma\acute{\iota}\alpha\nu$ (in essence); but as this was forbidden, he piled up synonymous expressions, $\kappa\alpha\tau\grave{\alpha}$ $\tau\grave{\eta}\nu$ $\dot{v}\pi\acute{o}\sigma\tau\alpha\sigma\iota\nu$ $\kappa\alpha\grave{\iota}$ $\kappa\alpha\tau\grave{\alpha}$ $\tau\grave{\eta}\nu$ $\ddot{v}\pi\alpha\rho\xi\iota\nu$ $\kappa\alpha\grave{\iota}$ $\kappa\alpha\tau\grave{\alpha}$ $\tau\grave{o}$ $\epsilon\hat{\iota}\nu\alpha\iota$. The unhappy man snatched at the branches. At bottom, the only thing that mattered was his signature, and the official text: amendments did not count.

Not only was the doctrinal task for the two councils prepared beforehand in this careful fashion: it was also decided [1] that, when their work was finished, each of them should appoint a deputation of ten members, and that the two deputations should meet in the emperor's presence for the final declaration of agreement. Thus the prince and his theological advisers were really

---

[1] Letter of May 27, *Continent priora* (Hil. *Frag. hist.* vii. 1, 2).

the beginning and the end of this great consultation.
The episcopate was shut in on both sides. It was also
enacted that, with regard to questions as to persons, each
of the two councils should deal only with its own part
of the empire—the Eastern prelates with Eastern disputes,
the Westerns with those of the West.

The Council of Ariminum[1] was the first to open,
about the beginning of July 359. It was very numerously
attended. Imperial agents had beaten up all the provinces,
and had recruited voluntarily or by force more than
four hundred bishops. The supporters of the Council of
Nicæa were in an enormous majority; they took up
their quarters in the church of the city; the others,
eighty at the most, in a separate building. With them
were Ursacius, Valens, Germinius, Auxentius, Epictetus,
Saturninus, etc. On the orthodox side, the most distinguished person seems to have been the Bishop of
Carthage, Restitutus. The Roman Church was not represented; at this moment the government was recognizing
two Popes, between whom it was difficult for it to make a
choice. After several fruitless conferences, the two parties
in the council decided to send separate delegates to the
emperor. The orthodox party entrusted to their representatives a very clear and firm protest[2] against any idea
of touching the Creed of Nicæa, and repudiated the
declaration of May 22. Four bishops, Ursacius, Valens,
Germinius, and Gaius,[3] who had presented it to them,
had been excommunicated by them. Their opponents,
on the other hand, sent in their agreement with the
emperor's formula. Constantius was then in Thrace,
drawing slowly near the frontiers of Persia, whither other

[1] A narrative account is given in Sulpicius Severus, *Chron.* ii.
41, 45; *cf.* Jerome, *Adv. Lucif.* 17, 18; documents in Hil. *Frag. hist.*
vii.-ix.; *cf.* Athan. *De synodis.* This book was written in the
autumn of 359, when Athanasius still knew nothing about the two
Councils of Ariminum and Seleucia, except their orthodox manifestoes,
and was ignorant of the defections which followed them.

[2] Hil. *Frag. hist.* viii. 1-3; *cf.* vii. 3 *et seq.*

[3] St Athanasius adds here the names of Auxentius and Demophilus (*De syn.* 9).

affairs were calling him. He gave a good reception to the delegates of the opposition, and, on the contrary, put off those of the majority.[1] The latter had at their head the Bishop of Carthage; neither he nor they were equal to the importance of their mission. They were so surrounded and lectured that they ended by betraying their trust, and took upon themselves not only to resume communion with the four deposed bishops who formed part of the opposing deputation, but to rescind, broadly speaking, everything done by those who had sent them. This proceeding, though strangely irregular, was confirmed by a protocol dated from a posting station called Nicæa, near Adrianople, on October 10.

It remained to secure its acceptance by the council itself. The twenty delegates returned to Ariminum in a condition of unexpected unanimity. Their example soon caused many defections; the meeting in the church began to grow thinner, to the benefit of the other building. The prætorian prefect Taurus, to whom was entrusted the duty of looking after the council and bringing it to the point the emperor wished, accomplished his task successfully. The bishops, penned up for seven months in the narrow limits of a small town, where they had nothing to do, grew weary, and demanded permission to go. Taurus remained deaf to their appeals. They would be allowed to go when everyone had signed. Also, his orders were, not to wait for absolute unanimity; when the number of those who refused to sign fell below fifteen, he was to send them into exile, and to set the others at liberty.

There was no one left to exile. The opposition, reduced to about twenty, under the leadership of Phoebadius, Bishop of Agen, and Servasius of Tongres, yielded at last to his exhortations. They were given further a sort of half-concession, by being allowed, provided they signed the formula, to expand it in the declaration of their adhesion. They took advantage, with more or

---

[1] See the emperor's letter addressed at that time to the council, and the reply of the latter, at the end of the *De synodis* of Athanasius.

less cleverness, of this concession; but they signed without exception. Ten new delegates, chosen this time by the whole council, went to carry to Constantinople, the documentary proof of this falling away.[1]

In the meantime, the other Council at Seleucia[2] was beginning its deliberations. Leonas, "quæstor of the sacred palace," like the prefect Taurus at Ariminum, represented the emperor, and exercised official oversight; the military governor[3] of the province, the Dux Lauricius, had orders to assist him with troops if necessary. About a hundred and fifty bishops were present, among others the two intruded primates of Alexandria and Antioch, George and Eudoxius; Acacius, the metropolitan of Palestine, a very influential person; Basil of Ancyra, Macedonius of Constantinople, Patrophilus, Cyril of Jerusalem, Eleusius of Cyzicus, Silvanus of Tarsus, etc.   Hilary of Poitiers had also been sent there. The *vicarius* of the *diocese* of Asia, whose business it was to despatch the bishops to the council, had not taken into consideration Hilary's position as an exile, and had packed him off with the others.

From the very first sitting (September 27), the parties were clearly defined. After a confused debate upon the order of proceeding, they decided to begin with the question of faith. Basil was absent on this particular day. He found himself afterwards among the number of persons in dispute, an accusation having been laid against him. Furthermore, he played scarcely any part in the council; it was Eleusius and Silvanus who directed his party at that time. Silvanus proposed that no new creed should be accepted, and that they should adhere to that of Antioch, which was called the Dedication Creed. In this way everything was set aside that had been done

---

[1] Hil. *Frag. hist.* ix.

[2] Socrates gives (*H. E.* ii. 39, 40) an analysis of its Acts which he had read in the collection of Sabinus. Sozomen (iv. 22) read them subsequently, and drew from them several new details; *cf.* Hil. *Adv. Const.* 12-15.

[3] Isauria, a province thinly populated, had no civil governor; it was administered by a dux.

at Court since Easter 358, whether at Basil's instigation
or that of the Arians. His proposition was accepted
by a hundred and five votes: Acacius then retired with
his followers; they were nineteen in all. Apart from
these two groups, there were some Egyptian bishops
who, like Hilary, adhered to the Council of Nicæa; but
in such surroundings they could scarcely have any
influence.

On the next day, while the hundred and five, shut up
in the church, proceeded to sign the formula of Antioch,
the Acacians, protesting strongly against this sitting *in
camera*, presented to the quæstor a declaration agreeing
with that of Sirmium, but so far amended that in it was
condemned the *anomoios* no less than the *homoousios* and
the *homoïousios*. This document,[1] adorned with thirty-two
signatures, was discussed on the two following days, by a
sitting of the whole council, but nothing was decided;
Silvanus, Eleusius, and their party remained inflexible,
and refused to hear of any other creed but that of the
Dedication.[2] Seeing this, Leonas declared that he had
been delegated to a unanimous council, and not to a
divided one. He took leave of the bishops, saying to
them: "Now, go and quarrel with each other in the
church." Following his example, the Acacians refused to
take any part in the subsequent meetings.

The majority, however, met together, and discussed
the questions affecting individuals. Cyril of Jerusalem,
who had been deposed two years before by his metropolitan, Acacius, had lodged an appeal, and the emperor
had referred his case to the Council of Seleucia: he was

---

[1] Athan. *De syn.* 29; Epiph. *Haer.* lxxiii. 25, 26, with the
signatures, to the number of 43. The number of the supporters of
Acacius varies, as we see, according to the documents.

[2] They refused explicitly to endorse the formulas of 358 and 359,
i.e., those of Basil and that of Mark. "If Basil and Mark," says
Eleusius, "have done anything in their private capacity, if they and
the Acacians choose to go on accusing each other on one point or
another, that is no business of the synod; it has not to examine if
their exposition of the Faith is or is not satisfactory." Sozomen,
H. E. v. 22, p. 165.

II　　　　　　　　　　　　　　　　　　Q

restored. On the contrary, George, Eudoxius, Acacius, Patrophilus, and five others were declared to be deprived of their episcopal rank; in the case of nine others, the council confined itself to breaking off relations with them, until they should have satisfactorily answered the accusations laid against them. A bishop was even consecrated for Antioch, in place of Eudoxius; but the candidate selected by the council, Annianus, immediately he was consecrated, was carried off by the Dux Lauricius and sent into exile.

Finally, the assembly separated, after having nominated its ten delegates to the emperor. The Acacians, as one may imagine, were already on the way to Constantinople.

Acacius, their leader, was a person of no small importance. Already mixed up, for many years, in all the theological intrigues of the Court, he now assumed the principal part. He was an intelligent, eloquent, and persevering man. To his personal gifts was added a high ecclesiastical position. Metropolitan of Palestine, successor of the illustrious Eusebius, heir to the famous library of Origen, he passed as being himself also a person of great learning. His opinions at bottom differed very little from those of Arius and Aetius; but he knew how to clothe them with an impressive and sparkling style, and above all how to disguise them under learned formulas. When he arrived at Constantinople, the first delegates from Ariminum had already yielded, and steps were being taken to deal with the Western council. While this operation was in process, Acacius conceived the idea of bringing Aetius to court, and trying if it would not be possible to manage a success for him, which would have greatly forwarded the affairs of the party. Constantius was favourable to his proposals. An Areopagus of laymen, presided over by Honoratus, the prefect of Constantinople, and sometimes by the emperor himself, listened to the arguments of the famous sophist, who, on this occasion, made but a poor figure, and thus disappointed the expectations of his patrons. They then formed a plan of making a scapegoat of him, and of proving their own good intentions by the anathemas with which they loaded him.

Meanwhile there arrived the delegates from Ariminum. Those of Seleucia were counting upon their support in a common resistance ; they hastened to inform them of the plot which was hatching [1] : the person of Aetius was to be condemned, but not his doctrine ; the Latins, they argued, ought to abstain, as they themselves were going to do, from any ecclesiastical relations with the supporters of the intrigue. The good Easterns were only wasting their time. Guided by their new leaders, Ursacius and Valens, the delegates from Ariminum at once proceeded to join the party of Acacius.

Hilary himself had also come to Constantinople. He saw the despair of the delegates from Seleucia ; he saw his fellow-countrymen, those Western bishops, whose orthodoxy he had so highly extolled, betray it before his very eyes, and deliver themselves over to the court party. He lost his patience, and lashed them soundly : " What ! " he said, " On arriving at Constantinople after the Council of Seleucia, you go at once and join yourselves to the heretics, which it has condemned ! You do not delay a moment, you do not take time to deliberate or to gain information ! The delegates of the Eastern synod, who hold no communion with the bishops here, come in search of you ; they try to put you in possession of the facts, and show you that the heresy has just been condemned. Was it not the time then, at any rate, to hold yourselves aloof, to reserve your judgement ? . . . A slave, I do not say a good slave, but an average one, cannot bear to see his master insulted : he avenges him, if he can do so. A soldier defends his king, even at the peril of his life, even by making for him a shield of his own body. A watch-dog barks at the least scent, he flies out at the first suspicion. But you—you hear it said that Christ, the Very Son of God, is not God ; your silence is an adhesion to this blasphemy, and you hold your peace ! What am I saying ?

---

[1] Letter in Hil. *Frag. hist.* x. 1.

You protest against those who cry out, you join your voices with those which wish to stifle theirs."[1]

Hilary did not confine himself to this eloquent invective. He demanded an audience of the emperor,[2] he insisted upon it, twice, and thrice. He was not heeded. The delegates from Seleucia, who stood alone in the breach, were attacked individually. They made a long resistance; they were pressed more and more forcibly. The 1st of January was approaching. Constantius wished to inaugurate his tenth consulate by the proclamation of religious peace. He just managed to succeed. It was not until the night between December 31 and January 1, that the last signatures were obtained by force.

Nothing more remained to be done but to clothe with conciliar authority the decisions agreed upon with the delegates, and to settle certain personal questions. This was the task of the Council of Constantinople,[3] which was held during the first days of January 360, with the co-operation of various bishops of Thrace and Bithynia; about fifty members in all. Acacius presided over the debates. Among those who were present we may notice the aged Maris of Chalcedon, one of the Fathers of Nicæa and of the protectors of Arius, and Ulfilas, the national bishop of a colony of Goths established on the banks of the Danube, who happened to be present in the capital just then; he too was an Arian, and one of long standing.

The formula of Ariminum was approved: it declared that the Son is like to the Father, forbade the terms "essence" and "substance" (hypostasis), repudiated all earlier creeds, and condemned beforehand all those which might be suggested subsequently. It is the official formulary of what was henceforth known as Arianism, in particular of that Arianism which spread itself among the barbarian peoples. The two creeds of 325 and 360, those

---

[1] Hil. *Frag. hist.* x. 2-4.   [2] *Ad Const.* ii.

[3] Upon this council, see Sozomen, iv. 24, who has gleaned from official documents. Only one of these has been preserved, a letter to George of Alexandria upon the condemnation of Aetius (Theodoret, ii. 24).

of Nicæa and Ariminum, are in opposition and each excludes the other. We cannot, however, say that the Creed of Ariminum contains an explicit profession of Arianism. It does not reproduce any of the technical terms of the primitive heresy; and as to the new Arianism, —Anomœanism—it expressly excludes it: it is not the ἀνόμοιος, the unlike, which is proclaimed, it is the ὅμοιος, the like, its contrary. Nevertheless, the vagueness of the formula allowed it to be understood in the most different and even the most directly opposite senses: with a little complaisance, Athanasius and Aetius might have repeated it together. This is why it was so perfidious and so useless, and why no Christian worthy of the name, holding truly to the absolute Divinity of his Master, could hesitate for a moment to condemn it.

Aetius was deposed from the diaconate, and excommunicated conditionally, that is to say, if he persisted in his opinions, "as having, in his books and discussions, made a display of a philosophy full of quibbles and foreign to the ecclesiastical mind, of having made use of blasphemous expressions, and so troubled the Church."

This sentence, however, was not universally approved: about ten[1] bishops who were frankly Anomœan refused to throw Jonah into the sea[2]; they were given six months to make up their minds.

So much for the treatment of friends. Now came the turn of the others; it was a wholesale slaughter. Sentence of deposition was pronounced against Macedonius of Constantinople, Eleusius of Cyzicus, Heortasius of Sardis, Dracontius of Pergamum, Basil of Ancyra, Eustathius of Sebaste in Armenia, Sophronius of Pompeïopolis in Paphlagonia, Helpidius of Satala, Neon of Seleucia in

---

[1] Sozomen, iv. 25; *cf.* Philostorgius, vii. 6; viii. 4.

[2] These were, first, Theophilus the Indian, the wonder-worker of the party (Aetius too, in spite of his scholastic learning, sometimes posed as inspired), next Seras of Paraetonium in Libya, Stephen of Ptolemais, and Helidorus of Sozousa in Cyrenaica; a Phrygian, Theodulus of Keretapa; three Lydians, Leontius of Tripoli, Theodosius of Philadelphia, Phœbus of Polycalanda, and two others.

Isauria, Silvanus of Tarsus, and Cyril of Jerusalem. The
reason assigned for their condemnation had nothing to do
with doctrine; apart from the general reproach of having
in the past two years gravely troubled the peace of the
Church, each of them was made the object of special
complaints of a disciplinary character. Basil, in particular,
found thrown at his head all the strong measures and undue
exercise of authority, which he had allowed himself during
the few months he was in favour.[1]

The government took action in its turn. Aetius was
imprisoned at Mopsuestia, and his works were proscribed.
Basil was despatched to Illyria, the others to different
places of exile. They were provided with successors. For
Constantinople choice was made of Eudoxius, whom it
would have been difficult to re-establish at Antioch; and,
without delay (on February 15, 360) they proceeded with
the dedication of the great Church of the Divine Wisdom
(St Sophia), which had been building for the last twenty
years. The council took part in the ceremony. Eudoxius
was spokesman; "The Father," he said, "is impious
($\dot{a}\sigma\epsilon\beta\dot{\eta}s$), the Son is pious ($\epsilon\dot{v}\sigma\epsilon\beta\dot{\eta}s$)." To the murmurs
which followed this strange language, he replied by
explaining that the Son reverences the Father, while the
Father has no one to reverence. This miserable quip, the
memory of which was preserved in Constantinople, gives
us a fair idea of the situation. We see what kind of
priests were filling the higher positions in the Church
of the East.[2]

Hilary was still in Constantinople, overwhelmed and
exasperated. To give vent to his anger, he set himself to

[1] The details of all this are contained in Sozomen, *H. E.* iv. 24,
who here summarizes the official Acts.

[2] Eudoxius, moreover, clung to this idea. We meet with it again
in his profession of faith, published by Caspari, *Alte und neue Quellen
zur Geschichte des Taufsymbols* (Christiania, 1879), p. 179. We must
even restore there the word "impious," the omission of which in
Caspari's text makes the passage incoherent: [$\dot{a}\sigma\epsilon\beta\hat{\eta}$] $\ddot{o}\tau\iota$ $\mu\eta\delta\dot{\epsilon}\nu a$ $\sigma\dot{\epsilon}\beta\epsilon\iota\nu$
$\pi\dot{\epsilon}\phi\upsilon\kappa\epsilon\nu$. Cf. *Bulletin critique*, vol. i. p. 169. It was undoubtedly on
the occasion of his installation at Constantinople that Eudoxius pro-
duced this singular formula.

write his book " Against Constantius," a terrible invective, which he had the good sense to keep to himself. He was allowed to return to the West.

The formula of Ariminum-Constantinople was carried from one bishopric to another, in order that those who had not taken part in the councils might have an opportunity of setting their signatures to it. In the West, this was scarcely necessary, so numerous had the representation of the episcopate been at Ariminum. In Asia Minor, in Syria, and in Egypt, the case was different. It was then that St Athanasius, from the recesses of some desert, addressed to the bishops of Egypt and of Libya, an urgent exhortation to remain true to their duty, and to refuse their signatures. We do not know what was the result of this step. There is small probability that the official agents could have had much success within the jurisdiction of Athanasius. The clergy remained devoted to him; in Libya, a considerable part of the episcopate had passed over to Anomœanism; and they too were hardly more likely to sign.

At Cæsarea in Cappadocia, the aged Bishop Dianius, who had held the see for twenty years and scarcely ever took a prominent part, was accustomed to sign all the official formulas; he signed this one too.

At Antioch the see was vacant: it was necessary to elect a new bishop. The choice fell upon Meletius, an unattached bishop. Meletius belonged to Melitene, in Armenia Minor. A council held in that city in 358 had deposed from the episcopate the Bishop of Sebaste, Eustathius, a man who was prominent on account of his zeal in propagating the ascetic life and monastic institutions. In his youth he had studied them in Egypt. It was said that he had been intimate with Arius, and had imbibed his teaching. However this may be, it is certain that at the time when the sentence of the Council of Melitene struck him in his episcopal position, Eustathius, like Basil of Ancyra, professed doctrines closely approximating to Nicene orthodoxy. Meletius, then one of the clergy of Melitene, agreed to replace him. He was a

man in high repute for his piety, his gentle affability
and his uprightness of mind. But Eustathius himself
also was very popular; the people of Sebaste refused,
to accept the successor whom it was proposed to give
them. Meletius had to retire; he settled at Berea in
Syria (Aleppo). In the following year (359) Eustathius
took part in the Council of Seleucia, in the ranks of
the homoïousian majority; Meletius, either at the
council[1] or afterwards, signed the Acacian formula. He
was thus, at the time when (in the winter of 360-361)
the see of Antioch was entrusted to him, the man of the
Council of Ariminum - Constantinople, like Acacius of
Cæsarea and George of Alexandria who assisted at his
installation. On that occasion he pronounced a very
clever discourse in which, while adhering to the official
formulas, in that he spoke neither of essence nor hypostasis,
he allowed it to be seen that at bottom he was not far
from thinking like the Nicenes.[2] The latter did not
conceal their joy. The Arians understood; and at the
end of a month they had found means to rid themselves
of the new bishop. Without subjecting him to a suit
on points of doctrine, they attacked him upon certain
acts of his administration, especially with regard to the
restoration of clergy ejected by his predecessors. In
his place they put Euzoïus, the former companion of
Arius, who had been deprived of the diaconate forty years
before by Alexander of Alexandria.

The Emperor Constantius had returned to Antioch,
and was presiding over these changes. The victory
remained with him—with him and his ecclesiastical
counsellors. Nicæa and Ancyra—Athanasius and Basil—
were overwhelmed in the same disaster. "The world
groaned," says St Jerome, "and was astonished to find
itself Arian." It was not astonished for very long. The
yoke under which the episcopate bent itself was soon to be
broken. At the end of the previous winter, in April 360,

---

[1] Socrates (ii. 44) expressly mentions him.

[2] St Epiphanius, who has preserved to us this discourse (*Haer.*
lxxiii. 29-33), does not find much in it to correct.

the finest troops in Gaul had been summoned by Constantius to serve on the Persian frontier. They had been assembled in Paris. When the time came for them to set out, the soldiers refused to leave Gaul. One evening they left their camp,[1] advanced towards the palace where the Cæsar was living, and acclaimed him Augustus, in spite of his resistance and his protests. Constantius had ceased to reign in the West. The high officials who represented him in the entourage of the young Cæsar withdrew, and Julian wrote to his imperial cousin to excuse himself for what had happened. Constantius was at Cæsarea in Cappadocia when he received these letters. The war with the Persians occupied him during this year and for the greater part of the following one. However, Julian, Augustus in spite of himself, made up his mind to defend by force of arms his enforced usurpation. In 361 he set out on his march towards the East. Constantius, free at last to act, left Antioch to fight the rival whom the West was sending him. But sickness stayed him at the foot of the Taurus. Euzoïus, the official Bishop of Antioch, was on the spot to baptize him, for this great composer of theological formulas was still only a catechumen; he died on November 3, 361. Julian received the news in Thrace; on December 11 he entered Constantinople: the destinies of the whole empire were placed within his grasp.

[1] Situated on the western slope of the hill since called Montagne Sainte-Geneviève, under the present Rue Soufflot. As to Julian's palace, considerable ruins of it still remain.

CHAPTER IX

JULIAN AND THE PAGAN REACTION

Paganism under the princes of the house of Constantine. The
sacrifices forbidden. Decline of the ancient religions. Julian's
youth. His religious development. On becoming Emperor, he
declares himself a Pagan. Retaliation of the conquered religion.
Murder of George of Alexandria. Writings of Julian : his piety,
his attempt to reform Paganism. His attitude towards the
Christians. Recall of the exiled bishops. Withdrawal of
privileges : teaching prohibited. Conflicts and acts of violence.
Rebuilding of the temple at Jerusalem. Julian and the people
of Antioch. His death.

ALREADY, under Constantine, especially after he became
sole emperor, the State had sided against paganism.
However, no general ordinance had closed the temples :
the State no longer offered sacrifices in them ; but, except
perhaps at the end of his reign, private persons had
retained their liberty to celebrate them. This toleration
was not destined to be long in disappearing, for the sons
of Constantine showed themselves even more determined
than their father to have done with the old religion. In
the year 341, Constans had addressed the following
rescript to the *Vicarius* of Italy : " Let superstition cease !
Let the folly of the sacrifices be abolished ! Whoever,
contrary to the law of the divine prince, our father, and this
present command of our Clemency shall dare to celebrate
sacrifices, must be judged and punished." [1] Other decrees

---

[1] " Cesset superstitio, sacrificiorum aboleatur insania. Nam
quicumque contra legem divi principis parentis nostri et hanc nostrae
mansuetudinis iussionem ausus fuerit sacrificia celebrare, competens
in eum vindicta et praesens sententia exeratur." *Cod. Theod.* xvi. 10, 1.

repeat this prohibition, specifying that the temples must everywhere be closed, and the sacrifices forbidden, under pain of death and confiscation.[1] Magnentius, although himself a Christian, had allowed, as an exception, that sacrifices might be celebrated during the night; but Constantius revoked this permission.[2]

However, we may notice that the only act of worship proscribed by this legislation is sacrifice. But the pagan religions comprised also many other religious ceremonies, and these do not appear to have fallen under the ban of the law. An imperial rescript of 342[3] expressly specifies that suburban temples connected with the circus and other games are not to be touched; it was the superstition that was attacked, and not the amusements of the public. The processions, the sacred feasts, the mysteries, and many other religious celebrations, went on as before. In Rome, the *Taurobolia* were celebrated down to the time of Theodosius. The initiations connected with Eleusis were practised in the reign of Constantius, and even after Julian's death. At Antioch, the famous sanctuary of Daphne was still thronged, and that with purposes the very reverse of austere. Instead of forbidding it absolutely, as public morality seemed to demand, the Cæsar Gallus confined himself to setting up a rival to it. He translated to the sacred grove the remains of St Babylas, the martyr bishop; henceforth, respectable people might venture to take the road to Daphne.

Moreover, the question for consideration here is much less the legislation than the actual practice. Of the legislation we can say at least that the terrible threats of the Emperor Constantius did not produce, so far as we know, a single victim. We never hear of pagan martyrs. Undoubtedly, there were in many places conflicts between the supporters of the two cults; certain histories of Christian martyrs are accounts of disturbances on a

---

[1] *Cod. Theod.* xvi. 10, 4 and 6; the exact date of law 4 is a subject of dispute; law 6 belongs to 356; it was promulgated in the name of Constantius and Julian.

[2] *Cod. Theod.* xvi. 10, 5, of 353.   [3] *Cod. Theod.* xvi. 10, 3.

religious pretext. Too zealous preachers, going to preach
the Gospel to rural populations little prepared to receive
it, are subjected to rough handling, and sometimes
murdered. Battles took place around temples which
bodies of fanatical Christians took upon themselves to
destroy; the buffets, of course, were distributed among
assailants and defenders. At Tipasa, in Mauritania, a
little girl, called Salsa, crept into a temple, seized a bronze
god and threw him from the top of a cliff; the pagans
caught her and sent her to rejoin the idol at the bottom
of the sea. Such occurrences have evidently nothing to
do with the laws; they are mere accidents.

As to the laws themselves, their application naturally
varied very much. When any district passed over entirely
to Christianity, it was quite natural that it should dispose
as it pleased of the buildings of the ancient cult. The
temples were then closed without any difficulty, the priesthoods were abolished, the gods appropriated to the adorn-
ment of public places, or stored in some corner. The
property of the temples reverted to the municipalities, if
it was not seized upon by the State, as often happened.
In other parts, on the contrary, in towns or country
places which refused to hear of Christianity, temples
and priesthoods were preserved; they kept up the festivals,
the games, the processions, and other external manifestations; as to the sacrifices, if they ever ventured to hold them,
they took good care to arrange matters so that the police
should know nothing about it. The police, in fact, often
shut their eyes when they did not connive. Towards the
end of Constantius' reign, Tertullus, prefect of Rome,
disturbed at the delay of a convoy of corn, offered in a
temple at Ostia a sacrifice to Castor and Pollux.[1] Most
often, and especially in large cities, opinions were divided
between the two forms of worship. There were certainly
many people who were interested in both at once. The
Christian assemblies, the vigil, the liturgy were rather
exacting, and did not offer much food for excitement.
The populace found more to enjoy in the meetings which

[1] Ammianus Marcellinus, xix. 10.

were held outside the town, near the tombs of the martyrs.
These included the *agapes,* from which, in spite of all the
efforts of the clergy, a certain cheerfulness, often proceeding to excess, was not excluded.   But all this could
not be compared with the pomp of pagan ceremonies.
The latter continued to exist, as a rule, so long as no
means of replacing them could be found, so long as those
of the religious ceremonies which appealed most to the
heart of the people had not been adapted by them to the
religion of Christ.

Generally speaking, and taking the empire as a whole,
paganism was in a deep decline.   It was giving way under
imperial dislike, and the prohibition of its form of worship.
Of the many educated writers who still professed it, not
one undertook its defence.   On the contrary, there was
found one of them who, having recently abandoned it,
drew up a terrible indictment of it.   Firmicus Maternus
was an advocate of Syracuse, who sought distraction from
the cares of his profession in the study of astrology.
Towards the end of Constantine's reign, he went to
Campania, where he published a treatise upon that science.
Some ten years later, having in the meantime renounced
paganism and the study of the stars, he addressed to
the Emperors Constantius and Constans, a book upon
" The Falsehood of the Profane Religions," in which, with
doubtful learning and the use of strange etymologies, he
draws up an accusation against the pagan cults.[1]   He
demands their abolition, an abolition final and without
mercy : " For we must make an end of them, Most Sacred
Emperors, you must cut short all this by severe legislation.   It is for this cause that God has given you the
empire, and has led you on from one success to another.
Remove, remove without fear, the ornaments of the
temples ; send the gods to the mint, and appropriate for
yourselves their possessions. . . ."   Such are the exhorta-

---

[1] Thus he professes to find in Serapis a reproduction of the
patriarch Joseph.   The sheaf of corn which the god bore on his head
seems to him to be a memorial of the ministrations of Joseph during
the years of plenty and of famine.

tions which reappear on every page under this fanatical
pen. We are far from the time when Justin was content
with imploring the emperors not to shed the blood
of the Christians.

At this period, it seemed scarcely possible that such
a state of things could ever return : the victory of
Christianity was a brilliant one, and the total disappearance of the old religions might be considered as near at
hand. Suddenly, however, the wind changed; the
forsaken gods again ascended the altars, and the
Christians felt themselves threatened anew by the power
of the State which had once more become hostile.

Julian [1] was born at Constantinople in 331 ; he was
the son of Julius Constantius, Constantine's brother, and
of Basilina, a Roman lady of high family, who died shortly
after his birth. He was six years old when his father and
one of his brothers perished in the massacres which
followed the death of Constantine. He himself escaped,
with his other brother Gallus. He was reminded later on,
that, in this hour of danger, he had had reason to be
grateful for the devotion of certain ecclesiastics. When
calm was restored, and Constantius had decided to take
the two children under his protection, Julian was entrusted
to Eusebius, Bishop of Nicomedia, a distant relative, who
had already exercised influence over his mother. He
remained with him, at Nicomedia and at Constantinople,
for five years. On the death of Eusebius, Julian and
Gallus, hitherto separated, were reunited and placed in a
villa called Makellon, at the foot of Mount Argeus, not
far from Cæsarea in Cappadocia. They remained there
nearly eight years, until the time (351) when Gallus was
appointed Cæsar, and went away to reign at Antioch.
As for Julian, he was allowed to finish his education by
attending the lectures of distinguished masters. For
this purpose he stayed in Constantinople, in Bithynia,
and in Asia. Being implicated in the affair of Gallus,
in 354, he was summoned to Italy, to the presence of the
emperor. The Empress Eusebia interceded in his favour;

[1] P. Allard, *Julien l'Apostat* (1900-1903).

and he was allowed to resume his studies. It was then that he visited Athens, and made the acquaintance of Gregory and Basil, two young Cappadocians, destined to win distinction as bishops. He did not remain there long, and was recalled in 355 to the court at Milan, to be associated in his turn in the government of the empire, and was charged to watch over the defence of the Western provinces. We know that he acquitted himself conscientiously and successfully of this task, that he shrank from none of the duties, great or small, which it imposed upon him, and that the impression which he left in Gaul was a favourable one.

Yet, under this defender of the Roman fatherland, was concealed a Greek sophist; this representative, this colleague of the pious Emperor Constantius was at heart a convinced and devout pagan. His inward development, known or suspected by a few persons only, was a thing of long standing. The circumstances of his education explain it in some degree.

His parents were Christians, like all the imperial family. When quite a little child, he had danced on the knees of Constantine, "the external Bishop" of the Christian Church. He was baptized while still young, and, until he left the villa of Makellon, we see him always surrounded by ecclesiastical personages. It is true that these were distinguished members of the Arian group, and that, in this school of religious sophistry, the Gospel was largely concealed by metaphysics. Occupied incessantly with questions as to the Divine relationships and processions, they lost sight of the message of Christ, of His history, and of His work of salvation. In the conflict of the creeds, in the intrigues of the court bishops, and their eagerness to overthrow each other, the Church lamentably frittered away its prestige. Men like Eusebius, George, and Aetius did but feebly commend Christianity. Yet the convictions of the faithful were, as a rule, stronger than this state of things; it did not check the progress of conversions, even among the well-educated classes. And besides, Julian's criticism of the Christian religion did not attack this or that particular shade of opinion. It was with the whole of it that he found fault; it was from Christianity as such that he broke himself free. And he broke himself free, because he had developed a different religious conscience.

He knew Latin, and spoke it "sufficiently," says Ammianus.[1] We should scarcely suspect it in reading his books and his letters; learned as he was in literature, he never quotes a Latin author, not even Vergil. Rome scarcely seems to exist for him; it is Athens which is the centre of things.

In heaven he saw only the gods of Greece; and in this world only the memories or the present interests of Hellenism, and of religious Hellenism. Julian was a devotee of the old cult, an enthusiastic adept in the mysteries and the pagan theology. Of the ancient poets, he knew scarcely any save the sacred poets, Homer and Hesiod. More eclectic in philosophy, he at first read Plato, Aristotle, and other authors; but as soon as he gained some measure of freedom from his teachers, his natural bent diverted him from the logicians and led him to the mystics, to the neo-Platonists; and even in this, not to those among them who, like Ædesius of Pergamum and Eusebius of Myndos, followed the philosophy of Plotinus, but rather to the disciples of Iamblichus, to those who practised magic and occultism. It was in this way that he fell into the hands of Maximus of Ephesus, who introduced him into the secret mysteries of his own philosophy, and put him in touch with the gods. Julian was twenty years old; his life, having always been carefully watched over by trustworthy persons, had remained serious and even austere. He had no passion save for the mystery of things, especially of things unseen. And in these pursuits the remainder of his Christianity vanished away. He had been instructed in its doctrine; he had been made to read the Bible, and to listen to catechetical lectures. But now, Moses, Jeremiah, Luke, and Matthew seemed to him but fustian

[1] xvi. 5, 7.

authors in comparison with Homer, Plato, and Iamblichus.
His relations with the philosophers having caused some
talk, his brother Gallus, disturbed with good reason as
to their consequences, thought it expedient to send to him
the most celebrated of the Christian sophists, Aetius, who
was then astonishing Antioch by the success of his
disputations. It was a mere waste of time. Against the
mysticism which enthralled the soul of Julian of what
avail was the arid and empty scholasticism of the masters
in Arianism?

The disciple of Maximus of Ephesus endured the
disputations of Aetius as he endured many other things:
Constantius, as he knew well, was not a man to be trifled
with in that quarter. Julian detested his cousin, whom
those about him had not failed to represent to him as the
assassin of his family. But this hatred did not prevent
him from dedicating to Constantius a fulsome panegyric;
he composed another in honour of the Empress Eusebia.
In these compositions, it was still the fashion[1] to make
use of pagan legends. This was a consolation to Julian:
he extolled his cousin—a thing most distasteful to him;
but he was also able to extol his gods, and this delighted
him.

With the exception of these formal exercises, he was
obliged, notwithstanding his ardour as a neophyte, to
continue to profess himself a Christian—a Galilean, as he
began to say—to take part in the religious assemblies
presided over by the official clergy, and to conceal his
devotion to the proscribed gods under an apparent zeal
for the religion which persecuted them. It was a difficult
and cruel position; for there is no doubt whatever that
Julian's new convictions were profoundly sincere. God
knows what would have been the issue of this inward
struggle, if it had been protracted as long as the respective
ages of Julian and Constantius seemed to foreshadow.
The circumstances, which soon brought the two cousins

---

[1] This lasted for a very long time. In the 5th century, the
panegyrics of Sidonius Apollinaris still make the *corps* of ancient
Olympus perform their customary manœuvres.

into conflict, allowed Julian to show himself in his true colours. He was not in any hurry. On January 6, 361, he was still to be seen at Vienne, where he was spending the winter, taking part in the Christian mysteries. It was for the last time : the following summer, in his march through Pannonia, he threw off all disguise, and celebrated with full ceremonial, before the whole army, the sacrifices which hitherto he had concealed in the secrecy of his private life. His enthusiasm for the ancient gods quickly burst forth in his speeches and in his official correspondence, as did also his rage against Constantius.[1]

The two cousins were marching against each other. The situation was becoming tragic. They were approaching to a second battle of the Milvian Bridge, to an encounter between a pagan and a Christian army. However, things took another turn. The death of Constantius allowed Julian to enter Constantinople in peace (December 11, 361). Instead of joining battle with his rival, Julian presided over his obsequies.

He took his revenge upon the ministers. A special court was set up, and balanced with much severity the accounts of the new Augustus. Among his victims figured the prefect Taurus, the hero of the Council of Ariminum, and the high chamberlain, Eusebius, whose baleful figure crosses now and again the story of St Athanasius and of Pope Liberius. Eusebius was put to death; he had played a part in the affair of Gallus which Julian did not forgive. Taurus was only exiled.[2]

But the chief care of the new sovereign, the ruling conception of the reign which was beginning, was to give paganism its revenge. Julian at once outlined his policy, and displayed in his person the Constantine of the old religion. An edict ordered the re-opening of the temples, and the renewal everywhere of the sacrifices.[3] This ordinance could not fail to be received with a wide divergence of opinion. There were some places in which it gave pleasure to the populace, which had remained

---

[1] See especially his letter to the Athenians.
[2] Ammianus, xxii. 3.   [3] *Ibid.* xxii. 5.

faithful to the gods of old. Elsewhere, it appeared ill-timed, the majority of the people having passed over to Christianity. Many municipalities had begun to demolish the temples; their endowments in land and their furniture had been either confiscated by the State, or alienated by the local authorities. Julian soon ordered everything to be put in the same position as before. A similar order had been given in 312 by Constantine and Licinius, in favour of the Christian churches. We do not gather that at that time it raised any serious difficulties; besides, when it was a question of private persons being dis-possessed, the emperors, in 312, indemnified them. Julian considered himself dispensed from doing so much. According to his ideas, the fact of having concurred in the destruction and spoliation of the temples constituted a crime for which it was natural to take vengeance. He did not go so far doubtless as to enjoin personal punish-ment for this; but he showed great harshness in his claims to restitution, condemning bishops, who had more or less favoured the destruction of the temples, to rebuild them, if necessary; and above all showing the greatest indulg-ence towards popular riots in favour of his pagan reaction.

The first victim was the intruded Bishop of Alexandria, George the Cappadocian. Driven from Alexandria in 358, this not ve.y attractive individual had trailed from council to council, mixing in every intrigue against orthodoxy and its defenders. Finally, just at the moment when Con-stantius was leaving Antioch to pursue hostilities against Julian, he regained possession, after three years' absence, of the metropolis of Egypt, where the police had prepared the way for him. Quite apart from the horror which he inspired in the adherents of Athanasius, George was universally detested. Many Alexandrians had cause to complain of his denunciations to the government and his acts of greed. The temples, which were still standing, exasperated him; he never ceased to utter threats regarding them. It was on November 26, 361, that the Alexandrians once more beheld the bishop whom they

loathed. Four days later, the prefect published the news
of the death of the emperor, and the accession of Julian
Instantly, the population rose in rebellion. George was
not killed that day, but only imprisoned. On December
25, another outbreak tore him from his prison. He was
murdered, with an official named Dracontius, against
whom the pagans had had cause of complaint. The dead
body of the bishop was hoisted upon a camel; several
fanatics harnessed themselves to the body of Dracontius.
Both corpses were thus dragged round the town; then
they were burnt, and the ashes were scattered to the
winds. Such was at Alexandria the ceremonial of
executions, when the populace took them into their
own hands.

Julian, on being informed of the affair, confined
himself to scolding the people of Alexandria. They
ought to have reserved George for the justice of the
courts. Apart from this question of procedure, he could
not but approve of their action: George was an enemy of
the gods. Afterwards he remembered that the deceased
prelate possessed a very fine library, of which he had
formerly profited to cheat the tedium of Makellon: the
officials were ordered to recover it, and send it to the
court.[1]

The emperor in Julian had not destroyed the man of
letters. He always loved books; he found time to read,
and even to write. His nights, which were not shortened
by worldly festivities, were for the most part consecrated
to study. It is from this time, the time when he was
burdened with the empire, that there dates almost all his
literary work, his theological treatises upon the King Sun,
and upon the Mother of the Gods, his writings against the
Cynics and the Christians, his satires, the Cæsars, the
Misopogon, and lastly, letters of importance, such as that
to the Athenians, that to Themistius, and a long religious
manifesto, of which only fragments remain. From the
outset he had summoned to his court rhetoricians and
philosophers, Libanius, Themistius, Maximus of Ephesus,

[1] *Juliani epp.* 9, 10, 36.

and honoured them as demi-gods.   To converse with them
was his greatest pleasure.   It was of no moment that he
had reached his thirtieth year; he was always a disciple.

He was also a religious zealot.   There had been other
emperors who were attached to the old national religion,
and some of them had even busied themselves with ardour
in trying to bring back to it the Christians who had strayed.
But such piety, such eagerness for holy things, for the
sacrifices, the processions, and the temples, no one had
ever displayed.   The only one of his predecessors who
could be at all compared with Julian in this respect was
Maximin, the Maximin after the time of Galerius, who could
no longer persecute openly, but who found means of doing
so indirectly, by exciting the religious zeal of the municipalities.   Julian made it known throughout the empire
that his favour would be proportioned to the enthusiasm
shown for the service of the gods.   If people would rebuild the temples, provide the ministrations in them and
frequent them, they could obtain anything they wished;
if not, they should have nothing, not even a garrison to
protect them when the enemy was approaching.

Like Maximin again he was to be seen organizing the
priestly colleges, grouping the priests of the different
sanctuaries around a high priest for each district, and
above these establishing provincial high priests; in other
words, creating pagan bishops and archbishops.   But—and
here there is a striking difference which it is only fair to
notice—whilst Maximin chose for these positions people
who were rich and ennobled, Julian desired a body of
men who were virtuous.   He required from them good
examples; the high priests were to watch over the conduct
of their subordinates, to reprimand, and to punish them, if
necessary.   His bishops were to be pious and of good
character, like those of the Christians.   He even went so
far as to urge them to organize charitable foundations
and systems of relief, such as existed everywhere in the
Christian communities.

These were the dreams of a student!   Paganism,
especially in the East, did not lend itself to such reforms.

The idea which Julian formed for himself of the priesthood and its duties was a Christian idea. Never did a pagan priest dream that he was under an obligation to live a more ascetic life than other men, or that the care of the needy had a special connection with his functions. Julian was pouring the new wine into the old bottles, and seeking to introduce the Christian spirit into the disinterred corpse of paganism. His success was indifferent. Those about him soon grew weary of his devotion, his pious exercises, his continual sacrifices. His clergy, among whom he had included several apostates from Christianity, were far from giving him satisfaction. When he had established himself at Antioch, he wished to conform to the religious observances of the country. But the cult of the Syrian gods was not made for people of austere morals. Julian appeared at the consecrated ceremonies with a retinue which would have deeply distressed his old teachers. He only made himself ridiculous, and compromised at one and the same time his philosophy and his dignity as emperor.

Of course this restoration of paganism excluded all Christians from the imperial favour, even before it rendered them outlaws. But they were numerous in the East, and Julian was obliged to proceed gradually in his manifestations of ill-will. The day after he entered Constantinople, the heads of the different Christian confessions—Arians, Anomœans, Macedonians, orthodox, and Novatians—were summoned to the palace, to listen to a declaration that there was no longer any official Christianity, and that no form of it was proscribed by the State. No more fair-sounding statement could have been found ; but the intention which dictated this toleration was to set the different sects by the ears, and in this way to weaken the resistance to paganism.[1] It was for the same end that the sentences of exile or imprisonment, pronounced as the sequel to the decisions of councils, were revoked. The orthodox

---

[1] It is Ammianus (xxii. 5) who discloses to us this intention. Julian knew, he says, that there are no savage beasts more ferocious than the Christians are one to another. Such was the impression given to enlightened pagans by the theological quarrels of that time.

bishops, those who adhered to the Nicene Confession of Faith, profited by this permission, and returned to their dioceses. So too did Basil of Ancyra and his friends, who had been so harshly treated by the Council of 360 ; and so did several stubborn Anomœans. We can readily imagine the disturbances likely to be caused by the return of these bishops, who found their sees occupied by successors. Such was not, it is true, the case of Alexandria, where Athanasius reappeared on February 21, and found his place vacant. But, in Africa, the return of the Donatist leaders was a veritable plague, which a statesman worthy of the name would never have thought of letting loose.

Unfortunately, in Julian, the statesman was stifled by the sectarian. The recall of the exiled bishops, whatever may have been the secret motive for it, was justifiable in theory ; and in practice, if some of its consequences were bad, others were good. But it was followed by other measures, justified by no theory of toleration. The Christian clergy, exempted from obligations of municipal service by Constantine, were now once more put upon the list; all their privileges were abolished. The bishops were deprived of the civil jurisdiction which Constantine had granted them.[1] Shortly afterwards, Christians were excluded from all positions in the imperial household, from all high administrative posts, and even from the army, so far as that was possible. Finally, the teaching of grammar and of rhetoric was forbidden to Christian masters.[2]

All these measures, the last especially, were cruelly felt. The prohibition to Christians of the teaching of literature and philosophy,[3] affected masters of distinction.

[1] We shall speak of this later on.

[2] Ammianus (xxii. 10) blames this measure very much : *Illud autem erat inclemens, obruendum perenni silentio, quod arcebat docere magistros rhetoricos et grammaticos ritus christiani cultores.*

[3] Philosophy is not mentioned in Ammianus' text given in the last note, but Julian expressly mentions it in his edict (*Ep.* 42) εἴτε ῥήτορες εἴτε γραμματικοὶ καὶ ἔτι πλέον οἱ σοφισταί. In this edict he leaves to young Christians permission to obtain instruction in the official schools. There are certain indications that he withdrew it afterwards. In any case such schools having necessarily, in his

Victorinus at Rome, Prohæresius in Athens descended from their professorial chairs, the latter in spite of the entreaties of Julian who would have made an exception in his favour.

All the cultured members of the Christian ranks felt themselves placed in a position of ostracism. In the emperor's name they were excluded from the Hellenic tradition and from intellectual culture. Two Christians of Laodicea in Syria, the two Apollinarii, father and son, endeavoured to replace the authors snatched from their hands, by compositions in verse and prose upon subjects derived from the Bible and the Gospel. Their zeal, seconded by an extraordinary facility of composition, was fortunately useless. They had not finished putting Genesis into the form of an epic, and the Gospel into Socratic dialogues, when the wind changed. They returned to Homer and Plato.

All this manifestation of ill-will on the part of Julian stopped short, however, of actual persecution. A Christian who had finished his education, who was neither an official nor a soldier, and who was able to live without asking anything from the government, was not threatened with death by the authorities of the State for the mere fact of professing the Christian religion. The churches still remained open, and worship was carried on there as in the past. But the attempt to revive paganism in a country where almost everyone was a Christian could not fail to produce numerous protests, and these were severely requited. This fact was responsible for executions, such as that of the priest Basil, at Ancyra,[1] the soldier Æmilianus, who was burnt alive at Dorostorum, on the Lower Danube, for an insult to pagan worship,[2] and of three Christians of Meros in Phrygia—Macedonius, Theodulus, and Tatian[3]—who were guilty of having broken

---

view, a religious character in a pagan sense, it would have been very difficult for Christians to attend them.

[1] Sozomen, *H. E.* v. 11.   [2] Jerome, *Chron.* a. Abr. 2379.

[3] It was to these that there was at first attributed the celebrated *mot* afterwards put into the mouth of the Roman deacon Laurence.

some newly restored idols. The people of Cæsarea in
Cappadocia had in the reign of Constantius destroyed
nearly all their temples: there still remained one of these,
the Temple of Fortune: they decided upon its destruction. The time was ill-chosen. The wrath of Julian
fell upon the audacious city, which lost its municipal
rights; upon the Church of Cæsarea, which he subjected
to an enormous fine; and upon the clergy, whom he
caused to be enrolled in the police bands, a laborious and
degrading service. Several citizens, who had been more
especially responsible for the destruction of the temple,
were exiled or put to death; among the latter have been
preserved the names of Eupsychius and Damas.[1]

Moreover, in those countries where pagans were in
the majority and now felt themselves the masters, they
had no obligation to restrain themselves in taking their
revenge upon the Christians for the slights of which their
own form of worship had been the object during the
preceding reigns. In Syria, where the proportion of
Christians varied very much in different places, we hear
of deplorable scenes. At Emesa, and at Epiphania,
Bacchanal processions streamed into the church bearing
a statue of Dionysos, which they installed upon the
altar.[2] The Christian cemetery at Emesa was given to
the flames.[3] The old Bishop of Arethusa, Mark, the
same who had saved Julian at the time of the massacres
of 337, found himself denounced to the emperor for
having ill-treated pagans and destroyed a temple. When
condemned to rebuild it he refused. He was then given
over to the mob, who dragged him through the streets,
tearing out his beard, and tormenting him in a thousand
ways; then he was given over to the school children,
who amused themselves by tossing him in the air to

Stretched upon a burning gridiron, they called out to the judge:
"We are cooked enough on this side; now turn us, and you will eat
us better done." (Socrates, iii. 15; *cf.* Sozomen, v. 11.)

[1] Sozomen, v. 4, 11. St Basil often speaks of them.
[2] *Chron. Pasch.*, pp. 295, 296.
[3] Julian, *Misopogon*, p. 461 (ed. Hertlein).

catch him on their sharp-pointed styluses; finally, he was smeared with honey, bruised as he was, and exposed to the wasps. Yet they did not finish him; he survived this abominable treatment. At Alexandria, Ascalon, Gaza, and Heliopolis, the pagan population was continually breaking out into disturbances. Priests and virgins were massacred with horrible refinements of cruelty; their bodies were cut open, and upon their quivering entrails barley was thrown that they might be devoured by swine. Julian did not interfere. He even encouraged the populace guilty of these atrocities. Constantine had made Maïouma, the port of Gaza, an independent city. Maïouma was Christian: Julian deprived it of its autonomy, and subjected it once more to the pagans of Gaza. The governor of Palestine, having tried to punish the instigators of a riot in which four Christians of that city had perished, the emperor deprived him of his position and sent him into exile.

Everything that could worry the Christians was good in his eyes. It was nearly three centuries since the temple of Jerusalem had been destroyed, and the Jews deprived of access to their former holy city; the new town of Aelia was peopled with Christians. The idea came to Julian of rebuilding the Temple of Israel, and reviving a cult for which personally he felt nothing but contempt. His intention was evident: he wished to do an injury to the great Christian pilgrimages, and to set up a rival to the beautiful churches of Constantine. The undertaking, though entrusted to an official of high rank and supported with large sums of money, had for all that no result. As soon as the foundations of the old building were disturbed, flames burst from them which burnt several of the workmen and, what is more, terrified the agents of Julian, who were apparently as superstitious as their master.[1]

At Antioch, where nearly everyone was a Christian, the emperor did not get much satisfaction. He tried to restore the vanished cults, especially that of Daphne. The

[1] Ammianus, xxiii. 1.

martyr Babylas, installed in the Sacred Wood by the
Cæsar Gallus, was an obnoxious neighbour for Apollo.
Julian ordered his remains to be carried back to the
cemetery. The Christians obeyed, but the translation
took place in the midst of a great gathering of the faithful,
and had the appearance of a formal protest. Antioch,
as its inhabitants boasted, remained loyal to the X and
the K, that is to say to Christ (Χριστός) and to Constantius
(Κωνστάντιος). The news soon followed that a fire had
broken out in the sanctuary of Daphne, and that the idol
was burned. Julian was furious, and gave orders for the
closing of the Great Church, the church which Constantine
had built, and which the council of 341 had dedicated.
It was even stripped of its sacred furniture. The officials,
who on this occasion invaded the sacred edifice, headed
by Julian, Count of the Orient, uncle of the emperor, and,
like him, a renegade, behaved themselves like blackguards,
and did not hesitate at indescribable profanations. The
aged Bishop Euzoïus tried to protest: they boxed
his ears.

These acts of violence did but increase the unpopularity
of the apostate emperor. He was conscious of it, but his
stubborn disposition resisted all opposition, even the
appeals of his most intimate friends, such as the prefect
Sallust, and the rhetorician Libanius. His hatred for the
Galileans overflowed into all his acts, his letters, and
his conversations. He ended by writing against them a
work in three books, afterwards refuted by Cyril of
Alexandria, who has thus preserved to us a part of it.
He also wrote, against the people of Antioch, his celebrated
Misopogon, in which he answers the criticisms of which
his personal appearance, and especially his long beard, had
been the constant butt. The people of Antioch loved him
little, and he returned their dislike. He concluded by
promising them that, on his return from the Persian War,
for which he was making preparations at the time, he
would deprive them of his presence, and would establish
himself at Tarsus.

This was as a matter of fact what happened; but not as

the emperor intended. Julian, after having invaded the Persian empire and led his army as far as the walls of Ctesiphon, found himself compelled to retrace his steps. In the course of a disastrous retreat, he was mortally wounded by an arrow, on June 26, 363; his body was carried to Tarsus. The leaders of the army immediately chose as his successor the commander of the guard, Jovian. The famous expedition ended in a shameful peace, by which the empire lost, not only part of the satrapies beyond the Tigris, annexed under Diocletian, but the fortress of Nisibis and the surrounding country, a district which had long been included in the province of Mesopotamia.

The new emperor was a Christian. Everyone realized that the festival of paganism was at an end. The supporters of the Hellenic restoration suffered many anxious moments. But they escaped with a good fright. Jovian persecuted no one; as to the Christians, they naturally saw the hand of Providence in the death of the apostate, and lavished on his memory the most heart-felt maledictions. But they went no further, and their leaders were the first to preach to them forgetfulness of injuries.

CHAPTER X

AFTER ARIMINUM

The Councils of Paris and of Alexandria. Restoration of the lapsed. Lucifer, Eusebius, and Apollinaris. Schism at Antioch : Meletius, and Paulinus. Athanasius exiled in Julian's reign. His relations with Jovian. The "Acacians" accept the Creed of Nicæa. Valentinian and Valens. The religious policy of Valentinian. Opposition of the Right wing : Lucifer and his friends. Opposition of the Left : Auxentius of Milan and the Danubian bishops. Valens and the formula of Ariminum. Negotiations between the Homoïousians and Pope Liberius. The question of the Holy Spirit : the party of Macedonius. The Anomœans : Aetius and Eunomius. Conflicts between them and official Arianism. The historian Philostorgius.

BETTER for the Church is a government which ignores or even persecutes it than a government which interferes too much in its affairs. Under Constantius the care of the Faith had entered more than it ought to have done into the province of the State. When the police were no longer at the service of the various formulas, and at the heels of the bishops, the bishops breathed more freely. The bent heads were raised, and the attitudes once more became natural.

It was at Paris that the first evidence of this was seen. The episcopate of the Gauls had in the last few years gone through many trials. The Emperor Constantius had urged the bishops, ever since the year 353, to subscribe to the condemnation of Athanasius, and to accept communion with the bishops of his court. As a rule, they had yielded, but with very bad grace. If some of them only had refused their signatures and accepted exile, as did the Bishops of Trèves, Poitiers, and Toulouse, the greater part had seen with disapproval the acts of violence used towards their colleagues. The Bishop of Arles, Saturninus, the instrument of the emperor's displeasure, was kept by them in quarantine. When they received from Sirmium the formula attributed to Hosius (357), with a request that they should approve it, they jibbed. The Bishop of Agen, Phoebadius, wrote to attack it. Signatures were refused, and they renewed the excommunication against Saturninus. Hilary, who was exiled in the heart of Phrygia, when informed of this state of things, warmly congratulated his colleagues on their attitude, and endeavoured to arrange an understanding between them and the semi-orthodox party, of which Basil of Ancyra was at this moment leading the triumph. This is the subject of his book on *The Synods*.[1]

Then followed the Council of Ariminum, where, thanks to the pressure put upon them by the prefect Taurus, and to the intrigues of the court prelates, the bishops of the Gauls allowed themselves to be led like the rest to a deplorable capitulation. Even the firmest among them, Servasius of Tongres and Phoebadius himself, compromised themselves, and co-operated either directly or indirectly in what was to be for a long time the formula of the Arian dissenters. When they returned home, very sad at heart, as we may well believe, they soon heard the news that Julian had been proclaimed Augustus, and that the high officials of Constantius, notably the prætorian prefect Florentius, with whom they had much more to do than with the Cæsar, had set out to rejoin their master. While these things were happening, Hilary arrived[2] with news from Constantinople, and letters addressed to the Western prelates by those of their Greek colleagues, upon whom

---

[1] *Supra*, p. 234.

[2] Hilary had not been pardoned ; this return to Gaul was, in the intention of the government, only a change of exile. They held that, being dangerous in the East, he would be less so in his own country. This, at least, is what Sulpicius Severus says, *Chron.* ii. 45 : *postremo quasi discordiae seminarium et perturbator Orientis redire ad Gallias iubetur, absque exilii indulgentia.*

Eudoxius, Acacius, and other victors of the day, had just been showering sentences of deposition. A meeting was held at Paris, probably in the summer of 360, and from thence an answer was despatched to the Easterns in a letter[1] full of sympathy, which censured Auxentius, Ursacius, Valens, and the other supporters of the intrigues at Ariminum, as well as the successors of the deposed bishops and, lastly, Saturninus, who was already condemned and always active on the side of wrong. They recognized, in accordance with the explanations of the Easterns, that they had been wrong in allowing themselves to be deceived[2] into the tacit suppression of the term "essence" ($o\dot{v}\sigma\acute{\iota}a$); henceforth, they promised to be more strict.

This letter represents apparently all that it was possible to do at a time when Constantius was still master in the East, and there was nothing to show that he would not also regain the mastery in the West. The orthodoxy of Nicæa possessed scarcely any representatives at that time. Paulinus and Rhodanius had died in exile; Athanasius had disappeared. In Rome, besides the fact that the political situation was not so free from complexity as in Gaul, Pope Liberius, who owing to unknown circumstances had remained aloof from the affair of Ariminum, was not entirely rehabilitated. Hilary could scarcely think of relying upon him. All that it was possible for him to do was to lead back the bishops of the Gauls into the right path, and make use of them to support the remnant in the East whose views were orthodox. The attitude adopted at the Council of Paris was a repudiation of the Council of Ariminum, a return to the position as it was before that assembly—the Nicene party in the West in alliance with the quasi-orthodox party in the East to fight against Arianism. It was little enough.

The position grew more clearly defined in 362, when

---

[1] Hil. *Frag. hist.* xi.

[2] "Cum ex litteris vestris in usiae silentio fraudem se passam simplicitas nostra cognoscat."

Julian, who had become sole emperor, had thrown over the official clergy, and recalled the exiles. Athanasius returned to Alexandria, Meletius to Antioch. It was on February 21, 362, that the Alexandrians beheld once more their indomitable bishop, after six years of absence and of outlawry. Other exiles, recalled by the same decrees, found themselves for the moment grouped around him. The greater part of them were Egyptians, but there was also one bishop from Palestine, Asterius of Petra, who had no doubt been imprisoned in Egypt, as Lucifer of Caliaris (Cagliari) and Eusebius of Vercellæ had been in the Thebaïd.

Lucifer, a man of ardent soul and indomitable character, had passed his time of exile in writing pamphlets of extreme violence. They were all aimed at Constantius, and the bishop took care that they should reach him. The Christian Ahab let the new Elias have his say. He had at first entrusted Lucifer to Eudoxius, Bishop of Germanicia; when Eudoxius was transferred to Antioch, Lucifer was sent to Eleutheropolis in Palestine, where the bishop, Eutychius, treated him harshly. Afterwards, as no one was able to silence him, he was finally sent to the recesses of the Thebaïd. The mere titles of his writings give an idea of his state of mind: "No agreement with heretics," "Apostate Kings," "No quarter for the enemies of God," "Let us die for the Son of God."

Eusebius was not less firm in his principles, but he knew how to control himself. He also had at first been placed under the charge of an Arian bishop, the aged Patrophilus of Scythopolis, who made incredible efforts to persuade his prisoner to enter into relations with him; but the Bishop of Vercellæ preferred rather to die of hunger than to submit to contact with his persecutors.[1] As a matter of fact, he did very nearly succumb. He was removed from Scythopolis, perhaps after the death of

---

[1] Letter from Eusebius to his flock in Italy, during his sojourn at Scythopolis (Migne, *P. L.*, vol. xii., p. 947).

Patrophilus,[1] and was transferred to Cappadocia, and finally to the Thebaïd.

The two Latin bishops were invited by Athanasius to stay at Alexandria, and to join himself and his council in settling certain urgent questions. Lucifer declined the invitation, but sent two deacons as his representatives. He was in a hurry to return to Antioch where, he said, the affairs of that Church required his presence. He was entreated not to aggravate, by untimely measures, the troubles which divided it. He promised what they asked, but with such a man, and in such a state of irritation, there was everything to fear.

Two other persons, also absent, caused themselves to be represented at the council, the Bishop Apollinaris of Laodicea in Syria, and the priest Paulinus, head of the little Eustathian Church of Antioch. Of the latter body we have spoken already. It now remains to explain the ecclesiastical position of Apollinaris.

Towards the end of the 3rd century, Alexandria had provided Laodicea with two very distinguished bishops, Eusebius and Anatolius.[2] Shortly after the Council of Nicæa, another Alexandrian, the grammarian Apollinaris, took up his abode there, after having taught for some time at Berytus. He met with a good reception, and was even ordained priest; his son, called like himself Apollinaris, also entered the ranks of the clergy, in the capacity of a reader. This did not prevent either of them from continuing the cult of the Muses; they even pursued it with some degree of exaggeration. They were always to be seen at the lectures of a pagan sophist, named Epiphanius,[3] and their example brought thither many of the faithful. The Bishop Theodotus looked upon this with a disapproving eye. One day, Epiphanius began to recite a hymn in honour of Bacchus, and, according to

---

[1] Patrophilus, although he died before Constantius, had to suffer from the pagan reaction under Julian. The pagans of Scythopolis disinterred his body, scattered his bones, and made a lamp of his skull (*Chron. Pasch.* a. 362).

[2] Vol. i., pp. 354-5.

[3] Often mentioned by Eunapius, in his *Lives of the Philosophers.*

custom, he began by enjoining unbelievers to retire.
No one stirred, the Christians any more than the rest.
Theodotus, being informed of this scandal, censured the
action so far as concerned the ordinary Christians present,
but he took rigorous measures against the two Apollinarii;
he reprimanded them publicly, and excommunicated them.
The culprits gave evidence of their repentance, did
penance, and finally the bishop pardoned them. Theodotus was soon succeeded (about 335) in the see of
Laodicea by a priest named George, also an Alexandrian,
who had formerly been deposed by Bishop Alexander, and
had come to seek his fortune in Syria. Theodotus had
been one of the first defenders of Arius. George was, or
had become, more moderate in his theological opinions: in
358 we find him among the opponents of Eudoxius and
of the Anomœan party. But he was an inveterate enemy
of Athanasius. At the Council of Sardica he appeared on
the list of the bishops deposed by the Westerns. When,
three years later, Athanasius, being recalled to Alexandria
in spite of the sentences of George and his friends, stopped
at Laodicea, there were no exchanges of courtesy between
them.[1] The two Apollinarii, on the other hand, made a
show of welcoming to their home the outlaw of the
Council of Tyre, and posed henceforth as upholders of
Athanasius and of Nicæa. As soon as Athanasius was
gone, they had to reckon with George, who excommunicated them once more. This time, the separation was
decisive. But the moral support of Athanasius enabled
them to resist this blow. A Nicene party was organized
around them, and Apollinaris the younger became its
bishop. We do not know exactly when, but it was probably
after the death of George and of Constantius, for we can
scarcely conceive that in the lifetime of the latter such a
proceeding could have been risked.[2]

[1] Athanasius had a special horror of George, and even with his
own party, he had not a good reputation. Ζῶν ἀσώτως οὐκ ἔλαθεν, ἀλλὰ
καὶ παρὰ τῶν οἰκείων καταγινώσκεται, τὸ τέλος τοῦ ζῆν καὶ τὴν εὐθυμίαν ἐν
τοῖς αἰσχίστοις μετρῶν (Athan. De fuga, 26).

[2] We hear no more of George after the Council of Seleucia (in
359) The Council of Constantinople (360) would certainly have

Thus the body of persons united or represented, in 362, round Athanasius was exclusively composed of pure Nicenes, who had never wavered, and who on that account had had more or less to suffer under Constantius. They fully realized that they and those of their opinion formed but a very feeble minority in the empire, but that, now that religious liberty was restored, many others, who had not exhibited the same constancy, would be desirous of joining them and resuming the old tradition. On what conditions ought they to welcome such persons? Here there presented itself a question both of practice and expediency, precisely analogous to that raised at the end of the persecutions by the repentance of the apostates. Already, in the West, Hilary had seen no objection to associating with those who had fallen into error at Ariminum as soon as they openly disclaimed their weakness. A like solution was adopted by Athanasius, Eusebius, and the rest. They decided that all the bishops of orthodox faith from whom signatures had been extorted, could, on repudiating them, still be maintained in their former positions. As to their leaders, they should be pardoned, if they repented, but they should be excluded from the ranks of the clergy.[1]

This measure could have but little effect outside the West and Egypt.[2] There, all or very nearly all were Nicenes at heart and supporters of Athanasius. Violence alone had made them yield. It was coming to an end: they returned quite naturally to their former attitude, like

deposed him, if he had been still living. But as there is no mention of its having done so, there is ground for thinking that George died about that time. The George of whom St Basil speaks (*Ep.* 251, 2) in connection with the Council of Constantinople is certainly George of Alexandria. Philostorgius (v. 1) says that Acacius of Cæsarea, on returning from that council, ordained bishops for the vacant sees; amongst them he mentions Pelagius for Laodicea. Pelagius was Bishop of Laodicea in 363, in the reign of Jovian. It would be in opposition to him, therefore, that Apollinaris created a schism.

[1] Athan. *Ep. ad Rufinianum.*

[2] However, there were in Palestine, in the island of Cyprus, in Lycia, in Pamphylia and in Isauria, a certain number of supporters of Athanasius.

those Christians, whom persecution forced into sacrificing,
but whose hearts, in no way separated from the Church,
returned to it at the first glimmer of peace.　In Syria, in
Asia Minor, and in Thrace, the case was different.　Nearly
all the bishops there had assailed Athanasius and supported
formulas more or less heterodox, which conflicted one with
another, but agreed at least in passing over in silence
the essential formulas of Nicæa.　The fact that Constantius
was no longer there to impose the Creed of Ariminum-
Constantinople did not entail in these countries the
return to pure orthodoxy.　They reverted, not to the
position of 325, but to that of 359.

In this Eastern world, the most interesting situation
was that of the Church of Antioch, as much on account of
the importance of the town as of the complexity of the
position.

There was at Antioch a group of Anomœans, as
determined opponents of the Council of Ariminum as
they were of the Council of Nicæa, and irreconcilable
supporters of Aetius.　The leaders had been exiled ; the
rest did not enjoy, under Constantius, the right of holding
assemblies.　After them, on the doctrinal ladder, came the
official Church, attached to the confession of Ariminum-
Constantinople, and presided over by the aged Euzoïus,
one of the original Arians, who had retracted under
Constantine, and had never ceased since to appear in the
ranks of the opportunists.　These, at the time of Julian's
accession, kept possession of the Great Church, the
cathedral of Antioch.　Next came the orthodox party,
who had long submitted, and down to the time of Leontius
inclusively had accepted bishops pleasing to the court
and to the Arianizing party, without, however, abandoning anything of their correctness of doctrine.　Rallied at
first by Flavian and Diodore, they had accepted with
enthusiasm the election of Meletius, and remained faithful
to him, despite the fact that exile had separated him far
from them.　They no longer took part, as they had formerly
done, in the congregations of the official Church ; they
formed a group apart, and met together in the most ancient

church in Antioch—the Apostolica, the Ancient, the Palaea
(παλαιά) as it was called—which Constantine's beautiful
Basilica had robbed of its rank as the Cathedral. Last
of all, came the group of Paulinus, separated from the
official Church for a very much longer period than the
preceding one, ever since the deposition of Eustathius
(about 330). Between these two varieties of orthodox
Christians there were several shades of difference in regard
to formulas: the first held to the three hypostases, the
others did not approve of this mode of expression. At
bottom they were in agreement. They were only separated
because they had been so, because circumstances had led
them to live apart from each other for some thirty years.
It only needed a little tact and consideration to secure
undoubtedly a complete reconciliation between them.
And this was the more easy, because only one of the two
parties was provided with a bishop.

The council held by Athanasius devoted itself very
seriously to this situation. The only one of its documents
which has come down to us is a letter relating to the
differences at Antioch.

It is addressed, so far as its form goes, to the Nicene
bishops who happened to be in Antioch, or were about
to go there—Eusebius, Lucifer, Asterius, Cymatius,[1] and
Anatolius—but in reality to Paulinus and his community.
The council indicates on what conditions the dissenting
party of the Palaea (Meletians), and even the Arians, may
be received to communion. They must accept the Creed
of Nicæa, and condemn those who say that the Holy
Spirit is a creature, a being separated from the Essence
of Christ.[2] That was all. The representatives of the
council were to admit anyone to communion who would
accept this programme, and to unite them to the followers

---

[1] Cymatius was Bishop of Paltus, a small port on the Syrian coast;
it was more than twenty years since the Arians had deprived him of
his see (Athan. *De fuga.* 3; *Hist. Ar.* 5). As to Anatolius, he is
styled, at the end of the letter, Bishop Εὐβοίας. There was at Berea in
Syria a bishop called Anatolius, who signed in 363 a letter to Jovian;
but he did not belong to the same party as Cymatius and the others.

[2] Κτίσμα εἶναι καὶ διῃρημένον ἐκ τῆς οὐσίας τοῦ Χριστοῦ.

of Paulinus. Paulinus himself must not exact anything more; above all, no mention was to be made of a spurious Creed of Sardica in which the unity of hypostasis is affirmed. This Creed had been presented to the council, it was true, but it was rejected by it, in order not to set up any rival to that of Nicæa, the only one which ought to be recognized. Besides, Athanasius and his supporters had satisfied themselves that those who spoke of *three* hypostases were in agreement with those who only acknowledged *one*, the one party applying the term, "hypostasis" to the Persons, the other to the Divine Essence.

Another dispute was beginning to divide men's minds at Antioch and elsewhere. It was the prelude to the celebrated controversies of the 5th century upon the Incarnation of the Son of God. Some seemed to admit only a moral union between the historic Christ and the Divine Word; others maintained that the Word exercised, in Christ, the functions of a thinking soul ($\nu o \hat{v} s$). The council listened to representatives of each opinion.[1] It came to the conclusion that everyone was really agreed upon two points: first, that the Incarnation was quite a different thing from the indwelling of the Word in the soul of the prophets, and secondly, that the Saviour possessed an animate body, endowed with feeling and intelligence. Under these conditions, there was no occasion for division. All these questions, moreover, ought to be laid on one side that they might adhere to the faith of Nicæa, and thus restore unity to the Church.

This programme of doctrine was simple, and the plan of union seemed quite natural. There were in Syria some faithful adherents of Nicæa; it was these who ought to form the rallying-point. The difficulty was, that these Nicenes were very few in number, and that they were represented principally by the two Little Churches of Antioch and of Laodicea, hitherto considered as schis-

---

[1] The council gives no names, but the first explanation was understood to be represented at Antioch by the Meletian priest Diodore, the other by Vitalis, one of his colleagues, and especially by Apollinaris of Laodicea.

matical by the bishops of the country and by the generality of the faithful. Instead of addressing themselves directly to Meletius and Pelagius and negotiating with them for a collective reunion, the council tried to detach from them their followers in order to rally them round Paulinus and Apollinaris. It was a fatal error, the consequences of which made themselves felt for more than half a century at Antioch, and for very much longer by the Church at large.

Perhaps, Eusebius and Asterius might on the spot have succeeded in understanding this situation, and in finding some remedy. But when they arrived at Antioch, they found the position seriously changed for the worse. Lucifer, without waiting for the decision at Alexandria, had compounded with Paulinus, and had ordained him Bishop of Antioch. After that there was no longer any means of coming to an understanding with Meletius, whether by recognizing him as sole bishop, or persuading him to renounce the bishopric of Antioch, in order that they might proceed in concert to a new election. Although deeply grieved, Eusebius did not think it incumbent on him to condemn this action of Lucifer. He recognized neither Paulinus[1] nor Meletius, and returned to Italy, making public, on his way, the merciful provisions of the Council of Alexandria in regard to those who had fallen into error at Ariminum. As to Lucifer, furious at the indirect censure entailed upon himself by the action of Eusebius, and embarrassed by the adhesion given by his deacons to Athanasius' Council, he also retired from the scene, fortified in his uncompromising attitude and no longer disposed to hold communion with anybody. According to him, by accepting the repentance of the lapsed, the confessors themselves had participated in their fall. Certain fanatics, very few in number, adopted the same attitude.

---

[1] Paulinus signed the Tome of Alexandria, but with lengthy explanations. Other signatures were, no doubt, affixed to it. We now possess only that of Carterius, Bishop of Antaradus, long ago deposed by the Arians (Athan. *De fuga*. 3 ; *Hist. Ar.* 5).

However, the severe measures of Julian soon put an
end to these private quarrels. We have seen how
Euzoïus was treated at Antioch. Athanasius had scarcely
been reinstalled, when the emperor ordered him to be
driven out upon the pretext that a man loaded with
condemnations could not return without a special order;
and further that it was all very well for the exiled
bishops to have been recalled, but it was not lawful for
them to resume their official duties.[1] The magistrates,
however, required much urging: the proceeding was too
unpopular. Julian was angry; he was greatly incensed
against Athanasius who had dared "in his reign to baptize
noble ladies."[2] The prefect, being frightened, submitted
and published the edict of proscription, which Athanasius
immediately obeyed (October 21, 362). Some time after
two priests, Paul and Astericius, were exiled on the
representations of some influential pagans. A petition
addressed to the emperor in favour of the bishop had
no other result but to draw down upon those who had
signed it a very severe rating, and upon Athanasius an
order of expulsion, not from Alexandria only as before,
but from the whole of Egypt.[3]

Athanasius remained in concealment. Everywhere in
the East Christians had several trying months to pass
through. On August 18, 363, the news of Julian's death
was published at Alexandria, together with an announce-
ment of the accession of his successor. Athanasius was
at Antinoë. He immediately re-entered Alexandria, and,
without making any stay there, embarked on a voyage
to Antioch.

Jovian had hastened to recall him from exile by a
decree couched in very flattering terms, the text of which
has been preserved[4]; he gave Athanasius a most cordial
welcome. About the same time a certain number of
bishops belonging to Syria and Asia Minor, headed by
Meletius and Acacius of Cæsarea, were collecting at
Antioch to discuss the situation. Finally, Basil of Ancyra

---

[1] Julian, *Ep.* 26.
[2] *Ep.* 6, to the prefect Ecdicius.
[3] *Ep.* 51.
[4] Migne, *P. G.*, vol. xxvi., p. 813.

and his party[1] sent a petition there. The new emperor, beginning a reign which opened so sadly, found himself as a climax to his trials involved in theological disputes. He had no intention of bringing together in one assembly all this crowd of bishops. Athanasius presented him with a memorial in which he commended the Creed of Nicæa to the exclusion of all others, with one small addition relating to the Holy Spirit. Acacius, Meletius, and their section also declared to him that the best thing to do was to adhere to the faith of Nicæa; however, they went on to explain that if the term *homoousios* had excited scruples, it was because people had not at first seen clearly what it meant, namely, that the Word proceeds from the Essence of the Father, and is like to Him in Essence.[2] The Homoïousians, who were not present in person, demanded either a return to the first decisions of Ariminum and of Seleucia—those before the capitulations, *i.e.*, a return to the *homoousios* and the *homoïousios*—or that all should be granted freedom to hold religious meetings.

The proceedings of these last two groups prove in short that the fusion had taken place between the two shades of doctrine. The sympathy of Hilary and of Athanasius for the opinions of Basil, Eustathius, Eleusius, and others was clearly shown at the Council of Paris first, and afterwards at that of Alexandria. We cannot say that the *homoïousios* had triumphed over the *homoousios*. The Nicene term was in no way ousted; it was even it which prevailed to the exclusion of the other. But the idea which the *homoïousios* accentuated was admitted,

---

[1] Socrates (*H. E.* iii. 25) mentions Basil of Ancyra, Silvanus of Tarsus, Sophronius of Pompeiopolis (in Paphlagonia), Pasinicus of Zela, Leontius of Comana, Callicrates of Claudiopolis, Theophilus of Castabala. This is the last time we hear of Basil of Ancyra. The subject of the letter is badly described by Socrates. Sozomen (vi. 4) gives a detailed analysis of it.

[2] This explanation appeared suspicious to Paulinus and his party. It was clearly from this quarter that there originated the protest entitled "Refutation of the hypocrisy of Meletius and Eusebius of Samosata," which is preserved in the appendices to St Athanasius (*P. G.*, vol. xxviii., p. 85).

under another formula—that of the three hypostases—as a useful and even necessary explanation of the *homoousios*. Orthodoxy thus expressed was that soon to be represented by Basil of Cæsarea and his friends, Gregory of Nazianzus, Gregory of Nyssa, and Amphilochius of Iconium.

But if there was a tendency to a *rapprochement* between doctrines, it was not so with regard to persons. There was a fine opportunity for reconciliation when, in October 363, Athanasius came into contact at Antioch with Meletius, Acacius, and the rest. The overture of peace was made by the Bishop of Alexandria ; he held out his hand to the representatives of that Eastern episcopate which had persecuted him for thirty years. Acacius and his friends had the bad taste to stand upon their dignity, and not to accept at once a reconciliation so desirable. Athanasius, deeply grieved, re-embarked without having been admitted to communion with them.[1]

The favour of Jovian was plainly bestowed upon all these representatives of the orthodoxy, whether of yesterday or to-morrow. In a pre-eminent degree Athanasius was his favourite. None the less he refrained from taking a side, and demanded only one thing—peace. We cannot see that he ever did anything to disturb Eudoxius, Euzoïus, and other representatives of the settlement of Ariminum-Constantinople. They found themselves diminished in number by the defection of Acacius and his section, who had passed all at once over to the side of the Council of Nicæa. The positions which they had, they kept ; they retained in particular the important sees of Antioch and Constantinople which were long to remain in their possession. The Anomœans in the same way were not interfered with. The Arians of Alexandria, with a certain Lucius at their head, made an attempt to secure the ear of the emperor and to excite him against Athanasius. They wasted their time and were even dismissed with some manifestation of displeasure.[2]

---

[1] Basil, *Ep.* 89, 258.

[2] See the very curious records of their interviews with the emperor

During his brief stay in Antioch,[1] the new emperor had hardly time to go very deeply into these questions. He set out for Constantinople but died on the way, on February 17, 364, and was immediately replaced (February 26) by Valentinian, an officer of his guard, who like him had been harassed in the reign of Julian for his religious opinions. Valentinian, on his arrival in Constantinople, associated his brother Valens with himself (March 28), and entrusted him with the government of the East, with the same area as had been possessed by Licinius (314-323), and by Constantius (337-350). Thus, there was once more an Emperor of the West and an Emperor of the East. If both maintained practically the same attitude towards paganism, they did not agree as to the course to be pursued in face of the parties which divided the Christian Church.

Valentinian, like Jovian, was personally attached to the faith of Nicæa, so far as a soldier whose first thought was his profession and his career, could have a preference in that kind of thing. He, too, wished before everything for peace. He had not the slightest intention that this peace should be disturbed for the sake of disputes about creeds, nor *a fortiori* that the civil power should be made to take part in these questions. His attitude much resembles that of the Emperor Constans. If, during the last months of the year 363, the attitude of Jovian had given rise to some hope of an official restoration of the Council of Nicæa, Valentinian for his part opened up but moderate prospects. Some significant words, soon translated into definite actions, taught the religious world that it must rely, not upon the emperor, but solely on itself, and that before all things, it must arrange its affairs in such a manner as not to compromise public order.

annexed to the letter of St Athanasius to Jovian (Migne, *P. G.*, vol. xxvi., p. 820).

[1] Scarcely a month ; he was at Edessa on September 27 ; and by November 12 we find him at Mopsuestia on his way to Constantinople (*Cod. Theod.* vii. 4, 9 ; xi. 20, 1).

The position in the West was, generally speaking, simple enough. In the year 360, the bishops of the Gauls, assembled in Paris, had, at Hilary's instigation, settled matters as they were to be settled two years later at Alexandria by Athanasius and Eusebius of Vercellæ. Pope Liberius who, as we have seen, had had no share in the Council of Ariminum, hastened for his own part also to make use of the new liberty, in order to quash the decisions of that assembly. Like Hilary, he conceded that their position should be preserved to those bishops who should rehabilitate themselves by adherence to the Creed of Nicæa.[1] On hearing what had been done at Alexandria, the bishops of Greece and of Macedonia[2] declared themselves to the same purpose: Pope Liberius wrote to the Italian bishops,[3] and they, in their turn, to those of Illyria.[4] Councils were held in Gaul, Spain, and almost everywhere. The Western episcopate breathed again and resumed its normal attitude, which had been completely upset by the interference of the Emperor Constantius and the prelates of his court.

The centres of opposition were very few indeed. There were two of them, one on the Right wing, as we should say, and one on the Left. The opposition from the Right were represented by Lucifer, who returned from the East in a humour of inflexible obstinacy, and refused absolutely any relations with those who had erred at Ariminum, and with those who accepted their repentance. He shut himself up in his own diocese of Caliaris (Cagliari), "contenting himself with his own communion." His attitude was imitated in Spain by the Bishop of Illiberris (Granada), a certain Gregory, who even before the Council of Ariminum had found himself in conflict with Hosius.[5] In

---

[1] Jaffé 220, a lost letter, but presupposed by that contained in the twelfth Fragment of St Hilary (J. 223); cf. J. 255, a decretal of Siricius, c. 1.

[2] Basil, *Ep.* 204, 5 ; cf. Athan. *ad Rufin.*, and J. 223.

[3] Jaffé 223.

[4] Hil. *Frag. hist.* xii.

[5] Upon this affair, see the narrative (strongly coloured and already containing legendary elements) in the *Libellus precum Marcellini et*

Rome, several persons held the same opinions; they rallied round the deacon Hilary, the man whom Liberius had sent with Lucifer to the Council of Milan. Like Lucifer, he had just returned from exile. He was the most uncompromising of all, for he even went so far as to require that the transgressors of Ariminum and their supporters should be subjected to a second baptism.

On the Left there were several determined Arians. In Gaul, we hear of Saturninus of Arles and Paternus of Périgueux; Hilary succeeded in obtaining their deposition, and it appears that these sentences were carried out. In Milan, Auxentius still held his own. Eusebius and Hilary set themselves to dislodge the Cappadocian intruder from his see.[1] But they had to deal with one who was more than their match. The former bishop, Dionysius, whom Auxentius had replaced, had died in exile: hence Auxentius had no Catholic rival. Moreover, he was a clever man; he had almost been accepted at Milan. The Emperor Valentinian had just arrived in that city; and everyone knew that he did not like clamour. But Hilary and Eusebius could not forego making it. Their only method of action was an uprising of the populace against the bishop. At the first outburst, an imperial edict commanded silence; then, as Hilary continued to protest, treating Auxentius as a blasphemer and an enemy of Christ, Valentinian ordered the quæstor and the Master of the Offices, assisted by about ten bishops, to hold an inquiry on this point. Auxentius began by declaring that there was no occasion to go back on the decisions arrived at by six hundred bishops,[2] and especially at the request of persons who had been condemned for the last ten years.[3]

Faustini (Collectio Avellana, No. 2, p. 14 (Ed. Günther); *cf.* Migne, *P. L.*, vol. xiii., p. 89). Letter from Eusebius of Vercellæ to Gregory (about 360) in Hil. *Frag. hist.* xi.

[1] Valentinian spent at Milan the last two months of 364, and the following year until the autumn. It was during that time that the conflict took place between Auxentius and St Hilary.

[2] That is, the councils of Ariminum and Seleucia added together and considered as favourable, *en masse*, to the theology of Auxentius.

[3] Hilary and Eusebius.

However, since the emperor insisted on it, he did not
hesitate to declare that Christ was truly God, of the same
Divinity and Substance as God the Father.[1] He was
made to repeat this profession of faith, quite unexpected
from the lips of a notorious Arian; he was even required
to put it in writing. He did so, but his edition of it was
so cleverly put together that it was capable of meaning
the contrary to what he had been made to say.[2] Hilary
perceived the equivocation, and protested energetically.
But the emperor showed himself satisfied, accepted communion with Auxentius, and commanded Hilary to leave
Milan. The intrepid bishop was obliged to abandon the
struggle; but he did not do so without a solemn warning
to the people of Milan that their bishop was an ill-disguised
heretic, and they should flee from him as they would
Antichrist.[3] Eusebius, who in this business had only
played the second part, had already left Milan. He
confined himself henceforth to the care of his enormous
diocese, which included the whole of the present Piedmont,
as far as the Alps, and even beyond. Auxentius, on his
part, contented himself with governing his Church of
Milan, without posing as a party leader. Besides, he
seems to have been, in Italy, the sole representative of the
tradition of Ariminum; we hear no more of Epictetus,
the Arian Bishop of Centumcellæ, so disgracefully involved
in the affair of Pope Liberius; he was no doubt dead.

By way of retaliation, in Pannonia and in the Latin
provinces of the Lower Danube, the episcopal body
remained faithful to their attitude in the time of the
Emperor Constantius. Ursacius and Valens always
possessed much influence there; Germinius still held the
most important episcopal see, that of Sirmium. The
orthodox party, in these countries, had a hard life. St
Martin, who belonged to Pannonia, visited about that

---

[1] *Christum Deum verum et unius cum Deo Patre divinitatis et
substantiae est professus* (Hil. *Adv. Aux.* 7).

[2] *Christum ante omnia saecula et ante omne principium natum ex
Patre Deum verum filium ex Deo Patre* (*Ibid.* 14). According as one
puts a comma before or after *verum*, the sense is Arian or Catholic.

[3] This is the subject of his *Liber contra Auxentium.*

time his native country of Sabaria. A disciple of St
Hilary, he did not hesitate to declare his orthodox
opinions, and to protest against the heresy taught by the
clergy. He was beaten with rods, and driven from the
town.[1] At Sirmium, three Catholics, Heraclian, Firmian,
and Aurelian were imprisoned for the same reason. We
still possess a curious record[2] of their appearance before
Bishop Germinius, and of the dispute between Heraclian
and the bishop. The document is dated January 13, 366.
" It is Eusebius," said the bishop, " that returned exile, and
Hilary, who has also been in exile, who have put these ideas
into thy head." And as Heraclian tried to defend himself,
Germinius said : " See what a long tongue he has. You
will not be able to break his teeth." Immediately, a
deacon and a reader flew at the accused and struck him
in the face. However, the conversation was resumed :
" Tell me, Heraclian—it was I who baptized thee ; how
didst thou receive baptism ? " Heraclian answered : " You
gave it me, in the Name of the Father, of the Son,
and of the Holy Ghost, and not in the name of one God
who is greater and one God who is lesser and created."
This Heraclian was well known in Sirmium ; he had in
former days opposed Photinus. Germinius at bottom did
not wish him much harm. He tried to win him over to his
own side, even pretending that he had had an explanation
in regard to his faith with Eusebius, who had declared
himself satisfied. At the end of the audience, the clergy
of Germinius spoke of indicting the dissentients before the
Governor (Consularis) of Pannonia, and demanding their
heads. The bishop contented himself with presenting to
them the Creed of Ariminum and, when they refused to
sign it, with giving them his blessing, to receive which
they consented to bow their heads.

Perhaps there was some element of truth in what

---

[1] Sulpicius Severus, *Vita Martini*, 4 ; Auxentius also drove him
from Milan.

[2] *Altercatio Heracliani laici cum Germinio episcopo Sirmiensi*,
published by C. P. Caspari, *Kirchenhistorische Anecdota* (Christiania,
1883), p. 133.

Germinius told them of his communications with Eusebius of Vercellæ. He did not go so far as the others; his ideas seem to have somewhat resembled those of Basil of Ancyra. We still possess a formula,[1] which he drew up, apparently shortly after the affair of Heraclian. Without employing the term *substance*, he teaches in this the likeness in Divinity, splendour, majesty, power, etc., and in everything, *per omnia similem*. This language disturbed the Arians. Valens and another bishop, called Paul, demanded explanations. Germinius began by not giving any, confining himself to saying that he remained united in heart with his colleagues. Still, they were not satisfied. Four of them, Ursacius, Valens, Paul, and Gaius,[2] meeting at Singidunum, insisted[3] upon his retraction of the *per omnia similem*. But the Bishop of Sirmium held his ground. He wrote to another group of bishops in the district[4] to explain his doctrine to them, and to protest against Ursacius and his three colleagues. He knew at first hand, he said, exactly what had been agreed upon before the Council of Ariminum, because he was present at the preliminary conference, at which the formula of agreement had been discussed. It was Mark of Arethusa who had held the pen: and it certainly tolerated the words, *Filium similem Patri per omnia*.

While in the West they were thus returning to the faith of Nicæa, and the fires of opposition were decreasing or gradually cooling down, the Eastern empire continued to pass from one crisis to another. We have already seen that in Western Asia Minor and the neighbouring districts a good many bishops, united round Basil of Ancyra and Eleusius of Cyzicus, professed a doctrine

---

[1] Hil. *Frag. hist.* xiii.

[2] This Gaius had played a part at the Council of Ariminum by the side of Ursacius and Valens (Hil. *Frag. hist.* vii. 4 ; viii. 2, 5 ; x. i.).

[3] Hil. *Frag. hist.* xiv.

[4] Hil. *Frag. hist.* xv. Those to whom it is addressed are: *Rufianus, Palladius, Severinus, Nichas, Heliodorus, Romulus, Mucianus,* and *Stercorius.* The Palladius here named is doubtless the Bishop of Ratiaria, who will be heard of again in the time of St Ambrose.

equivalent on the whole, apart from certain qualifications, to the orthodoxy of Nicæa. Persecuted and exiled, in 360, by the exertions of the official clergy, that is to say of more or less avowed Arians who sheltered themselves behind the confession of Ariminum, they profited in their turn from the circumstances of the time. Already they had sent their profession of faith to Jovian. At the moment when Valentinian, escorted back by his brother Valens, was leaving Constantinople for the West, they sent as a deputation to him Hypatian, the Bishop of Heraclea in Thrace, to ask for permission to assemble in council.[1] Valentinian declared that he saw no objection. They therefore met together at Lampsacus, on the Hellespont. As the result of these deliberations which lasted for two months, there issued a new condemnation of the Council of Ariminum-Constantinople, its formulas and its decisions against individuals. They proclaimed once more the *homoïousios*, necessary, as they said, to indicate the distinction between the Divine Persons; and the Dedication Creed of Antioch was canonized afresh. They also took measures with a view to ensuring, without the assistance of the government, the restoration of those bishops who had been superseded in their sees as a consequence of the council of 360. Eudoxius and his followers were invited to rejoin them, retracting of course all that they had done contrary to the opinions of the present council.

The Bishop of Constantinople, as no one could doubt, was not a man to submit to be condemned without defending himself. He had forestalled his opponents, and his credit was already assured with the Emperor Valens when the latter saw the arrival of the delegates from the Council of Lampsacus. They were unfavourably received. Valens exhorted them to come to an understanding with Eudoxius. He had taken up his position, and was determined to consider as official the doctrine of the Council of Ariminum. This, at first sight, may seem

---

[1] The best account is that of Sozomen, *H. E.* vii. 7, who here reproduces for us the documents of Sabinus better than Socrates.

extraordinary. It would have been more natural, so it seems, that Valens should have acted like his brother, and preserved neutrality amidst the various Christian confessions. Still, for Valentinian the problem was far more simple than for him. In the West—save at Milan, where the dispute had been cut short in the way we have seen—the differences of confession did not entail any serious discord. There was no Catholic rival against Ursacius or Germinius, any more than there was any Arian rival against Eusebius or Hilary. It was not so in the East. There, the division of the parties had given rise in many places to local schisms; several bishops disputed among themselves the same see. Valens may have thought that the public welfare required that he should take a side, and adopt one of the conflicting confessions. That of Nicæa had up to that time scarcely had any supporters but the Egyptians. In the reign of Jovian, it is true, a certain number of bishops of Syria or Asia Minor had signed the Nicene formulary. But they still remained on distant terms with Athanasius and his followers. In Asia Minor, there had just been witnessed the coalition against Eudoxius of all the opponents of Anomœanism, but amongst the party thus formed there still existed distrust of the *homoousios*. As a formula of conciliation between so many dissenting factions the Creed of Nicæa was scarcely recommended. Valens thought it preferable to make up his mind in favour of that of Ariminum, of which the official ratification was still fresh, while those who professed it occupied the great sees of Constantinople and Antioch, not to speak of many others. It was in this way that support was continued to the tradition of Constantius.

In the spring of 365 appeared an edict, commanding all the bishops who had been deposed under Constantius and reinstated under Julian, to withdraw once more. This edict was published at Alexandria on May 4. It imposed a fine of 300 pounds in gold upon the municipal authorities who should fail to obey it. The Alexandrians pleaded as a ground of exception the peculiar position of Athanasius.

It appeared that the author of his last expulsion was not Constantius but Julian, and that the last decree for his recall bore the name of Jovian. The prefect temporized, for the populace were weary of all these intrigues. Athanasius on his part offered no resistance, and withdrew (October 5). Finally, it was decided to recall him once more. On February 1, 366, an imperial notary formally reinstated him in the Church of Dionysius. This was the last time. In the following year, it is true, Lucius attempted to show himself in Alexandria, and to pose as a rival; but he had scarcely arrived, when he was nearly torn to pieces: the police had great difficulty in saving his life, and sending him back to Palestine. Athanasius remained master of the field of battle. After forty years of struggle, the old warrior was to spend in peace the few years which remained to him of life.

Meletius at Antioch was evicted,[1] as Athanasius had been. Paulinus, being of less importance, was left undisturbed. He was on fairly good terms with Euzoïus, who was henceforth the official bishop of the metropolis of the East.

However, the Homoïousians of the Council of Lampsacus did not resign themselves to their discomfiture. Being repulsed by the Emperor Valens, they decided to appeal to his colleague the Emperor Valentinian and to the bishops of the West.[2] It was the course adopted by Athanasius, twenty years before. The bishops of Asia assembled at Smyrna; other meetings took place in Lycia, in Pamphylia, and in Isauria.[3] Three

---

[1] Meletius was three times driven from Antioch; this is expressly mentioned in his funeral oration by St Gregory of Nyssa (Migne, *P. G.*, vol. xlvi., p. 857). The first exile is that which followed almost immediately his election in 361; the third that which lasted till the death of Valens (378); we are not quite certain where to place the second, perhaps in Julian's reign, perhaps under Valens, in which case Meletius would have been, like Athanasius, first driven out, and then recalled. Later on, he would then have been driven out again.

[2] Socrates, iv. 12; Sozomen, vi. 10, 11.

[3] These southern provinces of Asia Minor are mentioned several times by St Athanasius as containing bishops in communion with him.

delegates were chosen: Eustathius of Sebaste, Silvanus of
Tarsus, and Theophilus of Castabala in Cilicia. They were
given letters to the Emperor Valentinian and to Pope
Liberius. Valentinian at that time happened to be in
Gaul; they were not able to join him, probably because
he did not consent to receive them. Liberius, however,
gave them a reception, not without some hesitation, and
received the letters that they brought. The three envoys
had been authorized by those who commissioned them to
accept the Creed of Nicæa, which was known to be the
indispensable condition of communion with the Roman
Church. They did this in a document couched in
very explicit terms, in which they condemned besides
the Sabellians, the Patripassians, the Marcellians, the
Photinians, and the Council of Ariminum. Liberius, on
his part, wrote to the bishops whose names appeared
on the papers which had been presented to him (they
were sixty-four in number),[1] and to all the orthodox
prelates of the East.[2]

Communion was re-established with Rome. On their
homeward journey,[3] the delegates halted in Sicily, where
the bishops of the country, assembled in council,
fraternized with them; in like manner they received
testimonies in sympathetic terms from those of Italy,
Africa, and Gaul. Fortified with these documents, they
held a meeting at Tyana, in conjunction with certain
bishops of Syria or Eastern Asia Minor, several of whom
had already accepted the *homoousios* in 363.[4] The fusion

---

[1] Among these prelates appears a certain Macedonius, Bishop of
Apollonias in Lydia, whose epitaph I have identified and commented
upon. He was, like many other bishops of that party, a great ascetic;
he had much to endure at the hands of the Anomœans (*Bulletin de
correspondance hellénique*, vol. xi. (1887), p. 311).

[2] These two documents are given by Socrates, iv. 12 ; *cf.* Sozomen,
vi. 11. In the letter of Liberius the Sabellians and Patripassians
appear "with all the other heresies" in the list of persons to be condemned ; but the Marcellians and Photinians are not mentioned by
name.

[3] For what follows, see Sozomen, vi. 12.

[4] Sozomen (vi. 12), who gives us information as to the Council of
Tyana, evidently following Sabinus' account, mentions Eusebius of

between the neo-Catholics of the East and the old Homoïousians of Asia was in a fair way of being accomplished, under the auspices of Rome and the Latin episcopate. The assembly at Tyana despatched to all quarters the documents brought from the West, and summoned all the bishops to a great council which was to be held at Tarsus in the following spring. But Eudoxius put himself in the way of this project. The Emperor Valens forbade the council.[1]

In addition to the acceptance of the Creed of Nicæa, there was yet another point upon which difficulties were now beginning to show themselves. Amongst those persons who were willing to grant to the Son likeness absolutely and in essence to the Father, and even to accept, with regard to the first two Persons of the Trinity, the term consubstantial, there were some who refused to make the same concession as to the Holy Spirit. Gradually, as the dispute spread itself from this side, the positions adopted grew more definite in character.

The question was first raised in Egypt. Athanasius, during the last years of the reign of Constantius, had dealt with it fully in his letters to Serapion. He had cut it short in 362, by the Council of Alexandria ; in the following year, he had declared to the Emperor Jovian that the Creed of Nicæa must be completed, so far as concerns the Holy Spirit. Following his example, the neo-orthodox of Syria and Asia Minor laid stress upon this point, either by expressly affirming the consubstantiality of the Holy

Cæsarea in Cappadocia, Athanasius of Ancyra, Pelagius of Laodicea, Zeno of Tyre, Paul of Emesa, Otreos of Melitene, and Gregory of Nazienzus (the father).

[1] There is a little uncertainty as to the exact date of these last councils. That of Lampsacus belongs certainly to 364. It is possible that the journey of the three bishops to Rome may have been deferred till 366. Liberius died in that year, on September 24. But it is difficult to suppose that such a step should have been taken just at the time of, or immediately after, the rivalry of Procopius (September 28, 365-May 27, 366). I should be inclined to think rather that the bishops set out in the summer of 365, before Procopius had created his disturbance.

Spirit, or by producing formulas calculated to establish the dignity of the Third Divine Person. St Basil took up both attitudes in turn, teaching the consubstantiality in his books, but not going quite so far in his discourses in church. The creed then in use at Jerusalem, that which is still in use under the name of Nicene Creed, is not more explicit than the official eloquence of St Basil. It says of the Holy Spirit, that He is "the Lord and Life-giver, that He proceeds from the Father; that He is adored and glorified with the Father and the Son, that He has spoken by the prophets." Nothing more; it is not a vote inscribed against the "Enemies of the Holy Spirit."

This term (Pneumatomachi) was speedily made use of to describe the new party. They were also called "Semi-Arians," which meant that, while orthodox in the main as to the Second Person of the Trinity, they were Arians so far as concerned the Third Person. But the title which continued in general use is that of Macedonians, from the name of Macedonius, the former Bishop of Constantinople. This came about as follows. Macedonius had been elected in earlier days in opposition to Bishop Paul by the Eusebian party, and had been imposed, not without difficulty, upon the populace of Constantinople. At first, he made life very hard for the defenders of Nicene orthodoxy, who remained faithful to his predecessor. When the anti-Athanasian party became divided (in 357), he took up a decided position in favour of the moderates, and supported the opinions of Basil of Ancyra. We have no proof that he was distinguished by any special doctrine with regard to the Holy Spirit. He died in retirement in the neighbourhood of the capital, shortly after his deposition by the council of 360. But his followers did not all abandon him. There were a great number of them who did not wish to join themselves to Eudoxius, and who organized themselves, as well as they could, in a community of their own. The pure Nicenes, since the deposition of Bishop Paul, in 342, formed a group apart, without a bishop of their own, a position closely resembling that of the Eustathians of Antioch,

before the ordination of Paulinus. The supporters of
Macedonius, the Macedonians as they were called, did
not merge themselves with them. They had, outside
Constantinople, the support of a large number of bishops,
especially in the provinces of Thrace, Bithynia, and
the Hellespont. In these countries the Nicenes were
scarce: nowhere did they possess churches. It was the
Macedonians who represented in those quarters the
opposition to official Arianism.

This was not their sole recommendation. The best
known of this group of bishops were, owing to the dignity
of their lives, their asceticism and their zeal in organizing
works of charitable relief, the objects of high esteem
among the common people. From this point of view,
they were honourably distinguished from votaries of
ambition and of pleasure like Eudoxius and his associates.
Among them we have the names of two of Macedonius'
former clergy, Eleusius of Cyzicus, a man much esteemed
by St Hilary, and Marathonius of Nicomedia.[1] The
latter was a man of great wealth: after having made his
fortune in the offices of the prætorian prefect, he founded
at Constantinople hospitals and refuges for the poor;
afterwards, by the advice of Eustathius of Sebaste, he
embraced the ascetic life and established a monastery,
which long retained the name of its founder.[2]

Eleusius was adored by the people of Cyzicus. We
are told that, Valens having succeeded, by dint of entreaties
and threats, in extorting from him a discreditable signature, the bishop on his return home protested before his
people that violence had been used towards him, but

---

[1] We must add to the list the name of Macedonius of Apollonias
in Lydia, according to the inscription quoted above, p. 292, note 1.

[2] Sozomen, iv. 27. Socrates (ii. 38, followed by Sozomen, iv. 20),
on the authority of a Novatian source, apparently, says that he had
been installed by Macedonius at Nicomedia. We cannot quite see
where to place him. Cecropius was Bishop of Nicomedia from 351
to 358, when he was killed in the great earthquake on August 24,
which destroyed the town. Acacius in 360 ordained a successor
to him called Onesimus (Philostorgius, v. 1). Tillemont, vol. vi.,
p. 770, proposes to place him in Julian's reign; this would make him

that he no longer thought himself worthy to remain in office ; and that they must therefore elect another bishop in his place. His flock refused to listen any further to the suggestion ; they declared that they wished for no one but him, and that they would keep him. And so they did.[1]

The Homoïousian bishops on either side of the Bosphorus were thus in communion with the group at Constantinople, to whom it was customary to give the name of Macedonians. At the time of which we are now speaking, they had, for the most part, adopted the formula of Nicæa, and found themselves on terms of friendship with the Roman Church. A day came when the question of the Holy Spirit which had not been presented to them by Pope Liberius, brought them into conflict with the neo-orthodox of Upper Asia Minor. Being thus formed into a dissenting party, they were designated by the name of Macedonians, which was borne by their supporters at Constantinople. It was in this way that Macedonius became, after his death, the patron who gave his name to a special form of dissent, of which he had probably never dreamed.

It was not only with these dissentients on the right wing that the official clergy had to reckon. The irreconcilables on the extreme left also troubled their peace. After the council of 360, Aetius, as we have seen, had been exiled to Mopsuestia ; as he was treated too well there by the bishop, he was transferred to Amblada, a gloomy and unhealthy place in Lycaonia. As to Eunomius, his

---

an anti-bishop set up in opposition to Onesimus by Macedonius or by his party. However this may be, the activity of Marathonius was exercised rather at Constantinople than at Nicomedia ; whether because being prevented for one reason or another from residing in the latter city he had established himself in the capital, or because there has been attributed to his name the influence exercised by his monastery. The "semi-Arians" of Constantinople have been called Marathonians as well as Macedonians, which gives some ground for thinking that Marathonius may have been the real author of the doctrine of the Pneumatomachi.

[1] Socrates, iv. 6 ; Sozomen, vi. 9 ; Philostorgius, ix. 13.

celebrated disciple, he consented to sign the formula of
Ariminum-Constantinople, and in consideration of this
Eudoxius caused h.m to be installed as Bishop of Cyzicus,
in place of the exiled Eleusius.   Between Eudoxius and
Eunomius there had been, so it was reported, secret
agreements; the new Bishop of Constantinople had
pledged himself to bring about the reinstatement of Aetius;
in return, Eunomius had consented to moderate his
language.   He did not succeed in doing this sufficiently;
the people of Cyzicus travelled to Constantinople to
denounce him, and, as Eudoxius did not make up his
mind to rid them of their bishop, they complained to
the Emperor Constantius.   Eunomius relieved all parties
of trouble by abandoning his bishopric.   He then fell
into the hands of Acacius, who looked with an unfavourable eye upon Eudoxius' dallyings with the Anomœans.
Being summoned to Antioch, he was subjected to an
enquiry, but his trial was still going on when Constantius
died.

The accession of Julian gave liberty to the sectarians.
Aetius, who had had former relations with the new
emperor, was summoned to court[1]; and Julian, in spite
of his scant sympathy with the "Galileans" of any description, made him a present of a small estate in the island
of Lesbos.   The Anomœan party found itself better off
than the official clergy to whom the support of the government was now lacking.   Eudoxius and Euzoïus, after
having often cursed those tiresome persons, now thought
it prudent to draw closer to them.   Eudoxius would
have wished Euzoïus to reinstate them; Euzoïus that
Eudoxius should do so; they kept on passing from one to
the other this compromising task.   At length the Bishop
of Antioch made up his mind to annul everything that
had been done by the Council of Constantinople against
the Anomœans.   But he was in no hurry to publish his
decision; so little so that Aetius and his followers, growing impatient, decided to organize themselves separately
and to create a schism.   Aetius was ordained bishop; other

[1] Julian, *Ep.* 31.

members of the party also received episcopal consecration, and were sent into the provinces to preside over the adherents of Anomœanism. Eudoxius took no notice. Besides, what hindrance could he have offered? They went so far as to set up a rival to himself, by organizing in Constantinople itself an Anomœan Church, the first bishops of which were Pœmenius and Florentius. Towards Euzoïus they used rather more ceremony: Theophilus, the saint of the party, was sent to Antioch to try to arrange matters with the bishop, in default of which he was to organize against him all the Anomœans that the great city contained.

This fine frenzy was allayed when, at the end of 364, Eudoxius had succeeded in installing himself in the good graces of Valens, and in inducing him to return to the tradition interrupted by the death of Constantius. At Antioch, Euzoïus took up a hostile attitude; he no longer hesitated to call Theophilus a blackamoor, and his disciples emissaries of darkness. Eudoxius himself called them plagues. Aetius returned to his island of Lesbos; Eunomius retired to an estate which he possessed at Chalcedon. They had both renounced the exercise of sacerdotal functions; but they remained none the less the leaders and, as it were, the prophets of the party.

A little later came the usurpation of Procopius.[1] The pretender, at the time (363 to 364) when he was leading the life of an adventurer, had found refuge with Eunomius at Chalcedon. When he had gained possession of power,

---

[1] Procopius, a distant kinsman of Julian, was raised by him to important offices of State, and even, rumour said, chosen as his eventual successor. He appears to have been a pagan, or at least to have posed as such, for the time, to please his cousin. Shortly after the accession of Jovian, he thought it well to conceal himself for fear of being considered as a pretender to the throne, and treated accordingly. After many adventures, he ended by causing himself to be proclaimed emperor at Constantinople (September 28, 365) and secured at the outset some successes, which caused him to be acknowledged in the Asiatic provinces nearest to the Bosphorus. In the spring of 366, Valens gained the mastery over his rival, who was taken prisoner and beheaded on May 27.

several of the friends of Eunomius and Aetius himself
were accused of having sided against his usurpation;
Eunomius intervened and succeeded in clearing them.
But Valens returned, and they had to pay dearly for
this momentary enjoyment of favour. Hardly used by
the reaction, the Anomœan leaders invoked the support
of Eudoxius, who, having no longer any need of them,
treated them with disdain; far from commiserating them,
he told them that they deserved much worse punishments. Aetius, who had retired some time before to
Constantinople, to the company of Florentius, now died:
Eunomius closed his eyes, and his supporters gave him
a magnificent funeral.

As to Eunomius himself, being implicated in a political
case, he was exiled to Mauritania. On his journey
thither, he passed through Mursa in Pannonia, where
Bishop Valens, a former disciple of Arius, took him
under his protection. This protection was so successful
that Eunomius was recalled. But it was not for long.
Eunomius did not know how to keep himself quiet. He
continued to direct and to defend his party, engaging in
an incessant polemic with the orthodox doctors—Didymus,
Apollinaris, Basil, and the two Gregorys. Under Valens,
the prefect Modestus, with whom St Basil also had to deal,
banished him, as a stirrer-up of ecclesiastical disturbances,
to an island in the Archipelago. Under Gratian and
Theodosius, the Eunomians lost the right of holding
assemblies. Their leader was exiled anew to Halmyris
on the Lower Danube, and afterwards to Cæsarea in
Cappadocia, where the remembrance of his conflicts with
St Basil brought upon him so much unpleasantness that
he was forced to retire to Dakora, in a country place. He
was still living in 392, when St Jerome published his
catalogue of ecclesiastical writers. After his death, he
was buried at Tyana. It was in Cappadocia Secunda,
of which this place was the metropolis, that there was
born, in the little town of Verissos, the historian
Philostorgius. His parents were Eunomians. He was
brought up in the doctrines of that sect, and it was from

their point of view that he wrote during the reign of Theodosius II. an ecclesiastical history, of which only some extracts remain. During his youth he had known Eunomius, who made a deep impression upon him. Though afflicted with a slight stammer, and with a face disfigured by a skin disease, the prophet none the less possessed charm and eloquence. Aetius, keen in intellect and quick at repartee, was a master in debate; Eunomius himself was renowned for the lucidity of his exposition.

It is thanks to Philostorgius that we know the history, and even the *historiettes*, of Anomœanism. Notwithstanding the religious reputation enjoyed by some of its leaders, such as Aetius, Eunomius, and Theophilus, this party had never much practical importance. However, as it represented, from the doctrinal point of view, the clearest expression of Arianism, it figured for a very long time in the discourses and writings of controversialists, prone even from those far-off days to try their skill against the dead.

CHAPTER XI

BASIL OF CÆSAREA

State of parties in the east of Asia Minor. The youth of Basil and
of Gregory of Nazianzus. Eustathius, master in asceticism,
afterwards Bishop of Sebaste. Basil, a solitary, afterwards
priest, and Bishop of Cæsarea. The religious policy of Valens.
Death of Athanasius : Peter and Lucius. Valens at Cæsarea.
Basil and Eustathius. Basil negotiates with Rome. His rupture
with Eustathius. Arian intrigues. Dorotheus at Rome. Affairs
at Antioch. Paulinus recognized by Rome. Vitalis. The
heresy of Apollinaris. Eustathius goes over to the Pneumatomachi. Dorotheus returns to Rome. Evolution of the Marcellians. The Goths. Death of the Emperor Valens.

THE ancient provinces of Galatia and Cappadocia, which
under the early empire included the whole of Eastern
Asia Minor, had been carved up under Diocletian. Out
of their mountainous districts and those on the sea-board—
in fact the part known as Pontus—three provinces had
been made, Paphlagonia, the Pontus of Jupiter
(*Diospontus*),[1] and the Pontus of Polemon, their capital
cities being respectively Gangra, Amasia, and Neocæsarea. In the interior, Ancyra continued to be the
Galatian metropolis, and Cæsarea that of Cappadocia ;
but, to the east of Cappadocia, Armenia Minor formed a
special province, of which Sebaste was the capital.[2]

Christianity, since the days of Firmilian and Gregory
Thaumaturgus, had made great progress in these countries.

[1] Later Helenopontus, or Pontus of Amasia.
[2] All these cities have preserved their names, under forms slightly
altered by Turkish pronunciation : Kanghri, Amasia, Niksar,
Angora, Kaïsarié, Sivas.

Yet, as towns there were few, there were not a great number of bishoprics. It is with difficulty that, in an extent of country as large as the Italian peninsula, we can prove or presume the existence of as many as forty episcopal sees. The most important were always those of Cæsarea and Ancyra. As in the third century, the bishops of Upper Asia Minor were always ready to assemble in council, with the co-operation of their colleagues of Syria. We have spoken above of the synods of Ancyra and of Neocæsarea, earlier in date than the great Council of Nicæa. Later on, other councils were held at Gangra, at Ancyra again, at Melitene, Tyana, and Zela.

Arianism did not, so far as we know, make any very notable recruits among this body of bishops. Cappadocia whose hour had come, rather late in the day, to attract attention to itself, produced at that time a great number of ecclesiastical adventurers, who distinguished themselves elsewhere, under the protection of the imperial police: men like Gregory and George, the two anti-popes of Alexandria, and Auxentius of Milan. Asterius, the lecturer in the time of Arius, and Eunomius, the last oracle of the sect, had seen the light in Cappadocia. But these worthies do not seem to have attracted much sympathy in their native country. The men whom election called to the exercise of episcopal functions were of less advanced views. At the time of the Council of Nicæa, the Bishops of Ancyra and Cæsarea, Marcellus and Leontius, showed themselves the determined opponents of Arius. In the Churches of Tyana, Amasia, Neocæsarea, Sebaste, and in general throughout Pontus and Armenia Minor, the same doctrinal standpoint was maintained.[1] After Marcellus of Ancyra, who pushed consubstantialist doctrine too far, they elected Basil, who at first fought in the ranks opposed to St Athanasius, but ended by

---

[1] Athan. *Ep. ad episcopos Aeg. et Libyae*, 8. The testimony of Philostorgius upon the quarters from which Arius is alleged to have met with support at the Council of Nicæa (Migne, *P. G.*, vol. lxv., p. 623), is quite destitute of value.

becoming the leader of a reaction against Arianism, and was persecuted for that reason. His successor, another Athanasius, took the first opportunity to declare his fidelity to the faith of Nicæa, and never wavered in that attitude. At Cæsarea, Bishop Leontius had been replaced by one of his clergy, Hermogenes,[1] the man who had been entrusted at Nicæa with the task of drawing up the famous creed.[2] Dianius, who succeeded him (before 340), was not a man of strong character ; he was orthodox at bottom, but was never able to refuse his signature when it was demanded in the name of the party or of the government. He figures at the head of those "Easterns" who wrote from Antioch an insolent letter to Pope Julius, in 340, and who deposed him at the schismatical Council of Sardica.[3] We do not hear that he put himself forward either for or against Basil of Ancyra, in 358 ; but, two years later, he signed, like so many others, the formula of Ariminum-Constantinople. One of his suffragans, also a very worthy man, Gregory, Bishop of Nazianzus—the father of that Gregory who afterwards made the name of this little place immortal—was guilty of the same weakness.

When, in 355, Julian was staying in Athens, he made the acquaintance there of two young Cappadocians of high distinction, Gregory and Basil, both destined to become shining lights in the Church. The first was the son of the Bishop of Nazianzus, of whom I have just been speaking. His father was a saintly man of an original turn of mind, who had been at first a member of a confraternity of Hypsistarians, or worshippers of Zeus Hypsistos[4] ; he had been converted by the entreaties of

---

[1] Eulalius, of whom Socrates speaks (ii. 43 ; cf. Sozomen, iv. 24), was not Bishop of Cæsarea, but of Sebaste. His name appears among the signatories of the Councils of Nicæa and of Gangra.

[2] Basil, *Ep.* 81.

[3] In this same council there took part the Bishops of Juliopolis in Galatia, of Sinope and Neocæsarea.

[4] On this cult, in which we can recognize elements derived from Jewish Monotheism, see E. Schürer, *Die Juden im Bosporanischen Reiche*, in the Proceedings of the Berlin Academy, vol. xiii. (1897), p. 200, *et seq.* ; and Fr. Cumont, *Hypsistos* (Brussels, 1897).

his wife Nonna, and had been elected bishop very soon after his baptism. At that time, celibacy was not yet obligatory everywhere, even for the bishops. Gregory and Nonna continued to live together, and it was then that their son Gregory was born. The family of Basil came originally from Neocæsarea in Pontus, and had long been Christian. His grandmother Macrina had witnessed the persecution of Diocletian, during which she had fled to the woods with her husband; she had many memories of long ago, and had many things to tell of St Gregory Thaumaturgus. The father, Basil, was an advocate of high repute; the mother, Emmelia, was the daughter of a martyr; one of St Basil's uncles was a bishop at the same time as himself. Like his friend Gregory, the future Bishop of Cæsarea was born in 329. The two young people met first of all in the schools of Cæsarea, and later found themselves together in Athens, where they were united in close friendship.

At that time, a great deal was heard in Asia Minor of an ascetic named Eustathius,[1] who was propagating everywhere the practices, then quite novel, of the monastic life. In his youth he had stayed in Alexandria, and had attended the preaching of Arius[2]; also, and this was the most important fact, he had been initiated into asceticism. On his return to his own country, his father Eulalius, who was bishop at Sebaste,[3] displeased at seeing him parade an extraordinary costume, drove him from his Church. Eustathius then attached himself to Hermogenes, Bishop of Cæsarea, who, having doubts as to his orthodoxy, made him sign a profession of faith. After the death of Hermogenes, Eustathius sought the company of Eusebius of

---

[1] In regard to this personage, see Fr. Loofs, *Eustathius von Sebaste und die Chronologie des Basilius-Briefe* (Halle, 1898) and the article, "Eustathius of Sebaste," in Hauck's *Encyclopädie*. In some places, the author goes a little too far, being led on by his great desire to rehabilitate Eustathius.

[2] Basil, *Ep.* 130, 1; 223, 3; 244, 3; 263, 3; *cf.* Athan. *Hist. Arianorum* 4.

[3] Socrates, ii. 43, and Sozomen, iv. 24, say that Eulalius was Bishop of Cæsarea. See p. 303, note 1.

Nicomedia, with whom he fell out on account of matters of administration. His mode of life and his propaganda of asceticism gave offence to everyone, and raised up enemies against him everywhere. He had already been condemned by a council held at Neocæsarea. Eusebius pursued him before another assembly of bishops which was held at Gangra in Paphlagonia, about 340. We still possess the letter which this council addressed on the subject of Eustathius to the bishops of Armenia Minor. To judge from this document, Eustathius had gone beyond all bounds, and had revived the exaggerated practices, already condemned, of the ancient Encratites. But the subsequent development of his career gives ground for thinking that the council is extravagant in its censures, either because it was ill informed as to the abuses which it condemns or, more probably, because it attributed to Eustathius the excesses of too zealous followers. By dint of discrediting marriage, the innovators had made the faithful believe that there was no possibility of salvation in that state; hence came separations, and then falls. They despised assemblies in church, but held private ones, at which they dispensed special instructions. They had invented extraordinary costumes; the women clothed themselves in these like the men, and cut off their hair; when the slaves adopted this style of dress, their masters were no longer able to secure respect. In the matter of abstinence, they despised the rules of the Church, fasting on Sundays, and eating on fast-days. They dissuaded the faithful from making offerings to the Church, inviting them to assist their own communities instead. Some of them refused to eat meat, and would have no religious communion with married people, especially with married priests; they despised meetings for devotion at the tombs of the martyrs, and proclaimed to the rich that, if they did not rid themselves of all their wealth even to the last stiver, they had no hope of salvation. The council censured in vigorous terms these extravagances and others of the same kind, for they saw in them a criticism of the religious life as it was practised in the Church.

II   U

This attitude of dislike is always the consequence of undertakings such as that of Eustathius. He, no doubt, made some promises of submission ; but he can only have kept them very imperfectly, for he was afterwards condemned as a perjurer by a council at Antioch.

The movement, for all that, did not cease to advance. Eustathius, powerfully assisted in Constantinople by Marathonius, a former official, introduced into the capital the monastic forms of the ascetic life.[1] Marathonius had become deacon to Bishop Macedonius. Eustathius, absorbed in his propaganda, scarcely thought of troubling himself at that time about the theological preferences of the official clergy, or about the war which they were waging against St Athanasius. Athanasius knew him, and did not love him.[2] Years passed away. Finally, about the year 356, Eustathius was elected Bishop at Sebaste, the metropolis of Armenia Minor. It was about this time (357) that Basil returned from Athens to Cappadocia. He had often heard Eustathius spoken of ; perhaps he had already had some communication with him. At this moment he was hesitating between the world and the religious life. It was no doubt by the advice of the Bishop of Sebaste that he undertook a long journey in Egypt, Syria, and Mesopotamia, to visit for himself the most renowned solitaries. Fascinated with this ideal of life, he returned to his own country, and attached himself definitely to the man who was venerated there as the great master of asceticism. Eustathius was, and long remained, for him a mirror of perfection, a being almost divine. His relations and friends, especially his sister Macrina, who was already a religious, and Gregory, his companion in study, also urged him to forsake the world. He found in the valley of the Iris, not far from Neocæsarea, a solitude green and wild, where he took up his abode with several companions. Eustathius came from time to time to see his new disciples, and together they paid a visit to Emmelia, Basil's mother, who was living in a neighbouring town.

[1] *Supra*, p. 295.　　[2] *Ep. ad episcopos Aeg. et Libyae*, 70 ; *Hist. Ar.* 5.

War at this time had broken out in the Eastern episcopate: Eustathius, obliged by his new position as a bishop to take a side, played a very active part in it. In conjunction with Basil of Ancyra and Eleusius of Cyzicus, he led the Homoïousian Right Wing, and contended with the greatest energy against Aetius and his supporters. After a brief success, he saw the opposing party regain its foothold, and he received one of the first attacks. A council, assembled at Melitene in 358, under the influence of Eudoxius, declared him to be deposed from the episcopate, we know not for what reason, but no doubt on some pretext furnished by his ascetical extravagances. A priest of Melitene, Meletius, agreed to succeed him, and was ordained in his place. But the people of Sebaste would have none of it, and Eustathius remained bishop, declaring that, as those who had deposed him were heretics, there was no need for him to pay any attention to their sentences.

A crisis which affected him more severely was that which ended, at the beginning of the year 360, in the condemnation of the *homoïousios*, and the deprivation of its adherents. Like the other leaders of his party Eustathius was forced to submit at the last minute, and to put his signature at the end of the formula of Ariminum; like them, in spite of this sacrifice, he was deposed for other reasons. With him fell Sophronius, Bishop of Pompeïopolis in Paphlagonia, and Helpidius, Bishop of Satala in Armenia Minor, the latter guilty, like the Metropolitan of Sebaste, of having paid no attention to the sentences of Melitene. Eustathius was exiled to Dardania. The young Basil, who had followed him to Constantinople, returned to his own country. He had the grief of seeing the Bishop of Cæsarea, Dianius, for whom he professed a respectful affection, sign like everyone else the confession of Ariminum. Deeply distressed at this exhibition of weakness, he fled to his solitude in Pontus, and only returned to Cæsarea to be present at the last moments of the old bishop, who declared to him that, notwithstanding his signatures, he remained in his heart loyal to the faith

of Nicæa. It was then the year 362; Julian was emperor;
even if he had been well, Dianius could without danger
have confessed himself a Homoïousian. He died, regretted
by his disciple, and in his place there was finally elected,
after disorderly debates, one of the notabilities of the city,
named Eusebius, a man estimable for his uprightness and
piety, but still a catechumen and very little versed in
ecclesiastical affairs. Basil was still only a reader;
Eusebius raised him to the dignity of priest, to the great
satisfaction of everyone, especially of the monks and their
following. It was difficult for a priest so distinguished not
to excite jealousy; his enemies succeeded in stirring up
strife between him and his bishop. The monastic party
was already taking their stand at his back, when he wisely
made up his mind to leave Cæsarea and to take refuge
once more in his beloved solitude of Pontus. However,·
the times were once more beginning to become difficult.
Everywhere there was being published the edict of Valens
against those prelates who had been restored to their sees
in spite of their deposition in the time of Constantius.
This was the case with Eustathius, but not with Eusebius.
·But the emperor and his immediate circle, whether
episcopal or secular, were openly conducting a propaganda
in favour of the confession of Ariminum. Valens, on his
way to Antioch, appeared at Cæsarea. The bishop
recalled Basil, who, aided by his friend Gregory, gave
him energetic support at this delicate crisis. The storm
passed, and peace was preserved. Basil was concerned
in the negotiations of Eustathius with the West. They
went together to see the Bishop of Tarsus, Silvanus, in
order to come to some understanding with regard to the
Council of Lampsacus; Eustathius even wished to take
Basil there with him. He remained at Cæsarea, but on
the return of Eustathius and Silvanus from Rome he
followed his bishop to the Council of Tyana, at which the
letters of Pope Liberius were presented.

Several years passed away, during which Basil, who
from this time had enjoyed the confidence of Eusebius,
governed in his name the Church of Cæsarea. At last, in

370, the bishop died, and Basil, after numerous oppositions, was elected in his place. The aged Bishop of Nazianzus and Eusebius of Samosata figured among his consecrators.

It was impossible to make a better choice. Basil had everything in his favour: personal holiness, which was widely recognized, a highly cultivated mind, eloquence, Christian knowledge, and political ability. From the point of view of orthodoxy, he was absolutely irreproachable, never having been compromised by parties or signatures. He represented the old and simple faith of Pontus, transmitted and practised in the piety of his home. His ordination was perfectly regular. In his episcopal house at Alexandria, the illustrious Athanasius leapt for joy at the news; at the first opportunity he was heard to give thanks to heaven for having given to Cappadocia such a bishop as should be desired everywhere, a true servant of God. The old champion of the faith could now leave this world; he had someone to whom to hand on the torch.

If the man himself was of the highest order, the position, by reason of the difficulties which it presented, was worthy of him. Valens was about to return to Cæsarea. In 365, he had been suddenly called away from it by the rival claims of Procopius; when this business was ended, he had been obliged to carry on a war for three or four years on the Lower Danube. Now, his hands were free, as regarded the pretenders and the Goths; he intended to settle at Antioch. Valens was a man, masterful, brutal, and dogged. In the conflict between various religious parties, he had made up his mind from the first year of his reign; he remained to the end faithful to this attitude, and resolutely supported Eudoxius, Euzoïus, and their followers. The see of Constantinople became vacant in 370, about the same time as that of Cæsarea; he summoned to it the Bishop of Berea, in Thrace, Demophilus, the man who had been at one time the evil angel of Pope Liberius. This choice did not pass without opposition. When the name of Demophilus was pronounced in the presence of the faithful of the capital, in place of the usual acclamation "Worthy," there were heard many voices which cried "Unworthy!" Those who thus protested were punished with great severity. Some of them having decided to go to Nicomedia and to appeal to the emperor in person, he answered them by a sentence of exile. Eighty of them were put on board a ship; then, when they were out at sea, the crew set fire to the vessel and escaped in the boats.

Such an execution might well excite alarm in the episcopate of Asia Minor. The Goths were subdued; it was now the turn of the bishops; it was evident that they might expect harsh treatment. The method of procedure, as we can see from a large number of instances, was very simple. The prelates were presented, if they had not already signed it, with the formulary of Ariminum-Constantinople, and steps were taken to make sure that they accepted communion with the leaders of the party. In case of refusal, the churches were taken from the recalcitrant clergy; they lost all their privileges, especially with regard to municipal service; the monks were sent to the barracks. If there were disturbances, or if there were any reason to apprehend these, the bishops and the clergy were deported to distant provinces. Local opposition was broken down by force. The result was deplorable scenes, churches attacked and profaned, bloodshed, and sentences of extreme severity.

This *régime* was applied everywhere, not however at the same time. In Egypt, they waited for the death of Athanasius (May 2, 373). The clergy and faithful of Alexandria had made haste to elect in his place his brother Peter,[1] whom he had marked out as his successor. But the government refused to ratify this choice: they meant to secure the induction of Lucius, the leader of the Arians of Alexandria. To this end, the police, under the command of the prefect Palladius, and reinforced by the vilest of the rabble, once more invaded the Church of

---

[1] Peter was forthwith recognized by St Basil (*Ep.* 133) and by Pope Damasus.

Theonas. The consecrated virgins were insulted, assassinated, violated, and carried naked through the city. A
young man, rouged and dressed as a woman, was hoisted
on to the altar, where he performed suggestive dances,
while another youth, seated stark naked upon the throne
of Athanasius, gave utterance from it to obscene homilies.
Thus profaned, the venerable basilica welcomed the
nominee of Valens. Lucius made his entry into it,
escorted by the Count of the Largesses, Magnus, and
the aged Euzoïus. The latter had come post haste from
Antioch to be guilty of this final outrage against the
Church of Alexandria; it was thus that he took his
revenge for the sentence by which, fifty years before,
Bishop Alexander had expelled him in company with
Arius. On the following days, formal proceedings were
taken against the clergy. Some twenty priests and
deacons, several of whom were over eighty, were thrown
into prison, and then despatched by sea to Syria, where
they were confined in the pagan town of Heliopolis
(Baalbek). The populace protested, more especially the
monks; the most enthusiastic of these, to the number of
twenty-three, were arrested and sent to the mines of
Phæno and of Proconnesus. Amongst those who went
to Phæno was a Roman deacon, an envoy from Pope
Damasus to congratulate Peter on the occasion of his
accession.

These severities extended throughout the whole of
Egypt. Magnus, acting as imperial commissioner, went
from one bishopric to another to compel the recognition
of the official patriarch, meting out ill-usage with a
generous hand to anyone who offered resistance. Eleven
bishops were removed from their sees and despatched to
Palestine, to Diocæsarea, a town of Galilee, where there were
only Jews. Some of those who protested, having travelled
to Antioch to appeal to the emperor, received a decree
of exile which banished them to Neocæsarea, far away
in Pontus. Bishop Peter, a despairing witness of these
horrors, did not long succeed in remaining concealed in
Egypt; he made up his mind to take refuge in Rome,

where he waited in the society of Pope Damasus for the return of happier days. So had his brother Athanasius acted, at the time of Gregory's usurpation (339); Peter initiated him further by bringing to the knowledge of the Catholic episcopate the violent measures which had compelled him to leave his see of Alexandria.[1]

With regard to other countries we have fewer details; but the Catholics were everywhere treated with the same severity. Meletius, for the third time,[2] was driven from Antioch. Flavian and Diodore, now ordained priests, undertook the government of his Church. The places of worship had been handed over to Euzoïus and his clergy. The Catholics, hunted from one cover to another, ended by meeting in the open country, to which they owed the name given to them of "countrymen" (*Campenses*). Their courage was sustained by the exhortations of their brave leaders and of several celebrated monks, who hastened from the neighbouring deserts to join in the resistance. Pelagius of Laodicea, Eusebius of Samosata, Barses of Edessa, Abraham of Batna, and others besides were exiled together with numbers of the inferior clergy. The desolation was universal.

Nevertheless there were but few complaints from Western Asia Minor, or from Bithynia. In these countries the "Macedonians" held the upper hand; we do not know what was their attitude, nor if they were persecuted like the others.[3] In Galatia and in Paphlagonia the resistance does not seem to have been strong. The Bishop of Gangra, Basilides, was an Arian; Athanasius of Ancyra who died about this time (371) was provided with a successor agreeable to the government. Thence-

[1] See the letter preserved to a large extent in Theodoret, *H. E.* iv. 19; *cf.* Socrates, iv. 22. Upon these events, see Rufinus, ii. 3, 4; *cf.* Socrates, iv. 20-24; Sozomen, vi. 19, 20.

[2] His first exile was that in the time of Constantius (361); the second must doubtless have been caused by the edict of 365. It lasted but a short time, for the story of St John Chrysostom presupposes the presence of Meletius at Antioch from 367 to 370.

[3] See, however, the epitaph of Macedonius of Apollonias cited above, p. 292, note 1.

forward the bonds of communion were broken between
Galatia and Cappadocia. In the latter country Basil,
taken in hand first by the prefect Modestus, and then
by the emperor in person, opposed them with admirable
determination during the winter of 371-372. Tempering
his firmness with prudence,[1] strong in his personal dignity,
his unsullied character and his popularity, he succeeded
in preserving the government of his Church. Valens did
not impose upon him either formulas or communion with
bishops who were suspected. He confined himself to
being present in person at the religious services presided
over by the Archbishop of Cæsarea. He deemed no
doubt that such a bishop would have been very difficult
either to depose or to replace. But whatever his reason
may have been, an exception was made for Basil[2]; he
was allowed to live at Cæsarea, as Athanasius had been
allowed to die at Alexandria. He even received an
official commission in 372 to set in order the religious
affairs of the kingdom of Armenia and to ordain bishops
there. It also appears that, in the early days at least,
they left in peace the other bishops of Cappadocia, those
of Armenia Minor and of the Pontic provinces. We do
not find, for example, that they disturbed Eustathius
of Sebaste at that time, who was most certainly not in
line with the council of 360; nor the bishops of Neocæsarea and Nicopolis who were still less so.

In the spring of 372 Valens set out for Antioch,
and the people of Cæsarea breathed more freely. It
was not only on account of religion that they were
harassed. The government of Valens was engaged at
this time in altering the boundaries of the provinces.
Cappadocia, at the expense of which they had already

---

[1] It appears that his refusal was rather temporizing than cate-
gorical. In 375, in a letter to the *Vicarius* Demosthenes (*Ep.* 255),
he begs him not to force a meeting between himself and bishops,
with whom "we are *not yet* (οὔπω) in agreement on ecclesiastical
questions." The reference is to Arian bishops who accepted the
confession of Ariminum.

[2] Basil was treated by Valens very much as Auxentius had been
treated by Valentinian.

created the province of Armenia Minor and those of
Pontus, was now to be divided yet again. A Cappadocia
Secunda was formed, comprising the western and
southern part of the ancient province, with the
cities of Tyana, Colonia (Archelaïs), Cybistra, Fausti-
nopolis and, to the north of the Halys, the districts of
Mokissos and of Doara. To this same division belonged
also the postal stations of Sasima, Nazianzus,[1] and
Parnassos, the last two of which already possessed
bishoprics. Another postal station, Podandos, situated
in the middle of the Taurus, at the opening of the
Cilician Gates, remained outside the new province. It
was decided to create a new city there, to which were
to be attached a certain number of the municipal magistrates of Cæsarea. But these persons, not at all pleased
at going to live in such an out-of-the-way place, had
recourse to the influence of their bishop, who succeeded in
causing the proposal to be withdrawn. Podandos, therefore,
always remained a district or region (ρεγεών) belonging to
Cappadocia Prima.

Basil might have intervened in this last business,
which directly affected his own flock; but he had
evidently no valid reason to oppose to the division of
the province, and so refrained.[2] Tyana thus became
a civil metropolis. Its bishop, Anthimus, lost no time
in availing himself, in the ecclesiastical sphere, of the
consequences of this administrative separation: he set
up to be the metropolitan, the ecclesiastical superior of
the bishops included in the new civil jurisdiction.
Basil set himself in opposition. Hence arose a quarrel,
in which the Metropolitan of Cæsarea defended himself
to the best of his ability, especially by organizing new

[1] Nazianzus had perhaps possessed, under the name of Diocæsarea,
a municipal organization.

[2] It has often been said that this dismemberment of Cappadocia
was a blow aimed at Basil, whose sphere of influence it was sought
in this way to limit. But the influence of such a man could not be
confined to the greater or less extent of his metropolitical jurisdiction.
The government had more direct and more effectual ways of being
disagreeable to him.

bishoprics. Nazianzus remained faithful to him; he installed his brother Gregory at Nyssa, a little place to the west of Cæsarea; in the south he wished to have a bishopric at Sasima, on the road to Cilicia, and forced his friend Gregory to accept that title. The Church of Cæsarea possessed considerable property in the Taurus, the natural products of which had to pass through the new province in order to reach Cæsarea. Anthimus intercepted these convoys. It was in vain that Gregory protested that he had no wish to interfere in the matter, or to make war upon Anthimus in defence of Basil's chickens and mules: the Bishop of Cæsarea was determined, and "laid hands upon" his unwilling friend. But he could not induce him to fulfil his episcopal duties at Sasima. Gregory never celebrated divine service there, nor ordained a single clerk. He had a horror of Sasima. It was a desolate place, only a few houses round a posting station. There was no water, no vegetation: nothing but dust, and the never-ceasing noise of passing carts.[1] As to inhabitants, there were only vagabonds, strangers, or executioners with their victims who could be heard groaning and clanking their chains. This melancholy bishopric was naturally the cause of many troubles to the unhappy Gregory.

As for Basil, at first he met with some unpleasant opposition among the bishops of Cappadocia, but in the long run he triumphed over this. At Cæsarea his position was very strong. It became still more so when he had endowed that great city with an enormous establishment for relief, the buildings of which formed in the suburbs practically a new town; it was known as Basilias. The Emperor Valens had assisted him in its construction by granting him demesne lands.

Basil had kept on very good terms with Eustathius, his neighbour at Sebaste. Eustathius himself had also founded near his episcopal city, a kind of "grand hospice," which served as a model for the Basilias at Cæsarea. At the beginning of his episcopate, he had

---

[1] Greg. Naz., *Carm. de vita sua*, vv. 439-446.

entrusted the charge of it to a certain Aerius;[1] one of his companions in the ascetic life, who, it was commonly said, bore a grudge against Eustathius because he had been preferred before himself for the office of bishop. Their relations, far from improving, became so greatly embittered that one fine day Aerius finally threw up his duties and set himself to uttering abuse against Eustathius, accusing him of avarice, and assailing him for the most legitimate acts of his administration. Aerius had supporters; they joined him in creating a schism, and followed him to the meetings which he held in the caves of the neighbourhood. He taught them that priests were not inferior to bishops, that the Paschal Feast (Easter) was only an old remnant of Judaism, that there ought to be no fixed times for fasting, and that it was useless to pray for the dead.

The Aerians must have been few in number, for at a time and in a country where many pens were active, St Epiphanius is the only author who mentions them, lamenting their errors, it is true, but well pleased in his heart of hearts at having, thanks to them, one item more for his collection of heresies. In his estimation, undoubtedly too severe, Aerius and Eustathius were both of them Arians, Aerius openly, Eustathius with some measure of circumspection. It is certain that Eustathius was regarded with sufficient disfavour not only by the old Nicenes, such as Athanasius, Epiphanius, and Paulinus, but by the neo-orthodox themselves. The latter, with Meletius at their head, had accepted all Athanasius' conditions, i.e., not only the Creed of Nicæa, but also an explicit profession of the absolute Divinity of the Holy Spirit. Eustathius, always fond of compromise, did not say that the Holy Spirit was a created being, but neither did he affirm that He was God. It is possible that such a reserve appeared to him necessary. I have already said that it was observed by many others, and that Basil himself, although holding a very definite doctrine on this point, was accustomed to a certain economy in presenting it to his flock.

[1] In regard to Aerius see Epiphanius, *Haer.* 74.

This similarity of attitude was calculated to strengthen, in the eyes of the colleagues of the Bishop of Cæsarea, the bad impression already produced by his great friendship for his neighbour at Sebaste. Eustathius, who looked upon Basil as his disciple, had lent him several of his monks to assist him in the organization of his projects. Through these agents, Sebaste kept a watchful eye upon Cæsarea. Eustathius' monks soon allowed themselves to criticize Basil; this gave rise to various cases of friction, with reports more or less truthful.[1] The final result was a situation of considerable difficulty, which became more and more strained and, as we shall see, ended in a rupture between the two friends.

The religious policy of the Emperor Valens was a melancholy contrast to that of his brother Valentinian.[2] Many people in the East might well say that they lived there under an evil star. Even in the now far-off times of the Great Persecution, the West had scarcely had two years of suffering; in some countries, persecution had hardly touched them at all; whilst the East, from Diocletian to Galerius, from Galerius to Maximin, had had ten years of misery. Licinius and Julian had only shown their severity in the East. The Western bishops had only had to endure Constantius in the last years of his reign. And from the time of Julian's accession no one any longer thought of molesting them. Was it not natural that, being thus favoured by Providence, the Westerns should set themselves to work to rescue from affliction their brethren in

---

[1] *Ep.* 119.

[2] We must not judge of this, however, from the letter reproduced by Theodoret, *H. E.* iv. 7, a letter plainly apocryphal as well as the synodal epistle (iv. 8), which follows it. The imperial letter, headed with the names of the Emperors Valentinian, Valens, and Gratian, is addressed to the Pneumatomachi of Asia, and preaches to them the Trinity consubstantial in three hypostases, with a proclamation of anathema, which is scarcely in the imperial style. It incites the subjects of Valens to despise the commands of their sovereign, whom the forger apparently looks upon as the special protector of the heresy against the Holy Spirit. It is strange that Tillemont should have accepted such incongruities.

the East? When persecuted by Constantius, Athanasius had found among them refuge and support. They had interested in his cause their own Emperor Constans. Was there not ground for hope, now that Constantius was living again in Valens, that Valentinian too might intervene effectually with his brother? He would certainly do so, if the Western episcopate made energetic representations on behalf of the persecuted. And they certainly owed it to them to do so, for after all the orthodox and the well disposed had done their duty at Seleucia, and, if they did yield at Constantinople, it was because the other side had been able to urge upon them the appalling defection at Ariminum. In the West, they had reversed their opinions the moment a respite came, and in this new attitude perseverance was easy. It was upon the East that the error at Ariminum was pressing; and it was pressing severely.

Full of such thoughts as these, Basil, from the beginning of his episcopate, took measures to excite the Western Church to interest herself in the sufferings of her sister in the East. The best intermediary for such negotiations was plainly the Bishop of Alexandria. Athanasius does not appear to have had very friendly relations with Pope Liberius during the Pope's last years.[1] He found himself on better terms with the new Pope, Damasus, from whom in 371 he demanded the condemnation not only of Ursacius and Valens, but also of Auxentius, Bishop of Milan, who of all the adherents of Ariminum stood highest in the favour of the Emperor Valentinian. Basil wrote to Athanasius,[2] begging him to stir up the West in favour of an improvement of the general state of things, and to bring about, as he alone could do, the union of the orthodox at Antioch. Antioch was, in his eyes, the Mother-Church of the East.[3] Universal reconciliation

---

[1] If they had been on good terms, Liberius would not have given so warm a welcome to the envoys of the Council of Lampsacus. Damasus showed himself far more circumspect in his dealings with the Easterns.   [2] *Ep.* 66.

[3] Even of the whole world, if one were to press too closely one of his expressions: Τί δ' ἂν γένοιτο ταῖς κατὰ τὴν οἰκουμένην ἐκκλησίαις τῆς

depended upon its internal unity, which had been gravely
compromised by the schism between Paulinus and Meletius.

The reply of Athanasius was conveyed by one of his
priests. It encouraged Basil to decide definitely upon
his course. He took counsel with Meletius; a Meletian
deacon of Antioch, Dorotheus, was chosen to go to Rome.[1]
He was the bearer of a letter,[2] couched in general terms,
in which the Romans were reminded of their duties
with regard to the Churches of the East, assisted in bygone days by Pope Dionysius.[3] What they asked of
them at the present was the despatch of orthodox and
peaceable persons, capable of restoring the concord which
had been disturbed. Dorotheus was commended to the
Bishop of Alexandria,[4] to whom Basil confided his desires.
The Westerns were to send all the documents relating to
the steps they had themselves taken since Ariminum, to
condemn Marcellus, and to settle the difficulty at Antioch.
Up to the present, they had only condemned Arius; this
they continued to do on every occasion; but of Marcellus
they said nothing. As to Antioch, it must be understood
that the only term of reconciliation admissible was the
recognition of Meletius.

In the meantime, Athanasius was entreated to grant
to the Eastern bishops the privilege of communion with
himself.[5] To make quite sure of not compromising him,
he was to send his letters of communion to Basil, who
would only deliver them to the right persons.

But all this seemed to have remained fruitless.
Dorotheus, on arriving at Alexandria, was dissuaded from
embarking for Italy. The condemnation of Marcellus
would have been, for the Westerns, a formal revocation
of their previous judgment.[6] As to recognizing Meletius,

Ἀντιοχείας ἐπικαιρώτερον; the context shows that he was speaking
especially of the East.

[1] *Ep.* 68.   [2] *Ep.* 70.   [3] *Cf.* Vol. I. p. 311.
[4] *Ep.* 69, 67.   [5] *Ep.* 82.

[6] Basil is fully conscious of this, when he says (*Ep.* 69, 2) that
the heresy of Marcellus is proved by his books; but it was after
having taken cognizance of these books that the Councils of Rome
and Sardica had reinstated him.

they might as well not recognize Athanasius, who, it was well known in Rome, openly lent his support to Paulinus.

However, Athanasius thought it possible to bring about intercourse between Rome and Basil. A deacon of Milan, evidently unattached, for he was not in the service of Auxentius, landed at Alexandria, bearing a synodal letter in which Damasus, at the head of ninety-two bishops, notified to Athanasius the condemnation of Auxentius and of the Council of Ariminum. Sabinus, as the deacon was called, was sent on to Cæsarea with his document. It was not calculated to please Basil; for it said that the Father, the Son, and the Holy Spirit are all of one sole Divinity, one sole virtue, one sole image, one sole *substance*. But the word *substance* in Latin is equivalent to *hypostasis* in Greek. The Bishop of Cæsarea could not possibly admit this statement except by a liberal interpretation. But Basil knew that Latin was a comparatively poor language, and in particular that the term *essence* (οὐσία) was lacking in it. Instead of raising objections, he took time by the forelock, and gave Sabinus a packet of letters,[1] addressed to the Westerns in general, to Valerian of Aquileia, and to the Bishops of Italy and of Gaul. The last letter was in the name of Meletius, Eusebius of Samosata, Basil, Gregory of Nazianzus (the father), Anthimus of Tyana, Pelagius of Laodicea, Eustathius of Sebaste, Theodotus of Nicopolis, and others, thirty-two Eastern prelates in all. They had taken great care, this time, to avoid awkward refinements of expression, and to confine themselves to invoking the compassion of their Western colleagues, simply asking them to send some persons authorized to investigate the position and to bring about peace.

Basil did not fail to urge Meletius to adopt a respectful attitude towards Athanasius; he would have liked Meletius also to despatch an envoy to the West[2]; but Meletius sent no one.

Sabinus set out once more in the spring of 372. A year, at least, passed away, and no news came from the

---

[1] *Ep.* 90, 91, 92.   [2] *Ep.* 89.

Western Church.   At last, in the summer of the following
year (373), they saw the arrival from Italy of a priest
of Antioch, Evagrius, who, eleven years earlier, had
followed to Italy the celebrated confessor, Eusebius of
Vercellæ.   After the latter's death, Evagrius was returning
to his own country.   He brought back with him from Rome
a formula for signature, in which not a single word might
be changed ; and also the letters which had been entrusted
the year before to Sabinus : they had not given satisfaction.   These proceedings, we must admit, were scarcely
friendly.   They were not softened by a demand that the
Eastern prelates should themselves repair to Rome,[1] in
order that there might be some reason for making them a
return visit.

Basil was offended ; from that time forward he had
only a poor opinion of the Westerns, and their chief,
Pope Damasus, impressed him as a man of haughty and
merciless temper.   And moreover, the death of Athanasius
had just deprived him of his best base of operations.
Alexandria was in the hands of the Arians, and the
episcopate of Egypt was a prey to the most cruel
persecution.   The negotiations with the West were
broken off.   And, to crown all, Evagrius, on his arrival at
Antioch, refused to ally himself with the Meletians, and
entered into communion with Paulinus.[2]

It was at this moment that there took place at last the
complete rupture between Basil and Eustathius.

Eustathius, apart from Basil, had few friends.   One
party detested him on account of his monks, another
because of his doctrine.   It was impossible to get him to
take a side in the dispute about the Holy Spirit ; notwithstanding his reticences, it was seen that he inclined to
the opinion adverse to His absolute Divinity.   In the
provinces of Asia, the Hellespont, and Bithynia, he would
have been in agreement with the other bishops.   In the
heart of Pontus, however, the loudest voices were in favour
of the opposite doctrine, and some who would not, perhaps,
of themselves have defended the Holy Spirit with so

---

[1] *Ep.* 138, 2.   *Cf.* 140, 156.   [2] *Ep.* 156.

much vigour, ranged themselves on His side in order
not to be on the side of Eustathius. Basil, to whom this
dangerous friendship caused every day fresh anxieties,
made up his mind to put an end to it, and to induce
Eustathius to explain himself clearly. In the spring of
372 he repaired to Sebaste and, after prolonged conferences, persuaded his old master to embrace his own
opinions. He proposed to continue his journey and to
visit Theodotus, Bishop of Nicopolis, the declared
opponent of Eustathius, in order to arrange with him
and Meletius, who happened to be in that neighbourhood,
a formula which should be signed by the Bishop of Sebaste.
But, from information which reached him, he had reason
to fear that Theodotus, disturbed by the conference at
Sebaste, would give him an unfavourable reception. He
therefore returned home, only to resume the same journey
a few weeks later, the emperor having sent him on a
mission in Armenia Major. For the business of this
mission Basil needed the co-operation of Theodotus. He
therefore had an interview with him, at the country house
to which Meletius had retired ; they succeeded in coming
to a temporary understanding in the matter of Eustathius.
But Theodotus, after he had returned home, changed his
opinion completely ; and when Basil came to conduct him
to Armenia Major, he would not even admit him into his
church.

The mission to Armenia failed on that account. But
Basil and Theodotus ended by being reconciled ; they
even came to an agreement as to the formula [1] which was
to be presented to Eustathius, and the latter consented to
sign it.

One might think that everything was accomplished,
and that nothing remained but to shake hands. A
meeting-place was appointed : Eustathius was to be there
with Basil and his friends. They waited for him in vain.
His companions had turned him back ; it is quite possible,
too, that Basil's friendship for Meletius, his former rival,
may have seemed to him inordinate ; one fact is certain,

[1] *Ep.* 125.

that thenceforward he entertained a deadly hatred for his former disciple. On his return from a journey in Cilicia which he made at this time, he wrote to Basil, declaring that he renounced all communion with him.

The pretext was a letter from Basil to Apollinaris, a letter twenty years old, which contained no question of dogma whatever. Apollinaris and Basil were still laymen at the time of this correspondence. No matter : Basil had written to Apollinaris ; therefore, he was an Apollinarian, a heretic. Another letter, soon spread broadcast throughout the whole of Asia Minor, denounced Basil as an intriguer ; it painted in the blackest colours the part he had played in the matter of the signature. Thus began a deplorable controversy, in the course of which Basil and Eustathius exchanged the bitterest accusations. Basil was treated as a Sabellian, on account of his relations with Apollinaris. There was even circulated under his name a document in which his orthodoxy, on this head, was considerably compromised.[1] Basil, on his side, revived the old story of the relations of Eustathius with Arius, and recalled that he had been the master of Aetius ; as if anyone could be responsible for his masters or for his disciples.

The Arian party profited by this quarrel. From the outset Eustathius had found in the Cilician episcopate supporters whose orthodoxy was doubtful. In the following year (374) the Bishop of Samosata, Eusebius, the friend and adviser of Basil, was exiled to Thrace. Shortly afterwards, the *Vicarius* of Pontus, one Demosthenes, who did not love Basil, and with reason,[2] undertook a campaign against the orthodox Churches of Cappadocia and Armenia Minor. There was held in Galatia, towards the end of the year, a council of official bishops, under the direction of Euhippius, one of the influential members

---

[1] *Ep.* 129. The complete text was published at Rome, in 1796, by L. Sebastiani, *Epistola ad Apollinarem Laodicenum celeberrima,* etc., and reproduced by Loofs, *Eustathius von Sebastia,* p. 72.

[2] At the time of Valens' visit to Cæsarea, Demosthenes was still only *chef* of the imperial kitchens. As he made a show of meddling in the affairs of the Church, Basil had sent him back to his pots and pans. This was the cause of much talk at Cæsarea.

of the synod of 360. The Bishop of Parnassos, Hypsis, the nearest at hand, was deposed, and replaced by Ecdicius, a safe man. Gregory, Bishop of Nyssa, Basil's brother, being accused by a private individual, was summoned to appear and was brought under escort; but he escaped on the way. Demosthenes next visited Cæsarea, where he sentenced the clergy to municipal service; then he went to Sebaste, and did the same to those who supported Basil against Eustathius. Finally, he called together at Nyssa a council of bishops of Galatia and Pontus, who deposed Gregory and appointed his successor. The same proceeding was carried out at Doara.

Just at this time, Theodotus, Bishop of Nicopolis, died. The official council transferred itself to Sebaste: Eustathius, who had already had at Ancyra itself some relations with these prelates, now fraternized openly with them. From Sebaste, they pushed on to Nicopolis. There, with Basil's approbation, the Bishop of Satala had already installed his colleague of Colonia, Euphronius[1]; Eustathius had another candidate, a priest called Fronto. Euphronius was sent back to Colonia, and Fronto was put in possession of the churches; those who objected were evicted and had to hold their meetings in the open country, as the Meletians were wont to do at Antioch.[2]

It was while under the impression of these melancholy occurrences that Basil wrote a letter[3] to the bishops of Italy and of Gaul. After the reception given to his correspondence, he was scarcely disposed to resume negotiations with Rome. Nevertheless, in the preceding year (374)[4] he had assisted with his recommendation a

---

[1] Nicopolis, Satala, and Colonia formed part of the province of Armenia Minor, of which Eustathius was metropolitan.

[2] *Epp.* 225, 237-240, 244, 251.   [3] *Ep.* 243.

[4] The date is given by *Epp.* 120 and 121, which show us Sanctissimus as in Armenia Minor, at the time when Anthimus, Bishop of Tyana, had just ordained Faustus, τὸν συνόντα τῷ Πάπᾳ. This Papas is none other than the Armenian King Pap, called Para in Ammianus Marcellinus (xxx. 1), who was assassinated in 374. The

certain priest Sanctissimus, who was very well informed
as to the state of feeling in the West, and was travelling
through Armenia Minor and Syria,[1] collecting signatures.
Basil gave him his patronage.   When he had finished his
round, he set out for Italy (375), accompanied by
Dorotheus, now promoted to the priesthood.   They
carried with them, fortified by the signatures collected
by Sanctissimus, the formula which Evagrius had brought
over in 373 and Basil's letter.

The result was not that which was desired.   No one
came from the West; however, Dorotheus brought back
a letter[2] in which his zeal was acknowledged, and it was
stated that a strong effort had been made to assist him.
So far as doctrine was concerned, the letter condemned
the errors of Marcellus and of Apollinaris, but without
mentioning them by name.   The term *una substantia* was
no longer employed; for it was substituted that of *una
usia*, in Greek, since Latin did not possess the equivalent
of this term.[3]   Attention was also called to the fact that
the canonical rules as to the ordination of bishops and
clergy (*sacerdotum vel clericorum*) must be observed, and
that those who failed to do so could not be admitted
easily to communion.   This seems clearly aimed at
Meletius.

To show this intention more plainly, a letter was
written to Paulinus, and he, when he received it, hastened
to make a boast of it.[4]   Peter, the new Bishop of
Alexandria, was installed in Rome; and although he,

fact that Faustus "was with Pap," gives reason for thinking that he
had followed that prince in his journey to Cilicia, and that he was
living with him at Tarsus.   Sanctissimus then set out for Armenia
Minor, where he made a long stay with Meletius.   He did not go
to Syria until the following year.   I do not think that this chronological *datum* has been made use of previously.

[1] *Epp.* 120, 121, 132, 253-256.

[2] Constant, *Ep. Rom. Pontif.*, p. 495 : "Ea gratia."

[3] Basil (*Ep.* 214, 4) mentions this change.   Henceforward, the
Western Church will be found making the distinction between *usia*
and *hypostasis*.

[4] *Epp.* 214, 216.

personally, was on good terms with Basil,[1] he in no wise shared Basil's sympathies with Meletius.

The letter[2] received by Paulinus was, I think, brought to him by Vitalis, a priest of Antioch, who down to that time had been one of Meletius' clergy, but who had now decided to forsake him, because his ideas as to the Incarnation were not well received in that quarter Vitalis was an adherent of Apollinaris. I have explained above what constituted the peculiar doctrine of that learned man. Since the time of the Council of Alexandria (362), the opposition between the two opinions represented by Apollinaris and by Diodore had not ceased to accentuate itself.

In the Church of Meletius, Apollinarianism was energetically repudiated. Apollinaris, although bishop at Laodicea, kept school for all that at Antioch. Among his hearers he had had in the course of the preceding years a Latin monk of considerable scholarship, named Jerome, who, after having studied in the schools at Rome and cultivated asceticism with the clergy of Aquileia, had made up his mind to make trial of the hermit's life in the deserts of the East. But before burying himself there he stayed some time at Antioch, where he initiated himself in exegesis under the guidance of Apollinaris while avoiding his theological views. He had not thought it his duty to take a side between the two rival churches, and had confined himself in the matter of ecclesiastical communion to that of the Egyptian confessors, exiled to Syria for the Catholic Faith. At Rome also there had been a long hesitation between Meletius and Paulinus; but it was inevitable that the Alexandrian connections of the latter should turn the scale in his favour. This actually happened in the same year, 375. Through "his son" Vitalis, Pope Damasus had written officially to Paulinus, giving him power to deal with questions of communion. Damasus was badly informed; he did not know at this time that Vitalis was on the side of Apollinaris.

---

[1] *Epp.* 133, 266.   [2] A lost letter, mentioned in Jaffé, 235.

Pieces of information reached him, perhaps through Dorotheus; and he changed his mind. While Paulinus was boasting at Antioch that he had been recognized by Rome, new messengers were on their way to him; one, to warn him that difficulties had supervened[1]; the other,[2] to give him in relation to Vitalis more complete instructions. Vitalis and his followers must only be admitted into communion after an explicit repudiation of the doctrine according to which Christ had not been a perfect Man—the Divine Word having taken the place in Him of the intelligent soul (*sensus*, νοῦς). Apollinaris was not mentioned by name. Rome and Alexandria still retained some feelings of respect for the illustrious theologian.[3] The affair of Vitalis brought matters to a crisis. The Meletians already considered Apollinaris and Vitalis as heretics; after the letter of Damasus it was impossible for Paulinus to receive them into his

---

[1] *Per Petronium presbyterum*, Jaffé, 235.

[2] Jaffé, 235, but of course without the anathemas, and only as far as the words *in suscipiendo tribuat exemplum.* Following this letter, certain collections of canons (see Maassen, *Quellen*, vol. i., p. 232 *et seq.*) give a document, also addressed to Paulinus of Antioch: *Post concilium Nicaenum.* Other collections place it after the Council of Nicæa; Theodoret (*H. E.* v. 11) gives it by itself, translated into Greek. This document contains two series of anathemas; the first mentions by name Sabellius, Arius, Eunomius, the Macedonians, and Photinus. Without naming Eustathius or Apollinaris or Marcellus, it proscribes their principal errors, and concludes with a censure of those who migrate from one Church to another; it is no doubt Meletius who is aimed at. The second part of the document: *Si quis non dixerit*, etc., has in view neither Marcellus nor Apollinaris; it is concerned almost entirely with the Holy Spirit. I think that we have here before us two documents of different date which have been joined together later, without any regard to the chronological order. The second is really earlier than the first. It might well go back to the time (about 371) when St Athanasius wrote his letter to Epictetus. The errors with regard to the Incarnation which are mentioned in it are more closely akin to those that he refutes in that letter than to Apollinarianism properly so-called.

[3] We must remember that Apollinaris belonged to the "Little Church," and was the rival of Pelagius at Laodicea, as Paulinus was of Meletius at Antioch.

Church. They founded another Church, and Vitalis himself became its bishop.

While these things were happening at Antioch, Eustathius, isolated in his own country where his suspicious dealings with the official bishops had still further deprived him of sympathizers, conceived the idea of making overtures to his old friends, the "Macedonians." This party held in 376 a council at Cyzicus; Eustathius went to it. At this meeting a new confession of faith was adopted, in which the *homoousios* was repudiated afresh and replaced by the *homoïousios*; the Holy Spirit was also placed by it in the number of created beings. Eustathius signed this formula, and thus defined his attitude by ranking himself among the Pneumatomachi.

From Basil's point of view, these events were well suited to enlighten the Westerns as to the worth of the persons who were sheltering themselves in the East under their patronage. Eustathius had been received at Rome by the previous Pope; he had bragged of it for a very long time. Apollinaris and Paulinus, the heads of the Little Church, were *protégés* of Rome; so was Vitalis. No party was untarnished save Meletius and his followers, the very persons with whom the Romans would have nothing to do. Advantage was taken of this position of affairs to try a new course of action. In the spring of 377 Dorotheus and another priest, perhaps Sanctissimus again, set out for Rome with a letter addressed "to the Westerns," in the name of the Easterns collectively.[1] This time things were stated exactly. The Romans were informed that it was no longer the Arians who needed to be repudiated; their excesses were rendering them more odious than ever. Other enemies were threatening the Church, enemies all the more dangerous because to treat them kindly was to allow doubts to rise as to the pernicious nature of their doctrine. It was necessary to condemn in express terms Eustathius, the chief of the Pneumatomachi; Apollinaris, who taught the Millenial reign and disturbed everyone by his doctrine

---

[1] *Ep.* 263; cf. *Ep.* 129, in which Basil explains to Meletius the plan of this new step.

as to the Incarnation; and finally, Marcellus, whose disciples found too much support from Paulinus.

This new embassy of Dorotheus had only, and could only have, partial success. That the Roman Church repudiated the errors attributed to Eustathius, Apollinaris, and Marcellus, there could be no manner of doubt. It had already expressed itself clearly on that point. It had done so especially in the letter which Dorotheus had brought back to the East. It did so once more, to satisfy the Easterns, in another letter which Dorotheus carried back on his return from this new journey.[1] As to condemning by name absent persons, such as Eustathius, Apollinaris, or Paulinus, without even giving them a chance of explaining themselves in a debate in which both sides were heard, this could scarcely be asked of the Apostolic See. The utmost that it could have done would have been to ratify a sentence pronounced after such a discussion by the lawful authorities of the East. But this debate had not taken place, nor did such a sentence exist.

The situation was one from which there was no way out. On the men of this time who were well intentioned there weighed the consequences of the long war in which Eusebius of Nicomedia had embroiled the Easterns, first against Alexandria, and then against the Roman Church. Moreover, everyone was not well intentioned. Paulinus ought to have retired. But even when rid of the embarrassment of his personality, the position would have remained critical, for opinion in Egypt would still have seen, behind Meletius, the shades of his former patrons, Eudoxius and Acacius and their like. However, as Meletius was personally very popular, things would have settled themselves at Antioch, and elsewhere people would have ended by taking his side in the matter. In any case, Rome and Alexandria would have ceased to tow in their wake the cumbersome wreck of the old Marcellian party; and union would have been restored between them and the Churches of the East. This may be said in order to

---

[1] The Fragments, *Illud sane miramur* and *Non nobis quidquam* (Constant, *Ep. Rom. Pont*, pp. 498, 499).

indicate more clearly the lines and necessities of the situation, for I do not consider that it is the province of the historian to occupy himself with things which might have happened: he has quite enough to do with those that did happen as a matter of fact.

The interviews which Meletius' envoy had in Rome with Pope Damasus were not always of a very peaceable character. Peter of Alexandria was present at them. When it was a question of Meletius and of Eusebius of Samosata, he did not hesitate to display his aversion for them, and went so far as to treat them as Arians. Dorotheus at last lost patience, and attacked the Pope of Alexandria with some vehemence. Peter complained of this to Basil. Basil expressed his regret,[1] but at the same time drew his attention to the fact that Meletius and Eusebius, two confessors of the faith, who had been exiled by the Arians, deserved the respect of their colleagues; as to their orthodoxy on all the disputed points, he was certain of it, and would guarantee it.

Meletius, Basil, and their party represented, generally speaking, an evolution to the right by the old party of opposition to the Council of Nicæa. It was not the only party which circumstances had led to moderate their first attitude. At the opposite extreme, the old adversary of the " Easterns," the man against whom, from Eusebius of Cæsarea to St Basil, they had never ceased to fight, Marcellus of Ancyra, Marcellus the " Sabellian," was going through an evolution on his side or, rather, an evolution was going on around him. He was not yet dead when Basil became bishop. He was living in retirement at Ancyra, with a few clergy and a certain number of adherents, who formed around him a Little Church. The official bishop, Athanasius, he who gave his adhesion, in 363, to the Council of Nicæa, thought it his duty to harass this little group. Marcellus had long been estranged from the Bishop of Alexandria, his former companion in the struggles at Rome and at Sardica. But this did not hinder him from appealing to him. One of his clergy,

[1] *Ep.* 266.

the deacon Eugenius, was sent to Alexandria with recommendations furnished by the Bishops of Greece and of Macedonia. He presented a profession of faith,[1] in which the former doctrines of Marcellus were either toned down or cloaked; however, it did not go so far as to speak of the three hypostases. Athanasius, as we have seen, if he did not rule out this expression, certainly did not lay stress on it. He gave letters of communion to Marcellus' deacon and to his Little Church. This happened, I think, at the same time as the Council of Alexandria, in 362. Marcellus died about the year 375; he must have been over ninety,[2] and it is perhaps on account of his great age that we hear no more of him in these latter days. Thus deprived of its head, and repulsed by Basil and his supporters, who continually invoked against it the anathemas of the West, his party addressed themselves to the Egyptian bishops, who were living in exile at Diocæsarea in Palestine. These confessors, to whom they presented, together with a profession of faith,[3] the letters of communion given them in former days by St Athanasius, made no difficulty about admitting them. But Basil, to whom they next addressed themselves, thought that the exiles had been too hasty in the matter, and such was also the opinion of Peter of Alexandria.[4] Basil asked for nothing better than to welcome the Galatians; but he wished them to come to him, and not that they should presume to draw him to themselves.

This affair, like several others, was still pending, when, in 378, events of great importance occurred to modify the political and religious situation in the Eastern empire. Two years before, the Goths established beyond the Danube had found themselves attacked by the Huns who came from the Ural. Driven back by these savage hordes, they had asked for shelter on imperial territory, and had been allowed to settle in Thrace, upon certain conditions,

[1] Mansi, *Concilia*, vol. iii., p. 469.
[2] He was already bishop in 314, at the time of the Council of Ancyra.
[3] Epiphanius, *Haer.* lxxii. 11.   [4] Basil, *Ep.* 266,

among which was a promise to furnish them with means of support. The government of Valens organized this supply with so little conscience and humanity, that the immigrants revolted (376). It was necessary to undertake a regular campaign against them, which finally took such a turn for the worse that Valens was obliged to intervene in person. Before he left Antioch, moved by a wise clemency, he revoked the sentences of exile pronounced against ecclesiastical persons.[1]

Valens arrived at Constantinople on May 30, and[2] set out again a few days later to direct the military operations in Thrace. On August 9 he delivered battle. The Roman army suffered a terrible defeat, in which the emperor disappeared — either because his corpse could not be recognized among the dead, or because, according to a rumour which gained credence, he had perished in the burning of a cottage, to which he had been carried in order that his wounds might be cared for.

[1] Jerome, *Chron.:* "Valens de Antiochia exire compulsus sera poenitentia nostros de exilio revocat."—Rufin. *H. E.* ii. 13: "Tum vero Valentis bella quae ecclesiis inferebat in hostem coepta converti, seraque poenitentia episcopos et presbyteros relaxari exiliis ac de metallis resolvi monachos iubet."

[2] According to a legend related by Sozomen (vi. 40), and adopted also, with some alteration, by Theodoret (iv. 31), a monk of Constantinople, Isaac, had in vain adjured him to restore the churches to the Catholics. This story, doubtful enough in itself, cannot be set against the testimonies of St Jerome and Rufinus, who were living at that time in the East, as to the recall of the exiles by Valens himself; besides, the recall of the exiles is quite a different thing from their reinstatement in the place and position of the official clergy.

CHAPTER XII

GREGORY OF NAZIANZUS

Gratian and Theodosius. Return of the exiled bishops. **Death of Basil.** The Easterns accept the conditions of Rome. Attitude of Theodosius. Situation at Constantinople. Gregory of Nazianzus and his church, the " Anastasis." Conflicts with the Arians. Alexandrian opposition : Maximus the Cynic. Gregory at St Sophia. The Second Œcumenical Council (381)· Obstinacy of the Macedonians. Installation of Gregory. Death of Meletius : difficulties with regard to his successor. Resignation of Gregory. Nectarius. The canons. Hostility against Alexandria. Flavian elected at Antioch. Protests of St Ambrose. Roman Council in 382. Letter from the Easterns.

GRATIAN, warned of the danger, but detained in Gaul by an invasion of the Alamanni, which was stayed by the battle of Colmar, arrived in time, in spite of all difficulties, on the Lower Danube. Valens should have awaited his arrival, in order that the Goths, being caught between the two armies, might have been easily overcome. After the disaster, the young emperor of the West—he was not twenty—first of all took steps to improve the situation; and then, not feeling strong enough to govern by himself both parts of the empire, shifted the burden of the East from his own shoulders to those of one of his generals, Theodosius, who was proclaimed Augustus at Sirmium on January 16, 379. Some time ere this Gratian had hastened to ratify and to extend the measures already taken by Valens for the recall of the exiled bishops. Meletius reappeared at Antioch, Eusebius at Samosata ; all the confessors reassumed the government of their churches.

One of the first to return was Peter of Alexandria.
Before allowing him to leave Rome, Damasus had
caused him to be present at a council, at which it was
finally decided to condemn by name Apollinaris and one
of his principal lieutenants, Timothy, who had just been
made Bishop at Berytus.   Peter set out immediately
after.   No sooner had he disembarked at Alexandria
than a popular outbreak drove Lucius from the city;
he hastened to take refuge at Constantinople, where,
although the Emperor Valens was gone, he found at
any rate the hospitality of the Bishop Demophilus, still
as always holding his position, and determined not to
give it up till the last moment.

It was just at this time that Basil died, on January 1,
379.   He had not completed his fiftieth year; his career
might well have been a more protracted one; his endur-
ance of adversity gave reason to look forward to what he
would have been in prosperity.   But his health, always
poor, had not been made any stronger by the imprudences
of asceticism and the fatigues of his episcopate.   Among
all his sufferings, he complains specially of a liver
complaint, which we might suspect, apart from this
testimony, from the restless and embittered tone of his
correspondence.   Exposed to the often brutal ill-will of
the government, to opposition from ecclesiastics, opposition
for the most part stupid but arising from several different
causes, and, for that very reason, difficult to overcome;
deprived of coadjutors of any value, for notwithstanding
their friendship and their ability, his brother Gregory of
Nyssa and his friend Gregory of Nazianzus were more
of a hindrance than a help to him; Basil brought to the
service of a programme of reconciliation, a natural
temperament at once too sensitive and too pugnacious.
Hence arose an endless series of failures.   In the affair
of Eustathius, we see him, to satisfy the fierce consubstantialists, holding a knife to the throat of an old friend, a
venerable bishop, and the result which he achieved was
that, in spite of this sacrifice, the irreconcilable Atarbius
of Neocæsarea could not endure him, fled at his approach,

and kept his flock in such a state of terror by his
threatening dreams, that they revolted against the
Bishop of Cæsarea, their compatriot and the glory of
their country.   Basil desired that Meletius should be
recognized as Bishop of Antioch, and fought doggedly to
that end, without considering the difficult position in
which such an event would place the Churches of Rome
and Alexandria.   He was opposed; and he lost his
temper, and expressed himself in no measured terms.
Even in his own country and his own ecclesiastical circle,
his influence was vigorously opposed.   Some people have
wished to see in him the founder of a kind of Patriarchate,
with a jurisdiction corresponding to the "diocese" of Pontus.
But it is evident that he had no authority in the Western
provinces, those of Bithynia, Galatia, and Paphlagonia.
The bishops of the sea-board of Pontus[1] did not
trouble themselves about him.[2]   In the interior, when
the sees were not occupied by Arians, as at Amasia and
in the Armenian Tetrapolis, their occupants were quarrelling with each other; some approved of the monks, others
would have none of them; some thought that, on the
question as to the Trinity, Basil inclined too much to
the right; others deplored his making concessions to
the left.   Had he been blessed with good health, the
noble soul of the Bishop of Cæsarea might perhaps have
risen above all these miseries.   But the bodily machine
refused to act; the pilot died, worn out, just when the
tempest was abating.

It was a bitter day for the pontiffs of official Arianism
when they heard of the recall of their exiled rivals!
Besides, this was only a preliminary measure.   They
knew the sympathies of the young emperor, and they
had doubts as to what would come next.   At Antioch,
Meletius, confronted by special difficulties, quickly grasped
a situation now much simplified.   To come to an understanding with Rome had been, under Valens, a thing
greatly to be desired; under Gratian and Theodosius, it

---

[1] Sinope, Amisos (Samsoun), Polemonion, Kerassond, Trebizond.
[2] *Ep.* 203.

was the one and only solution. Basil, who perhaps
might have had scruples, was no longer there to suggest
conditions. A council of one hundred and fifty - three
bishops assembled in the. Syrian metropolis during
the autumn[1] of 379, and voted an unqualified adhesion
to the Roman formularies.[2]

They thus anticipated the intentions of Theodosius.
The new emperor had settled at Thessalonica. He fell
ill there during the winter, and was baptized by Bishop
Acholius, a decided Nicene. In an edict,[3] dated February
27, 380, Theodosius declared to his people that they must
all profess the religion which "the Apostle Peter had
taught in days of old to the Romans, and which was now
followed by the Pontiff Damasus and by Peter, Bishop of
Alexandria, a man of Apostolic sanctity." That party
alone had any right to the title of "Catholics"; all others
were heretics; their conventicles were not regarded as
churches, and they were threatened with penalties.

---

[1] Nine months after the death of Basil, says Gregory of Nyssa,
De vita Sanctae Macrinae (Migne, *P. G.*, vol. xlvi., p. 973).

[2] We still possess (Constant, *Ep. Rom. Pontif.*, p. 500) the
signatures (seven formally set out, the others summarized) which
were appended to this document. There is no doubt about the
meaning of the formulary. As to the terms of it, that is not so easy
to decide. The signatures are attached, in the MSS. where they are
found, to a collection composed of the letter of Damasus, *Confidimus
quidem*, and of the three fragments, *Ea gratia, Illud sane miramur*,
and *Non nobis quidquam* (see above, pp. 320, 325, 329). But this
collection of documents is very incoherent. It is clear that it only
represents an extract from a more extensive collection. The Easterns
would assuredly not have signed the letter *Confidimus* if it stood
alone, for in it we find the term *una substantia* ($=\mu ia\ \dot{\upsilon}\pi\dot{o}\sigma\tau a\sigma\iota s$),
against which they had always protested. But this term might be
considered as explained by the subsequent letters, in one of
which it is replaced by the expression *una usia*. It is possible,
therefore, that they may have given their adhesion to the views
contained in the *dossier* as a whole. In any case their adhesion
must have been drawn up in a special formula, which the author of
our extracts has neglected. The formula by which he introduces
the signatures, and the *explicit* which comes after, presuppose a
close connection between the Council of Antioch and the Roman
documents which precede it.

[3] *Cod. Theod.* xvi. 1, 2.

At Antioch, the orthodox, both those who belonged to the Great Church (the party of Meletius) and those who belonged to the Little Church (the party of Paulinus) were numerous.   They could await with quiet confidence the executive measures which would hand over to them the ecclesiastical buildings still held from them, no longer by Euzoïus, who had been dead some time, but by his successor, Dorotheus.   The situation was not so clear at Constantinople.   There, the Arian party was strong.   Its leader, Demophilus, was enthroned at St Sophia; the clergy under his orders were in possession of all the churches.   Those in opposition to him, whether Macedonians or Nicenes, were rigorously excluded from them, just as the adherents of Meletius and Paulinus were at Antioch.   At the advent of Demophilus, the Nicenes had tried to appoint a bishop of their own, in the person of a certain Evagrius ; he was immediately seized by the police, and imprisoned at Berea, where he seems to have died, for we hear of him no more.   Now that the times had become more favourable, the Nicenes felt the necessity of union and organization.   The neo-orthodox party of the East hastened to assist them, being anxious that the place of Demophilus should be given to one of their own friends, and above all to prevent the Apollinarians, who were already on the move, from seizing upon it for themselves.   Negotiations followed, at the conclusion of which, Gregory, the son of the old Bishop of Nazianzus, was chosen as the Shepherd of this little flock.

Ever since the death of his parents in 375, Gregory, free at last to follow his vocation to asceticism, had fled from Nazianzus.   Leaving Basil to extricate himself as best he could from the difficulties which besieged him on every side, he had taken refuge in the monastery of St Thecla at Seleucia in Isauria.   It was there that he heard of the defeat of Valens and the death of Basil.   After refusing many entreaties, he at last consented to the request made to him, and went to Constantinople, where he opened a Little Church in the house of one of his relations.   The orthodox party gathered round him.

II   **Y**

His signal uprightness of character and, above all, his wonderful eloquence, soon drew together a considerable body of hearers. The Church of Constantinople, oppressed for forty years by violence and intrigue, came to life again in that humble edifice. Gregory himself had given to his chapel the name of *Resurrection* (Anastasis). It was there that, among so many other homilies, he pronounced his five Discourses upon the Trinity—classic specimens of Greek theology. The dissenting oratory, thanks to the golden eloquence of this first of Chrysostoms, became more frequented and better attended than the official basilicas. The Arians were much disturbed. During the night before Easter Sunday (379) a furious crowd rushed from St Sophia to attack the Anastasis, where Gregory was baptizing his neophytes. The crowd consisted of the virgins and monks of the Arian Church, drawing in their wake the poor assisted by their charity, a docile following of the dominant clergy. It seemed to Gregory as if he saw a party of Corybants with Fauns and Mænads. Stones flew through the air against the Catholics; some of them struck the bishop; one of his people was beaten and left for dead.[1] Yet none the less he himself was held responsible for the disorder, and dragged before the courts.

He could make light of this ill-treatment from a quarter from which it was only to be expected. But far more grievous to him were the internal disputes of his little community. The reaction from the schism of Antioch was felt there. Gregory, who held strongly to the three hypostases, found himself treated as a tri-theist. He was asked if he were for Paul or for Apollos, *i.e.*, for Meletius or for Paulinus. He would have preferred to be only for Christ; but that was difficult.

Far away in Alexandria, the Patriarch Peter was keeping a watchful eye upon what was happening at Constantinople, and, being always dominated by his old resentment against the Easterns, the former persecutors of his brother Athanasius, he was disturbed to see the

---

[1] Details in *Or.* 35; *Ep.* 77; *Carmen de Vita*, vv. 652-678.

Cappadocian orator, the friend of Basil and of Meletius, in a fair way to inherit at Constantinople the succession of the Arians. At the outset he had written to Gregory in very friendly tones; Gregory, on his part, preached a panegyric on Athanasius. At the Anastasis, they felt quite secure about Alexandria. Hence they gave a warm welcome to a person, albeit a very extraordinary one, who came from that country. This was a certain Maximus, a Cynic philosopher, who had found a way to combine the observances of his sect with the profession of Christianity. Athanasius had corresponded with him.[1] He had had in more than one place difficulties with the police; but, as he said that he had been persecuted for the faith, that fact only gave him another claim on the good-will of guileless people. Among their number, we must admit, might be included the illustrious man whom circumstances had placed at the head of the Catholics of Constantinople. In spite of his staff, his philosopher's cloak, and his long hair, Maximus was treated by Gregory as a confessor of the faith, and as an intimate friend; he took him into his house, gave him a place at his table, and trusted him with his complete confidence. That nothing might be wanting to these friendly demonstrations, Gregory also honoured him by a fine panegyric, pronounced in church in the presence of its hero.[2] On his side, Maximus was most attentive to Gregory's sermons, applauded him in church, and supported him outside by the popularity which he enjoyed in certain circles.

Now this Maximus was Bishop Peter's candidate for the see of Constantinople. If he was now with Gregory, it was to rob him of his bishopric. One night the doors of the Church of the Anastasis, thanks to the complicity of a priest, were opened to give admission to a strange assembly. Sailors from the corn ships, just arrived from Alexandria, escorted a group of bishops of their country, who at once proceeded to the task of the election and consecration of Maximus as Bishop of Constantinople.

[1] *Ep. ad Maximum philosophum* (Migne, *P. G.*, vol. xxvi., p. 1085).
[2] *Or.* 25.

Gregory, some distance away, was sleeping uneasily, for he was ill; his faithful clergy too were slumbering. The ceremony began. The custom of that day did not allow clerics to wear their hair long. It was necessary, therefore as Gregory said when he told the story later in the language of satire, "to shear the dog upon the episcopal throne." The result of this operation was the discovery that much of this celebrated head of hair was artificial, The ceremony was not over when the dawn brought people to the church. A fine tumult ensued. The Egyptians, terrified, retired in disorder, and only found refuge with a musician in the neighbourhood. There, in a wretched hovel, they finished their ceremony.

One can imagine the position of Gregory. He was, greatly distressed, angry with himself for his simplicity. and he wished to go away. But his faithful flock watched him carefully. In one of his discourses, they thought they discovered an intention to fly. They surrounded him and beset him with a thousand entreaties. As he still seemed determined, they said, "If you go, you will take the Trinity with you." Gregory understood, and remained. In the meantime the new bishop, accompanied by his consecrators, repaired to Thessalonica to obtain the recognition of Theodosius. He was quite mistaken. The emperor knew everything, and repulsed him harshly. Maximus then embarked for Alexandria, where he solicited the support of Bishop Peter. The latter was in a very difficult position. The matter had not gone well at Constantinople; the emperor was displeased; and, as a climax, Pope Damasus, being informed by Acholius and his Macedonian colleagues, protested strongly against the attempt.[1] Peter's punishment came from the same quarter as his sin. His Bishop of Constantinople stirred up a riot against him at Alexandria to force his support. The prefect had to intervene, and banished the episcopal Cynic to a place where he could no longer disturb the tranquillity of the streets.

We learn from these events that Gregory, notwith-

[1] Jaffé, 237, 238.

standing his indisputable sanctity and his eloquence, was
a little wanting in practical common sense. He was
certainly not pleasing to Peter of Alexandria, whose merits
the imperial rescript of February 27 had so highly praised.
Was he really the man needed, just then, at the head
of the Church of Constantinople? Theodosius, a strong
man himself, must have had doubts like these. But, for
the moment, he refrained from settling the matter. He
could not, however, allow an indefinite prolongation of
the state of uncertainty which existed in the capital
with regard to religious affairs. He had hitherto been
detained at Thessalonica by his military operations
against the Goths. As soon as his hands were free there,
he turned towards Constantinople, which he entered on
November 24, 380.

Two days afterwards, the churches were taken from
the Arians and restored to the Catholics. Demophilus
showed no more inclination at the last moment than
previously to accept the Creed of Nicæa. He left the
city. On November 26, the emperor conducted Gregory
to St Sophia. An enormous crowd congregated on the
route—not altogether a friendly crowd, far from it, but a
large display of military force secured order. Behind the
vigorous and imposing prince, the blue bird of Cappadocia
led the triumph of orthodoxy. The weather was grey;
autumn clouds veiled the morning sky. Was the rain
going to fall upon the Council of Nicæa? Arians and
Catholics looked up to the heavens with very different
desires. Gregory entered the darkened basilica, and,
while the imperial procession took its place in the
tribunes, he sat down in the apse beside the episcopal
throne. Just at that moment, the sun, bursting through
the clouds, shed its rays through all the windows; it
saluted the victory. Shouts rang out: "Gregory, Bishop!"
But Gregory, bewildered and speechless, proved unequal
to the greatness of the occasion. In his stead, another
bishop called upon all those present to recall their thoughts
for the celebration of the sacred mysteries.

From that day forward the Anastasis was abandoned;

it was at St Sophia that the eloquence of orthodoxy resounded. Under the roof which had once sheltered Eudoxius, the Saint of Nazianzus set in order his life of austerity and devotion. It was not without difficulty that he could set his hand to the reorganization of his great church. Many interests found themselves injured; and Gregory was the object of an attempt at assassination. But the local opposition was gradually disarmed; and the illustrious bishop saw the moment arriving when his position was finally to be regularized and strengthened. Theodosius had decided to gather together in a great council the episcopate of the Eastern empire. To this assembly he had committed the task of providing, in a definite manner, for the government of the Church of Constantinople.

Notices of convocation were sent out. There is every appearance that at first invitations were not sent to the bishops of Egypt, nor to those of Eastern Illyricum, of whom the most distinguished was the metropolitan of Thessalonica. At all events these bishops did not arrive till much later than the others. Paulinus did not appear at all; nor did the few bishops in communion with him, such as Diodore of Tyre and Epiphanius of Salamis. Meletius arrived early, escorted by seventy bishops from the "diocese" of the Orient. Helladius, the new Bishop of Cæsarea in Cappadocia, also came, with the two brothers of Basil, Gregory and Peter; then came his friends, Amphilochius of Iconium and Optimus of Antioch in Pisidia; and last, some fifty bishops from Southern Asia Minor, Lycia, Pamphylia, Pisidia, and Lycaonia. On the whole, this assemblage of bishops represented fairly well the immediate followers of Basil. His bodily presence was wanting to his victory; but his spirit pervaded the assembly. From Galatia and from Paphlagonia, where the bishoprics were still occupied by Arians, there came no one. Neither do we find among the signatories the name of any bishop of Western Asia Minor. In these countries there prevailed the semi-Arian or Macedonian confession, promulgated anew in the recent councils held at Cyzicus

and at Antioch in Caria.[1] Yet Theodosius had thought
it his duty to summon also the bishops of that shade of
opinion. Some of them came, thirty-six in all, headed
by their old leader, Eleusius of Cyzicus, the famous
champion of the *homoïousios*, and by his colleague, Marcian
of Lampsacus. Eustathius of Sebaste was no longer alive
to join them. His death took place either shortly before
or after that of his old friend Basil; it was Basil's youngest
brother, Peter, who had replaced him as Bishop of Sebaste.

It was in vain that the orthodox party discussed
matters long and amicably with their opponents, and that,
in a homily[2] delivered at St Sophia on the Feast of
Pentecost (May 16), Gregory treated with the utmost
circumspection the subject of the Holy Spirit; Eleusius
and his followers obstinately maintained their attitude.
It was necessary to make up one's mind to a separation
from them. This was done with all the more regret,
because, whether at Constantinople or elsewhere, the
"Macedonians" numbered in their ranks many estimable
persons.

The question of the Bishop of the see of Constantinople
was easily settled in a friendly assembly. It was only a
matter of form, for Gregory was very evidently, and had
long been, the candidate of Meletius; the support of all
the Easterns was assured to him. We can imagine how
glad the brothers and the friends of Basil were to give him
their votes. No opposition was manifested. No one
could take seriously the claims of Maximus the Cynic,
repudiated as he was in the East by everyone, even by
the Egyptians. As to the forced consecration which
Gregory had received from Basil, everyone knew that it

---

[1] On the Council of Cyzicus (*supra*, p. 328) see Basil, *Ep.* 244, § 9.
That of Antioch in Caria is placed by Socrates (*H. E.* v. 4, with the
mistake τῆς Συρίας) and by Sozomen (*H. E.* vii. 2) shortly after the
accession of Gratian. Sozomen mentions elsewhere (vi. 12) another
council held in Caria by thirty-four bishops, at the time fixed for the
meeting of the Council of Tarsus (*supra*, p. 293), *i.e.*, about twelve
years earlier. It is probable that these two assemblies were really
only one, and that it should be placed in 378 or 379.

[2] *Or.* 41.

had not been followed by any taking possession of his diocese; that the so-called Bishop of Sasima had continually protested against the violence done to him; that he had never exercised any episcopal functions at Sasima; and that, if he had exercised them at Nazianzus, it was only as assistant to his father, never as bishop of the see. It could not therefore be said that he was transferring himself from one diocese to another. It was from solitude, and not from another bishopric, that he had come to Constantinople.

All this was clear as daylight. Gregory was fully installed by the council, and by its chief, Meletius. Twenty years had passed away since the latter had himself been called to the see of Antioch by the leaders of the Arian party of that time, the friends of Euzoïus and of Acacius, of Dorotheus and Demophilus. If Gregory had not signed the Creed of Ariminum, his father, the Bishop of Nazianzus, had done so. If the council was not an assembly of converts, at least many of its members must have had embarrassing memories. As a whole, they were returning from afar. But they had suffered enough under Valens not to be troubled under Theodosius by a past which was already distant. Although they had formerly been obliged either to keep silence or to sign, they had none the less kept the true faith; they had known how to maintain it at the cost of the severest sacrifices; and it was with sincere hearts that they acclaimed it in times of peace. And what they had done, they had done quite alone, kept at a distance and distrusted by the Western Church and the Egyptians. They were even conscious of having defended against their misgivings the formula of the three hypostases, the necessary complement to the *Homoousios* of Nicæa. Basil was victorious all down the line. When his friend Meletius, whom he had so perseveringly defended, took the hand of Gregory to lead him to the episcopal throne of St Sophia, how many must have called to mind the great Bishop of Cæsarea! The Church of Antioch paid its debt to Basil, while making a magnificent atonement for its former persecution of his heart's brother. No better honour could have been paid to his illustrious memory.

Meletius died during these days of triumph. The installation of the Bishop of Constantinople was the last ceremony over which he presided. His obsequies were celebrated with the greatest pomp; Gregory of Nyssa pronounced the funeral oration.

His removal from the scene re-opened a question of the greatest difficulty. On his return to Antioch, towards the end of the year 378, Meletius had tried to come to an arrangement with Paulinus. As to the proceedings or agreements which resulted in this connection, our information is derived only from legends.[1] Is it true that Meletius suggested to Paulinus that they should sit together, with the Book of the Gospels between them? Or that, at any rate, it was agreed that the first of them to die should have no successor? We do not know. As to the last point, the pious desires of sensible persons of every opinion must have agreed. It is certain that suggestions to that effect had come from the West, especially from the circle of St Ambrose.[2] But in the West they only concerned themselves with theoretical right, and with regard to details they accepted the Alexandrian views of the situation. On the spot, it was evident that the community attached to Paulinus was of little importance, that Meletius was the real bishop, and that the rival Church only existed by the favour of Alexandria and of the West.

The fact that the question of the succession to Meletius was raised at Constantinople, and during a great council, composed almost entirely of his partisans, was not calculated to

---

[1] Socrates, *H. E.* v. 5 (*cf.* Sozomen, *H. E.* vii. 3), combines together two accounts—one favourable to Paulinus, the other in which his followers are treated as Luciferians. Theodoret (*H. E.* v. 3) gives us no firmer ground. It is not even certain that the *magister militum* Sapor, who was instructed to conduct the restoration of the churches of Antioch to the Catholics, acted in the time of Meletius, rather than in that of Flavian.

[2] Letter of the Council of Aquileia, Ambrose, *Ep.* 12, 5; *cf.* 13, 2.

advance the solution which was desired, not only by the
Western Church but by sensible people in the East.   The
latter found a spokesman in the new Bishop of Constantinople.   Gregory insisted strongly that they should unite
themselves to Paulinus.   He was not listened to.   The
circumstances of the Meletians, the new favour shown to
them, the successes they had obtained, all served to enkindle
them.   As in the days of Eusebius of Nicomedia and the
Council of Sardica, they vaunted their points of superiority
as contrasted with the West.   "Was it not in the East,"
they said, "that Christ was born?"   "Yes," replied
Gregory ; "and it was in the East also that He was
slain."   His efforts were in vain ; the bishops decided that
Paulinus should not be recognized, and that a successor
must be appointed to Meletius.   Gregory was much distressed.   This council, over which he had presided since
the death of Meletius, was beginning to irritate him.   "The
youngest of them," he said,[1] "chattered like a flock of jays,
and were as furious as a swarm of wasps ; as to the old
men, they made no attempt to control the others."

In these ungrateful surroundings his beloved solitude
returned to his mind, with memories of peace and religious
meditation.   He began to declare that, since no one
would listen to him, it was better for him to go away.
But this was not the wish of the bishops ; they insisted
strongly upon his remaining at the post where they had
placed him.   In the meantime, there arrived the Bishop of
Thessalonica, Acholius, and the new Pope of Alexandria,
Timothy, who some months before had succeeded his
brother Peter.   "They blew with the rough wind of the
West," said Gregory,[2] meaning that they favoured
Paulinus.   From that point of view, it was the arrival of
a reinforcement for the Bishop of Constantinople.   But
unfortunately they did not quite like Gregory, or rather
they could not resign themselves to the fact that the see
of Constantinople had been filled up by the successors of
Eusebius of Nicomedia and Leontius of Antioch.   They
took their stand on ecclesiastical rules, raised objections

[1] *Carmen de Vita*, vv. 1680-1699.   [2] *Ibid.*, verse 1802.

as to Sasima and Nazianzus, and protested against translations from one bishopric to another.

These absurdities exasperated Gregory. Enough of these triflings, enough of these hypocritical disputes! In a final address, he gave an account of his spiritual stewardship, and bade a most touching farewell to his people, to the city of Constantine, to his Church the Anastasis, to St Sophia, to the Holy Apostles, to the Council, to the East, and to the West—the West, for which and through which he suffered persecution. Then he set out for Nazianzus. Acholius and Timothy had done a fine piece of work!

To his vacant place there was elected a man of the world, a certain Nectarius, a Cilician by birth, who had been a government official at Constantinople. His past had not been distinguished for austerity; but his beard had grown white; he was now both affable and grave. The Bishop of Tarsus, Diodore, a celebrated ascetic, thought that he had a sacerdotal mien, and added his name to the list of candidates presented to the emperor. Theodosius nominated him.[1] It was then discovered that he had not yet been baptized. It was the case of St Ambrose over again, minus the lofty virtue and the capabilities of the Bishop of Milan. Perhaps the emperor thought that Nectarius would turn out a second Ambrose. If so, he was mistaken; but, at a moment when the Church of Constantinople, after so many dissensions, had so great a need of rest, Nectarius, who was not inclined to fret himself too much about delicate shades of difference, was perhaps, in spite of or even on account of his deficiencies, the man demanded by the situation.

Under his presidency, evidently an honorary one, the council concluded its labours. These may even have been finished earlier. The four canons in which they are summed up show no signs of Alexandrian influence. We can scarcely believe that Timothy had had a share in their composition.[2]

[1] Sozomen, *H. E.* vii. 8.

[2] Nevertheless, his name appears, with that of a Bishop of Oxyrhynchus, in the list of signatories, which is in some places of a rather artificial character.

The first of these canons proclaims once more the faith of Nicæa, and anathematizes all heresies, mentioning by name those of the Eunomians or Anomœans, of the Arians or Eudoxians, of the Semi-Arians or Pneumatomachi, and of the Sabellians, Marcellians, Photinians, and Apollinarians. The second canon forbids prelates to meddle with the affairs of other civil "dioceses" than their own; the Bishop of Alexandria must confine his anxious care to Egypt; the religious administration of the East concerns only the bishops of the Orient, who shall bear in mind what was decided at Nicæa with regard to the prerogatives of the Church of Antioch; the same shall hold good of the dioceses of Asia, Pontus, and Thrace. As for Christian bodies situated beyond the frontiers of the empire, they shall be governed according to established custom. By the third canon, the Bishop of Constantinople finds himself attributed the pre-eminence of honour ($\tau \grave{\alpha} \ \pi \rho \epsilon \sigma \beta \epsilon \hat{\iota} \alpha \ \tau \hat{\eta} \varsigma \ \tau \iota \mu \hat{\eta} \varsigma$) after the Bishop of Rome "because Constantinople is a new Rome." Finally, the last canon decides the case of Maximus the Cynic: he is not recognized as a bishop, and all his acts, especially his ordinations, are declared null and void.[1]

For anyone who can read between the lines, these decisions of the council represent so many acts of hostility against the Church of Alexandria and its claims to hegemony. It is orthodox in tone—there is no doubt of that, and it condemns all the heretical movements of the time; but care is taken, in enumerating them, to include among them the Marcellians, old dependants of Alexandria, to whom it had still, quite recently, extended its protection. If so much stress is laid on each bishop occupying himself only with his own affairs and remaining within the "diocesan" area to which he belongs, it is from a desire to prevent the interference of the Egyptian Pope in the affairs of Constantinople, Antioch, and other places. If the pre-eminence of Constantinople is asserted, without disputing that of Rome, it is in order to escape from that of

[1] The three canons, which follow these in collections of canons, represent later additions.

Alexandria. It might have seemed perhaps of little use to allude to the blundering affair of Maximus; but, as the recollection of it was disagreeable to the Alexandrians, the council did not fail to bring it to life again.

In fact, old quarrels were remembered too well. Gregory had been quite right to flee; it was not a time for peaceful souls. If the members of the council had been wiser, they might have asked themselves from which quarter—Alexandria or the East—interferences with the affairs of others had been more frequent and more harmful. Was it not an Egyptian affair, that matter of Arius? Who had added venom to it? Eusebius of Nicomedia, and his accomplices in Bithynia and Syria. Were they Egyptian bishops who had led the chorus at the Council of Tyre? Whence came the rivals of Athanasius, men like Gregory and George? In this outbreak of passion against him, had Athanasius ever given a pretext by entrenching upon the rights of others? They mistrusted the superior power of Alexandria. Had they not used and abused that of Antioch?

But all this was forgotten under the influence of present resentment. They even sacrificed the ancient prestige of Antioch. The traditional metropolis of the East, the second cradle of Christianity, weakened at that moment by schism, did not seem to be a sufficient bulwark against the Alexandrian peril. As a rallying centre, they preferred to it Constantinople, the city of Constantine, the new Rome. Constantius, Julian, and Valens had usually resided at Antioch: military exigencies called them on the side of the Persian frontier. But now the Danube was a greater cause for anxiety than the Euphrates; and it was easy to foresee the abandonment of Antioch for Constantinople. The bishop of this great city was called upon to profit, so far as his influence was concerned, by the vicinity of the imperial court and the chief seat of government. From this point of view, he inherited the position of the Bishop of Antioch. Never did he forget this origin. The ecclesiastical history of the East was long to resound with his rivalry with his colleague of Alexandria.

Besides these practical decisions, the bishops drew up a doctrinal statement, which we no longer possess. It no doubt took the form of a letter addressed either to the whole episcopal body, or to certain churches.[1]

While the bishops were on their way home, Theodosius published, on July 30, 381, a law ordering the churches to be restored everywhere to the orthodox party, and, that there might be no occasions for doubt, he specified, in each civil "diocese," those prelates with whom communion would be a guarantee of orthodoxy for the guidance of his officials. For Thrace, besides Nectarius of Constantinople, there were the Bishops of Scythia and Marcianopolis; for Egypt, Timothy; for Pontus, Helladius of Cæsarea, Otreius of Melitene, and Gregory of Nyssa; for Asia, Amphilochius of Iconium and Optimus of Antioch in Pisidia; for the Orient, Pelagius of Laodicea, and Diodore of Tarsus. The capital cities of the dioceses of Asia and the Orient—Ephesus and Antioch —had no bishop, or rather the Bishop of Ephesus was a "Macedonian," and in Antioch they were still waiting for a successor to Meletius. One was elected shortly afterwards: this was Flavian, the former companion in conflict of Diodore, who himself was now Bishop of Tarsus. Flavian had every possible claim and every necessary quality. But unfortunately his election took place under such conditions that it was not possible for either Rome or Alexandria to accept him.

However, the wind from the West, the roughness of which was so unpleasant to the Easterns, began to blow once more. The Emperor Theodosius received letters[2]

---

[1] The synodal letter of 382, which will be quoted presently, is the only document which mentions this statement (τόμος). It presupposes, as it seems to me, that Pope Damasus had the text of it. There is certainly no connection between this document, which contained anathemas against the new doctrines (those of the Anomœans, Macedonians, and Apollinarians), and the creed called Niceno-Constantinopolitan, which is now sung in the Mass. The latter has nothing to do with the council of 381. Upon this often debated question, see the article of Harnack, in Hauck's *Encyclopädie*, vol. xi., pp. 12-28.   [2] Ambrose, *Ep.* 12, *Quamlibet.*

from a council held at Aquileia almost at the same time as that of Constantinople. This council had been attended by a certain number of bishops from North Italy, amongst others Valerian of Aquileia and Ambrose of Milan, with delegates from the episcopate of the Gauls and from that of Africa. They thanked the Eastern emperor for having restored the churches to the Catholics, but they deplored the fact that there was still no peace amongst the latter. Timothy of Alexandria and Paulinus of Antioch, who had always been in communion with the orthodox party, had cause of complaint against those " whose faith had, in the past, shown itself unstable."[1] It was desirable that this matter should be decided by a great council : and it might be held in Alexandria itself.

Shortly afterwards, the wretched Maximus arrived at Aquileia, where the council was still assembled[2]; he succeeded in insinuating himself into the good graces of Ambrose, showed him letters from Peter of Alexandria, and told him in his own way the story of his ordination. The Bishop of Milan did not wait for information from Rome : he believed what he was told, and new letters[3] from the bishops of Italy conveyed to Constantinople a protest in favour of this strange client, whose rights, in the eyes of Ambrose, exceeded those of Gregory of Nazianzus. According to Ambrose, the council assembled in the capital of the Eastern empire ought at least to have suspended its judgment until the great council, demanded in the previous letter. No attention was paid to him; perhaps his protest arrived too late. He soon heard that Maximus had been deposed, Gregory installed, and even provided with a successor in the person of Nectarius. In like manner at Antioch Meletius had been replaced, in spite of all agreements or suggestions in a contrary sense. For the third time, Ambrose addressed himself

---

[1] " Quorum fides superioribus temporibus haesitabat."

[2] This seems implied by the letter, No. 13, of St Ambrose, (*Sanctum,* c. 4), the text of which is corrupt.

[3] A lost letter, mentioned in the following one, *Ep.* 13, *Sanctum animum.*

to Theodosius, in his own name and in the name of the
bishops of the "diocese" of Italy,[1] by the advice, as he
said, of the Emperor Gratian. He declared that such
affairs ought not to be decided apart from the Western
episcopate, which had a right to know with whom it
ought to be on terms of communion.

These protests, probably supported by Pope Damasus
and by the Emperor Gratian, induced[2] Theodosius to
accept the idea of a joint council, in which should be
united the two episcopates of the East and the West.
He invited the Eastern episcopate to send delegates to
Constantinople, with that intention; and it was decided
that the meeting should be held in Rome.

We have but little information with regard to this
council. Paulinus of Antioch was present, accompanied
by Epiphanius, the metropolitan of the island of Cyprus.
Acholius of Thessalonica also went to it. We may
conclude that the Bishop of Alexandria was, at least,
represented. As to the "Easterns," properly so called,
the people who had held a council the year before at
Constantinople, they avoided it, as their spiritual ancestors
had done at Sardica forty years before. However, we
must acknowledge that they did so more formally.
Three of them were sent to Rome, bearing a letter in
mingled tones, the text of which we still possess.[8] It
opens with a description of the melancholy state to which
the religious policy of Valens had reduced the Eastern
Church; then comes a delicate reminder that the Westerns
had troubled themselves little about their unfortunate
brethren; then they are thanked for the interest which,
in happier days, they are beginning to evince. The

---

[1] *Ep.* 13, *Sanctum animum.* By its title and its text, this letter
betrays a date subsequent to the Council of Aquileia. The group of
bishops in whose name Ambrose writes is that of the bishops of the
'diocese" of Italy, which we must carefully distinguish from the
group of bishops of the suburbicarian diocese, who depended directly
upon the Pope, and had nothing to do with the Bishop of Milan.

[2] He seems to have made some objections; Letter 14 of St
Ambrose, *Fidei tuae*, has preserved a trace of this.

[8] Theodoret, *H. E.* v. 9.

Eastern delegates would have had much pleasure in attending the Council of Rome; but they had come to Constantinople without suspecting that it was a question of so long a journey, for which they had no instructions from their colleagues. It was now too late to consult them. "These reasons, and many others, prevent us from coming to you in a greater number. Nevertheless, to improve the position, and to show our affection for you, we have entreated our brothers in the episcopate, Cyriacus, Eusebius, and Priscian, to be so good as to undertake this journey. Through them, we manifest to you our desires as being peaceable and in the direction of unity,[1] as well as our zeal for the true faith." At this point there was set out the faith of the Eastern Church, in conformity with the Creed of Nicæa, the Trinity consubstantial with three hypostases, the Incarnation of the Word perfect with a perfect humanity. For details, the Westerns were referred to the confession (τόμος) of Antioch,[2] and to that of the "Œcumenical" Council, held the year before at Constantinople. As to questions relating to individuals, they had been decided according to traditional rules and the decree of Nicæa, which committed the care of them to the bishops of the different provinces. It was in this way that Nectarius had been established at Constantinople, Flavian at Antioch, and that Cyril had been recognized at Jerusalem. All this had been done in a regular manner, and the Western Church had only to rejoice thereat.

It came to this, that the Easterns, while showing that no difference with regard to the faith any longer divided them from the Westerns, refused the latter any right to interfere in their internal affairs. And it is true that the circumstances were calculated to justify in their eyes such an attitude. The peace of the East could not be indefinitely compromised for the sake of Paulinus and his Little Church. They had been wrong perhaps not to win over this old irreconcilable by giving him the succession to Meletius;

---

[1] Τὴν ἡμετέραν προαίρεσιν εἰρηνικὴν οὖσαν καὶ σκόπον ἐνώσεως ἔχουσαν.

[2] That of 379; *supra*, p. 336.

but was it possible to forget that, if he had become so troublesome, it was the fault of the Westerns who had consecrated and supported him? It was for them to get rid of him and to rid others of him. It would, besides, have been very dangerous to go and plead against Paulinus before those who were defending him with a firm determination not to reverse their own action. Were they, in a matter which concerned Constantinople, to face the decision of Ambrose, who, only the year before, had allowed himself to be deceived by that imposter of a Maximus, and who had not yet dreamed of abandoning him? No, no. People capable of supporting Paulinus against Meletius, Maximus the Cynic against Gregory of Nazianzus; people whose dependents had been Marcellus, Eustathius, Apollinaris,[1] and Vitalis — could not really be conversant with Eastern affairs and persons. The best thing to do was to arrange matters among themselves, and to allow Time, that wise physician, to heal the wounds which here and there were still bleeding.

So thought the Easterns. Hence, the Council of Rome, being held without them, could have no effect. Yet it does not appear that this assembly supported the demands of Ambrose in favour of Maximus the Cynic. We must conclude that the Bishop of Milan, when better informed, had abandoned them himself. Theodosius insisted at this time, I think, that Nectarius should be recognized at Rome. High officials from his court, supported by the delegates from the Eastern episcopate, took the necessary steps with the Pope, and induced him to send letters of communion to Constantinople.[2] As for the business at Antioch, things remained as they were.

[1] In his letter *Fidei tuae* (*Ep.* 14), Ambrose still claims for Apollinaris judgment after a full hearing of the case.
[2] A fact recalled by Pope Boniface, in a letter belonging to the year 422 (Jaffé, 365).

CHAPTER XIII

POPE DAMASUS

WITH the exception of Africa, where irreligious discord still raged, peace reigned in the Churches of the Latin West down to the time when the Emperor Constantius transferred to it the quarrels of the East. It had previously been quietly occupied in binding up the wounds made by persecution, in restoring the sacred edifices, enlarging them to contain the very numerous recruits whom Christianity was receiving; and finally, in completing what was lacking in organization. New bishoprics were being founded almost everywhere in proportion as the bodies of Christians increased in importance. Councils were undoubtedly held, though we only hear of those convoked on account of the Donatists and the Arians. The Council of Arles, in 314, was of special importance. It was a kind of Œcumenical Council, as was speedily said, in which the bishops assembled from all parts of Constantine's empire. The Pope was not present; he sent in his stead two Roman priests. This was the

inauguration of a practice which was long observed.
Very few were the Popes who quitted Rome, especially
for ecclesiastical affairs : *maior a longinquo reverentia.*

At the time of the Council of Arles, Pope Miltiades[1]
had just been succeeded by Silvester. The latter held
the see almost to the end of the reign of Constantine.
He appears as an important figure in legends, but his
real history is unknown. All that we know of him
is that he was accused by "sacrilegious persons," and
that the emperor removed the case to his own personal
tribunal.[2]   Julius, who replaced him after the short
episcopate of Mark, would be not less forgotten if he
had not been mixed up with Eastern affairs. The
internal history of the Roman Church during this first
half of the 4th century seems to have run its course
without incident. The number of the Christians increased
to an enormous extent. The ancient places of worship,
hastily restored when the persecution was over, received
constant additions by the erection of new churches.[3]
Search was made in the cemeteries of the suburbs for the
tombs of the martyrs; the faithful delighted to adorn
them; often, they even erected over them chapels of
more or less magnificence. In these were celebrated
their anniversary feasts, of which a calendar was soon
drawn up.[4]   As the number of believers increased, there

[1] Miltiades, July 2, 311-January 11, 314; Silvester, January 31,
314-December 31, 335; Mark, 336 (January 18-October 7); Julius,
February 6, 337-April 12, 352.

[2] Letter of the Roman Council of 378 to the Emperors Gratian
and Valentinian II. It undoubtedly refers to some criminal process
instigated by the Donatists. It was a very ordinary move on the part
of persons who disagreed with their bishops on religious grounds, to try
to bring obloquy upon them by dragging them before secular tribunals.

[3] *Titulus Equitii* (S. Martino ai Monti), under Silvester; *titulus
Marci* (S. Marco) under Mark; *titulus Julii* (S. Maria in Trastevere),
with another basilica (SS. Apostoli) near the Forum of Trajan, under
Julius; *basilica Liberiana* (S. Maria Maggiore), under Liberius;
titulus Damasi (S. Lorenzo in Damaso) under Damasus.

[4] The Philocalian "Ferial" belongs to the year 336; it is probable
that the one which is included in the compilation of the Hieronymian
martyrology went back still earlier.

naturally resulted also a great development in religious observances and in the number of ecclesiastics.

St Athanasius, who came to Rome in 339, made a great sensation in the best society. He was in a position to relate to the Roman ladies the extraordinary life of the hermits Antony and Pacomius and their followers.[1] So was sown the first seed of many aristocratic vocations which soon bore fruit.

The Roman Church had received in the days of Silvester, official intimation of the condemnation of Arius by the Bishop of Alexandria. Being invited to the Council of Nicæa, the Pope had sent there, as in the case of the Council of Arles, two priests to represent him. With regard to doctrinal questions, the Roman Church was at peace. The days of Hippolytus, Callistus, and Tertullian were now far away. In the matter of formulas, when any need was felt for making use of them, there was that of Tertullian and of Novatian, "One Substance, Three Persons," which seemed sufficient for every need. Formerly, when Greek was spoken, the term *homoousios* had been made use of; it was now translated by *consubstantialis*, thus identifying the two words οὐσία and ὑπόστασις. This was the terminology which Silvester's legates recommended to the Council of Nicæa, and of which they secured the adoption.

When, in 340, the Roman Council, presided over by Pope Julius, saw the appearance before it, in one of the basilicas of the city, of the Bishops of Alexandria, Ancyra, and Gaza, the question of dogma raised no difficulty. Of the three appellants, Marcellus of Ancyra was the only one who had been condemned in the East for his doctrine. And he, also, upheld the Unity of Substance

---

[1] It was said afterwards that he brought some of these ascetics to Rome. Palladius (*Historia Lausiaca*, i.) mentions Isidore, the hospitaller of Alexandria, and Socrates (*H. E.* iv. 23) mentions Ammonius Parotes. But, even from the account of Palladius, Isidore could only have been twenty-one years of age at the time of the journey of Athanasius; and Ammonius, who died in 403, could not have been much older.

and the Trinity of Persons; the Romans had no difficulty about coming to an understanding with him.

All this produced no effect on Roman, we may almost say on Latin, opinion, unless it were in producing the impression that the Church in the Empire of Constantius, just as in Africa, was troubled by profound dissensions. And it was impossible to devote an unlimited amount of attention to these distant troubles. However, certain differences of opinion had been brought officially before the Roman Church: the bishops of the West began to realize that it would be necessary for them to concern themselves with these Eastern affairs. A certain number of them took part in the Council of Sardica, the result of which, as we have previously seen, did not answer to the hopes of those who had called it together. Being angry with the defenders of Athanasius, the Easterns pronounced sentences of deposition against Pope Julius, against Maximin, Bishop of Trèves, Hosius of Cordova, and several others. It is true that these sentences had no effect; neither they nor the counter ones pronounced from the side of the Latins prevented the resumption of negotiations, in the following year, between the two episcopates. The bishops went and came from Milan to Antioch, and from Antioch to Milan. These negotiations, however, were the business of the leaders; the episcopate as a body was but scantily concerned in them; and the general mass of the faithful and of the clergy took absolutely no interest in them.

The position was no longer the same from the beginning of 353 when the Emperor Constantius, master of both halves of the empire, sought to engage the Western episcopate in the crusade then going on in the East against Athanasius and against the Creed of Nicæa. He succeeded, but not without exciting opposition in some cases which was severely put down. Ever since the Great Persecution, people had been accustomed to see the bishops govern their churches in peace. The list of exiles and of confessors was unrolled once more under the government of Constantine's son. Several churches found themselves deprived of their heads; for instance—in Gaul, those of Trèves, Poitiers, and Toulouse; in Sardinia, that of Cagliari; in Italy, those of Milan and Vercellæ. The exiles were sometimes replaced by persons who came from Cappadocia or some other Eastern country who could scarcely speak Latin. Auxentius of Milan was the most celebrated of these immigrants. We must also mention Epictetus, who was installed at Centumcellæ (Civita-Vecchia), and who was a very undesirable character.

But the place where the trouble was most grievous was Rome. At the moment when Constantius entered Italy, during the summer of 352, Pope Julius had just been succeeded by Liberius (May 17). We have already seen what his attitude was in this melancholy business, how he was banished from Rome, and exiled to the remote parts of Thrace.

The violence shown to him was much resented by the Christian populace. At first, the clergy made great demonstrations of fidelity. In a solemn assembly, priests, deacons, and other clerics took an oath in the presence of the faithful that, so long as Liberius lived, they would accept no other bishop.[1] Among the most determined figured the archdeacon Felix, and the deacon Damasus, the latter of whom had set out with Liberius, but had returned shortly after. This fiery zeal soon died out. The Court resolved to appoint a successor to Liberius. This time it was not considered wise to have recourse to the Cappadocian band: the new Bishop of Rome was chosen from the ranks of the Roman clergy. The archdeacon Felix was summoned to Milan and, notwithstanding his oath, accepted the succession to the exile. Acacius of Cæsarea superintended the whole affair[2]; Epictetus was also mixed up in it.[3] They no doubt figured at the ordination ceremony, performed, says Athanasius, by three spies[4] in

---

[1] Upon this, see *Collectio Avellana*, n. 1: *Quae gesta sunt inter Liberium et Felicem episcopos*. The oath is attested also by St Jerome, in his *Chronicle*, a. Abr. 2365.

[2] Jerome, *De viris*, 98.   [3] Athan. *Hist. Ar.* 73.

[4] Κατάσκοποι, a play upon words, in contradiction to ἐπίσκοποι.

the palace, in the presence of three eunuchs, who filled the
part of the Christian people. On his return to Rome,
Felix was welcomed by the majority of the clergy; but
the people would not hear of him, and held aloof, seizing
every opportunity of expressing their displeasure and
demanding the return of Liberius. In May 357,
Constantius visited Rome. Then their efforts increased.
Christian matrons presented themselves at the palace[1];
and in the circus the crowd demanded their bishop.
"You shall have him," replied the emperor; "and he
will return to you better than he left you." He knew
already that Liberius had not held out, and that the
Bishops of Aquileia and Berea had persuaded him to forsake Athanasius and accept communion with the Easterns.

But this proceeding on the part of Liberius put the
government in a position of very great embarrassment.
He might now be reinstated at Rome, since he had done
what he was asked to do. But what was to be done with
Felix?[2] After long hesitation, the Court at last decided
to entrust the government of the Roman Church to two
bishops at the same time. I have said before that this
scheme was refused by the people who, now that Liberius
was restored to them, made it their own business to get
rid of his rival. This solution, however, was not
accomplished without scenes of brawling.[3] Somewhat
confused recollections[4] represent Liberius to us as installed
on the Via Nomentana near Sta Agnese, and Felix as
taking refuge on an estate which belonged to him, on
the road to Portus. It is certain that the former Pope
gained the victory, that the faithful flocked to his presence,
and arranged for him a triumphal entry.[5] Shortly after-

[1] Theodoret, *H. E.* ii. 14.

[2] A law as to the immunities of the inferior clergy (*Cod. Theod.* xvi.
2, 14) was addressed to him. The date which it bears in the
Theodosian Code (December 6, 357) is open to challenge.

[3] Regrettable incidents, which occurred on this account, were
referred to, in 360, in the condemnation of Basil of Ancyra (Sozomen,
H. E. iv. 24).

[4] *Liber Pontificalis*, Lives of Liberius and of Felix II.

[5] Jerome, *Chron.* a. Abr. 2365; *Coll. Avell.*, loc. cit.

wards, Felix returned to contest the position, and tried to regain possession of the basilica of Julius, in Trastevere, with the assistance of the clergy of his party. But the faithful, including both the aristocracy and the common people, interfered a second time, and the intruder, being decisively repulsed, made up his mind to take no further steps.[1]

One serious indication of this troubled state of things was that the Roman Church was not represented at the Council of Ariminum. This was a piece of good fortune for it, since the result was that, when the council broke up, it had had no share in the " falling-away " of that assembly. The year 360 passed by without Liberius having recognized its decrees, against which protests were already being uttered in Gaul. In the spring of 361 the officials of Constantius disappeared: the reign of Julian was beginning. The West was scarcely aware of it. There, Christians were accustomed to live with pagans, who were still numerous and influential and were largely represented in government offices and in the ranks of the aristocracy. Besides, the Christians seldom allowed themselves to be carried away into those excesses of zeal which, in Julian's reign, served as a pretext for so many reactions. Liberty was restored completely under Jovian and Valentinian. On December 22, 365, Felix died. His party was wise enough not to give him a successor, and Liberius to show the greatest indulgence towards those persons who had taken his rival as their leader. The unity of the clergy was re-established. Yet bitter memories remained : everyone had not approved of the merciful conduct of Liberius; Liberians and Felicians continued to look at each other askance. The death of Liberius (September 24, 366), following almost immediately after that of Felix, opened the

---

[1] We know that legend gave Felix a striking revenge, and that it even sacrificed to him the memory of Liberius. Upon this, see my edition of the *Liber Pontificalis*, vol. i., p. cxx. ff. In this pontifical chronicle Felix figures, as the result, I think, of a later editing, in the number of the Popes. He is also included in the same way in other catalogues of rather earlier date. Of all the anti-popes of antiquity, Felix is the only one to be so favoured.

conflict between the two currents of opinion. Scarcely
was the Pope buried than two parties formed themselves.
The one established itself at the end of the Campus
Martius, in the basilica of Lucina (S. Lorenzo in Lucina);
the other in the basilica of Julius (S. Maria) in Trastevere.
The latter were the irreconcilables, the adversaries of the
pacific policy of the dead Pope.   They included only
seven priests and three deacons; and one of the latter,
Ursinus, was acclaimed as bishop and ordained on the
spot by the Bishop of Tibur. It was on Sunday, and the
custom already existed of choosing that day for episcopal
ordinations.   In the Church of Lucina, the deacon
Damasus, an adherent of Felix who had come over to the
other side, was elected by a large majority of clergy and
laity. Damasus was a Roman. His father before him had
passed through all the degrees of the hierarchy.[1] He was
a man of high character and some literary knowledge,[2] and
was favourably regarded by the Christian aristocracy. His
enemies were wont to cast at him as a reproach the
popularity he enjoyed with the matrons[3]; they had not
forgotten his readiness to accept Felix, after having made
some show of zeal at the moment of the departure of
Liberius.   Once elected, he took no immediate steps to
obtain ordination: no doubt, it was too late in the day.
The ceremony was therefore deferred until the following
Sunday.

The meeting in the Church of Lucina had hardly
broken up, when news was brought of what had just taken
place in Trastevere. Feelings, as is always the case
in these popular elections, were in a highly excitable
condition. The most ardent, among whom were included,
we are told, the circus-drivers and other persons of the
same type, rushed *en masse* towards the basilica of Julius.
The followers of Ursinus offered resistance. A battle

---

[1] Inscription (Ihm. No. 57) in S. Lorenzo in Damaso, a church
which was erected, it would seem, upon the site of his father's house.

[2] His verses display some knowledge of Vergil. We shall have
to speak later of his relations with St Jerome.

[3] They called him the ear-scratcher of the ladies, *auriscalpius
matronarum* (*Coll. Avell.*, loc. cit.).

ensued : cudgels were brought into play, some were wounded, some even killed. The riot lasted three days. On the following Sunday, October 1, the basilica of the Lateran which had been put in a state of defence by the adherents of Damasus witnessed the consecration of the lawful bishop. It was the Bishop of Ostia who, according to custom, took the chief part in this ceremony.

What were the forces of authority doing in the midst of all this disorder ? The Prefect of Rome, Viventius, was a wise and conscientious man, but of a disposition not easily roused to action. He made laudable efforts to appease the populace; but failing of success, he made up his mind to leave the city and retire to a country-house some way off, hoping, no doubt, in this way to shelter his person and his authority. Gradually, his mind regained the calm which had been disturbed ; he recognized the regularity of the ordination of Damasus, and decided that Ursinus should be exiled from Rome, with the two deacons, Amantius and Lupus, who were, after him, the chief leaders of his party. This was done. But the dissenting party held out ; the seven priests who were with them continued to bring them together in schismatical meetings. Damasus then appealed to authority. The seven priests were arrested ; but, as the guards were conducting them out of Rome, the partisans of Ursinus fell upon the escort, set the prisoners free, and led them in triumph to the basilica of Liberius,[1] where they installed themselves as in a fortress.

But the adherents of Damasus did not leave them to enjoy their success. On October 26, an opposition mob, in which several of the clergy were mixed up, proceeded to lay siege to the basilica on the Esquiline. The doors were closed and strongly defended. While these were being assailed with hatchets and fire, the most nimble of Damasus' supporters climbed on to the roof, effected an opening in it, and through this poured down a hail of

---

[1] In its main structure, including the colonnades and the mosaics which crown them, the basilica of Liberius has been preserved down to our own day.

tiles upon the partisans of Ursinus. At last the doors
gave way; and an appalling conflict ensued. When order
was re-established, a hundred and thirty-seven dead
bodies were taken up.[1] We may well believe that the
Ursinian party made the most of these victims; it was
admitted that the besiegers had not lost a single man.
Although much damaged, the basilica continued to be
the scene of schismatical meetings: in these protests
were made against the violence done, the assistance of
the emperor was invoked, and a council was demanded.
But gradually the guards of the prefect succeeded in
restoring outward order.

A year after these events, Valentinian, thinking that
the passions of the parties were now sufficiently allayed,
allowed Ursinus and the other exiles to return to Rome.
On September 15, 367, the anti-pope made a solemn
re-entry into the city, amid the acclamations of his
supporters, who lost no time in renewing the disturbance,
with the result that the emperor, finding his hopes were
mistaken, caused Ursinus to be expelled again (November
16). The prefect Viventius had been replaced by Vettius
Agorius Prætextatus, a man much esteemed for his amiable
character and highly cultivated mind. He was a pagan,
and a very zealous one. The inscriptions which mention
him, together with his wife Aconia Paulina,[3] extol his
piety towards the gods, and enumerate in stately terms
the priestly offices which he held. It was he who, when
Pope Damasus urged him to be converted, replied:
'Willingly, if you will make me Bishop of Rome."[4]
Ammianus Marcellinus makes a similar reflection, in close
connection with the rival claims of Ursinus. He thinks
it very natural that there should be a contest for such a
position as that of bishop of the capital, "for," he says,
'if that post is once gained, a man enjoys in peace a

---

[1] This is the number given by Ammianus Marcellinus; the *Gesta*
speaks of one hundred and sixty dead; the *Chronicle* of St Jerome
(a. Abr. 2382), mentions only *crudelissimae interfectiones diversi sexus.*

[2] *Coll. Avell.* 5. Letter to the prefect Prætextatus.

[3] *Corpus Inscript. Lat.*, vol. vi., Nos. 1777-1781.

[4] Jerome, *Contra Joh. Hieros.* 8.

fortune assured by the generosity of the matrons ; he can ride abroad in a carriage, clothed in magnificent robes, and can give banquets, the luxury of which surpasses that of the emperor's table." He adds that it would be better to imitate the poverty and simplicity of certain provincial bishops, whose virtue is a recommendation for Christianity.[1] Ammianus was not the only man to deplore the progress of comfort among the Roman clergy. St Jerome has censured with much vigour the strange abuses which the increasing prosperity of the Church of Rome introduced into its midst. But we must return to the schismatics.

The basilica of Liberius had remained in their hands. Damasus laid claim to it through the "protector" of his Church, and Valentinian, who did not wish for disorders in Rome, caused this edifice to be restored to him.[2] At the same time, the priests, who presided over the meetings of the Ursinians, were banished.[3] But the ferment took some time in subsiding. They assembled, on Sundays and Feast-days, in the cemeteries in the outskirts of the city, and the Office was celebrated as well as it could be in the absence of clergy. The Church of St Agnes, on the Via Nomentana, was one of the meeting-places of the dissentients. One day, a terrible affray took place there, in which the Ursinians got the worst of it, and were ejected. After this it was necessary to forbid to the promoters of disturbance, not only the city but the outskirts as well, within a radius of twenty miles.[4] Ursinus himself was sent off to Gaul. Some time afterwards, permission was granted to him and to certain of his supporters to reside in Northern Italy[5]; but they were forbidden to come near Rome. The imperial rescripts relating to this affair show us Valentinian for ever divided between a dread of interfering too vigorously in a religious dispute and his anxiety for public tranquillity, which was very difficult to maintain in the midst of the unoccupied and restless populace of the ancient capital.

---

[1] Ammianus, xxvii. 3, 14.   [2] *Coll. Avell.* 6 (end of 367).
[3] *Ibid.* 7, January 12, 368.   [4] *Ibid.* 8, 9, 10 (end of 368).
[5] *Ibid.* 11, 12 (end of 370 to summer of 372).

As for Damasus, his victory had cost him too dear :
his promotion had been accompanied by too much police
action, too many imperial rescripts, too many corpses.
The whole of his Pontificate felt the effects of it. And
besides, Ursinus had never laid down his arms; as long
as he lived, he never ceased his implacable hostility to
his rival. As he could not dethrone him, he tried to
get rid of him by means of criminal prosecutions. There
was already a question of an attempt of this kind about
the year 370,[1] and another, as we shall see, happened later.

It was not only with the schism of Ursinus that the
Pope had to deal. Rome was full of 'Little Churches.'
Not to speak of such remnants as there might be of old
sects, such as Valentinians, Marcionites, Montanists, and
Sabellians, the Novatian Church still continued to exist,
governed by a series of bishops, who linked themselves
on to the old episcopal succession, from St Peter to
Fabian. The African Christians, who had found a home
in Rome, if they belonged to the Catholic confession, that
of Cæcilian, attended the same churches as the Catholics of
Rome ; but the Donatists were organized separately, under
bishops of their own country.[2] They were called Mountaineers, *Montenses*, no doubt on account of some local
peculiarity. There were also the Luciferians, so-called,
those who had taken the same attitude as Lucifer of

[1] Gratian alludes to this in his rescript to Aquilinus (*Coll.
Avell.* No. 13, p. 57, Günther): *iudiciorum examine exploratum
mentis sanctissimae virum* (Damasus), *ut etiam divo patri nostro
Valentiniano est comprobatum.* It is no doubt to this affair that
Rufinus alludes, in the passage (ii. 10) in which he speaks of the
ill-will of the prefect Maximin. This official was Præfectus Annonæ
in 369-370 ; he replaced the prefect of Rome who was ill, and showed
a severity during this provisional tenure of office which made him
hated by everyone. A little later (371-372), he was Vicar of Rome,
i.e., of the *Diœcesis suburbicaria.*

[2] This episcopal succession was known to Optatus, ii. 4. It
began with a certain Victor, who was present as Bishop of Garba at
the Council of Cirta (305) and later on established himself in Rome.
He was succeeded by Boniface, Encolpius, Macrobius, known by
some of his writings, Lucian, and Claudian. This Claudian gave a
great deal of trouble to Damasus, as we shall see later.

Caliaris (Cagliari) and Gregory of Illiberris against the defaulters of Ariminum, men to whom Liberius, Hilary, Eusebius of Vercellæ, and even Athanasius himself, were palterers with the truth. They had a bishop who was named Aurelius; but the most renowned personage of their party was a priest called Macarius, whose austerities were famous. The meetings of these dissentients were held, for lack of churches, in private houses. The police, stimulated by denunciations from the Lateran, made life hard for the schismatics. Macarius, who was arrested during a religious service, suffered much from the brutality of the common people. Being condemned to exile, he died at Ostia from a wound which he had received when he was arrested. The Bishop of Ostia, Florentius, apparently more moved by his virtues than shocked by his uncompromising obstinacy, gave him honourable burial in the basilica of the martyr Asterius.[1] His party rallied again under the leadership of a certain Bishop Ephesius. Damasus had some trouble in getting rid of this new rival.[2]

The Bishop of Ostia, although he had presided at the ordination of Pope Damasus, does not seem to have had much taste for his continual appeal to the secular arm. We can easily understand what would be thought of this, alike by those who had consecrated Ursinus and by the other bishops who had approved of his ordination. Damasus had therefore to struggle, not only against a Roman party, determined and always ready for disturbance, but also against a strong opposition among the Italian bishops. He tried, we are told, to obtain the condemnation of Ursinus from a council assembled in honour of his *natale*, in 367 or 368; but the bishops, although remaining in communion with the Pope, seem to have refused to pronounce a sentence against an absent man.[3]

---

[1] *Libell. precum.* 77-82.

[2] *Ibid.* 84-91, 104-107. The prefect Bassus, mentioned in this account, belongs to the year 382.

[3] *Gesta inter Lib. et Fel.* 13, an Ursinian document, we must remember.

Also, as the favour of the government was so necessary to him, he was not disposed to cause difficulties in that direction. The Emperor Valentinian, as we have seen, would not admit that the State was justified in taking measures against those prelates who had remained faithful to the confession of Ariminum. It would have been a delicate matter for Pope Damasus to set himself counter to this policy of pacification. Athanasius also had some difficulty in inducing him to take action against the few Arian bishops who remained in the Western Empire. He tried it first[1] with regard to Ursacius, Valens, and the other " Illyrians." It was a more difficult matter as to Auxentius, who had been specially authorized by the Emperor Valentinian. At last the Pope made up his mind to act, and in a second council, held at the instigation of Athanasius, he declared[2] that the Creed of Nicæa was the only authorized Creed, and that that of Ariminum could not replace it. In an incidental phrase he speaks of a condemnation already pronounced against Auxentius, quoting as authorities the Bishops of Gaul and Venetia, behind whom he entrenches himself. At the end of the synodical letter, he expresses a hope that the irreconcilables will speedily lose the title of bishops, and that their churches will be delivered from them.

This was not very explicit. But perhaps Damasus was right not to run any risk. What would have been the use? It was certain that Valentinian would take no steps to dispossess bishops already recognized by him, and accepted by their people. Therefore, the best thing to do was to wait till they died, and then replace them by orthodox successors.

Auxentius did not put the patience of the Pope to too long a test: he died in the autumn of 374. The business of replacing him gave rise to serious conflicts between the orthodox party, determined to secure possession of the bishopric, and the Arians, equally determined to keep it.

---

[1] Athan. *Ep. ad Afros* 10.

[2] Jaffé, 232, *Confidimus quidem*; *cf.* Sozomen, *H. E.* vi. 23; Theodoret, *H. E.* ii. 22.

The province of Æmilia-Liguria had as its consular at
this time a Roman nobleman named Ambrose.[1]   At the
time of his birth, his father, also called Ambrose, was
prætorian prefect of the Gauls.   He already had other
children, a daughter, named Marcellina, and a son, Satyrus.
The young Ambrose was brought up in Rome by his
mother and sister, his father having died soon after his
birth.   The family, one of the most illustrious in Rome,
had long been Christian; one of its members, St
Soteris, had suffered martyrdom in the time of Maximian.
The Pope sometimes came to their house; the ladies
received him with the greatest respect, and kissed his
hand.   As soon as he had departed, young Ambrose,
still at a roguish age, would begin to imitate his grave
walk and his stately gestures; he even attempted to make
Marcellina kiss his hand, but his sister laughingly refused
As soon as his education was finished, he became attached
to the secretariat of the prætorian prefect, Probus, the
most important Christian nobleman in Rome.   Probus
appointed him governor of Æmilia-Liguria, advising him
to treat the people under his administration with gentleness, like a bishop, not like a magistrate.   Probus was a
prophet.   The episcopal election having, as I said before,
much excited the minds of the populace, a great commotion took place in the church, and the governor thought
it his duty to go there.   Suddenly, a child's cry was
heard: "Ambrose Bishop!"   Both parties at once took up
the cry with a united acclamation.   It was in vain that
Ambrose protested, and employed every effort to escape
from the popular favour, declaring that he had not been
baptized.   He was not listened to.   The bishops who
were present deemed that his name was the only one on
which agreement was possible.   They passed over the
rules which forbade the ordination of neophytes.   Ambrose
was baptized on November 30, and ordained eight days
afterwards (December 7).

[1] *Aurelius Ambrosius.*   The biographical details as to St Ambrose
come to us through his secretary, the deacon Paulinus, who wrote
the life of his master at the request of St Augustine.

Thus suddenly raised to the episcopate, he had much
to learn, if not of Christianity in general, at any rate, of
theology. As he had studied Greek, he set himself to
read the works of Philo, Origen, Basil, and Didymus.
Immediately after his consecration, he had occasion to
correspond with the illustrious Bishop of Cæsarea, who
congratulated him upon his appointment.[1]   The Church of
Milan had soon cause for satisfaction at having secured
such a pastor.   But it was not only to this Church that he
had been given; it was to the whole body of Christians of
that time. This soon became evident.

However, the Emperor Valentinian died suddenly at
Brigetio, in Pannonia, on November 17, 375. He left two
sons: Gratian, the elder, aged sixteen, who had been
associated with his father in the Empire for some years,[2]
was at Trèves when his father died; the other, Valentinian,
still quite young, was living at Sirmium with his mother,
the Empress Justina.   The army on the Danube, without
consulting Gratian, associated his younger brother with
him in the government; Gratian confirmed this arrangement, but without depriving himself of the government of
the whole of the West. Ambrose, whose election had
been received by the dead emperor with great satisfaction,
remained always devoted to his family.   So long as
Gratian lived, the bishop was his trusted adviser.

Italy was still disturbed by the obstinacy of Ursinus.
The suburbicarian provinces being forbidden to him, he
stirred up strife at Milan, joining his efforts to those of the
Arians, who had now passed into the condition of dissenters, troubling Ambrose in his official duties, and
thwarting his plans. His hand was seen once more at
Rome in various intrigues. In 374, the emperor was
obliged to write on this subject to the *Vicarius* Simplicius.[3]
Powerless, in spite of all his efforts, to gain possession of
the Lateran, the anti-pope set himself to drive his rival

---

[1] Basil, *Ep.* 197.

[2] Gratian was born on April 18, 359; he was associated in the
empire on August 24, 367.

[3] The letter is lost, but it is quoted in *Coll. Avell.* No. 13.

out of it. A criminal process was undertaken against
Damasus by Isaac, a converted Jew. At this time, the
Roman magistrates prided themselves, following the example of Valentinian, on their extreme severity. We do
not know of what crime Damasus was accused,[1] but it
was evidently of some capital offence, and the affair, being
vigorously pursued before the prefect of Rome, was threatening to end in a condemnation, when Gratian was induced
to intervene. The emperor tried the case himself, gave
judgment, and sent the venerable Pontiff away acquitted
of the charge. Isaac was exiled to Spain; Ursinus
was imprisoned at Cologne. Isaac shortly afterwards
renounced Christianity and returned to the synagogue.[2]
Such attempts were characteristic of the ethics of the time.
We may judge what security could be enjoyed by bishops,
especially bishops of great towns, exposed as they were,
in the exercise of their multifarious functions, to the
danger of offending so many people and of making so
many enemies.

Damasus was not satisfied with the testimony which the
imperial decision had just given in favour of his innocence;
he wished the whole affair to be discussed in a council. A

---

[1] The legend of the *Liber Pontificalis* speaks of adultery; but, as
Damasus was nearly eighty years of age, such a charge would have
been far too improbable.

[2] This Isaac, during his Christian period, published several works
of theology and exegesis. Gennadius (*De viris*, 26) knew of, and we
still possess (Migne, *P. L.*, vol. xxxiii., p. 1541), a small treatise on the
Trinity and the Incarnation. To Isaac must also be attributed an
"Explanation of the Catholic Faith," published in 1883 by Caspari
(*Kirchenhistorische Anecdota*, vol. i., p. 304). Dom G. Morin (*Revue
d'hist. et de litt. relig.* 1899, p. 97 *et seq.*) has proposed to attribute
to him two important works, the Commentary known as Ambrosiaster's
upon the Epistles of St Paul, and the *Quaestiones V. et N. Testamenti*,
both written in Rome in the time of Pope Damasus. This hypothesis
is very probable, and still remains so, although (*Revue Bénédictine*,
1903, p. 113) its author has abandoned it. I think, with Martin
Schanz (*Gesch. der röm. Litteratur*, part iv., p. 455), that Dom Morin
has not succeeded in refuting himself, and that the new solution
which he proposes for this literary problem is far from possessing the
same value as the first.

meeting of bishops from all parts of Italy assembled in
Rome in 378.[1] They presented to the emperor a petition,
which we still possess as well as Gratian's reply. The
bishops reminded him that, during an earlier phase of the
affair of Ursinus, the sovereign had decided that, while the
police concerned themselves with the banishment of the
author of the disturbances, it was the Pope's function to
take measures against the bishops who had espoused
his cause. This was perfectly just. Granted the attitude
adopted in religious matters by the Emperor Valentinian,
the State could have no idea of interfering in ecclesiastical
decisions; its special duty was to guard against public
order being compromised. Nevertheless, contingencies
might arise, when the efficacy of ecclesiastical sentences,
and the services which they were called upon to render
from the point of view of good order, might be compromised by too complete an abstention on the part of the
State. Therefore, the bishops demanded the assistance of
the strong arm of the law, first in securing the appearance
of the rebellious prelates, and afterwards in preventing
the deposed bishops from stirring up strife in the churches
which the ecclesiastical judge had withdrawn from their
jurisdiction. Several cases are specified. The Bishops of
Parma and Puteoli refused to submit to the sentences of
deposition passed against them; an African Bishop,
Restitutus, and Claudian, the Donatist Bishop of Rome,
are also mentioned.

But this council was chiefly occupied with Isaac's
affair, still quite recent. It endeavoured to secure that the
Pope at any rate should be protected against such attempts.
The emperor, it said, has investigated the conduct of
Damasus; false accusers ought henceforward to be forbidden to drag him before the magistrate. If there was
any occasion for a trial, and if the case was not within
the competence of the council, at least it ought to be
carried before the emperor in person. In addition to
the recent case, there was another precedent: Pope

---

[1] In the collections of councils; see also Constant, *Ep. Rom.
Pont.* p. 523.

Silvester, being accused by sacrilegious persons, was judged by the Emperor Constantine.

In consequence of these representations Gratian addressed to the Vicar Aquilinus a rescript,[1] in which on all these points he expresses agreement with the views of the council. However, so far as regards the exceptional jurisdiction claimed for the Pope, he confines himself to enjoining that the accusations or testimony of persons of doubtful character or well known as calumniators are not readily to be admitted.[2] This is equivalent to a refusal. The Pope remained, like his flock, subject theoretically to the jurisdiction of the prefect of Rome. We must add, however, that after the pontificate of Damasus there is no mention of such jurisdiction being exercised over any of his successors.

It might have been thought that things were now arranged, and that Ursinus would remain quiet. But it was not so. The young emperor was good-natured and weak, and he allowed himself to be appealed to and beguiled. The agents of the anti-pope, in particular a eunuch called Paschasius, were furiously active in Rome. In 381 the prefect sent to Court a report, in which the whole matter seemed to have been reopened. Just at that time a council met at Aquileia. Ambrose, who was its moving spirit, obtained from it a very urgent application to Gratian.[3] It is the last time we hear of Ursinus. He died, no doubt, soon afterwards.

When appealed to, as he constantly was, by the Eastern bishops to pity their position, Damasus might well have replied that his own was scarcely to be envied, and that he found himself no more than they on a bed of roses!

The Council of Aquileia,[4] of which I have just been

---

[1] *Coll. Avell.* n. 13 : *Ordinariorum sententias*, in the last months of 378.

[2] "Ne facile sit cuicumque perdito notabili pravitate morum aut infami calumnia notato personam criminatoris assumere aut testimonii dictionem in accusationem episcopi profiteri."

[3] Ambrose, *Ep.* 11.

[4] Upon the Council of Aquileia, see the record preserved amongst the letters of St Ambrose (after letter 8), letters 9-12 of the same

speaking, is connected with a whole campaign, undertaken
and resolutely carried out by Ambrose, to extinguish
in the Western empire the last fires of Arianism. We
have seen that the Emperor Valentinian's neutrality
in regard to creeds allowed certain bishops who had
remained loyal to the "faith" of Ariminum to retain
possession of their sees. The orthodox bishops had to
protect themselves as well as they could. In Spain, in
Gaul, and in Italy, from the days of Eusebius of Vercellæ
and of Hilary, the orthodox party had held council after
council, and had multiplied declarations in favour of
the Creed of Nicæa; it was everywhere proclaimed
as the only one to be accepted. When Damasus had
solemnly taken up his position against Ursacius, Valens,
and even Auxentius, other episcopal meetings were held
in Sicily, Dalmatia, Dardania, Macedonia, the two Epiri,
in Achaia and in Crete[1]; in short, in all the provinces
of Illyricum, always excepting those nearest to the
Danube,[2] where the movement in favour of Nicæa was
thwarted by a certain amount of resistance. In Africa
also there seems to have been some hesitation. The
Bishop of Carthage, Restitutus,[3] had played an important
part in the "betrayal" of 359; the Creed of Ariminum
had its defenders in Africa, and Restitutus himself seems
to have remained attached to it for a long time. Athanasius was uneasy at this state of things. Although the

author, and the fragments of Maximin's book against Ambrose in
Fr. Kauffmann, *Aus der Schule des Wulfila* (Strassburg, 1899).

[1] Athan., *Ep. ad Afros.* 1.

[2] The two Dacias, Upper Mesia, and the Pannonian provinces.

[3] This is, I think, the same Restitutus mentioned in the council's
letter to the emperor (c. 6 see above, p. 372). It is generally allowed
that the person referred to there is a Donatist; but the Donatists
are mentioned separately in the phrase which follows. The rescript
to Aquilinus does not speak of him and could not have done so, because
the case of that bishop belonged to the jurisdiction of the African
authorities, and had nothing to do with the Italian officials. Besides,
if the Bishop of Carthage had once more become favourable to the
Creed of Nicæa, there would have been no need for St Athanasius
to interfere; at any rate he would not have failed to mention in his
letter so important a fact.

affairs of Africa belonged rather to the jurisdiction of
Rome than to his own, he thought it his duty to come
to the assistance of Pope Damasus, and wrote a celebrated letter "to the Africans" in which he inculcated upon
them the necessity of abandoning the formula of Ariminum
and adopting that of Nicæa. Restitutus refused to be
convinced and maintained his position. Proceedings
were taken against him from Rome; an attempt was
made to compel him to appear before a tribunal of
bishops, and a rescript was even obtained to that effect
from the Emperor Gratian; but the accused disobeyed
and did not appear. The matter, however, was arranged
shortly afterwards, either by the death of Restitutus
or by his return to orthodoxy.

There remained the Danubian provinces where the
opposition to Nicæa was deeply rooted, and was maintained
in spite of all exhortations from councils. It would only
have been labour lost if Athanasius had written to them
But gradually death thinned the ranks of the opposing
bishops; and the new holders of the sees were of con-
forming opinions.

When Germinius died, Ambrose succeeded in placing
in the important see of Sirmium an orthodox bishop
named Anemius. It was not without difficulty that he
achieved this; for the Empress Justina, who lived at
Sirmium, was an enthusiastic Arian and fought with
all her might against the intention of the Bishop of
Milan. Even before the consecration of Anemius, two
Danubian bishops, Palladius of Ratiaria,[1] and Secundianus,
who had been disturbed apparently on account of their
doctrine and threatened with the loss of their bishoprics,
had obtained the consent of Gratian to their cause being
judged by an Œcumenical Council which was to be held
at Aquileia. Delayed for some unknown reasons, amongst
which, however, we may certainly include the ravages
made by the invasion of the Goths, the council opened
at last on September 3, 381. It included a certain number
of bishops from Upper Italy (*dioecesis Italiae*) and from

[1] Artcher, south of Vidin, in the modern Bulgaria.

the "diocese" of Pannonia; from three other "dioceses,"
Africa, Gaul, and the Five Provinces, representatives had
been appointed by the body of bishops. Pope Damasus,
seeing no necessity for such a display of ecclesiastical
forces, sent no representatives, and even opposed the idea
of his own immediate suffragans taking part in the
council. No one came from Britain or from Spain, or
from the Orient either, although an invitation couched in
general terms had been circulated there. The Eastern
prelates had just held a meeting at Constantinople; they
did not disturb themselves. From Eastern Illyricum,
which included the "dioceses" of Dacia and of Macedonia,
there came only the two bishops concerned whose sees
were in the "diocese" of Dacia. Acholius of Thessalonica,
and no doubt several other prelates from his district,
had already taken part, as we have seen, in the Council
of Constantinople.[1]

After several rather confused discussions, the debates
— presided over by Ambrose, with the decision and
clearness of an official judge—were concentrated upon

[1] They took part in it, however, on a special and, in some ways,
an unusual summons. The manner in which Gregory of Nazianzus
speaks of them, calling them "Westerns" (*Carm. de vita sua*, line
1802; *cf.* Ambrose, *Ep.* xiii. 7), and their relations with Pope
Damasus (Jaffé, 237, 238) clearly places them among the Western
episcopate. This is still more evident with regard to the bishops
of the diocese of Dacia; from documents of the Council of Aquileia
it is plain that Palladius and Secundianus had their sees *in partibus
Occidentalibus*, and even that the secular authority which could maintain them there or banish them thence by force was that of the
Emperor Gratian. It is admitted on the evidence of Sozomen (*H. E.*
vii. 4) that Gratian entrusted to Theodosius the care of governing
Illyria with the Orient: Ἰλλυριοὺς καὶ τὰ πρὸς ἥλιον ἀνίσχοντα τῆς ἀρχῆς
Θεοδοσίῳ ἐπιτρέψας. Sozomen in speaking of Ἰλλυριοί was undoubtedly
thinking of the *Illyricum Orientale* of the *Notitia Dignitatum;* but
there is nothing to show that the boundaries established on that side
betweeen the imperial jurisdictions of Arcadius and Honorius date
back to the time when Theodosius was associated in the empire.
In July 381 Gratian issued enactments in Mesia, at Viminacium
(*Cod. Theod.* i. 10, 1; xii. 1, 89). Moreover, these provinces, although
they belonged politically to the Eastern empire, continued none
the less to form part of the ecclesiastical body of the West.

an Arian document, a letter of Arius himself, in which his
heretical doctrine was set out without any ambiguity.
This letter was read, and upon each of the disputed points
the dissentients were required to declare whether they
accepted or rejected the expressions of the arch-heretic.
They lost themselves in evasions, in subtle distinctions, in
disputes as to the competence of the tribunal, which they
did not consider of sufficient importance.   Ambrose told
them that it was impossible for all that to put hundreds of
bishops to inconvenience, as had been done at the time of
the Council of Ariminum, merely to clear up an individual
case which was so simple.   As to the root of the matter,
what Palladius and Secundianus said and what they left
unsaid alike combined to disclose their real opinions.   It
is evident that they were Arians: that, for them, the
Father was the only true God; and the Son and the Holy
Spirit were beings clearly inferior to Him.   The council
decided that there was reason for deposing the two
bishops.   They informed the emperor of their sentence,
begging him to carry it out.

The Eastern prelates, whose presence Palladius and
his colleague demanded at Aquileia, would not have
treated them otherwise.   They had not condemned the
Arians or Eudoxians, replaced Dorotheus by Meletius
and Demophilus by Gregory of Nazianzus, to give anyone a ground to claim their support against Latin
orthodoxy.   From this time forward, there was no longer
any loophole through which it was possible to creep
between the Churches of the East and those of the West
in order to introduce or to support the heresy of Arius:
both were agreed to get rid of it.

There still remained, however, between the two
Churches some personal disputes, which were very difficult
to smooth down.   I have already mentioned in the last
chapter, how Ambrose had been the means of bringing
about the assembling at Rome of a great council in which
he hoped that these matters would be settled.   This
council was actually held, but without result, unless it
were to exhibit to the pious curiosity of the Romans an

assemblage of celebrated bishops, Acholius of Thessalonica, Paulinus of Antioch, Epiphanius of Cyprus, and Ambrose of Milan. This time, Marcellina had good reason to kiss her brother's hand.[1] Other noble ladies were eager to offer to the foreign prelates the hospitality of their luxurious mansions. Besides the bishops, much notice was taken of a Latin monk, named Jerome, who had just been spending several years in the East. A native of Dalmatia,[2] he had come to Rome to pursue his studies, and after a somewhat dissipated youth had been baptized there.[3] In the course of a journey in Gaul, when he stopped for some time at Trèves, he felt himself called to a life of retirement, prayer, and intellectual work. One of his companions in study, Rufinus, who was from Aquileia, induced Jerome to visit his native town, and there he met with several persons possessed by the same desires as himself—the priest Chromatius, Heliodorus of Altinum, Bonosus, Rufinus, Niceas, and others. In their company, he imagined himself already "in the kingdom of the blest."[4] In 373, this edifying company broke up—for what reason we do not know. Whilst Bonosus went to lead a hermit's life upon a rock on the Dalmatian coast, Rufinus embarked for Alexandria, and Heliodorus, Jerome,

---

[1] It was not the first time that Marcellina had seen him since his elevation to the episcopate. She was with him at Milan in 378 during a severe illness which he had in that year. Marcellina had been consecrated as a virgin by Pope Liberius, one Christmas day, in the basilica of St Peter (Ambrose, *De Virginibus*, iii. 1). She died at Milan, after Satyrus and Ambrose.

[2] Stridon, his native town, was destroyed during his lifetime, about the year 378, by the Goths. Its situation remains uncertain ; see, however, *Corpus Inscriptionum Latinarum*, vol. iii., No. 9860 ; and Bulic, *Bull. Dalm.* vol. xxii. (1899), p. 137. Upon St Jerome, see the excellent monograph of George Grützmacher, in the *Studien zur Geschichte der Theologie und der Kirche*, vols. vi. (1901) and x. (1906).

[3] It is impossible to admit that the indiscretions, the memory of which troubled Jerome in after years, could have been subsequent to his baptism. In that case, he would never have been ordained priest.

[4] "Aquileienses clerici quasi chorus beatorum habentur." *Chron. a. Abr.,* 2390.

and several others fixed their choice upon the Syrian
desert. There also there were famous solitaries, of whom
they must have heard from Evagrius, a priest of Antioch,
who had just made a long stay in Italy. At this time he
was returning to his own country ; perhaps they travelled
together. In any case, it was from him that, on his arrival
at Antioch, Jerome received hospitality. As to his
companions, two lost courage and returned to Venetia ;
two others died ; Jerome himself fell sick. It was then
that he had his celebrated dream, in which he heard
himself reproached for his attachment to pagan authors,
and promised never again to open any book by a profane
orator or poet. As soon as his health was restored, he
hastened to learn Greek, and began the study of exegesis
under the guidance of the famous Apollinaris. Finally,
screwing up his courage, he buried himself in the desert of
Chalcis, and at first attempted to imitate the extreme
asceticism of the most renowned monks. But he was not
of the stuff of which fakirs are made[1] ; he returned to his
books. Shortly afterwards, he compiled the Life of Paul,
the first hermit of Egypt—a composition with a large
element of myth—and began his exegetical works by inter-
preting the prophet Obadiah. He also devoted himself
to Hebrew, a hard penance for a disciple of Cicero.

His relations with Apollinaris had not led him into
heresy, nor had it even made him a theologian. He was
a rhetorician and not a philosopher, and theology had but
little attraction for him. Upon that subject he always
depended on the opinion of someone else. But dogmatic
disputes followed him even into the desert. The Meletians
tormented him about the three hypostases. For a Latin
such as he was, three hypostases meant three substances
—in other words, three Gods. Such polytheism was
repugnant to him in the last degree. These perplexities
were increased by his uncertainty as to the ecclesiastical
position. He repudiated, needless to say, the official
Church of Antioch, that of the Arians, which was then

---

[1] Upon the extreme austerities of the monks of this country, see the
next chapter.

strong in the favour of the emperor. But among the others, to which was he to go? There were three Bishops of Antioch—Meletius, Paulinus, and Vitalis, all anti-Arians, all claiming to be in communion with the Apostolic See of Rome. Jerome did not hesitate to make direct appeal to Pope Damasus,[1] who did not reply to his first letter, perhaps not to his second, but who let it be seen plainly enough by his actions that Paulinus alone enjoyed his confidence. The Meletian clergy redoubled their importunities. Worn out with these continual suspicions as to orthodoxy, Jerome made up his mind to abandon the desert, leaving the monks to their chains, their dirt, and their claim to rule the Church from the depths of their caves.[2] At Antioch, Paulinus wished to ordain him priest. He submitted, but with the stipulation that he should remain a monk, and be free to go wherever he might think fit. Shortly afterwards (380-381) he was in Constantinople, with Gregory of Nazianzus, who was his second master in exegesis. Gregory was a great admirer of Origen; Jerome became one also, under his teaching, and set himself to translate the works of the celebrated Alexandrian. It was at this time also that he translated the *Chronicle* of Eusebius, completing it and continuing it down to the death of Valens. It is surprising that he never makes any mention of the council of 381, which took place during his stay in Constantinople. This council, which had repudiated Paulinus, and disgusted Gregory of Nazianzus, could certainly not have enlisted his sympathies in any way. It was in these circumstances that, Pope Damasus having obtained permission from the emperors for the assembling of a new council in Rome, Jerome once more beheld the old metropolis. Damasus knew him. In addition to his letters from the desert, he had received from him a little exegetical treatise on

---

[1] *Ep.* 15, 16.

[2] *Ep.* 17: "Pudet dicere: de cavernis cellularum damnamus orbem. In sacco et cinere volutati, de episcopis sententiam ferimus. Quid facit sub tunica poenitentis regius animus? Catenae, sordes, et comae non sunt diadematis signa, sed fletus."

the vision of Isaiah.[1] The Pope had his curiosity awakened as to the difficulties of Scripture. No one was better qualified than Jerome, steeped as he was in the knowledge of languages and the study of interpreters ancient and modern, to give him the necessary information. When the Pope had Jerome in Rome entirely at his beck and call, he began to overwhelm him with questions upon the difficult points of the Bible ; he encouraged him, with an eagerness that was almost indiscreet, to translate the Greek interpreters ; he urged him to revise or rewrite—on the basis of the Hebrew or Greek originals— the Latin version of Holy Scripture. Jerome gently protested, but he did it ; and in doing it, he enjoyed the purest pleasure possible to persons of his character— that of seeing his learning of some use. As he was well acquainted with the East, both with regard to men and books, the Pope had recourse to him for his correspondence with those lands. In the whole life of Damasus, nothing makes him more pleasing to us than this friendship with Jerome, and the broadness of mind which it betokens. But we must add at once that such favour, and for such a reason, was eminently calculated to expose the learned monk to the jealous malevolence of the Roman clergy. They concealed it at first ; for Jerome was in favour. Compliments were paid him ; he was called saintly, humble, eloquent ; he was spoken of for the papal chair. But this did not last long. Objections were discovered to his renderings ; they upset what had become familiar. He was envied for the success he met with in high society. Christian matrons of real devotion looked with favour upon this austere and learned man, who without any falling away in doctrine or in conduct guided them with sincerity and dignity in the most exalted paths of the religious vocation. Amongst these ladies was Marcella, left a widow when quite young, who lived in retirement in a palace on the Aventine ; another widow, Lea ; a virgin, Asella ; and lastly, Paula, also a widow. Paula had several children : one of them, Eustochium,

[1] *Ep.* 18.

remained a virgin, and lived always with her mother; another daughter, Blæsilla, after a short married life, hesitated for some time between the world and retirement. Jerome was the friend of these holy women. He explained the Scriptures to them, and encouraged them in their pious exercises. Could any further reason be wanted? The worldly set was speedily hostile to him: the fashionable ladies, who even in those far-off days, knew how to reconcile pleasantly the Gospel and a life of amusement; the curled and scented ecclesiastics who were attached to their society, who flocked to their *petits levers*, were the eager recipients of their presents, and lived in expectation of their property; in short, "the whole council of the Pharisees" was all agog. We must, however, confess, that it was not only Jerome's virtues which so exasperated them. He had his faults also, and very patent ones, amongst others an extreme irritability, which made him intolerant of the slightest criticism, and led him into extreme violence of language. The blows which were struck at him, he returned with enormous interest. He fought with words, as well as with his pen, allowing himself to be drawn into disputes, in which the parties grew so warm that they ended by spitting into each other's faces.[1] Marcella was frightened sometimes: such proceedings offended her dignity. Paula, on the contrary, never made any objections; she was a model sheep. Nothing alarmed her. One day, Jerome addressed to her daughter Eustochium a treatise on virginity, marked by an extraordinary freedom of style.[2] Other mothers were scandalized at it; Paula approved of everything, and allowed herself to be called the

---

[1] It is Jerome himself who gives us this piece of information (*Ep.* l. 4): *Quoties me iste* (he is speaking of another monk) *in circulis stomachari fecit et adduxit ad choleram! Quoties conspuit et consputus abscessit!*

[2] *Ep.* 22; see especially c. 25. *Omnia munda mundis;* but we are astonished at some of the language which this holy man uses to a young girl of eighteen. The pagans, as we may well believe, read these pamphlets with zest, and were highly amused by them.

"mother-in-law of God," since her daughter was, by her vow, "the spouse of Christ."

It was during this period also that Jerome wrote his dialogue against the Luciferians, in which he makes a formal indictment against the Little Church, founded more or less intentionally by the celebrated Bishop of Sardinia. He also attacked a certain Helvidius who, as a protest against the attraction of vocations to virginity, had set himself to prove that Mary, the Mother of the Lord, had had other children afterwards by her marriage with Joseph. It cost him dear, for Jerome, thus attacked on a tender spot, made him atone very severely for his hasty exegesis.

So long as Pope Damasus lived, Jerome was able to labour, to teach, and to fight, as he pleased. But he had only lived three years in Rome when his protector, who had attained a very advanced age, passed from life to life beyond (December 11, 384).

Pope Damasus is very popular with the archæologists of our own days, on account of the beautiful inscriptions with which he adorned the tombs of the Roman martyrs. Pilgrims, at the beginning of the Middle Ages, copied them eagerly; several of them have been preserved entire; others are found in fragments in the excavations of the catacombs. Everyone knows their admirable caligraphy. Never have worse verses been transcribed so exquisitely. And if the verses were only bad! But they are empty of history, they are obscure, and contain scarcely anything but commonplaces. Thus, they bear witness that the local tradition with regard to the martyrs was almost obliterated at the time when the pious pontiff sought to preserve it. Nevertheless, his intention deserves praise. Stoutly opposed as he was, and bitterly assailed by persons who prided themselves on their superior zeal, Damasus felt the necessity of conciliating the feeling of the common people. Now the populace was beginning to take more and more interest in the heroes of ancient days. To recover their true history would have been almost impossible. And besides, it had been almost always

the same. But the ecclesiastical authorities were in a
position to know where the martyrs had been buried; it
was their duty to guide in the direction of the authentic
tombs a pious enthusiasm which might have wandered
elsewhere; and by associating themselves closely with
it, they maintained an indispensable communion of feeling
between themselves and the generality of the faithful.

On the death of Damasus, a former deacon of Liberius,
named Siricius, was chosen as his successor. This new
Pharaoh had not known Joseph, or rather was not at all
inclined to be friendly to him. Jerome soon saw that to
stay in Rome would become difficult for him. In the
meantime, Blæsilla, after some months as a fashionable
widow, had been induced by him to embrace, as her
mother and sister had done, a life of retreat and privation.
She only lived four months afterwards. Her "conversion"
had already been a shock to her worldly friends; her
death was a desolation. Society was furious against the
monks. It was then that Jerome experienced a revival of
the former attraction of the Holy Places, which twelve
years before had carried him from Aquileia to Antioch,
but without inducing him to complete the journey.
Paula also had wished, for many years, to follow the
example of Melania, and to visit the monks of Egypt
and the sanctuaries of Palestine; she told Jerome that
she would follow him. Jerome sailed first; Paula and
Eustochium followed in another ship. In Cyprus they
met once more Bishop Epiphanius, and at Antioch
Paulinus, two friends dating from the last council. It was
at Antioch that they made their preparations, under the
guidance of Paulinus, for the journey to the Holy Places.

CHAPTER XIV

THE MONKS OF THE EAST

Egypt, the fatherland of the monks. Antony and the Anchorites. The monks of Nitria. Pacomius and Cenobitism. Schnoudi. Monastic virtues. Pilgrimages to the Egyptian solitaries. The monks of Palestine: Hilarion and Epiphanius. Sinai and Jerusalem. Monks of Syria and of Mesopotamia. Monasticism in Asia Minor: Eustathius and St Basil. Attitude of the Church and of the Government.

THE heresy of Arius, the schism of Meletius, the long conflicts and the fidelity of Athanasius, make Egypt stand out in special relief in the Christian history of the 4th century. The great Councils of Nicæa, of Tyre, of Sardica, and of Ariminum; the Church torn by divisions, bishops deposed, exiled, and hunted down by the police of the Most Christian Emperor; the Faith betrayed by creeds; religion perverted amid inexpiable strife; all these calamities took their origin in the land of the Nile. And yet, Egypt was not a byeword and a scandal; in spite of all the difficulties which he caused, Athanasius by reason of his lofty and unruffled virtue, above all by his indomitable courage, ever remained the object of universal admiration. All respectable people flocked round him by instinct. It was well known that he did not stand alone; that all the bishops, all the faithful of Egypt supported him by their devotion, and that this devotion cost them dear; that they had paid for it by persecutions incessantly renewed, from the time of Constantine to the end of the reign of Valens. Egypt was the sanctuary of orthodoxy, the classic ground of confessors of the faith.

But it had another title to respect: it was the fatherland of the monks. To the revered name of Athanasius
were united in pious stories the names of Antony and
Pacomius, of Ammon, of the two Macarii, and those of
many other personages in whom piety soon embodied
the ideal of Christian heroism. The country in which
these holy men lived, and where the institutions which
sprang from them flourished, soon became a second Holy
Land. Pilgrimages were made there, not to visit
celebrated tombs, or places which bore witness to the
great facts of Bible history, but to venerate living saints,
to gaze upon their faces emaciated by austerity, and to
listen to their edifying conversation. In the year 373, a
great Roman lady, Melania the elder, inaugurated in this
respect the series of Western pilgrims. But long before
this, Hilarion, Eustathius, and Basil had travelled
thither from Palestine and Asia Minor. As a result of
these journeys, the renown of the Egyptian monks was
spread abroad; their example encouraged imitation, their
way of living inspired the reforms which were already
beginning to influence the old form of asceticism, more or
less everywhere.

Indeed, there were almost everywhere Christian ascetics;
there had been so from the outset. I have already said
that asceticism is not a peculiarity of Christianity; it
existed before it, and apart from it, among certain religious
or philosophical sects[1]; and the Church has never accepted
it as an essential and obligatory form of the Christian
life; she has always shown herself mistrustful of it when
there was the slightest reason for suspicion that austere
practices were connected with unorthodox doctrines.[2]

[1] The Therapeutæ of Philo, if the book "On the Contemplative
Life" is really his, were Jewish ascetics, living in communities. Some
thirty years ago, an attempt was made to connect all Egyptian forms
of monasticism with certain cases of voluntary seclusion from the
world which are known in the worship of Serapis. This absurd idea
had some success at first; no one maintains it now.

[2] An instance of this kind was represented in Egypt by the
asceticism of Hieracas of Leontopolis, who, about the beginning of
the 4th century, founded a sect into which no one could be

Far from condemning such practices, however, in themselves, she has considered them as meritorious, edifying,
and worthy of honour.   In the 3rd century there were
many ascetics of either sex living in their families, or at
least in ordinary society, and having no idea of separating
themselves from it in order to lead a life of isolation.
Here and there, they did group themselves together,
either for religious exercises, or for a community life.[1] In
Egypt, as elsewhere, there were both men and women
who embraced a life of celibacy, "apotaktikoi" as they
were sometimes called; they are often mentioned,
especially the virgins, in the stories of martyrs, and the
accounts of religious disturbances.   They dwelt in towns
and villages, sometimes in the suburbs, in some quiet
place, where they lived alone; but they took part in the
ordinary religious life and especially in meetings for public
worship, where they showed themselves more regular than
others.

The first person[2] who conceived the idea of isolating
himself entirely, of fleeing from the inhabited world and

admitted unless he renounced marriage, and adopted a vegetarian
diet. According to his teaching, marriage, which was permitted in
the Old Testament, is forbidden in the New, because the teaching of
the New Testament must be higher than that of the Old. Hieracas
was a very learned man, well acquainted with Egyptian and Greek
literature.   He had also cultivated medicine, astronomy, and other
sciences. In theology, he depended in some respects upon Origen,
in rejecting the Resurrection.   Children according to him could
not be saved. He had strange ideas with regard to the Trinity:
he identified Melchizedec with the Holy Spirit. Arius quotes a proposition of his which would seem somewhat akin to Modalism (letter
to Alexander, Epiph. *Haer.* lxix. 7). St Epiphanius, who gives us
information (*Haer.* lxviii.) upon the heresy of Hieracas, was acquainted
with commentaries by him upon the six days of Creation and on
other parts of the Bible. He also composed many sacred poems in
Greek and Egyptian. He died at the age of ninety, still exercising
his profession as caligraphist.

[1] Such was the παρθενών in which St Antony placed his sister
(Athan. *Vita Ant.* 3).

[2] I pass over St Paul of Thebes, who, according to St Jerome,
must have fled to the desert in the time of the Emperor Decius.
This story is not very well established.

even from the ordinary society of the faithful, was St Antony.[1]

He was born in 251 in a village of the *nome* of Heracleopolis, in Middle Egypt. His parents were not poor. From his earliest childhood he showed a great aversion to intercourse with his fellows; he could never be persuaded to go to school; and hence he remained all his life an unlettered man, not understanding Greek, and not knowing how to read even in Coptic. On the death of his parents (about 270) he sold his property, placed a sister who remained to him and who was younger than himself in a house of consecrated virgins (εἰς παρθενῶνα), and began to live as an ascetic, first at the door of his own house, afterwards in the outskirts of the village, and finally in a tomb at a great distance from it. Fifteen years passed away, during which time, although preferring the intercourse with hermits in the neighbourhood or those passing by, he yet kept in touch with the people of his village. But in 285, yielding to the attraction of a more complete solitude, he crossed the Nile and directed his steps towards the mountains on the right bank (the Arabian chain), where, in the heart of a terrible desert, he discovered the ruins of a fortified castle. A spring of water gushed near. The name of the place was Pispir[2]; and there he took up his abode. Every six months his provision of bread was brought to him. He passed his time in prayer or in making mats. Separated from men he lived with God, and also with demons whose assaults hold a prominent place in his history.

After twenty years of solitude, Antony found himself

[1] After a great deal of dispute as to the authenticity of the life of St Antony, critics have ended by accepting it once more. And it is upon that document that the account which follows is based. As to the other testimonies to St Antony, see Dom E. C. Butler, *The Lausiac History of Palladius*, i. p. 220, in the Cambridge *Texts and Studies*, vol. vi.

[2] Der-el-Meimoun, on the right bank of the Nile, between Atfih and Beni-Souef (Amélineau, *Géog. de l'Egypte*, p. 353; cf. *Anecd. Oxon., Semitic series*, part vii. map).

one day besieged in his fortress; his door was forced; they were disciples who came to him and thus vanquished their master. His example had been contagious. Many Christians, abandoning family, country, and Church, and flying also from judges and tax collectors,[1] now populated the desert of Pispir and the neighbouring mountains. Antony gave them a welcome and plenty of good advice.

This happened at the time of the Great Persecution. The solitaries were too far off to be affected by it. They went to meet it: in the reign of Maximin, Antony went down to Alexandria with several of his disciples, and busied himself in serving and encouraging the confessors. This journey did not fail to increase his fame. He soon found that there were too many monks at Pispir, and certainly too many visitors. A caravan of Bedouin Arabs passed by, going in the direction of the Red Sea: he joined them. After a journey of several days he discovered in the mountains near the seashore a spot which possessed water, palm-trees, and a small tract of land which could be cultivated. This was his second and last refuge.[2] To go and look for him in such a place, it was necessary to undergo more than ordinary fatigue. And so he was left there in peace. Sometimes, however, he descended towards the Nile valley and went to spend a few days at Pispir.

He lived to a very great age; he did not die until 356, at the age of a hundred and five. When he was almost ninety he took a second journey to Alexandria, in 338,[3] to greet Athanasius on his return from his first exile and to lend him aid against the Arians. They were old acquaintances. Athanasius had been for some time Antony's disciple, and afterwards they had met again several times. In the ecclesiastical quarrels which tore Egypt asunder, the great solitary had always taken the part of his friend: neither Arians nor Meletians had ever been able to

---

[1] *Vita Ant.* 44.

[2] This is the monastery of St Antony, still in existence, as is also that of St Paul at some distance from it.

[3] This date is supplied by the *Chronicle of the Festal Letters*.

detach him from his side.   When Antony died, he showed
a last mark of regard for Athanasius and bequeathed to
him, besides an old tunic of sheepskin, the well-worn
mantle which had long served him for a bed, and which
had been in the first instance Athanasius' own gift.
Serapion, Bishop of Thmuis, also received a remembrance
of the same kind.

These relics were a symbol of the perfect and cordial
agreement which existed between the heads of the
Egyptian Church and the patriarch of the anchorites.
Neither of them seems to have realized that these flights
to the desert might have had some drawbacks.   Yet,
when we look closely into the matter, the hermit was
a living criticism of ecclesiastical society.   The mere fact
of his retirement proved that in his estimation the Church
had become an impossible dwelling-place for anyone
who wished to lead a really Christian life, and this judgment was founded upon an ideal of religious life which
differed markedly from that of the Church.   For him the
very essential of Christianity was asceticism.   Fraternal
union, meetings for public worship, the liturgy, and
instruction from the bishop, all these things were of
secondary importance in comparison with that cultivation
of the soul which consists above all in personal mortification and continual prayer.   We cannot see how Antony,
during his twenty years of seclusion, can ever have been
enabled to receive the Eucharist.

Such a mode of life would have astonished St Ignatius
of Antioch and St Clement of Rome.   Even in the 4th
century the exodus to monasticism alarmed in more
places than one the representatives of tradition.   The
Bishops of Alexandria, Peter, Alexander, and Athanasius,
were not disturbed by it; they even looked with favour
upon this new form of piety, which preached so eloquently
to the general run of lukewarm Christians.   The ecclesiastical danger could be guarded against by keeping the
hermits under the direction of episcopal authority.   This
was a matter of organization.   Those recluses who were
out of reach were, and could only be, exceptions to the

rule. The general body of hermits were not too much scattered; each of them had his hut or his cave, his cell as it was called, but they were not very far from one another. It was easy to arrange a spiritual centre for them—a church—round which they organized themselves into a sort of country parish.

Thus in Egypt there was no difficulty about the matter: bishops and monks arranged things between themselves, and the new kind of life soon became very popular. As early as the reign of Constantine, there were monks throughout the whole of Egypt. One of their most celebrated colonies was that of Nitria. To the west of the Delta, at a considerable distance south of Alexandria, a large valley opens out from the north-west to the south-east, at the bottom of which are salt lakes which produce nitre. It is a very melancholy place, and its name in our day is Wadi-Natroun, the Valley of Nitre. Here, about the time of the Council of Nicæa, a certain Amoun[1] came to lead the life of an ascetic. He had left behind him in Egypt a wife with whom he had lived for eighteen years in a celibate union. His wife collected virgins around her; while Amoun on his part soon saw solitaries flocking to his retreat in Nitria. Twice a year the husband and wife visited each other. When Amoun died, St Antony, who was still alive, saw the angels descend from heaven and receive his soul. His spiritual posterity soon increased to considerable proportions: forty years after his death there were more than five thousand monks in the grim valley of Nitria. Like Antony's hermits, each lived in a separate cell; in the middle of the valley rose a church where they all assembled on Saturday and Sunday; eight priests, who owed obedience to the Bishop of Hermopolis Minor, were attached to this church. It was the centre of government and discipline. Three palm trees shaded

---

[1] *Historia Lausiaca*, 8. This work is always quoted here according to Dom Butler's edition. See below, p. 402 (note). But I put in parentheses the numbers of the chapters in the old editions when they differ from the new numbers.

the court of the church; to each of them was attached
a whip, which was made use of to chastise the evil doings
of offenders from outside or, if there were need, of the
solitaries themselves. With the exception of their weekly
meetings, the monks passed their time as they liked
in their cells, working for their living at basket-work,
sometimes two together, sometimes three together,
often alone. Morning and evening there sounded
from one end of the valley to the other the chanting of psalms. Beyond the Wadi-Natroun stretched a
still more frightful desert, that of the Cells where the
more courageous had made their retreat. Farther still,
the solitude of Scetis, a country of sand and of
hunger, received the most renowned connoisseurs of
Nitrian asceticism.

For there was a certain connoisseurship, a *virtuosité* in
asceticism, an open rivalry between the monks, not only of
this district but throughout the whole of Egypt. Pambo,
Or, Nathanael, Benjamin, Macarius of Egypt and Macarius
of Alexandria, appear in the number of Nitrian celebrities.
Macarius of Alexandria could never hear of any feat of
asceticism without at once trying to surpass it. The
monks of Tabenna ate no cooked food during Lent;
Macarius thought fit to observe this rule for seven years,
from one end of the year to another. He was to be seen
frantically endeavouring for twenty consecutive nights to
keep himself awake. He was already an old man when
he conceived the idea of visiting Tabenna itself, to give
a lesson to those famous ascetics, who spent their nights
standing upright, and during Lent only ate once in every
five days. He presented himself, disguised, at the door of
a monastery and, when Lent came, passed the whole
of it standing upright, without even bending his knees
either by day or night, without drinking and even without
eating, except that on Sundays he swallowed, quite
uncooked, a few cabbage leaves. During the whole of this
fast he continued to work with his hands at the trade of
basket-making, and when he was not working, he prayed.
The monks of Tabenna rose in revolt against this formid-

able rival, but their superior thanked him for having humbled the pride of his disciples.[1]

It was not always the mere attraction to asceticism which drove men into the desert. Some came there to do penance. In Nitria, a certain negro called Moses was long spoken of; he had formerly been a slave whom no one would put up with and, being driven away by his masters for that reason, he then became a brigand-chief. In this latter capacity he acquired a terrible reputation. At last he decided to change his life, and took possession of a cell in the holy valley. One night he was attacked there by four robbers. They had come to the wrong man: the recluse had not lost his former vigour; he knocked his assailants down, tied them up, took all the four upon his broad shoulders, and went like this to the church, asking what he should do with them. During the explanations which followed, the name of Moses was pronounced. Moses for the brigands was the great celebrity of their profession. Without hesitation they too became monks.[2]

In those days, the desert was supposed to be full of demons. The hermits, notwithstanding their austerities, often experienced attacks from them. We have already seen what a place is filled in the life of St Antony by the struggle against the temptations of evil spirits. In Nitria, in the same way, the monks complained of them greatly; the demon of avarice prowled round the alms sometimes left by well-to-do pilgrims; but it was especially the demon of the flesh which came to trouble the nights of the ascetics. They fought it as best they could, sometimes by means scarcely sane. One of them, Pachon, thought he would seek to be devoured by wild beasts. So he sat down at the entrance to a cave which he knew to be inhabited by hyenas. At night-fall, these animals really did come out, and smelt him for a long time; but they went away without doing him any harm. Another day, he applied a serpent of a venomous kind to his stomach; but he was not bitten.[3]

[1] *Hist. Laus.* 18 (19-20).   [2] *Ibid.* 19 (22).   [3] *Ibid.* 23 (29).

The disciples of St Antony, the monks of Nitria, and of many other places in Lower or Middle Egypt, were not, strictly speaking, subject to any rule or any superior. The priests who served their churches had only liturgical functions: they were not monastic superiors. The whip which hung from the palm-tree, near the Church of Nitria, was merely an instrument of general government, in no way a symbol of conventual discipline. New-comers attached themselves to some experienced hermit, who guided their first steps in the ascetic career; afterwards, they arranged themselves how they liked, sanctifying themselves according to the received methods, and perfecting these according to their taste.

Such independence made access to the desert-life easy for persons of every variety of culture and condition. Among the monks of Nitria were men of the world, former members of the clergy, people of high and distinguished education. In certain cells were to be found not only copies of the Sacred Books, beautifully transcribed by the solitaries themselves,[1] but the works of the ancient doctors —of Clement of Alexandria,[2] and above all of Origen, who although he was not regarded with favour, it is true, in Pacomian monasteries,[3] preserved elsewhere many faithful adherents. These later on, under the patriarch Theophilus, had to endure evil times.

Far away from Nitria, and even from Pispir, in the heart of Upper Egypt, there sprang up about the time of Licinius another efflorescence of monasticism, which finally developed in institutions widely different from the primitive form of hermit life. A young peasant named Pacomius, (Παχούμιος) who had been called up for military service and disbanded shortly afterwards (314), had occasion, during his short stay in the army, to experience the charity of the Christians. His family were pagans, and

---

[1] It is highly probable that the fine MS. H of the Epistles of St Paul, of which we still possess some fragments, was the work of Evagrius of Nitria. Upon this, see A. Ehrhard, *Centralblatt für Bibliothekswesen*, 1891, p. 385, and Armitage Robinson in the *Historia Lausiaca* of Dom Butler, vol. i., pp. 103-106.

[2] Palladius, *Hist. Laus.* 60.   [3] *Life of Pacomius*, c. 21.

lived in the neighbourhood of Esneh (Latopolis), to the south of Thebes. He never saw them again. As soon as he was free from the army he asked for baptism, and then devoted himself to asceticism under the direction of a solitary named Palaemon, who had his hermit's cell upon the right bank of the Nile, opposite Denderah. Soon he felt himself drawn to gather other ascetics round him, and to lead with them a life in community. He was the inventor[1] of what we wrongly call the monasteries,[2] and of the cenobitic life. The first monastery was founded at a place called Tabennesis.

Disciples flocked there in hundreds; whole groups of hermits—this form of asceticism was very widespread in that district—placed themselves under the discipline of the new master. A second monastery was organized, at an hour's distance from the first, at a place called Pebôou (Παβαῦ, now Faou); but that soon proved insufficient. Other monasteries were built, either in the neighbourhood, or a little lower down or higher up the river, in the outskirts of Achmîn (Panopolis) and Esneh (Latopolis). In the lifetime of Pacomius there were at least nine of them. These monasteries were not independent of each other; they formed what we should now call an Order, a Congregation. All of them followed the same mode of life, were subject to the same rule, to the same temporal administration, and obeyed the same superior. The superior, after having at first resided at Tabennesis, soon fixed the seat of his government at Pebôou.

Each of the monasteries comprised a closed area, in which were built several houses, each sheltering some forty monks, grouped according to the nature of their manual labour.[3]

[1] An attempt of this kind had been made before him, but without success, by a certain Aotas (*Vita Pachomii*, 77).

[2] Μοναστήριον means properly a place where one lives alone; this is exactly the contrary of the usually received meaning; Κοινόβιον, of which we have no literal equivalent in French, means a place where men live in common; this is the correct term, but it is Greek.

[3] Upon the documents relating to St Pacomius and his monasteries, see Ladeuze, *Étude sur le cénobitisme Pakhomien*

Their Rule, which we still possess, was comparatively
endurable. The Pacomian monks worked with their
hands, and even with their heads, for they were obliged
to learn by heart at least the Psalter and the New
Testament. They were allowed to feed themselves as
they liked, that is to say, to eat more or less often, though
of course of fare which had small claim to be called
delicate; those who fasted more, worked less. While
eating, they covered their heads with their hoods; in this
way they disguised an operation which apparently seemed
to them unbecoming, or, at any rate, kept to themselves the
secret of the privations which they voluntarily endured.
Pacomius was soon joined by his sister, who, on her
brother's advice, established for her part monasteries for
women.

Pacomius had many visions, of which the monks,

pendant le IVe siècle et la première moitié du Ve. The best
biographical document is the Greek Life, published (shockingly:
this work ought to be done again) by the Bollandists (*Acta SS. maii*,
vol. iii., p. 22* *et seq.*) ; it has been supplemented and retouched,
subsequently, in Coptic as well as in Greek (Boll. *loc. cit.*, pp.
44*-53*, and 54*-61* [letter of Ammon to Theophilus]). The other
accounts (*Hist. mon.* 3 ; *Hist. Laus.* 32-34 ; *cf.* 7, 18 ; Sozomen, iii.
14 ; vi. 28) are only of minor importance, and can scarcely count with
regard to the earliest beginnings. As to the text of the Pacomian
Rule, many recensions of it exist ; but these documents are liable to
be modified considerably in the course of time. It is very difficult to
distinguish, in those which we possess, what goes back to Pacomius
himself from what has been added gradually by the care of his
successors. A considerable number of texts of it go back to a
summary given by Palladius (*Hist. Laus.* 32) ; according to him
(*cf.* Gennadius, *De viris*, 7) an angel brought this text to St Pacomius,
engraved upon a table of brass. Sozomen (iii. 14) even says that this
table was preserved in his own time at Tabennesi. The best edition
is still that which has come down to us in a Latin version by St
Jerome (Migne, *P. L.*, vol. xxiii., p. 61), which had certainly not been
translated from the original Coptic, but from a Greek text coming
from the monastery of Canope. Upon all this, see Ladeuze, *op. cit.*,
p. 256, *et seq.* Jerome also translated twelve letters of Pacomius
(Migne, *op. cit.*, p. 87), in which we meet with Greek characters
employed as cryptographic signs. According to Palladius (*loc. cit.*)
these characters seem to have served also to designate various classes
of monks ; but this is not absolutely certain.

naturally, made a great deal. He was conscious of possessing in certain cases the power of sounding the consciences of people, and treated them in accordance with the impression he thus received. The bishops of the neighbourhood were disturbed in mind by this singular gift, and Pacomius had to explain himself before a synod held at Latopolis. Apart from this, the episcopate does not seem to have thrown any obstacle in the way of the development of his communities; far from it. The " Pope," Athanasius, was their friend : he visited Tabennesi, in 333, during his pastoral journey through the Thebaïd. The monks kept up a regular communication with Alexandria : they had boats which plied between their various colonies and went down the river as far as the capital, in order to sell the produce of their labour there, and to buy things of which they were in need. In 346, several of them found themselves just in time to welcome the bishop on his return from exile. On their way, they had disembarked at Pispir, to visit St Antony. Pacomius had only been dead a few months : the patriarch of the anchorites received them warmly, and extolled the merits of the founder of monastic houses. Later on, when exile had brought Athanasius back to Upper Egypt, the monks saw him once more among them, proscribed and pursued by the police of Constantius. Pacomius had been succeeded, after a short interval, by Orsisius, one of his first disciples, an excellent man, but one who found himself somewhat disconcerted when for the first time centrifugal tendencies began to manifest themselves in the congregation. He at once chose a coadjutor in the person of another Tabennesian monk of the early days, one Theodore, thanks to whom the Pacomian foundations multiplied. Soon they reached as far as Hermopolis Magna, opposite Antinoë. It was there that in the reign of Julian, Theodore, while on a tour of inspection, met for the last time Athanasius, the perpetual exile. Foreseeing that this might happen, he had brought many followers with him. Athanasius was received in triumph, with the chanting of psalms. The " Abbot "

Theodore conducted him, holding the bridle of his ass. Acclamations echoed from shore to shore. In this land of the upper river, there was no occasion to trouble oneself about the police of Alexandria.

It was another world. The people from the great town were like foreigners there ; they were called the Alexandrians, the city folk ($\pi o\lambda\iota\tau\iota\kappa o i$), the Hellenes. In the monasteries, they were treated as guests, and grouped separately. Their first care, if they wished to join the community, was necessarily to learn the Coptic of Thebes (Sahidic).

Theodore died about 368. The aged Orsisius, who had taken him as coadjutor, was still alive. Athanasius advised him to resume the reins of government. Here we come to an end of the information furnished by the Life of Pacomius, an interesting document, which seems to have been compiled immediately after the death of Theodore, by one of the few Greek or Greek-speaking monks then living in the chief monastery. Later on, a colony of Pacomians was established close to Alexandria, at Canope. It was from this colony that St Jerome got his information with regard to Pacomius and his Rule ; and it was from this that the greater part of the visitors, whether Greek or Latin, were able to form a judgment on the Pacomian institutions.

Monasticism continued to flourish in the country of its origin ; but it appears that, gradually, people came to think of it as capable of realization apart from the grouping of communities, which was the ideal of St Pacomius. He was still living, when, about the year 343, a child of nine years of age, called Schnoudi, embraced not far from Tabennesi the profession of a monk. This child was destined to become one of the most original figures in the history of Egyptian cenobitism.

Upon a spur of the Libyan chain, opposite the town of Achmîn (*Chemnis*), there stands a kind of fortress of imposing appearance with its high and massive walls. This is the White Monastery — the monastery of St Schnoudi. In former days there was near it a village

called Atripe. Towards the middle of the 4th century,
an anchorite called Bgoul allowed several disciples to
gather round him there, and amongst them his nephew
Schnoudi was soon to be found. Bgoul had organized his
followers into a monastery, adopting the cenobitic system
of Pacomius. After his death, about 388, the government
of the community passed into the hands of Schnoudi,
under whom it assumed extraordinary proportions. On
the outskirts of the great monastery arose branch-
establishments; convents for women were added to the
congregation. A man of ardent soul, served by a will
of iron and most remarkable common sense, Schnoudi
was a born leader of men. His monks, who were
numbered by hundreds, were entirely in his hands. He
led them with severity ; any infringement of the Rule was
punished with blows of whip or of stick. Schnoudi was
himself the operator, and he struck hard ; one day he
struck so hard that the sufferer died in consequence, a
circumstance which was not allowed to trouble him. His
influence soon extended throughout the whole countryside,
where his hand, when it was kind, was stretched out to
every sort of suffering to relieve it ; when it was angry,
it fell with terrible force upon evil-doers, upon bad priests,
upon unjust judges, upon any pagans who still existed,
and upon their temples. He lived to the incredible age
of one hundred and eighteen years, venerated and feared
by all the Thebaïd and even by the barbarians, against
whom his monastery offered to the Roman soldiers an
unassailable retreat. Antony had given good example
and advice ; Pacomius rules ; Macarius at Scetis and
John at Lycopolis astonished the world by marvels of
austerity ; Schnoudi, in his White Monastery, was like
Elijah on Carmel, an inspired administrator of justice, a
redoubtable man of God. In the social and political
confusion which prevailed in those desolate regions, it
was not difficult for him to assume a kind of divine
lieutenancy, and to exercise it in his own fierce way.[1]

---

[1] In addition to his Life, by his disciple Besas (Amélineau,
Mémoires de la mission archéol. du Caire, vol. iv. 1), we possess letters

It was not only in Nitria, upon St Antony's mountain, and in the Pacomian or Schnoudist monasteries, that asceticism flourished. Egypt was filled with monks. In the reign of Theodosius, the entire town of Oxyrhynchus[1] belonged to them. Their cells invaded the towers of the encircling walls, the gates of the town, the temples and other unused public buildings. In Antinoë, Palladius counted as many as twelve convents of women.[2] From Syene to the Delta, in the deserts that lie between the cultivated lands and the barren mountains which enclose them to east and west, hermitages succeeded one another in an unbroken chain. Many were to be seen also in Lower Egypt, towards the desert of Suez and of Pelusium as far as Lake Menzaleh and the sea. Here and there, famous characters attracted attention. Some of the anchorites had lived retired from the world ever since the days of persecution or the first years of peace. To begin with, they had lived on roots amid frightful solitudes; then disciples gathered around them. These they directed, teaching them, by brief maxims or long conversations, the discipline of a solitary life, and giving them by their own life the most eloquent of examples. Their austerity shone throughout the neighbourhood, serving as a lesson to the clergy and the faithful who remained in the world, and also as an argument to overcome the obstinacy of the pagans. Every kind of miracle was of course attributed to them; some, like John of Lycopolis, were reputed to be prophets. Their renown even reached the Court, which did not disdain, when necessity arose, to consult them as though they were oracles.[3]

---

and sermons of Schnoudi himself which help us to form a good idea of this personage. All these documents are in Sahidic Coptic. Schnoudi knew Greek, but he only spoke it when necessary. His surroundings were essentially Coptic, and so was his literature. This is why Greek and Latin authors, even those who, like Palladius, visited the Thebaïd in his lifetime, betray no knowledge of him. The best monograph on Schnoudi is that of Herr Joh. Leipoldt, *Schenute von Atripe*, in the *Texte und Untersuchungen*, vol. xxv. (1903). See also Ladeuze, *op. cit.*

[1] *Hist. mon.* 5. [2] *Hist. Laus.* 59 (137).

[3] John of Lycopolis was supposed to have predicted to Theodosius

We must not think that austerity was their only virtue. Their maxims, many of which have been preserved to us, indicate a great concern for interior perfection; they can readily be adapted to conditions of life very different from the terrible asceticism from whence they proceeded. Many generations of holy souls, in every class of Christian society, have profited by them for centuries, and still do so. They knew well, or if all of them did not, at least some of them did, that their fasts and mortifications of every kind were after all but one way amongst many others; and that even those people who remained in the world could sanctify themselves in another manner.

Paphnutius of Heracleopolis[1] or, rather, of the desert near that town, had mortified himself for a long time, when the idea came to him to ask God to what degree of merit he had attained. The answer was that he had arrived at the same stage as a man who followed in the nearest village the profession of a flute-player. Paphnutius wished to see him; the man told him that, before cultivating music, he had been a brigand. This was not very reassuring. However, the hermit, by dint of questioning his flute-player, learned that once, during his career as a brigand, he had been able to save the life and the honour of a virgin consecrated to God. Paphnutius returned to his desert and renewed his mortifications, accompanied by his brigand musician, whom he had made his disciple. The disciple became an excellent monk, but he died. Left alone, his master made an effort to lead a life even more severe than before. After long years had passed, he again felt the desire to estimate his progress, and again asked God to tell him how far he had gone. "Exactly as far," he was told, "as the mayor of such and such a village." This man was a good peasant, an excellent father of a family, an upright and benevolent administrator who enjoyed universal esteem. A third attempt carried Paphnutius to the same level as a merchant

his victories over Maximus and over Eugenius; and also, after the latter victory, his approaching end.

[1] *Hist. mon.* 16.

II   2 C

of Alexandria, an honest and charitable man, who was not unmindful of the hermits and used to make them presents of dried vegetables.

Such lessons were not thrown away upon a humble and intelligent monk such as Paphnutius was. He took pleasure in impressing upon others the doctrine derived from his own experiences, and in proclaiming the truth that in every state of life it is possible to please God and attain to a high degree of holiness. When he died, his disciples saw him enter Heaven, and receive a welcome from the angels and the prophets.

Visitors, as I have already said, were not lacking to these holy people.[1] Some came from far—from Constantinople, Rome, Gaul, and Spain. All of these did not go so far as the Thebaïd. As a general rule, they confined themselves to the valley of Nitria and to the monasteries of Lower Egypt. This was what was done by the two Melanias, and Silvania, the half-sister of Rufinus, the celebrated minister; and by St Paula and St Jerome himself—the latter, I fear, being rather more attracted by the libraries and learned men of Alexandria than by the heroes of the desert. Cassian went no further. With

[1] Besides the lives of Antony, Pacomius, and Schnoudi, the Egyptian monks of the 4th century are known to us from the following documents: 1st—The journey of 394, the Greek text of which, separate and entire, has not yet been published, although several manuscripts of it have been noted; Sozomen derived information from it; it is also to be found, blended with that of Palladius, in what was called until recent days the *Historia Lausiaca*. Rufinus made a translation of it, under the title *Historia Monachorum*, which gave it wide currency among the Latins. 2nd—The *Historia Lausiaca* of Palladius, the story of a hermit who later became a bishop, after having spent eleven years in Egypt (388-399), chiefly among the monks of Nitria. Dom Butler has succeeded in distinguishing the true text of Palladius from the interpolations of the *Historia Monachorum* (See *The Lausiac History of Palladius*, vol vi. of the Cambridge *Texts and Studies*, 1898-1904). 3rd—The "Institutes" and "Conferences" of Cassian who was living in Egypt at the same time as Palladius, and who, like him, waited at least some twenty years before publishing his recollections. 4th—In these narrative documents we have already a good many mentions of the holy monks, and anecdotes concerning them. Others have come to us directly, in the letters of Pacomius

greater determination Rufinus of Aquileia, who, besides, spent six years in Egypt, pushed on as far as Pispir. Posthumianus, one of the speakers in the Dialogues of Sulpicius Severus, was not satisfied even with that: he desired to visit the far-distant monasteries of St Antony and of St Paul, near the Red Sea.

The Thebaïd of that day comprised the present Fayoum, which from the time of Theodosius possessed, under the name of *Arcadia*, a separate provincial organization. Rufinus and Posthumianus went to the Thebaïd. The pilgrim Etheria (or Eucheria[1]), whose account of her journey has unfortunately not come down to us in a complete form, also visited the Thebaïd. In 394, a party of travellers ventured as far as Lycopolis; Rufinus has translated an account of their journey. About the same

and of Schnoudi, and above all in what is called "The Maxims of the Fathers," several collections of which are extant: one, in the alphabetical order of the "Fathers" (Migne, *P. G.*, vol. lxv., pp. 72-440), has been preserved in Greek; two others, Rosweyde's *Vitae Patrum*, Books v.-vi. and Book vii. (Migne, *P. L.*, vol. lxxiii.) are known to us through ancient Latin versions. These collections belong to a time well on in the 5th century; but in many cases they are taken from older collections. Upon this, see Butler, *op. cit.*, part i., p. 208. Indeed, for the whole literature of this subject, recourse should be had for information to Dom Butler's book. It must be added, however, that a synthetic work, and even a clear and convenient classification of the sources of information still remains a want to be supplied. This subject, treated with marvellous perception, but without a clear conspectus of the matter as a whole, by the venerable Tillemont, has been complicated in recent times by unjustifiable hypotheses and allegations as absurd as they are ill-natured. It has been necessary also to fight against the tendency of the upholders of Coptic to claim originality and authority exclusively to the advantage of documents in the Egyptian language, and to depreciate the Greek texts.

[1] It is she who was at first confused with the Silvania or Silvia, mentioned above. On this question, see the memoir of Dom Férotin, in the *Revue des Questions historiques*, 1903, vol. lxxiv., p. 367. In the *Revue augustinienne*, 1903 and 1904, Père Edmond Bouvy, starting from the spelling Eucheria (the MSS. give the readings *Etheria, Echeria, Eiheria, Egeria*) identifies the pilgrim with a daughter of Fl. Eucherius, who was consul in 381, and uncle of Theodosius. In any case, Dom Férotin has proved that she was a native of Galicia, and belonged to a community of religious in that country.

time, Palladius himself went to see John the prophet. Later on, the persecution which he had to suffer as the friend of Chrysostom, forced him to make a closer acquaintance with Upper Egypt. Being banished to Syene, he embraced the opportunity of visiting several Pacomian communities, notably that of Panopolis.

These journeys were not very easy ones. All along the marshes of the Nile, the pious travellers were liable to encounter sleeping crocodiles, which woke up at their approach and frightened them terribly. Leviathan and Behemoth then still dwelt in the great river : hippopotamuses sometimes came out of it, and roamed about the fields. In the deserts, certain caves gave shelter to enormous serpents. And lastly, the whole country was more or less infested with brigands. The severity of the imperial taxes ruined so many folk that the desert was peopled with starving highwaymen. When there was no one else to pillage, they pillaged the abodes of the solitaries. The monks converted some of them from time to time; and several of these recruits even attained to a high degree of sanctity. But many remained in the world, and upon the roads.

What most contributed to render the pilgrimage to Upper Egypt difficult was the barbarians of the south. In the reign of Diocletian, the Empire had retreated before them from the Second Cataract to the First. Not content with this success, they continued to extend their ravages into the part of the country which the Romans had reserved to themselves. In spite of the garrisons which the military commandant (*dux Thebaïdos*) had established all along the river-bank and in the oases, they were everywhere to be seen, from Syene to Lycopolis. It was not without reason that the Pacomian monasteries were surrounded by high walls.

Visitors, if they were rich, willingly left alms behind them. But the hermits were men of few wants; and besides, it was seldom that they had not some form of manual labour, the product of which sufficed to supply the cost of such needs. In return for the marks of respect shown to them, they offered exhortations, good advice,

and sometimes little presents.   The elder Melania, who
was very generous to them, brought back with her from
Egypt many tokens of remembrance.   Pambo of Nitria,
whose death she witnessed, made her a present of a basket,
the last work which had occupied his hands.[1]   The gift of
Macarius the Alexandrian to her was a sheep-skin, which
had a very strange history.   One day, the hermit had
seen a hyena enter his cell, carrying her little one between
her teeth ; she laid it at his feet, and gave him to understand by her attitude that she desired some favour of
him.   Macarius looked at the little creature, perceived that
it was blind, and restored its sight.   The hyena took it up
again, and departed ; but some time after she returned to
the hermit's abode carrying a sheep-skin, as a proof of
her gratitude.[2]

Melania found Egypt a prey to a very grave religious
crisis.   It was just at that time that the government
of Valens was endeavouring to secure to the Arians
the succession to Athanasius, and to impose its candidate
Lucius as Bishop of Alexandria.   The monks of Nitria
were prominent among the opponents of this course.
Several of the most venerable Fathers were arrested, and
transported to an island in the middle of one of the
great lakes on the coast.[3]   Others were joined to the
company of the bishops deported to Diocæsarea.   Melania
accompanied them, and provided for their material wants.
Her zeal attracted attention ; the *consularis* of Palestine being
ignorant of her rank had her arrested, meaning to extort
money from her.   The Patrician lady allowed herself to be
put in prison ; but as soon as she was there, she disclosed
her rank ; the government officials abased themselves.

Egypt did not long preserve the monopoly of
anchoritism and cenobitism.   The East soon entered
upon the paths opened by Antony and Pacomius.

It was Hilarion who first introduced into Palestine
the mode of life of the Egyptian solitaries.[4]   He was

---

[1] *Hist. Laus.* 10.   [2] *Ibid.* 18 (19-20).   [3] Rufinus, *H. E.* ii. 4.
[4] Upon St Hilarion, see his life written by St Jerome.   *Cf.* Sozomen,
H. E. iii. 14.

born in a pagan family at Gaza, and sent to Alexandria to pursue his studies. He became a Christian; and then as he heard a great deal of Antony, who had just left his fortress at Pispir and begun to receive disciples, Hilarion visited him, and, after a short stay, returned to his own country accompanied by a few companions who, like himself, were attracted by a hermit's life.[1] He took up his abode on the lonely coast to the south of Gaza, and lived there a long time in the practice of extraordinary asceticism. From time to time he preached to the pagans of the Philistine country, waged war against the temples, and converted the Arabs of the neighbouring tribes. His disciples soon numbered several thousands.

Like Antony, Hilarion was a hermit, the master and director of hermits. Not far from him Epiphanius of Eleutheropolis organized a real monastery, following the model of Pacomius. He, too, had formed his projects in Egypt, where he had made some stay during the last years of Constantine's reign. His monastic colony was established in the place called Old Ad, near his native village of Besandouk.[2]

[1] According to St Jerome's account, Hilarion would seem to have been born in 291; at the time of his stay with St Antony he could only have been fifteen years of age. This visit would thus be placed in 306, when the persecution was in full vigour. It is strange that the persecution should not have left any trace in the narrative.

[2] Hilarion and Epiphanius, who had no doubt already been acquainted with each other in Palestine, met much later in the island of Cyprus, where Epiphanius became a bishop about 367. Hilarion, being disturbed in his austerities by the constant influx of visitors, betook himself to Egypt about 356. Some years after, Julian's police, excited by the people of Gaza, who were no friends of a hermit opposed to the gods, forced him to fly to a greater distance. He then stayed in Sicily, afterwards in Dalmatia, and finally at Paphos in Cyprus. The pretty legend of his meeting with Epiphanius was well known. The bishop having set before him some fowl, the hermit protested that never in his life had he touched such food. To this Epiphanius is said to have replied that he himself had never lain down to rest without being reconciled to any person with whom he might have had some disagreement. "My father," said Hilarion, "your philosophy is worth more than mine. . . ." (*Vitae Patrum*, v. 4.)

Farther to the south, the holy mountain of Sinaï attracted pilgrims and solitaries. To these the intricate valleys at the end of the peninsula offered retreats suitable to their manner of life. They quickly multiplied. The Biblical memories of which these places were full could not fail to be eagerly cherished by these holy people. They soon set themselves to discover the exact situation of all the scenes of the Exodus. The sacred topography of Sinaï was fixed for centuries.

Very soon the summit of Djebel Mousa was crowned by a chapel: another oratory arose on the place of the burning bush, the spot on which visitors now find the celebrated monastery of St Catherine.[1] In the present Wadi-Feirân, the inhabited place which used to be called the town of Pharan was, alike for the wandering tribes of the peninsula and for the hermits, a centre of commerce and administration. Hermitages and chapels were to be found even as far as the seashore, in terrible places where nevertheless, thanks to some poor little stream of water and to the modesty of their requirements, the monks succeeded in supporting life.

It was in this maritime region that there lay the desert of Raïthu, the monks of which were massacred in 373 by Blemmyan pirates who came from the extreme end of the Red Sea.[2] On the same day, we are told, a band of Saracens fell upon the hermitages above Pharan; some of the solitaries were able to take refuge in a tower; the others were butchered.[3] Such raids were frequent. They produced but little booty. But

---

[1] The publication of the *Peregrinatio* has definitely put an end to the theory according to which these identifications only date back as far as the time of Justinian, Serbal having been, before the Djebel Katarin, the sacred mountain visited by Christian pilgrims. The lady pilgrim of the time of Theodosius does not trouble herself about Serbal; the holy places she visits are the same that we visit now.

[2] These pirates did not attack the monks only. The people of Pharan who tried to stop them were beaten by them, and their wives and children made prisoners.

[3] So the account of Ammonius, an eye-witness, in Combéfis, *Illustrium martyrum lecti triumphi* (1660), p. 88. *Cf.* the story of

the monks themselves had a certain marketable value
for the Bedouins.   They sold them as slaves, or sacrificed
them to their goddess Ouazza, the Morning-Star.

In Palestine and in Syria, as in Egypt, the district
of the monks was also that of the brigands.   From the
Red Sea to the Euphrates, solitaries and Bedouins encountered each other in the deserts on the frontier.
From time to time, incidents such as I have just been
describing took place as the result.   By degrees, however,
their relations improved.   The virtues of these holy men,
their austerity and their charity at last ended by making
an impression, at any rate to some extent, even
upon barbarians, who were little enough disposed to
gentle emotions.   Little by little the monks led them
to Christianity.   But of this we shall have to speak
later.

Jerusalem and the whole of Palestine[1] were filled
with monks.   In the Holy City, the *monazontes et
parthenae*, whom we find such regular attendants at the
services of Bishops Cyril and John, represent undoubtedly
an efflorescence of the ancient local asceticism.   But very
early, around Jerusalem, there were monasteries where
the religious lived in community, and swarms of hermits
of the Egyptian types.   There were some of all languages.
The Latin establishments over which Rufinus presided
on the Mount of Olives, and Jerome at Bethlehem, are
representatives to us of many others of the same type,
inhabited by male or female religious of Greek language
or Syriac speech.

In Phœnicia, where Christianity had still made but
little progress, settlements of ascetics were much less
frequent.   A few isolated hermits, however, were to be
found there; amongst them we hear of two disciples of
St Antony, Cronius and James the lame.   In this country

Theodulus, the son of St Nilus, related by his father himself
(*Narrationes*, Migne, *P. G.*, vol. lxxix., p. 589).   This history belongs
to the early years of the 5th century.

   [1] Palladius, *Hist. Laus.* 43-46 (103, 104, 113, 117, 118), 48-55
(106-112); Sozomen, *H. E.* vi. 32.   See also the *Peregrinatio*.

the monks had much to suffer; they encountered continually
the ill-will of the pagan population.[1]

It was otherwise in Northern Syria, around the
Christian cities of Antioch, Berea, and Chalcis; and in
the country beyond the Euphrates, in the neighbourhood
of Edessa, Batna, and even Harran. Although the
inhabitants of this town had remained unsubmissive to
the preaching of the Gospel, the places consecrated by
memories of Abraham, Laban, and Rebecca possessed
their chapels, just as did those of Moses and Elias. The
Syrian desert, from Lebanon as far as the mountains of
Armenia, was full of solitaries. Aones was considered the
oldest of all these. He lived for a long time near Harran,
by the well at which Jacob and Rachel had first met.
These solitaries led a life still more severe than their
brethren of Egypt; some of them were to be found who
lived like wild beasts, in the heart of the forest, without
any provisions, their only food being uncooked herbs.
They were called shepherds ($\beta o \sigma \kappa o i$) by their neighbours—
a charitable name, for they might more justly have been
described as sheep. Others bound themselves to chains
made fast in the rock, carried enormous weights, and gave
themselves up to all the extravagances of Indian fakirs.
Sometimes the bishops tried to persuade them to
moderation; but they were scarcely listened to. As a
contrast, the Arabs of the desert and the Syrian peasants
had the greatest veneration for these extraordinary beings.
Their popularity even extended to the towns. In times
of crisis, the clergy did not fail to avail themselves of
their prestige. It was thus that, in the reign of Valens,
we find Aphraates and Julian Sabbas leaving their
solitudes in Mesopotamia, and going to Antioch to take
sides with Flavian and Diodore, and to assist them in
their struggle against heresy in official quarters.[2]

---

[1] Palladius, *Hist. Laus.* 47 (90-95); Sozomen, *H. E.* vi. 34.

[2] Upon Aphraates, see Theodoret, *Hist. relig.* 8; upon Julian, see
his panegyric by St Ephrem (Assemani, *S. Ephraemi Syri Opera*, gr.-
lat., vol. iii., p. 254); Palladius, *Hist. Laus.* 42 (102); Theodoret,
Hist. relig. 2; Sozomen, *H. E.* iii. 14. It is especially from the

Several highly cultivated men, such as Jerome and Chrysostom, carried their admiration for this mode of life so far as to wish to practise it themselves. Jerome soon lost his taste for it ; Chrysostom only left the desert when illness, the natural consequence of his ascetical indiscretions, finally triumphed over his courage.

We do not find that the pious extravagances of the solitaries of the East had any definite connection with the movement in Egypt. The Eastern monks were not much inclined to a life in common. The grouping in monasteries or colonies of anchorites was only established amongst them by slow degrees. We never hear of any actual rules by which they were guided. It is not surprising that, having no superiors to direct them, living far from one another, and each of them according to his own will, they should have allowed themselves to be carried into real excesses.

Quite otherwise was the form of monasticism which we meet with in Asia Minor. Here, Egyptian influence is evident. Eustathius first, and Basil afterwards, were disciples of the Egyptian monks. In the hands of Eustathius asceticism immediately assumed distinctive forms, which, whether through the master's own fault or that of imprudent disciples, offended the customs of the country and excited very lively protests. The nature of the country, in Pontus and Cappadocia, did not allow of the same liberty as in Egypt and in the Orient. In those regions, the desert was never very far off; and when once persons had found their way there, they could practise any extremes in the way of asceticism that they wished, without incommoding anyone else. Cold, too, was a hardship which they seldom had to fear, and the temperature in those parts moderates the appetite. If necessary, it is quite possible to live there on a few dates. It was quite different north of the Taurus. In that cold climate, the desert meant the bare mountain-side, fatal to human life in winter. It was absolutely necessary that the ascetics

Historia religiosa of Theodoret that we derive our information as to the monks of Syria

should not go very far from inhabited places, and, as their wants were not so few as those of their brethren in the Thebaïd, they were obliged to enter into closer communication with the rest of mankind.

Eustathius, notwithstanding his Egyptian experiences, does not appear, at first, to have propagated either monasticism nor anchoritism. The criticisms addressed to him by the Council of Gangra, about 340,[1] are directed, not against an exotic form of asceticism, nor even against a gross exaggeration of the ancient and traditional asceticism, but rather against a tendency to represent it as obligatory, as the Encratites did. Whether Eustathius was judged too unfavourably at that time, or whether he corrected his ideas afterwards, one thing is certain, namely, that at the time when he allied himself with St Basil, his asceticism no longer excited on the part of the Church any objection founded on principle. Upon that ground master and disciple always walked hand in hand. The quarrel which separated them in their later years did not affect this point. A large number of ascetical works,[2] Great and Little Rules, Constitutions, etc., were soon collected together, under the name of St Basil,[3] in a special collection, which was afterwards considerably enlarged by numerous additions. In the time of Sozomen,[4] some people attributed the paternity of them to Eustathius. This is extremely doubtful. But, whatever may be the truth about this question of literary history, the spirit, being assuredly that of Basil, can scarcely differ from that of Eustathius. What is of importance, though for quite other reasons, is that we possess in these books the monastic code of the Byzantine East. It is under the Rule of St Basil that all the monasteries of the Græco-Slavonic world have lived for centuries, and still live at the present day.

In spite of its Egyptian connections, Basilian monas-

---

[1] See above, p. 305.   [2] Migne, *P. G.*, vol. xxxi.

[3] The ἀσκητικόν of Basil is already mentioned, in 392, in the *De viris* of St Jerome (c. 116).

[4] iii. 14, § 31.

ticism marks a great progress towards moderation and
discipline. A strong point is made of the life in community; the inspiration of Pacomius prevails over that
of Antony. The monks have a superior, whose office
is to maintain discipline, to preside over admissions and
novitiates, to instruct and direct the whole community.
Their time is to be divided between meetings for prayer,
the reading of the Bible, and manual labour, especially
working in the fields. The austerities appointed by
the Rule are of a simple character and comparatively
moderate.

From Pontus and Cappadocia, as also from the colonies
of Constantinople,[1] this new type of asceticism soon spread
with the greatest rapidity. Public opinion, and especially
episcopal opinion, could not fail to show more favour
towards it than to Eastern eccentricities. It was even
grateful to it for gradually absorbing the more ancient
form of asceticism, that of the religious living in the world.
In the monasteries, the enthusiasm of celibates and
consecrated virgins found a discipline which the limits of
the local Church could not have imposed upon them
without difficulty. The monasteries themselves, it is
true, had some trouble in the early days in reconciling
themselves with the earlier ecclesiastical organization:
there were clashings, tentative steps, some disputes.
Gradually, however, the balance was attained, and the
new relations were formally sanctioned by canonical
legislation.

As to the civil law, its intervention scarcely ever made
itself felt in these early days, except occasionally and to
meet particular circumstances. Valens, being angry with
the monks of Nitria, who resisted the usurpation of
Lucius, punished a certain number of them, and even
made a law imposing upon them military service.
This law, which St Jerome mentions in the year 377,
could not have had any lasting effects. And besides, we
have good reason for believing that it only affected those
monks who had given cause for complaint. Theodosius

[1] See above, pp. 295 and 306.

also took measures against the monks; for some time he forbade them to live in the towns,[1] where their presence was often prejudicial to good order. Pious as he was, this emperor had little taste for the interference of the monks in the affairs, even the religious affairs, of the world which they claimed to have renounced. And indeed we do not see what administration could have consented to allow the wandering through the towns and on the high-roads of these undisciplined bands of professed redressors of wrongs, who were always ready to interfere with sentences and with the application of the laws, to ill-use anyone who did not share their opinions, and to destroy with violence the edifices of proscribed forms of worship. *Monachi multa scelera faciunt*, said[2] Theodosius to St Ambrose. It was a still more serious matter that, with their austerity, their freedom of speech and their boldness, they were extremely popular. From this point of view, the government could not but look with a favourable eye upon their confinement in monasteries, where, thanks to the Rule and to the authority of the superiors, there was reason to hope that they would preserve the spirit of their vocation, and not transform themselves into disturbers of the public peace. But, in the time of Theodosius, the institution of the monasteries was very far from being sufficiently widespread, to produce these salutary effects everywhere. It was still necessary for a considerable time to reckon with the enthusiasm of the monks and their popularity.

[1] *Cod. Theod.* xvi. 3, 1, a law revoked two years later (xvi. 3. 2).
[2] Ambrose, *Ep.* 41, § 27.

CHAPTER XV

THE WEST IN THE DAYS OF ST AMBROSE

St Hilary and his writings. St Martin of Tours. Council of Valence. Priscillian and his asceticism. Spanish disputes: Council of Saragossa. Attitude of Damasus, of Ambrose, and of Gratian. Maximus in Gaul; the trial at Trèves. The Ithacians. Reaction under Valentinian II.; the schism of Felix; the rhetorician Pacatus. Priscillianism in Galicia. Council of Toledo: dissensions in the Spanish episcopate. The Priscillianist doctrine. St Ambrose and the Court of Justina. Ambrose and Theodosius. Pope Siricius. Jovinian and St Jerome.

HILARY of Poitiers died in 366,[1] leaving behind him a great memory. Of all the bishops of the West, it was he who, throughout the final struggles, had played the greatest part, and that not only in Gaul but in the East and in Italy. He derived no special authority from the situation of his see, but his soul was the soul of a leader of men; and in times of crisis they rallied round him as by instinct. High-spirited and determined, able to form a quick and confident judgment of a situation, he knew how to resist, and his resistance was not to be overcome; he knew also how to open up ways of arrangement when any were to be found. The impression made by his actions was strengthened, for later generations, by the witness of his writings. To Christianity, which he did not embrace till the prime of life, he had brought a culture which was already very considerable. When banished to Asia, he found in study an employment for his enforced leisure: it was then that he made himself familiar with

[1] On January 14, following the tradition of the liturgical anniversary.

the Greek language, and gained acquaintance with the
Doctors of the East, especially with Origen, whose
figurative exegesis, always concerned to rediscover the
New Testament in the Old, squared with what Hilary
was familiar with in others and had himself attempted.
But it was in theology especially that Hilary learnt from
the Easterns. He had left Gaul with very vague ideas
on the controversies of the day[1]; he returned, bringing
not only his *De Synodis*, in which are treated questions
of great subtlety, but also a great work, in twelve books,
on the Trinity. These compositions display a very
considerable advance upon his "Commentary on St
Matthew," which was written before 356. In that,
Hilary was still influenced by the ideas of Tertullian
and Novatian: the Word is Eternal as Word, not as
Son.[2] The difficulty of this language of a bygone age
was revealed to him by a deeper examination. We meet
with it no more in the writings of his exile.

Hilary also took an interest in poetry. He had composed a collection of hymns. One of these compositions, at
least, has come down to us: it is an alphabetical
canticle,[3] in the Horatian metre *Sic te diva potens Cypri.*
I have already mentioned his requests to the Emperor
Constantius, and the terrible pamphlet he directed at him,
in 360, during a moment of despair. It was at that
time, too, that Hilary determined to expose to the public, in
a narrative well supported by proofs, the origin and actual
state of the episcopal disputes. Of this work, analogous
in form and intention to the Apology of Athanasius
against the Arians, we only possess now a few fragments[4]
and a prologue, evidently imitated from the *Histories* of
Tacitus.[5] And even the fragments which have survived are
those of a revised edition, for we find in them documents

---

[1] "Regeneratus pridem et in episcopatu aliquantisper manens,
fidem Nicaenam numquam nisi exsulaturus audivi" (*De Synodis*, 91).

[2] *In Matth.* xvi. 4 ; xxxi. 3.

[3] Published by Gamurrini, from a MS. at Arezzo (*Sancti Hilarii
tractatus*, etc., Rome, 1887, p. 28).

[4] These are what are called his *Fragmenta historica*.

[5] Cf. *Fragm.* i. 4, with Tacitus, *Hist.* i. 2.

of a date later not only than 360, but also than Hilary's death.

It is a singular thing that this great champion of Nicene orthodoxy, who fought and suffered so much for Athanasius, seems to have remained unknown to him. Not once is he mentioned in the writings of the Bishop of Alexandria. The other Easterns are not less ignorant of him. Theodoret never speaks of him; if Socrates, and Sozomen after him, tell us something about Hilary, it is thanks to Rufinus whose ill-constructed history was translated into Greek. It was quite otherwise in the West. The memory of the struggles against the Arians upheld by the Emperor Constantius soon passed into oblivion; but Hilary's books did not perish. He was always considered a master in doctrine, even when men had Ambrose, Jerome, and Augustine.

Among the friends of Hilary there had long been found a strange ascetic called Martin, who, after having served in the army, discharged for some time at Poitiers the office of exorcist. Martin's parents were pagans; his father, an officer in the army, made him serve under the standards; later he retired of his own accord from the service and settled at Sabaria, in Pannonia, of which he was a native. Martin, when only twelve years old, had secured admission as a catechumen, at Pavia, where his parents then resided. We find him, later on, at Amiens,[1] and then at Worms, where he asked for his discharge from the army, acting under an inward prompting to renounce the world and lead the life of an ascetic. Shortly after his establishment at Poitiers, he repaired to Pannonia in the hope of converting his parents. In the case of his mother he succeeded; but the old tribune remained faithful to his gods. It was during this time that Hilary was beginning his journey into exile. Martin protested with as much vigour as he could in his position, strenuously undertaking the defence of his master, of the others who were proscribed, and of the faith of

---

[1] It is with Amiens that the celebrated story of the divided cloak is connected.

Nicæa. He had much to endure on this account, for the bishops of Pannonia were all more or less on the opposite side. In Milan, where he wished to settle, Auxentius made his life so hard that he sought refuge in the little island of Gallinaria, on the coast of Liguria. On Hilary's return he rejoined him at Poitiers, where he was allowed to live as he liked. In the neighbourhood of the town he chose for himself a hermitage, round which other ascetics soon gathered. This was the origin of the monastery of Ligugé, the first of the kind in Gaul and even in the West. These holy people, and especially their master, soon attracted attention. Seven years after the death of Hilary (in 373), the Church of Tours having lost its bishop, the voice of the people made itself heard to acclaim the Saint of Poitiers as his successor. There was some opposition, especially among the bishops, who did not like the idea of having as a colleague a monk who did not wash himself or dress properly. In this we see already the conflict between popular enthusiasm—which thinks more of character than of appearance—and the worldly considerations which prevail, and will do so more and more, with the superior clergy. Martin was consecrated in spite of this opposition, albeit reinforced by his own ; but he found means to combine the monastic life with the duties of his new position. Another monastery was founded by him near Tours, on the cliffs which overhang on the north the bank of the Loire.[1] There he took up his abode with his disciples, and there he spent all the time which was not occupied by his pastoral cares. In his life, which we owe to the enthusiasm of one of his friends, Sulpicius Severus, a great nobleman who had been converted to asceticism, we find mention, in the midst of many miracles, of a characteristic trait— the war which he waged against the rural paganism. Martin had a difficult task in endeavouring to Christianize the peasants of Gaul, who were strongly attached to their ancient religious usages, to the worship associated with their rustic temples and the sacred trees.

[1] This is Marmoutier (*Martini monasterium*).

This struggle against declining paganism was at this time the chief concern of the bishops. In other respects we do not find that in these districts of the Far West the twenty years which followed the Council of Ariminum were fertile in incident. Of the island of Britain we hear nothing until the 5th century. In Gaul, Martin was already a bishop, when a council assembled at Valence (in 374) to settle some dispute of which we know no particulars. We only possess some disciplinary regulations communicated in the form of a letter to the bishops of the two administrative dioceses [1] between which the Gallican provinces were divided. The first of the signatories, among whom appear the Bishops of Trèves, Vienne, Arles, and Lyon, is the Bishop of Agen, Fœgadius or Phœbadius, of whom we have heard in the time of the Emperor Constantius.

In Spain, the little fire of schism which Bishop Gregory was feeding at Illiberris (Granada) [2]—it was not a fire which burnt very brightly—was extinguished with him. Certain Novatians afforded occupation to the pen of Pacian, [4] Bishop of Barcelona. All this was of little consequence. But the moment was approaching when Spain would attract men's attention and set all the West in commotion.

About the beginning of the reign of Gratian, a great deal was heard of an ascetic movement of a peculiar character, directed by an expert theologian called

---

[1] "Fratribus per Gallias et quinque provincias constitutis episcopis."

[2] See above, p. 284.

[3] When St Jerome wrote his *De viris* (in 392) Gregory appears to have been still alive.

[4] Three letters to a Novatian called Sympronianus (Migne, *P. L.*, vol. xiii., p. 1051 *et seq.*). Pacian also left two homilies, one on baptism, the other on penitence. In a work which is lost, the *Cervulus*, he preached against certain pagan superstitions, in particular against the masquerades of January 1. His success was small; we even find him lamenting that his descriptions had given a taste for the Carnival to persons who had never heard of it before (*Paraenesis*, c. 1; Migne, *op. cit.*, p. 1001).

Priscillian.[1] He was a rich man, distinguished by birth and education, well versed in Christian and other literature, even in astrology and the occult sciences, endowed with a keen intellect and a persuasive eloquence ; and all these gifts were at the service of an ardent zeal for the propagation of his own ideas. These were chiefly connected with the right mode of life : Priscillian was a preacher of asceticism.

Asceticism was not unknown in Spain. The Council of Elvira speaks much of celibates (*confessores*) and consecrated virgins, meaning by those terms persons who practised continence and abstinence according to the already time-honoured customs of the Church, and within the bounds of its organization. The disciples of Priscillian went further in marking themselves out as distinct from these. In the first place they were disciples of a particular man, and of a man who had no mission to teach from the Church, who claimed to some extent an inspiration of his own and took his stand in his teaching, not only upon the received Scriptures, but also upon the apocryphal writings, and notably upon those lives of the Apostles Peter, John, Andrew, and Thomas, which were so strongly imbued with the Encratite spirit opposed to marriage, to wine, and to any kind of substantial food. Moreover, there prevailed among them a tendency to despise other Christians. They separated themselves at certain times of the year, during Lent and in the days before the Epiphany[2] ; at such times they disappeared from sight ; no one saw them ; they kept themselves

---

[1] Upon the Priscillianist movement, see Sulpicius Severus, *Chron.* ii. 46-51 (cf. *Dial.* ii. 6, 11), whose account must be corrected sometimes by notes of Priscillian himself, in his apologetical memoirs, especially the second treatise addressed to Pope Damasus [*Corpus script. eccl.* (Vienna), vol. xviii.] ; cf. the Council of Saragossa in 380 ; letter of Maximus to Pope Siricius (*Coll. Avell.* 40) ; Philastrius, *De Haeresibus*, 84 ; Pacatus, *Panegyric of Theodosius*, 29 ; Jerome, *De viris*, and letter 75 ; Council of Toledo in the year 400.

[2] From December 17 to January 6, says the Council of Saragossa (canon 4). It is possible that at the time of the council the feast of Christmas had not yet been introduced into Spain.

shut up in their own houses or in the mountains. It
was known that they held secret meetings in lonely villas,
and it was remarked that they generally walked bare-
footed. They fasted on Sundays. If they came to
Church they allowed the Eucharist to be given to them;
but no one saw them communicate. Finally, and this
was a more serious matter still, women who are always
delighted with any novelty, even and especially of a religious character, fluttered continually round the celebrated
teacher. He held meetings for women only, over which
he presided, either in person or by means of his assistants.

All this was calculated to cause anxiety. A proselytiz-
ing asceticism has always excited ill-feeling on the part of
ordinary Christians. And, at the time of which we are
now speaking, the clergy lent it little support or rather
offered resistance to it, whether from bad motives,
through attachment to a somewhat self-indulgent form of
life, or from good, such as a care for unity, and a fear lest
such observances might conceal some reprehensible
doctrine. On this last point their fears were not without
foundation ; from the very beginning, discreditable
rumours were in circulation with regard to the new sect.
Nothing, however, was as yet proved : criticism could only
take hold of what was seen from the outside—seclusion,
teachers without authority, meetings of women, and the
use of apocryphal books.

The first protest came from the Bishop of Cordova,
Hyginus, who set in motion his colleague of Emerita,
Ydacius. The latter at once entered upon a campaign.
Among the adepts of the movement there was prominent
a woman of considerable position, a certain Agape, who,
in conjunction with a rhetorician named Helpidius, had
communicated to Priscillian, so it was rumoured, the
doctrines of a Gnostic, Mark of Memphis, an emigrant
from Egypt to Spain. The Priscillianists were not without supporters among the episcopal body, Two of their
friends, Instantius and Salvian, had become bishops and
openly supported the party ; Symposius, Bishop of Astorga
in Galicia also joined them, and soon the number was

reinforced by the adhesion of the Bishop of Cordova, who had changed his mind and had finally convinced himself that the new ascetics were in no way dangerous.   It was in the Western provinces, tnose of Lusitania and Galicia, that the movement appears to have been most definite. Ydacius, Metropolitan of Lusitania, thought it his duty to inform Pope Damasus.   The Pope replied in a letter which we no longer possess; in this, foreseeing that the Spanish bishops would assemble to deal with the matter, he advised them not to deliver any personal condemnation in the absence of those accused, and without having heard their explanation.[1]   A council was actually held at Saragossa in 380; we possess a formal account of its decisions aivided into disciplinary canons, which have in view the points on which complaint was made of the Priscillianists.   Two bishops from Gaul, Fœgadius of Agen and Delphinus of Bordeaux, took part in its meetings and signed first.   With them were ten Spanish prelates, one of whom, Symposius, was favourable to the innovators.

The latter, meanwhile, not being attacked by any direct condemnation,[2] suffered their adversaries to say what they pleased, and continued their propaganda.   They even assumed the offensive.   The bishopric of Avila, in Ydacius' province, having become vacant, they secured the election of Priscillian there, and tried in other places to obtain colleagues who shared their opinions.   Accusations were laid against Ydacius; and these excited great scandal in the Church of Emerita.   Priscillian and his two friends entertained the charges, denounced Ydacius to the Spanish episcopate, and even went to Emerita to

---

[1] "Ne quid in absentes et inauditos decerneretur" (*Priscill.*, Treatise ii., p. 35).

[2] Sulpicius Severus (*Chron.* ii. 47) says in so many words that the council condemned the Bishops Instantius and Salvian, as well as the laymen Helpidius and Priscillian.   But this is refuted by the account which the latter has left of this stage of the business.   However, it is possible that something of the kind was attempted, for a rumour of the condemnation was circulated in Spain (*Priscill.*, Treatise ii., p. 40).

declare themselves openly against him. There was already talk of a new council. Ydacius took the initiative; and, thanks to the support of Ambrose, whose sympathy he had managed to win, he obtained from the emperor a rescript, couched in general terms, against "the false bishops and the Manicheans." He prepared to make use of this against his opponents, although they were not mentioned by name in the rescript. Priscillian and his two colleagues, uneasy at the turn which affairs were taking, made their way in person to Milan, furnished with letters testimonial from their clergy and flocks, to prove that they were true bishops; as to the accusation of Manicheism, they would be able to get rid of that by the language they adopted. The imperial Quæstor listened to them and answered them kindly; but Ambrose remained ill-disposed to them: no settlement was arrived at. They pushed on to Rome, and sent to Pope Damasus a memorial of justification, which we still possess. Damasus refused to receive them. One of them, Salvian, died in Rome. Instantius and Priscillian returned to Milan, where, in spite of Ambrose's opposition, they succeeded in obtaining, through Macedonius, the Master of the Offices, a decree with which they returned to Spain, and reinstalled themselves in their bishoprics.

The Bishop of Emerita had now to act with energy. In his campaign against the Priscillianists he had enlisted the assistance of his colleague of Ossonova, Ithacius, who claimed to have been commissioned by the Council of Saragossa to follow this matter up. Ithacius was by no means a model prelate; he was worldly, luxurious, shameless, addicted to the pleasures of the table, just the kind of person, in fact, to be obnoxious to holy people. Priscillian set the proconsul Volventius in motion against him, and the latter, on an accusation of attempting to disturb the public peace, was about to take steps against Ithacius when he succeeded in escaping to Gaul. There he was warmly welcomed by the prætorian prefect. This high official, whose name was Gregory, was taking steps to call the matter before his own tribunal, when a new rescript arrived from Milan, due, like the preceding one, to the friendly intervention of Macedonius. This time, the decision was ordered to be given in Spain; the case was referred to the Vicarius of this "diocese"; and an order was given for the banishment of Ithacius beyond the Pyrenees. The Bishop of Ossonova found himself in a most critical situation; he vanished from the scene.

It was the best thing he could have done. At that very moment, Maximus was declaring himself emperor in the island of Britain; shortly afterwards he landed in Gaul; Gratian, deserted by his troops, was killed at Lyon on August 25, 383. The "tyrant" made his entry into Trèves, and his authority was recognized from the Ocean to the Alps.

It was a disaster for the Priscillianists. Their friends in Milan could no longer avail at the new court at Trèves.[1] The bishop of that place, Britto by name, had been a helper of Ithacius; he lent him support with the new emperor. Maximus naturally desired to make himself popular, especially with the bishops, whose influence over the people he knew. He had practised every sort of cajolery with St Martin. Ithacius profited by these inclinations, and persuaded Maximus to regard his adversaries as the most dangerous of evil-doers. The leaders of the Spanish movement were invited to appear before a council assembled at Bordeaux. Ithacius there assumed the part of accuser; the document which he presented against his adversaries was long preserved.[2] The accused replied in the same manner: Tiberianus, Asarbus, and several others read a defence; we still possess that of Priscillian and of Instantius.[3] The tribunal showed itself unfavourable to them: Instantius was deposed from the episcopate. They were about to turn to Priscillian, when he conceived the fatal idea of

---

[1] Macedonius, besides, had fallen into disgrace (Paulinus, *Vita Ambr.* 37). He was not a friend of Ambrose.

[2] Isidore, *De viris ill.* 15. It was undoubtedly from this source that Sulpicius Severus obtained the information which he relates as to Mark of Memphis as the master of Priscillian.

[3] *Priscilliani tract.* i.

appealing to the imperial tribunal. The bishops consented,[1] and the trial was transferred to Trèves.

The Gallican episcopate at that time showed no enthusiasm for asceticism; and the Priscillianist bishops, compromised as they were by the disputes to which they had given rise in Spain, had against them, besides suspicions more or less clearly defined, the distrustful attitude of the two great ecclesiastical authorities of the West—Pope Damasus and Bishop Ambrose. Their propaganda was considered dangerous; it had already made inroads into Aquitaine. In the district of Bordeaux, a great lady, Euchrotia, and her daughter Procula,[2] lent it substantial patronage. The faithful of Eauze, so it was complained, had embraced Priscillianism in a body. Such circumstances as these produced a state of opinion which was not of a character to enlist for the innovators the sympathies of the new government.

Supported by his metropolitan Ydacius, the Bishop of Ossonova played once more at Trèves, before the criminal magistrate, the part of accuser. Now that he felt himself the stronger, he adopted a high tone; it was not only against the Priscillianists that he inveighed; every form of asceticism was detestable to him. He even found fault with St Martin and attempted to accuse him of heresy. Martin, on his side, besought Ithacius to abandon a hateful part, and protested to the emperor against the intervention of a criminal judge in a question of doctrine. "No shedding of blood!" he said, "Ecclesiastical penalties, such as deposition, are quite enough." Maximus finally promised him that no extreme measures should be taken. And therewith St Martin departed. Freed from his presence, the bishops resumed their unhallowed work; two of them, Magnus and Rufus, succeeded in converting the emperor once more to their opinion. An enquiry was

---

[1] There were involved in the matter accusations belonging to the ordinary criminal law, which were not within ecclesiastical jurisdiction.

[2] With regard to Procula, Sulpicius Severus does wrong in relating a petty story which is improbable and incapable of verification (*Chron.* ii. 48).

decided upon; it was entrusted to the prætorian prefect, Euodius,[1] a harsh and severe man, who succeeded in convicting Priscillian of witchcraft. He made his report to the emperor, and Maximus decided that the accused deserved the penalty of death.

The trial was formally resumed. It was not without difficulty that they succeeded at last in tearing Ithacius away from the accusers' bench. Priscillian was condemned to death and executed with six others, the deacons Asarbius and Aurelius; then Felicissimus and Armenius, who had quite recently joined the sect; finally, Latronianus, a distinguished poet,[2] and the matron Euchrotia. Bishop Instantius escaped with sentence of exile, as did also the rhetorician Tiberianus[3]; they were banished to the Scilly Isles.

The affair did not end there. A military commission was appointed to go to Spain, with instructions to seek out the accomplices of Priscillian on the spot, and to try them summarily. Such atrocities filled all good people with loathing. Against the feeling of the majority of the bishops, one of their number, Theognis, ventured to excommunicate Ithacius. Martin returned to Trèves. Bishop Britto had just died; his colleagues assembled to choose his successor; the choice had fallen upon a certain Felix, who was personally of good repute. On his arrival at the imperial Court, Martin refused to hold communion with the bishops, amongst whom he saw the blood-stained Ithacius. The latter tried hard to compromise Martin along with the condemned, but it was not possible for him so to deceive the emperor. Martin never ceased to protest against the

---

[1] *Is* (Euodius) *Priscillianum gemino iudicio auditum convictumque maleficii nec diffitentem obscenis se studuisse doctrinis, nocturnos etiam turpium feminarum egisse conventus nudumque orare solitum nocentem pronuntiavit* (Sulpicius Severus, *Chron.* ii. 50). The crime of witchcraft by itself was a capital crime. For the rest we must remember that all extreme doctrines easily become *obscenae*, and women *turpes*, when malevolence is concerned in the matter; the *nudus orare* might have been a form of asceticism. Besides, none of this was any concern of a secular judge.

[2] Jerome, *De viris*, 122.   [3] *Ibid.* 123.

blood which had been shed, and to demand that there a
stay should be finally made, and that the tribunes should
not be sent to Spain. He absolutely refused on any
consideration to listen to any proposal for entering into
communion with those who were already beginning to
be called the Ithacians. He yielded, however, when he
was given the choice between his participation in the
ordination of Felix and the immediate despatch of the
commissioners. But to the end of his life he lamented
this necessity of interrupting for a moment his protest
against the blood which had been shed.

He was not the only one to protest. The new Pope
Siricius seems certainly to have asked for explanations,
for we find Maximus in a hurry to offer them, by pretending to liken the Priscillianists to the Manicheans,
which made them fall under the penalties of extremely
severe laws. He also ordered all the documents of the
trial to be sent to the Pope to show him that there had
not been a condemnation of innocent men.[1] Notwithstanding these explanations, Siricius did as St Martin had
done, and refused communion with himself to the supporters
of Ithacius. Ambrose adopted the same attitude.[2] This
was plainly to be seen when he visited Trèves, in 387,
as ambassador from Valentinian II. He presented himself at the Court of Maximus, but not at the Church of
Felix, as he did not wish to have any relations with bishops
"who had demanded the death of the heretics."

But Ambrose, as the representative of a prince against
whom armed preparations were already being made in
the Gauls, was not in a position to put a stop to the
severities ordered at Trèves. The pursuit of Priscillianists
continued. On his journey home, the Bishop of Milan
met an old man, who was being led into exile; it was his
colleague of Cordova, Hyginus, the man who, having first
denounced the Priscillianists, had ended by showing them
goodwill. In vain Ambrose entreated that at least
respect should be shown to his age, that he should

---

[1] *Coll. Avell.* n. 40.
[2] Council of Turin, c. 6. *Cf.* Ambrose, *Ep.* 26.

be given proper clothing and other necessaries. He was rebuffed.

As long as Maximus lasted, *i.e.*, until the summer of 388, the Priscillianists continued to be harassed, and the ascetics in general to be looked upon with suspicion. It was not wise, at that time, to appear with a face emaciated by fasting, or to devote one's nights to pious reading. The worldly prelates—Ithacius at their head—were on the alert and suppressed devotion. But all this was changed when Valentinian II. was restored in 388. There was a reaction as well; and Ithacius was attacked. In vain he protested that he had not been the only one to take proceedings against Priscillian: his former accomplices made haste to desert him, and suffered him to be deposed from the episcopate. Ydacius of Emerita, his Metropolitan, had not waited for this, but had sent in his resignation. Unfortunately for him he changed his mind, and wished to return to his Church, which gave rise to disturbances The government imprisoned the two bishops at Naples.[1]

However, the friends of those who had been put to death obtained permission to give them honourable burial. The remains of the Priscillianist leaders were transported to Spain, and buried with the greatest pomp, amid the enthusiasm of their followers. In Gaul, Priscillianism retained adherents in certain parts of Aquitaine; but the most serious consequence of the whole affair was the discord it introduced among the bishops. Felix of Trèves, ordained by the Ithacians, possessed the sympathies of the prelates who were hostile to asceticism. The others, without having any objection to him personally, avoided him as though he had the plague. It would have been better for him if he had been exiled, like the bishops of Emerita and Ossonova. In his own country, party-spirit had transformed him into a scapegoat; the blood of Euchrotia and of Priscillian appeared to many eyes to

---

[1] Ithacius (*Ithacius Clarus*) seems certainly to have written besides the memorandum already mentioned, a treatise on Arianism, in which he refuted an Arian deacon named Varimadus (Migne, *P. L.* vol. lxii., p. 351*)*.

stain his episcopal mantle, and could never be removed.
Siricius and Ambrose[1] would have nothing to do with
him; they had declared in express terms, by letter, that
people must choose between communion with them and
with him.[2] The schism was still existing in 396, for it
was with the main object of remedying it that there was
held, in that year, a great council at Nimes[3]; and in 401,
just when Sulpicius Severus, who complains bitterly about
it, was finishing his *Chronicle*. Several years later the
Italian Council, assembled at Turin, repeated the condemnation. The quarrel was only stilled with the death
of the unhappy Felix.

Of course political matters played their part in this
affair, and the Ithacians had to suffer for having been
protected by Maximus. In 389, the rhetorician Pacatus
Drepanius, an envoy from the Gauls to Theodosius,
pronounced before that prince and before the Roman
senate a panegyric in which the execution of the Priscillianists, especially of the matron Euchrotia, figured among the
crimes of the usurper. With what were these people
reproached? For being too pious: *nimia religio et
diligentius culta divinitas*. It was for that reason they
were persecuted, and by informers who were priests only
in name, and whom men saw, not without feelings of
horror, pass from the trials by torture to sacred
ceremonies.[4]

In Spain, the reaction against Maximus had very
different consequences. Priscillian became a demi-god;
his followers now swore only by his name. It was
especially in Galicia, where, apparently, his tomb was
situated, that the enthusiasm of his disciples broke forth.
The anniversary of the new martyrs was celebrated, their

---

[1] The matter appears to have been investigated in a council at
Milan, held in 390, *propter adventum Gallorum episcoporum*
(Ambrose, *Ep.* 51).

[2] Council of Turin, c. 6.

[3] Upon the Council of Nimes, besides the Synodal Letter
(Hefele, *Conciliengeschichte*, vol. ii., p. 62), see Sulpicius Severus,
Dial. i. 13.

[4] Pacatus, *Paneg.* 29.

books were eagerly read, and their doctrines openly preached. Several bishops joined the movement, some from conviction, others because they were forced to do so, that they might not offend their fanatical people. The most important among them was Symposius of Astorga, the bishop who had been present at the Council of Saragossa; with him were Vegentinus, Herenas, and some others as well. As soon as a bishop died, the people acclaimed a Priscillianist candidate. Symposius, who was apparently the senior or the metropolitan of the province, lent his co-operation for the ordination. Thus he consecrated Paternus in the important town of Bracara Augusta (Braga); other bishops, such as Isonius, Donatus, Acurius, Æmilius, and his own son, Dictinius, received imposition of hands from him. These comprised almost the whole episcopate of Galicia[1]; the province seemed lost to orthodoxy.

Such a scandal could not last long. It excited no doubt the attention of Theodosius who, having been born in Galicia, could not fail to take an interest in his native country. The bishops of the other provinces assembled at Saragossa,[2] and afterwards at Toledo, and summoned their Priscillianist colleagues to appear before them. They refused. In the interval between the two councils, Symposius and Dictinius, who until then had only received priest's orders, travelled to Milan, hoping that Ambrose, so severe to the Ithacians, would give them some help. They were deceived. Ambrose decided that they must condemn Priscillian and his doctrine; and in

---

[1] We do not know at this particular time of any other orthodox bishop besides Ortygius of *Aquae Celaenae*. And even he was driven away by the sectaries. He was present at the Council of Toledo in 400, when his restoration to his see was determined upon.

[2] We must not confound this new Council of Saragossa with that of 380, the attitude of which obliged Symposius and Dictinius to have recourse to St Ambrose and the Pope. The Pope at that time was Siricius, and no longer Damasus; among the conditions imposed by St Ambrose on the two Galician bishops was a provision that they should erase Priscillian and his companions from the number of the Martyrs. All this indicates a date later than 385.

return for this they might be received to communion; also Dictinius must give up all idea of being made a bishop. They promised to comply. Ambrose and Pope Siricius then wrote to the Spanish bishops to receive them on the conditions agreed upon. But such conditions were easier to accept in Milan than to keep in Galicia. On his return home, Symposius attempted to remove the name of Priscillian from the catalogue of the Martyrs, and Dictinius pretended to refuse the episcopate. But the people protested; and so things were restored to the old footing, and letters from Dictinius were even soon found in circulation, in which the proscribed observances were more or less justified.

Ambrose died in 397, and two years afterwards, Pope Siricius followed him to the grave. In the following year, the orthodox bishops of Spain met once more at Toledo. This time, the prelates of Galicia put in an appearance; the secular authority had no doubt intervened. The situation was a very complicated one. Among the accused, some gave signs of repentance; they condemned Priscillian, his books, and his doctrine, signed every retractation which was asked of them, declared that they had only sinned by mistake, and that, although their opinions remained orthodox, they had been forced to yield to the violence of the people. Others declared that Priscillian was a martyr, the victim of the jealousy of the bishops, and they would never forsake him. Vegentinus and Symposius were the leaders of the first party; the other rallied behind Herenas. As to the orthodox party, they were themselves greatly divided; the bishops of Betica and the district of Carthagena would not hear of a compromise; they demanded the deprivation *en masse* of the whole Galician episcopate, or at all events that they should be put in a state of siege. The Lusitanians and the Tarragonese, though less implacable, were, nevertheless, not greatly inclined to leniency. After much consideration, they began by deposing the refractory bishops—Herenas at their head. As to the others, one alone was admitted to communion, Vegentinus, who

appeared to have compromised himself least. The Bishop
of Bracara, Paternus, was allowed to enter into relations
with him ; Paternus was thus admitted by an intermediary.
The others, Symposius, Dictinius, Isonius, and all those
in communion with Symposius, were invited to sign a
formula, and, if they did so, they were to be allowed to
retain their sees. But as it was impossible to come to an
understanding on the question of what kind of relations
were to be held with them, it was decided that the
question should be referred to the new Pope, Anastasius,
and to the new Bishop of Milan, Simplicianus. Until
their decision was received, the reconciled bishops were
to refrain from holding ordinations.[1]

The reply[2] of the two Italian primates was not long
delayed ; it was favourable to the moderate orthodox
party and to the penitent prelates. Communion was
therefore re-established between them and the rest of
the Catholic world. But there always remained in Galicia
a nucleus of unyielding Priscillianists ; they held their
ground there in spite of the imperial laws which quickly
fell upon them[3] ; and, moreover, the Swabian invasion
soon gave them full liberty. We still hear of them
for a long time afterwards. Gradually, the cult of
Priscillian was concentrated towards the extremity of
the province, in the diocese of Iria Flavia, where some
adherents were still to be found towards the end of the
6th century. It was in this very country, the last refuge
of Priscillianism, that the Spaniards in the time of the
Asturian kings were to "re-discover" the tomb of the
Apostle James, the son of Zebedee, and to found a
celebrated cult.

As to the orthodox bishops, the reconciliation of the
Priscillianists was to them "a stone of stumbling." The
prelates of Baetica and of the district of Carthagena,

---

[1] The document for all this is the Council of Toledo in 400, the
record of which has come down to us only in fragments, inserted in
the formal minute of another council held in 447. *Cf.* the *Chronicle*
of Idacius, under the year 399.

[2] Presupposed by a letter of Pope Innocent, Jaffé, 292.

[3] *Cod. Theod.* xvi. 5, 40, 43, 48.

irritated at the indulgence shown by the Italians, refused all relations with those who accepted communion with the reconciled party. The spirit of Gregory of Illiberris moved them. In vain did Pope Innocent intervene[1] to censure the rigorists. They paid no attention to him; their schism lasted until the invasion of the barbarians in 409.

Such is the external history of the Priscillianist movement. At the present day, how are we to think precisely of the doctrine taught by Priscillian? Sulpicius Severus condemns it very harshly, but without explaining himself. He seems to see in it a species of immoral Gnosticism. Since the rediscovery of several writings of Priscillian, it is the custom to oppose them to Sulpicius, and to represent Priscillian as a mere preacher of asceticism, who can be reproached at most only for his taste for apocryphal writings; his affair was merely an episode in the continual battle between an episcopate corrupted by worldliness and the ascetic party. I cannot accept such a vindication. Undoubtealy, no heretical thesis is maintained in the writings of Priscillian which have come down to us. But it is well to remember that this literature is composed of three memoirs of self-justification, written for presentation to the ecclesiastical authorities, and of a few sermons preached to the faithful of Avila, at a time when the teaching of Priscillian was already looked upon with suspicion, and could scarcely have been exposed to the public.[2] It is not in compositions of this kind that we can expect to find definite heresies. The author, it is true, declares repeatedly that he condemns all heresies—the Ophites, the Nicolaitans, the Patripassians, the Manicheans, etc.; but his anathemas always avoid the real point of the matter. Thus, for example, he sees in Manicheism only the worship of

[1] Jaffé, 292.

[2] What are called the *Canones Priscilliani* were already known; these are a sort of exposition of Christian doctrine in ninety articles, with a note of the texts from St Paul which prove them. But we have only an orthodox recension of them due to a bishop called Peregrinus.

the sun and moon; and the Patripassians are for him people who could not discover in the Gospel any mention of the Son of God. A man must be a mere tiro in investigation, if he allows himself to be taken in by such anathemas. Ambrose, Damasus, and Martin, persons whom no one would rank among the enemies of asceticism, regarded Priscillian with mistrust. The reception which they gave to the Spanish mystics is in this respect very significant, even though we do not quite understand what exactly they reproached them with. It is certain that it was not easy for them to be enlightened. The sect was a very mysterious one; it was, not merely from the time when it had to endure suffering but from the outset, a secret society. In the meetings of the initiated clearly things were said which it was not considered proper to entrust to ordinary believers, even to ascetics of the old type. More than this, the Priscillianists admitted that they lied to disguise the doctrines of their sect. Dictinius, before his conversion, had composed a treatise called "The Scale" (*Libra*), in which is explained the theory of useful lying.[1] People do not take so many precautions unless there is something to conceal.

It is certain also that the Priscillianist initiates— like the Valentinian "pneumatici" and the Manichean "elect"—formed, according to the views of the sect, a class superior to the rest of the faithful. They alone possessed the fulness of the doctrine and perfection of life. The latter was realized in asceticism, an asceticism resting on a dualistic basis. In man there is an element which is divine in the proper sense of the word; by this element God and man are of the same nature.[2] The world is the work of another principle. It was in vain that Priscillian condemned Patripassianism; the doctrine of the *Filius innascibilis*, professed by his

---

[1] St Augustine speaks of it at great length in his book *Contra mendacium*.

[2] Dictinius, at the council in 400, expressly admitted that he had held that doctrine.

disciples,[1] presupposes a Trinity purely nominal; and I do not see in what other sense we can interpret the formula *tres unum sunt in Christo Jesu*, which appears in one of his apologies.

It is not without reason that the first persons who have described Priscillianism have presented it as a form of asceticism inspired by Gnostic ideas. It is thus that it is spoken of by Philastrius of Bresica[2] shortly after the events at Trèves. St Jerome in 392 had not yet studied the question for himself.[3] He only knew that Priscillian had left certain writings; that some persons represented him a Gnostic, and others defended him from that error.[4] Very little was then known of the Councils of Saragossa and Bordeaux, in which the questions of doctrine must have been discussed. The sect still kept its books secret.

But it did not always do so. Orosius and St Augustine were acquainted with them[5]; the extracts which they give from them and the information which they derive from them agree entirely with the idea of an ascetic Gnosticism. Little by little opinion gained in precision in regard to them. Direct study came to strengthen the impression left by the proceedings of the Council of Toledo, and by the recantation which it secured from several Priscillianist leaders. It would be vain to allege a development in doctrine, presumably produced in the sect after the death of its founder. The bishops Symposius

---

[1] Symposius, at the same council, repudiated the doctrine of the two principles, and that of the *Filius innascibilis*, but admitted that they were accepted in the sect.

[2] *Haer.* 84.   [3] *De viris*, 121.

[4] Several years afterwards, about 399, St Jerome, writing to a noble Spanish lady, takes sides definitely against Priscillian; but he does not seem to have studied his doctrine very deeply. What he says of it refers only to the memoir of Ithacius; and in regard to this he makes a strange blunder, confusing Mark of Memphis, of whom Ithacius speaks, with Mark the Gnostic, a contemporary of St Irenæus. Jerome, *Ep.* lxxv. 5; cf. *Adv. Vigilantium*, 7, and *In Esaiam*, lxiv. 5.

[5] See the *Commonitorium* of Orosius, and the reply of St Augustine, *P. L.*, vol. xlii., p. 665 *et seq.*

and Dictinius who abjured in 400 were not recent initiates; there is nothing to prove that their Priscillianism differed in any respect whatsoever from that of Priscillian himself.

In fact, horrible as the executions at Trèves were, and strongly as they have been condemned in the Church it was impossible for the Church to recognize its own traditions in the religious system of the victims.

Ambrose at Milan was, for the whole of the West, a kind of oracle; even in the East his was a power to be reckoned with. He was truly the *sacerdos magnus* of the Bible, the "gran prete" of the poet. A Roman by birth, by tradition, and by education, government was natural to him. He governed the Church fearlessly, as he would, had need been, have governed the State. Bishop of the Latin capital, he had the emperor within reach of his exhortations. And all went well in that quarter so long as Gratian lived. That amiable prince was to him an obedient son. War, the chase, and State affairs did not prevent him from taking an interest in matters of religion. He plied Ambrose with questions, and the bishop, absorbed as he too was by many cares foreign to pure speculation, was called upon to find time to write whole treatises of theology[1] for the information of his imperial disciple.

It was a terrible blow for Ambrose, when he heard that Gratian, forsaken by the army of the Gauls, had been treacherously assassinated. To regret for the loss of the young and sympathetic emperor were added grave fears alike for the empire and for orthodox religion. Now, it was with Valentinian II. that he would have to deal, or rather with his mother, Justina, the friend and patroness of the Arians. However, at first, Justina had more serious anxieties than that for the Creed of Ariminum. Ambrose saw her come to him with her son, a child of twelve years old; she put the child forward and placed him in his arms. The bishop promised to go over the mountains to negotiate with Maximus, and to save what

---

[1] Treatises, *De fide, De Spiritu Sancto, De incarnationis dominicae sacramento.*

could still be saved. Maximus just then showed himself
in a very haughty mood; and the negotiations were
somewhat stormy. However, they came to an understanding at last; the envoys of Valentinian II. consented to
recognize the usurper, who, for his part, promised not to
cross the Alps.

On his return to Milan, Ambrose had at first no cause
for anything but satisfaction with the court. He was
energetically supported in his dispute with Symmachus
(384) in the matter of the altar of Victory. But, in the
following year (385), the Arian question came forward
again, and relations became gravely strained. There had
remained at Milan, ever since the time of Auxentius,
several persons who were attached to the confession of
Ariminum, including even some clerics, although the new
bishop had been wise enough to accept *en bloc* the
ecclesiastical *personnel* of his predecessor. Ursinus, the
pretender to the see of Rome, had made use of these people
to stir up scandal against Ambrose[1]; an unattached
Pannonian Bishop, Julianus Valens, busied himself in the
same quarters, at Milan and in the neighbouring towns.
He had been ordained at Pettau (Poetovio) by the Arian
party, in opposition to Mark, the Catholic bishop of that
place. When the Goths showed themselves upon the
Upper Drave, Valens put himself on their side and helped
them to make themselves masters of his episcopal city.
He had made himself half a Goth, and wore a necklace
and bracelets, in the manner of the barbarians. The city
was pillaged, but the people of Pettau continued to refuse
to have anything to do with Valens, and he was obliged to
take his departure.[2] Peace was concluded with the Goths
in 382: many of them then gained a footing in Court
circles; the army was recruited more and more from
among the barbarians; their leaders attained the highest
dignities. All this tended to form round the empress an
Arian circle which was a cause of much anxiety to

[1] Ambrose, *Ep.* 11; see above, p. 370.
[2] Ambrose, *Ep.* 12. This letter and the preceding one are written
in the name of the Council of Aquileia (381).

Ambrose. It became still more so when circumstances
provided the party with a religious leader, in the person
of a second Auxentius. This man, I think, must be
identified with Auxentius, the Arian Bishop of Dorostorum on the Lower Danube.[1] He was a disciple of
Ulfilas, and had even written the Life of that famous
personage. If he was to be found at the Court of Milan,
it was no doubt because the determined attitude of
Theodosius would not allow a prelate who was notoriously
Arian to continue to exercise his office in the Eastern
Empire.[2] Auxentius wished to have a church of his own ;
the Court asked Ambrose for the Portian Basilica (St
Victor *ad corpus*), which was situated outside the walls.
Ambrose refused. The demand was pressed ; it was even
proposed, at one time, to take from him the new Basilica,
i.e., one of the buildings of his own cathedral.[3]

The Feast of Easter (385) was approaching. The
emperor caused the Portian Basilica to be seized, and then,
in face of the attitude of the bishop and the people,
relinquished his design.[4] This defeat exasperated the
Court extremely. Auxentius took advantage of this
fact to obtain a law granting the right of meeting to
the faithful who adhered to the Creed of Ariminum ; the
opposing party, *viz.*, the Catholics, thus suffered a
severe rebuke.[5] On the other hand we find Maximus
intervening in the matter—Maximus, the usurper of

---

[1] See below, Chapter XVII.

[2] I am not aware that this identification of Auxentius of Dorostorum
with the Auxentius of Milan—the contemporary of St Ambrose—has
been made before. Ambrose says (*Sermo contra Aux.* 22) that he
came from Scythia, where he was called Mercurinus. Dorostorum
was in Lower Mœsia, but on the frontier between that province and
that of Scythia.

[3] There were at this time in Milan two cathedral basilicas ; the
ancient church, which was preserved down to the 16th century,
bore the name of St Thecla : it was demolished in 1548 to enlarge
the piazza of the Duomo ; the other was quite new in the time of St
Ambrose ; it was the predecessor of the present cathedral.

[4] All this is related, with profuse detail, in a letter of Ambrose to
his sister Marcellina (*Ep.* 20).

[5] *Cod. Theod.* xvi. 1, 3.

Gaul, the murderer of Gratian. The Court of Milan
received from him a letter, in very vigorous terms, in
which he took up the defence of the persecuted Catholics.[1]
Such a proceeding could not fail to embitter the dispute.
When the Easter celebrations came round again (386),
Ambrose was once more summoned to give up one of his
churches, and was then formally bidden to leave Milan.
He refused to abandon his flock, who, besides, were
determined not to allow him to go, and remained on the
alert, spending whole days and nights in the church. He
also refused to take part in a conference with Auxentius.[2]
There was nothing for it but to leave him in peace. And
it seemed also as if Heaven itself came to his aid. On
June 17, 386, he discovered the remains of two Milanese
martyrs, Gervase and Protasius; no sooner were they
exhumed than they caused miracles of so signal a
character that not only the city of Milan, but the whole
of Christendom rang with the tidings.[3] Ambrose acquired
in matters of this kind an unexpected success. Before
his time, only three martyrs had been known at Milan—
Victor, Nabor, and Felix; but, after Gervase and Protasius,
he discovered at Bologna, in 393, the tombs of SS. Vitalis
and Agricola, and again at Milan, in 395, those of SS.
Nazarius and Celsus.[4]

In the meantime, Maximus, the by no means disinterested protector of the Catholics of Italy, was causing
the Court of Milan more and more serious uneasiness.
In the spring of 387,[5] Ambrose, who had been reconciled
with Valentinian and his mother, made his way once more
to Gaul, with the ostensible object of recovering Gratian's
remains, but evidently with the view to arrange matters, if

[1] *Coll. Avell.* 39.   [2] *Ep.* 21 ; *Sermo contra Aux.*   [3] *Ep.* 22.
[4] Paulinus, *Vita Ambrosii*, 14, 29, 32. Ambrose, *Exhort. virgin.* 1.
—On the Saints of Milan, see the works of P. F. Savio, *Ambrosiana*,
1897 (Nazarius and Celsus) ; *Nuovo bull. di archeol. crist.*, 1898,
p. 153 (Gervase and Protasius) ; *Rivista di scienze storiche*, Pavia,
1906 (Victor, Nabor, and Felix).
[5] After Easter, which fell that year on April 25 ; it was at this
time that Augustine received baptism at Milan, from the hands of
Ambrose.

it were still possible to do so. But it was no longer possible. Some months later, Maximus entered Italy; Valentinian, Justina, and the whole of their court fled by sea, and found refuge at Thessalonica.

Theodosius received them kindly, and set himself to put in order again the affairs of his youthful colleague. This he succeeded in doing in the following summer. Maximus, being defeated on the Save and the Drave, took refuge at Aquileia ; the troops of the Eastern emperor came up with him there, and made themselves masters of his person. He was executed without delay, on July 28, 388, and Valentinian II. was recognized as Emperor of the whole of the West. It was about this time that he lost his mother, the last hope of the Arian party : Valentinian now passed under the moral guardianship of Theodosius, and under the religious influence of Ambrose.

Moreover, Theodosius stayed nearly three years in the West. During this time he held frequent communication with Ambrose. The esteem which they professed for each other did not prevent them from finding themselves sometimes at variance. The people of Callinica[1] on the Euphrates had sacked a synagogue, at the instigation, so it appeared, of their bishop. In the same country, a procession of monks having encountered a party of Valentinians, a fight took place, at the end of which the monks, having vanquished the heretics, fell upon their temple and burnt it to ashes. Theodosius ordered that the disorder should be severely repressed, and was especially urgent that the Bishop of Callinica should rebuild the synagogue at his own expense. Ambrose intervened, and succeeded in putting a stop to all reprisals. In these cases Theodosius allowed himself to yield, but he did so with much ill-temper, and complained bitterly of the monks.[2] Ambrose declared that Jews and pagans had been guilty of many acts of the kind in Julian's reign, and no one had interfered with them. It was, it must be confessed, a poor argument.

[1] Upon this affair, see letters 40 and 41 of St Ambrose.
[2] *Ep.* 41, § 27.

On the other hand, he had reason on his side when
he protested against the massacre of the people of
Thessalonica who had been guilty of sedition, and
required the emperor to do penance.[1] Theodosius consented; he had, indeed, been the first to regret his
outburst of passion, and to deplore the frightful consequences which had resulted from it. Before he set out
on his return to the East in 391, Ambrose again made
strong representations to him in order to obtain a settlement of the affair at Antioch, in which he had never
ceased to take an interest. The result of this application
was that a great council assembled at Capua in 391.
Pope Siricius must have been represented there, and the
Bishop of Milan must have been the moving spirit in it;
but with regard to this assemblage we have only a small
number of pieces of information which refer quite as much
to certain local affairs, of which we shall hear later on, as
to the principal business.

In the following year, the young Emperor, Valentinian
II., was assassinated in Gaul. His place was taken by a new
usurper, Eugenius, under whose patronage a last revival of
paganism was beginning to take shape, at any rate at
Rome,[2] when Theodosius reappeared on the scene in 394.
Ambrose, broken-hearted at Valentinian's death, had held
himself aloof from the new government. He did not long
enjoy the pleasure of seeing Theodosius again, for that
prince died on January 17, 395. His remains were
transported from Milan to Constantinople.

The great bishop followed him soon afterwards, on
April 4, 397, which was Easter eve. Ten years before,
at the same Paschal festival, he had poured the water of

---

[1] *Ep.* 51. This story has been very dramatically told by Sozomen
(*H. E.* vii. 25), and especially by Theodoret (*H. E.* v. 17). These
authors add, following Rufinus (*H. E.* ii. 18), that Theodosius after
this affair ordered by a special law that the execution of imperial
sentences should always be deferred for a month, if they involved
severe penalties (*vindicari severius*). This is the law, *Cod. Theod.* ix.
40, 13, which is wrongly dated in the Theodosian Code, as is shown
by the observations of Mommsen with regard to another law, vii.
18, 8.   [2] See below, Chapter XVII.

baptism on the forehead of Augustine. At the time of his death, his neophyte was already Bishop of Hippo : one light succeeded the other. And, moreover, Ambrose did not entirely pass away. Besides the brightness of his memory, he left many books—pastoral works, sermons on the Bible, transformed for publication into exegetical treatises; funeral orations; hymns and liturgical commentaries; theological dissertations against Arianism, upon the Divinity of the Holy Spirit, upon the Incarnation; moral exhortations on the duties of the clergy and on the profession of virginity ; and letters on the questions with which day by day his experience was called upon to deal. All these were written quickly in the midst of the cares of a devoted ministry. Ambrose did not mind availing himself of assistance from previous works. He knew Greek very well, and borrowed largely from Origen, Didymus, and Basil. In his treatise on duties he set himself to follow Cicero. He had no literary vanity. In his writings, he thought only of their practical utility, not at all of the lustre they might bring him. Whether they were of greater or less originality, he cared little, provided that they fulfilled the purpose for which he published them. Who could blame such a man for having saved his time for action?

Although somewhat eclipsed by his distinguished colleague, Pope Siricius was worthily administering the Apostolic Church. Like the majority of the Popes of these early days, he seems to have been of moderate abilities, abilities which were above all practical. At Rome it was the custom to choose the bishop among the local clergy; the Pope invariably came from the professional ministry. An election like that of Ambrose was impossible. This system involved the loss of the chance of obtaining leaders of wide range of ideas, but it was almost certain that they would be always wise and experienced. The schism of Ursinus was suppressed. When assembled to choose a successor to Damasus, the faithful of Rome had protested against the usurper.[1] The Roman Church

Letter of Valentinian II. to the Prefect Pinianus (*Coll. Avell.* 4), Feb. 24, 385.

under Siricius lived almost in peace, recruiting itself more and more at the expense of paganism, and multiplying or enlarging its sacred buildings. It was at this time that the Basilica of St Paul[1] was rebuilt, with the proportions in which we see it at the present day. With regard to internal conflicts, we hear of none except quarrels between the monks and their opponents. Siricius, a man who loved order, supported the general principles of Christian asceticism, but looked with no favourable eye upon people who caused disturbance. In the very first days of his Pontificate, Jerome had felt that the air of Rome was becoming unhealthy for him. But he was not the only one who might be a cause of uneasiness. Jerome, at least, was an honest man; his austerity was not feigned, his life was pure, and occupied in useful work. But at a time when no monastery existed in Rome, when the monks were left to themselves, and wandered all day long through the streets, we can imagine the eccentricities, and even the disorders, against which the ecclesiastical authorities had to keep a watchful eye. So-called celibates (*continentes*) were to be seen vieing with the most exquisitely scented clerics in the assiduity with which they danced attendance upon great ladies, and in the skill with which they angled for legacies.[2] It became necessary to repress abuses of this kind by a law,[3] which was posted up in all the churches in Rome; and this severe law, which forbade anyone to make a will in favour of Christian priests and monks—while pagan priests preserved the right of inheritance—was declared by the ecclesiastical authorities of the time to be just and necessary.

These abuses, however, had not the effect of bringing the religious profession into disrepute. Quite the contrary; for the bishops, manifestly supported by public

---

[1] Letter of Valentinian II. to the Prefect Sallust. (*Coll. Avell.* 3).

[2] It is with this, I think, that there is connected the composition of certain liturgical forms included later in the collection called the "Leonian Sacramentary." See my *Origines du culte chrétien*, 3rd edition, p. 142.

[3] *Cod. Theod.* xvi. 2, 20 ; *cf.* Ambrose, *Ep.* xviii. 14 ; Jerome, *Ep.* lii. 6.

opinion, had never set themselves more eagerly to raise it.
They continually repeated that, all things being equal in
other respects, virginity is superior to marriage, represents a higher condition, and is more meritorious for the
life to come.   I have said "all things being equal in other
respects," for no one dreamed of placing a bad monk or
an indiscreet virgin above a father or mother of a family,
who was faithful to his or her duties.   But, with this one
reservation, there is no kind of praise which was not
bestowed on a life of continence and abstinence; and,
as was inevitable, the enthusiasm displayed for it sometimes passed all bounds.   Hence arose in some persons a
tendency to reaction, which, when translated into words,
was liable in its turn to be lacking in restraint.

At the period at which we have arrived (about 390),
this tendency was represented at Rome by a certain
Jovinian,[1] who, after having lived for many years as a
monk — dishevelled in hair and in clothing, absorbed
in fasting and mortification — had ended by convincing
himself of the uselessness of his observances, and by
returning to the ordinary conditions of life, without going
so far, however, as to marry.   If he had stopped there,
there would have been nothing to say; but he soon
passed from practice to theory and to spreading his ideas
abroad.   According to the teaching of himself and his
disciples to anyone who would listen to them, there was
no moral difference between the life of celibates and that
of married people; abstinence and other ascetic practices
were equally useless; in the other world no special
recompense would reward these observances; all this,
they declared, clearly followed from the stories of the
Bible in regard to the patriarchs, the prophets, and the
apostles themselves; as to the Virgin Mary, she had
ceased to be a virgin in bringing her Son into the world[2];
after Him, she had had other children.   All this was
consistent enough, once the premises were granted.

---

[1] Upon Jovinian, see Haller, *Iovinianus* in the *Texte und
Untersuchungen*, vol. xvii. (1897).

[2] Jovinian did not deny the Virginal Conception of Christ.

Jovinian had another doctrine, according to which true Christians could not possibly sin; those who do so have not been truly baptized; they have only received the outward part of the Sacrament, without experiencing its inward efficacy.[1]

These ideas were propagated by disputations and addresses; at last they were set forth in a book, and this was a misfortune for Jovinian, because henceforth his opponents had a basis for operations against him. Among the most active opponents were the friends of Jerome, especially the Senator Pammachius, a very pious man, who had renounced the world and devoted himself to works of charity. They denounced Jovinian to Pope Siricius; he in his turn gathered his clergy together; and when it had been proved that the new doctrines were incompatible with the "Christian Law," Jovinian and eight of his followers were excommunicated as propagators of heresy. News of this sentence was immediately given to Milan by three Roman priests, whom Siricius entrusted with the duty of carrying thither a sort of circular letter.[2] Jovinian was already there, hoping no doubt to arrange matters in his own favour with the assistance of the Court. He was mistaken. Ambrose needed little rousing against the enemies of virginity. He assembled some bishops around him, and pronounced against Jovinian an additional condemnation.[3] The emperor, warned by the legates, gave no reception to the heretics; they were even driven from Milan.[4] A little later,

[1] Thanks to this doctrine, Jovinian (or rather, his memory), played a part later on in the controversies between Pelagians and anti-Pelagians, who each hurled him at the others' heads

[2] Jaffé, 260.

[3] Letter 42, addressed to Pope Siricius. The Council of Milan goes a little too far in comparing the opinions of Jovinian to Manicheism. So far as we are informed, there is nothing in common between the two systems.

[4] In a law of the Theodosian Code (xvi. 5, 53), Jovinian is represented as holding meetings in the outskirts of Rome. Orders are given for the deportation of himself and his adherents to different islands. The law is dated in 412; but the name of the prefect to whom it is addressed would point rather to the year 398. Besides,

in 396, two monks of Vercellæ, having broken their vows, began to preach against asceticism. Ambrose wrote to the Church of Vercellæ in the severest terms, speaking of the innovators as Epicureans.[1] Augustine also had occasion to write against the doctrines of Jovinian.[2]

But these refutations were of somewhat later date. At the time, Pammachius, whom the sentences of Rome and Milan had not sufficed to appease, took it into his head to secure the intervention of Jerome. Of the latter, for several years nothing had been heard. He was immersed at Bethlehem in his Biblical studies, and seemed to have turned his back for ever upon the Babylon of Italy. If he ever wrote there it was to implore his friends to rejoin in Palestine the colony he had founded in it with Paula and Eustochium, and to extol the sanctity of the Holy Places. However, there still remained to him memories. Neither St Paul, nor the prophets, upon whom he was diligently commenting, nor Origen, whom he was translating so eagerly, caused him to forget Cicero; and loudly as he celebrated the charms of the Holy Land or the virtues of the hermits of Palestine,[3] Rome ever lived in the background of his memories. Pammachius sent him Jovinian's book.

What a piece of good fortune! Virginity, and asceticism as a whole to be defended, and that before the Roman public, and against an adversary who did not know how to write![4] Jerome let himself go. In a few weeks he had composed his two books against Jovinian, and Rome soon rang with them. Unfortunately, he had gone too far, and it was not against Jovinian, already crushed by official sentences, that public opinion was excited, but against the imprudent controversialist, who,

the name of the heretic in the MS. tradition is *Jovianus*, not *Jovinianus*. It is, in fact, very doubtful if our Jovinian is in question here.

[1] *Ep.* 83, about 396.

[2] This is the subject of his *De bono coniugali.*

[3] His Lives of Malchus and of Hilarion belong to this period.

[4] He quotes from Jovinian, while refuting him; his extracts really give the impression of an author who cared little about his style.

under pretext of defending asceticism, placed married people in a most awkward position. Pammachius was sorry for having invoked such a helper. He did all he could to withdraw the unfortunate philippic from circulation. The priest Domnio, another of Jerome's friends, for his part removed from it the most objectionable passages, and both of them wrote to the hermit. Jerome at once assumed the defensive. He began by modestly explaining to his friends that his books were not the kind which could be suppressed or expurgated at pleasure; that the public gave them so great a reception that they were no sooner written than they were in everybody's hands. As to the objections made against him, he was naturally of opinion there was no common sense in them.

In Jerome, the "old man" died hard. At the moment when he was embarking on the campaign against Jovinian, he had just published his *De viris illustribus*, in which his literary judgments manifest so strongly his friendships and his animosities. Thus he contents himself with mentioning Ambrose by name, without saying one word about his writings, "for fear he might be accused of flattery or suspicion cast upon his veracity." There was no fear of flattery, for, apart from a few common-place mentions, he never spoke of Ambrose except to decry him. Amply provided himself by the pens of Origen and of Eusebius, he finds fault with Ambrose's borrowings from Greek authors. He had even taken the trouble to translate the work of Didymus upon the Holy Spirit, in order that the Latin public might judge what, on a similar subject, a miserable crow (*informis cornicula*, for which read "St Ambrose") owed to the Alexandrian Doctor. It was with an equally charitable intention that he had translated into Latin the homilies of Origen upon St Luke. In his *Chronicle* he had abused Cyril of Jerusalem and St Basil, treating the first as an Arian, and asserting that the merits of the Bishop of Cæsarea were annihilated by his pride. Of John Chrysostom, whose eloquence at the moment when Jerome was writing his *De viris* held Antioch spellbound and illuminated the whole of the East, he knew only a little treatise on the Priesthood. Later on, he was to aggravate in a signal degree the injustice of which he was guilty towards that illustrious man. But Basil had been the friend of Meletius, and Chrysostom was one of Flavian's priests: the relations of Jerome with the Little Church of Antioch would explain, in some measure, the bad temper which he displays when they are concerned. It is more difficult to understand why he showed so little goodwill to the Bishop of Milan, who was himself a supporter of Paulinus, himself a champion of asceticism, and a patron of virginity. Could there have been some unpleasantness between the pious salons of Marcella and of Marcellina? Or could Ambrose, who went to Rome in 382, at a time when Jerome was also there, have inadvertently inflicted a scratch upon that most sensitive of skins? Of all this we know nothing.

Very discreet in his mention of Ambrose's literary efforts, and in general as to those of authors who did not please him, Jerome is fortunately less reserved as to his own. His *De viris* concludes with a long chapter, in which he draws up a complete catalogue of all that he had published down to the year 392. It was no small amount. If Jerome was bad-tempered, at any rate he did not waste his time.

CHAPTER XVI

CHRISTIANITY IN THE EAST UNDER THEODOSIUS

Christian settlements north of the Danube. Ulfilas and the conversion of the Goths. The sects. The assembly in 383. Divisions among the Arians and Eunomians. The Novatians. Fanatical sects: the Massalians. Amphilochius, Bishop of Iconium. Gregory of Nyssa. Gregory of Nazianzus. Epiphanius and the heretics. Apollinaris: his teaching and his propaganda. Diodore of Tarsus. Flavian and Chrysostom. The schism at Antioch: Council of Cæsarea. Eusebius of Samosata. Edessa and its legends: St Ephrem. Palestine. Cyril of Jerusalem. Pilgrimages: visit of Gregory of Nyssa. Rufinus and Jerome. Arabia: the cult of Mary. Titus of Bostra and his successors. The Council of 394.

1. *Arianism among the Goths.*

CHRISTIAN propaganda in the West had scarcely extended beyond the frontiers; there still remained too much to be done in the interior without engaging in distant missions. Besides, the Scots and Picts to the north of Roman Britain, the Saxons, Franks, and Alamanni, in independent Germany, were in a state of continual hostility to the empire. There was quite enough difficulty already in preventing them from ravaging it, without thinking of going to them in order to preach the Gospel. At certain points, in Upper Germany (*Agri Decumates*) and beside the Carpathians (Mœsia and Dacia), Roman settlements had already passed the line of the Rhine and of the Danube; but they had all been swamped by the invasions in the middle of the 3rd century; and then, finally, the empire had abandoned positions which stood out of all relation to the centre of government. It is possible that Christianity had already been planted there in a few places; but of this we have neither indication nor testimony.

Such was the state of things down to the end of the 4th century. Except near the mouths of the Danube, we hear nothing of the establishment of churches beyond the frontiers, but much on the other hand of churches destroyed on Roman territory by the invasions of barbarians.

Beyond the Lower Danube, the *legatus* of Mœsia Inferior had long watched over the passage between the south-east angle of the Transylvanian plateau and the Black Sea. His protection extended along the shore of the latter to various Greek settlements, such as the towns of Tyra and Olbia, at the mouth of the Tyras (Dniester) and of the Borysthenes (Dnieper), the town of Cherson (Sebastopol), and the little kingdom of Bosphorus (Kertch) at the entrance to the Sea of Azov. Tyra and Olbia, ancient colonies of Miletus, were, under the empire, in a state of great decay. Hellenism there found itself more and more ground down by barbarism. We hear nothing more of them after the reign of Alexander Severus, which leads us to conclude that they were destroyed by the Goths. It was not so with Cherson and Bosphorus: these two cities, so different in their origin and institutions—the one democratic, the other monarchical—had no doubt to suffer a good deal from the new barbarians, both in their commerce and in the political influence which they exercised with the Scythians and Sarmatians; but they held their ground and continued to exist until the Middle Ages. Christianity was established there at an early period: a Bishop of Bosphorus was present at the Council of Nicæa in 325,[1] a Bishop of Cherson at that of Constantinople in 381.

---

[1] Κάδμος Βοσπόρου. Another bishop of this see perished in 358 at Nicomedia, under the ruins of the church which was overthrown by an earthquake. Sozomen (*H. E.* iv. 16) mentions him without giving his name. Upon the Christian antiquities of Kertch, see the article of J. Kulakowsky, in the *Römische Quartalschrift*, vol. viii. (1894), p. 309 *et seq.*

The Goths themselves were reached by the spreading
of the Gospel as soon as they began to live in the
neighbourhood of the Black Sea. We might almost say
that the beginning of their Christianity dated from the
terrible invasions by which they harassed the empire
towards the middle of the 3rd century. From their
expeditions into Asia Minor they brought back with
them, amongst other captives, several Christians who
taught them with success the doctrine of Christ.[1] Clergy
were to be found amongst the captives; and these
organized the first groups of converts. The churches
of Bosphorus and Cherson, as well as those on the Lower
Danube, could not fail to serve as bases for propaganda.
At the Council of Nicæa there was a bishop of "Gothia,"
called Theophilus. Certain indications lead us to connect
him with a group of Germanic peoples who finally
established themselves in the Crimea, abandoning their
wandering life, while the main body of the Goths and
their dependents flowed towards the West.[2]

[1] Philostorgius (ii. 5) and Sozomen (ii. 6) agree as to this. One
of these captives perhaps was the Eutyches of Cappadocia who is
mentioned in a letter of St Basil (*Ep.* 165).

[2] In the time of St John Chrysostom, these Goths received their
bishops from Constantinople. He himself consecrated for them one
of these who was called Unila, and of whom he speaks very favourably (*Ep.* 14). Unila died during his exile, which caused Chrysostom
much anxiety, because he did not wish the successor to be consecrated
by the intruder Arsacius (*Epp.* 206, 207). This mission was connected
with a Gothic monastery at Constantinople—that of Promotus. In
547, certain Goths of the Crimea, whom Procopius calls Tetraxites,
(*Bell. Goth.* iv. 5) asked a bishop from Justinian. They lived on the
shores of the Sea of Azov. Other Goths are mentioned by the same
writer (*De aedif.* iii. 7) as settled peoples, agriculturists, and allies
of the empire, to which they were able to furnish 3000 fighting-men.
They lived in the maritime region, in the neighbourhood of a place
called Dory. It was on this side, *i.e.*, to the east of Cherson, that
there was situated the bishopric of Gothia which is noticed in
Byzantine annals from the 10th century onwards (Νέα τακτικά); more
ancient records do not mention it. It is possible that all these
pieces of information refer to one and the same bishopric, which,
since the time of Theophilus, may have represented the religious
organization of the Goths and other barbarians who had settled in the

Several Mesopotamian ascetics had been exiled to
Scythia during the last years of Constantine's reign,
perhaps a little later. Their leader was a certain Audius.
The official clergy charged them (apart from their extraordinary mode of life) with an insolent insubordination
towards the hierarchy, with various erroneous doctrines,
anthropomorphism amongst others, and, finally, with their
opposition to the Paschal decree of the Council of Nicæa.[1]
They were very zealous folk; the idea of evangelizing
the Goths attracted them. They threw themselves into
it with enthusiasm, and obtained considerable success; they
even went so far as to organize monasteries. After the
death of Audius, another Mesopotamian, Uranius, undertook the government of the sect. Both of them were
bishops, although by irregular ordination. They also in
their turn ordained some of their own converts, notably
a certain Silvanus.

But the most considerable effort was that made by
Bishop Ulfilas. Notwithstanding his Germanic name, he
was descended from a family of Cappadocian captives,
carried away from their homes in the reign of Valerian.[2]
At about the age of thirty, Ulfilas was fulfilling the duties
of a reader, no doubt in some mission-church, when he
was chosen by the king of the Goths to form one of an
embassy to the Court of Constantius. Eusebius of
Nicomedia saw him, and thinking that his abilities gave
hope for the future, consecrated him bishop for his nation.
When Ulfilas returned home, he set himself to fulfil his
duties with the most intelligent ardour. It was he who

Crimea. But this is not certain; and in any case we should have
to allow change of residence and perhaps interruptions in the
succession.

[1] This decree was again confirmed by the Council of Antioch
(canon 1). On the Audians our best source of information is
Epiphanius (*Haer.* lxx.). Theodoret (*H. E.* iv. 9) adds some new
particulars which apparently correspond to a further development.
Upon the attitude of the Audians on the Paschal question, see my
memoir, "La question de la Pâque au concile de Nicée," in the
Revue des questions hist., vol. xxviii. (1880), p. 29.

[2] In the little town of Sadagolthina, on the skirts of Parnassus.

initiated the Gothic nation into Roman and Christian civilization. He formed an alphabet, which replaced with considerable advantage the old Runic script; and he translated into Gothic the greater part of the Holy Scriptures.[1] A large number of his fellow-countrymen embraced Christianity. King Hermanaric at length grew uneasy at seeing so many of his companions-in-arms pass over to the religion of the Romans. He grew angry, and ordered all the missionaries, those of Audius as well as those of Ulfilas, to recross the Danube. The Audians returned to the East; Ulfilas and his disciples, who had followed him in great numbers, were permitted to settle in the province of Mœsia Inferior, near the town of Nicopolis. This exodus took place in 349 or thereabouts. Ulfilas lived thirty-three years longer. He was an Arian. In 360, he was present at the Council of Constantinople, and gave his vote with those who approved of the Creed of Ariminum. In 383, being summoned by the Emperor Theodosius, with the leaders of other dissenting groups, he again travelled to the capital, and died on his arrival there. The confession of faith which he had prepared, and which was his spiritual testament, we still possess. It is Arianism pure and simple.[2]

The step taken by the king of the Goths against Bishop Ulfilas did not completely put an end to the

[1] Philostorgius, ii. 5. He seems only to have omitted the Books of Kings, thinking it would be unwise to put so many descriptions of battles before the eyes of people who were only too much inclined to warfare. This is what Philostorgius says. If this was really the case, Ulfilas must have had to make other "cuts" in the Old Testament.

[2] To the information gained from historians of the 5th century (Philostorgius, ii. 5 ; Socrates, *H. E.* ii. 41, iv. 33 ; Sozomen, *H. E.* iv. 24, vi. 37), we can now add contemporary documents, preserved in the treatise of the Arian Bishop Maximin against St Ambrose. This treatise, transcribed in the margins of the Paris MS. 8907, was first studied by Waitz, *Ueber das Leben und die Lehre des Ulfilas,* Hanover, 1840 ; then by Bessell, *Ueber das Leben des Ulfilas,* etc., Göttingen, 1860. It has been published entirely—so far as the state of the MS. permits—by Fr. Kauffmann, *Aus der Schule des Wulfila,* in vol. i. of *Texte und Untersuchungen zur altgermanischen Religionsgeschichte,* Strassburg, 1899. It contains (pp. 73-76) a long extract from a letter

propaganda beyond the Danube. The Bishop of Thessalonica, Acholius, took an effective interest in it. But the times became more and more difficult. The Goths near the Danube had supported the claims of Procopius against Valens; hence, when the latter had got rid of his rival, ensued a war which lasted for three years (367-369). The preachers of the Roman religion bore the brunt of the recoil of these hostilities. Several stories of martyrs belong to this period. The best authenticated is that of a St Sabas, who was drowned in the river Buseu[1] in 372. Others were burnt, sometimes *en masse*, in the tents which served them for churches.[2]

The way being thus prepared, a general conversion to Christianity took place as the consequence of a grave political event. The Huns, crossing the line of the Don, forced the Goths back, upon the Dniester first, afterwards upon the Sereth, threatening to drive them still farther. Being brought to a stand at the Danube, the vanquished Goths determined to ask for a refuge in the Roman empire. They were welcomed there as guests and auxiliaries (376); but very soon they conducted themselves in it like masters; and after the disaster at Adrianople, in 378, their history follows them, no longer to the vicinity, but into the very heart of the empire. At the time when they penetrated there, the confession of Ariminum represented official Christianity; the Church of

in which Auxentius, Bishop of Dorostorum and a disciple of Ulfilas, relates the life of his master. It is at the end of this little document that we find the "Credo" of Ulfilas: "Ego Ulfila episkopus et confessor semper sic credidi et in hac fide sola et vera transitum facio ad dominum meum."

[1] Μούσεον, a tributary on the right of the Sereth. This event took place on April 12, which is the day of his Feast.

[2] Socrates, *H. E.* iv. 34; Sozomen, *H. E.* vii. 37; Basil, *Ep.* 164, 165; Ambrose, *Ep.* 15, 16; *in Luc.* ii. 37; Aug. *De civ. Dei* xviii. 52; see also the hagiographical traditions relating to SS. Bathusius and Vereas (March 26), St Nicetas (September 15), and St Sabas (April 12). The remains of these martyrs were translated respectively to Cyzicus, to Mopsuestia, and to Cæsarea in Cappadocia. The remains of St Sabas were collected and sent to St Basil by the *Dux* of Scythia, Junius Soranus, his fellow-countryman.

Constantinople was governed by an Arian bishop. But this only lasted for a short time; the government of Gratian and of Theodosius took up a decided position on the side of the faith of Nicæa. From that quarter the barbarians would not undergo any serious pressure. But the members of the episcopate were divided amongst themselves. If the Bishops of Tomi[1] and Marcianopolis[2] were pillars of orthodoxy, Auxentius of Dorostorum[3] was a fervent disciple of Ulfilas; Palladius of Ratiaria[4] had long records of service in the Arian camp; and they were not the only ones. But it is Ulfilas more than any one else who has to be reckoned with in this matter. What instructor could commend himself more highly to the Gothic nation and to its leaders? With him, Christian worship was clothed in national forms; it was conducted in Gothic; Gothic was the language for preaching and for prayer. It was true that, as regarded the Creed, he was not in agreement with the actual possessors of imperial authority; but he had been so under the government of Constantius and Valens. Who could say that a new change was impossible? And after all, was it such an urgent matter to obliterate all religious distinction between Goths and Romans?

Whether or no people reasoned in this way on the situation, the fact remains that it settled itself in such a way that Arianism in proportion as it lost ground among the subjects of the empire gained it amongst its "allies."

It was not only upon the Lower Danube that this was the case. Along the whole length of that river the barbarians who lived on the frontier passed over, one after another, to Christianity, and to Christianity in an Arian[5] form. The circumstances were almost exactly

---

[1] The Bishop of Tomi was the only bishop in his province of Scythia.   [2] Cod. Theod. xvi. 1, 3.

[3] Upon Auxentius, see above, p. 437.   [4] Supra, pp. 375 et seq.

[5] We must notice, however, the story of Fritigil, Queen of the Marcomanni, to whom St Ambrose had given religious instruction by letter (Paulinus, Vita Ambr. 36). She persuaded the king, her husband, to give himself to the Romans, and went herself to Milan, where St Ambrose had just died.

the same. In Pannonia, as in Mœsia, the churches had long been governed by Arian prelates. If on this side we do not find any bishop who was equal to Ulfilas, we must certainly acknowledge that the example of the Goths contributed greatly to determine the views of the other Germanic nations. Arianism enters at this moment upon a new career. Goths of the West and of the East, Burgundians, Swabians, Vandals, and Lombards begin to make it their national religion; in the provinces wrested from the empire they are to restore to honour the confession of Ariminum; down to the 6th and 7th centuries we shall see it holding the faith of Nicæa in check. But these are later and Western developments. For the moment all that we need notice particularly is that even in the interior of the empire, whether in the East or in the West, and among Roman populations, Arianism was to profit by the prestige of its new adherents. It was useless to think of eradicating it from the army; the Goths henceforth added themselves to this as auxiliary troops, and that under the command of their national chiefs; and besides, even in the ranks of the regular army and its senior staff, they were largely represented. The Goths had to be reckoned with in this respect as in so many others.

2. *Theodosius and the Sects.*

The barbarian adherents of Arianism were not the only ones to demand the attention of the Emperor Theodosius. It had been comparatively easy to restore the churches to the orthodox prelates, and to rain the condemnations of councils upon the followers of Demophilus and of Eunomius. Agreement in spirit between the two parties was not secured so quickly. Banished from the official buildings, the heretical teaching was still carried on in conventicles; the spirit of Aetius still breathed there; it was useless to exile Eunomius; he found means everywhere to carry on the controversy. It was at Constantinople more than anywhere else that it raged.

People were beset with it in the streets and in the public squares. There was not a street-corner at which men were not to be found furiously discussing the most abstruse matters. The money-changer whom you asked for some money spoke to you of the Begotten and of the Unbegotten; the baker, instead of telling you the price of bread, declared that the Father is greater than the Son, and that the Son is subject unto Him. If you asked for a bath, "the Son comes certainly from nothing," would be the reply of the bath-keeper—an Anomœan.

Theodosius had a great desire to put an end to these divisions, instead of having to punish the dissentients, who, after all, were mostly conscientious and peaceful folk. He persuaded himself that by his personal intervention he would obtain some results.[2] After the two councils of 381 and 382 he convoked a third in 383, which was to take the form of a conference between the leaders of the different confessions; the emperor was to take part in it, and to endeavour to arrange an understanding.

The meeting actually took place[3]; it was held in the month of June. Ulfilas, notwithstanding his great age, travelled to Constantinople, where he died on his arrival. We still possess the confession of faith which he intended to present to the emperor. Eunomius at this time was living at Chalcedon; he came to present his own confession of faith, which has also been preserved.[4] The others, Demophilus, on behalf of the Arians, and Eleusius, on behalf of the Macedonians, did the same. To judge from the documents of Eunomius and of Ulfilas, each of them confined himself to stating his own belief,

[1] Gregory of Nyssa, *Or. de Deitate Filii et Spiritus Sancti* (Migne, *P. G.* vol. xlvi., p. 557).

[2] A legendary account related by Sozomen (*H. E.* vii. 6) and Theodoret (*H. E.* v. 16), who makes Amphilochius of Iconium take part in it, represents Theodosius as hesitating, even at that time, between Arianism and orthodoxy. Nothing is more improbable.

[3] Kauffmann, *Aus der Schule des Wulfila*, p. 76.

[4] Migne, *P. G.* vol. lxvii., p. 587, note 34 ; Mansi, *Concilia*, vol. iii., p. 645.

without making the slightest step towards conciliation. The explanations by word of mouth gave no more sign of any desire for an understanding. There is a tradition that the orthodox party proposed that they should adhere to that formula, out of all of them, which should represent the teaching of the ancient Fathers, *i.e.*, of those who lived before the appearance of Arianism ; and that this proposal was not accepted.[1] In these circumstances there was nothing to be done but to persevere in severe measures; and this is what actually happened. A new law [2] forbade all meetings for worship — public or private—of the Eunomians, Arians, and Macedonians, in exactly the same way as those of the Manicheans and similar sects. The Novatians alone obtained toleration for their churches.

There is every appearance also that, if not in law at any rate in fact, it was the same with the Macedonians and the Arians. Their meetings were prohibited; but they held them all the same, and the police shut their eyes [3] in spite of the complaints of some of the bishops. What object was to be served by severity? The sects of themselves were journeying to their end. Every day they were losing adherents; those who remained got excited among themselves, quarrelled, and created new schisms. When Demophilus died they sought for his successor in Thrace, a certain Marinus; other Arians acclaimed Dorotheus who had been dispossessed of his bishopric of Antioch. At one on the fundamental principle of Arian dogma, the two parties had discovered points on which they could not agree. Before the creation of the Son could God have been called Father? Yes, said Marinus: No, declared Dorotheus. A Syrian pastry-cook, Theoctistus, warmly defended the ideas of Marinus; hence the disciples of the latter received the nickname of pastry-

---

[1] Socrates, *H. E.* v. 10, who evidently exaggerates the part played at that time by the Novatians.

[2] *Cod. Theod.* xvi. 5, 11, of July 25, 383; *cf.* xvi. 5, 12, and 13, which belong to December 3 and January 21 following.

[3] Socrates, *H. E.* v. 20.

cooks (*Psathyriani*). They had also the support of the
Bishop of the Goths, Selenas, the successor of Ulfilas.
This gave them a certain standing, but did not prevent
them from forming fresh divisions. The Psathyrian
Bishop of Ephesus, a certain Agapius, had disputes with
Marinus. It was not until 419 that these internal quarrels
were reconciled.[1]

The Eunomians, who indeed were no less divided
amongst themselves, were pursued with more severity. I
have spoken before of the successive periods of exile of
their prophet, Eunomius. His followers seem to have
taken pleasure in increasing the differences which separated
them from orthodoxy. They even went so far as to change
the ritual of baptism, from which they eliminated both the
triple immersion and the enumeration of the Divine Persons.
No sooner were they provided with a special baptism,
than they hastened to declare it to be the only efficacious
one, and to rebaptize those who joined them from the
other sects. It was against them that legislation was
directed, in rescripts continually renewed,[2] and that
orthodox theologians directed their efforts from all sides,
St Basil of Cæsarea had inherited this controversy from
Basil of Ancyra and his friends; his brother, Gregory of
Nyssa, took it up after him.[3] Chrysostom, at Antioch,
pronounced a large number of discourses against the
Anomœans.

[1] Socrates, *H. E.* v. 23.

[2] *Cod. Theod.* xvi. 5, 8, 11-13, 17, 23, 25, 27, 31, 32, 34, 36, 49, 58,
60, 65.

[3] The *Apologeticus* of Eunomius, an explanation of doctrine,
published by that doctor during the early years of his career as a
theologian, was refuted by St Basil, who has thus preserved the text
of it for us, before his elevation to the episcopate. Eunomius replied
to Basil; but he took his time, and his reply had only just been
published when Basil died. In it, the Bishop of Cæsarea was
attacked personally and with much bitterness. His brothers, Peter
of Sebaste and Gregory of Nyssa, thought there was occasion for an
answer. This was the origin of the twelve books of Gregory against
Eunomius. Apollinaris and Didymus had also written against the
Apologeticus.

3. *Asia Minor.*

It was not only with these recent forms of dissent, all more or less derived from the heresy of Arius, that Theodosius' bishops had to concern themselves. The old sects which had been organized since the second and third centuries, continued to exist and to divide the Church. The Novatians, who had enjoyed toleration for a considerable period,[1] were very numerous in Constantinople and in the Asiatic provinces of Bithynia, Paphlagonia, and Phrygia. In these countries of simple habits a severe form of religion was always popular. The most powerful Novatian communities, those which influenced all the others, were those of Constantinople, Nicomedia, Nicæa, and Kotyæon (Kutahié). The historian Socrates, who is very well informed as to this religious sect, relates various particulars of the Novatian bishops of Constantinople— Acesius,[2] who was alive at the time of the Council of Nicæa, and who had, it appeared, borne testimony to the *homoousios*; and afterwards Agelius, persecuted as well as the Catholics during the reigns of Constantius and Valens. Agelius was still living in 383; he took part in the religious conference in that year.[3] In this little circle of rigorists there were a few distinguished men, who, either through family tradition, or from an attraction to a more refined form of piety, found themselves more at home there than among the multitudes of the Great Church. During Valens' reign one of them, Marcian, after a career in the imperial palace, was elevated to the priesthood; he was very learned, and his beliefs did not prevent the emperor from entrusting to him the education of his daughters, Anastasia and Carosa. Marcian profited by this favour to secure a mitigation of the severe measures from which his co-religionists were at that time called upon to suffer.[4] His son Chrysanthus was also a prominent man; under Theodosius, he filled

---

[1] With regard to their position under Constantine and Constantius, see the next chapter.   [2] Socrates, *H. E.* i. 10.

[3] *Ibid.*, ii. 38 ; iv. 9 ; v. 10.   [4] *Ibid.*, iv. 9.

the office of *Consularis* of Italy, and *Vicarius* of the Britains.[1] Another Novatian priest, Sisinnius, had formerly attended in company with Julian the lectures of Maximus of Ephesus. Agelius, before his death, consecrated Marcian and Sisinnius bishops, stipulating, however, that Marcian should exercise episcopal functions first, and that Sisinnius should be his successor.

The plan was carried out. Marcian had a good deal of difficulty with one of his priests, Sabbatius, who set himself to create a schism with regard to the date of Easter. This was an old quarrel. Among the Novatians, as among the Catholics before the Council of Nicæa, there had been two ways of fixing the Paschal date: some persons decided it by the equinox, and these were the more numerous; on this point, the Novatians of Rome and of Constantinople were in agreement with the Great Church; others, like the Easterns before Nicæa and the Audians afterwards, followed the calculations of the Jews. This latter use had been accepted, in the time of Valens, at a council held in the little town of Pazos, near the sources of the Sangarius, by a certain number of Novatian bishops belonging to the Phrygian region. Marcian dared not put himself in conflict with them; he caused it to be decided in a synod, that each might celebrate Easter according to the use which he preferred.[2]

In Phrygia, the Montanist centre at Pepuza still existed; its influence even extended far enough to provoke repressive legislation. The Montanists, Priscillianists,[3] Phrygians, Pepuzians, and Tascodrugitee are mentioned from time to time in the Theodosian Code.[4] Every year they celebrated, on April 6, a great ceremony, which was their Feast of Easter.[5] Some of them were converted from time to time [6]; but the further progress was made, the more these old sects tended to shut themselves off in

---

[1] Socrates, *H. E.* vii. 12.   [2] *Ibid.*, iv. 28; v. 21.

[3] Disciples of the prophetess Priscilla : not to be confounded with the Priscillianists of Spain.

[4] xvi. 5, 10, 40, 48, 57, 65.   [5] Sozomen, *H. E.* vii. 18.

[6] Basil, *Ep.* 188.

grim exclusiveness. There were also the devotees of compulsory encratism, isolated at first, but now grouped together in propagandist confraternities, varying in nomenclature and in observances—Encratites, Hydroparastatae, Apotactici, Saccophori.[1] These last, as their name indicates, were clothed in sacks. Another species of fanatics appeared at the time of which we are now speaking. These were the Massalians or Euchites. These two denominations, the first of which was Semitic, the other Greek, may be defined by the name Prayers (those who pray). The movement which they represent came originally from the region where the country of Syria borders on Armenia, and their numbers rapidly increased in Syria and in Asia Minor. Epiphanius mentions them in his *Panarion*, written before the death of the Emperor Valens. At the outset, the Massalians had no organization. They were people who had renounced all their possessions; they lived entirely upon alms, and came and went, always praying and doing nothing else. When night came they slept anyhow, men and women together, and in the open air as far as possible. With the offices of the Church and its fasts they concerned themselves not at all. It was by prayer alone, and by an absolute detachment from the goods of this world, that they held communion with God and His saints—a communion so close that they did not hesitate to attribute to themselves the designations of angels, prophets, patriarchs, and Christs. According to them, baptism only effaces past sins; it does not prevent the indwelling in every man, from the time of his birth, of an evil spirit with whom he has to struggle incessantly. This struggle against the evil spirits filled their minds to the exclusion of everything else; when it became very violently within them, they were seen to make gestures as though shooting arrows, or to jump into the air with enormous leaps, sometimes even beginning to dance.

These Christian dervishes were eminently calculated to cause alarm to the episcopate of that day, the whole energies of which were devoted to the task of restoring

[1] Basil, *Epp.* 188, 199.

peace to the Church, and keeping it in good order. The first bishop to concern himself with them was the Metropolitan of Iconium, Amphilochius. Presiding over a council held at Side in Pamphylia, he severely condemned such a manner of life. Information of this condemnation was given to Flavian, the Bishop of Antioch, who with the support of several bishops summoned before him one of the Massalian leaders, Adelphius, an old man of very advanced age. Flavian succeeded by strategy in making him disclose his secrets, for the sect had secrets and disguised them with the greatest care. For the second time the Massalians were condemned. Flavian besides took the necessary steps to secure the acceptance of his sentence by the bishops of Mesopotamia and Armenia Minor, the country in which this strange sect had first taken root.[1]

But these disciplinary measures, and the legal prohibitions which followed them, were far from putting an end to Massalianism. This heresy still flourished in Pamphylia and in the east of Asia Minor; and in Armenia also it long gave cause for anxiety.

Amphilochius of Iconium, whom we have just seen appearing in this affair, was during the reign of Theodosius the most important ecclesiastical personage in the whole of Asia Minor. In him, far more than in his own kin, Basil had found an heir. And, in fact, it was Basil who had made Amphilochius what he was. Educated in the school of Libanius, who always preserved a great affection for him, and afterwards an advocate at Constantinople, Amphilochius did not remain long in the world. He was living in retirement in Cappadocia with his invalid father, when, towards the end of the year 373, Basil was begged by the people of Iconium to choose for them a bishop. His choice fell upon Amphilochius, who had scarcely passed his thirtieth year. Just at this time, the town of Iconium became the metropolis of a new province, that of Lycaonia, formed at the expense of Pisidia and

---

[1] Upon this affair see Photius, cod. 52, who gives the gist of a collection of official documents ; cf. Theodoret, Haer. fab. iv. 11.

Isauria. This gave rise to certain special difficulties, which obliged the new bishop to have frequent recourse to the wisdom of his illustrious protector. Basil did not fail him. A number of his letters are addressed to Amphilochius, notably his three synodical letters,[1] which were included later on in the Greek codes of canons with an authority similar to that which clothes, in the Latin collections, the Decretals of the Popes. The Bishop of Cæsarea, besides finding in this direction food for his zeal, was glad to have, in the heart of Asia Minor, a man whom he could thoroughly trust, and who was full of energy and devotion. Through him, Basil could command the persons of goodwill scattered throughout Phrygia, Pisidia, and even in the more distant provinces of Lycia and Pamphylia. Amphilochius came from time to time to Cæsarea, in spite of the difficulty of a journey across the central steppe of Asia Minor. Basil also put in an appearance at Iconium. In 376, he sent there his Treatise on the Holy Spirit, which was read in synod, and sent by Amphilochius' exertions to the most distant provinces, as a preservative against the propaganda of the Pneumatomachi.

Under such guidance, Amphilochius, who before becoming a bishop had scarcely troubled himself at all about theology, soon developed into a man of large doctrinal knowledge, and became a kind of oracle. Of his writings, however, we possess little more than fragments.[2] As we saw, in 381 he was chosen, with his neighbour Optimus, the Metropolitan of Pisidia, as the centre of all ecclesiastical relations in the western "diocese" of Asia Minor. They both appear to have lived to the end of the reign of Theodosius.[3] They were closely allied friends with Basil's brothers and also with Gregory of Nazianzus; and in Constantinople they also enjoyed a valuable friendship,

---

[1] *Epp.* 188, 199, 217.

[2] Upon Amphilochius, see the monograph of Karl Holl, *Amphilochius von Iconium*, Tübingen, 1904. *Cf.* G. Ficker, *Amphilochiana*, part i., Leipzig, 1906.

[3] Amphilochius was also present at the council of 394.

that of the celebrated matron Olympias, who afterwards rendered so many services to Chrysostom.[1] It was in her house that Optimus died.

In Cappadocia and the neighbouring countries, the memory of Basil was always cherished, being represented by his family and his friends. Emmelia had lived long enough to see her son a bishop; when she was gone, her eldest daughter, Macrina, was superior of the monastery of Annesi, on the Iris, which had been established by them both, opposite the place where Basil himself had his hermitage. Macrina survived her mother for several years, but only lived a few months after Basil's death. Her youngest brother, Peter, had been brought up under her care, and shortly after her death he was elected Bishop of Sebaste. Her other brother, Gregory of Nyssa, was present during her dying hours; their last conversations formed the groundwork for his dialogue on "The Soul and the Resurrection."

The Bishop of Nyssa who, up to that time, had been treated somewhat loftily by his great brother, Basil, now obtained considerable importance. He was an orator, and was much in request for great funeral orations, and other ceremonial discourses. He, whom Basil had thought too simple to be sent to negotiate with Pope Damasus, found himself entrusted by the Council of 381 [2] with an extremely confidential mission to the bishops of Arabia and Palestine; it is true that he returned from it without having met with success. He was a theologian: he wrote against Eunomius [3] and against Apollinaris; we owe to him a remarkable exposition of doctrine, called the Great Catechism, and many other slighter treatises. His Lives of Saint Gregory the Wonder-worker, and of Saint Macrina, gives him a place among hagiographers.

Like all the preachers of that time, he discoursed much

---

[1] Palladius, *Dial.* 17.

[2] It is not quite certain if this mission was from the Council of Antioch in 379, or from that of Constantinople, two years later. I think it was from the latter.

[3] *Supra*, p. 458, note 3.

upon Holy Scripture. In exegesis, all the Cappadocians were debtors to Origen. Basil and Gregory of Nazianzus had compiled together, under the title of Philocalia, a collection of the choicest passages of the great Alexandrian Doctor. However, they had abstained from adopting those of his opinions which went beyond the accepted teaching. Gregory of Nyssa was less careful. He allowed himself to be led astray by the doctrine of the final restoration (ἀποκατάστασις), *i.e.*, of universal salvation as destined to extend at last to the worst of men, and even to the evil spirits themselves.

The other Gregory, the ex-Bishop of Constantinople, had retired to his own country of Nazianzus. Before leaving the capital, he had made his will — a curious document, which is preserved amongst his works. There was no bishop then in Nazianzus. Since the death of the elder Gregory, the see had remained unfilled. His son had not the least idea of establishing himself in it: his alleged translations from one see to another had brought him too many vexations for him to dream of allowing himself another. Nevertheless, it was impossible to him not to take an interest in this Church. He governed it from Arianzus, an estate belonging to his family, where he usually lived. His ill-luck had eaten into his heart. The bitter memory which he retained of it is reproduced in his letters and verses. For he wrote a great deal; nearly all his letters belong to these closing years. He now had to spend Lent without uttering a single word, and this was certainly a heavy penance both for himself and for others; but his pen was never at rest.

Among the clergy of Nazianzus there was an Apollinarian party: and this complicated the situation. The bishops of that region—with Theodore, the new Metropolitan of Tyana, at their head—saw no objection to the vacancy being prolonged under such an administrator, and it was this which made it so difficult for Gregory to find a successor to his father; but there was further the fear that even if the bishops consented to an election, a candidate would be proposed to them whose

II   2 G orthodoxy was doubtful. It was in these circumstances that Gregory wrote to Cledonius, one of the priests of Nazianzus, two letters in which he deals, in opposition to the Apollinarians, with the subject of the Incarnation. These letters became later as famous as his discourses upon the Trinity; in the controversies of later centuries we find them continually appealed to. But, at the time, they produced no effect at Nazianzus. The Apollinarians, taking advantage of an illness which kept Gregory at a distance, succeeded in appointing a bishop of their own. This was too much: Gregory protested; the governor rid him of the intruder, and the bishops of Cappadocia at length filled up the vacancy in the threatened Church.

Gregory lived for some years longer in retirement and the practice of austerities, but never ceasing to interest himself in local affairs, nor even in the general interests of the Church. By his poetical compositions he sought to counteract those of Apollinaris; he ever kept a watchful eye upon that party, which was then very active in spite of all the condemnations which had been heaped upon it. The Apollinarians took advantage of the toleration of Theodosius, who gladly allowed the laws with regard to heretics to lie dormant, and of the indolence of Nectarius, who seemed never inclined to reawaken them. Gregory thought it his duty, from the depth of his retirement, to address expostulations to his successor [1] for this. It was undoubtedly to his intervention that the Apollinarians owed the law made in 388 by which their religious organization was once more proscribed. Gregory died in 389 or 390.

The island of Cyprus held constant communication with Southern Asia Minor. At the time of which we are now treating, this island formed in civil matters a province by itself, and its metropolis, Salamis, had as bishop, Epiphanius,[2] a holy man, who was renowned throughout the East. The unanimous vote of the Cypriots, in 367, had drawn him from his monastery at Eleutheropolis in Palestine, where he had long led a life of austerity and

[1] *Ep.* 202.   [2] *Supra*, p. 406.

study. I have already told how this monastic foundation
was the result of quite a long stay which Epiphanius had
made in Egypt in his early youth. It was not only with
solitaries that he had been in touch there; he had also
come across many heretics, whose eccentricities attracted
his attention. He even came very near forming too
intimate an acquaintance with them. Some Gnostic ladies
took an interest in him, and wished to initiate him in their
redemptive ceremonies. But fortunately he began by
reading their books, which enlightened him as to the
intentions of these female doctors: Joseph, once again,
escaped from the harem of Potiphar! He took his
revenge for this adventure by denouncing to the bishop
of the place all the sectaries he knew; the bishop put the
matter in the hands of the police, and eighty persons were
driven out of the town.[1]

It was clearly to this time that Epiphanius' intense
hatred for heretics went back. He soon began to seek
information as to their history, and to collect books and
documents likely to instruct him thereon. But he did not
write anything on the subject until he became bishop. It
was at the request of certain people at Syedra in Pamphylia that he composed first (on the Trinitarian heresies
of the day) a treatise called *Ancoratus*, at the end of which
appeared, for the first time, the Creed which we now use
under the name of the Creed of Nicæa. Shortly afterwards, two Syrian hermits, Acacius and Paul, exhorted
him to undertake a general refutation of all heresies. He
laboured at it for several years, from 374 to 377; this
second compilation received the name of *Panarion*.
Eighty heresies are there described and controverted.
The series opens with the philosophical sects—Stoics,
Platonists, and Pythagoreans; then he passes on to the
Samaritan and Jewish sects; and finally, beginning with
Simon, we arrive at the Christian heresies. The ancient
authors of heresiologies, especially Irenæus and Hippolytus,[2]
are laid very largely under contribution; certain refutations
of special heresies, and even some heretical books, have also

---

[1] *Haer.* xxvi. 17.　　　　[2] See Vol. I., p. 227.

been ransacked. And finally, on a great many points, especially in connection with contemporary forms of dissent, Epiphanius speaks from his own personal experience. In more than one passage he makes use of stories or of facts collected by himself during his stay in Egypt. At that time, already long past, he was the same simple and artless man that he remained all his life. It was not only with ladies who were adherents of Carpocrates that he came into contact. The Meletians laid hold of him in their turn and romanced to him about their early history. With regard to Origen also many stories were palmed off on him. And although it would have been so easy for him to discover the true history of that eminent man from the writings of Pamphilus and of Eusebius, he relates to us absurd legends in connection with him. Of course we have no reason to reproach Epiphanius for his dislike of Origen's opinions. Many others before him had condemned them, especially Methodius, whose polemics he appropriated. But for Epiphanius Origen was the responsible author of all the heresies which were distracting the Church as he saw it; hence he lost no opportunity of attacking him with a fury which amounted to mania. Epiphanius knew five languages[1]; and he set himself to use them, in order to slander Origen throughout the whole world.

Thoroughly orthodox, and a most enthusiastic admirer of Athanasius, Epiphanius necessarily took the part of Paulinus against Meletius. But this did not hinder him from being on good terms with Basil, and accepting the three hypostases.[2] Although he inveighed against Hellenic culture as represented by Origen, he was in no wise an enemy of learning: he held Apollinaris in great veneration, and was a friend of St Jerome. The fall of Apollinaris was a deep grief to him; but he had no

---

[1] Greek, Egyptian, Syriac, Hebrew, and Latin. As to his Latin, Jerome (*Adv. Ruf.* ii. 22) says that he knew this last language *ex parte*. In actual fact, he never wrote except in Greek, and that very badly.

[2] Basil, *Ep.* 258.

hesitation in giving to the Dimœrites, as he called the Apollinarians, a place in his gallery of heretics.

4. *Apollinarianism.*

Apollinaris, as we saw above,[1] was at Laodicea, bishop of a Little Church closely resembling that of Paulinus at Antioch. He was a man of very wide culture. Of all the highly educated Christians in the East at that time, he was by far the most prominent, and certainly the most prolific in his writings. He had fought for the common faith against Porphyry and against Eunomius[2]; in Julian's reign, he had written a whole series of classic stories taken from the Bible, to replace the authors of Greek antiquity who were then forbidden to the Christians. His exegesis was famous. Repudiating the ancient allegorizing, which Origen and his imitators had so greatly abused, he explained the Sacred Books in their natural sense. This new departure was gladly welcomed, although it was not without its inconveniences. By following this method, Apollinaris found himself led to deduce from the Apocalypse the promise of the Reign of a Thousand Years, and of an earthly restoration of the Temple and of the Law. The time when such ideas as these had been popular was long past; in the East, they were quite out of fashion. These Judaizing ways of regarding it had done injustice to the Apocalypse itself: many Churches refused to it the status of a Canonical Book.

But it was especially by his theology that Apollinaris laid himself open to criticism. The friends of Meletius, who looked upon the Church of Paulinus as tainted with Sabellianism, had no hesitation in attributing to Apollinaris language which was compromising from this point of view.[3] It appears, however, that upon the question of the Trinity there was nothing serious with

---

[1] *Supra*, p. 273.
[2] According to Epiphanius, *Haer.* lxxvii. 24, he would seem to have been exiled by the Arians.
[3] Basil, *Ep.* 129.

which to reproach him. It was upon another point that his doctrine raised difficulties. And here some explanations are necessary.

At the time when Apollinaris appeared upon the scene, the Church had settled upon the terms in which thenceforth it was to explain the sense in which it understands the relationship between the Unity of God and the Divinity of Jesus Christ. The Divine Being manifested in Jesus is absolutely identical with the One and Only God recognized by Christianity; He is distinguished, however, by a differentia (*spécialité*), obviously mysterious and incomprehensible, which, in the language of the New Testament, by which that of the Church guides itself, is expressed by the relationship of Son to Father. Hence arises the distinction of " Persons," to use the terminology of the West—of " Hypostases," in that of the East. To the two Hypostases or Persons of the Father and the Son is added, by an analogous distinction, the third Hypostasis or Person of the Holy Spirit. In this way is constituted the " Trinity " of theology ; thus the Christian tradition is formulated, as clearly as such a mystery allows, in the philosophical language of the time.

Another problem remained to be solved. What is the exact relationship between the human form of Jesus and the Divine Being which is united to it? What degree of human reality must be acknowledged in the Christ whom the Apostles knew, and with whom they lived and conversed? Christians of Hellenic education, whose numbers were swelled by the early preachings to the heathen, found themselves quite at the outset attracted by an explanation which was very natural from their point of view. The human form, the human life of Christ, including in that His Passion and His Resurrection, was only a succession of appearances. Was it not thus that the gods made themselves visible? Jupiter and his companions, when they showed themselves upon earth, assumed a material form, most frequently the human form. Everyone had become familiar with the magical operations which changed the exterior of beings, and allowed invisible spirits to manifest themselves. In the Bible itself divine apparitions were frequently mentioned; stories like that of Tobit and his journey with the angel Raphael popularized the idea of beings, invisible in their proper nature, but clothing themselves on occasion in human semblances, and seeming then to belong to humanity. We must not be astonished that, in the time of Trajan, St Ignatius of Antioch had so much difficulty with the theory of "apparent" Incarnation—Docetism, as it was called. A hundred years later, his successor Serapion discovered at Antioch a sect of "Docetae," with an organization and sacred books of its own. Moreover, the Gnostics and the Marcionites had immediately appropriated this conception, which fitted in wonderfully well with their dualist ideas. In the 4th century there were still Docetae at Antioch, and we find the interpolator of the letters of Ignatius waging war against the Christology of "apparent" manifestations. In certain places, it had taken special forms : some said that the flesh of Christ came from Heaven, that it represented a physical humiliation (anéantissement) of the Divinity, and that it owed nothing to the natural development by which the child originates from its mother. Athanasius, when already near the end of his life, wrote on this subject to Epictetus, the Bishop of Corinth, in whose diocese these ideas had become prevalent. Shortly afterwards, we find them contested by St Basil, in a letter addressed to the people of Sozopolis in Pisidia. At the root of this system was always to be found the assumption of the incompatibility between human infirmities and the Divine Majesty: this assumption did not disappear: we meet with it again in the controversies of the centuries which followed.

Far from being dismayed at such a conception, Christian mysticism, as St Athanasius so happily formulated it, enthusiastically embraced the idea that God willed to clothe Himself with all our weaknesses, that He might transform them into Divine strength ; that He willed to become Man, in order to make us divine: αὐτὸς γὰρ ἐνηνθρώπησεν ἵνα ἡμεῖς θεοποιηθῶμεν. But if it

is possible to speak of such matters as these in the
language of religion, it is difficult to express them in the
terms of philosophy. There were not wanting people, in
the 4th century, who thought that they could settle everything by saying that the Divine Word had taken in Jesus
the place of the soul, and that Christ was composed of a
human body and a Divine soul. So thought Arius, and
he was not the only one. Even among uncompromising
Catholics, even among the associates of Apollinaris, this
combination found supporters. Apollinaris himself had
arrived at a somewhat different solution. Starting from
the distinction between body, soul, and mind, he admitted
that Jesus had received from humanity a body inspired by
a soul (*un corps animé*), but that the human mind (*νοῦς*) had
been replaced in Him by the Divine element. Apart from
this collocation, he saw no means of preserving the Unity
of Christ. Those who represented Him to themselves as
formed of the Divinity and of a complete humanity,
seemed to him madmen, capable of believing in centaurs,
the hippogriff, and other fabulous creatures.

This assertion which Apollinaris treated as absurd
was nevertheless maintained in Antioch itself by a great
many persons who were by no means strangers to theological culture. For Diodore and his followers, the mind
in Jesus was a human mind. But they did not on that
account deny the Unity of Christ, and tried to reconcile
it with their way of thinking. Perhaps their explanations
left something to be desired; they had to be completed
later on. Just then it was the system of Apollinaris
which offended traditional feeling.

It took, however, some time before matters arrived at
a crisis. At the time of the Council of Alexandria in 362
the theory was already known; Athanasius, who earnestly
desired peace just then, seems to have changed his tactics,
and to have been satisfied with ingenious explanations.
Apollinaris had conceded to him that Christ possessed
a soul and a mind, without specifying whether this mind
were human or Divine. Athanasius had asked no more
of him. Apollinaris was so much respected, the old

Nicene party in the East thought themselves so fortunate in possessing a scholar of such distinction, that there was a tendency on their part to shut their eyes to anything in his teaching which was possibly open to criticism. So long as Athanasius lived, it does not appear that the Christology of Laodicea caused any scandal in Alexandria.[1] Even in Syria it was some time before anyone began to consider carefully what objection there was to it.

It seems, too,[2] that with Apollinaris himself the question long remained in the sphere of academic disputations. Diodore and Flavian exchanged refutations with him; and he maintained his own opinions in various explanatory treatises. In spite of all the trials to which they were exposed during Valens' reign, the Catholics of Antioch found time to argue fiercely on the matter both for and against. The dispute did not assume an ecclesiastical character until one of the friends of Apollinaris—Vitalis a priest of Meletius like Flavian and Diodore—left that party and joined the Church of Paulinus. To this Church he rendered a great service at the outset by obtaining for it the alliance of the Roman Church. He travelled to Italy, saw Pope Damasus, and obtained from him letters recognizing Paulinus. I have already told how Damasus, uneasy on account of what others told him of Vitalis, changed his mind, and ordered that he was only to be received under certain conditions. To accept them would have been, for Vitalis, to betray his former attitude. He remained faithful to Apollinaris. Being expelled by Paulinus, and

---

[1] The writings of Athanasius against Apollinaris are entirely unauthentic.

[2] The history of Apollinaris is full of obscurities; his contemporaries tell us but little about him; and as to his writings, they have been suppressed for the most part, or placed under false names. Dräseke, *Apollinarios von Laodicea* in the *Texte und Untersuchungen*, vol. vii. (1892), has tried to reconstruct his work in dogmatics; but all the attributions are not equally certain. The most important of these writings are the treatise, περὶ τῆς θείας σαρκώσεως τῆς καθ' ὁμοίωσιν ἀνθρώπου, reconstructed by Dräseke from quotations, *op. cit.*, p. 381; and the profession of faith Κατὰ μέρος πίστις (p. 369) placed under the name of St Gregory Thaumaturgus.

having no longer any position in the Church of Meletius, he did not hesitate to found another Church: through his exertions, and in his own person, Antioch possessed a third bishop, not to mention of course the official Bishop Euzoïus, who was an Arian. It was at this time that Epiphanius, who, from his island of Cyprus, was following all these movements with care, made up his mind to visit Antioch, and to find out what truth there was in the reports which reached him. He conversed with Paulinus, who was represented as a Sabellian by Vitalis; Paulinus had no difficulty in clearing himself. As to Vitalis, Epiphanius saw with pleasure that he repudiated the absurd doctrines put forward by Docetae of various types, but with regret that he adopted a theory representing Christ as imperfectly man—the Word performing in Him the functions of the mind.[1] Epiphanius reasoned with Vitalis in vain, and was obliged to return home in great distress.

However, Pope Damasus, without mentioning Apollinaris by name, condemned his Christology, at the same time reprobating all those who divided Christ into two persons—the Son of man and the Son of God. For this latter theory no one in the East held himself responsible; but the Apollinarians were always trying to drive their adversaries into it. The Egyptian bishops exiled in Palestine had declared in their turn against Apollinaris.[2] The new dogma had thus against it both Rome and orthodox Egypt. It is strange that Vitalis and Apollinaris should have thought of resisting. What could they expect? All those who in the East were supporters of Meletius and Basil had long mistrusted them : did they not belong to the "Little" Church? Now, when even the Little Church rejected them, and when its protectors in the West and in Egypt expressly condemned them, upon what support could they count?

Nevertheless, they braved the risk. Besides the

---

[1] See a curious account of this interview in Epiphanius, *Haer.* lxxvii. 20-23.

[2] Basil, *Ep.* 265.

two Churches of Antioch and Laodicea, they also organized another at Berytus, of which a certain Timothy became bishop. Other bishops were consecrated and sent to a distance. From the year 377 onwards, Basil complains bitterly of their propaganda; their emissaries were everywhere abroad, trying to divide the Churches. We have seen that immediately after the death of Valens this party endeavoured to lay hands upon the Church of Constantinople, and that it was daring enough to make an attempt at Nazianzus itself in opposition to the illustrious Gregory.

It was impossible that such attempts could meet with success. Rome, Alexandria, Antioch (both the Little Church and the Great one) multiplied their condemnations; the Œcumenical Council of 381 placed the Apollinarians in the catalogue of heretics, at the same time as it ensured in the East the predominance of their most avowed enemies. Then came finally, in 383 and later, the imperial laws,[1] which classed them with the Eunomians, Arians, and Macedonians; they were forbidden to hold meetings and to have clergy of their own.

Being thus repressed, the movement was arrested or, rather, it disguised itself. An Apollinarian Church was no longer possible, if it ever had been; it remained a mere School, without any apparent organization. Its master lived on for some years, in a shadow which we cannot succeed in penetrating. He seems to have continued to write. When he was dead, his disciples, to preserve his compositions, adopted the plan of dissembling them under borrowed names. In this way, their circulation was maintained; Gregory Thaumaturgus, Athanasius, and Popes Dionysius, Felix, and Julius, were invoked to shield with their patronage the works of Apollinaris and his school. This fraud met with great success: it made many victims in the next century.[2]

---

[1] *Cod. Theod.* xvi., 5, 12, 13, 14, 33.

[2] Leontius of Byzantium (?) *Adv. fraudes Apollinaristarum*, Migne, *P. G.* vol. lxxxvi.², p. 1948.

5. *Syria.*

Diodore and Flavian, the two champions of the orthodox faith in the gloomy days of Constantius and Valens, were now presiding over the Churches of the East, the one as Bishop of Tarsus and Metropolitan of Cilicia, the other as Bishop of Antioch. Until his promotion to the episcopate in 378, Diodore nad lived at Antioch, where he was much honoured. He was, like Apollinaris, a learned man, nurtured in the philosophy of Aristotle, and well versed in exegesis of the most solid kind. He wrote a great deal upon all kinds of subjects, provided always that they had a religious interest. It was not only against the Arians and against Apollinaris that he directed his polemics; pagans and philosophers also employed his pen. Amid the frivolities of the great town, he managed to practise the most rigorous asceticism. His thinness was talked of far and wide; he looked like a skeleton. The Emperor Julian, who knew him and did not love him, alleged that it was a punishment inflicted by the gods of Olympus.[1]

At the time when Julian gave currency to this idea, Diodore the thin had still more than thirty years to live. Before leaving Antioch, he trained there two young people, both of whom were called to great renown: Theodore, who like his master transferred himself later to Cilicia, where he died Bishop of Mopsuestia; and John, afterwards surnamed Chrysostom, who was destined to so much success as an orator, and to be the centre of such pitiable tragedies. Theodore of Mopsuestia was the father of Nestorianism; Diodore was its grandfather. A bitter enemy of Apollinaris, he had succeeded in maintaining against him the absolute and integral Humanity of Christ, and in thus saving for future generations the historical sense of the Gospels. But he had not succeeded in finding, to express the relation between the Humanity of Jesus Christ and His Divinity, a formula which could

[1] Julian, *Ep.* 79.

satisfy the religious requirements of that grave problem. Between the two "natures"[1] he admitted only a moral bond. The terms, "two Sons," "two Persons," were avoided; but in reality, Diodore and his followers represented Christ to themselves as a prophet "possessed" by the Divinity—not in a transitory and partial way like the old prophets of Israel, but in a manner which was permanent, perpetual, and complete. With such ideas, they could not reach that contact, that penetration, which is demanded alike by the language of the Gospel: "The Word was made Flesh," and by the mystical formula: "God became Man to make us divine." They approached rather to the conceptions which had been defended in bygone days at Antioch itself by Paul of Samosata.

But, pending criticisms which were soon to follow, and not only from the Apollinarian side, Diodore was for the moment the oracle in theology of the dominant Church.

Flavian, when he became Bishop of Antioch, was already far advanced in years, for he could remember the discourses of Bishop Eustathius. He has left no reputation as a writer. Like Nectarius at Constantinople, he was a good and peace-making pastor. For his flock the time of acute struggle was over; the old warrior took his rest. He could do so with the greater security, because he soon found himself provided with an admirable fellow-worker in the person of Chrysostom. Like Diodore, Theodore, and Flavian himself, John had sprung from a distinguished family. Libanius had had him as a pupil: it was a fact on which he long congratulated himself; we are even told that at the hour of his death the famous rhetorician named his Christian disciple to succeed him in his chair of eloquence. But John had other aims. Meletius had baptized him, and ordained him reader; he lived for some time with his bishop, and afterwards with

---

[1] "Two Natures" was the technical phrase of Diodore; "A single Nature," that of Apollinaris (μία φύσις τοῦ Θεοῦ Λόγου σεσαρκωμένη), who left it as a legacy to Cyril of Alexandria and the Monophysites.

his mother, when Meletius had been sent into exile. One fine day he fled to the desert, and went to live among the monks, in the mountain near Antioch. It was about the same time that Jerome was mortifying himself, not far from there, in the deserts of Chalcis. Their impressions of the Eastern anchorites are very different. Just in proportion as Jerome is bitter,[1] John shows himself enthusiastic. His beautiful soul — young, pure, and trustful—could see nothing but holy men and edifying actions. But the hard life of the desert was not suited for him; at the end of six years, his shattered health brought him back to Antioch in 380. Meletius had just returned there. He received him again as one of his clergy, ordained him deacon, and in 386 Flavian raised him to the priesthood. John was already known by several writings, On the Priesthood, On the Monastic Life, On Providence; his talent for speaking was revealed in several trials. Flavian gave him a pulpit, and installed him in the old cathedral, the " Palaia," as it was called. It was from thence that, for twelve years, there flowed upon the people of Antioch a stream of lucid eloquence— exquisite in its simplicity, adapting itself marvellously to the needs of the time, to the taste of the Antiochenes and to their feelings at the moment. The Bible, explained without allegorical refinements, was the usual theme; sometimes the orator would attack the Anomœans, who were still numerous and active; sometimes the Jews, or rather Christians who were enticed by the attraction of Jewish festivals. The High Days of the Christian year, the anniversaries of the martyrs, varied from time to time the arrangement of his sermons. Sometimes, too, there occurred unusual events, moments of strong feeling when the anxiety of a whole people seemed to pass into the soul of the orator and, coming there into contact with the deep peace of the saints, was transformed into speech of thrilling grandeur. Thus in 387, on the occasion of some new taxation, the people rose in revolt, threw down the statues of the Emperor Theodosius and the Empress

[1] *Supra*, pp. 380 *et seq.*

Flaccilla, dragged them through the streets, and began to acclaim Maximus the Western usurper. It was easy to foresee the kind of vengeance which would ensue. The people had not yet the example of Thessalonica before their eyes; for that did not happen till the following year. But they already knew the severity of Theodosius and the violent outbursts of his anger. Whilst the venerable Flavian set out in the depth of winter on the way to Constantinople, Chrysostom occupied the minds of the Christians of Antioch, comforted them, and took advantage of their present distress to make them listen to wholesome exhortations. Later on, in 395, the news came that the Huns were invading Roman Asia; they even appeared as far as the outskirts of Antioch. It was a good opportunity for preaching repentance : John was not unequal to it.

But the time was drawing near when, as the victim of his own great renown, he was to be torn from the devotion of his fellow-countrymen, and transported to play his part in the capital. In 398, John succeeded Nectarius as Bishop of Constantinople.

The schism which divided the Catholics of Antioch was not yet at an end. Paulinus still maintained his position against Flavian, being strong in the support of the Westerns and the Egyptians. Some time after the passing visit of Paula and Jerome,[1] he felt his death approaching. Fearing, no doubt, that his group of adherents would not survive him, and that a serious appeal to the heart and the good sense of his flock would unite them once more to the Great Church, he made arrangements for a successor to himself. With this end in view, he cast his eyes upon Evagrius, the former friend of Eusebius of Vercellæ,[2] and consecrated him himself before he died. What is more, he performed this ordination alone, without the assistance of any other bishop.[3] All

---

[1] Supra, p. 384.   [2] Supra, pp. 321, 379.

[3] It would doubtless have been difficult for him to find other bishops in Syria, where everyone was in union with Flavian. To have recourse to Epiphanius or the Egyptians would have been

this was irregular to the last degree. However, the
"Eustathians" were so deeply rooted in Antioch, and
had so many supporters outside it, that the action was
not condemned: Evagrius was accepted by the Little
Church.

Of course, the Little Church gained as recruits all the
malcontents of the Great Church. Anyone who had
cause of complaint against Flavian and his clergy at once
joined Evagrius. The women especially flitted continually
from one communion to the other. Both sides believed
themselves to be Catholics; preference for one or the
other could only base itself on very elusive shades of
difference. But this did not prevent constant disputes,
abuse, and anathemas. Flavian's clergy were much disturbed about the matter.[1] But what was to be done?

Evagrius was not recognized either by the Bishop of
Alexandria or by those of the West. The latter, even if
his ordination had been regular, would have shown too
great an inconsistency if, after having protested so strongly
against the idea of appointing a successor to Meletius,
they had approved of filling up the place of Paulinus·
However, they did not come over to the side of Flavian'
and continued to regard his rights as problematical·
Ambrose led this campaign with his usual determination.
In 382 he had wished to summon Flavian and Paulinus
to appear: now, he wished Flavian and Evagrius to be
sent to Italy, and lost no opportunity of appealing to
Theodosius on the subject. But Flavian had no intention
of allowing his rights, so evident to himself, to be discussed

difficult, on account of the distance. Besides, they would not have
lent themselves to an ordination which uselessly perpetuated the
schism. They did not support Evagrius.

[1] Chrysost. *Hom.* xi. *in Eph.* 5, 6 (*P. G.*, vol. lxii., pp. 85-86); *Hom.
de Anathemate* (*P. G.* vol. xlviii. p. 945 *et seq.*). Cavallera (*Le Schisme
d'Antioche*, p. 16) attributes this latter homily to Flavian, on account
of a passage of Ignatius of Antioch, indicated by the words ἅγιός τις
πρὸ ἡμῶν τῆς διαδοχῆς τῶν ἀποστόλων γενόμενος. But in this passage the
orator simply expresses the idea that Ignatius had lived in a past
generation, near the days of the apostles; he does not seem to me to
represent Ignatius as his predecessor in the apostolic see of Antioch.

by others.   He always found some way of escaping
summons.[1] In 391, Ambrose thought he had got hold of
him. He had secured the summoning of a great council
at Capua, and Theodosius, who had returned to the East,
had sent for the Bishop of Antioch to come to him. He
gave Flavian a lecture, and wished to send him off to Italy ;
but Flavian pleaded the winter and his great age : to cut
the story short, he succeeded in obtaining leave to return
to his Eastern diocese.   The Council of Capua took place
without him.   For the sake of peace, all concurred in
agreeing to resume relations with all the orthodox bishops
of the East; while, as to the affair at Antioch, it was
decided to entrust to Theophilus a settlement of it on a
definite basis.   Theophilus then summoned the two
parties before him ; but once more Flavian managed to
avoid putting in an appearance, and entrenched himself
behind the imperial edicts.[2]

It was not such a simple matter as Ambrose imagined.
Flavian and Evagrius were not persons to be placed on
the same level, either in respect of importance or of
legitimacy.   Theophilus put the matter on a proper footing, and Pope Siricius agreed to certain arrangements
which made a solution very much less difficult.   The
Bishop of Alexandria summoned a council at Cæsarea in
Palestine.   He was to have presided over it, but at the
last moment he discovered that the exigencies of the war
he was waging against the heathen gods retained him in
Alexandria : the assembly, consisting of Syrian bishops,
adopted naturally enough the peace-making views of
the Pope.   He had said, when sketching the course to be
followed, that there must be no infringement of the canon
of Nicæa, by which several bishops are required for the
consecration of one.   This meant the condemnation
of Evagrius.   Siricius had also said that there ought only
to be a single bishop in Antioch, legally installed, in
conformity with the canons of Nicæa.   In this description

---

[1] Theodoret, *H. E.* v. 23, can only give us here general outlines,
for his account is inexact and confused.

[2] Ambrose, *Ep.* 56.

the council recognized Flavian, and signified the decision
to Theodosius.[1]

Shortly afterwards, in 394, Flavian, Nectarius, and
Theophilus met in brotherly intercourse with each other
at a council in Constantinople.[2]   It is natural to believe
that Rome made no more difficulties than Alexandria,
and that friendly relations with the West were re-established without delay. A deputation from the clergy of
Antioch, headed by Acacius, Bishop of Berea, repaired
to Rome.[3]   At the same time Theophilus despatched
there a venerable priest of his own Church—Isidore.   The
welcome they received and the letters which they brought
put an end to this protracted strife. But the Little Church
still continued to exist.   It is true that Evagrius died, and
Flavian succeeded in preventing a successor being
appointed; but the flock still gathered around their dis-

---

[1] This Council of Cæsarea has only lately been known, by the
publication of a letter in which Severus of Antioch mentions it ; he
even quotes an important passage from a report addressed by this
assembly to the Emperors Theodosius, Arcadius, and Honorius. We
learn from this document that the council had taken cognizance of
three letters ; one, from the "brethren" (of the West ?) to Theophilus ;
another, from the Council of Capua to the bishops of the East ; and a
third, from Siricius, Bishop of Rome, in conformity with which the
council gives its judgment (E. W. Brooks, *The Sixth Book of the Select
Letters of Severus*, vol. ii. (English translation), part i., 1908, p. 223 ;
the text will also be found, in French, in Cavallera, *Le Schisme
d'Antioche*, p. 286, in which, for the first time, this document has been
made use of. It goes without saying that the council must have
informed, not only the emperor, but also Pope Siricius and
Theophilus of its decision ; but of these letters we have no account.

[2] *Infra*, p. 494.

[3] Theodoret, *H. E.* v. 23. This historian does not connect this
reconciliation between Rome and Antioch with the installation of
Chrysostom at Constantinople ; nor does Socrates (*H. E.* v. 15). It
is only Sozomen (*H. E.* viii. 3) who groups the two events together.
It is a mistake to confuse the two journeys of Acacius of which
Palladius speaks (*Dial.* 4 and 6). Isidore was certainly not entrusted
with carrying to Rome the documents relating to the election of
Chrysostom, whose rival he had been ; Theophilus at that time would
not have wished to impose upon him so bitter a task. It would
be better, perhaps, in order to fix the date of his journey to Rome, to
keep, though with a slight correction, the story which Socrates relates

sentient clergy. We must admit that Flavian did not
smooth the way for reconciliation. He refused to receive
among his clergy those who owed their ordination to
Paulinus and to Evagrius. Such ordinations were in his
eyes null and void. His uncompromising attitude was
not favourably regarded in Rome ; Theophilus again
intervened, and wrote letters to his colleague of Antioch,
begging him to be more conciliatory. He quoted various
precedents, notably that of Ambrose of Milan, who had
not hesitated to receive the clergy of Auxentius.[1] We
have now reached the time of Pope Anastasius (400 or
401); Flavian died shortly afterwards, the local schism
being still unhealed.

The Syria of the Euphrates, or Euphratesian province,
had known in the reign of Constans the celebrated
Eudoxius, Bishop of Germanicia, whose intrigues conducted him in turn to the great sees of Antioch and
Constantinople. In the days of the Emperor Valens it
possessed an episcopal celebrity of a very different kind
in Eusebius, Bishop of Samosata,[2] the friend of Meletius
and of Basil, and as closely concerned as they were in
the movement whereby the East was drawing closer to
Nicene orthodoxy. This attitude of Eusebius caused
him to be exiled to Thrace in 374. He was not a
writer, but he was a man of wise counsel and much
practical common sense. Being deeply convinced of the
importance that Churches should be provided with good
bishops, he took a great interest in all ordinations. He

(vi. 2), according to which Isidore carried to Italy two letters from his
bishop, addressed, one to Maximus, and the other to Theodosius, but
one only of these was to be delivered to whichever of the two the
fortune of war should have favoured. This supposes that Isidore
came to Rome in 388, the year in which Palladius saw him at
Alexandria. Socrates perhaps confused the war against Maximus
with that against Eugenius : such errors are frequent with him. In
that case the journey of Isidore and Acacius must have taken place in
394, a date which fits in well with those of the Councils of Capua,
Cæsarea, and Constantinople.

[1] Brooks, *loc. cit.*, p. 303 *et seq.* ; Cavallera, *loc. cit.*, p. 290.
[2] Often mentioned in the letters of Basil and Gregory of Nazianzus ;
cf. Theodoret, *H. E.* iv. 12, 13 ; v. 4.

assisted in 361 at the ordination of Meletius at Antioch; later on, at that of Basil of Cæsarea; and after the death of Valens he himself consecrated a bishop at Edessa[1]; it was on one of these occasions that he perished at Dolicha, whither he had come to ordain the new Bishop Maris. As he was passing along the street, an old woman who was an Arian threw a tile at him, which struck him on the head and wounded him mortally.

Eulogius, who had been ordained by Eusebius at Edessa, was, like his consecrator, one of those who returned from the persecution. He had been banished from Edessa at the same time as the Bishop, Barses, who, however, never returned from far-off Phile, his place of exile. The Christians of that generation could remember the holy deacon Ephrem (Aphreïm) of Nisibis, a poet and exegete of great distinction.[2] When Nisibis was given up to the Persians in 363, Ephrem had retired into Roman territory and settled at Edessa, where he continued his literary work. His commentaries on the Bible, which enjoyed a great reputation in those days, were soon translated into Greek and later on into Armenian. For the Gospels, the text that he followed was the Diatessaron, a compilation in which the texts of the four Evangelists were blended into a single narrative.[3] This arrangement was very ancient; it dated back to the famous apologist Tatian, a native of those

---

[1] Theodoret, *H. E.* v. 4, mentions many other ordinations which he performed.

[2] The history of St Ephrem, which is told with considerable minuteness in certain authors, and even in Tillemont, rests upon various biographical or even autobiographical documents of a highly circumstantial but extremely suspicious character. I pass them over and confine myself to a few essential and well-authenticated details. *Cf.* Rubens Duval, *La littérature syriaque*, Paris, 1899, p. 332 *et seq.* There is still much to be done with regard to this author, his history, and his work. The latter has only been preserved very incompletely in Syriac; and there is mixed with it a very large proportion of apocryphal matter. *Cf.* Jerome, *De viris*, 115; Palladius, *Hist. Laus.* 40 (101); Sozomen, *H. E.* iii. 16; Theodoret, *H. E.* ii. 26 and iv. 26.

[3] The commentary of Ephrem on the Diatessaron is only extant in Armenian.

Syriac-speaking countries. The Churches of Osrhoene had early adopted it for liturgical use. Basil knew the "Syrian" scholar and held him in great esteem.[1] He owes his celebrity chiefly to his poetry. At Nisibis he had sung of the exploits of his fellow-citizens when besieged by the Persians; at Edessa, he set himself especially to rival the heretics. Bardesanes and his son Harmonius had left behind them a substantial legacy of popular songs, which perpetuated their teaching and made it widely known. Ephrem composed other songs in a metre marked by lines of seven syllables, in which he assails with vigour not only the followers of Bardesanes, who were still numerous, but also Marcionites, Manicheans, and other heretics, and inculcates at the same time Christian virtues and the true faith of the Church. He died in 373, just when the blast of persecution was making itself felt, which drove on the road to exile both his own Bishop, Barses, and so many other prelates of Osrhoene.

When the storm was past, the Church revived once more. While the monks of Harran cherished the memory of Abraham, the people of Edessa were devoted to that of King Abgar and to the cult of St Thomas. During the period of more than a hundred years that it had been in vogue, the legend of Abgar had entered the domain of accepted facts. In the ancient palace of the kings of Edessa there were shown the sculptured portraits of Abgar and his son Manou; here also was to be seen the celebrated spring which had gushed out miraculously during a siege, to take the place of the aqueducts which had been cut by the Persians; sacred fish swam there then as they do now. And, above all, there was preserved a notable relic, the famous letter of Jesus to King Abgar. Pilgrims of distinction were allowed to see it and even to make a copy of it. If the Persians drew near to Edessa, the bishop was wont to mount the ramparts and solemnly to read out the sacred words. Nothing more was necessary: the enemy retired forth-

---

[1] Basil, *Hexam.* 2 ; *De Spiritu Sancto*, 29.

with. As to St Thomas, his body was preserved in an enormous and magnificent basilica. Where did it come from? It would perhaps have been indiscreet to ask; in after years it was admitted that it had been brought from India.[1]

Few pilgrims risked themselves in this far-off country of Mesopotamia, situated beyond the Hellenized world, and incessantly ravaged by war. On the other hand the roads which led to Palestine were more and more frequented. It was like a fulfilment of the ancient prophecies: all the nations were coming to Jerusalem.

After Macarius, in whose episcopate imperial piety had done so much for the Holy Places, the see of Ælia had been occupied by Maximus, an old confessor, lame and blind in one eye since the days when the Emperor Daïa had sent him to the mines. Ælia remembered that it had once been at Jerusalem. How could it have forgotten the fact, above all now when the basilicas of Constantine and of Helena, besieged by enormous crowds from all quarters, were reviving and exalting its venerable traditions? The Bishop of Jerusalem was a very overpowering suffragan for the Metropolitan of Cæsarea; their relations to each other bear evidence of the fact: it is true that these relations had been settled by the Council of Nicæa, but somewhat vaguely, and this arrangement had not diminished the rivalry between the two sees. In the dogmatic disputes of the 4th century, the irrespective bishops were rarely to be found on the same side. Macarius does not seem to have carried away from the Council of Nicæa the same feelings of disappointment as Eusebius of Cæsarea. In 346 Maximus gave a public welcome to Athanasius on his return from the West, and even assembled for the occasion a council of sixteen bishops of Palestine. This demonstration was not likely to please Acacius, the new Metropolitan. At that time Cyril, one of the priests of Maximus, enjoyed a great reputation for eloquence; we

---

[1] On the pilgrimage to Edessa, in the time of Theodosius, see especially the *Peregrinatio*, c. 19.

still possess a whole series of catechetical lectures of his, which were delivered during one Lent for the instruction of candidates for the Easter baptism. Upon the Trinitarian question, the orator shows great prudence: he avoids the disputed term *homoousios*, but his doctrine is correct and devoid of any compromise with Arianism. About the year 350,[1] Cyril was elected successor to Maximus, and then installed in due form by the bishops of the province, and, needless to say, with the consent of the Metropolitan.[2] In 351 Cyril wrote to the Emperor Constantius to inform him of a celestial phenomenon— a cross of light which had appeared on the horizon at Jerusalem.[3] Shortly afterwards we find him engaged in conflict with Acacius upon questions of jurisdiction. The quarrel became so bitter that the Metropolitan cited his suffragan to appear before his council, and even deposed him for contumacy. This was in the year 357. Acacius of Cæsarea was very popular at Court. Cyril appealed from this decision, but could not succeed in retaining his see, which was immediately bestowed on an intruder. Retiring to Tarsus, to Bishop Silvanus, he joined the group of the semi-orthodox—Basil of Ancyra, George of Laodicea, and other opponents of pure Arianism. Restored to his see in 359 by the Council of Seleucia, which adjudicated upon his appeal, he was again deposed a few months later by the Council of Constantinople, presided over by Acacius.[4] We find him again at Jerusalem in Julian's reign[5]; but Valens ordered him to

---

[1] This is the date given in St Jerome's *Chronicle*.

[2] Letter of the council of 382 (Theodoret, *H. E.* v. 9, p. 1033). Socrates, *H. E.* ii. 38, says that Maximus had been deposed by Acacius and Patrophilus ; this is a mistake.

[3] The conclusion of this letter is certainly not authentic.

[4] Amongst the ostensible charges brought up against **him was** the following :—During a time of famine, Cyril had caused **several** valuable articles from the treasury of his church to be sold ; amongst other things a richly embroidered vestment, the gift of Constantine to Bishop Macarius. Passing from purchaser to purchaser, the precious stuff fell into the hands of some one connected with a theatre, who displayed it on the stage (Sozomen, *H. E.* iv. 25).

[5] Rufinus, *H. E.* i. 37.

be expelled once more, and it was not until 378 that he was able to return. He took part in the Council of Constantinople in 381, and that assembly solemnly acknowledged him as a legitimate bishop. From that time forward he was left in peace. He was able to reassume the government of his own Church and even of the neighbouring Churches, for we find him installing in the see of Cæsarea one of his nephews, whose name was Gelasius.

The state of religion at Jerusalem suffered from these disturbances. After Cyril's deposition, for more than twenty years various usurpers, under the protection of the Arians, had succeeded one another in the religious administration of the Holy City. There was a party in opposition to them, and not only among the native population, but also among the colonies of monks, who were becoming daily more numerous. This body of opponents had connections with Egypt, with the West, and, in Syria, with the party which was led by Paulinus and Apollinaris. The usurpers were naturally regarded among them with detestation; but Cyril himself met with but little sympathy from them. He was not sufficiently above suspicion for them; they reproached him with his relations with the circle of Basil of Ancyra and of Silvanus,[1] with his communications with Meletius and Flavian. Jerome, from whom we hear all the scandal of these zealots, does not hesitate to put into the same boat both Cyril and his rivals; according to him, they were all Arians.[2] Besides, even had the monks been united in a common devotion to Cyril—which was far from being the case—they would still have found themselves in disagreement in regard to Paulinus and to Apollinaris, especially

---

[1] There were also the Pneumatomachi, whose opposition rested on different grounds (Palladius, *Hist. Laus.* 46 [118]); but they do not appear to have been very numerous. Melania and Rufinus brought them back to the fold.

[2] *Chron.* a. Abr. 2364. This was written before his journey to Palestine, and after his stay at Antioch; it was, I think, from those about Paulinus that he collected the information, very hostile and very inaccurate, which he gives us with regard to Cyril.

to the latter, whose propaganda was then agitating the
cells on the Mount of Olives. The situation became so
much embittered that the council of 381 thought it
advisable to send Gregory of Nyssa on a special mission
to Palestine as well as to Arabia, where there were also
troubles.

Gregory saw at close quarters this famous place of
pilgrimage, of which there remain to us so many roseate
accounts. In his heart, bishop as he was, enthusiasm for
Biblical places could not swallow up anxieties of a higher
order. After his return home, he showed no zeal for the
Holy Places. Like the author of the *Imitation* in later
days, he deemed that those who run from place to place
on pilgrimages are not on the road to sanctification.
Nowhere had he met with so many rascals as at
Jerusalem: theft, adultery, poisoning, and assassination
were common occurrences there. Instead of taking
journeys to risk his virtue on the highways, and his life
among such cut-throats, why should a man not remain in
that good land of Cappadocia, where churches were not
lacking, and where rogues were fewer than honest men?

We ask ourselves, what would have happened if the
Bishop of Nyssa, instead of confiding his impressions to
select correspondents,[1] had expressed them in the presence
of Melania, Paula, Silvania, Etheria, and other enthusiastic pilgrims. Fortunately, they heard nothing of it, and
the popularity of the Holy Places suffered in no wise from
his criticisms. The more visitors came, the more these
sacred sites multiplied. There was not a single village in
Palestine which did not possess some Biblical reminiscence.
Of course a great many of these were authentic, at least
in the sense that the places mentioned in the Bible could
be identified with towns, villages, rivers, and mountains,
which really existed. But the curiosity of the pilgrims
demanded more details; and, as the supply could not fail
to correspond with the demand, at last everything was
rediscovered—even the most problematical things, such
as the tomb of Job and the palace of Melchisedech. Once

---

[1] Greg. Nyss. *Epp.* 2, 3.

created, the sanctuary attracted the monks, and the legend flourished.

Amongst the Latin colonies, that of the Mount of Olives and that of Bethlehem attracted attention and even made some stir. The first was the more ancient. It dated back to the last years of the Emperor Valens. Melania and Rufinus lived there, each surrounded by a group of pious persons of their own sex, sanctifying themselves by fasting, prayer, and the study of the Sacred Books. Some ten years later Jerome and Paula established themselves at Bethlehem, under the same conditions. Rufinus and Melania had at first made a stay in Egypt; the new-comers, arriving by way of Antioch, did not neglect to make also a pilgrimage to the hermits of the Nile. Jerome profited by this visit to converse at Alexandria with the old and venerable Didymus,[1] who, although blind from his earliest years, had none the less found means of instructing himself so profoundly in the branches of sacred knowledge, that Athanasius had confided to him the direction of the Catechetical School. Didymus justified his bishop's trust. With a calm untroubled by noises from without, acutely as they made themselves heard around him, he taught the doctrine of the Trinity in accordance with the most recent and most orthodox formulas; at the same time upholding, on the whole, the system of Origen, which was already strongly assailed. Didymus was a great ascetic: St Antony, who had visited him long before Jerome did, had shown him marks of his esteem; he had also many admirers amongst the solitaries of Nitria. However, even in his own country, he did not please everyone: his attachment to Origen caused uneasiness.

Certainly it had caused no uneasiness to Rufinus, who before Jerome's visit had attended Didymus' instructions. Nor did Jerome again feel any trouble about it. The blind sage of Alexandria added one more to the Greek

[1] On Didymus and his theology, see the excellent monograph of J. Leipoldt, *Didymus der Blinde* (*Texte und Untersuch.* vol. xxix., 1905).

masters of whom he boasted already,[1] Apollinaris and
Gregory of Nazianzus. Origen continued to be in his
eyes a great light of the Church; without compromising
himself with Origen's peculiar teaching any more than he
had done with that of Apollinaris, Jerome professed an
admiration for him which knew no bounds, and, with his
customary gentleness of temper, treated as a "mad dog"[2]
anyone who allowed himself to criticize the Alexandrian
master.

It was in this frame of mind that he returned from
Egypt, and resumed in his retreat at Bethlehem his
labours upon the text and interpretation of the Bible.
Between whiles he translated Origen and Didymus.
Rufinus, so far as regards Origen, held the same view as
his friend. They agreed also on the question of Apollinaris,
whom they both condemned alike for his teaching and his
propaganda, and they even agreed about the business at
Antioch: they were both on the side of Paulinus, without,
however, thinking themselves entitled to turn the cold
shoulder upon Bishop John, the successor of Cyril, and
like him in communion with Flavian. There was thus
no reason for disagreement between the two men, except
that there were two of them, at the head of two colonies
of the same origin, and so exposed to the temptations of
rivalry. Moreover, close to Rufinus lived Melania, a
personality at once dominating and unyielding; Rufinus
himself, with all his piety and his learning, was a man
who showed himself from time to time lacking in tact and
moderation, although it would have needed a large share
of both qualities to avoid collision with the extremely
irritable man whom circumstances had given them as a
neighbour.

In the province of Arabia, beyond the Jordan and the
Dead Sea, the body of bishops had, with a few rare
exceptions, followed the various evolutions of their
Eastern colleagues. Since 363, they had given their

---

[1] *De viris*, 109, where Jerome lays stress upon his literary
relations with Didymus.

[2] Passage quoted, Vol. I., p. 252, note 1.

adhesion, as Acacius and Meletius had done, to the Creed
of Nicæa.   The metropolitical see of Bostra was occupied
at that time by Titus, a distinguished writer, to whom we
owe a treatise against the Manicheans.[1]   Titus and his
clergy had much to put up with from Julian the apostate.
In connection with some disturbances which had taken
place at Bostra, the bishop was led to protest to the
emperor that although the Christians around him were as
numerous as the pagans were, he felt confident of being
able to keep order in the city.   Julian imputed to him
as a crime what he described as a piece of presumption
which reflected upon the people of Bostra, and tried to
lead them to rise against their bishop.   It was certainly
not his fault that they did not treat Titus with violence.[2]

At the time when Apollinaris was agitating the East,
there took their birth in Arabia certain striking innovations, which were not, perhaps, of great local importance,
but which are interesting to observe, because they throw
a light upon a certain working of men's minds.   For the
first time we find a mention of a *cultus* devoted to Mary,
the Mother of the Saviour.   Naturally, it was the women
who inaugurated it.   They had imported it, it would seem,
from Thrace and from Scythia.   This cult consisted in an
annual festival.   The people assembled around a kind
of throne, mounted on wheels, and offered to the Virgin
Mother cakes specially prepared, which were called
"collyrides."   There was a complete liturgical rite, which
women alone could celebrate.   Epiphanius, so well
informed in matters of this kind, deduced from it the
heresy of the Collyridians, and carefully refuted it, both
in a special letter addressed to Arabia, and in his great
treatise against all heresies.   But at the same time and
in the same documents he had also to concern himself
with another manifestation, perhaps called to life by the

[1] Migne, *P. G.*, vol. xviii., p. 1069; but the text is interpolated and
incomplete; we must take account also of the Syriac version, edited
in 1859 by Lagarde.   As to Titus, see Jerome, *De viris*, 102; *Ep.*
lxx. 4; Sozomen, *H. E.* v. 15; and a recent monograph of J.
Sickenberger in the *Texte und Unt.*, vol. xxi., 1901.

[2] Julian, *Ep.* 52.

previous one, but at any rate of an opposite tendency.
This is what he calls the heresy of the Antidicomarianites.
These, briefly, were persons who thought, like Helvidius
and Jovinian, that from the time when the Gospel mentions
the brethren of the Lord, and speaks of Jesus as the "first-
born," Mary must have had other children after Him.

A more serious dispute arose with regard to the
successor of Titus. A certain Bagadius, who had been
elected and ordained Bishop of Bostra, soon found himself
confronted by a very strenuous opposition, which was
upheld by an episcopal tribunal, composed of two
bishops, Cyril[1] and Palladius. These two prelates deposed
Bagadius; he was ejected, and in his place another bishop
named Agapius was consecrated. But Bagadius did not
accept his deprivation: he presented himself in 381 at
the great Council of Constantinople; Agapius did the
same. The council, seeing no way to a decision between
them, instructed Gregory of Nyssa to visit Bostra and
arrange the matter. Gregory did not succeed in this,
and the quarrel continued. The parties concerned carried
the matter to Rome, whence they returned to the East
with a letter from Pope Siricius, directing Theophilus of
Alexandria to effect a final settlement of this interminable
dispute.

During the last years of Theodosius, the most
prominent personage in the Eastern Empire was the
prætorian prefect, Rufinus, a man who was at once
ambitious, grasping, and cruel. Theodosius, however,
trusted him entirely. It was to his care that he entrusted
his family and his Eastern possessions, when in 394 he
was obliged to set out for Italy in order to repress the
usurpation of Eugenius. The ambitions of Rufinus were
unbounded. He was supposed to aim at the Imperial
throne, and it certainly seems that he had chosen Arcadius
—the eldest of Theodosius' sons, who had long been
associated with his father in the empire — to be the
husband of his own daughter. While Theodosius was
waging war against Arbogast and Nicomachus Flavianus,

[1] Perhaps Cyril of Jerusalem.

Rufinus devoted his leisure to great festivals in his own honour. As he made a parade of extreme devotion, he had built in his villa at Drus (the Oak), three miles from Chalcedon, a magnificent basilica in honour of the Apostles Peter and Paul. The Pope had sent him some relics of them. When the building was completed, he determined to celebrate its dedication by a great festival, to which he invited the chief bishops of the East, Nectarius of Constantinople, Theophilus of Alexandria, Flavian of Antioch, Amphilochius of Iconium, Gregory of Nyssa, Theodore of Mopsuestia, the Metropolitans of Cæsarea in Cappadocia, of Ancyra, of Tarsus, of Cæsarea in Palestine, and many others—thirty-seven prelates in all. He took advantage of the occasion to have himself baptized, and wished to have as his godfather one of the most venerated of the solitaries of Nitria, Ammonius, the man who had cut off one of his ears to avoid being made a bishop.[1] This holy man was brought from Egypt, and played in Rufinus' festivities the part which had been assigned to him.[2]

As to the bishops, they took advantage of their meeting to hold a council. For this purpose, they transported themselves to Constantinople, and to the Baptistery of St Sophia. Of the matters with which they dealt we know only of one—that of the see of Bostra. The two claimants were present. Theophilus, in fulfilment of the commission given him by Pope Siricius, laid this celebrated dispute before the meeting. The conduct of those bishops who had deposed Bagadius was severely censured; some even spoke of passing condemnation on their memory. But the leaders did not think that a sentence of any kind ought to be pronounced against the dead.

How exactly the affair of Bostra was settled, we are left in ignorance by the few lines which remain to us of the formal record of the proceedings.[3] And, moreover,

[1] Palladius, *Hist. Laus.* 11 (12). *Cf.* p. 357, note 1.

[2] He died shortly afterwards, and was buried in the Church of the Oak, where his tomb remained an object of much veneration.

[3] Until recent times they had been known from an extract preserved in a collection of Byzantine canon law; this extract appears

the real importance of this meeting of bishops is found neither in the ostentatious ceremony which was the pretext for it, nor in the decisions which emanated from it; but in the testimony it gives us of the religious pacification which had been accomplished in the East. There is agreement everywhere: Flavian sits down with Theophilus. Theophilus with his Eastern brethren defers to the wishes of Pope Siricius. The schism in Arabia is settled; and that of Antioch reduced to the proportions of a local disagreement of which we catch no echo, henceforth, in the relations between the great churches. It was a festival of peace, destined, alas! to be followed by a very cloudy future. Scarcely one year was to elapse before Rufinus, the promoter of these solemnities, was to fall the victim of a political assassination. In 403 his basilica was to witness the deposition of Chrysostom, and from that crime were to issue terrible divisions. Once more those, too, were destined to be reconciled. The name of Theodore of Mopsuestia reminds us of others, the echo of which was to ring through long centuries. Rufinus' Council was only a halt on the mournful road.

in the collections of councils. I have since found another extract from the same document in a treatise (still unedited) of the Roman deacon Pelagius, against the condemnation of the Three Chapters. This extract has been published in the *Annales de philosophie chrétienne*, 1885, p. 281. It is in this that there is a reference to Pope Siricius; the other extract does not mention him.

CHAPTER XVII

CHRISTIANITY, THE STATE RELIGION

Paganism after Julian. Attitude of Valentinian and of Valens.
Gratian. The Altar of Victory. Pagan reaction in Rome
under Eugenius. Theodosius : the temples closed. The temple
of Serapis at Alexandria. Popular disturbances. Position of
the Christian sects at the accession of Constantine. Laws of
repression. The Novatians. The Catholic Church alone
recognized. Alliance of the Church with the State. Liberty,
right of property, privileges. Intervention of the State in
religious disputes, in the nomination or the deprivation of
bishops. Episcopal elections. Civil jurisdiction of the bishops.

1. *The End of Paganism.*

THE dynasty of Constantine, by a strange irony of fate,
came to an end with a prince who was at once an apostate
and a pagan. But Julian's reign lasted only a short time ;
his restoration of Hellenism had taken no root ; and
the memory which remained of it was that of a foolish
attempt, a kind of religious masquerade. With the exception of a few hierophants, genuine pagans do not seem to
have lent to it as much support as had been desired by
the stage-manager. Of Julian himself they preserved a
pious remembrance, but without any very deep regrets.

His proceedings, indeed, could only have the effect of
throwing ridicule, and even odium, upon the melancholy
but inevitable decline of the old religion. Henceforth, its
fate was sealed ; the current was too strong for the State
itself, with all its power, to be able to swim against it.
Whether the emperor were favourable or not, Christianity
was certain of success. When we remember that it did not

cease to make progress in Africa, in spite of the stumbling-block of Donatism; that the Arian crisis, and bishops like Eusebius of Nicomedia, Stephen of Antioch, Gregory and George of Alexandria, and Eudoxius of Constantinople, did not prevent its conquest of the East, we can judge how much could be effected against it by official hostility or even by persecution.

The Christian princes who succeeded Julian—Jovian, Valentinian, and Valens—had all been members of his military staff. Far from concealing their faith, they had professed it with sufficient energy to incur the displeasure of their sovereign, and even temporary disgrace. When they came into power, they simply closed the pagan parenthesis and things returned to the course they had followed during the time of Constantius, although with less severity. The properties restored to the temples by Julian were taken from them again for the benefit of the imperial revenue,[1] but the liberty of everyone in matters of religion was loudly proclaimed. It seems that at first the absolute prohibition of sacrifices was allowed to drop. On a few points only were there restrictive measures[2]: nocturnal ceremonies were forbidden—with some exceptions, however, for the mysteries of Eleusis, which were celebrated by night, received a dispensation.[3] Augury without being proscribed or even censured was closely watched, as also were the other religious practices connected with the divining of the future—i.e., of course, the political future. Being themselves new men, the heirs of a dynasty which had been deeply rooted, and the last representative of which had left sympathizers, Valentinian and Valens felt strongly the necessity of making their own position secure, and not allowing themselves to be opposed by rivals of the stamp of Procopius. Procopius was really a kinsman of Julian's, and not without personal sympathies with paganism.

---

[1] *Cod. Theod.* x. 1, 8.

[2] Laws alluded to in *Cod. Theod.* ix. 16, 9; *Cf.* Ammianus Marcellinus, xxx. 9.

[3] *Cod. Theod.* ix. 16, 7, a law of 364; *cf.* for Eleusis, Zosimus, *H. E.* iv. 3.

In the Empire of the East, the Catholics, driven from
their churches and forced to meet in secluded places,
envied the pagans the publicity of their worship. Whether
because the latter abused the liberty which was left to
them,[1] or for other reasons, the two imperial brothers at
length showed themselves more rigorous. Sacrifices were
once again forbidden, but not the act of burning incense
upon the altars.[2]   Gratian did not at first show himself more severe. However, we do not find that after the
death of his father in 375 he took the title of *Pontifex
Maximus*, which the emperors had always borne since the
time of Augustus, and which, thenceforward, none ever
bore again. Zosimus[3] tells a story on this subject, according to which the *pontifices* of Rome offered to Gratian, on
his accession, a sacerdotal robe in his capacity of head of
their college; the emperor is represented as refusing it
for religious reasons. This anecdote is more than doubtful; but it sufficiently expresses the more decided attitude,
from a personal standpoint at first, and afterwards as
legislator, which Gratian adopted in these matters. This
young prince, who had been brought up in a genuinely
Christian household, had had as his instructor the famous
Ausonius, who had grounded him in ancient literature,
and assuredly had not inculcated in him any prejudice
against Hellenism. When he became emperor, he had
very close relations with St Ambrose, relations which
swayed him in a different direction. In the main, however,
it was by his own conscience and by circumstances that
he was chiefly guided. In spite of all professions of
toleration, none of the emperors of the 4th century, and
Julian no more than the rest, had ever renounced the
dream of religious unity. Gratian inherited from his
father the conviction that paganism was destined to

---

[1] The Council of Valence in 374 (c. 3) is still concerned with
baptized Christians who offer sacrifices or suffer themselves to undergo
the Taurobolium.

[2] Libanius, *Oratio pro templis*.

[3] iv. 36. The story is told in such a way as to explain a prophetic
pun upon the usurpation of Maximus.

[4] *Cod. Theod.* xvi. 10, 7, 9.

disappear, and that the State must assist in this end,
without, of course, compromising itself by violent measures.
He continued to prohibit sacrifices, but he went no
further, at all events in his legislation. Theodosius also,
although the position was riper in the East, stopped there
during the early years of his reign. In the long run, the
distinction so long recognized between sacrifice and the
other acts of worship was finally abandoned. Every
external manifestation of the pagan religion was rigorously forbidden, whether in the temples, or on the highways and on private property.[1]

Such measures involved, or practically involved, the
closing of the temples. These buildings were almost
everywhere the chief ornament of the towns. Several
of them, imposing from their vast proportions and the
majesty of their architecture, were able to defend themselves in addition by the religious awe which they had
inspired for so many centuries. Many of them contained
works of art of the greatest value. What was to become
of them? The legislator seems to have been anxious, and
that from the time of Constantine onwards, to protect the
interests of art, and to preserve their monuments to the
cities.[2] At various times, laws were made for the preserva-
tion of the temples, and even for keeping them open,
especially when they could be adapted for public use, for
instance, for the meetings of the councils and of the local
magistrates. Besides, even if the ancient worship was
proscribed in itself and in its religious practices, no one
dreamed for a moment of depriving the public of the
games and other festivities to which it had given rise. In
many places the people continued to assemble around the
temples, even when they had been emptied of their idols.
The religious ritual of the ancient festival was suppressed,
but everything else was preserved, even the priesthood,
which still had a reason for existence, because it remained

[1] Laws of 391 and 392 ; *Cod. Theod.* xvi. 10, 10-12.
[2] *Cod. Theod.* xvi. 10, 8, in 382 (the law deals with a temple
situated in Osrhoene ; I think that it refers to the town of Harran) ;
xvi. 10, 15-18, in 399.

entrusted with the duty of presiding over and organizing the public festivals.[1] Of course in many places somewhat more was retained than the rigorists would have admitted. In secluded places, in the heart of the country, or on large private estates, the temples, the sacred groves, and the mysterious springs long retained their prestige. The last victim was not sacrificed for several centuries after the prohibitions of Constantius and of Theodosius.

Moreover, we must take care, in matters of this kind especially, not to confuse the law and the application of it. Even in the large towns where the State was supreme, it was some time before paganism, though theoretically proscribed, ceased actually to hold an important position. Constantius visited Rome in 357; he saw the temples still standing and thronged as of old. He knew (for how could he have been ignorant?) that in spite of his laws, incense was still smoking there, and also the blood of victims; and that the expenses of the religious processions were still borne by the State. He showed no approval, for he was of marble, and prided himself upon never betraying his feelings; but neither did he condemn. Julian had not to raise up again the altars of Rome : they had never been thrown down. They still stood under the Christian princes who came after him. However, the continual progress of Christianity deprived the old religion of the favour of the populace. With every advance, there was a further shrinkage of the circle of worshippers. The aristocracy who clung to the ancient traditions did their best to maintain them; but it was not without effort. The sacred colleges and the priesthoods were recruited with difficulty. Certain great nobles accumulated sacred offices, evidently because so few people were in a position to fill

---

[1] The *sacerdotes* or *coronati* are still mentioned, for a considerable time, in the imperial laws. These offices were even, as at the time of the Council of Elvira, sought after by some Christians little troubled by scruples. Legislation was necessary before they could be excluded from them (*Cod. Theod.* xii. 1, 112). Although no longer involving the obligation to sacrifice, the priesthoods were none the less too closely connected with paganism for it not to be unseemly that they should be seen exercised by Christians.

them. In such circumstances, we can imagine that the
State would ask itself whether it ought to continue to
defray the expenses of a cult which was, comparatively
speaking, little practised. Here, we must explain a little.
Under the pagan *régime*, when the State asked for
sacrifices, it was the State which defrayed the expenses.
This under Christian emperors no longer happened:
Gratian found nothing to alter in this respect. But the
temples were provided with endowments consisting both
of personal and real estate, which served to pay the
expenses of the ordinary maintenance of the cult. On the
other hand, the officials, when their services were not
gratuitous and purely honorary, were remunerated by the
municipalities, and in Rome by the State, which, as a
general rule, also had charge of the administration of the
patrimony of the temples, and had at last come to consider
itself as the real proprietor of it. When the population
passed over to Christianity, either entirely or by a great
majority, the municipalities had been obliged to take steps
to clear up this position. Although we have no information as to details, we can well imagine that they did not
succeed in doing this everywhere at the same time, or in
the same way, and that many abuses and encroachments
were the result. Gratian made a general rule, but the
text of it has not been preserved[1]; it applied not only to
religious establishments, which, having been deserted by
their congregations, had really no longer any reason for
existing, but to institutions which were still living, and
the end of which it was intended in this way to hasten.
It was then that the great Roman colleges, the pontiffs,
vestal-virgins, quindecemvirs, and others received the
fatal blow.

This law was already in force when, in 382, there
occurred the incident of the Altar of Victory. Augustus,
after the battle of Actium, had placed in the meeting-
place of the Senate a statue of Victory, which had formerly

[1] Often alluded to in the discussion between St Ambrose and
Symmachus with regard to the Altar of Victory ; cf. *Cod. Theod.* xvi.
10, 20.

been brought from Tarentum at the time when the
Roman Republic had made itself master of that town.
Beneath it an altar was placed, and as the members of the
Senate entered they threw on it a few grains of incense;
oaths and vows, when there was any occasion for making
them, were consecrated by the presence of the goddess.
When there were Christian senators, they soon found
themselves scandalized by this idol. The Emperor
Constantius had it taken away; Julian replaced it; after
him, it was allowed to remain, thanks to the comparative
toleration which ruled during the reigns of Jovian and
Valentinian. But the Christian senators increased in
numbers every day; their scruples found their way to
the ears of Gratian, who ordered the removal once more
of the goddess who gave rise to the dispute. This decision
was the occasion for a famous debate; the pagan senators
protested by the mouth of Symmachus, one of their most
distinguished members; they claimed to be the majority,
and demanded that, in the Senate at least, the Roman
religion should be respected. Gratian refused to receive
their envoy: he had learnt, from a protest of the Christian
senators presented to him by Pope Damasus, that
Symmachus did not represent the real opinions of the
assembly. But Gratian died in the following year (383),
and Valentinian II. allowed Symmachus to plead his
cause before the Imperial Council. During the interval
he had been appointed Prefect of Rome. His speech[1]
made a great sensation. Ambrose then intervened, asked
for a full account of the memorial, and discussed it step
by step.[2] It was not only the restoration of the Altar of
Victory that was demanded by the old Roman; he protested
also against the laws of spoliation, which had deprived the
temples of their revenues and the priests of their stipends;
the vestal-virgins, especially, were defended by him with
the greatest warmth. Ambrose had an answer to everything; but we must confess that, after the lapse of so
many centuries, we receive a strange impression when
comparing his arguments with those of Symmachus, and

---

[1] *Symm. rel.* 3.   [2] Ambrose, *Epp.* 17, 18.

thinking of the lips which reproduce the same arguments
for and against in our own day in a similar conflict.[1]

The demand of Symmachus had no result: things
remained as they were. In this year (384) the gods
lost one of their most faithful servants, in the person
of Vettius Agorius Prætextatus. He had been prætorian
prefect at the same time that Symmachus was prefect
of Rome.[2] Another distinguished pagan, Nicomachus
Flavianus, had also been prætorian prefect in 383.
Such a state of things serves to show us that if the laws
were severe towards paganism, the government itself bore
no malice to its defenders. In 387 Maximus invaded
Italy, and compelled Valentinian II. to take refuge with
Theodosius. His authority was recognized in Rome for
several months, and Symmachus, who was by no means
a novice in the art of panegyric, pronounced yet another
in honour of the new prince. It cost him dear, for
Theodosius lost no time in reinstating his young colleague.
Maximus, after being defeated in several battles, was
given up to the Emperor of the East and finally put
to death, and those who had espoused his cause found
themselves in a very difficult position. Symmachus took
refuge in a church.[3] He was pardoned; he suffered
neither in his person, nor in his goods, nor in his dignities.
Theodosius and Valentinian came to Rome in 389.
Flavian and Symmachus reappeared at their sides.
Flavian became once more prætorian prefect; as for
Symmachus, he was designated for the consulship, and
actually inaugurated his tenure of the office on January 1,
391. The government evidently wished to win over to
its side by personal favours all that still remained of
the old pagan aristocracy, which was more and more
thwarted in its religious views. But the struggle was
against convictions tenaciously held. The pagan party
refused to resign itself to the disestablishment of the

---

[1] With regard to this affair, which has often been described to
readers, see especially Boissier, *La fin du Paganisme*, pp. 267-338.

[2] See above, p. 364.

[3] It was a Novatian Church placed under the authority of the
Novatian Pope, Leontius (Socrates, *H. E.* v. 14).

Roman worship, or to the removal of the Altar of Victory. They never ceased to besiege the princes with their protests. Theodosius received at Milan[1] a deputation from the Senate; when he had set out for the East, Valentinian II., who had betaken himself to Gaul, was attacked there by another embassy.[2] All this, however, produced no effect.

But on May 15, 392, Valentinian was assassinated at Vienne, at the instigation of Count Arbogast, a too powerful general. The murderer cast the purple mantle upon the shoulders of an official of the imperial chancery, Eugenius by name, who in bygone days had won some renown as a professor of literature. He was a Christian; Arbogast, his patron, was not. When Eugenius saw, as he very soon did, that Theodosius would not recognize him, he thought it to his advantage to rely upon the pagan party, the party of opposition, exasperated by so many failures, and especially by the recent laws which had just forbidden absolutely all practice of the old form of worship. At that time the Prætorian Prefect of Italy was Nicomachus Flavianus, the cousin and son-in-law of Symmachus, and like him zealously devoted to the gods. The great pagan nobles had every scope to carry out what they desired to effect. The restoration of the grants-in-aid to the old religion met, it is true, with some obstacles. Eugenius needed much persuasion; it became him but ill as a professing Christian to take such a responsibility. At last a way out was found; the possessions and stipends were restored, not directly to the temples, but to the

[1] Probably in 389 before his journey to Rome. The author of the *De promissionibus*, who wrote towards the middle of the 5th century, relates (iii. 38) that Symmachus, in a panegyric officially delivered (*praeconio laudum in consistorio recitato*), having asked Theodosius to restore the Altar of Victory, the emperor drove him from his presence and packed him off at a moment's notice a hundred miles away in a peasant's cart. This is, in my opinion, a legendary transformation of one of the fruitless applications made by Symmachus and the Senate, to Gratian, Valentinian II., or Theodosius.

[2] Upon these appeals from the Senate, see Ambrose, *Ep.* 57. The Bishop of Milan seems to have feared for a moment that Theodosius would give way.

pagan senators. As to the Altar of Victory, liberty to sacrifice and to celebrate all pagan ceremonies, the wishes of Symmachus and his friends were granted full and complete satisfaction. Yet Symmachus appears[1] to have accepted this unexpected change with a certain amount of reserve. It was Nicomachus Flavianus who came to the front. Up to that time although strongly attached to the worship of the gods, and showing little affection for Christians whenever his official duties gave him an opportunity of being obnoxious to them,[2] he had not displayed a devotion so extreme as Prætextatus did, nor had he declared himself with so much urgency as Symmachus had done in favour of the old traditions. Now, however, we find him exhibiting the very utmost zeal. The possessions of the temples served to organize festivities of great pomp and noise. Cybele, the Mother of the Gods, was carried in procession; the ceremonies of Isis were once more performed; sacrifices were offered with great magnificence to Jupiter Latialis; the temples of Venus and of Flora, of which so many hard things had been said, were once more opened for their licentious rites; and, finally, a complete lustration of the city, according to the ancient ritual of purification occupied for three months those who still followed the old religion, and provoked exceedingly, as we can well imagine, the adherents of the new. Amongst the latter some, disconcerted at their want of favour with the new administration

---

[1] The collectors of his correspondence have eliminated from it the letters belonging to this period.

[2] Aug. *Ep.* 87, 8; *cf.* the law of 377, *Cod. Theod.* xvi. 6, 2 (*Cod. Just.* i. 6, 1). In the new edition of the Theodosian Code it is a mistake to dispute that the law was addressed to Flavian, the Vicarius of Africa; the subject in itself excludes the reading *Flaviano vic. Asiae.* It is besides clear that this law was not dated from Constantinople, where neither Gratian, nor Valens, nor Valentinian II. were to be found in 377. St Augustine says that Flavian was the Donatists' man (*partis vestrae homini*). If he has not made a mistake, and I scarcely think that he has, this means that Flavian favoured them, not that he was himself a Donatist. Nicomachus Flavianus had translated into Latin the work of Philostratus upon Apollonius of Tyana (Sidonius Apollinaris, *Ep.* viii. 3).

and debarred from the public offices, began to feel within themselves some drawings towards apostasy. What Antioch had seen under Julian, Rome now passed through under the efforts of its aristocracy.[1]

Theodosius interrupted the festivities. He set out again, as in 388, on the road to Italy. Arbogast and Flavian marched to stop him. On their departure from Milan, they had promised to turn Ambrose's Cathedral into a stable. They did not return. Flavian, who had been entrusted with guarding the passage of the Julian Alps, allowed it to be forced, and killed himself in despair. In the battle which ensued, near the River Frigidus,[2] Eugenius was defeated and taken prisoner; Theodosius had him beheaded. Arbogast, like Flavian, committed suicide. The banners of the conquered bore the image of Hercules; once more Christ remained master on the field of battle.

And this was the end. The laws which forbade pagan worship were once more put in force. There was no persecution of individuals, even of those who had been most deeply implicated in the usurpation and in the pagan reaction: Symmachus lived for many years, and the family of Nicomachus Flavianus, without showing the slightest sign of embracing the victorious religion, still held high offices of State. But the pagan form of worship was forbidden, and the temples were closed.

We must not imagine that they were handed over to the Christians to be transformed into churches. In many places, and most particularly in Rome, where the two religions had existed side by side during the whole of the

---

[1] For a detailed account of these events, we may refer to the "Invective against Nicomachus Flavianus," *Dicite qui colitis*, discovered by M. L. Delisle, in a celebrated MS. of Prudentius (Paris, 8084) and published by him in 1867 in the *Bibl de l'École des Chartes*. Other editions have appeared since, notably those of Haupt, in *Hermes*, vol. iv., p. 354, and of Riese, in the *Anthologia Latina* (Coll. Teubner), n. 4. It is a declamation in verse against the pagan reaction of 394, written at Rome immediately after Flavian's death. Among the commentaries which have been made upon it, see especially that of De Rossi, *Bull.* 1868, p. 49 *et seq.*

[2] The River Wippach, to the east of Goertz.

4th century, the Christians were quite sufficiently provided with buildings, and had no wish to claim the temples. It is not until the 7th century that we find them appropriating one, and turning it into a church: the transformation of the Pantheon, about the year 612, is the earliest fact of this kind which can be established. Now, this took place at a time when the State no longer knew what to do with the ancient monuments of Rome. They were no longer of any use; the public treasury had been drained in order to repair them; the best thing to do to preserve them or to turn them to account was to give them to the Church. Like all the fine monuments of Rome, the temples had suffered much both from Alaric's Goths and from the Vandals of Genseric, who had despoiled them of their ornaments of precious metals and other valuable materials; but they remained standing so long as they were able to resist the encroachments of time and the violence of storms.

Besides, the transformation of the temples into churches was not without drawbacks. The enormous temple of Cælestis at Carthage, after being closed for some time, was overgrown with brambles. The authorities allowed Bishop Aurelius to use it for Christian worship, so that on one Easter Day the bishop's throne was erected on the very spot where the ancient idol had formerly stood. In the crowd which thronged round the primate of Carthage was a young man of observant mind, who, while following the offices, looked about him. An inscription in fine letters of gilded bronze attracted his attention. On the façade of the temple ran the inscription: AVRELIVS PONTIFEX DEDICAVIT. It seemed like a prophecy. However, it was soon discovered that the second Aurelius and the form of worship over which he presided did not succeed in obliterating the old traditions. Many of the neophytes, scarcely emancipated from their paganism, combined in their prayers the worship of the Tyrian goddess with that of Christ. This sealed the fate of the old temple; an order was given for its destruction.[1]

---

[1] Pseudo-Prosper, *De Promissionibus*, iii. 38; Salvian, *De gubern. Dei*, 8.

It appears that in many places the closing of the temples was accomplished, as at Rome, without disturbances. But it was not so in the East, and especially in Syria, where certain important districts remained unalterably attached to their old forms of worship. At Alexandria, as in Rome, it had been necessary to tolerate not only the opening of the temples, but the continuance of the sacrifices. In the country districts, and perhaps also in certain towns, every effort was made to evade the law. On the customary days, the people assembled in front of the temple; without offering a sacrifice in the strict sense, they killed the animal enjoined by the ritual and ate it together, in a kind of feast, the religious character of which was manifested by hymns in honour of the gods. In this way they professed to be acting strictly within the bounds of the law. But the law had, amongst the ranks of the Christian population, many voluntary defenders who were but little disposed to be content with pleasing fictions, and whose zeal was apt to pass all bounds. The black swarm of monks swooped down upon the festival; with blows of sticks and fists they scattered the unbelievers, then fell upon the temple and sacked it. Such things were often to be seen in the neighbourhood of Antioch. The pagans complained to the bishop, and scarcely obtained a hearing. Libanius took their cause in hand, and composed in this connexion, at the beginning of 384, his plea for the temples,[1] addressed to the Emperor Theodosius. The illustrious rhetorician was much too late in the field. He really imagined that the authorities would confine themselves to the prohibition of the sacrifices, and allow the rest to continue. At the conclusion of his appeal, meaning to enunciate an absurd hypothesis, he thus addresses the emperor: "You might, sire, have decreed as follows: That none of my subjects shall henceforth believe in the gods nor show them honour ; that none shall ask ought of them, either for himself or for his children, unless in silence and in secret; that everyone shall accept the religion which I honour (the Christian religion), shall join in its

---

[1] Ed. Richard Foerster, *Libanii opera* (Teubner), vol. iii., p. 80.

worship, pray according to its rites, and bend his head
beneath the hand of those who preside over them, and that
upon pain of death."

This was, however, really what Theodosius wished,
with the exception of having recourse, I do not say to the
pain of death, but to any penalty at all. Apart from these
means, the use of which it strictly denied itself, the
extirpation of paganism was pursued by every method at
the disposal of the government. If no one was attacked
in his fortune or even in his occupation, on the other hand
a vigorous assault was made on the worship itself and on
its temples. When closing the temples proved insufficient,
there was no hesitation in proceeding to their destruction.
The law forbade this in general terms, but recourse was
had to special edicts. In the same year that Libanius
wrote his appeal, the Prætorian Prefect of the Orient,
Cynegius, was sent to Syria and Egypt, with a special
mission to close effectually all the temples which had
either not been closed at all, or only partly so.[1] This
meant, for Alexandria, the end of the *régime* of toleration.
Some years afterwards a conflict of the most violent
character broke out in that great city between the pagans
and the Christians. The new Bishop Theophilus (385)
had secured from the emperor the gift of an ancient
building, which had already in the reign of Constantius
been handed over to Arian worship. In order to change
it into a church, he made some alterations in it, and
these brought to light various objects associated with the
cult; there had been there, in bygone days, a temple of
Bacchus or of Mithra; the votive offerings associated with
this were rediscovered, some of them of a very unseemly
kind. Theophilus, to spite the pagans, caused these
things to be paraded all through the town. This
exhibition evoked a riot; and, after a protracted conflict
in the streets, the pagans, under the leadership of a
philosopher, Olympius, took refuge in the Serapeum, and
fortified themselves there. This enormous temple was
built upon an artificial mound; it was reached by means

[1] Zosimus, *H. E.* iv. 37.

of a staircase of a hundred steps; upon the platform, besides the *naos* itself and the porticoes, there were erected various buildings devoted to the services of the sanctuary. From this stronghold the rioters made sorties, often returning with prisoners; these they compelled to renounce Christianity; and some of them died in this way, meeting an unexpected martyrdom. Being powerless to subdue this rebellion, the local authorities consulted together, and it was decided to write to the emperor. Theodosius replied. He pardoned the outbreak, and even the tortures inflicted on the Christians[1]; but he ordered the abolition of the worship of Serapis. It was only the idol which was destroyed. And even then it was not easy to find anyone to raise his hand to it. The colossal statue of the god occupied the centre of the temple; upon his head rested the famous "bushel," the emblem of fertility. Facing it was a window, cleverly arranged so that on certain days it directed upon the gilded lips of the god the first rays of the rising sun. Other marvels besides were to be seen in this temple, venerated and feared above all others. The pagans declared that if anyone laid hands upon Serapis, the world would be instantly destroyed. However, a soldier ventured to hurl his javelin at the head of the god; and the charm being thus broken, Serapis was hewn in pieces and dragged through the streets of Alexandria. The Patriarch, Theophilus, continued his excavations which once more put him in possession of "exhibits" of a scarcely edifying character; he was not the man to keep them to himself.[2] The emperor had given orders that the idols made of precious metal should be melted down, and

---

[1] The leader of the revolt, Olympius, retired to Italy; two others, two men of letters, Helladius and Ammonius, who were pagan priests, became teachers of grammar at Constantinople. The historian Socrates attended their lectures. Helladius in later years used to tell of his own free will how, at the time of the troubles in Alexandria, he had killed with his own hand as many as nine Christians.

[2] On all this, see Rufinus, *H. E.* ii. 22-30; *cf.* Sozomen, *H. E.* vii. 15, and Socrates *H. E.* v. 16.

that what they yielded should be distributed to the poor. Theophilus took care to reserve one of these images, which was specially curious, and to put it in a conspicuous place, always with a view to annoying the pagans. The other temples of Alexandria shared the same fate as the Serapeum. In Canopus also Serapis possessed a famous sanctuary; he was dislodged from it; and a colony of Pacomians came to establish in this place the " Monastery of Penitence."

In Syria, as in Egypt, paganism defended itself, and even more successfully. At Petra, at Areopolis in the ancient Idumæa, at Gaza and at Raphia, on the seaboard of Palestine, at Heliopolis, in the Lebanon, the population resisted stoutly the decrees for the closing of the temples. These were, however, successfully carried out. Even at Gaza, Marnas, the celebrated local god, found himself imprisoned in his own sanctuary.[1] In Northern Syria, the Bishop of Apamea, Marcellus, obtained orders to demolish the temples. He succeeded, not without difficulty, in destroying the principal temple of his episcopal city: the old building defended itself by its massive size and the strength of its construction. When it was levelled to the ground, the bishop attacked the other temples within his jurisdiction. One day, at a place called Aulon, where an armed resistance had been organized, he appeared accompanied by soldiers and gladiators. A battle ensued; the pagans observed the bishop who was praying in a place apart. They seized him and burned him alive. Of course, his flock regarded him as a martyr. The murderers were discovered; but the bishops of the province prevented any prosecution.[2]

The crisis lasted for some time longer. Shut up though he was in his temple, Marnas often received there stealthy visits from his devotees in Gaza. Porphyry, the bishop, obtained from Arcadius, though not without difficulty, an order for destruction. In the early years of the 5th century, Chrysostom let loose the Syrian monks upon the sanctuaries of the Lebanon. Harran, in spite of all

---

[1] Jerome, *Ep.* 107.   [2] Theodoret, *H. E.* v. 21.

efforts, remained pagan. We have no proof that, in these
countries of old religions, the gods of Aram did not retain
until the Moslem conquest, and even later, a few belated
worshippers.

It is impossible for me to trace in all its details the
final conflict between the two religions. Too often, as at
Apamea and Alexandria, there were scenes of bloodshed.
St Augustine speaks of sixty Christians massacred at
Suffecta in revenge for the destruction of an idol.[1] In
397, three clergy who were sent to the Val di Nona,
above Trent, to convert the mountaineers there to
Christianity, were massacred by them.[2] The adventures
of St Martin in his struggle against the paganism of the
country districts are known of all men. In Gaul and
elsewhere, many legends of martyrdom, which we cannot
succeed in fitting in with the official persecutions, are
founded upon facts of this kind, upon sanguinary disputes
brought about by the ill-timed zeal of certain Christians
and by the persistent attachment of the people to the old
forms of religion. The only victims that we know of are,
it is true, Christians ; but only the Christians have written
the story, and it is quite natural that they should not
have taken account of the deaths of their opponents.

Whatever may be the proper division, or even the
number of human lives which were sacrificed at that
time, paganism was in the end stamped out. By dint of
laws and of edicts, by the natural progress of Christianity,
or by the violent struggle between adherents of the old
religion and those of the new, the latter ended by gaining
the day both legally and in actual fact.

2. *The Proscription of the Sects.*

For the Imperial government the conflict between the
old faith and the new represented only one side of the
religious problem. Within Christianity itself, there were

[1] *Ep.* 50.

[2] Letters of Bishop Vigilius of Trent to Simplician of Milan and
to St John Chrysostom (Migne, *P. L.*, vol. xiii., p. 549 ; they are also
contained in the *Acta sincera* of Ruinart).

quite sufficient varieties, divisions, and disputes, to try the patience of the rulers and to put their tact to a severe test.

With Manicheism, which was not Christian at all except in certain external forms, and which really represented a religion quite different from any other, their relations were very simple, and had already become traditional. It was Diocletian who had proscribed this strange religion[1]; and that at a time when he was not yet persecuting Christianity. His terrible law does not seem to have been carried out to the letter under the Christian emperors.[2] Manicheism is often condemned in their legislation, and more severely than other sects. We hear of Manicheans being sent to prison or to exile; but we do not find that the penalty of death which had been ordered by Diocletian was ever applied to them.

As to the Christian sects, the law, under the pagan emperors, had distinguished between them and the Great Church. The edicts of persecution or of toleration were applied indifferently to every variety of Christians. But after Constantine it was no longer so.

We have seen before that in addition to the right of existence, which was recognized to the Christian communities by the edicts of Galerius, Constantine, and Licinius, and even in addition to measures of restitution decreed by these last two emperors, privileges, exemptions, and favours, pecuniary and otherwise, were very soon bestowed upon the Churches, first in the West, and afterwards in the East, as soon as Constantine became master there. This prince, who was very well informed as to the internal divisions of Christianity, decided from the outset that his favours should go only to the Great Church, which had been recognized by him as true and legitimate. This preference showed itself at first in his acts: it was finally expressed in legislation: we find it ratified in a law of 326.[3]

---

[1] See Vol. I., p. 410.

[2] The *summum supplicium* only reappeared once in the Theodosian Code (xvi. 5, 9), in connection with certain classes of persons who appear to correspond to the Manichean "elect."

[3] *Cod. Theod.* xvi. 5, 1.

But, apart from this question of privileges, heretics had had in the beginning, like all Christians, the right to re-establish their churches and to resume their meetings. The most ancient Christian church which is still standing is a Marcionite church, situated, it is true, in a country which was subject at that day to Licinius.[1] In Africa, Constantine tried to deprive the Donatists of their churches[2]; but that was a case of a sect just coming to the birth, and of buildings which might be considered as being diverted by it from their lawful attachment, and taken away from their true owner, the Catholic Church of the district. This distinction is clearly revealed in a law of 326,[3] which, while it authorizes the Novatians to possess churches and cemeteries, makes an exception for the real property which the sect might have usurped from the Great Church at the time of their separation. The authorization here granted to the Novatians purports to relate only to them, as representing a special position, better than that of the other sects.[4] This agrees entirely with the comparative respect which the Council of Nicæa shows towards these dissenters, or rather to those of them who were resuming connection with the Catholic Church.

They are mentioned, however, with the other sects, in an edict, several years later in date, the text of which Eusebius[5] has preserved to us. It is a kind of exhortation, addressed directly by the emperor to the heretics—Novatians, Valentinians, Marcionites, Paulinians, Montanists, and others—calling upon them to return to the Church. There is a reference in it to a law, despatched to the governors of provinces, according to which religious

---

[1] In the present village of Deir-Ali, to the south of Damascus (the ancient Ituræa). We may still read, above the door, the inscription Συναγωγὴ Μαρκιωνιστῶν κώμης Λεβάβων, τοῦ κυρίου καὶ σωτῆρος Ἰησοῦ Χριστοῦ, προνοίᾳ Παύλου πρεσβυτέρου, τοῦ λχ´ ἔτους. This year 630 of the Seleucid era corresponds to the year 318 of our own era.

[2] *Supra*, p. 93.

[3] *Cod. Theod.* xvi. 5, 2.

[4] "Novatianos non adeo comperimus praedamnatos ut his quae petierunt crederemus minime largienda."

[5] *Vita Const.* iii. 64, 65.

assemblies were forbidden to the dissenters, even in private
houses ; their places of meeting were taken from them to be
handed over to the official Church ; and finally, their common possessions were confiscated by the State. Eusebius
assures us [1] that these severities, reinforced by sentences of
banishment directed against the leaders, had the effect of
bringing back to the Church a large number of dissenters.

Such laws, as we see from the striking example
of the Donatists, could not always be carried out.
In fact, the Little Churches continued to exist. The
Novatians had one at Constantinople. During the reign
of Constantius, Bishop Macedonius, a man little given to
toleration, compelled them to transfer it to the other side
of the Golden Horn (Galata). Under this bishop the
supporters of his predecessor Paul and of the *homoousios*
were treated as dissenters, and even worse used than the
Novatians. They followed the latter to the suburbs,
attended their churches for lack of others, and a fusion
very nearly took place between the two bodies under
the pressure of a common persecution.[2] At Cyzicus also,
the Novatian Church was destroyed at that time by the
efforts of Bishop Eleusius. In Paphlagonia, where they
were very numerous, they had to suffer from the consum-
ing zeal of the Bishop of Constantinople. Macedonius,
availing himself of his influence with the authorities,
succeeded in bringing about the despatch to this district of
quite a formidable military expedition. The Novatians,
excited no doubt by previous annoyances, had assembled at a
place called Mantineion. The four *numeri*, who were marching against them, did not dismay them. Armed with axes
and scythes, these peasants cut to pieces the imperial troops.[3]

Undertakings of this kind on the part of the official

---

[1] *Vita Const.* iii. 66.

[2] The details collected by Socrates (*H. E.* ii. 27, 38 ; *cf.* Sozomen,
H. E. iv. 2, 3) upon the ill-treatment to which the followers of Paul
were exposed at this time, refer rather to private acts of violence than
to formal acts of the government.

[3] Julian alludes to these facts in his letter 52, in which he speaks
of massacres of heretics which took place under Constantius
ἐν Σαμοσάτοις καὶ Κυζίκῳ καὶ Παφλαγονίᾳ καὶ Βιθυνίᾳ καὶ Γαλατίᾳ.

bishops presuppose that they had the law on their side,
that the edict spoken of by Eusebius was in no way
imaginary, and that the Novatians themselves had not
long enjoyed the exceptional conditions which Constantine
had granted them at first. They recovered them under
the successors of Constantius, and down to the beginning
of the 5th century they appear to have been left in peace.
In Constantinople, Rome, Alexandria, and in many other
places, we hear of Novatian churches, the existence of
which was neither disturbed nor concealed.

The other dissenters also held their ground, in spite of
legislation which grew less and less favourable to them.
Abrogated for a moment under Julian, the laws which
relate to them had speedily been revived. Officially they
were forbidden [1] to hold meetings for worship, and that
under pain of confiscation of the building in which the
assembly had taken place. But the very fact that this
prohibition had to be repeated over and over again, and
that new laws had again and again to be drawn up
against the sects, proves that they continued to exist.
Not to speak of the Donatists, who were masters in their
own country and to whom no one dared to speak of the
Code, many dissenting communities were able to defend
themselves, almost everywhere, by their numbers and
their influence. When they could not frighten the
magistrates, they found other means to ensure that they
should leave them in peace—the venality of these officials
here played its part—and, except for a few anxious times,
they managed to get off scatheless.

Yet, serious and numerous as might be these infringe-
ments of it, the legislation remained, was constantly
renewed, and was more and more clearly defined, being
influenced invariably by the principle that there was only
one way of being a Christian—that which was recognized

---

[1] Prohibition referred to in a law of Valens and Gratian (375-378),
Cod. Theod. xvi. 5, 4. Apparently suspended for a short time, it was
re-established by a law of August 3, 379 (*Cod. Theod.* xvi. 5, 5).

[2] The title *De Haereticis*, in the Theodosian Code (xvi. 5), contains
no less than sixty-six laws, and that is not all.

by the State and directed by the official Church. That Church alone had the right to exist and to perform the worship—the collective worship, the worship of the community—which all Christians, whatever their denomination, considered as essential to their religion, as constituting for them a duty. As to individual convictions, so long as they do not show themselves by outward actions, and especially by participation in forbidden meetings, the State respects them on the whole. We do not find that it ever forced heretics to recant. Nevertheless, especially when it was a case of sects looked upon with peculiar disfavour, such as the Manicheans at first, and afterwards the Eunomians and some others, too, at different times— the mere fact of belonging to them produced consequences more or less serious : disqualification for public offices and for military service, limitation of the right to dispose of their possessions by will or by gift, or to acquire them by the same means, denial of rights of residence, and banishment.

We must also take notice of the proscription of books. Those of Arius were declared by Constantine to be similar to the treatise of Porphyry against the Christians, and as in the case of that work it was forbidden, under pain of death, to preserve them.[1] The same prohibition, with the same penalty was extended to the books of the Eunomians.[2]

3. *The Church in the State.*

But this Christian religion to which all the ancient traditions of worship were sacrificed, this Catholic Church in which alone the government consented to recognize genuine Christianity — what were its exact relations with the State ? The local Church in each city, the grouping of Churches throughout the empire as a whole, could only represent, when compared with the State, a private society. Such had been the position at the time of the laws of persecution ; and such it remained under

---

[1] Letter of Constantine Τοὺς πονηρούς, Socrates, *H. E.* i. 9, p. 31.
[2] *Cod. Theod.* xvi. 5, 34.

the Christian emperors. In allowing it to live, the emperors of 311 recognized implicitly that its existence could be reconciled with the working of the State. It was a kind of approbation, from an external and administrative point of view, of the fundamental statutes of the Christian community. If the State had confined itself in its dealings with the Church to the simple toleration of a little regarded power, its relations with it would have remained very simple, analogous, for example, to those which it maintained with the Jewish communities. But in the first place, the Church, local or universal, was already exceeding in importance, and exceeded to an ever-increasing extent, all other organized associations that the empire contained. Even if the emperor had remained a pagan, it would have been difficult for him not to give special attention to a society of such wide range; the mere exercise of his autocracy would have led him to concern himself in its internal affairs. The conversion of the prince strengthened this tendency. Who had a greater interest than he had in knowing where, among so many shades of difference, was the true Christian tradition? To which of them, in case of disputes, was it, I do not say more legitimate but more tempting, to address himself? Was it not the Donatists and the Arians who introduced Constantine into the realm of canon law and of theology? Even apart from public order and the just solicitude which any emperor must have for it, was not a Christian prince led quite naturally to see to it that peace should reign amongst his brethren in Jesus Christ, and that the guidance of them should be entrusted to worthy pastors?

Here are many motives for interference in religious matters! But this was not all. Once a Christian, the emperor wished forthwith to convert the empire also, and not only to convert it, but to make the new religion what no one had ever been able to make the old one, a universal and official institution, a State religion.

Such a design naturally presupposed that the State would make an effort to hasten the disappearance of the

old pagan form of worship, and that it would employ—
if not every possible means—at least a great deal of zeal
to hinder divisions of opinion which were capable of
dislocating the Church. But it also presupposed that the
government would often intervene in ecclesiastical affairs,
and that the high favour which elevated the Church from
being a proscribed sect to the position of a kind of
State institution, would be recompensed by conspicuous
demonstrations of loyalty.

The Church resigned itself to this. We nowhere find
that it raised any objections on the ground of principle.
It was considered very natural. The triumph of Christ,
of His religion, His Church, and of His followers had
been foretold by the Prophets, announced in the Gospel,
and claimed by the Christian conscience. In the days
of old, Christians had cursed the Babylon of the Seven
Hills ; now they were conquering her and were going
to convert her. What triumph could be more desirable ?
Undoubtedly there were evil times during which Babylon
baptized though she was, still made them feel her heavy
hand. It was then that Donatus said: "What has the
emperor got to do with the affairs of the Church ?"
It was then that Athanasius discovered in Costyllius all
kinds of resemblances to Antichrist. But when things
went smoothly, no one was scandalized to see the
emperor's intervention. That he should intervene only
in the good sense, that was all that was asked of him.

These ideas appear to us simple-minded, because our
education in matters of this kind has become singularly
subtle. But in the time of Theodosius no one thought
otherwise, not even those who had reason to complain
of the Imperial interference. We may take it for granted
that if Donatus and Eunomius had been in favour, they
would not have hesitated to secure for their dogmas the
stamp of official approval, and to procure for them the
support of the police.

To the changes in their legal position brought about
in 311 and in 313, the Christians owed, before everything
else, the liberty of their associations, now recognized for

what they really were, and released from the shackles imposed by the law upon associations which were concerned with morals. Christians had the right of possessing in a corporate capacity, not only a common fund but also the real property which provided them with a centre of meeting, *i.e.*, churches and their dependent buildings, the bishop's house, hospitals, and other charitable institutions; also their cemeteries, and even landed property at a distance. The ecclesiastical patrimony might be augmented by gift and by will. The State recognized the bishops, the elected heads of the communities, as the administrators of their temporal possessions, and as their spiritual governors.

To this liberty which had been granted from time immemorial to the Jewish communities, and which the Christian churches had also themselves enjoyed in fact long before Constantine, in the interval between persecutions, were soon added several minor privileges, such as exemption from municipal office,[1] from forced labour, from the land-tax in the case of public churches,[2] and from that of the "chrysargyrium" (licence) for the inferior clergy who were engaged in some small trade.[3]

But one fact of special importance is that the position recognized to the Great Church—to the Catholic Church —was not conceded to the dissenting bodies. Hence resulted a State orthodoxy. The State was obliged to know which among the parties in conflict was the one that represented genuine Christianity, the one which it ought to acknowledge and to protect as such. In theory, it would seem, the State had no advice to give; it was for the Christian communities to settle their own

---

[1] *Supra*, p. 50. The exemption dates from 313; see *Cod. Theod.* xvi. 2, where it is often mentioned.

[2] In the law of Constantius (*Cod. Theod.* xi. 1, 1, wrongly dated 315; it should rather be 360) which mentions this exemption, we must not take the words *ecclesias catholicas* as meaning orthodox churches in opposition to nonconformist churches; it refers to public churches for the use of the whole community, as opposed to private churches, domestic oratories, monastic chapels, etc.

[3] *Cod. Theod.* xiii. 1, 1, 11, 14; xvi. 2, 8, 10, 36.

disputes. But, as a matter of fact, apart from occasional appeals to his arbitration, care for public order, care even for the welfare of the Church induced the sovereign to intervene in these disputes, and to take whatever means he judged advisable in order to put an end to them. Hence we find the emperors organizing religious inquiries, gathering together councils, taking a very close interest in their labours, drawing up the programme for them, intervening even in the composition of formulas and in the choice of bishops.

When the points in controversy did not go beyond the domain of the local Church, it was possible still to settle them by the intervention of superior ecclesiastical authorities, to whom, in case of need, the government lent material support. But if the episcopate were divided, what means could be found of producing agreement, and which side ought to be taken? If there had been, in the Church of the 4th century, a central authority recognized and active, it would have offered a means of solution. But it was not so. Antioch and Alexandria are at variance; the Egyptian episcopate supports Athanasius, the Eastern episcopate opposes him. How was the matter to be decided? By doing as Aurelian did, and putting oneself on the side taken by the Roman Church? For that, it would have been necessary that there should be in this respect a tradition, a custom; that it should have been usual to see the Roman Church intervening in these matters. But in reality it was a very long time since anything had been heard of that Church in the East. A century before, the authoritative ways of Pope Stephen had offended many people, among them some of those most held in honour. The deposition of Paul of Samosata was notified to the Church of Rome, as it was to that of Alexandria, but it had not had to take any share in it. It played but a minor part at the Council of Nicæa. Athanasius, when deposed by the Council of Tyre, does not seem to have had any idea that an appeal to Rome might restore his fortunes. It was his adversaries who, when seeking support for the usurpers of Alexandria,

made the first approaches to Pope Julius. Further, so
soon as they met with opposition from him, we find them
assuming a disdainful attitude towards the Pope, and
even taking upon themselves to depose him. Even in the
West, we have seen what concern the Donatists had for
the Church over the sea in general, and for the Roman
Church in particular.

There was not there a guiding power, an effective
expression of Christian unity. The Papacy, such as the
West knew it later on, was still to be born. In the place
which it did not yet occupy, the State installed itself without
hesitation. The Christian religion became the religion
of the emperor, not only in the sense of being professed
by him, but in the sense of being directed by him. Such
is not the law, such is not the theory; but such is the
fact.

The emperor, it is true, did not himself determine
the formularies of faith; that was the business of the
bishops. If he feels the necessity of fixing exactly, on some
particular point, the theological language, it is to them
that he addresses himself. Whether they are assembled in
councils, more or less œcumenical, in one or in two divisions ; or whether they meet in smaller gatherings on individual summonses despatched at will, it is always to the
emperor that the meeting owes its formation, it is to him that
it looks for its programme, for its general direction, and above
all for the sanction of its decisions. If, like Theodosius, the
emperor distrusts formulas, and has recourse more readily
to persons, it is he who decides with whom it is right to
hold communion. And upon what grounds does his
decision rest? Upon his own personal estimate of the
situation. Theodosius was a Nicene, like all the Westerns ;
when he was called to govern the East, he indicated to it
as standards of orthodoxy the Bishops of Rome and of
Alexandria. Later on, when he knew his episcopal world
better, he perceived that these authorities were not so
decisive as was necessary, and he indicated others.

The emperor again does not assume, in theory, the
right of deposing a bishop. That is the business of the

Church which alone is in a position to know whether such an one of its representatives has or has not violated its internal statutes. In proceedings taken against bishops and other clergy, the State does not interfere, provided such proceedings relate only to statutory obligations, and do not affect the common law of the State. Thus, if a bishop teaches heresy, or a clerk breaks the law of celibacy (provided it was not a case of adultery), it is for the Church, and not the State, to recall him to his duty, and to apply to him its own penalties, dismissal, (deposition) and exclusion (excommunication). Where the State intervenes, and at the request of the Church, is in relation to the consequences which may be produced in regard to public order by the execution of the ecclesiastical sentence. Then the State, by ordinary police measures, would eject, banish, or imprison such and such a bishop, or such and such a claimant as should be pointed out to it, either by its own officials or simply by episcopal authority, after a trial in due form.

Such is the theory. In practice, it is evident that the government would have no difficulty in finding in the divisions amongst the episcopate, and the weaknesses of individual members, a basis of operations against any persons who presumed to displease it. Moreover, the common law, with its crimes of *lèse-majesté* and rebellion, provided it in certain cases with other means of action. In fact, a bishop, especially a bishop of important position, who wished to live a quiet life, had to be careful not to oppose the official dogmas and, generally speaking, the manifestations, even when they affected religion, of the will of the government. However, we must not go too far, and assimilate the bishops to the State officials. The " army of the Church " is always distinguished from the " army of the world," not only by the nature and dignity of its functions, but also by its origin. The bishops are, and remain, the elected of their Church ; they invest each other, without the State having anything to do in the matter. To face the hierarchy of government officials who all owe their existence, either directly or indirectly, to the will of the emperor, there rises the ecclesiastical hierarchy which, for its part, holds its powers by election.   And this election remains generally free.   We are not forbidden to suppose that in certain cases, where the choice of persons was of further importance to him—at Antioch, and at Constanti-nople, for instance—the suggestions of the sovereign may have assisted the electors in their decision.   But at Rome, at Alexandria, and elsewhere, so far as our knowledge goes, the choice of the electors was respected.[1]   At the most, in case of doubt, as in a case of ambiguity in dogma, the government only intervened to ascertain the truth of the matter, not to impose a candidate.

There was in this no small advantage for the Church. In it alone was the right of election exercised.   We may even say that, by means of its councils, it showed some marks of a government in accordance with opinion and of representative institutions.   Outside the Church, in the civil and political domain, there were only the governors and the governed.   This special position the Church held by its essential condition—that of a private society, independent of the State, when once it had come to terms with its legislative decisions.   The State having, after trial, admitted its existence, had no longer any right to interfere in its internal government, and it was compelled to respect the element of liberalism which that government contained.

These two societies, which tended more and more to include the same persons, and were scarcely distinguish-able any longer save by their aims, could not fail to multiply their points of contact, to rely upon each other, and to lend each other support.   A conflict between them produced the effect of something absurd.   A heretic prince, or a rebellious bishop, remained possibilities, but they were abnormal.

One of the most ancient and most significant testi-monies to this mutual understanding is the institution of

---

[1] Of course there were certain exceptions, in times of crisis, like those in which it imposed the usurpers Gregory, George, Felix, and Lucius.

the episcopal tribunal in the 4th century. Here, let it be
said at once, it is not a question of judgments given by
the bishops and their priests in the disputes between
Christians. That goes back to the very beginning of
Christianity. The members of the primitive Christian
communities, like those of the Jewish communities, readily
carried their proceedings before their religious leaders.
They continued to do so in the 4th century, and even
afterwards. The decisions thus given were binding upon
the conscience, but could only be upheld by statutory
means. In order to claim the weight of public authority, it
was necessary that the judgment should have been given
by way of arbitration, with a preliminary agreement
between the parties. But what I mean to call attention to
now, is the right granted to litigants by the Christian
emperors to carry their civil disputes, and to cite their
opponents, before the bishops, and then to demand the
execution of their decision without any previous compromise.[1] Recourse to this ecclesiastical tribunal was not
limited to causes between Christians; any persons might
avail themselves of it, and that in whatever state their
suit might be, even if it had been thrashed out before a
secular judge, and he had begun to deliver his judgment.
It was not a tribunal of appeal; it was a special court,
which was considered able to inspire more confidence than
the ordinary court, and the access to which was made easy.
The bishop thus possessed the jurisdiction of an arbitrator; fortified by the decision given by him, one could
claim that it should be officially enforced. In fact, the State
admitted that the episcopal procedure was simpler, more
honest, and less costly than that of its own judges, offered
to disputants special advantages, and it had no hesitation
in securing these for them. It is a testimony which is
very honourable to the Church: we may be allowed to
call attention to it since the jurisdiction has given rise to
so many disputes and scandals.

Such was the position of the Church in relation to the
State at the close of the 4th century. What a change

[1] *Cod. Theod.* i. 27, 1 ; *Const. Sirm.* 1.

since Diocletian! Not only was it persecuted no longer, but it was protected, it was imitated, it had become like a public institution. Religious unity—so long the dream of statesmen—had become through its means a reality. It is useless now to speak of syncretism: all religions were now deserted in favour of one alone, and that, the very one against which it had formerly been desired to unite them. Absorbed in some degree by the Roman State, the Church absorbed it in its turn, permeated it with its principles, made of it the Christian State.

But what had been the result for Christianity of this great external change? How far were the tradition of the Gospel and the inner life of the Church affected by the accession of multitudes and the favour of the powers of the world? It is this that we have now to estimate.

INDEX

ABGAR, King of Edessa, 485
Ablavius, Prætorian Prefect in Nicomedia, assists Athanasius, 135
murder of, 154
Abraham of Batna, exile of, 312
Acacius, the Metropolitan of Palestine, lat the Counc. of Seleucia, 240-244
description of, 242
the Councs. of Con^ple, 244, 245, 482
and Athanasius, 282
and Eunomius, 297
troubles in Rome, 359
Bp. of Beroea, 482
and Cyril of Jerusalem, 487
Acesius, Novatian, Bp. of Con^ple, 459
Acholius, Bp. of Thessalonica, and Gregory of Nazianzus, 346
and the Goths, 453
Ædesius, his condemnation and escape, 34
Aelia Capitolina (Jerusalem), colony of—description, 63
sites at, 65
prerogatives of Bp. of, 120, 486
monks at, 408
disturbances at, 486-488
Aelia, Church of, supposed site of the Last Supper, 62
Aerius and Eustathius, 316
Aetius, a Christian sophist, and Julian, 220, 257
his doctrine, 221, 242, 245
banishment, 235
deposed at Counc. of Con^ple, 245
imprisonment, 246, 296
release, and ordination as bp., 297
and Eunomius, 297-300
death, 299

Africa, persecution of Christians in, 5, 38
dissensions in, 53, 355
the Donatist schism, 79, 190 et seq.
the Creed of Nicæa, 374
the Counc. at Aquileia, 376
Agapius, Bp. of Cæsarea in Palestine, 32
Agapius, Bp. of Ephesus, 458
Agelius, Novatian, Bp. of Con^ple, 459
Agonistics. See CIRCUMCELLIONS
Alamanni, invasion of the, 333
Alexander, Bp. of Con^ple, and Arius, 146
Alexander, Bp. of Cæsarea in Cappadocia, 62
Alexander, Bp. of Alexandria, 98
and Arianism, 102, 106
disciplinary canons, 119
death, 132
Alexander, Vicarius of Africa, 79
Alexandria, martyrs of, 37
churches of, 98, 202
clergy of, 99
Arianism at, 102-104, 156, 157
date of Easter, 111
disturbances, 211, 310, 311
paganism in, 508
Alfius Cæcilianus and Bp Felix, 90, 91
Ambrose, St—De Virginibus, 40 n.
childhood, 369
ordained Bp. of Milan, 370
and the Counc. of Aquileia, 373 et seq.
the West in days of, 414 et seq.
and Ydacius, 422
and asceticism, 424
at Trèves, 426
and Felix of Trèves, 428
and Priscillianism, 429

II   2 L